Visual Studio® 2008 All-in-One Desk Reference For Dummies

Cheat Sheet

D0565647

Visual Studio 2008 Keyboard Shortcuts for General Development Environment

Task You Want to Perform	Feature	Keyboard Shortcut
Browse data types	Class View	Ctrl+Shift+C
	Object Browser	Ctrl+Alt+J
Edit code	Format Document	Ctrl+K, Ctrl+D
	Comment Selection	Ctrl+K, Ctrl+C
	Uncomment Selection	Ctrl+K, Ctrl+U
	Insert Code Snippet	Ctrl+K, Ctrl+X
	Toggle Outlining	Ctrl+M
Expansion	Collapse to Definitions	Ctrl+M, Ctrl+O
	Toggle Designer and Markup	Shift+F7
	View Code	F7
Debug	Start Debugging	F5
	Start without Debugging	Ctrl+F5
	Step Into	F11
	Step Over	F10
	Toggle Breakpoint	F9
	Restart	Ctrl+Shift+F5
Find and replace	Find Symbol	Alt+F12
	Quick Find	Ctrl+F
	Quick Replace	Ctrl+H
Find help	Contents	Ctrl+Alt+F1
	Context-sensitive help	F1
	How Do I	Ctrl+F1
	Index	Ctrl+Alt+F1
	Search	Ctrl+Alt+F3
Manage project resources	Properties Window	F4
	Data Sources	Shift+Alt+D
	Server Explorer	Ctrl+Alt+S
	Solution Explorer	Ctrl+Alt+L
	Toolbox	Ctrl+Alt+X
	Add New Item	Ctrl+Shift+A
	Add Existing Item	Shift+Alt+A
	Build Solution	Ctrl+Shift+B
Open files and projects	New File Window	Ctrl+N
	New Project Window	Ctrl+Shift+N
	Open File Window	Ctrl+O
	Open Project Window	Ctrl+Shift+O
Navigate windows	Close Document	Ctrl+F4
	Close Tool Window	Shift+Esc
	Cycle Documents	Ctrl+F6
	IDE Navigator	Ctrl+Tab
	Cycle Tool Panes	Alt+F6

For Dummies: Bestselling Book Series for Beginners

BESTSELLING
BOOK SERIES

Visual Studio® 2008 All-in-One Desk Reference For Dummies®

Cheat Sheet

Technology and Terminology

Technology	Description
Assembly	A file for physically storing data types, including the DLL files where code is compiled
Base Class Library	A set of managed code that enables developers to create Windows and Web applications that target the Common Language Runtime
Common Language Runtime	A managed environment for running applications that prevents memory leaks
Common Type Specification	A set of rules for how programming languages use data types
Garbage Collection	A feature of the Common Language Runtime that manages memory
Global Assembly Cache	A repository that stores public versions of assemblies
Namespace	A unique identifier for the logical organization of data types

Common Visual Studio Item Templates

Item Template	Description
Application Configuration File	Stores application settings for a Windows application
Class	Empty class-definition file
Class Diagram	Model of new or existing classes
Crystal Report	Report using Crystal Reports
DataSet	Stores data using DataSet Designer
HTML Page	Web page using HTML
Icon File	A Windows icon file
Report	Report using SQL Server Reporting Services
Settings File	XML configuration file
Site Map	Describes flow of Web pages in a Web application
SQL Database	Empty database for storing local data
Style Sheet	Cascading Style Sheet
User Control (WPF)	Windows Presentation Foundation user control
User Control	Reusable custom control
Web Configuration File	Stores application settings for a Web application
Web Form	User interface for Web applications
Web Service	Code file for a Web service
Windows Form	User interface for a Windows application
Windows Script Host	A file containing script run as a Windows program
XML File	Empty XML document
XML Schema	Describes contents of an XML document
XSLT File	Contains a stylesheet used to transform XML documents

For Dummies: Bestselling Book Series for Beginners

Visual Studio® 2008
ALL-IN-ONE DESK REFERENCE
FOR
DUMMIES®

by Rick Leinecker and Vanessa L. Williams

WILEY

Wiley Publishing, Inc.

Visual Studio® 2008 All-in-One Desk Reference For Dummies®

Published by
Wiley Publishing, Inc.
111 River Street
Hoboken, NJ 07030-5774

www.wiley.com

Copyright © 2008 by Wiley Publishing, Inc., Indianapolis, Indiana

Published by Wiley Publishing, Inc., Indianapolis, Indiana

Published simultaneously in Canada

For general information on our other products and services, please contact our Customer Care Department within the U.S. at 800-762-2974, outside the U.S. at 317-572-3993, or fax 317-572-4002.

For technical support, please visit www.wiley.com/techsupport.

Wiley also publishes its books in a variety of electronic formats. Some content that appears in print may not be available in electronic books.

Library of Congress Control Number: 2008923599

ISBN: 978-0-470-19108-8

Manufactured in the United States of America

10 9 8 7 6 5 4 3 2 1

WILEY

About the Authors

Rick Leinecker has held a number of prestigious positions in companies such as IntraCorp, MCI, and Landmark Communications. He has written more than 20 books on technical subjects such as C++, C#, ASP.NET, and computer security. He has a thriving consulting practice in North Carolina's Triad area and innovates in fields such as imaging, podcasting, and artificial intelligence.

Vanessa L. Williams is a consultant and author specializing in Microsoft's Share Point and .NET technologies. Through her Midwest consulting business, Vanessa Williams Business Solutions, she provides custom development, systems implementation, hosting, and training services for SharePoint, .NET, and Visual Studio Team System. She has ten years of business information systems experience spanning several industries including transportation, petroleum marketing, manufacturing, retail, and motor-sports entertainment. Her nontechnical experience — including jobs as a shipping clerk, accounting clerk, and forklift driver — gives her the unique ability to view systems implementations from an end-user's perspective.

Vanessa grew up in Indianapolis, where she graduated from the Kelley School of Business at Indiana University with a Bachelor of Science degree in Business Management and Computer Information Systems. She is active in the online tech community and welcomes comments, feedback, and questions via her Web site, www.sharepointgrrl.com.

Dedication

Rick Leinecker: This book is dedicated to John and Tina.

Vanessa L. Williams: To Mel and Rosie.

Publisher's Acknowledgments

We're proud of this book; please send us your comments through our online registration form located at www.dummies.com/register/.

Some of the people who helped bring this book to market include the following:

Acquisitions and Editorial

Project Editor: Rebecca Huehls

Sr. Acquisitions Editor: Katie Feltman

Sr. Copy Editor: Teresa Artman

Technical Editor: John Mueller

Editorial Manager: Leah P. Cameron

Editorial Assistant: Amanda Foxworth

Sr. Editorial Assistant: Cherie Case

Cartoons: Rich Tennant
(www.the5thwave.com)

Composition Services

Project Coordinator: Erin Smith

Layout and Graphics: Claudia Bell, Stacie Brooks, Alissa D. Ellet, Melissa K. Jester, Christine Williams

Proofreaders: John Greenough, Susan Moritz

Indexer: Infodex Indexing Services Inc.

Special Help: Linda Morris

Publishing and Editorial for Technology Dummies

Richard Swadley, Vice President and Executive Group Publisher

Andy Cummings, Vice President and Publisher

Mary Bednarek, Executive Acquisitions Director

Mary C. Corder, Editorial Director

Publishing for Consumer Dummies

Diane Graves Steele, Vice President and Publisher

Joyce Pepple, Acquisitions Director

Composition Services

Gerry Fahey, Vice President of Production Services

Debbie Stailey, Director of Composition Services

Contents at a Glance

Introduction 1

Book I: Visual Studio 2008 Overview 11
Chapter 1: What Is Visual Studio? 13
Chapter 2: Exploring .NET 21
Chapter 3: Modern Software Development 31
Chapter 4: The Languages of .NET 55
Chapter 5: The Many Editions of Visual Studio 2008 67

Book II: Getting Started 79
Chapter 1: Installing Visual Studio Professional 81
Chapter 2: Browsing Visual Studio 89
Chapter 3: Making Connections with Visual Studio 103
Chapter 4: Upgrading .NET 115

Book III: Building Applications............................. 127
Chapter 1: Getting Smart about Smart Clients 129
Chapter 2: Building Smart Client User Interfaces 149
Chapter 3: Building Visual C++ Applications 175
Chapter 4: Building Web Applications 187
Chapter 5: Using AJAX For Rich Web Pages 213
Chapter 6: Laying Out Your Site 225
Chapter 7: Exploring ASP.NET Services 253
Chapter 8: Building a Mobile Application 271

Book IV: Getting Acquainted with Data Access 289
Chapter 1: Accessing Data with Visual Studio 291
Chapter 2: Show Me the Data... 309
Chapter 3: Working with Strongly Typed DataSets 345
Chapter 4: Working with XML 381
Chapter 5: Under the Hood with ADO.NET 399
Chapter 6: Using Visual Studio with SQL Server 437
Chapter 7: LINQ 467

Book V: Coding 473

Chapter 1: Programming with Visual Studio 2008.....................................475
Chapter 2: Understanding Data Types...493
Chapter 3: Get Some Class 525
Chapter 4: Wiring Up Events in the User Interface 551
Chapter 5: Getting Productive with Visual Studio 2008.............................569
Chapter 6: Exploring Web Services 595
Chapter 7: Handling Exceptions and Debugging 617
Chapter 8: Testing Code with Visual Studio..639

Book VI: Going the Extra Mile 657

Chapter 1: Building Solutions and Projects 659
Chapter 2: Deployment Options...675
Chapter 3: Checking Out Source Control 701
Chapter 4: Building Professional Reports with Crystal Reports.....................719

Book VII: Extending Visual Studio 737

Chapter 1: Exploring Visual Studio Extensions 739
Chapter 2: Being a Team Player with Visual Studio Team System.....................747
Chapter 3: Using Visual Studio with Vista and Office 2007 765

Index 781

Table of Contents

Introduction 1

Who Should Read This Book? 2
About This Book 3
Foolish Assumptions 4
Conventions Used in This Book 5
    Stuff you type 5
    Menu commands 5
    Display messages 5
How This Book Is Organized 6
    Book I: Visual Studio 2008 Overview 6
    Book II: Getting Started 6
    Book III: Building Applications 6
    Book IV: Getting Acquainted with Data Access 7
    Book V: Coding 7
    Book VI: Going the Extra Mile 8
    Book VII: Extending Visual Studio 8
About the Companion Web Site 9
Icons Used in This Book 9

Book 1: Visual Studio 2008 Overview 11

Chapter 1: What Is Visual Studio? 13

The Role of the Integrated Development Environment 14
    Tools beyond the basic three 15
    Enter Visual Studio 15
Visual Studio as the Hub 17
The Keeper of .NET 18
New Features in Visual Studio 2008 19

Chapter 2: Exploring .NET 21

Following the Evolution of .NET 21
Getting Acquainted with the .NET Components 24
    .NET freebies 25
    No free lunch 26
Peering into the Future of .NET 27
Using the New Features in .NET 29

Chapter 3: Modern Software Development 31

Software Engineering in Action 32
    Have process, will repeat 33
    Practicing what you preach 36

Building a developer's toolbox 38
Working with your partners in development 39
Components Defeat Monoliths 40
Architecture evolution 42
Component management in .NET 43
Managed Code Execution 46
Taking Out the Garbage 50
Allocating memory 52
Releasing memory 52

Chapter 4: The Languages of .NET **55**

Looking at the Languages of .NET 56
Visual Basic 57
Visual C# 59
Visual C++ 60
J# 61
Choosing the Right Language for the Job 62
Becoming a Good Programmer 63
Learn the syntax 64
Write your own code 65
Spend some time in other language studies 66

Chapter 5: The Many Editions of Visual Studio 2008 . . . .**67**

Making Sense of the Visual Studio Editions 67
Visual Studio Express Editions 68
Visual Studio Tools for Office 69
Visual Studio Professional 70
Visual Studio Team System 70
Choosing the Right Edition 71
Subscribing to the Microsoft Developer Network 71
Weighing your options 73
Developing When It's a Team Effort 74
Managing projects with Team System 75
Architecting software 76
Developing software with Team System 77
Testing with tools 77
Collaborating with Visual Studio Team Foundation 77
Taking a Visual Look Ahead 78

Book II: Getting Started *79*

Chapter 1: Installing Visual Studio Professional **81**

Installing Versions Side by Side 81
Taking a look at all the .NETs 82
Getting help from Visual Studio 2008 82

Meeting System Requirements 83
Stepping through the Installation 84
Launching Visual Studio for the First Time 85

Chapter 2: Browsing Visual Studio 89

Making Your Way around Visual Studio 89
Dealing with Windows Galore..90
    Docking windows 91
    Working with tabbed documents 92
    Working with multiple documents 92
    Managing windows...93
Building Solutions with Visual Studio 2008....................................94
    Using the Solution Explorer to manage solutions and projects 96
    Working with solution and project menus 98
Using the Properties Window..98
Browsing Servers 99
Writing Code with the Code Editor 100
Using the Forms Designer 101
Taking a Look at Other Designers 102

Chapter 3: Making Connections with Visual Studio 103

Getting Help 103
    Setting help viewing options..104
    Opening and navigating the help documentation.............105
    Searching and filtering search results 108
    Customizing Document Explorer search and home pages 109
    Customizing the start page 110
Staying in Touch with the .NET Community.................................111
    Pursuing certification 112
    Viewing Webcasts...113

Chapter 4: Upgrading .NET 115

Making the Case for an Upgrade 115
    What happens to Visual Studio code in an upgrade? 116
    What are alternatives to upgrading?..................................117
    How do you upgrade from pre-.NET languages? 117
Considering Your Conversion Strategies 118
    Converting Windows applications and class libraries 119
    Converting Web applications..120
    Running Web applications side by side...............................122
    Using Copy and Paste to control conversions...................124
    Using the Visual Studio converters 124
Using Visual Studio 2008 with .NET 2.0 125

Book III: Building Applications 127

Chapter 1: Getting Smart about Smart Clients 129

Switching from Fat Clients to Smart Clients 129
Designing Windows Forms 130
    Creating your first smart client project 131
    Saying, "Hello world!" 132
Taking Command from Control Central 133
    Introducing the control toolbox 134
    Customizing the toolbox 135
    Adding controls to your form 136
Manipulating Controls 138
    Formatting controls 138
    Seeing the snaplines 140
    Locking controls 141
    Setting the tab order 141
    Access a control's tasks with smart tags 142
Using the Properties Window 143
    Setting properties 146
    Responding to events 147

Chapter 2: Building Smart Client User Interfaces 149

Building the Windows Container 149
    Setting common form properties 149
    Creating dialog boxes 150
    Adding menus and toolbars 155
    Creating a Multiple Document Interface 162
    Taking advantage of visual inheritance 165
Laying Out Your Controls 166
    Grouping controls 166
    Setting layout properties 168

Chapter 3: Building Visual C++ Applications 175

Getting to Know Visual C++ 175
Introducing Visual C++ Templates and Wizards 177
Saying "Hello, Visual C++" 179
    Creating managed applications 180
    Creating unmanaged applications 182

Chapter 4: Building Web Applications 187

Getting to Know the Visual Web Developer 188
    Building better Web applications with ASP.NET 188
    Understanding how ASP.NET pages are served 190
    Creating Web sites 190
Saying "Hello, World Wide Web" 191
    Viewing ASP.NET syntax 193
    Adding content 194

Working with Web Sites 196
    Adding new pages 196
    Benefiting from the battle of the server controls........................198
    Changing your view..208
    Running your Web site...212
Using Starter Kits 212

Chapter 5: Using AJAX For Rich Web Pages **213**
AJAX Explained: What It Does and Why You Should Consider
  Using It 213
    ASP.NET postback architecture 214
    Partial page updates 214
Using AJAX Extensions 217
    Creating your first AJAX Web application.................................217
    Adding traditional ASP.NET controls to the form 218
    Using AJAX to implement a partial page update pattern............219
    Updating controls outside UpdatePanel 220
Using the AJAX Controls 222
    Adding the AJAX Control Toolkit to the Visual Studio toolbox....222
    Using AJAX controls from the Toolkit.....................................224

Chapter 6: Laying Out Your Site **225**
Keeping Track of Input with Validation Controls 225
    Adding a validation control...226
    Testing a validation control 227
    Handling multiple validation controls 229
Mapping Out Your Site Navigation 231
    Adding a site map 232
    Adding navigation controls 233
Managing Your Site's Appearance with Themes and Master Pages 234
    Using themes and skins 235
    Mastering master pages 240
Laying Out Web Pages with CSS 245
    Introducing CSS basics 246
    Adding and creating CSS styles 247
    Creating a page template with CSS..248
    Applying styles to controls 251

Chapter 7: Exploring ASP.NET Services **253**
What a Wonderful Provider!..253
Managing State 256
    Understanding view state...257
    Using session state...259
Providing the Perks of Membership 260
    Configuring the default database 260
    Running a site on IIS...261
    Securing membership content 263
    Setting up a login page..265

Getting Personal..268
   Saving visitor settings with profiles............................268
   Letting users customize with Web parts......................269

Chapter 8: Building a Mobile Application **271**

Developing Applications for Smart Devices 272
   Mobile everything 272
   Decisions, decisions...272
   Differences in smart-device development......................275
Saying, "Hello, Smartphone!" 276
   Getting your machine ready 276
   Creating a smart-device application 277
   Changing the application's target platform 280
   Setting up a C++ smart-device application....................280
Building Mobile Web Applications...281
   Setting up the mobile Web site.......................................281
   Exploring device emulators 283
   Automating your connection..285
Accommodating Special Considerations for Smart-Device
   Applications 287

Book IV: Getting Acquainted with Data Access.............289

Chapter 1: Accessing Data with Visual Studio **291**

Accessing Data with Visual Studio and .NET.......................292
   Meeting ADO.NET..292
   Exploring the Visual Studio data toolbox.....................296
Understanding Databases 296
   Introducing relational databases...................................297
   Understanding SQL 298
Dragging and Dropping Data..299
   Preparing your computer to work with data 299
   Adding data to Windows applications...........................300
   Adding data to Web Forms...304

Chapter 2: Show Me the Data **309**

Adding Data Access in Windows Applications.....................309
   Working with the Data Sources pane 310
   Viewing data source objects 311
   Adding data sources 312
   Connecting to databases 314
   Adding controls from the Data Sources pane 318
Getting Your Data in a Bind..321
   Using BindingSource to connect to other data 321
   Using BindingNavigator 323
   Binding by using the Binding property 324

Creating Web Forms That Access Data 326
   Meet the controls 327
   Customizing layout with templates 331
   Working with tasks and properties 334
   Updating data with the DataSet Designer 336
   Getting the view right with the GridView control 340
   Binding to expressions 342

Chapter 3: Working with Strongly Typed DataSets 345

Understanding the DataSet...345
   Discerning typed versus untyped DataSets 348
   Working with untyped DataSets 349
   Flexing your strongly typed DataSets.....................................350
   DataSets and XML, together at last...351
Creating Typed DataSets...352
   Creating a DataSet in a class library.......................................352
   Adding typed DataSets to existing projects............................354
Exploring the DataSet Designer..355
   Meet the players...355
   Building a DataSet of your own 356
   Adding database objects 360
   Going beyond database tables 362
Shepherding Data..364
   Using the TableAdapter Configuration Wizard......................365
   Using the TableAdapter Query Configuration Wizard..................371
Looking under the Hood of a Strongly Typed DataSet 374
   Viewing code...374
   Using partial classes 375
   Viewing the source...377
Using a Typed DataSet..378

Chapter 4: Working with XML 381

Storing Data the XML Way 382
   Creating a new XML file 384
   Describing data in an XML document......................................385
Creating an XML Schema 387
   Building an XML Schema...388
   Using XML snippets 389
Transforming XML with Extensible Stylesheet Language
   Transformations 391
   Writing an XSLT style sheet...392
   Linking an XSLT file to another document 394
   Staying on the path with XPath 395
XML and .NET 396

Chapter 5: Under the Hood with ADO.NET 399

Meet the Players...399

Picking a Provider 401
    Accessing providers..402
    Objectifying the providers 402
Making Connections 403
    Connecting to a database...404
    Closing your connection 407
    Stringing up connections..408
    Building connection strings 409
Using Commands 414
Reading Data with DataReaders.......................................417
    Stepping through data 420
    Retrieving data with the Get accessors............................421
    Retrieving schema info 425
Caching Data with DataSets 425
    Filling a DataSet 426
    Updating data with the Update method 428
    Using TableAdapters 430
    Using transactions..431
Supporting XML with ADO.NET 432
Using ADO.NET in Your Applications 433

Chapter 6: Using Visual Studio with SQL Server 437

Getting Acquainted with SQL Server 2005........................437
    Installing SQL Server Developer Edition 439
    Working with the SQL Server tools 443
    Using the Adventure Works sample 445
Creating Database Projects..446
    Managing scripts with database projects 446
    Handling data with SQL Server projects 453
Managing Your Database with Visual Database Tools.......458
    Using a local database 460
    Adding tables with Table Designer 462
    Adding queries and views 464

Chapter 7: LINQ 467

Using LINQ to Query Integers..467
Finding Active Processes 470
Creating New Objects in the Query 471

Book V: Coding *473*

Chapter 1: Programming with Visual Studio 2008 475

Using the Code Editor...475
    Simplifying your common tasks 477
    Using visual cues 484
    Browsing and navigating code..485

Exploring Visual Basic and C#...486
    Organizing programs...486
    Getting started...489

Chapter 2: Understanding Data Types 493

The Rules of Data Types...493
Making a Declaration 494
The .NET Framework's Common Type System 496
    Understanding the type hierarchy...............................496
    Throwing it on the stack or the heap 497
    Completing your assignments 498
    Popular value types 500
    Popular reference types 502
Creating Your Own Types 503
When There's More than One..506
    Using arrays 507
    Using System.Collections 509
    Iterating through arrays and collections.....................511
    Collections in the real world 513
Converting Types..513
Meet the Nullable Types...516
Browsing Types 517
    Setting the scope..517
    Setting the view 518
    Viewing data types 519
    Viewing source code...522
Accessing Types in Your Source Code 523

Chapter 3: Get Some Class 525

Bringing Programs to Life the Object-Oriented Way 525
What's with Objects? 526
Anatomy of a Class in .NET..530
    Inheriting the services of System.Object 533
    Using classes in your code...534
Using Class Designer..535
    Exploring Class Designer...536
    Designing classes 539
    Viewing existing classes 546
    Working with objects 548

Chapter 4: Wiring Up Events in the User Interface 551

Handling Events..552
    Discovering events...552
    Wiring up events and event handlers 556
Getting a Life Cycle 559
    Understanding life cycles in Windows applications 559
    Understanding Web page life cycles............................561

Chapter 5: Getting Productive with Visual Studio 2008 569

Sending Your Code to Boot Camp..569
    Attending the naming convention..569
    Calling all cars! FxCop to the rescue!..572
    Setting up FxCop as an external tool..576
It's Not Your Father's IntelliSense Anymore 577
    Using code snippets..577
    Stub it out with method stubs...580
    Adding using statements..581
    Objectifying your code..582
Creating XML Documentation..585
Factoring in the Refactoring...589
    Refactoring with Class Designer..591
    Refactoring C#...592

Chapter 6: Exploring Web Services 595

Saying Hello to Web Services..596
    Understanding ASP.NET Web services 597
    Adding a method 600
    Testing Web services 601
Consuming a Web Service...608
    Communicating with a Web service...608
    Finding Web services 609
    Using a Web service in your application.....................................612

Chapter 7: Handling Exceptions and Debugging 617

Structured Exception Handling to the Rescue 617
    Handling exceptions 618
    Using Visual Studio to manage exceptions 624
Understanding Debugging...626
    Enabling debugging...626
    Firing up the Debugger 627
    Debugging for those special circumstances 637
    Debugging generated code...638

Chapter 8: Testing Code with Visual Studio 639

Defining Unit Testing 639
Unit Testing in Visual Studio...641
    Creating unit tests 642
    Running a battery of tests..644
    Writing better code 646
Approaches to Unit Testing 647
    Letting stubs do the tough testing..648
    Simplifying testing with mocking objects...................................649
    The stubbies versus the mockers 650
Using the Object Test Bench 650
Automating Tests with Testing Frameworks 654

Book VI: Going the Extra Mile 657

Chapter 1: Building Solutions and Projects 659
Understanding Solutions and Projects...................659
    The anatomy of a build..................660
    Using the Build menu..................662
    Selecting the active build and platform..................663
    Dealing with compiler errors and output..................663
    Using Configuration Manager 666
    Setting project configurations 669
Managing Your Builds..................672
    Handling Lone Ranger builds..................672
    Creating master builds..................673
    Automating builds..................673

Chapter 2: Deployment Options 675
Understanding Deployment Basics..................675
Deploying Smart Client Applications..................677
    From No Touch to ClickOnce..................677
    Making a Windows Installer 688
Deploying Web Applications..................695
    Using the Publish Web Site utility 697
    Handling web.config files for testing and production 698

Chapter 3: Checking Out Source Control 701
Using Source Code Control with Visual Studio 701
    How source code control works..................702
    Getting ready for source control 702
Binding to a Source Control Provider..................704
    Adding a blank solution..................705
    Adding an existing solution..................705
    Adding a project to an existing solution 707
    Breaking a binding..................707
Performing Common Source Control Tasks..................708
    Retrieving files from source control 710
    Editing source-controlled files..................711
    Checking files into source control..................713
    Retrieving a solution or project from source control..................714
Source Code Control in the Real World..................715
Going Beyond Integration 716

Chapter 4: Building Professional Reports with Crystal Reports 719
Choosing the Right Crystal Edition 719
Creating Reports with Crystal Reports..................720

Connecting to Data Sources...725
    Getting to know your databases...725
    Using Database Expert...726
Using the Crystal Reports Report Designer 730
    Adding content to a report..730

Book VII: Extending Visual Studio 737

Chapter 1: Exploring Visual Studio Extensions 739

Extending Visual Studio...739
    Adding administration and troubleshooting tools......................739
    Downloading new programming tools for Vista and Office..........740
    Trying out development resources and new server products.....741
    Keeping up with developer blogs and other news sources..........743
Exploring AJAX and the Atlas Library...744
Looking Ahead to the Next Visual Studio....................................745

Chapter 2: Being a Team Player with Visual Studio Team System ...747

Introducing the Visual Studio Team System...............................747
Exploring the New Role-Based Editions 750
    Visual Studio Team System for Software Architects.....................751
    Visual Studio Team System for Software Developers 753
    Visual Studio Team System for Software Testers 755
    Visual Studio Team System for Database Professionals................756
Getting to Know Team Foundation Server....................................756
    Accessing Team Foundation Server...757
    Creating a new team project 759
    Browsing with the Team Explorer 761
    Creating work items with Excel 762

Chapter 3: Using Visual Studio with Vista and Office 2007 765

Exploring Vista 765
Getting Started with Vista..768
    Creating Vista applications 768
    Creating workflow applications...773
Getting Ready for Office 2007 775
Going Virtual...777

Index 781

Introduction

*I*f you're like a lot of folks, you were probably a little perplexed by the announcement of the new Visual Studio and .NET platforms. Your immediate reaction may have been, "Oh, no — not another set of tools to learn."

Even if you look forward to the new productivity that Visual Studio 2008 and the new version of the .NET Framework can offer, you may still be wary. Like many experienced developers, you have become comfortable with what you know. A comfortable developer is a productive developer. So you may have put off reading about the new tools as long as possible because you figured that you would find all your usual tasks hidden on new toolbars and menus.

Nothing could be further from the truth.

Visual Studio 2008 is more than just the next version of Visual Studio to use with the next version of the .NET Framework. Visual Studio 2008 continues Microsoft's attempt to position Visual Studio as a tool you can use for the upstream and downstream development activities that sandwich actual code writing. For example, you can use Visual Studio to visually model the entities you want to create in code. Unlike other modeling tools that have only a one-way relationship between the model and the code generation, your code stays synchronized with the model.

To be sure, Visual Studio still excels when it comes to writing code — whether you're writing it yourself or using one of Visual Studio designers to generate code for you. As with the designers in previous versions of Visual Studio, you drag and drop icons from a toolbox onto a design surface. Visual Studio generates the code for you in the background. You can then get up and running in using the new Visual Studio designers and code-generation features by simply reusing what you already know from using previous versions of Visual Studio.

If you're new to Visual Studio, you're getting to the party just in time. Whether you need to write mountains of custom code or create a simple application, Visual Studio 2008 can get the job done. Furthermore, Visual Studio supports the latest approaches to software development, including object-oriented design and programming, componentized applications, and model-driven development.

Visual Studio 2008 provides a dizzying array of editors, controls, designers, and supporting tools for developing software. Getting mired in the details of using these tools is a productivity killer. This book uses plain English to show you how to use Visual Studio 2008 to get busy building software while ignoring unnecessary details. Use this book to focus on the work that pays the bills and to

✦ Improve your individual efficiency and productivity as a developer.

✦ Display proficiency in selecting the right Visual Studio 2008 tools required to develop a solution.

✦ Employ Visual Studio 2008 to guide and improve your individual software-development practices or those of a team.

✦ Navigate the many project types, editors, and designers in Visual Studio 2008.

✦ Increase your confidence and professionalism in using the development environment of choice for developers of solutions based on the Microsoft platform.

✦ Determine the role of Visual Studio in your software development process, whether you're working solo or on a team of 20.

Who Should Read This Book?

A little something for everyone is in this book, whether you're brand-new to software development or an old pro. No matter what your skill level is, you need this book if you see yourself in any of these categories:

✦ **New application developers** — Whether you're a student, a graduate who just landed your first programming job, or a power user looking to expand your horizons, you'll find everything you need to get productive with Visual Studio 2008 Professional.

✦ **Existing .NET developers** — Not sure when you can make the jump to version 3.5 of the .NET Framework? Never fear. You can start using Visual Studio 2008 right now, with previous versions of the .NET Framework. I show you how, in Book II, Chapter 4. Plus, see how to convert your existing applications and use what you already know to get productive.

✦ **Existing developers using other technologies** — Whether you're coming from Visual Basic 6 or Java, you'll find lots of no-frills examples to help you get started with Visual Studio 2008.

✦ **Advanced developers on the bleeding edge** — Even if you've used the .NET Framework since it was in beta, this book shows you how to use Visual Studio 2008 for the latest guidance and best practices in software development.

Visual Studio 2008 Professional is a good development environment for developing software in organizations of all sizes. Use this book if you are any of the following:

✦ **A corporate developer** — Use this book to differentiate yourself or your team members from everyone else in the company. Keep yourself relevant — and your job protected from outsourcing — by demonstrating proficiency in using the latest Microsoft toolset.

✦ **A private consultant** — Use this book to improve your return on investment in the software you use to generate revenue. Visual Studio 2008 has many features to help you stay focused on delivering quality software that fulfills contractual obligations.

✦ **A commercial software developer** — Use this book to see how Visual Studio 2008 can help you improve your ad hoc processes and differentiate yourself from competitors.

Visual Studio 2008 isn't just for developers anymore. Increasingly, software is developed as part of a team effort. Visual Studio 2008 has increased its scope to encompass more aspects of the software development life cycle. As a result, all roles on the team are increasingly affected. Regardless of your role, you may find this book helpful if you fill any of these roles:

✦ Managers, leads, and supervisors need to understand the productivity gains and best-practices guidance offered by Visual Studio 2008. These gains can be useful for improving team processes, as well as for evaluating programmer productivity.

✦ Architects, designers, and analysts will find new tools designed to improve collaboration among analysis, design, and implementation steps.

✦ Developers, testers, and technologists use Visual Studio 2008 to develop and test software. As such, this integral part of the software development process requires you to know how to harness its many features into a set of steps that supports a specific project's development requirements.

About This Book

In this book, you find out how to use Visual Studio 2008 Professional Edition to build these types of applications:

✦ Windows applications

✦ Web sites and Web services

✦ Mobile applications

✦ Native applications using C++

You may be surprised that Visual Studio 2008 has moved way beyond building merely traditional applications. You can use it to build and manage solutions for SQL Server databases, SharePoint sites, Windows Workflow applications, BizTalk packages, and many other enterprise server solutions. Most of these topics are discussed throughout the book.

The message of this book is mostly how to use Visual Studio to improve your personal productivity as a developer, whether you're working solo or as part of a team.

The book focuses primarily on Visual Studio 2008 Professional Edition, although many examples work in other editions, too. Many developers, regardless of the size of their shops, use Visual Studio 2008 Professional Edition. Even if you're using one of the new role-based editions, it provides many of the same features as Visual Studio 2008 Professional.

You can't talk about Visual Studio 2008 without also covering the .NET Framework. This book covers the .NET Framework at a very high level and in the context of demonstrating the features of Visual Studio 2008.

The book is mostly "language agnostic," although (just like in real life) the language best suited for the job is used to demonstrate the material. In most Microsoft shops, there is a preference for either Visual Basic or C#. For that reason, many chapters use Visual Basic examples when they could have just as easily used C# examples.

Despite the preceding statement, this book isn't a learn-to-program book or a language-syntax book. If you're new to programming, consider checking out a beginning programming book or course. If you're a hobbyist or a new programmer, you may find all the tools in Visual Studio 2008 to be overwhelming or outside the bounds of your budget. In that case, consider using a Visual Studio Express Edition, which is free.

Foolish Assumptions

You'll get the most out of this book if you already know how to use basic programming constructs, such as `for` loops and `if ... then` statements. Even though this book doesn't teach you how to program, it does share guidance and tips on the use of best practices. Even if you have never programmed, you can still use the examples in this book to start creating basic Windows and Web applications using Visual Studio 2008.

Here are some other assumptions this book makes about you:

✦ **You have little or no experience with object-oriented programming (OOP).** Becoming an OOP whiz takes many years of hands-on practice.

This book can help lay the groundwork for your OOP training and show you the OOP features in Visual Studio 2008. Book V introduces you to OOP.

✦ **You have little or no experience in using Visual Studio or the .NET Framework.** If you have plenty of experience with Visual Studio or the .NET Framework, you can reuse that knowledge with this version of Visual Studio. Either way, you are walked through all the examples, step by step.

✦ **You don't have formal training in computer science.** This book offers technical explanations of what Visual Studio is doing behind the scenes when it's relevant to helping you understand the topic.

Conventions Used in This Book

This book uses a helpful set of conventions to indicate what needs to be done or what you see on-screen.

Stuff you type

When you are asked to type something, like a command or an entry in a text box, the text looks like this:

```
Type me
```

Menu commands

When you are given a specific set of menu commands to use, they appear in this format:

```
File⇨New⇨Web Site
```

In this example, you should click the File menu, choose the New menu item, and then choose the Web Site menu item.

Display messages

If a specific message is referred to that you see on your screen, it looks like this on the page:

```
This is a message displayed by an application.
```

All code in the book also looks like this.

How This Book Is Organized

This book is organized so that you don't have to read it from cover to cover. To get the most out of the book, use the Table of Contents or Index to find specific topics. The seven mini-books cluster common tasks for which you might use Visual Studio 2008 to develop software. This section provides a brief overview of what you can find in each mini-book.

Book I: Visual Studio 2008 Overview

Book I is a good place to start if you're new to Visual Studio or .NET, or just want a refresher. In Book I, you get the lowdown on the following Visual Studio 2008 and .NET Framework topics:

✦ What Visual Studio is and its role in application development

✦ What .NET is and its role in application development

✦ How Visual Studio and .NET play together

✦ How programming languages fit into the world of Visual Studio and .NET

✦ How to make sense of all the different editions of Visual Studio 2008

Book II: Getting Started

Use Book II to get up and running with Visual Studio 2008. If you already installed Visual Studio 2008 and are familiar with making your way around the Visual Studio interface, you can fast-forward through most of Book II. You find out how to

✦ Install Visual Studio 2008.

✦ Get the lay of the land in Visual Studio 2008.

✦ Use Visual Studio to stay in touch with the Microsoft community.

✦ Plan your upgrade strategy to Visual Studio 2008.

Book III: Building Applications

Visual Studio 2008 is all about creating applications. In Book III, you dig into the kinds of applications you can create. Here are some topics you find here:

✦ Develop Windows, Web, and mobile applications.

✦ Make your Windows applications look and feel like professional applications.

✦ Create applications with Visual C++.

✦ Design Web sites using themes, master pages, site maps, and Cascading Style Sheet layout.

+ Use AJAX for Rich Web Applications.

+ Explore the membership, profiles, registration, and Web parts providers in ASP.NET.

+ Create ASP.NET Services.

+ Create Windows applications and mobile Web sites for smart devices.

Book IV: Getting Acquainted with Data Access

Nowadays, all applications require access to data. Book IV surveys the vast array of data access features in Visual Studio 2008. Even a seasoned ADO.NET programmer should take a fresh look at the new data access code-generation features in Visual Studio because they can help you to

+ Explore data controls, including `BindingSource`, `BindingNavigator`, and the ASP.NET data source controls.

+ Use the Data Sources pane and the Data Source Configuration Wizard.

+ Create and manage connection strings.

+ Use the DataSet Designer to create and manipulate strongly typed datasets.

+ Understand and use `TableAdapter`s and stored procedures.

+ Access data by using objects in a class library.

+ Use XML documents, XML schemas (XSD), XML style sheet transformations (XSLT), and XPath with the XML Editor and the XML Designer.

+ Use the .NET Framework data providers with ADO.NET `DataReaders` and `DataSets`.

+ Explore SQL Server 2005 and SQL Server Projects.

+ Use Visual Database Tools and create database projects.

Book V: Coding

Book V shows you all the major Visual Studio features for designing, writing, and generating code. Whether you're an experienced or novice programmer, you're likely to come across something you haven't seen yet. Here are some topics discussed in this minibook:

+ Use the Code Editor to format and navigate source code.

+ Explore the basic language syntax of C# and Visual Basic.

+ Understand value types and reference types in the .NET Framework.

+ Create custom data types and work with collections.

+ Get a primer in object-oriented programming and explore the anatomy of classes in .NET.

+ Use the Class Designer to create new classes and explore existing ones.

+ Use Visual Studio to explore and consume events.

+ Understand the life cycles of Windows controls and Web controls.

+ Use FxCop to analyze your code.

+ Explore the new IntelliSense features, such as code snippets and method stubs.

+ Refactor code with the Class Designer and the C# Code Editor.

+ Create, test, and consume Web services.

+ Handle exceptions gracefully with structured exception handling.

+ Control code execution and view data with the Debugger.

+ Create unit tests and use the Object Test Bench.

Book VI: Going the Extra Mile

Visual Studio 2008 provides many features that take your productivity to new levels. At some point, all developers need to explore the topics covered in Book VI:

+ Configure and manage the build process.

+ Explore your deployment options for Windows applications and Web applications.

+ Use source-code control with Visual Studio.

+ Create reports with Crystal Reports and SQL Reporting Services.

Book VII: Extending Visual Studio

Visual Studio 2008 is the development platform for many exciting new technologies being introduced by Microsoft. In Book VII, you explore how to

+ Find add-ons from Microsoft and other third parties to extend the features of Visual Studio 2008.

+ Create a rich, Web-based user experience with Atlas.

+ Look ahead to future versions of Visual Studio and how you can start using them now.

+ Explore Visual Studio Team System and Team Foundation Server.

About the Companion Web Site

There is a companion Web site that provides additional material. It can be found at www.visualstudioallinone.com or www.dummies.com/go/visualstudio2008aio. What you'll find is a section for each mini-book. Inside each section are resources links, projects with the source code, and several podcasts. You can ask questions by e-mailing Rick at Rick@JSVentures.com.

Icons Used in This Book

In a book stuffed to the gills with icons, the editors have decided to use — you guessed it — more icons. Luckily, however, the book's icon set acts as visual signposts for specific stuff that you don't want to miss.

Tip icons point out advice that might save you time, trouble, and, quite possibly, cash.

These tidbits are completely optional, but if you're really into the technical side of things, you'll find loads of interesting info here.

Always read the information next to this icon! These icons highlight pitfalls to avoid as you deploy your applications or put the power of Visual Studio 2008 into action.

As its name suggests, this icon highlights stuff that you might want to, well, remember.

This icon points out resources that you can find on the book's companion Web site, which can help you further explore the topic being covered.

Book I

Visual Studio 2008 Overview

The 5th Wave   By Rich Tennant

"We should cast a circle, invoke the elements, and direct the energy. If that doesn't work, I guess we'll have to learn C++ after all."

Contents at a Glance

Chapter 1: What is Visual Studio? 13

Chapter 2: Exploring .NET 21

Chapter 3: Modern Software Development..31

Chapter 4: The Languages of .NET 55

Chapter 5: The Many Editions of Visual Studio 2008 67

Chapter 1: What Is Visual Studio?

In This Chapter

✔ Figuring out Visual Studio's role in software development

✔ Seeing Microsoft's vision for Visual Studio

✔ Saying hello to .NET

✔ Looking at the new features in Visual Studio 2008

What does it take to write software? You need, at minimum, three basic items:

✦ A text editor, such as Notepad

✦ A programming language, such as Visual Basic or C#

✦ A compiler that can convert the programming language into a language your computer can understand

A *programming language* is a language that humans can understand and use to write computer programs. Computers understand only machine language, which is why a compiler has to translate the program from the human-readable programming language into machine language.

If all you need is Notepad to write computer programs, why are so many software-building tools, as well as books about software-building tools, on the market? Why is the software-tools industry a multi–billion-dollar-per-year industry? The reason is that building software with tools such as Notepad would be slow because the code would have to be interpreted (similar to DOS batch files). And companies aren't paying their software developers to show off how well they can memorize language syntax. No, companies are paying software developers to build working software in the least amount of time possible and with the fewest resources, thus making quality development tools essential.

Have you ever opened a program up with Notepad? When you do, all you see is strange-looking characters. It's not human-readable. That's because someone wrote the program with a human-readable language and then compiled it into machine code.

Just to be completely accurate, .NET language compilers don't exactly create machine code. Technically, they create pseudocode (or Microsoft Intermediate Language; MSIL). It's an intermediate step to machine code that is still not human-readable. When the operating system (OS) encounters this pseudocode, it performs a compilation before the application actually runs. This process is known as just-in-time (JIT) compilation.

To be truthful, building software that does more than just say `Hello world` requires more than just writing a few lines of code in a text editor. Who knew that business software could be so complex?

That's where tools such as Visual Studio enter the picture. Visual Studio is a type of software development tool — an integrated development environment (IDE) — that enables you to build software more quickly by offering an advanced editor, compiler, and debugger in a single, easy-to-use package.

The Role of the Integrated Development Environment

Language compilers and all the tools you need to start writing computer programs are available for free. Most vendors provide software development kits (SDKs) that provide all the tools you need to

✦ Write code by using a text editor, such as Notepad.

✦ Convert the code into the machine code that your computer can understand.

✦ Use an integrated Debugger.

✦ Take advantage of online help and IntelliSense.

✦ Use the project templates.

After you run your text file through the compiler, you can execute the file to run your program.

One of the most popular SDKs for software development supports using the Microsoft family of languages, usually either C# or Visual Basic. You can download the Microsoft .NET SDK for free from the Microsoft .NET Framework Developer Center at

http://msdn.microsoft.com/netframework/downloads/updates/default.aspx

If you have Visual Studio 2008 installed, the SDK is already installed.

SDKs are an inexpensive way to play around with new tools or keep your skills updated in new or unfamiliar technologies.

Tools beyond the basic three

Developing software requires all kinds of tools. At the minimum, you need a text editor and a compiler, as described at the beginning of this chapter. As you might guess, however, other tools greatly assist development. In addition to an editor and compiler, you need tools for

✦ **Testing and debugging** — You can step through your code one line at a time to resolve errors with a debugger.

✦ **File linking** — Link all the files you need to build an entire application.

✦ **Configuration management** — Manage the configuration settings for everything from file locations to compiler settings.

✦ **Code editing** — Write code without having to memorize the syntax for a programming language. These tools, which have some intelligence about how to use the program language, can provide suggestions or context-sensitive help as you write code.

✦ **Deployment** — Easily deploy your compiled application to other computers, where it can be executed.

When you download an SDK, you get some of the tools just mentioned, as well as many others. These tools are independent of each other — and the problem you quickly discover is that managing all these individual tools is cumbersome. Plus, many of the tools are command-line tools — you get no point-and-click convenience here.

That's when the idea hits you: "Hey, wouldn't it be great if all these other tools were integrated into a single tool?" That's exactly what an IDE does: It puts all the individual tools — the intelligent Code Editor, the Debugger, and the Configuration Manager — into a single tool where they can interact with one another.

The *Visual Studio 2008 All-In-One Desk Reference For Dummies* companion Web site has a list of the most popular and common tools that you can download from Microsoft. See the Introduction for details about the Web site.

You can download Visual Studio 2008 Express at

```
www.microsoft.com/express/product
```

Enter Visual Studio

The Microsoft IDE is Visual Studio. Visual Studio 2008 is the latest version of this product. Some of the numerous editions of Visual Studio are better suited to individual developers, whereas others are geared toward developing software in a team setting. See Chapter 5 in this mini-book for more details on these editions and how to choose the edition that's right for you.

With Visual Studio 2008, you get these features:

✦ **Programming languages,** such as Visual Basic .NET and C#. See Chapter 4 in this mini-book for more details on the languages you can use with Visual Studio 2008.

✦ **Technologies for building high-quality software,** such as Windows applications, Web-based applications, Web services, and applications for mobile devices (such as smartphones). Book III shows you how to use Visual Studio 2008 to build applications.

✦ **Data access tools** that allow you to access data from any of the popular database management systems, such as Microsoft SQL Server or Oracle. You can also access text files and XML files. Book IV covers the data access capabilities of Visual Studio 2008.

✦ **Tools for debugging, designing, testing, and deploying applications.** Book VI covers many of these tools.

✦ **All the features of the Microsoft .NET Framework,** which provides a rich set of features that allows you to work at a higher level of abstraction. Chapter 2 in this mini-book discusses the evolution of .NET, and Chapter 3 describes the services of .NET.

You aren't restricted to using Visual Studio just for Microsoft .NET; nor is the popular open source editor, Eclipse, limited to Java. You can use Visual Studio to create Java applications, or you can create .NET applications by using Eclipse.

You can use multiple programming languages, thanks to the nature of IDEs. All the various tools that are integrated into an IDE can be created by multiple vendors. Instead of restricting you to just the set of tools that comes from a particular vendor, a *plug-in* allows you to use additional tools created by third-party vendors or the open source community.

To download the Visual Studio plug-in named Grasshopper (which allows you to create Java applications), go to

```
http://dev.mainsoft.com
```

You can find plug-ins for Eclipse at

```
www.improve-technologies.com
```

Why would you want to mix up your languages with your IDE? The answer is productivity. In the same way that using a single tool (such as an IDE) is better than using 12 different tools, using an IDE that you're already familiar with is more productive than switching to a new IDE. So, if you work in a company that develops Microsoft applications primarily using Visual Studio, you can also use it to create Java applications. You don't need to learn to use a whole new tool, such as Eclipse.

A podcast that talks about the compilation process is available on this book's companion Web site. See the Introduction for details about the Web site.

Visual Studio as the Hub

As if the integration of tools weren't enough, Microsoft has something else in mind for Visual Studio: It envisions Visual Studio as the hub for all the server applications with which a developer might interact.

For example, instead of accessing Microsoft SQL Server by using the tools for that server, you can access SQL Server features right inside Visual Studio. The same statement is true for BizTalk. In the future, Visual Studio will integrate with even more server applications. In this way, Visual Studio is the hub of all your interactions with your company's information technology environment — assuming, of course, that you're strictly a Microsoft shop.

Microsoft has another kind of hub in mind for Visual Studio. The company realized that software development involves more than just coding like a madman. In fact, writing code usually involves only one-quarter to one-third of the effort involved in building software. The rest of the project's time is spent gathering and analyzing requirements, creating models that explain those requirements, and refining those models into tangible designs that are ultimately translated into code. After the code is written, the software has to be thoroughly tested, and bugs tracked and maintained.

Many developers use everything from pen and paper to third-party tools to perform the rest of the tasks involved in building software. Microsoft saw an opportunity to bring all this activity under the Visual Studio umbrella. In the past, a developer might have used tools to create models and to automate code testing. Now, all these tools are integrated in Visual Studio, and they work together.

The tools work together so well that a model you create in Visual Studio can even generate code. Visio could do that, for example. The model in Visual Studio, however, updates to reflect changes that you make in the code itself!

Microsoft also realized that software development doesn't happen in a vacuum. The days of hotshot developers isolating themselves for weeks at a time to build the next big applications are long gone. Companies have finally realized that this approach to software development isn't sustainable.

Instead, a company usually has a team of developers, often with specialized roles, working on a project at the same time. By acknowledging that *software developer* means more than just *programmer,* Microsoft has expanded Visual Studio with its Team Foundation version to become the hub of a company's team development activities. See Chapter 5 of this mini-book for more information about the different versions of Visual Studio.

A team using Visual Studio can log a software bug, associate the bug with a section of code, assign the task of fixing the bug to a developer on the team, and track the resolution of the bug. All this happens in Visual Studio!

Microsoft's goal (in addition to increased profits) is for Visual Studio to become *the* personal productivity tool for software developers. In the same way that Microsoft Office has increased the productivity of office workers by freeing them from typewriters and calculators, Microsoft intends for Visual Studio to create a new standard of productivity for individual software developers and the teams on which they work.

The Keeper of .NET

The .NET Framework is the Microsoft platform for creating modern Windows, Web, and mobile software applications. Although the platform provides the steam that makes your applications go, the Visual Studio 2008 development environment allows you to harness that power. The power of .NET is made accessible by Visual Studio, and its widespread use wouldn't be possible otherwise.

Back in the good old days of software development, before frameworks like .NET existed, developers had to write a lot of code to do simple tasks, such as open a file and display its contents on the screen. In an effort to simplify repetitive tasks, many programming languages started providing helper functions that developers could call. Development environments, such as Visual Studio, were often tailored for use with a specific programming language, such as Visual Basic.

Helper functions were created to do just what their name implies: Help developers do something they needed to do. Instead of having to interact with the OS and telling it to find a file and open it for reading, all a developer had to do was call a helper function and then tell the function the name and location of the file to open. The helper function would then "talk to" the OS and return the file's contents. The developer could use another helper function to display the returned contents on-screen. If the developer then decided to give the user the option to print the file's content, another helper function handled all the details of printing the file.

These helper functions improved a developer's productivity and enabled that person to work at a higher level of abstraction. Over the years, companies such as Sun and Microsoft that make software development tools realized that developers needed a little more than just helper functions. Common software development problems had to be solved, such as how to

✦ Manage memory.

✦ Ensure that code is secure.

✦ Allow programs to be moved easily from one hardware platform to another, such as from Windows to Linux.

The solution to this problem was to create a virtual hosting environment in which software applications could run. This host, also known as a *virtual machine* or *runtime engine,* provides services such as file input/output (IO) and memory management to the software that is executed inside the host. The Sun version of the virtual machine is Java. The Microsoft version is the .NET Framework, also referred to as just *.NET* or *Microsoft .NET.*

The .NET Framework is more than just a simple set of helper functions. Applications that are created with the .NET Framework are hosted in a virtual machine called the *Common Language Runtime (CLR).* Therefore, before a computer can run an application that you build by using .NET, the .NET Framework must be installed on the computer. The version of the framework that's installed is the *.NET Framework Redistributable,* which is a free download from the Microsoft Web site. Many new computers have the .NET Framework Redistributable already installed, and most corporations are installing the Redistributable on all their computers.

By running your application in the .NET framework, your application can take advantage of the many services that .NET provides.

As mentioned earlier in this chapter, you can download the Microsoft .NET SDK to get the tools you need to start building software. To fully capitalize on all the development features of .NET, however, you need Visual Studio.

New Features in Visual Studio 2008

Visual Studio 2008 has many new features:

✦ **Support for version 3.0 and 3.5 of the .NET Framework** — Visual Studio 2008 was built to take advantage of all the new features of the .NET Framework. As a matter of fact, Visual Studio 2008 can target .NET Framework 2.0, 3.0, and 3.5. You find out how in Book II, Chapter 4.

✦ **Improved Web development** — In addition to introducing more tools for building and deploying Web applications, Visual Studio 2008 still sports the Visual Web Developer, which uses a local Web server to eliminate the need to have Microsoft Internet Information Services on the development computer. The addition of Ajax as an integral component allows rich, yet responsive applications. See Book III for more information.

✦ **Increased support for developing applications for mobile smart devices** — Visual Studio provides emulators for smartphones and PDAs that allow you to see what your application looks like.

✦ **The use of SQL Server 2005** — Although Visual Studio 2008 can work with older versions of SQL Server and competitors' database management systems, it works best with SQL Server 2008. You can even code stored procedures within Visual Studio. Microsoft SQL Server 2000 Desktop Engine (MSDE) has been replaced with a special developers' edition of SQL Server called SQL Server 2005 Express. There is also a new visual data modeler that makes creating and managing databases much easier.

You can download SQL Server 2005 Express at

```
http://msdn2.microsoft.com/en-us/sql/aa336346.aspx
```

✦ **New controls with smart tags** — Many new controls for Web- and Windows-based development are available, such as the new `ListView` control. Many new controls automate features that previously had to be coded by hand. All the controls feature smart tags that prompt you on how the control is intended to be used.

✦ **Improved code generation and IntelliSense** — New features, such as code snippets and method stub generation, provide intelligent code templates that allow you to fill in your application specification information. New refactoring tools help you transform your code from procedural to object-oriented.

✦ **The capability to work at a higher level of abstraction** — The new visual modeling features allow you to think about your software at a higher level. The models generate the underlying code, which allows you to concentrate on solving your business problems.

✦ **The use of Team Foundation** — In addition to the Professional edition, which is intended for individual developers, the Team Foundation edition of Microsoft Visual Studio provides all the features necessary to manage the entire software development life cycle.

✦ **More integration with MSDN** — Visual Studio 2008 is even more integrated with the Microsoft Developer Network (MSDN).

Chapter 2: Exploring .NET

In This Chapter

✓ Discovering how .NET has evolved

✓ Sneaking a peek at the components of .NET

✓ Looking into the future of .NET

In an attempt to mitigate the increasing complexity of building software, Microsoft released a new set of tools in 2002 (although the first beta was released in July 2000) for building software: the Microsoft .NET Framework.

The .NET Framework provided the plumbing necessary to write complex applications. Perhaps you've gotten some really tough assignments with the expectation that they would be done in a few weeks. Although the business logic seemed fairly easy, the infrastructure wasn't. Some of the more complicated assignments you might have encountered perhaps included programs that had to communicate over the Internet, create graphically appealing reports, or perform complex database access. At that time, those tasks were difficult. Now, the .NET Framework makes them easy — almost trivial.

.NET is a reflection of the latest thinking about, and best practices for, how software should be developed. *Visual Studio* is the premiere toolset that Microsoft created for developing software by using the .NET Framework. Although the road to Microsoft .NET and Visual Studio 2008 has been misunderstood by some at times, most developers agree that using Visual Studio to develop Microsoft .NET applications is a huge productivity boon.

Following the Evolution of .NET

Microsoft released the first version of .NET in 2002. Because Microsoft tried to append the .NET moniker to all its initiatives, from software development tools to enterprise servers to operating systems, .NET initially suffered from an identity crisis. Thanks to the ubiquitous use of the term by Microsoft, however, .NET is now as much a brand as it is a technology.

Five versions of .NET have been released:

✦ **Version 1.0** — Released in 2002, along with the Visual Studio .NET integrated development environment

✦ **Version 1.1** — Released in 2003; includes Visual Studio .NET 2003

+ **Version 2.0** — Released in October 2005 with Visual Studio 2005

+ **Version 3.0** — Released in November 2006 with the Windows Vista OS

+ **Version 3.5** — Released in November 2007 with Visual Studio 2008

Each of these versions represents a milestone in developing software with NET:

+ In version 1.0, all development — whether Windows-based or Web-based, and regardless of the language — was integrated into Visual Studio. Prior to the release of .NET, each Microsoft development tool was a separate product.

+ The object-oriented language C# was created as part of .NET. Visual Basic .NET was completely revamped to be object oriented. Many Visual Basic developers felt betrayed, and Microsoft has had a hard time convincing them to make the leap.

+ Data access was greatly simplified with ADO.NET, and ASP.NET was introduced for developing Web applications. Even though these technologies share the same names as their predecessors (ADO and ASP), that's where the resemblance stops. Like all .NET technologies, ADO.NET and ASP.NET are object oriented.

+ With version 1.1 of .NET, many 1.0 features that either weren't ready yet (such as the Compact Framework for devices such as the Pocket PC) or were available separately from Visual Studio (such as ASP.NET) were completely integrated into Visual Studio .NET 2003.

+ Version 1.1 was more stable and more widely accepted. During this time, the Microsoft .NET brand became diluted from overuse.

+ In the two years between the release of versions 1.1 and 2.0, the *dot-net community* — as the collective of .NET developers is often called — busily wrote applications that demonstrated how powerful .NET could be. Microsoft listened, and many of the suggestions for ways to extend .NET, which were written about in articles on Web sites such as `www.gotdotnet.com` and `www.4guysfromrolla.com`, were implemented as new features in the 2.0 version of .NET.

+ For the release of .NET 2.0, Microsoft dropped the .NET suffix from its non-development software. .NET now refers to just the application platform — the .NET Framework.

+ Visual Studio 2005 matured into more than a mere coding environment and can now manage many aspects of the software development life cycle. The Team System version of the product uses a server-based component as a data repository.

✦ C# established itself as a rock-solid, object-oriented language.

✦ MSDN, the Microsoft Developers Network, became more tightly integrated with the Visual Studio product.

✦ Version 3.0 combined version 2.0 with four new technologies:

- *Windows Presentation Foundation (WPF):* Gave developers the capability to create much richer applications by providing better controls. It helped separate the user interface (UI) from the business logic. It also assisted developers who wanted a consistent UI between desktop applications and Web-based applications.

- *Windows Communication Foundation (WCF):* Provided easier and more robust communications between connected systems. It is built on the Web services technology.

- *Windows Workflow Foundation (WF):* Enabled developers to create workflows by using a new XML-based language named XAML.

- *Windows CardSpace:* This security framework helped users manage identities that can be used in transactions such as Web site log ins.

✦ Version 3.5 builds incrementally on version 3.0. In addition, it adds the following:

- Language Integrated Query (LINQ)

- Integrated use of Asynchronous JavaScript And XML (AJAX)

- Full support for WF, WCF, and WPF

With the latest versions of Microsoft .NET, Microsoft developers can finally stand toe-to-toe with Java developers and know that they can use almost all the same language and development features. And, with Visual Studio 2008, many developers' favorite third-party tools are part of the integrated development environment (IDE), which boosts productivity immensely. At the same time, the Microsoft Team Foundation edition of Visual Studio 2008 draws a line in the sand, positioning Visual Studio and Microsoft .NET as the tools of choice for enterprise software development.

Some folks were skeptical when first encountering .NET. It was at the 2000 PDC (Professional Developers Conference) in Orlando, and nobody knew how to react. For Rick's ruminations about the first couple of years of .NET, you can listen to a podcast at this book's companion Web site. See the Introduction for details about the Web site.

Getting Acquainted with the .NET Components

To fully grasp how all the pieces of .NET work together, you first need a basic understanding of all those pieces. At a very high level, you can think of .NET in terms of

✦ **The .NET Framework** — All the software that makes Visual Studio possible

✦ **The .NET Software Development Kit (SDK)** — All the software that enables you to build software applications by using the .NET Framework

You can download both the .NET Framework and the SDK for free from Microsoft at

```
http://msdn2.microsoft.com/en-us/netframework/
    aa731542.aspx
```

✦ **The programming languages of .NET** — The four languages that Microsoft offers (in addition to dozens more that are available from third parties):

- Visual Basic

- C#

- C++

- J#

  J# is used often by Java programmers who want to do .NET programming right away.

See Chapter 4 of this mini-book for more on these languages.

A language that can be used to develop .NET applications is said to *target* the .NET Framework.

✦ **The technologies of .NET** — All the stuff you can build with .NET, such as Windows and Web applications, Web services, and applications for smart phones

✦ **Visual Studio** — The IDE that puts access to everything in this list at a developer's fingertips

The default languages of .NET are also free in the sense that you can learn the language syntax and use any text editor to write it. The tool that you need to convert the programming language to a language the machine can understand is a *compiler,* which is also free. The compiler is part of the .NET Framework.

To take full advantage of the languages and technologies of .NET in a seamless way, however, you need Visual Studio.

.NET freebies

To start developing .NET applications, all you need is

+ The .NET Framework
+ The .NET SDK

The .NET Framework provides the bulk of the functionality; however, you need the SDK in order to write code for the.NET Framework.

The Microsoft .NET Framework consists of these three components (all of which are free and become resident when the .NET Framework is installed):

+ **Common Language Runtime (CLR)** — The CLR provides a managed environment for running software applications. Developers access the features of the CLR through the Base Class Library (see its upcoming bullet). Some features of the CLR, such as automatic memory management, just happen. (The developer doesn't do anything.)

+ **Common Type System (CTS)** — The CTS sets the rules for how programming languages that use the .NET Framework must behave. New languages can then be developed for use with .NET.

+ **Base Class Library (BCL)** — The BCL is the part of the .NET Framework that developers get to "touch." The BCL enables developers to create Windows- and Web-based user interfaces and to access databases and services of the operating systems.

Because the .NET Framework is complex, a detailed discussion of every aspect of the Framework is beyond the scope of this book. Knowing all the details of the inner workings of the .NET Framework isn't necessary for most developers, anyway, which is part of the reason why Visual Studio is such a valuable tool. It allows developers to access the features of the .NET Framework at a higher level of abstraction and "hides" the implementation details.

If you really want to know more about the inner workings of the .NET Framework, see Chapter 3 in this mini-book.

The .NET Framework SDK provides developers with free tools they can use to access the .NET Framework. In addition to some general utilities, the SDK contains tools to help you

+ Manage configuration and deployment, and configure the .NET Framework.

+ Debug software and manage security.

Language compilers are installed with the .NET Framework.

If you're using Visual Studio 2008, the SDK is installed by default. You might still want to use some of the utilities in the SDK to automate build processes or perform other functions that aren't part of the Visual Studio interface.

If you really want to learn how the .NET Framework works, dig into the SDK and use the Framework command line compilers. In other words, do some development without using Visual Studio. You can gain a much better appreciation of all the time that Visual Studio saves, and you can better troubleshoot problems that occur in Visual Studio.

No free lunch

Yes, the fundamental components of .NET are free. However, if you expect to be productive, you might need to spend some dough. Specifically, get your hands on Visual Studio 2008. With Visual Studio, you're better positioned to take advantage of the languages and technologies of .NET.

Dozens of languages for .NET are available, although only these four are from Microsoft:

 ✦ **Visual Basic** — Visual Basic has a streamlined syntax that many developers find easy to learn and use.

 ✦ **C#** — C# is a rapid application development language. Some of the .NET Framework is written in C#.

   Although Rick likes to use Visual Basic for UI programming, he feels that C# works best for writing business logic.

 ✦ **C++** — You can use this more advanced language to build business applications, operating systems, and language compilers.

 ✦ **Visual J#** — This language is the Microsoft version of Java.

Here are a couple of third-party languages available for .NET:

 ✦ Borland Delphi

 ✦ Cobol

For more specifics on the languages of .NET and how to choose and learn one, see Chapter 4 of this mini-book.

The technologies of .NET are what allow you to build cool applications. With these technologies, you can

 ✦ Build Windows applications by using **Windows Forms.**

 ✦ Build Web-based applications by using **ASP.NET.**

✦ Access data from all different kinds of data stores by using **ADO.NET.**

✦ Share data between disparate systems by using **Web services.**

✦ Create software for mobile devices, such as smartphones, by using the **NET Compact Framework.**

Peering into the Future of .NET

The world of application development has changed significantly in the past decade. The concept of hosting software inside a runtime engine is now the de facto standard for building most software applications — and Microsoft .NET is a major player.

Visual Studio is all grown up from its days as a meager code editor. You can use it now to manage many aspects of software development. As the keeper of .NET, Visual Studio is poised to take .NET into more aspects of the software development life cycle, such as designing and testing.

As Microsoft looks to the future, it's placing its bets on its new OS, Windows Vista. Vista, which is completely different from any of the previous Microsoft operating systems, features these completely redesigned subsystems:

✦ A new presentation layer for building Windows applications, graphics, videos, and documents, called **Windows Presentation Foundation (WPF):** Applications that target the WPF are called Aero applications, the name of the new Vista user interface. Aero might eventually replace Windows Forms, but that replacement is several years away.

✦ A new communications subsystem called **Windows Communication Foundation (WCF):** This manages all communications and frees developers from having to handle the details. The subsystem also supports peer-to-peer communications. You can still use good old-fashioned Web services if you want, but all WCF communications are integrated with Vista.

✦ A new programming model using **version 3.5 of the .NET Framework** to easily access all features of Windows: Previous versions of Windows used a C library interface that was challenging to learn. Previous versions of the .NET Framework provided only limited access to the Windows OS. Microsoft is positioning version 3.5 of .NET as the programming model of choice for Vista applications, which makes it possible to

• Deploy applications to Windows computers and better manage updates to those applications.

• Provide more secure applications by using the security features of Windows.

• Develop more stable applications.

Version 3.5 of the .NET Framework was originally named WinFX. The *FX* is shorthand for the .NET Framework. Microsoft thought the name implied that .NET was "baked" right into Vista. Unfortunately, its customers didn't get it. Microsoft realized that .NET is a stronger brand than WinFX and decided to change the name.

You can download version 3.5 of the .NET Framework at

http://msdn2.microsoft.com/windowsvista/default.aspx

Another exciting area of development is Microsoft Office 2007. Microsoft has expanded the Office feature set to include new server products, such as SharePoint Portal Server. The new name for SharePoint Portal Server is Microsoft Office SharePoint Server 2007. Office includes servers for InfoPath forms and Excel reporting. Of course, all these features are extensible with Microsoft .NET.

Microsoft even released a special edition of Visual Studio: Visual Studio Tools for Office (VSTO). VSTO allows developers to create applications by using the .NET Framework and Office.

The next versions of Visual Studio are expected to more tightly integrate Visual Studio and Microsoft .NET with the new features of the OS. You'll still be able to do all the traditional business development by using Windows Forms.

Don't expect to see the version after Visual Studio 2008, code-named *Hawaii,* until somewhere after 2010. The expectation is that Hawaii will attempt to deliver on the vision behind the Microsoft software factories (without the unions and the time clocks). The idea behind software factories is that developers should be able to use a tool to stamp out similar kinds of software. For example, an invoicing application is an invoicing application. In how many unique ways can you manage invoices? Microsoft wants to build tools that allow developers to draw pictures or models of their software applications. In this example, you might drop a customer, an order, or an invoice on a modeling screen; Hawaii would then build a full-blown invoice application.

To read more about software factories, go to

http://msdn2.microsoft.com/teamsystem/aa718951.aspx

With Microsoft making the .NET Framework an important element of its new OS and Microsoft Office, the future looks bright for both the .NET Framework and Visual Studio. See Book VII for more details on Vista, Office, and the future of .NET and Visual Studio.

Using the New Features in .NET

Here is a list of a few new features in version 3.5 of the .NET Framework that have been long awaited:

✦ **Faster execution** — This includes faster garbage collection, 64-bit improvements, and thread pool performance.

✦ **New additions to the BCL** — Among these added features are the `BigInteger` type, anonymous and named pipes classes, and new `Addin` hosting features.

✦ **Workflow-enabled services** — Developers can build services with the new Workflow Framework. This gives them the capability to simplify development with less need to write communications code.

✦ **AJAX-enabled WCF services** — *AJAX* is a Web development technique for making asynchronous exchanges of small amounts of data between browser and Web service calls from the browser client script to the Web server.

Chapter 3: Modern Software Development

In This Chapter

✔ Understanding the professional approach to software development

✔ Building a software development toolbox

✔ Seeing why component-based software is superior

✔ Peeking at how programs are executed in .NET

✔ Discovering automatic memory management

Even if you've never worked in software development, you've no doubt heard about many of the problems associated with software development projects, such as

✦ Frequent schedule and budget overruns

✦ Software that doesn't do what it's supposed to do

✦ Software that's obsolete by the time it gets finished

✦ Software that ships with security flaws

Over the years, the software development industry has created a number of approaches and tools to help better manage software development. Several of these approaches are discussed later in more detail in the section "Have process, will repeat." However, some of these approaches can be categorized in one of these two main approaches. Most real life situations, though, are a hybrid of the two:

✦ **Ad hoc, or hotshot** — In this approach, characterized by nonexistent development practices, no standard exists for how software is developed. Hotshot programmers often work all night and come in at noon the next day. You usually get no documentation, and only the programmer understands how the code works.

✦ **Rigorous and slow** — As a rejection of the other approach, this one takes an engineering view of software development. The argument is that dotting all your *i*'s and crossing all your *t*'s, and then getting proper sign-off at each step along the way, gives software development a process that's repeatable and — most importantly — accountable.

Unfortunately, the engineering approach adeptly creates mountains of documentation but doesn't adeptly create working software on budget and on time. It also squelches the creativity that truly phenomenal innovations rely on.

After producing many failed projects, software developers have started to get the message that ad hoc approaches are too immature and the rigors of an engineering mentality probably too inflexible. At the same time, most companies have learned that relying on hotshot developers is a recipe for disaster. Instead, many firms now hire developers who write manageable code, rather than someone who can write code faster than anyone else.

Of course, in spite of everyone's best efforts, sometimes a superhuman effort might be required for several days. One particular project that comes to mind involved training that was to take place on Monday. On Saturday, several severe software flaws were discovered that had to be fixed. They were all fixed by Monday morning at 2 a.m. But, as you can likely guess, no one got a lot of sleep that weekend.

This chapter offers an abbreviated history of software development by discussing where the process now stands and how it got there. You also find out about some of the inner workings of .NET as it relates to modern development approaches.

Software Engineering in Action

Over the years, a number of methodologies and tools were created in an attempt to solve the problems involved in software development, with each solution promising to deliver software development projects from the evils of scope creep and second system syndrome. *Scope creep* occurs when additional features that weren't originally planned for find their way into the software.

If you've ever worked on the second incarnation of an existing system, you've no doubt experienced *second system syndrome*. In this case, the project quickly gets bloated because developers and users see so many opportunities to improve the existing system. Unfortunately, many methodologies and tools designed to keep projects on track are not only very expensive, but their implementation also requires significant overhead. As a result, companies spend a lot of money but don't always see results. And, on a personal note, any time that the marketing department has input, runaway feature creep is a real danger.

Now that software developers have had some time to see what doesn't work, they've started to create a living framework of what does work:

✦ **Create repeatable processes.** Rather than treat every project as if it's shiny and new, developers have started to acknowledge that they should take some common steps. Also, by acknowledging that different kinds of software development projects exist, developers are rejecting the notion of a one-size-fits-all process and are instead creating processes that can scale up or down to fit the project.

✦ **Follow best practices.** By creating a body of industry best practices, software developers are sharing and reusing their knowledge of how to solve problems.

✦ **Use more than one tool.** Developers have learned that no single tool can do the job. Instead, a toolbox of tools from many different vendors and the open source community is a better approach than putting all your eggs in one basket with a single vendor.

You can find a list of best practices at this book's companion Web site. See the Introduction for details about the Web site.

Have process, will repeat

When it comes time to start a new software development project, many developers aren't sure where to begin. Depending on your role in the project, the project might not actually start for you until after somebody else completes their responsibilities. Does the project start before or after the kick-off meeting? Should you even have a kick-off meeting — and, if so, who should attend? These questions are answered by the management style and processes that your company adopts for developing software.

Managing a software development project tends to fall somewhere between these two approaches:

✦ **Waterfall** — In the *waterfall* approach, one phase of the project completely ends before another phase can start. In this way, the project "waterfalls" through the stages.

✦ **Iterative** — Projects that are developed *iteratively* go through the same phases multiple times. Developers can move backward and forward through the development phases several times to iteratively develop their understanding of both the problem and the solution.

A process for developing software is like any other process: It's a set of steps you go through to achieve an outcome. Your company has a process for paying bills and entering into contracts. Some business processes are more strictly defined and closely adhered to than others. The same is true for developing software. Some companies have strict rules about how projects are initiated and how they progress. Other companies approach each project like it's their first. This list offers a few of the popular process approaches:

✦ **Software engineering** — The rigorous engineering approach brings an engineering mindset to software projects. A body of standards outlining the kinds of documentation and processes that should support a project is defined in the Institute of Electrical and Electronics Engineers (IEEE) software engineering standards.

✦ **Agile** — This approach embraces change as part of the software development process. In most approaches, *change* is usually considered a bad word. Agile developers work in pairs, create many prototypes of their solutions, and incorporate user feedback throughout the entire process.

✦ **Test-driven** — This newer approach to building software involves building test harnesses for all code. These tests, written from the requirements documentation, ensure that code can deliver promised features.

✦ **Rational Unified Process (RUP)** — The RUP commercial process uses the IBM suite of Rational tools to support software development. Its noncommercial equivalent is the Unified Process (UP). RUP and UP are iterative approaches.

What's common to all these approaches is the acknowledgment of a software development life cycle (SDLC). Most processes account for the fact that all software progresses through a life cycle that has similar stages:

✦ **Initiation** — Project planning and justification get the project up and running.

✦ **Requirements gathering** — After the project is approved, developers start talking with users about what they expect the software to do. Frequently, this phase requires reexamining the planning and feasibility efforts from the preceding stage.

✦ **Analysis** — At this stage, developers analyze the requirements they have gathered to make sure that they understand what end users want.

✦ **Design** — Developers start to work out models that describe what the requirements might look like in software.

✦ **Construction and implementation** — Developers write the programs that execute the models created in the design stage.

✦ **Testing** — The programs are tested to ensure that they work properly and meet the requirements that the end user specified.

✦ **Deployment** — Software is installed, and end users are trained.

✦ **Maintenance** — After the software has passed all its tests and been implemented, it must still be supported to ensure that it can provide many years of service to the end user community.

In a project that uses a waterfall management approach, the software is likely to progress through the stages of the life cycle in chronological order. A project managed iteratively cycles back through the phases while it makes forward progress. On larger projects, people usually fill specialized roles at different stages of the SDLC. One person often fills multiple roles. Table 3-1 lists some common roles in the SDLC.

Table 3-1	Roles in a Software Project
SDLC Phase	*Role or Job Title*
Initiation	Project manager, project sponsor
Requirements gathering	Analyst, subject matter expert
Analysis	Analyst, subject matter expert
Design	Designer, architect (possibly specialized, such as software architect or technical architect)
Construction and implementation	Programmer
Testing	Tester, quality assurance (QA) personnel
Deployment	Installer, trainer, technician, technical architect
Maintenance	Support personnel, programmer, tester

A software project generally doesn't flow like a waterfall through stages of the SDLC, so that's a big reason why the waterfall approach has fallen out of favor. In most cases, the stages of the SDLC are either

✦ **Iterative** — The stages are repeated multiple times throughout the project. For example, developers commonly loop through the initiation, requirements, and analysis phases several times until they get a handle on what they're expected to build. Each loop delves progressively deeper into the details. You'll frequently question the assumptions of the requirements and analysis stages after you start building models in the design stage.

✦ **Concurrent** — Stages often occur at the same time. For example, a group of developers might analyze requirements while another group starts to build the design models. The design group can start to validate (or invalidate) the analysis assumptions.

Choosing a process isn't an either/or proposition. Many teams like to combine the features they like best from several different approaches. For example, your team might like the change-management features of the agile approach. If you have doubts as to which way to go, you can refer to the IEEE software engineering standards.

Regardless of the approach you decide to take, here's some advice to take into consideration:

+ **Use a process — any process.** Homegrown processes are sometimes better than "store-bought" ones. If everyone gets to participate in creating a process, they're more likely to want to see it succeed.

+ **Repeat the process.** A process becomes a process only after it has been repeated multiple times. Doing something once and then abandoning it doesn't create a process.

+ **Improve the process.** You can't improve your process unless it has some means of providing feedback and metrics for measuring. Without metrics, you have no way of knowing when something has improved. If you're unsure how to do this, take a peek at other methodologies to get some ideas.

Practicing what you preach

A body of knowledge has started to develop around software development. Developers realize that many businesses are trying to solve the same kinds of problems. Rather than treat each project as a one-off experience, developers know that elements of the project are common to other projects that they need to develop. When a problem gets solved the same way over and over again, the solution is often referred to as a *best practice*. For a best practice to develop, many people must be trying to solve the same problem. For example, the following list includes several problems that Web site developers try to solve:

+ Providing secure access

+ Logging errors

+ Accessing data

Businesses also need to solve a common set of problems, such as the following:

+ Capture and fulfill orders

+ Manage customer information

+ Invoice and receive payments

Rather than try to solve all these problems on your own, an entire community of developers, authors, and companies are sharing their experiences and guidance on how to approach these problems.

This shared knowledge can be called best practices, design patterns, frameworks, or models. Microsoft's own vision for sharing knowledge includes patterns, practices, and software factories.

In fact, the underlying premise of runtime environments, such as the Microsoft .NET Framework and the Java Virtual Machine, is that all programs need common features, such as portability and memory management. Frameworks, patterns, practices, and models are all knowledge repositories that enable developers to reuse the work of other developers. Modern software development makes extensive use of all these knowledge-sharing tools.

According to Professor Joe Hummel, of Lake Forest College, some of the best practices for software development include these elements:

✦ **Object-oriented programming** — This style of programming makes programs easier to understand and test.

✦ **Components** — Software that's broken into components is easier to deploy. The upcoming section "Components Defeat Monoliths" expands on the benefits of using components.

✦ **Testing** — *Integration testing,* or repeated automated testing, is important in order to see how components work together.

✦ **Code reviews** — Standards are crucial for identifying how code should look. Having peers review each other's code enforces standards and exposes developers to new styles. (As the adage goes, "Two heads are better than one.")

✦ **Prototyping** — You should build your software frequently, not only to make sure that it works, but also to get it in front of end users early and often so that they can validate your progress.

✦ **Tools, tools, tools** — Use tools to help you manage your process and projects. See the next section for more about using tools.

Another best practice to keep in mind is that when it comes to developing software, less is more. A team of four to six developers can usually develop higher-quality software than larger teams can. As team size increases, so does the complexity of keeping everyone in the loop. Keep your team sizes small.

When you're using best practices, you have to keep things in context. The tools and processes you use for building commercial-quality software might not be the same tools and processes you should use to build software for an internal department that has a closed information technology environment.

Building a developer's toolbox

Just like plumbers and auto mechanics have toolboxes, software developers have toolboxes, too. Your software development toolbox should include all the usual suspects:

+ **Integrated development environment** (IDE), such as Visual Studio

+ **Third-party tools** that you like to use for testing or logging

  Many developers take advantage of open source software, such as NUnit for unit testing and Log4Net for logging application errors.

+ **Project management software,** such as Microsoft Project, or maybe even a simple spreadsheet program

+ **Collaboration software,** such as Windows SharePoint Services, that you can use to store your project's artifacts

+ **Source code-control software** so you can keep all your source code safe and secure

You should build a toolbox of resources to which you can turn for advice about how to handle security, build secure Web sites, and face any other kind of software challenge. Sure, you could just "Google" whatever you're looking for. You have more success, though, if you turn to a common set of resources. Here's a start:

+ **Software Engineering Institute (SEI)** — The SEI plays a huge role in defining software engineering. You can find SEI on the Web at `www.sei.cmu.edu`.

+ **Software Engineering Body of Knowledge (SWEBOK)** — The SWEBOK represents the consensus among academicians and practitioners for what the processes for software development should look like. If you have never thought about what it means to engineer software, the SWEBOK is a great place to start. You can download it at `www.swebok.org`.

+ **Microsoft patterns and practices** — A few years ago, Microsoft finally started sharing with the world how it thinks that software developed by using Microsoft tools *should* be developed. Microsoft patterns and practices is a combination of books, articles, software, and other resources that help you write software the way Microsoft believes it should be written. Find patterns and practices at

  `http://msdn.microsoft.com/practices/GettingStarted`

+ **Rational Unified Process (RUP)** — RUP is one of the more popular development processes. Tons of books and articles have been written on the subject, which you can find. Note that you can use the RUP without buying any of the tools that IBM makes to support the process.

✦ **Agile Manifesto** — The manifesto for agile software development can change the way you think about software development. Read the manifesto at `http://agilemanifesto.org`.

✦ **MSDN Webcasts** — The Microsoft Developer Network, or MSDN, presents Webcasts on every kind of software subject imaginable. You can find Webcasts at `http://msdn.microsoft.com/events`. Read more about MSDN in Book II, Chapter 3.

A Webcast that you might find valuable is the series Modern Software Development in .NET, by Professor Joe Hummel. Dr. Hummel has a series on C# and on Visual Basic; you can download his Webcasts from

`www.microsoft.com/events/series/modernsoftdev.mspx`

Much of the advice you find tells you how software *should* be developed, but not so much how it *is* developed. Become familiar with how things are supposed to be done as you continue learning the techniques that other developers use to solve real-world problems.

Working with your partners in development

The most important lesson that software developers have learned is that "it takes a village." Long gone are the days when hotshot programmers were expected, or allowed, to hole up in their offices for weeks while they created the next big application.

Now, software development is recognized as a team effort. Although some teams still place people in specialized roles, such as programmers, people are more commonly filling multiple roles on a project. The lines between analysts, designers, programmers, and testers are becoming more blurred.

The blurred roles are part of the reason that many developers objected to Microsoft's planned release of different versions of Visual Studio based on the roles of a development team. As roles blur, developers are expected to be more flexible. Many diehard programmers experienced the outsourcing of their jobs to India. Those programmers who were flexible enough to learn new languages or new roles found new jobs. Others weren't so fortunate.

Although it would be good to see programming jobs remain in the United States, the harsh reality is that most businesses' profit motives are much stronger than their loyalties to employees or even to the towns and cities where they get their start. The trend in development is for developers to think in higher levels of abstraction, which means being able to take on the role of a designer or analyst.

Not all developers work a 40-hour week, of course, although the length of that workweek is becoming the norm. Many consulting houses are becoming more reasonable about creating a work-life balance for their employees, and an increasing number of developers are maintaining reasonable hours. There are even rumors that developers at the company everyone loves to hate, Microsoft, are working regular hours.

Developers *are* sometimes expected to work extra hours, of course. Sometimes, during the software development life cycle, extra work is required, although it's becoming more of an exception than the norm.

Components Defeat Monoliths

Older software that was developed before the creation of modern software development techniques, or that uses outdated practices or obsolete development tools, is sometimes called *legacy software*. Almost all businesses support at least a few legacy applications. Sometimes, a company's legacy software is limited to a few non-essential utilities used by a single department. At other times, the legacy application is a mission-critical application that must be kept running. Either way, at some point, you'll be asked to support a legacy application.

Here are some of the challenges you might encounter in supporting legacy applications:

✦ **Minimal, missing, or out-of-date documentation** — Although documentation usually isn't the strong suit of most developers, the complexity of some legacy applications can be overwhelming. Newer development techniques favor simplicity and allow the code to be self-documenting. At the same time, more intelligent tools, such as Visual Studio 2008, can update modeling documentation to reflect changes made in the source code.

✦ **Components that are tightly coupled** — A legacy application sometimes has dependencies on other software that can cause the application to crash. Components are considered *tightly coupled* when you can't separate them from each other. If the software is broken into pieces, those pieces, or *components,* can't be reused for other software. New applications must be created, which leads to the same logic being deployed in multiple applications.

✦ **The use of nonstandard protocols** — Software that was developed before the creation of standards, such as XML, often use proprietary file formats and communications protocols. This situation makes it difficult for the software to interoperate with other software.

✦ **"Spaghetti" source code** — The emphasis in coding hasn't always been on readability. As a result, programmers write programs that are cryptic and hard to understand. This can happen for two reasons. One, as you might expect, is from poor planning and a low skill level. The second, though, is because developers sometimes have to write code with limitations that are imposed upon them by situations, such as hardware limitations.

✦ **General deployment and maintenance difficulties** — Many legacy applications were intended to be deployed in much simpler hardware configurations than the ones in use now. Software written in the mid- to late 1990s was probably never intended to be used over the Internet, for example.

You can, of course, find software developed by using all the latest tools and practices that have all these characteristics. However, developers who are paying attention to industry best practices and working with, rather than against, modern tools should find that they have to go out of their way to write bad software.

Software written with these drawbacks is *monolithic*. With a monolithic application, you can imagine the developer sitting down and writing one long piece of source code that does 25 different things. Although the software might work and be efficient, this approach is hard to maintain and scale.

Software developers now focus on

✦ **Readability** — Writing software shouldn't be a contest to see how cryptic you can be. Today's approach favors a programming style that avoids shortcuts and abbreviations, and instead uses an implementation designed to be transparent to future developers. This technique makes the code self-documenting because you don't have to write additional documentation that explains what the code does. One thing to note is that the compiler is very smart when it comes to optimizing the output. Most of the time, clearly understandable code compiles to the same thing that seemingly efficient but cryptic code compiles to.

✦ **Components** — Breaking down software into discrete, manageable components is favored over creating one huge application. Components can be reused in some cases and are easier to deploy.

One reason why these changes have come about is that management has realized that hiring and retaining people is expensive. Even though modern tools and practices might be more verbose and require more processing power than legacy code, using modern tools and practices is acceptable because the power of hardware has increased relative to its price. Buying more hardware is cheaper than hiring additional developers.

Another reason why components have become more important is the expanded use of networking and the Internet. Developers found that by breaking applications into components that could be deployed across multiple servers and connected by a network, they could get around the monolithic applications that didn't run.

Architecture evolution

The 1990s approach to component-based design was most often implemented in a physical, two-tier architecture: In this *client/server* architecture, some part of the application resides on the client, and another part resides on the server. A network connects the client to the server. In most cases, the data resided on the server, while the program to access the data resided on the client.

As time went on, developers became craftier at carving up their applications to run on multiple servers. This approach is generally referred to as *n-tier design* because an application can have any number, or *n* number, of tiers.

In reality, most applications stick with a two- or three-tier design. The standard for many applications is a logical three-tier design that looks like this:

✦ **Presentation layer** — The code for the graphical user interface

✦ **Business object layer** — The code that deals with the logic for your business domain, such as customers and orders

✦ **Data access layer** — The code that handles the process of moving data from the business objects into the data store, such as a database

One reason why this approach is popular is that it allows you to mix and match layers. Suppose that you create a business object layer that recognizes how your company manages its customers and orders. You can then create a Windows-based presentation layer and a Web-based presentation layer. Because all your business logic is specified only once in your business object layer, you have to maintain only one set of business objects. What's more, if you decide that users of smartphones need to be able to access your business object layer, you only have to create an additional presentation layer.

Contrast this approach with a monolithic application, in which you create separate applications for each user interface you need. You then have a Windows application, a Web-based application, and a third application for your smartphones. Each application has its own set of business logic for handling customers and orders. If you discover a bug or your business decides to changes its rules, you have to make changes in all three applications. With a tiered approach, the change is limited to your business object layer.

You still have to test your application before you roll it out. For example, you might need to modify the user interfaces so that they can handle a new field. Still, this technique is much preferred to having three sets of business logic.

This logical three-tier design can be implemented in several ways in the physical world:

✦ **Two tiers** — In this typical client/server model, the presentation and business object layers might reside on the client, while the data access layer resides on the server.

✦ **Three tiers** — In this model, each layer can be hosted on a different computer.

✦ **More than three tiers** — If any of the layers is especially complex or requires significant processing power, each of the layers can further be divided and implemented on multiple computers.

✦ **No tiers** — If all the code resides on a single computer, it can be said to have one tier or no tiers.

Component management in .NET

The unit of deployment in .NET is an *assembly.* In an application with three tiers (physical, business, and data access), as described in the preceding section, each tier would likely have its own assembly. Of course, that's not to say you can have only one assembly per tier. Each tier can have as many assemblies as necessary to adequately organize the source code. The application might look something like the image shown in Figure 3-1.

Figure 3-1:
Each layer in a multi-tiered application is an assembly.

Assembly MyWindowsApp.exe	Presentation Layer
Assembly MyBusinessObjects.dll	Business Objects Layer
Assembly MyDataAccess.dll	Data Access Layer

When an application is compiled, you can choose whether to compile it as an executable or a class library. In a three-tiered application, you might have the following assemblies.

✦ MyWindowsApp.exe — The file you would execute on a client PC. The file contains all the code for the presentation layer. The presentation layer consumes code from the other two layers by creating a reference to that code.

✦ MyBusinessObjects.dll — The class library that contains all the code for your business logic.

✦ MyDataAccess.dll — Another class library that contains all the code for getting data to and from the data store.

The reason that the business objects and data access layers are compiled as class libraries and not as executables is to prevent users from executing the files directly. Because no user interface is in those layers, users have no reason to execute them directly. The assemblies are just libraries of code that you can reference from other code.

To use the code that's in the business objects or data access class libraries, you create a reference in the executable file of the presentation layer, as shown in Figure 3-2.

Figure 3-2:
One
assembly
can use the
code in
another
assembly by
creating a
reference.

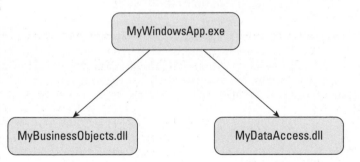

After you create a reference to the assembly, you can access the code inside the assembly. Suppose that MyBusinessObjects.dll contains code to get a customer's address. To display the customer's address on-screen in your application, however, the presentation layer must reference the MyBusinessObjects.dll so that .NET knows where to get the code that gets the customer's address. See Book IV, Chapter 3 to read about referencing a class library.

After the reference is created, your presentation layer can access the code, which might look something like this:

```
MyApp.MyBusinessObjects.Customer customer;
customer = new MyApp.MyBusinessObjects.Customer("Smith, John");
MyDataList.DataSource = customer.GetCustomerAddress();
```

The first line of this code asks that the Customer class in the MyBusinessObjects class library set aside some memory for the customer Smith, John. The code that asks the data record for Smith, John from the database is stored in the MyBusinessObjects class library. Herein lies the beauty of assemblies: You can use this logic to retrieve the customer information in any of the presentation layers you create. Figure 3-3 demonstrates how the presentation layer accesses the code in MyBusinessObjects.dll.

Figure 3-3:
The presentation layer assembly can access the code in the business objects layer.

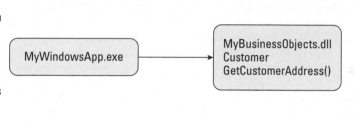

In the figure: MyWindowsApp.exe → MyBusinessObjects.dll / Customer / GetCustomerAddress()

What's in a namespace?

Notice that the code in the code sample is separated by dots, like this:

```
MyApp.MyBusinessObjects.
    Customer
```

Code is organized in .NET by using namespaces. *Namespaces* are a way to hierarchically organize code so that duplicate names can be used without creating confusion for .NET.

In this example, the top of the namespace hierarchy is named MyApp. Within the MyApp namespace is MyBusinessObjects. You might also find MyWindowsApp and MyData Access within the MyApp namespace. You access the code in those namespaces like this:

```
MyApp.MyWindowsApp
MyApp.MyWebApp
MyApp.MyDataAccess
```

Using namespaces this way allows someone else to have the same namespaces within a different namespace hierarchy. For example, if a co-worker has the namespace TeamApp, the namespace might look like this:

```
TeamApp.MyWindowsApp
TeamApp.MyWebApp
TeamApp.MyDataAccess
```

In reality, you probably wouldn't prefix your namespaces with the word *My*. You'd most likely use your company's name or the name of the application. The namespace should allow you to easily identify the code contained within the namespace. Can you guess what kind of code you'd find in the Microsoft.Word or Microsoft.Excel namespaces?

In the real world, you would probably use a customer identification number rather than the customer's name. What if the database had two entries for `Smith, John`? You would need some way to deal with the inevitability of having two or more different customers with the same name.

The second line of code tells .NET to use the customer name `Smith, John` from the preceding line to call the code that retrieves the customer address. The code then assigns whatever value is returned to a data list, which presumably is used to display the customer's address onscreen.

All the software that makes up the .NET Framework Class Library is made up of assemblies. Microsoft created a special place to store all the assemblies for .NET called the Global Assembly Cache, or GAC. (Yes, it's pronounced *gack.*) The GAC stores all versions of an assembly in a folder on your computer. You can store the assemblies you create in the GAC folder or in an application folder. See Book VI, Chapter 2 for more information on installing applications in the GAC.

Before the GAC came along, developers had no easy way to manage the versions of an application, so many people began to refer to the deployment of Windows applications as *DLL hell.* This term reflected the fact that the files that contain the code libraries — DLL files — could quickly become your worst enemy if you realized that you didn't have the right version of the file you needed in order to make your application work.

The term *DLL hell* was originally coined in an article entitled "The End of DLL Hell," which you can read at

`http://msdn2.microsoft.com/en-us/library/ms811694.aspx`

Managed Code Execution

One hallmark of modern software development is the way software is executed on a computer. Previously, software deployment and execution worked like this:

1. A programmer wrote source code, using some higher-level language, such as Visual Basic.

2. Before the computer could understand the source code, it had to be *compiled,* or converted to the native language that the machine understands.

3. Because each kind of computer has its own native language, the code had to be compiled each time the programmer wanted to use it on a different kind of machine. There wasn't much compatibility between machines, so the existing source code often had to be modified to address the subtleties of the new hardware environment, as shown in Figure 3-4.

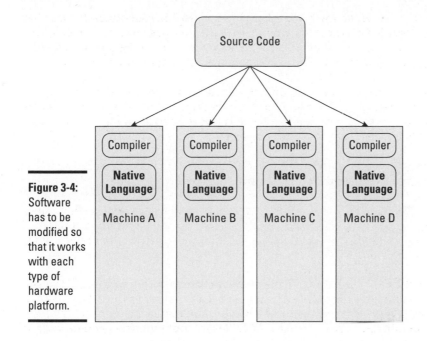

Figure 3-4:
Software
has to be
modified so
that it works
with each
type of
hardware
platform.

4. Because the code was converted to the native language of the machine, the code, when it was executed, had direct access to the operating system and the machine's hardware. This access not only made programming complex, but it also created an unstable operating environment.

The compiled .NET code that the CLR (Common Language Runtime) consumes is known as *managed code.* That's different than native code. *Native code* compiles into something that the CPU can directly use. Managed code must undergo the just-in-time (JIT) process by the CLR before the CPU can use it.

Back in the 1990s, the folks over at Sun had the bright idea of creating a programming language that could work on any machine. The Java Virtual Machine (JVM) that they built creates, on the hardware, a mini-environment that allows the software to be executed without touching the hardware, as shown in Figure 3-5. The JVM was smart enough to know how to make the software work with the hardware. Because of the resulting stable environment and simplified programming, Java was widely embraced.

Ever mindful of its competition, Microsoft sneaked a peek at the Sun JVM and liked what it saw. Over time, all the different Microsoft teams that were working on building development tools and languages started coalescing to work on their implementation of the virtual machine. The Microsoft .NET Framework was born.

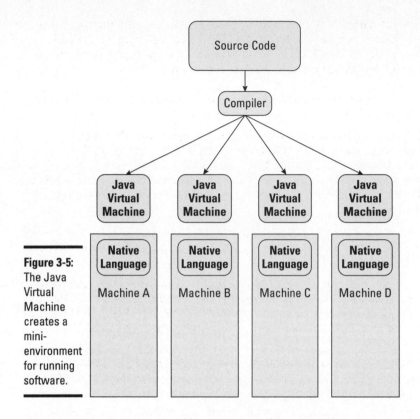

Figure 3-5: The Java Virtual Machine creates a mini-environment for running software.

The CLR virtual machine

Two big benefits of using the Common Language Runtime (CLR) virtual machine are that code is easily portable to multiple hardware platforms and the CLR provides a safer, more stable execution environment.

The CLR provides these additional services for managed code:

✔ Automatic memory management

✔ Verification that code will be executed as intended and hasn't been tampered with

✔ Assurance that managed code can interact with unmanaged code (code running outside the CLR)

✔ Support for multiple versions of the code

See the nearby section "Taking Out the Garbage" for more information on automatic memory management.

The Microsoft version of the virtual machine is slightly different in implementation from Java, although they're similar conceptually. The virtual machine in .NET is the CLR. These steps show how using virtual machines changed the deployment and execution of software:

1. A programmer writes source code, using a higher-level language, such as Visual Basic .NET.

2. The VB.NET compiler converts the source code into Microsoft Intermediate Language (MSIL), which is the native language of the CLR virtual machine. Rather than convert the source code into the hardware's native machine language, the compiler creates intermediate code that the CLR understands. Source code compiled into MSIL is *managed* code.

All language compilers that target the .NET CLR convert the source code into MSIL. Source code from multiple languages can then be used to create a single application.

3. The compiler also creates metadata about the source code. The metadata identifies to the CLR all the assemblies and other files that the source code needs in order to be executed properly. The CLR is responsible for resolving dependencies before the code is executed.

4. When the code's assembly is executed, it's compiled a second time from the MSIL into the native code for the hardware platform on which the code is being executed. This second compiler is the *just-in-time (JIT)* compiler because the MSIL code is compiled just before it's executed.

When code is compiled by using the JIT compiler, the compiled code is stored in memory. If the code is used again, it doesn't have to be compiled again. Rather, the copy of the code that's in memory is used. When the execution is complete, the code is removed from memory. If the code is called again after being removed from memory, it must be compiled into native machine code again by the JIT compiler.

5. Managed code (code that runs in the CLR) is executed within the CLR virtual machine. As a result, the code doesn't have direct access to the hardware and operating system. The code is more stable and less likely to crash the system. To read more about the benefits of running code in the CLR virtual machine, see the sidebar "The CLR virtual machine."

Figure 3-6 diagrams how code is executed by using the CLR.

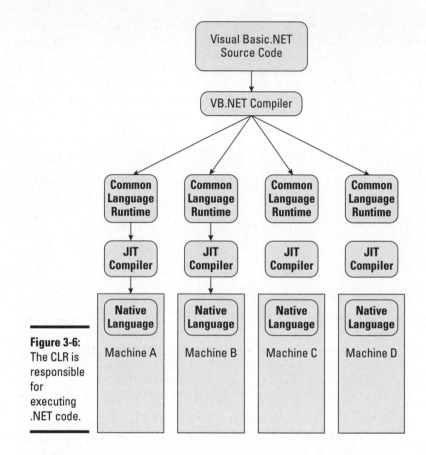

Figure 3-6:
The CLR is
responsible
for
executing
.NET code.

The architecture used by the JVM and Microsoft .NET are part of an international standard for how software execution should be managed. The languages of .NET are expected to conform to the Common Language Specification. The CLR of .NET is the Microsoft implementation of the Common Language Infrastructure.

Taking Out the Garbage

One big service of the .NET Framework is automatic memory management, or *garbage collection*. Microsoft didn't make up this term — it's an authentic computer science term that applies to computer memory.

Before a computer program can use a resource, such as a database, the program must request that the computer set aside memory for the resource. After the program stops using the memory, the data stored in the memory is referred to as *garbage* because it's no longer useful. To reclaim the memory for another use, the CLR determines when it's no longer in use and disposes of it.

A garbage collector, such as the one in the .NET Framework, takes care of the business of asking for memory and then reclaiming it after the program is done using it. The garbage collector collects the garbage memory and then makes it available for use again.

Memory is used to store the resources a program needs to complete tasks, such as

✦ Storing data, such as customer and order records

✦ Displaying information on the screen or sending it to a printer

✦ Opening network connections for sending data

✦ Opening a database connection

✦ Opening a text file

The garbage collector frees the developer from having to perform these tasks:

✦ Tracking how much memory is available and how much is used

✦ Assigning memory to program resources

✦ Releasing memory when resources are done using it

The garbage collector allows developers who are creating a program to focus on customers, orders, and other business domain entities, rather than on memory management. Using a garbage collector eliminates two common errors that developers make when they have to manage their own memory:

✦ **Forgetting to free memory** — When a program doesn't release a computer's memory after the program's done using it, the memory is quickly filled with garbage and can't be used for useful tasks. This is often called a *memory leak*. When a program runs out of memory, it crashes. What's worse is that memory leaks can cause other programs — and even your whole computer — to crash.

✦ **Trying to use memory that has already been freed** — Another common error that developers make is trying to access a resource that has already been removed from memory. This situation can also cause a program to crash unless the developer makes the program test whether the resource is still available. A developer who forgets that the resource is freed probably won't remember to test the resource before trying to use it.

Allocating memory

To prevent you from having to manage the memory yourself, the CLR allocates memory for program resources this way:

1. The CLR reserves a block of memory, which is the *managed heap*.

2. When you ask for resources, such as to open network connections or files, the CLR allocates memory for the resource from the managed heap.

3. The CLR notes that the block of memory is full so that it knows to use the next block of memory when you ask for a resource the next time.

Although you still have to tell the CLR that you need the resource, all the details about which memory addresses are occupied, as well as what they're occupied with, are handled by the CLR on your behalf.

Releasing memory

This section describes how the CLR knows when to release the memory.

The CLR divides the memory in the managed heap logically into manageable pieces, or *generations*. The garbage collector (GC) uses three generations: 0, 1, and 2. The GC operates under the assumption that newly created objects will have shorter life spans than older objects.

Whenever you ask for a new resource, memory is allocated from the portion of the memory block designated as Generation 0. When Generation 0 runs out of memory, the GC starts a collection process that examines the resources in memory and frees anything it deems as *garbage* (anything that's unusable to the application). After freeing as much memory as possible, the GC compacts the memory so that all the remaining resources are placed next to each other in a neat stack. Compacting memory is something the developer doesn't have to do.

How do resources get into Generations 1 and 2? If the GC can't reclaim enough memory from Generation 0 to accommodate your new requests, it tries to move the resources from Generation 0 to Generation 1. If Generation 1 is full, the GC tries to move them to Generation 2. This process is how older resources that are still in use graduate through the generations.

Garbage collection isn't something you should try to control — it happens automatically.

The GC doesn't know what to do with certain kinds of resources after it realizes that you aren't using them any more — for example, resources from the operating system when you work with files, windows, or network connections.

.NET provides you with special methods — named `Close`, `Finalize`, and `Dispose` — that you can use to tell the GC what to do with these resources.

The vast majority of resources you use in .NET don't require you to release them. If you're unsure whether you should make method calls before you're completely done with an object, go ahead and call the `Close`, `Finalize`, or `Dispose` method while the object is still in scope. See Book V, Chapter 3 to get the skinny on how to use methods such as Finalize.

Garbage collection isn't unique to .NET. Java also provides garbage-collection services to its developers. Read the article that describes how garbage collection works in Java at

`www.javaworld.com/javaworld/jw-08-1996/jw-08-gc.html`

You'll find that the process is remarkably similar to garbage collection in .NET.

Chapter 4: The Languages of .NET

In This Chapter

✓ Introducing the programming languages of .NET

✓ Finding the language that's right for you

✓ Figuring out the fundamentals of programming

*P*art of the draw to Visual Studio 2008 is that it has many tools that make software development a breeze. You can fire up Visual Studio 2008 and, in no time flat, have a Windows or Web application that looks very professional.

Take a look at the application shown in Figure 4-1. It looks like any other Windows application you use. Rick created it in about five minutes by using Visual Studio 2008. Even though it uses only two lines of code, it looks like an element from a full-blown Windows application.

Figure 4-1:
Create professional-looking Windows applications by using Visual Studio.

You can download this simple project from this book's companion Web site. See the Introduction for details about the Web site.

Visual Studio provided the Windows Form shown in Figure 4-1, and you just drag and drop the text boxes and buttons onto it. Behind the scenes, Visual Studio takes care of all the programming necessary to make this screen work by using *code generation,* which writes all the necessary code for you. All you have to do is use a designer (a graphical tool) to paint the screens and make them look the way you want. You can also use designers to generate code to build everything from DataSets to reports. Figure 4-2 shows a diagram of code generation.

Use Windows Designer to create a form.

Drag and drop items onto the form.

Visual Studio generates the code.

Generated program displays windows when executed.

Figure 4-2: Visual Studio works behind the scenes to generate the code to make an application work.

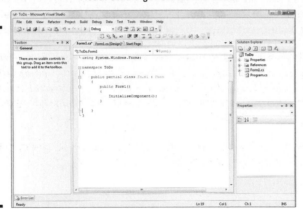

At some point, however, you need for your application to do more than just look pretty. When someone clicks a button or a menu item, your application should respond. This response takes place only when you write the code that tells the application what you want it to do, and that, my friend, requires programming. This chapter introduces the programming languages you're most likely to use.

Looking at the Languages of .NET

Even though Visual Studio can do a great deal for you, it can't write your program for you. When someone clicks a button, you have to provide code that carries out the desired action. The following list describes the kind of code you would have to create to perform a specific task:

✦ **Open a new window and display it to the user.** You have to write the code to open the new window.

✦ **Save a record to the database that the user entered.** You have to write the code to save the record to the database.

✦ **Perform a calculation based on data that the user entered.** You have to — you guessed it — write the code to perform the calculation.

Programming languages have come a long way since they were first created. Modern programming languages are higher-level languages than their predecessors because each line of code that you write gets translated into multiple lines of instructions for the computer.

Before the introduction of higher-level languages and after the era of punch cards and programming in hex codes, programmers wrote programs by using assembly language. *Assembly language* matches computer instructions line for line; in other words, each line of assembly language that you write is equal to one line of computer instructions. Writing programs in assembly languages is time-consuming and requires extensive knowledge of how computers work.

The need for higher-level languages that allow programmers to write one line of code that's translated into multiple lines of computer instructions had to be addressed. These higher-level languages allow developers to be more productive. Also, programmers don't have to be as knowledgeable about the inner workings of computers.

The languages of .NET are all examples of higher-level languages. Microsoft has four default languages for .NET:

✦ Visual Basic

✦ Visual C#

✦ Visual C++

✦ J#

Not all higher-level languages are created equal. Each of the languages of Microsoft .NET has its own set of advantages and disadvantages. The next few sections describe each of these languages, starting with the old standby, Visual Basic.

Visual Basic

In the area of Windows programming, Visual Basic has been around for quite awhile. This language has many devotees, and programmers love it because it's easy to learn, write, and debug. You can easily begin writing workable software very quickly.

You can use Visual Basic to build these types of applications:

✦ For Windows

✦ For the Web

✦ For mobile devices

To make Visual Basic work with the Microsoft .NET Framework, the language had to be totally rewritten. In the process, many long-time Visual Basic programmers felt that Microsoft betrayed the defining characteristic of Visual Basic: It's easy to use.

Even though Visual Basic.NET was introduced in 2002 (although the first beta was released in 2000), many new programs are still written in Visual Basic 6, the last version of VB before it was .NET-ized. Microsoft is aware that many developers still haven't made the move to Visual Basic.NET, so the company included a significant amount of documentation to help Visual Basic 6 developers take the plunge. You can find more information at

```
http://msdn2.microsoft.com/kehz1dz1.aspx
```

Even though the process of moving from Visual Basic 6 to VB.NET has been painful, it places VB on the same playing field as all the other .NET programming languages. Had Microsoft chosen not to rewrite Visual Basic, it might have been on its way to language obscurity.

Rewriting Visual Basic made the language more powerful by turning it into a true object-oriented language. VB.NET allowed Microsoft to implement

✦ Customer-requested changes, such as inheritance and threading

✦ Complete access to all the features of .NET

✦ Interoperability between Visual Basic and the other .NET languages

✦ The removal of features such as `GoSub/Return` and `DefInt`

✦ Consistency between Visual Basic and other languages and language standards

This Hello World code sample from MSDN was written in Visual Basic.NET:

```
' A "Hello World!" program in VB.NET
Module Hello
  Sub Main()
      MsgBox("Hello, World!") ' Display message
  End Sub
End Module
```

Notice how the syntax is simple. Neither extra braces nor punctuation are required. For more information about this code sample, see MSDN at

```
http://msdn2.microsoft.com/3cf7t4xt.aspx
```

Visual C#

Released in 2002 (although the beta was released in 2000) with the first version of the Microsoft .NET Framework, Visual C# was created especially to take advantage of Microsoft .NET features. C# has many characteristics in common with other languages in the C family of languages:

✦ All statements end with a semicolon.

✦ Blocks of code are enclosed in curly braces.

✦ The language is case sensitive.

Check out the C# version of Hello World:

```
using System;
// A "Hello World!" program in C#
namespace HelloWorld
{
    class Hello
    {
        static void Main()
        {
            System.Console.WriteLine("Hello World!");
        }
    }
}
```

The C# version of Hello World requires a few more lines than Visual Basic. Some find the braces a nice visual cue for grouping code together (ourselves included). Other developers see them as a waste of space. For more information on this code sample, see the MSDN documentation at

```
http://msdn2.microsoft.com/k1sx6ed2.aspx
```

The C# language is useful for writing object-oriented applications. In addition to showcasing the .NET Framework, Microsoft created C# to leverage the large numbers of Java, C, and C++ programmers who can easily learn the language. People with a strong C++ and Java background have learned C# is as little as two weeks.

In its attempt to lure Java developers, Microsoft also created the *Java Language Conversion Assistant* (JLCA), which converts Java source code into C#. This tool is good for converting fairly simple programs. Graphical conversions don't work, though.

Visual C++

Visual C++, the most complex language in the Microsoft .NET offerings, is used to develop systems-level software, such as graphical user interfaces (GUIs), device drivers, and mobile applications. Visual C++ is a development environment for creating Windows applications by using the C++ programming language. Visual C++ can create applications that produce native code, or applications that produce managed code.

Here's a C++ version of Hello World:

```
#include <iostream>
// A "Hello World!" program in C++
using  namespace std;
int main()
{
    cout << "Hello World! \n";
    return 0;
}
```

The C++ syntax is bit more cryptic than other high-level languages such as VB or C#. For example, cout is short for console output. C++ syntax isn't as intuitive as other languages.

You can find a simple Hello World example at

http://msdn2.microsoft.com/ms386445.aspx

Check out *C++ For Dummies,* 5th Edition, by Stephen Randy Davis and Chuck Sphar (Wiley), if you're interested in creating C++ applications. You have to get your mind around C++ before you can get any benefit from Visual C++.

You might think of Visual C++ as a development environment inside a development environment. Visual C++ allows you to use C++ syntax to write programs. Visual C++ provides several tools that shortcut the amount of effort required to create a standard C++ application, such as

+ **Compilers** — Target the .NET Common Language Runtime (CLR) and the x86, x64, and Itanium hardware

+ **Libraries** — Include Active Template Library (ATL), Microsoft Foundation Classes (MFC), standard C++, C Run-Time (CRT), and the C++ Support Library to support CLR programs

+ **A development environment** — Supports project management and configuration; source code editing and browsing; and debugging

Visual C++ can be used as part of the Visual Studio IDE, or you can use its individual tools on the command line. Although C++ is a powerful language, it's also the most difficult of all the .NET languages to learn.

J#

J#, which is the Microsoft implementation of Java, allows Java programmers to write Java programs that run in .NET. However, J# programs don't run on the Java Virtual Machine (JVM), and J# isn't supported by Sun, the maker of Java.

Here's a J# code sample of Hello World:

```
package HelloWorld;
// import java.lang.*;
class Program
{
    public static void main(String[] args)
    {
        System.out.println("Hello, World!");
    }
}
```

J# syntax uses curly braces and semicolons, like C# does. If you already know Java, you shouldn't have any problems picking up C#. For a line-by-line explanation of this code, see

```
http://msdn2.microsoft.com/ms240891.aspx
```

Here's what you get with J#:

✦ **A compiler** — Compiles Java-language syntax to Microsoft Intermediate Language (MSIL), the language of the .NET CLR

✦ **A binary converter** — Allows you to convert Java programs for which you don't have the source code to .NET assemblies

✦ **Class libraries** — Provide compatibility with Java Development Kit Level 1.1.4

Because J# syntax is Java syntax, you can use Visual Studio to debug Java applications.

One limitation of J# is that you can't access the features of the .NET Framework by using J# code. If your J# application needs to use the .NET Framework, you have to write an assembly by using another .NET language, such as C#.

For more information about whether to upgrade Java applications to J# or convert them to C#, see

www.javaworld.com/javaworld/jw-01-2003/jw-0103-migration.html

Choosing the Right Language for the Job

One key feature of Microsoft .NET is that in order for a programming language to work with .NET, its compiler must be able to translate the language into MSIL. Because all the languages can be converted to MSIL, all instructions that get executed by the computer should be similar, if not the same.

In other words, the computer doesn't care what programming language you choose when you're writing programs for .NET. MSIL equalizes all the languages as far as the computer is concerned.

Choosing a language should be motivated by human needs, not by the computer. Think about what you're trying to accomplish when you're making a decision. Your goal should be to write programs that do what you want them to do and that your teammates can read and maintain.

As you make your decision, keep these considerations in mind:

✦ **Microsoft has positioned Visual Basic as an easy entry point into Microsoft .NET.** If you're new to programming or new to .NET, Visual Basic is probably the way to go.

✦ **If you have experience with using Java, C, C++, or even one of the scripting languages, such as Perl or Python, you might appreciate Visual C#.** C# syntax is similar to these C-based languages.

AJAX attacks!

An exciting development for JScript is its new Web development methodology: AJAX (Asynchronous JavaScript And XML). It uses JScript and other technologies related to the Web to provide Windows-like user interfaces to Web pages. JScript is no longer just for accessing client-side content. With AJAX, you can use JScript to interact with the server, too.

Getting all the AJAX technologies to work together to create this rich Web experience is a daunting challenge. The Microsoft initiative named Atlas intends to provide a toolbox of Ajax controls. You can start using Atlas right now. Check out the Microsoft Atlas page for more information about Atlas and JScript: http://asp.net/ajax/default.aspx.

✦ **If you're primarily concerned about performance, you probably should choose unmanaged C++.** Beware, however, that you pay a steep penalty in complexity. Also, to truly gain the performance edge, you can't take advantage of the services of .NET.

Unless you have the formal training and practical experience to write tight code (code that doesn't waste any memory or processor cycles), you probably won't gain any performance edge by using C++ without .NET. Don't buy the hype that you can write faster programs with C++. Although that's possible, most programmers don't have the experience to do it. Furthermore, in the amount of time you spend trying to figure it out, you could already have the program finished in Visual Basic or C#.

✦ **If you ever build Web applications with ASP.NET, you already use JScript.** Many of the ASP.NET server controls generate JScript to make them work. You should also try JScript whenever you need to get something done in a jiffy, such as when you parse a text file. You might find that you like the laid back style of JScript better than its more buttoned-up brethren.

For a Microsoft comparison of the languages of .NET, see

```
http://msdn2.microsoft.com/czz35az4.aspx
```

Most people are choosing between Visual Basic and C#. Your historical use of one language over the other often dictates your choice. People who use Visual Basic tend to be less interested in aesthetics and more interested in getting the task done so that they can move on. C# programmers often speak of the purity and expressiveness of the language.

Having used both, we offer these highlights:

✦ Visual Basic is easy and fast to learn, but it is more verbose.

✦ C# lends itself well to object-oriented development, and far more code examples are available than for VB.

Typically, there are two parts to ASP.NET code. The first is the presentation page with the HTML-like objects. The second is the code that responds to page events, known as code-behind. Rick likes to use C# for all his ASP.NET code-behind files, as well as use C# for all his business objects.

Becoming a Good Programmer

Learning how to program is probably more important than choosing a language. By learning how to program, you can move fluidly among languages.

All programming languages share common themes, or *programming constructs*. You should become familiar with some of the common programming constructs:

✦ Declaring variables

✦ Understanding variable types

✦ Knowing when and how to use variables for loops

✦ Controlling the flow of your program by using conditional If...Then statements

✦ Using arrays to store a series of data, such as the months in a year

After you finish this book and have the skills, you can get more advanced information. If you're interested in moving beyond this book, start with the course catalog for the Computer Science department at your local college or university. You're more likely to find "what it means to program a computer" courses that cover programming fundamentals. Be careful about applied technology courses or books that teach a specific language, such as Visual Basic or Java. If possible, take a look at the syllabus or talk to the professor or lecturer before signing up. Explain that you want to get more out of the course than just language syntax.

Building software involves more than just writing code, and software development consists of several phases. This book shows you how to use Visual Studio 2008 in many of these different phases.

After the requirements gatherers gather, the analysts analyze, and the designers design, at some point, somebody has to write some code. If you want that person to be you, you need to learn language *syntax,* or the grammar of a programming language.

Learn the syntax

If you want to learn language syntax, consider *not* starting with Visual Studio because Visual Studio doesn't possess any special "magic" for creating applications. Visual Studio lets you develop software at a higher level of abstraction. As a result, Visual Studio generates a lot of code for you — code that you probably won't bother to take the time to understand. To be frank, the code that Visual Studio generates probably isn't the code you want to learn from.

Writing cryptic code isn't the goal. Rather, the goal is to write code that's easy to read and maintain. The code generated by Visual Studio can be complex and abstract. It's good code because it's highly reusable, but it can be hard to understand.

Some people argue that you shouldn't bother trying to memorize syntax. As long as you know the basic programming constructs, you should be able to program in any language. Don't forget that companies want developers with high levels of productivity, which usually translates into using some kind of tool, such as Visual Studio.

Write your own code

When Rick was in college, the recommended order for taking courses was to start by using a text editor and manual compiler in a language like C; learn a C-derivative scripting language, such as JavaScript or Perl; and then learn Visual Basic .NET with Visual Studio.

Many of Rick's classmates, however, chose instead to start with the VB.NET course and work their way backward. Unfortunately, they started with the easiest way to develop software. When they got to the harder courses, where you had to manage your own memory and create your own data structures, they were lost.

Rick had the same experience with *Structured Query Language* (SQL), which is the language of databases. When he first started working in information technology, he was doing a lot of report design, mostly relying on report-design software to graphically build his database queries. Report designers, such as Crystal Reports, generate the SQL necessary to pull the data out of the database.

When Rick started doing application development, he realized quickly that his SQL skills were deficient. He immediately started making himself write out all his queries by using a native SQL tool. After he stopped relying on code-generation tools and started writing his own SQL, he quickly learned the language. Now he gets to choose whether using a code-generation tool is the best way to go, given the task that he needs to accomplish.

Here's the bottom line: You need to know some language syntax if you expect to become more than a copy-and-paste coder. Here are some tasks you can undertake to become a better programmer:

+ Learn the principles of object-oriented design and programming.

+ Learn the basic programming constructs that are common across all programming languages.

+ Pick a language, and learn how that language implements object-oriented programming and basic programming constructs.

+ If you know that you will work with a specific technology, such as Windows Forms or Web services, commit yourself to learning as much as possible about that technology and its best practices development.

+ Practice, practice, practice.

If you invest in these techniques, your code will be well written, no matter what.

Spend some time in other language studies

If you want to separate yourself from the development pack, pick a language and spend four consecutive weekends working with that language outside the Visual Studio environment. This technique is also a good way to teach yourself a new language, such as Java.

You might also need to familiarize yourself with some of these other languages and technologies:

✦ **Standards for Web development** — such as HTML, Cascading Style Sheets (CSS), JavaScript, and AJAX — to help with troubleshooting

✦ **File formats,** such as XML and really simple syndication (RSS), so that you can transfer data between disparate systems

✦ **Query syntax** of SQL for writing stored procedures and queries for reading and updating databases

✦ **Regular expressions for manipulating text**

✦ **Windows Active Directory and security**

✦ **Object models for Office applications** (such as Word and Excel) and **server applications** (such as SharePoint and BizTalk)

Chapter 5: The Many Editions of Visual Studio 2008

In This Chapter

✔ Sorting out multiple editions of Visual Studio

✔ Deciding which edition is right for you

✔ Choosing the right MSDN subscription

✔ Getting acquainted with Visual Studio Team System

✔ Looking at the future of Visual Studio

Sorting out all the different editions of Visual Studio is mind-numbing. Microsoft provides a Visual Studio edition for developers at all levels of experience, from absolute beginners working on their own to large-scale development teams with thousands of members.

This chapter helps you make sense of the different editions of Visual Studio so that you can decide which one's right for you. Read on to discover the features of Visual Studio Team System and read about the future of Visual Studio.

Making Sense of the Visual Studio Editions

Although Microsoft still offers the stalwart Standard Edition and Professional Edition, the company expanded its offerings to reach out to everyone from novices all the way to high-end, large-scale development teams.

Visual Studio offers these editions, listed in order from the simplest to most complex features included in the edition:

✦ Visual Studio Express Editions

✦ Visual Studio Professional

✦ Visual Studio Team System

One of the major goals of Microsoft with Visual Studio is to enable personal productivity for all software developers. This list describes which edition you should use if you're in one of these groups:

✦ **You're a hobbyist, student, or novice.** Check out the Express Editions. You should also consider it if you don't know whether to upgrade from a previous version of Visual Studio.

✦ **You do occasional development work by yourself.** You should appreciate the get-down-to-business features of Visual Studio Professional Edition.

✦ **You create applications that use Office as their user interface (UI).** Visual Studio Professional Edition makes creating Office applications dead simple.

✦ **You're a professional software developer who works alone or on a small team.** Visual Studio Professional is geared toward you.

✦ **You're part of a larger development team.** Your team should check out Visual Studio Team System.

Visual Studio Express Editions

The Express Editions of Visual Studio, which are less feature-rich than the other editions, are perfect for students, hobbyists, and folks just getting started. Rather than have one large, overwhelming soup-to-nuts software development tool, the Express Editions come in many flavors, depending on what type of development you want to do:

✦ **Web** — Create Web applications and Web services by using Visual Web Developer 2008 Express. This edition enables you to write code by using C# or Visual Basic, and provides editors for HTML and XML. It has a built-in Web development server that you can use to build and test your Web application. Numerous starter kits are provided to help you jump-start your projects.

✦ **Database** — Most applications are data-centric. SQL Server 2005 Express Edition is a fully functional database management system that integrates with Visual Studio. You can use Visual Studio to create databases, write stored procedures, and add data. Although database sizes are limited to 4GB, the databases are compatible with SQL Server 2005. So, the skills you acquire are transferable to SQL Server 2005 and SQL Server 2008.

✦ **Windows** — Express Editions for Windows development includes editions for Visual Basic, C#, C++, and J#. Use Visual Basic, C#, and J# for building Windows applications, console applications, and reusable components. You can use C++ to create both managed and unmanaged code. To build Web applications, use the Web Developer Edition.

Most beginners will find that they make few compromises by using Visual Studio Express Editions. You get these benefits:

✦ **Your developed applications are fully functional.** They aren't watered-down versions.

✦ **As your needs grow, you can scale up to one of the higher editions.**

✦ **Your skills are transferable to other Visual Studio editions.**

✦ **The price is right.** You can download all the editions for Web and Windows development for free from the Microsoft Web site. Microsoft originally planned to charge $49 for the products after a period of being free for one year, but it decided to make the products free permanently. SQL Server 2005 Express Edition is also available at no charge.

Download these tools at

```
http://msdn.microsoft.com/vstudio/express
```

The Express Editions of Visual Studio are an excellent choice for students or anyone wanting to learn how to program. These choices weren't always available: As a result, students used tools like Microsoft Access, which is worlds away from enterprise-level database management tools, such as SQL Server. Kudos to Microsoft for providing these tools and making them affordable.

Visual Studio Tools for Office

Visual Studio Tools for Office is no longer a separate edition, as it was with Visual Studio 2005. Although VS Tools for Office is now part of Visual Studio 2008, it's worth talking about separately so that you can appreciate all that it brings to the table. Visual Studio Tools for Office (VSTO, pronounced *vis*-toe) is geared toward independent software vendors and systems integrators who build custom Windows and Web applications for the Microsoft Office system.

With VSTO, you get these features.

✦ Visual Basic and C# programming languages

✦ Integrated visual designers for working with databases

✦ Advanced debugging tools

✦ Designers geared toward building applications that use Word, Excel, and InfoPath as their UI

Visual Studio Professional

Visual Studio Professional is geared toward professional .NET developers. This edition provides even more advanced visual designers and a tightly integrated toolset. If you develop software for a living, this edition is the one you're most likely to use.

Visual Studio Professional provides these features:

✦ All the Microsoft .NET programming languages

✦ Integrated visual database tools

✦ Designers for XML schema design and XML style sheets

✦ Advanced debugging and deployment tools

✦ The ability to develop stored procedures, functions, and triggers for SQL Server 2005 or SQL Server 2008

✦ Crystal Reports

Visual Studio Team System

The Visual Studio Team System (VSTS) has created a lot of buzz. VSTS is important because

✦ It acknowledges the specialized roles that people play on large development teams.

✦ It's the Microsoft attempt to move into the tools space of the software development life cycle.

VSTS isn't a product; rather, it comprises four client editions of Visual Studio:

✦ Visual Studio for Architects

✦ Visual Studio for Database Professionals

✦ Visual Studio for Software Developers

✦ Visual Studio for Testers

The Team System also includes a server component — the Team Foundation Server (TFS) — that enables collaboration among the client editions of VSTS.

Because VSTS is a huge departure from the previous editions of Visual Studio, this chapter digs into it in more detail in the upcoming section "Developing When It's a Team Effort."

Choosing the Right Edition

With numerous editions of Visual Studio and numerous features strewn across these editions, finding an edition that's right for you can seem daunting. The answer almost always comes down to money (somebody else's, you hope).

Because pricing can change, specific prices aren't quoted here. However, here's a ballpark idea of how much these editions cost:

+ **Express Editions** — Free

+ **Professional Edition and Visual Tools for Office** — Between $550 and $800

+ **Team Editions** — Between $2,300 and $5,500; available only with a Microsoft Developer Network (MSDN) subscription

+ **Team Foundation Server** — About $3,000 for the required separate server license

The price you pay depends on whether you're upgrading or paying full retail price.

Helping you decide whether to choose the Team System is beyond the scope of this book. Chances are that your employer will make the decision. Nevertheless, as a .NET developer, you have a responsibility to understand the role of the Visual Studio Team System. Check out the later section "Developing When It's a Team Effort" for more information.

Subscribing to the Microsoft Developer Network

Microsoft changed its licensing for MSDN with the release of Visual Studio 2008. MSDN provides you with access to Microsoft operating systems, server software, and productivity applications for development purposes.

You can choose from three levels of MSDN subscriptions:

+ **Academic** — For about $800, you have access to all the Microsoft operating systems, such as Windows Server 2003 and Virtual PC.

+ **Professional** — For about $1,200, you get Visual Studio 2008 Professional Edition, SQL Server 2005, SQL Reporting Services Developer Editions, and Virtual PC, in addition to access to Microsoft operating systems.

✦ **Premium** — This provides you with the Virtual PC, SQL Server 2005 Developer Edition, and Visual SourceSafe operating systems; server products, such as BizTalk and SharePoint; and Microsoft Business Solutions software, such as Great Plains and Microsoft CRM. You also get to choose an edition of Visual Studio. The price you pay for a subscription depends on the edition of Visual Studio you choose:

- *Visual Studio Professional* — This costs about $2,500.

- *Visual Studio Team Edition for Software Architects, Testers, or Software Developers:* Choose one of these editions for about $5,500.

- *Visual Studio Team Suite* — For about $11,000, you get access to all three Team Edition editions of Visual Studio.

The Visual Studio Team Editions and Team Suite with MSDN Premium Subscriptions include the TFS Workgroup Edition with five client-access licenses. The full-blown TFS product requires an additional server license.

Check out the latest pricing at

http://msdn.microsoft.com/vstudio/howtobuy

For more details about what you get with each level of MSDN subscription, go to

http://msdn.microsoft.com/vstudio/products/subscriptions

MSDN subscriptions provide you with development and testing licenses only. You can't use the software you download from MSDN in a production environment. You can only test or develop.

A single MSDN subscription provides you with ten licenses for each product you download. You may install the software on ten computers one time or ten times on one computer. Only individuals with MSDN subscriptions may use the software. In other words, each member of your team needs an MSDN subscription if they plan to access software downloaded from MSDN. The licenses are valid forever, even if you choose not to renew your MSDN subscription. You may continue using the software for testing and development after your MSDN subscription expires.

Each developer requires a separate MSDN subscription. Just because a single MSDN subscription has ten licenses doesn't mean ten people can use it. Each person must have his own subscription.

Weighing your options

After you have an idea of what the pricing structure looks like and what you can get for your money, look at these scenarios to help you decide which edition of Visual Studio 2008 is right for you:

+ **If you want to save some money or mentor a young programmer:** Be sure to download all the Express Editions for free. Even if you think that you'll never need them, download them now at

    `http://msdn.microsoft.com/vstudio/express`

    You never know when you might need a free edition of a relatively powerful development tool.

+ **If you're a college student:** Check with your school bookstore or your department to see whether your school has an academic license with Microsoft. When Rick was in college, he could pick up a copy of Visual Studio Professional for $25 — only $5 per disc. Your school might have a similar license.

+ **If you work in a small- to medium-size business or have your own consulting business:** Choose Professional Edition if you want to use Crystal Reports Designer to create reports. If you don't mind having separate tools for Web-based and Windows-based development, you can save a few bucks and go with the Express Editions. If you intend to do more development work, choose the Professional Edition. You benefit from using Class Designer and being able to access remote databases.

+ **If you do extensive development work with Office:** Visual Tools for Office is a no-brainer — except, of course, that you get all the VSTO tools with the Visual Studio Team Editions. If you do only occasional Office work, stick with Professional.

Consider these scenarios as you decide whether to choose MSDN:

+ **You're a professional developer or have developers working for you.** Spring for the MSDN subscriptions. Consider it part of the cost of doing business. Most developers expect to have access to these tools.

+ **You're a one-person show or you're on a budget, so maybe you can get around buying an MSDN subscription.** In that case, buy a copy of Virtual PC or VMWare and then install evaluation versions of whatever software you need to work with. You can save images of the evaluation versions if you need to reuse them for other projects.

Evaluating your alternatives

Over the years, Rick has worked in a number of Microsoft shops. This type of shop tends to go with "all things Microsoft" and not even consider alternatives. Microsoft has many useful products, but they're not always the right choices for all situations. They're often the easiest choices, though, especially if your infrastructure and development efforts are heavily invested in all things Microsoft.

Before you commit yourself and spend huge sums of money, ponder some alternatives:

✔ Supplement Visual Studio Professional with open source tools, such as NUnit for unit testing and FxCop for static code analysis.

✔ Consider using *Project Mono,* an open source version of C#.

✔ Explore alternative development environments, such as Eclipse and NetBeans.

Nothing about using Visual Studio is inherently bad. Just remember that when you frame solutions by using Microsoft tools, or any vendor's tools, you narrow your choices and lose perspective. By evaluating alternatives, you can see whether Visual Studio is the way for you to go.

As you make your decision about which tools to use, remember that Microsoft has a profit motive for selling Visual Studio. Why is it giving away the Express Editions? The answer is that all marketers know that a trial offer is the best way to sell something.

When you decide to go with Visual Studio, you're not only getting a productivity tool, but you're also joining a community. Using Visual Studio and Microsoft .NET will no doubt shape how you approach solutions development.

Developing When It's a Team Effort

With Visual Studio 2008, Microsoft continues the move that Visual Studio 2005 started and moves into the realm of software development life cycle tools in a big way. The products that Visual Studio Team System comprise were tested on thousands of user projects. Although your project might not be as big, you might still benefit from the team collaboration features.

This section walks you through some of the features of Visual Studio Team System, starting with managing a project, defining its architecture, and building and testing the software. The features of Visual Studio Team System are expanded on in Book VII, Chapter 2.

Managing projects with Team System

Although the Team System doesn't include a special edition for project managers, it allows project managers to use Visual Studio to

✦ Create a project portfolio where all the project's artifacts can be accessed.

✦ Select a development methodology from predefined templates.

✦ Create a process-aware project portal complete with reports for evaluating progress.

A project manager views a project by using Portfolio Explorer in Visual Studio or the project's portal. By using Visual Studio Portfolio Explorer, you can

✦ Maintain source code control.

✦ Query work items, such as requirements, tasks, and bugs.

✦ View progress reports.

✦ View project documentation.

✦ Review build information.

Because the project portal is SharePoint-driven, you can open artifacts (such as requirements checklists) in Excel and modify them. Multiple people can then work on these artifacts and check out, publish, synchronize, and enforce data-validation rules.

Visual Studio Team System allows other team members to perform these tasks:

✦ **Create and edit work items, associate work items with source code, and view work item queues.**

✦ **Import work items into Microsoft Project and publish the updated project plan back to the project portal**

✦ **Sync updates from Project, Excel, and the portal to a team database.** This allows developers to use Visual Studio to view and update work items.

✦ **Work with the tools and views that make them productive** (analysts in spreadsheets, developers in Visual Studio, and project managers in Project). Other stakeholders can use the project portal to monitor progress.

✦ **View reports on scheduling, bug fixes, and requirements churning.** Project managers can also drill into the reports to see underlying data.

✦ **Collect data throughout the course of a project as developers work.** You don't need to hold numerous status meetings and have people fill out and compile paperwork.

Architecting software

By using the designers in Visual Studio Team Edition for Software Architects, architects can

✦ Model applications and the target technology environment

✦ Validate that the applications will run in the target environment

These tools are geared primarily toward service-oriented architectures, such as Web services.

One incredible tool in Visual Studio Team Edition for Software Architects is Application Designer. You can use it to

✦ **Lay out applications that provide and consume new or existing Web services.**

✦ **Connect applications to build multi-tier applications.**

✦ **Show how to map applications to the logical datacenter design.**

✦ **Turn the diagram into code.** Application Designer creates projects and classes, and stubs out methods.

✦ **Keep code synchronized with design in both directions.**

Application Designer is beneficial for these reasons:

✦ Architects can see the visual structure of an application.

✦ You can lay out the design without committing to code, also known as *whiteboarding.*

✦ You don't have to abandon design tools when you move to code.

✦ You can validate designs long before anything gets built.

The Software Architect Edition also provides a *Logical Datacenter designer,* which allows architects to map the applications they design to a technology environment that will host them. The Logical Datacenter allows architects to

✦ **Query their technology infrastructures.**

✦ **Define settings and constraints for the servers in their datacenters, such as what kind of authentication the server allows and whether the application needs scripting.**

✦ **Determine whether their applications will run in the target environment.**

✦ **Use graphical tools to change the configurations of applications or host environments.**

✦ **See communication pathways in the datacenter.**

✦ **Drag, drop, and validate.** The system does real-time validation to tell you what applications can be hosted on a given server.

✦ **Specify settings and constraints in Application Designer for a component.** Remember that models and validation work both ways.

The Application and Logical Datacenter designers open communications between designers, developers, and information technologists.

Developing software with Team System

The Software Developers Edition provides additional tools for testing and code analysis:

✦ **FxCop** — Enable code analysis and receive warnings as part of the build process.

✦ **Performance tools** — See which functions are called most often.

✦ **Unit testing and code coverage** — Test your code and use visual tools to see how much of your code is tested.

Testing with tools

The testing tools in Visual Studio Team Edition for Testers allows users to

✦ Record tests and generate scripts based on browser sessions.

✦ Play back scripts.

✦ Create validation rules to test for conditions on the Web pages.

✦ Bind data to tests so that you can use data-driven tests (for example, to search for keywords in a database).

✦ Use a load-test wizard that groups counters and offers guidance so that you're not guessing what each counter does and which one to use

Collaborating with Visual Studio Team Foundation

The Team Foundation Server enables the collaboration features for the Team Editions of Visual Studio Team System. With TFS, you get these features:

✦ Source code control

✦ Work-item tracking

✦ Build automation

✦ Team communications

✦ Reporting

The integrated check-in procedure using TFS includes

+ **Channels for managing source code, work items, check-in notes, and policy warnings**

   Check-in notes are fields the project manager creates that the developer is required to fill out before check-in.

+ **The option to create a standard check-in process that can be reviewed**

+ **Access to the compare feature so you can expedite code reviews by comparing two different versions of source code**

+ **Policy warnings notification**

   For example, that check-in must be associated with a work item

Taking a Visual Look Ahead

The Microsoft vision for the current editions of Visual Studio 2008 started culminating in 1999. While you're busy mastering the program's current set of tools, wisely look ahead at some technologies that will influence Visual Studio near and far:

+ **Visual Studio, code name** *Hawaii* — The next version of Visual Studio, due sometime in 2010, will provide tools for targeting the latest Windows OS and bring software development to a new level.

+ **Software factories, domain-specific languages, and dynamic services initiatives** — All these terms show Microsoft's direction for software development and information technology management.

+ **Windows Live, Office Live, Visual Studio Live** — These services are the latest move from Microsoft into subscription-based software.

See Book VII for more information on how you can start using preview editions of many of these technologies right now.

Book II

Getting Started

The 5th Wave — By Rich Tennant

"Our automated response policy to a large company-wide data crash is to notify management, back up existing data and sell 90% of my shares in the company."

Contents at a Glance

Chapter 1: Installing Visual Studio Professional 81

Chapter 2: Browsing Visual Studio 89

Chapter 3: Making Connections with Visual Studio 103

Chapter 4: Upgrading .NET 115

Chapter 1: Installing Visual Studio Professional

In This Chapter

✔ Using multiple versions of Visual Studio

✔ System requirements for Visual Studio

✔ Installing Visual Studio

✔ Launching Visual Studio

As long as you have adequate hardware resources to run Visual Studio, getting it up and running is a straightforward process. You might spend all day waiting for the software to install, but then you can stay up all night playing around with all its cool new features. This chapter gives you the details.

Installing Versions Side by Side

You can use any release version of Visual Studio, from Visual Studio 6.0 through Visual Studio 2008, on a single computer. Of course, we don't recommend opening all the versions at one time. Here are the versions:

✦ Visual Studio 6.0

✦ Visual Studio 2002

✦ Visual Studio 2003

✦ Visual Studio 2005

✦ Visual Studio 2008

If you installed beta versions or any other prerelease version of Visual Studio 2008 (code name Orcas) on your computer, you must uninstall them completely before installing the final version of Visual Studio 2008. For more information, see

http://msdn2.microsoft.com/vs2008/bb964521.aspx

As a rule, after you open an older version of a solution in the next version of Visual Studio, you can no longer open the solution in the previous version. For example, if you open a Visual Studio 2002 solution in Visual Studio 2003, you can no longer open the solution in Visual Studio 2002. Be sure to have backups of all your solutions before you start opening them in different versions.

Taking a look at all the .NETs

You can have multiple versions of the Microsoft .NET Framework installed on a single computer. These versions of .NET have been released:

✦ Version 1.0, released with Visual Studio 2002

✦ Version 1.1, released with Visual Studio 2003

✦ Version 2.0, released with Visual Studio 2005

✦ Version 3.0, released with Windows Vista, Windows 2008, and products such as System Center Operations Manager (SCOM)

✦ Version 3.5, released with Visual Studio 2008

Version 3.0 of the .NET Framework was released in late 2006 with Windows Vista. You'll be able to target version 3.5 with Visual Studio 2008. Book VII, Chapter 3 highlights some of the features of Windows Vista and the newest versions of .NET. In the past, the version of .NET released with its corresponding version of Visual Studio can be used with only that version of Visual Studio. With Visual Studio 2008, however, you can target any .NET version.

Chapter 4 of this mini-book talks about targeting multiple versions of the .NET Framework with Visual Studio 2008.

Getting help from Visual Studio 2008

Until now, each version of Visual Studio provided its own help collection. These collections were quite large, and often combining them with the Help Collection Manager was more convenient. Visual Studio 2008 features a local help database, but emphasis is placed on online resources. There is an option during installation if you want only local help. You can manage these with the following steps.

To use Help Collection Manager in Visual Studio 2008, follow these steps:

1. **Choose Options from the Tools menu.**

The Visual Studio 2008 Options dialog box opens.

2. **Expand the Environment folder and select Help.**

   General, Dynamic Help, and Online options are displayed.

3. **Open the Online options.**

4. **Choose your settings.**

   The Online Help dialog box for the Visual Studio 2008 displays, as shown in Figure 1-1.

5. **Select the online resources you want for your help system.**

Figure 1-1:
The Visual
Studio 2008
Combined
Help
Collection
Manager
shows you
how to
combine
your help
collections.

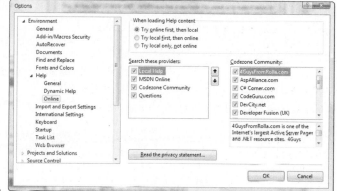

Meeting System Requirements

Here are the minimum requirements for installing Visual Studio 2008 Professional Edition:

✦ A 1.6 GHz Pentium III+ processor

✦ 1GB RAM

✦ 5GB disk space

✦ A CD-ROM or DVD-ROM drive

You also need one of these operating systems:

✦ Windows 2003

✦ Windows XP Professional

✦ Windows Vista Professional

As usual, the minimum requirements probably aren't where you want to be. Although Visual Studio will surely run on a computer using the minimum requirements, you'll probably be able to drink a cup of coffee between mouse clicks, which defeats the purpose of using productivity software. In reality, you probably want at least a 1.8 GHz dual-core processor with at least 2GB RAM. If you don't think that you have enough hardware and can't upgrade, consider using the Express editions of Visual Studio.

If you're stuck running Visual Studio 2008 on an older machine that doesn't meet the requirements, you can add more memory to the system. Rick is currently run Visual Studio 2008, SQL Server 2005 Developer Edition, and all the other software you see in this book on a machine with 2.4 GHz dual-core processor and 2GB of memory.

You must have Administrator rights to the computer on which you wish to install Visual Studio 2008. User rights are sufficient to run Visual Studio 2008.

Stepping through the Installation

Installing Visual Studio is fairly simple. After you insert the DVD or CD, you see the Visual Studio 2008 Setup screen.

Installing Visual Studio is more involved than clicking `setup.exe` and walking through a wizard. Visual Studio requires a number of components to install in order to be fully functional. Installation involves the following tasks:

1. **Install Visual Studio and version 3.5 of the .NET Framework.**

2. **Install the help documentation.**

3. **Check for updates at Windows Update.**

To start the Installation Wizard and install Visual Studio 2008, follow these steps:

1. **Click the Install Visual Studio 2008 option on the Visual Studio 2008 Setup screen.**

Setup loads the installation components and displays the Welcome screen.

2. **After the setup components are loaded, click Next on the Welcome screen.**

The Microsoft Visual Studio 2008 Setup start page is displayed.

The start page displays a list of components that are already installed and a list of components to be installed.

3. **On the start page, select the I Accept the Terms of the License Agreement check box to indicate that you read and agree to the license agreement.**

4. **Click Next.**

   The options page displays.

5. **On the Options page, select the radio button indicating whether you want the Default, Full, or Custom installation. Then specify the installation path.**

   In the lower-right corner, note the table that displays disk space requirements. This figure shows installing Visual Studio on the C: drive. You can, however, install to any active hard drive on a computer that has sufficient hard drive space. Visual Studio installs components on your system drive, even if you choose to install Visual Studio on another hard drive.

6. **Click Install on the Options page to start the installation.**

   The install page displays.

   If you chose the Custom installation from the Options page, you see the Next button rather than Install. After clicking Next, you can select all the individual components you want to install.

   The Install page displays the progress of the installation along with useful information about new features in Visual Studio 2008. After all the components are installed, the finish page is displayed.

   If everything installs properly, the Finish page displays a message stating that setup is complete. If any errors occur, they're displayed on this page.

7. **Click the Finish button to close the Installation Wizard.**

   After the wizard closes, the Visual Studio 2008 Setup window displays again.

8. **You can click the link to install the product documentation.**

   After the documentation is installed, the Setup window is displayed again.

9. **Click the link to check for service releases and install any service release that Windows Update displays for you.**

Launching Visual Studio for the First Time

When you launch Visual Studio for the first time, you see the Choose Default Environment Settings dialog box. You can choose a set of environment settings based on the kind of development work you do.

Your choices for development settings are

✦ General

✦ Visual Basic

✦ Visual C#

✦ Visual C++

✦ Web

The settings you choose determine the headings you see on the start page and the types of project templates you see when you create a new project and set your default programming language. The General option is a good choice because you might develop applications in more than one language. Development settings also let you customize menus, toolbars, and help documentation to suit the choice you make.

This book uses General Development Settings for all examples. In most cases, the keyboard shortcut commands are offered, when available. The keyboard shortcuts are pretty consistent across the development settings.

You can use the Import and Export Settings Wizard to change your development settings. To start the wizard, follow these steps:

1. **Choose Tools⇨Import and Export Settings.**

The Import and Export Settings Wizard displays, as shown in Figure 1-2.

2. **Select the Reset All Settings radio button, and then click Next.**

The Save Current Settings page is displayed.

3. **To save your settings so that you can reuse them later, click Yes and then specify the filename and directory. To discard your settings, click No.**

4. **Click Next to save or discard your settings.**

5. **On the next page that displays, choose a default collection of settings from the list there, as shown in Figure 1-3.**

6. **Click Finish.**

Visual Studio changes your settings.

You can also use the Import and Export Settings Wizard to import settings that you saved from another machine or that a friend sent you.

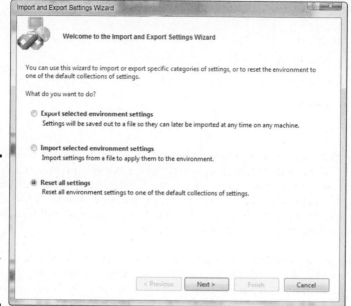

Figure 1-2:
Use the Import and Export Settings Wizard to change your default settings.

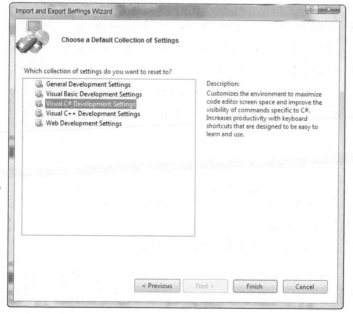

Figure 1-3:
Select a collection of settings to reset as your default settings.

Chapter 2: Browsing Visual Studio

In This Chapter

✓ Becoming familiar with the development environment

✓ Understanding solutions and projects

✓ Browsing properties, servers, and code

✓ Painting forms with visual designers

*W*ith Visual Studio 2008, you have access to hundreds of commands, tools, and designers. The Visual Studio Code Editor and Object Browser put the Microsoft .NET Framework's thousands of methods at your fingertips. You have everything you need to build powerful, world-class Windows applications and Web sites — if only you knew where to begin.

Making Your Way around Visual Studio

When you first open Visual Studio 2008, you see a screen that reflects a Visual Studio 2008 installation that uses the general development settings.

Note these feature:

✦ **Start page** — This page is your dashboard for navigating Visual Studio 2008 and connecting to resources in the .NET community. The start page includes these features:

- *Recent Projects* — A list of recently opened projects in Visual Studio 2008; also includes links to open and create new projects and Web sites

- *Getting Started* — A list of links to resources to help you get started using Visual Studio 2008

- *Visual Studio Headlines* — A list of news relevant to Visual Studio 2008

- *MSDN News* — A list of headlines from MSDN, the Microsoft Developer Network

✦ **Solution Explorer** — This task pane on the right side of the screen lists open solutions and the projects they contain.

✦ **Class View** — This tab on the task pane in the lower-right corner of the screen displays a tree view of classes contained in the open solution.

✦ **Server Explorer** — This task pane on the left side of the screen provides a tree view of the servers you're working with. The Server Explorer is automatically hidden by default, but it appears if you hover your mouse over it.

✦ **Toolbox** — This task pane on the left side of the screen provides groups of controls that you can drag and drop onto visual designers in Visual Studio 2008.

✦ **Menu bar and Standard toolbar** — These two elements provide access to additional tools and windows.

Because most of the task panes, windows, and menus in Visual Studio 2008 are *context sensitive,* they display different options depending on what kind of application you're developing. For example, the toolbox displays text boxes and buttons that work in Windows applications when you open them.

Visual Studio provides many windows in addition to the ones displayed by default. You can display all the windows by using the View menu, as shown in Figure 2-1.

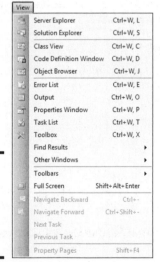

Figure 2-1:
Use the
View menu
to open
additional
windows.

Dealing with Windows Galore

Visual Studio 2008 displays content in two basic Window styles:

✦ Tabbed documents, such as the start page

✦ Task panes, such as Solution Explorer

You can treat anything that opens as a tabbed document like a task pane and vice versa. Here are your options for working with windows in Visual Studio 2008:

+ **Floating** — The window floats within the environment.

+ **Dockable** — The window can be docked in a certain area of the screen.

+ **Tabbed Document** — The window is placed in the tabbed-documents area.

+ **Auto Hide** — The window is toggled between minimized and restored.

+ **Hide** — The window is hidden from view.

To access the window options, follow these steps:

1. **Right-click the title bar of the window you want to manipulate.**

2. **Choose the window option from the contextual menu.**

You can also access the window options by using the Window menu.

If you change your mind or make a mistake and want to restore all the windows to their original states, follow these steps:

1. **Choose Window⇨Reset Window Layout.**

A confirmation box appears and asks you to confirm that you want the windows reset to the default layout.

2. **Click Yes.**

All windows are restored.

Docking windows

When you make a window dockable, you can use positioning anchors to position it on-screen. To dock a tabbed document, follow these steps:

1. **Right-click the tabbed document and choose Dockable from the contextual menu.**

The window appears as a floating window.

If the Dockable option is already selected (a check mark appears next to it), the window is ready to be docked. Go on to Step 2.

2. **Position your mouse over the title bar of the window and start dragging the window.**

While you drag, position anchors appear on-screen.

3. **Move the window toward a position anchor.**

   As you hover over a position anchor, a shadow is placed where the anchor will position the window.

4. **Release the window over the position anchor.**

   The window is docked.

Working with tabbed documents

You can display any window as a tabbed document by simply right-clicking the window's title bar and choosing Tabbed Document from the contextual menu. When more than one document is displayed, you also have the options of creating horizontal and vertical groups of tabbed documents. To create a vertical tab group, follow these steps:

1. **Right-click the tab of a tabbed document.**

2. **Choose New Vertical Tab Group from the contextual menu that appears.**

   The documents are displayed side by side in the viewing area.

 You can create horizontal groups by choosing New Horizontal Tab Group. To remove the groupings, right-click the tab of the tabbed document and choose Move to Previous Tab Group from the contextual menu.

Working with multiple documents

You can display tabbed documents as separate windows. To change this setting, follow these steps:

1. **Choose Tools⇨Options.**

   The Options dialog box appears. The General options in the Environment area are displayed by default.

2. **In the Window Layout section, select the Multiple Documents radio button, as shown in Figure 2-2.**

3. **Click OK to save your settings.**

Tabbed documents are displayed as separate windows. You can right-click the title bar of a document window to view a contextual menu with display options.

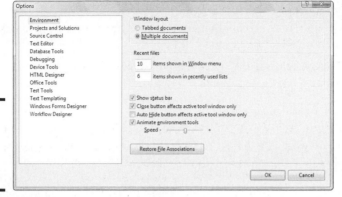

**Book II
Chapter 2**

**Browsing
Visual Studio**

Figure 2-2:
Display
documents
in separate
windows.

Managing windows

Whether you choose to display content in tabbed documents, separate windows, or floating task panes, you can always use the Window menu to manage your open windows. Figure 2-3 shows the list of commands available on the Window menu.

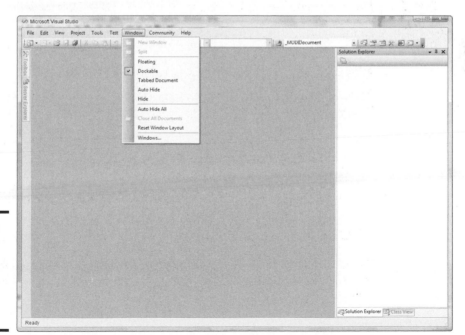

Figure 2-3:
Use the
Window
menu to
manage
your open
windows.

Building Solutions with Visual Studio 2008

Exploring Visual Studio without any files open is different from exploring it when you have an application open for editing. Most windows and task panes aren't populated with options until files are open. Although you can use Visual Studio to open individual files (such as XML files), in most cases, you use Visual Studio to create new Windows and Web applications, and edit existing applications.

Applications you create with Visual Studio 2008 require many different kinds of files in order to work properly. The files that make up an application are *items.* Examples of items include

✦ Source code files

✦ References

✦ XML and HTML files

✦ Visual designer settings

✦ Data files

The items that make up an application are grouped into containers so that the items are easier to manage. Visual Studio 2008 provides two types of containers:

✦ **Project** — A group of items that combine to create a component of a solution, such as a Windows project

✦ **Solution** — A collection of projects and items that combine to create a deployable solution

You use the New Project dialog box, as shown in Figure 2-4, to create new projects and solutions.

Here's how to invoke the New Project dialog box:

✦ Use the Recent Projects area of the start page.

✦ Choose New⇨Project from the File menu.

✦ Use Solution Explorer to add a new project to an existing solution.

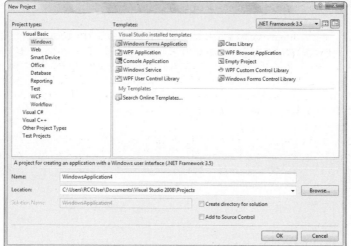

Figure 2-4:
Create new
projects and
solutions
from the
New Project
window.

Exploring the New Project dialog box gives you some idea of the kinds of applications you can create using Visual Studio 2008. To open the New Project dialog box by using the Recent Projects area, follow these steps:

1. **Click the start page. If it isn't displayed, choose View⟹ Other Windows⟹Start Page.**

2. **Locate the Recent Projects area of the start page in the upper-left corner of the screen.**

3. **Click the Project link, to the right of the Create option.**

The New Project dialog box appears.

The New Project dialog box (refer to Figure 2-4) has three areas:

✦ **Project Types** — Displays the programming languages and kinds of projects you can create for each language.

✦ **Templates** — Displays the list of project templates available for each type of project.

Visual Studio uses project templates to know what files to create when you tell it to create a certain kind of application. For example, when you use the New Project dialog box to create a new Windows application, the Windows Application project template tells Visual Studio to create a Windows project with a new, blank Windows Form.

✦ **Project and solution details** — Allows you to name the project and tell Visual Studio where you want it saved, and allows you to specify whether you want a solution created and what to name it. By default, Visual Studio always creates a solution to contain your projects.

Here's how to create a new project by using the New Project window:

1. **In the Project Types tree, expand the Visual Basic project type category.**

A list appears of project types that you can create by using the Visual Basic language.

2. **Click the Windows project type.**

A list of project templates that are available for Windows applications appears in the Templates window.

3. **Click the Windows Forms Application template.**

4. **Enter a filename for your new Windows application in the Name text box.**

5. **Accept the default file location or click the Browse button to select a new location.**

6. **Click OK to create the new project.**

A new Visual Basic project is created, and a blank Windows Form is displayed in the Forms Designer.

Using the Solution Explorer to manage solutions and projects

The *Solution Explorer* graphical tool helps you manage solutions and projects. When you open a solution or project, a graphical representation of the solution and the items within it are displayed in the Solution Explorer. In Figure 2-5, Solution Explorer displays the new Windows application created in the preceding section.

Solution Explorer provides many commands you can use to manage your solution. To view a list of commands available for managing a solution, follow these steps:

1. **Right-click the solution in the Solution Explorer.**

The solution is the topmost item in the tree. A contextual menu appears.

2. **Choose a command from the menu.**

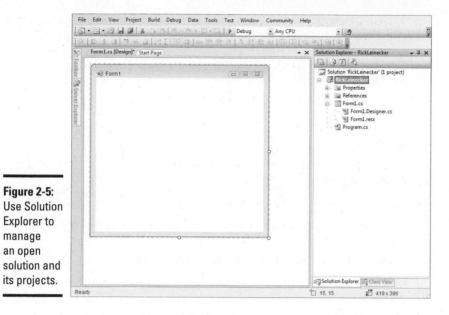

Figure 2-5:
Use Solution
Explorer to
manage
an open
solution and
its projects.

You can also right-click a project in Solution Explorer to view a contextual
menu of project commands. Figure 2-6 shows the contextual menus for solutions (left) and projects (right).

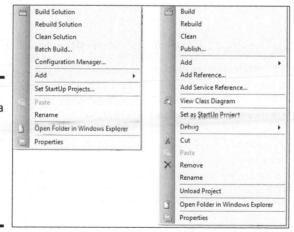

Figure 2-6:
Right-click a
solution
(left) or
project
(right) to
display its
contextual
menu.

On each of the contextual menus, the Add menu item expands to display a list of items you can add to your solution or project. Items you can add to a solution include

✦ New and existing projects

✦ New and existing Web sites

✦ New and existing items, such as XML files

✦ Folders for organizing items

Items you can add to a Windows project include

✦ New and existing items, such as Windows Forms, classes, and XML files

✦ Folders for organizing items

The items that you can add to other kinds of projects are specific to the type of project. For example, you can add Web Forms to Web sites.

You can right-click the items within a project to display contextual menus, too. For example, when you right-click a Windows Form, you see a menu that displays the following commands to

✦ View Code

✦ View Designer

✦ View Class Diagram

Working with solution and project menus

When you open a solution in Visual Studio 2008, the menu bar displays project-specific menus, including these three:

✦ **Project or Website** — Manage Windows projects or Web sites.

✦ **Build** — Build and deploy your solution.

✦ **Debug** — Use the Debugger.

Depending on the kind of project you open, you might also see menus for Data, Format, and Layout. When you're using Visual Studio 2008, don't forget to look up at the menu bar occasionally to see additional commands that you might not have known exist.

Using the Properties Window

Almost everything in Visual Studio — from controls to solutions — has properties. Properties can be quite simple, such as a few settings options, or can be composed of complex configuration wizards. The Properties window is displayed by default as a task pane on the right side of the screen.

You can view the properties of an item in several ways:

✦ Right-click an item and choose Properties from the contextual menu.

✦ Click an item and choose View⇨Properties Window.

✦ Click an item and press F4.

Figure 2-7 shows the Properties window for a text box control for a Web site. To read more about using properties, see Book III, about building applications with Visual Studio 2008.

Book II
Chapter 2

**Browsing
Visual Studio**

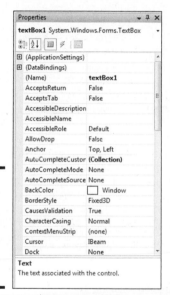

Figure 2-7:
Set the properties for an item via the Properties window.

Browsing Servers

Use Server Explorer to view server configuration details and to connect to data sources. Server Explorer is displayed by default as a task pane on the left side of the screen. You can use Server Explorer for these tasks:

✦ Create and manage data connections.

✦ Drag and drop items, such as event logs and message queues, from a server to the design surface.

✦ View configuration details about services running on a server.

Figure 2-8 shows an example of Server Explorer. See Book IV, Chapter 3 for more information about using Server Explorer to manage data connections.

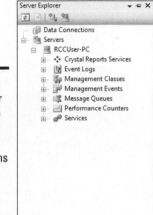

Figure 2-8: Use Server Explorer to manage data connections and other server resources.

Writing Code with the Code Editor

Building applications requires writing code. For this purpose, Visual Studio 2008 provides a *code editor,* which is a special kind of word-processing program. Unlike the word processor used to write this book, a code editor is tuned to write programs. Although a regular word processor includes features like table formats and bullet points, the Visual Studio 2008 Code Editor has these features:

✦ **Auto-complete** — The Code Editor provides an intelligent authoring and editing auto-complete tool named IntelliSense. It provides you with a list of programming commands that are appropriate for the context in which you're writing. Figure 2-9 shows the Code Editor with IntelliSense in action.

✦ **Formatting** — Write consistent-looking code using features such as indenting, word wrapping, and placing tabbed blocks of code.

✦ **Outlining** — Collapse blocks of code so that they're out of view.

✦ **Macros** — Visual Studio 2008 provides helper tools, such as code snippets and comment/uncomment features.

Visual Studio 2008 provides intelligent code editors for

✦ .NET programming languages, such as Visual Basic, C#, and J#

✦ Web-based files, such as HTML, CSS, and XML

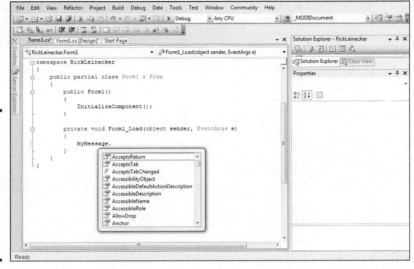

Figure 2-9:
The Code
Editor is a
special
word
processor
for writing
computer
programs.

To open the Code Editor, use one of these methods:

✦ Open a file that uses any of the .NET languages just mentioned.

✦ Double-click a code file in Solution Explorer.

✦ Add a new programming file to a solution.

Book V shows you the Code Editor in action.

Using the Forms Designer

One key feature of Visual Studio 2008 is that you can build a Windows application or Web site by dragging and dropping controls, such as text boxes and labels, onto a design surface. The designer generates, behind the scenes, the code that's necessary to create the user interface you're painting with the designer. Visual Studio 2008 provides two distinct forms designers:

✦ Windows Forms Designer
✦ Web Forms Designer

The forms designers are displayed by default when you create a new Windows application or Web site.

Two windows that go hand in hand with the forms designers are the toolbox and the Properties window. (See the section "Using the Properties Window," earlier in this chapter.) The toolbox, displayed by default as a task pane on the left side of the screen, provides a list of the controls you can drag and drop onto the forms designer to create a Windows or Web Form. Figure 2-10 shows the Windows Forms Designer and the toolbox.

See Book III for examples of the visual forms designers.

Taking a Look at Other Designers

Visual Studio provides many visual designers that are intended to increase your productivity. Here are a few:

✦ **Class Designer** — Model existing code or create new code by building models. Book V, Chapter 3 describes the Class Designer.

✦ **DataSet Designer** — Drag and drop tables from a database to create programmable datasets. See Book IV, Chapter 3.

✦ **Crystal Reports** — Visually build reports for Windows or Web applications. Book VI, Chapter 4 demonstrates how to use the Crystal Reports Designer.

✦ **Smart devices** — Create applications for smartphones and use emulators to see what the software does. Start building applications for smart devices in Book III.

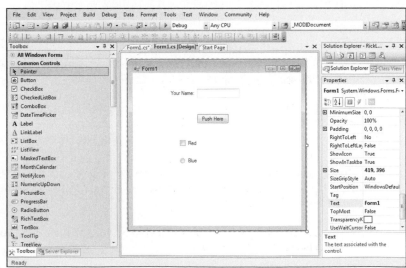

Figure 2-10:
Use the toolbox to drag controls and drop them on the forms designer.

Chapter 3: Making Connections with Visual Studio

In This Chapter

✔ Exploring the help features of Visual Studio 2008

✔ Reaching out to the .NET community

✔ Keeping up with certifications and Webcasts

*W*hen you use Visual Studio, you're not just using a development tool — you're joining a community. This statement is true, no matter what development tool you use. The technologies people use often cluster them into communities, such as

✦ Java

✦ Linux and open source software

✦ Mac

✦ .NET

That's not to say that people don't cross over — because they do. Many .NET developers are also closet Linux folks. Nevertheless, as a .NET developer, you're likely to run in the same circles as other .NET developers. This chapter shows you some of the ways you can use Visual Studio to keep in touch.

Getting Help

When you install Visual Studio, help files are installed on your hard drive. The help documentation is a combination of local offline and online resources, including

✦ Online and offline Microsoft Developer Network (MSDN) documentation for Visual Studio and .NET

✦ Online content, such as community forums, from the Microsoft Web site

✦ Online content from third parties approved by Microsoft to provide content

MSDN includes a library full of documentation, as well as a Knowledge Base. A paid subscription to MSDN allows you to download software for development purposes. For more information about MSDN subscriptions, see Book I, Chapter 5.

Setting help viewing options

You can view help content within Visual Studio or as a separate window. To set your options, follow these steps:

1. **Choose Tools⇨Options in Visual Studio 2008.**

The Options dialog box is displayed.

2. **In the options tree on the left side of the dialog box, click the plus (+) sign next to the word Environment.**

The list of environments is expanded.

3. **Click the Help option in the tree.**

The general Help settings are displayed.

4. **From the Show Help Using drop-down list, choose your preference for whether you want help content displayed in an integrated viewer within Visual Studio or in an external window, as shown in Figure 3-1.**

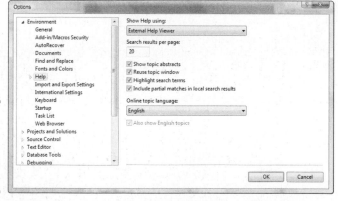

Figure 3-1:
Set your preferences for how help is displayed.

5. **Click OK to save your choices.**

You have to restart Visual Studio for your preferences to take effect.

Some folks like to configure help to open in an external window. The Visual Studio 2008 interface is already cluttered with windows. By opening help in an external window, you can focus on the documentation.

Opening and navigating the help documentation

You can access the Visual Studio help documentation in several ways, including the ones in this list:

✦ Use the Help menu in Visual Studio.

✦ Press F1 to view dynamic help topics based on the context in which you're working in Visual Studio.

✦ Use the features on the Community menu.

The Visual Studio help documentation is displayed in the Microsoft Document Explorer, which is a specialized Web browser. Document Explorer has all the features you expect to see in help documentation:

✦ **Search** gives you search options, as you'd expect, and is discussed in more detail a little later in this section.

✦ **Index** displays an alphabetized index of topics.

✦ **Contents** shows you a tree of topics, from which you can drill down to find out more about a topic of feature.

You also filter the help contents and index by using categories such as .NET Framework, Web development, or a specific .NET language, as shown in Figure 3-2.

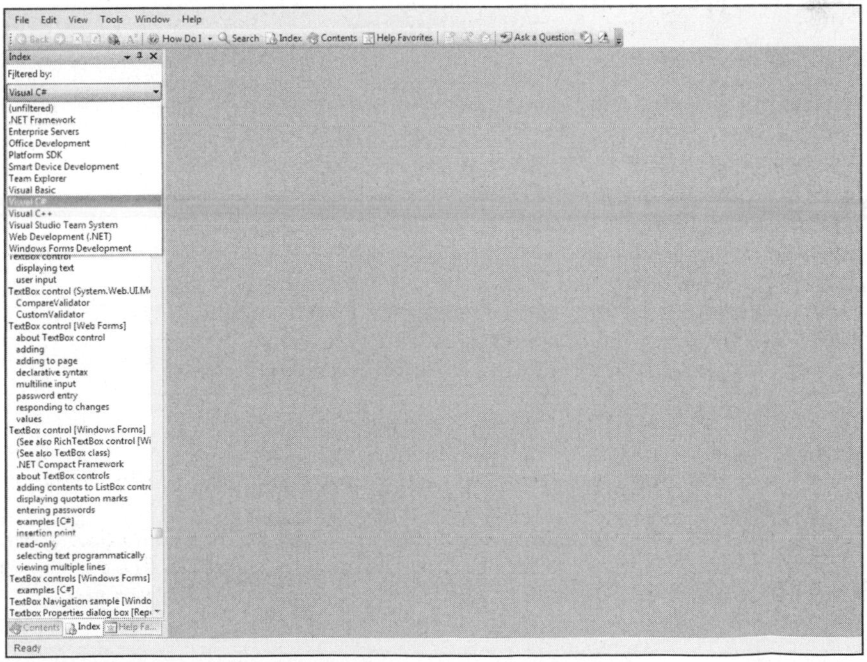

Book II
Chapter 3

Making
Connections with
Visual Studio

Figure 3-2:
Filter help contents and the index to narrow the choices.

✦ The **Favorites** feature creates a bookmark to your favorite help topics. To add a favorite help topic, right-click the topic and choose Add to Help Favorites from the shortcut menu.

Your help favorites are saved when you exit Document Explorer. If your computer crashes, any favorites that you created are lost. *Hint:* Periodically restart Document Explorer if you don't want to lose your favorites.

In addition to the preceding key features, the following tools across the top of the window are also helpful when searching for an elusive answer to a question:

✦ Use special **How Do I?** topics covering everything from Crystal Reports to Visual Studio Tools for Office.

✦ **Ask a Question** enables you to search Microsoft online forums, ask questions, and check for answers. Figure 3-3 shows the Ask a Question feature, where you can search public forums for answers. You can post questions to the forums if you can't find the information you need.

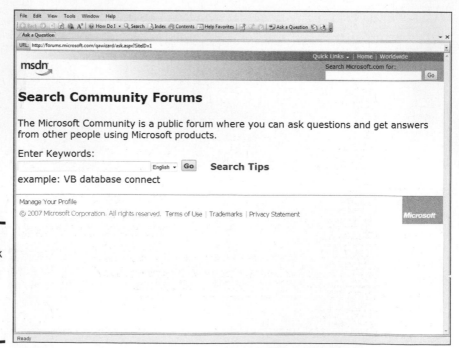

Figure 3-3:
Use the Ask a Question feature to search public forums.

- ✦ Use **the Ask a Question button** to submit suggestions or report bugs to Microsoft.

- ✦ Another feature you'll definitely want to check out is the **Sync with Table of Contents** button. After you locate a topic by using search or the index, click Sync with Table of Contents to display the topic in the Contents pane. Displaying the topic in this pane gives you the context in which the topic is used. Figure 3-4 shows the Sync with Table of Contents button.

The Visual Studio help documentation includes topics for .NET, Visual Studio, programming languages, and many other technologies. It's easy to get overwhelmed when using the Index or Search features. By synchronizing a topic with the Table of Contents, you can quickly see the domain in which the topic belongs.

See the section about discovering events in Book V, Chapter 4 for an example of using help to locate a topic.

Book II Chapter 3

Making Connections with Visual Studio

Sync with Table of Contents

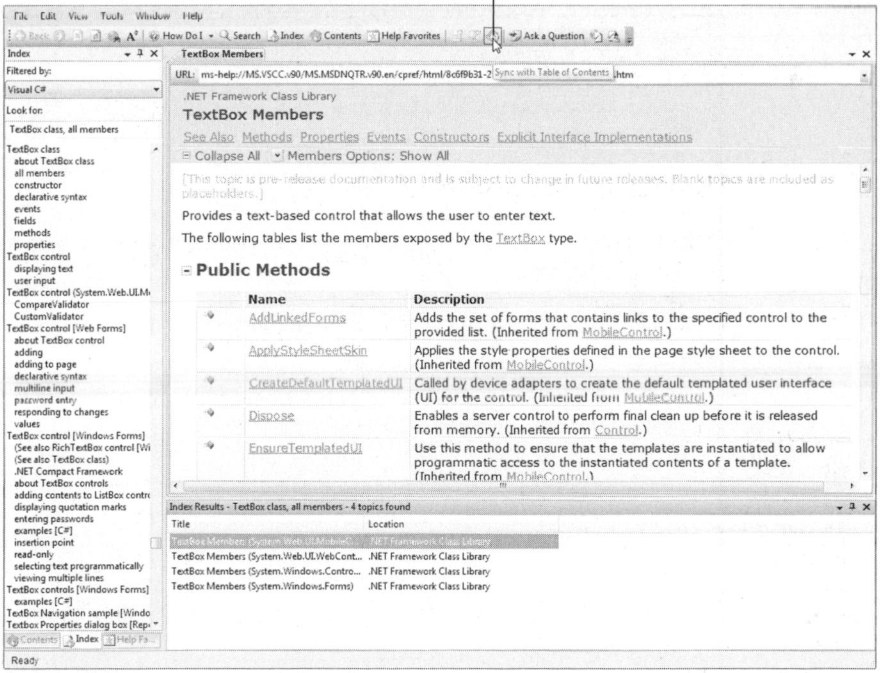

Figure 3-4: Use the Sync with Table of Contents button to place a help topic in context.

Searching and filtering search results

You can use the Search feature to search the Visual Studio documentation, as well as online content from third-party Web sites. In the Search window, you can filter your results by these criteria:

✦ **Language** — Visual Basic or C#, for example

✦ **Technology** — Team System or Windows Forms, for example

✦ **Content type** — Controls or code snippets, for example

Four major providers are searched for results, as shown in Figure 3-5:

✦ MSDN Online

✦ Codezone Community

✦ Questions

✦ Local Help

You can change the order in which the providers are displayed and remove providers by choosing Tools⇨Options.

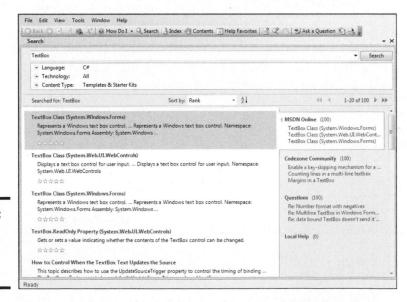

Figure 3-5:
Searches use four major providers.

Customizing Document Explorer search and home pages

As mentioned earlier, Document Explorer (in which you view help) is a Web browser. Like most Web browsers, it has search and home pages that you can set to any Web page you wish. By changing the search and home pages, you can create shortcuts to resources on the Web that you use frequently while researching problems. For example, you might set your home page to your My Yahoo! page and your search page to the Microsoft search page, which allows you to quickly access these resources from within Document Explorer.

To change your search and home pages in Document Explorer, follow these steps:

1. **Press F1 to open Visual Studio help.**

2. **Choose Tools➪Options.**

The Options dialog box appears.

3. **Click Web Browser.**

4. **Type the URLs you wish to use for your home page and search page, as shown in Figure 3-6.**

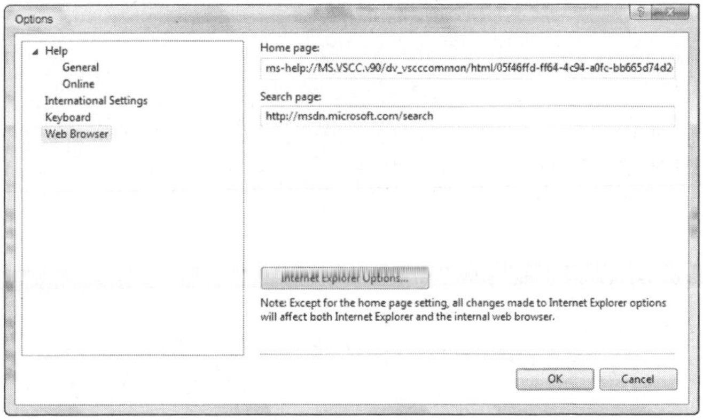

**Book II
Chapter 3**

**Making
Connections with
Visual Studio**

Figure 3-6:
Type URLs
to use for
Document
Explorer
home and
search
pages.

5. **Click OK.**

To access the search and home pages in Document Explorer, choose View➪Web Browser➪Search or View ➪Web Browser➪Home, respectively.

TIP

The Document Explorer Standard toolbar has a button to open the search page. You can add a button to open the Home page by choosing Tools⇨ Customize. Drag and drop the Web Browser Home command in the View category onto the toolbar, as shown in Figure 3-7.

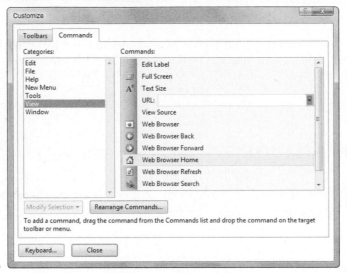

Figure 3-7: Add the Web Browser Home command to the toolbar.

Customizing the start page

Another useful help feature in Visual Studio is the start page. When you open Visual Studio, the start page automatically displays headlines from MSDN. These pages are helpful because they cover topics that developers often need help with. The start page is actually a supplementation to the normal help mechanism.

The news that's displayed on the start page uses really simple syndication (RSS) for displaying news feeds. You can set the news feed on the start page to any RSS feed. For example, to set the start page to display the top stories from CNN, follow these steps:

1. **Choose Tools⇨Options in Visual Studio.**

2. **Expand the Environment options by clicking the plus (+) sign in the options tree.**

3. **Click the Startup option.**

4. Type the URL for top CNN news stories in the Start Page News Channel field:

```
http://rss.cnn.com/rss/cnn_topstories.rss
```

5. Click OK to save your changes.

Your start page is updated with the top stories from CNN.

Some developers don't want the RSS information to show when they first run Visual Studio. They might not have an Internet connection, or they might not want to wait for it to update. You can turn the startup page off by going to the Tools menu and choosing Options, and then making your change on the Startup tab.

Staying in Touch with the .NET Community

Visual Studio puts a major emphasis on using the online community. Part of what makes .NET so valuable is the community that comes along with it. You can use the .NET community to get

+ Help on a topic

+ Code samples and starter kits

+ Controls and add-ins that extend Visual Studio

The Visual Studio Community menu (located in the MSDN item in the Help menu) is another means for you to access the .NET community. Use the Community menu in Visual Studio 2008 to

+ **Ask a question.** Search Microsoft community forums for answers. You can post questions to the forums if you can't find answers to your questions.

+ **Check question status.** Check the status of a question you asked in a forum.

+ **Send feedback.** Make suggestions and report bugs to Microsoft.

+ **Check out the Developer Center.** Visit the Developer Center Web page (on the Microsoft Web site), which provides access to additional Visual Studio resources.

+ **Hang out in the Codezone Community.** See links to additional online community Web sites where you can find code samples and tutorials.

✦ **Look at the partner-products catalog.** Search an online catalog for tools, components, add-ins, languages, and services that you can buy to extend or use with Visual Studio.

✦ **Do a community search.** Set the filter on the help search function to one of these five predefined filters:

- Template and Starter Kits

- IntelliSense Code Snippets

- Samples

- Controls

- Addins and Macros

When you access the features of the Community menu, as shown in Figure 3-8, the content is displayed via Document Explorer, which also displays help for using Visual Studio.

Pursuing certification

As you make your way out and about in the .NET community, you likely want some way to show that you're not a poser. Microsoft provides a certification series designed to demonstrate, to all who care, that you know your stuff.

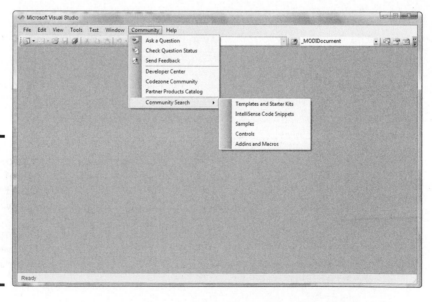

Figure 3-8:
Access the .NET community from the Community menu in Visual Studio.

Microsoft offers three levels of certification:

✦ **Technology** — These entry-level certifications demonstrate your proficiency in a specific Microsoft technology, such as.NET Framework, SQL Server, or BizTalk.

✦ **Professional** — This more-comprehensive set of certifications is geared toward professional software developers and information technology (IT) specialists.

✦ **Architect** — This peer-reviewed certification requires at least ten years of advanced information technology experience.

Each level of certification accommodates specific certifications. For example, these certifications are available in the Professional series:

✦ **Microsoft Certified Technology Specialist** — Tests your knowledge of developing software by using .NET and Visual Studio 2008

✦ **Microsoft Certified Professional Developer** — Focuses more on specialized job roles, such as Web and Windows developers

✦ **Microsoft Certified Applications Developer** — Geared toward people who develop applications by using .NET and Web services

✦ **Microsoft Certified Solutions Developer** — Intended for people who build enterprise-level solutions

To read more about Microsoft certifications, go to

`www.microsoft.com/learning/mcp/newgen`

You can get an updated list of resources at the companion Web site for this book. Look for that URL in the book's introduction.

Viewing Webcasts

In the past few years, the quality of content on MSDN has improved substantially. Not only is the content more accurate, but Microsoft also introduced more kinds of content in addition to plain old documentation. One area that's especially exciting is *Webcasts,* which are free Internet broadcasts of training, tutorials, and presentations.

You can participate in live Webcasts, or you can watch prerecorded Webcasts. An advantage of watching Webcasts live is that you can pose questions to presenters.

You can watch Webcasts about topics ranging from Windows Server 2003 to DotNetNuke to unit testing in Visual Studio 2008. Webcasts are a useful way to dig deeper into the core technologies that you use every day or to get an overview of topics.

Here are some Webcast resources you should check out:

✦ The MSDN Events and Webcasts page features Webcasts for Visual Studio and SQL Server:

    `http://msdn.microsoft.com/events`

✦ The TechNet Events and Webcasts page helps you keep up with technical topics:

    `www.microsoft.com/technet/community/webcasts`

✦ View Webcasts related to Visual Studio Team System:

    `http://msdn2.microsoft.com/teamsystem/aa718763.aspx`

Chapter 4: Upgrading .NET

In This Chapter

✔ Deciding when to upgrade

✔ Converting Windows applications and class libraries

✔ Exploring conversion options for Web applications

✔ Using Visual Studio 2008 with previous versions of .NET

W hat does it mean to upgrade to Visual Studio 2008? Two tasks are required for an upgrade:

✦ Move to the Visual Studio 2008 toolset.

✦ Use version 3.5 of the .NET Framework.

Depending on your situation, you might decide to

✦ Start using Visual Studio 2008 and .NET 3.5 right away for all new development.

✦ Upgrade all your existing Windows and Web applications to Visual Studio 2008 and .NET 3.5.

✦ Leave all or some of your existing applications in the versions of Visual Studio with which they were created.

✦ Upgrade your existing applications to Visual Studio 2008 while still using a previous version of the .NET Framework.

This chapter talks about these scenarios and walks you through some conversion processes.

Making the Case for an Upgrade

When you make the decision to upgrade to Visual Studio 2008, your existing applications must be converted to work with Visual Studio 2008 before they can be opened. In most cases, the conversion process doesn't change your code. Instead, it merely updates configuration files, such as project and solution files. The changes that are made depend on whether you're converting

✦ Windows applications

✦ Web applications

✦ Class libraries

Visual Studio 2008 uses version 3.5 of the .NET Framework by default. The syntax of programming languages, such as C# and Visual Basic, changes incrementally with each new version of the .NET Framework as new features are added and existing features are improved. The conversion process doesn't update your code to the latest syntax. Rather, the newer versions of .NET continue to support the syntax of previous versions. Most of the time, no change is necessary to your code. In almost every case, the newer versions add features rather than change existing features. It's up to you to determine whether new and improved syntax is available and decide whether you want to change your code to use the new syntax.

When you make the decision to upgrade to Visual Studio 2008, you have lots of choices. In the sections that follow, you find out more specifics about what happens to code when you upgrade, alternatives to upgrading, and what you need to do to upgrade programs in pre-.NET languages.

What happens to Visual Studio code in an upgrade?

As you think about whether you should upgrade, consider these issues:

✦ **Windows applications and class libraries aren't changed much by the conversion process.** Even though configuration settings are updated, your code stays the same.

✦ **Any code or controls that were *deprecated* (made obsolete) in version 3.5 of the .NET Framework still work.** You can't use the visual designers for deprecated controls, although you can use the Code Editor.

✦ **Your class libraries aren't optimized to take advantage of the latest features in .NET 3.5.** You have to figure out whether you should change your code.

✦ **After converting applications to Visual Studio 2008, analyze your code by using FxCop.** It offers you suggestions for improving your code. See Book V, Chapter 5 for more information about FxCop.

✦ **Web applications require some finesse to get all their components converted properly.** You need to do some preparation work before you convert them.

✦ **Applications that are especially complex can be difficult to convert.** If you can't convert the entire solution, you might have to convert individual projects one at a time and then add them to your Visual Studio 2008 solution.

+ **Clients running your applications must have the .NET 3.5 Framework installed.** You can convert your applications to work with Visual Studio 2008 and deploy applications to work with previous versions of the .NET Framework. You see how later in this chapter.

+ **You can't "un-convert."** You can restore your backups, however, and discard the converted application if you don't like the results.

What are alternatives to upgrading?

You have several alternatives to performing an outright upgrade of your application to Visual Studio 2008:

**Book II
Chapter 4**

+ **If it ain't broke . . .** You might not have any compelling reason to upgrade your Visual Studio 2002, 2003, and 2005 applications to Visual Studio 2008. Unless you plan to take advantage of the new Visual Studio 2008 features in your Visual Studio 2002, 2003, and 2005 applications, you probably don't need to upgrade.

+ **Go "side by side."** You can run all three versions of the .NET Framework and Visual Studio on a single computer. Your existing version 2.0 applications then work alongside any new version 3.5 applications you create.

+ **Step up to the 3.5 Framework.** Chances are that your .NET 2.0 applications will run on the 3.5 Framework, even without converting them to work with Visual Studio 2008. You can take advantage of the new security and performance features of .NET 3.5 without touching your code.

+ **Mix and match.** If you have relatively stable parts of your application that use previous versions of the .NET Framework and you want to do new development in Visual Studio 2008, you can mix and match. Just reference your older components in your new Visual Studio 2008 solution.

+ **Take the brute-force approach.** You can manually re-create your applications in Visual Studio 2008 by choosing to copy and paste your old code into newly created Visual Studio 2008 solutions.

+ **Indulge in the best of both worlds.** You can target the .NET 2.0 runtime with your existing applications in Visual Studio 2008. You can read how later in this chapter.

How do you upgrade from pre-.NET languages?

All this assumes that you're converting from a previous version of the .NET Framework to the current version. If you're upgrading from a pre-.NET language, such as Visual Basic 6, you need to jump through a few hoops to get your application converted. After they're converted, you'll still likely need to finesse the converted code to make it work.

You might be able to reuse stable components created in Visual Basic 6.0 by using a feature of the .NET Framework called COM Interop. With COM Interop, you can consume your Visual Basic 6 code from your .NET applications.

In the case of ASP.NET, you have additional considerations when you choose to upgrade to Visual Studio 2008 and ASP.NET 3.5:

+ **ASP.NET uses a new, simplified model for managing resources, such as code and Web pages.** Project files are no longer needed because all the configuration settings are moved to `web.config`, which is an XML-based configuration file.

If you're really attached to using project files, you can use the Web Application Projects extension for Visual Studio 2008. Download the extension for free from Microsoft's Web site at

   `http://msdn2.microsoft.com/en-us/asp.net/aa336618.aspx`

+ **You can execute your Web sites on local development machines by using the ASP.NET Developer Server.** Using the ASP.NET Developer Server requires less configuration and is more secure than using Internet Information Services (IIS) as your local Web server.

+ **ASP.NET 3.5 offers a new code-behind model, new controls for laying out Web pages and working with data, and improved deployment options.** Your productivity is greatly improved with ASP.NET 3.5.

See Book III for more information on creating Web applications with ASP.NET 3.5.

Considering Your Conversion Strategies

Visual Studio provides a conversion wizard for migrating projects from previous versions of .NET to the .NET 3.5 version. The conversion process itself is fairly straightforward: You just open your Visual Studio 2002, 2003, or 2005 solution in Visual Studio 2008, and the Conversion Wizard automatically opens and walks you through the conversion process.

Before you convert any applications, you need to do some preparation work on them:

+ Make sure that you have good backups in case you decide to roll back to the unconverted version.

+ Make sure that all your source code compiles *before* you convert.

✦ Take the time to clean up any extraneous files that don't belong with the application.

✦ Make sure that the .NET 3.5 Framework is installed on all client machines that will run your application.

Converting Web applications requires more preparation than converting Windows applications because the conversion process is more involved. See "Converting Web applications," later in this chapter, for more details.

Converting Windows applications and class libraries

As a rule, you should try to convert an entire solution first, rather than convert each of the projects in a solution individually. If the conversion process can't convert all the projects in your solution, you should

✦ Allow the Visual Studio Conversion Wizard to convert the solution and as many projects as it can.

✦ Open individual projects that don't convert in Visual Studio 2008. Walk through the Conversion Wizard for each project that doesn't convert with the solution.

✦ Add the converted projects to the converted solution.

To convert Windows solutions and projects, follow these steps:

1. **In Visual Studio 2008, choose File⇨Open⇨Project/Solution.**

   The Open Project window appears.

2. **Browse to your Visual Studio 2002, 2003, or 2005 Windows application and click the Open button. If you have a solution file, you should open it.**

   The Visual Studio Conversion Wizard appears.

3. **Click Next to start the wizard.**

4. **Select the Yes, Create a Backup Before Converting radio button, specify a backup location, and then click Next.**

   A summary of the solution and projects to be converted is displayed.

5. **Click Finish to start the conversion.**

   After the conversion is done, a completion window appears. Any errors that occur during the conversion process are listed.

6. **To display a conversion log, select the Show the Conversion Log When the Wizard Is Closed option, and then click Close.**

The conversion log, as shown in Figure 4-1, appears in Visual Studio 2008.

Follow these steps again to convert class libraries.

After the conversion, build your application in Visual Studio 2008 to make sure that all converted projects are compiled. If you have multiple projects in your solution, you should build your class libraries first and work your way through any dependencies until all your components are built.

Converting Web applications

The conversion process for Web applications is more involved than for Windows applications and class libraries. Coverage in this section uses IIS 6. The Visual Studio Conversion Wizard performs several additional functions when converting Web applications, including these:

✦ Moving project file configuration settings into the `web.config` file

✦ Creating new folders, such as App_Code, and moving standalone class files

✦ Updating the code-behind attributes to reflect new attributes

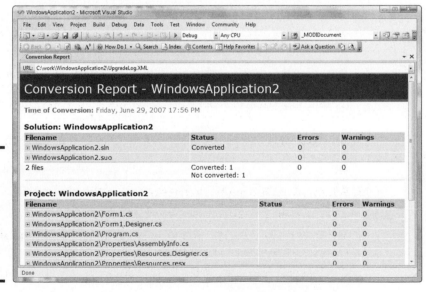

Figure 4-1:
View the conversion log for details about the conversion process.

Because the Web application conversion process is more involved, the preparation requires that you do a few more tasks, as well:

+ **Make sure that all files that need to be converted are included in the project.** The Visual Studio Conversion Wizard converts only those files.

  To include in a project any files that were previously excluded, open the project in Visual Studio 2002, 2003, or 2005; right-click the file; and then choose Include in Project from the contextual menu.

+ **Remove any files from your project directory that aren't part of the project.**

+ **When you convert multiple projects, make sure that no overlap occurs in the files that each project references.** For instance, if projects share resources — such as images — you should create unique copies of each for the projects.

+ **When you convert multiple solutions, make sure that no overlap occurs in the projects contained in the solutions.**

+ **Remove references to other Web projects.** In other words, your `Import` and `using` statements at the beginning of the source code shouldn't refer to other Web projects.

Book II
Chapter 4

Upgrading .NET

To convert a Web application, follow these steps:

1. **Choose File➪Open➪Web Site.**

The Open Web Site window appears.

You must open your Web site using the Open Web Site window in order for the conversion wizard to work properly.

The Open Web Site window gives you several sources from which you can open your Web site. In most cases, you'll open your site from a local IIS site. You can also choose to open a site from a File Transfer Protocol (FTP) site, remote Web server, or source control.

Don't select File System as your source. Converting a Web application from a file system causes the Web site to lose data about the site's structure.

2. **Select Local IIS from the list of sources in the left pane.**

A list of Web sites on the local computer appears.

3. **Navigate to the Web site you want to convert, select it (as shown in Figure 4-2), and then click Open.**

The Visual Studio Conversion Wizard appears.

Figure 4-2:
Open an
existing
Web site by
using the
Local IIS
option.

4. **Click Next to start the wizard.**

5. **Follow the steps in the Visual Studio Conversion Wizard to complete the conversion.**

If errors occur in the conversion, read the conversion log and determine which files weren't converted. Remember that class files aren't converted. They're copied to the solution directory as-is.

Check the `ConversionReport.webinfo` file to view the steps taken to convert the application. The file is named `ConversionReport.txt` if you haven't installed the Conversion Wizard upgrade.

Build your applications by making sure that all dependent projects are built first. Always open your converted project by using the Local IIS option.

After the conversion, you have an ASP.NET 3.5 Web application that you can edit in Visual Studio 2008. The folder structure and code-behind model are updated to the new ASP.NET 3.5 model.

Running Web applications side by side

You can specify which version of the .NET Framework you want a Web application to use. Version 3.5 of the Framework is backward-compatible with versions 2.0 and 3.0. You can then run your existing applications in version 3.5 and take advantage of improved security and performance features without recompiling.

Configuring your Web application to use version 3.5 of the .NET Framework requires that the .NET Framework version 3.5 is installed on the server where the application is hosted. If that version isn't installed, browse to the Windows Update site on the server and install it.

To configure a Web application to use version 3.5 of the .NET Framework, follow these steps:

1. **Launch the IIS Manager on the server.**

In Windows Vista, you can find the IIS Manager by choosing Administrative Tools from the Control Panel.

2. **Select Application Pools.**

3. **Right-click in the Application Pools window and choose Add Application Pool.**

4. **Name the new Application Pool and select the .NET version you desire.**

5. **Expand the Web Sites folder and navigate to the Web site you want to configure.**

6. **Right-click the Web site and choose Advanced Settings from the contextual menu.**

7. **Select your newly created Application Pool, as shown in Figure 4-3.**

8. **Click OK.**

Book II
Chapter 4

Upgrading .NET

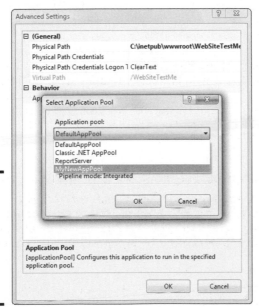

Figure 4-3:
Set the
version of
the .NET
Framework
you want
the site
to use.

You can repeat these steps for all the Web sites hosted on the server to specify whether you want the site to use version 2.0, 3.0, or 3.5 of the Framework.

Using Copy and Paste to control conversions

If you like to take control of your conversions, you can re-create your applications manually in Visual Studio 2008. Here's the overview:

1. **Create new Windows or Web solutions.**

2. **Use the visual designers to manually re-create your forms, pages, user controls, and any other elements that are in your existing application.**

Make sure to keep your naming style consistent with your old application.

3. **Copy any code that you want to bring over from your old solution.**

Your code should work as long as you re-created all your Windows and Web forms properly.

4. **Build your applications and deal with errors.**

Using the Visual Studio converters

Visual Studio 2008 provides two converters for converting Visual Basic 6.0 applications to Visual Basic.NET and for converting Java and J++ 6.0 applications to C#:

✦ Visual Basic Upgrade Wizard

✦ Java Language Conversion Assistant

To open either of these converters, follow these steps:

1. **Choose File⇨Open.**

The Open fly-away menu appears.

2. **Choose the Convert option.**

The Convert dialog box appears.

3. **The only conversion assistant available right now is for Visual Basic, as shown in Figure 4-4.**

4. **Select the Create New Solution radio button.**

5. **Click OK to start the wizard and then follow its steps.**

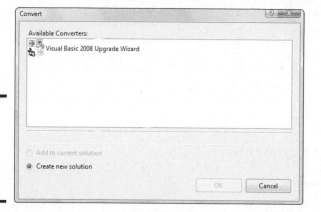

Book II
Chapter 4

Upgrading .NET

Figure 4-4:
Choose a
converter
from the
Convert
dialog box.

Using Visual Studio 2008 with .NET 2.0

Suppose that you want the best of both worlds. You want to take advantage of the exciting new features in the Visual Studio 2008 development environment, such as the Class Designer and code snippets, and you still need to target the .NET 2.0 runtime environment. Well, my friend, that option is available to you.

Note that you can't use any of the features of the .NET 3.5 Framework, such as generics and master pages. If you try, you receive an error message when you build your solution. Also, you can't use this trick with Web applications. ASP.NET uses a completely different build model than Windows applications and class libraries do. You can still get the lay of the Visual Studio 2008 land, though, while continuing to target previous versions of the .NET Framework.

See Book III, Chapter 4 for more information about master pages and Book V, Chapter 3 for more information about working with generics.

To target a previous version of .NET 2.0 with your application, follow these steps:

1. **Open your Visual Basic or C# application in Visual Studio 2008 from the File menu.**

If you're opening an application created in a previous version of Visual Studio, you need to walk through the Conversion Wizard steps before you can open the application.

2. **Choose Options from the Tools menu and then click the Application tab.**

3. Choose .NET Framework 2.0 from the Target Framework drop-down list, as shown in Figure 4-5.

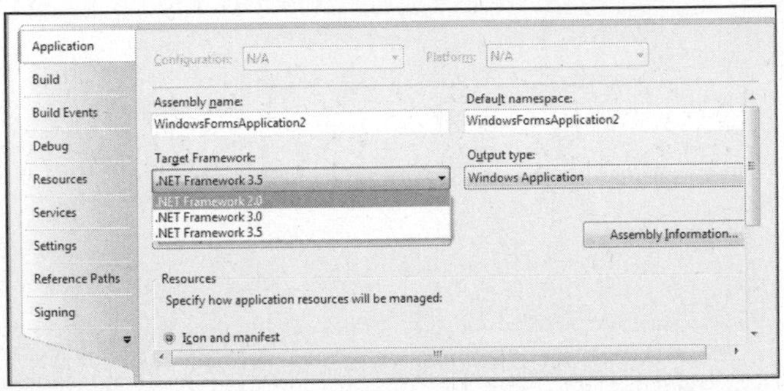

Figure 4-5:
Select .NET
2.0 from
the list of
available
platforms.

4. Click OK.

The platform for your project is updated to .NET 2.0 in the Configuration Manager. When you build your application, Visual Studio 2008 targets the .NET 2.0 version of the .NET Framework.

5. Click the Close button to close the Configuration Manager.

6. Build your application by choosing Build➪Build Solution.

Verify that your application is compiled using the .NET 2.0 compiler by viewing the contents of the Output window, at the bottom. Notice that Visual Studio used the Visual Basic and C# compilers vbc.exe and csc.exe, respectively, for the version 2.0 Framework.

The Microsoft team responsible for MSBuild is also working on its own tool for using Visual Studio 2008 with the .NET 2.0 compiler. Its project is named MSBee, which stands for MSBuild Everett Environment. MSBee works similarly to the MSBuild Toolkit. The main difference is that you can't use MSBee using the Visual Studio 2008 Build menu. Instead, you have to manually build your applications using the command line. You can download MSBee for free at

www.codeplex.com/Wiki/View.aspx?ProjectName=MSBee

You aren't restricted to using these two applications. The .targets files are what makes it possible to create .NET 2.0 and .NET 3.0 assemblies using Visual Studio 2008.

Book III

Building Applications

Contents at a Glance

Chapter 1: Getting Smart about Smart Clients 129

Chapter 2: Building Smart Client User Interfaces..149

Chapter 3: Building Visual C++ Applications 175

Chapter 4: Building Web Applications..187

Chapter 5: Using AJAX For Rich Web Pages 213

Chapter 6: Laying Out Your Site 225

Chapter 7: Exploring ASP.NET Services 253

Chapter 8: Building a Mobile Application..271

Chapter 1: Getting Smart about Smart Clients

In This Chapter

✔ Getting acquainted with Windows Forms

✔ Creating your first smart client application

✔ Working with controls

✔ Setting properties and responding to events

*V*isual Studio has all the tools you need to build everything from the simplest to the most complex Windows applications. By using the Microsoft .NET Framework, Visual Studio provides the visual designers that make building Windows applications a breeze. For example, Visual Studio gives you the following elements to accomplish common tasks:

✦ Project Templates help you set up your project.

✦ Visual designers help you lay out Windows Forms.

✦ The control toolbox makes adding user interface (UI) elements to your Windows Forms a breeze.

✦ Wizards, property-setting windows, and shortcut task lists enable you to easily configure UI elements.

This chapter walks you through some of the tools that Visual Studio provides for building managed Windows applications that use either Visual Basic or C#.

Switching from Fat Clients to Smart Clients

The Windows operating system (OS) and applications that run on Windows have been around for more than 25 years. With ubiquity, early Windows applications became bloated and hard to deploy. In response, developers snubbed their noses at these newly dubbed *fat clients* and started using a combination of client and server resources to create leaner applications.

Proving that the grass isn't always greener, folks quickly learned that thin clients had their problems, too. Although thin clients were easier to deploy, they weren't all that feature rich, and they didn't work when the network went down. Then came the Internet, and the world went crazy for Web-based applications. Many talented developers found innovative ways to twist and contort simple Web pages into what seemed like full-blown desktop applications. They used a combination of server-side code and JavaScript. Although developers had modest success in this arena, many diehard Windows programmers cringed at the lack of UI sophistication in Web-based applications.

Thanks to inexpensive, fast hardware and the maturity of Windows application development, the Windows application is again being redefined — this time as the smart client. Although a smart client might look like any old Windows application, you can use its key differences to

✦ Create rich user experiences.

✦ Deploy and maintain applications with greater ease.

✦ Enjoy more security than in a traditional Windows application.

Smart clients still provide all the same features as earlier generations of Windows applications:

✦ You can build data-centric, interactive applications.

✦ You can access the local computer.

✦ They don't require a server in order to run.

Windows applications are all about creating an intuitive, visually appealing, and interactive user experience. If user experience weren't important, we all would still be running good old-fashioned, character-based applications in DOS.

Smart clients aren't the last word in Windows applications. The next wave of Microsoft products for Windows and Visual Studio will usher in even more opportunities for Windows developers to enhance the user experience. See Book VII, Chapter 3 to read more about the next generation of Windows applications.

Designing Windows Forms

The basic building block of a smart client Windows application is the Windows Form. Windows Forms, a key technology of the .NET Framework, provide

✦ Libraries for creating a UI

✦ Libraries for common tasks, such as reading and writing to the file system

✦ A set of controls that provide common UI elements

The *Windows Forms Designer* is the Visual Studio visual design surface for working with Windows Forms. Use the Windows Forms Designer for these tasks:

✦ Visually lay out your UI.

✦ Configure UI attributes.

✦ Write custom code that's executed when users interact with your form.

Figure 1-1 displays the Windows Forms Designer in Visual Studio. The next section walks you through creating a new Windows application and using the forms designer.

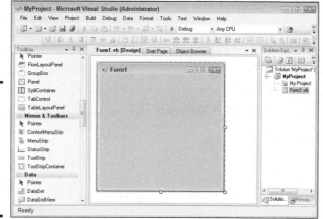

Figure 1-1: Use the Windows Forms Designer to lay out your user interface.

**Book III
Chapter 1**

Getting Smart about Smart Clients

Creating your first smart client project

Visual Studio uses Solutions and Projects containers to organize all the files necessary to build an application. When you create a new Windows application, Visual Studio creates all the files you need and prepares the development environment with the windows, designers, and editors that you need to work with your new project.

To create a new smart client project in Visual Studio, follow these steps:

1. **Choose File⇨New⇨ Project.**

The New Project window appears.

You can also open the New Project window by pressing Ctrl+Shift+N.

2. **In the Project Types hierarchy, click the programming language you want to use.**

   A list of project templates that are available for that programming language appears on the right.

   Windows applications created by using Visual Basic, C#, managed C++, and J# use the .NET Framework. Although the examples in this chapter use Visual Basic, you can create Windows applications by using any language. See Chapter 3 in this mini-book for more details about creating Windows applications with C++.

3. **Click the Windows Application icon.**

4. **Enter a unique name for your application in the Name text box.**

   Although you can give your application any name you want, you probably should choose a name that describes your application. Many developers include the word *Windows* or the abbreviation *Win* in an application's name to distinguish it from other kinds of applications, such as Web or mobile applications.

5. **Click OK to create the application.**

Visual Studio creates a new solution with a Windows project. A new Windows Form is added to the project, and Visual Studio displays the form in the Windows Forms Designer.

Saying, "Hello world!"

When you create a new Windows application, Visual Studio generates all the code necessary to display the Windows Form on the screen when you run your application. To run your new Windows application, press Ctrl+F5. Visual Studio builds your Windows application and displays a blank Windows Form.

Most Windows applications use menus, text boxes, and buttons. These types of user interface elements are *controls*. Follow these steps to add controls to make your application say, "Hello world!":

1. **Open the control toolbox by pressing Ctrl+Alt+X.**

2. **Drag and drop a label control from the toolbox onto the forms designer.**

3. **Drag and drop a button control onto the forms designer.**

4. **Double-click the button control.**

   Visual Studio creates a block of code to handle the button's `Click` event. The Code Editor appears with the cursor flashing in the block of code.

5. Type this line in the Code Editor:

- *VB*

```
Label1.Text = "Hello World!"
```

- *C#*

```
Label1.Text = "Hello World!";
```

6. Press Ctrl+F5 to run your Windows Form.

When you click the button on your form, `Hello World!` appears on the label you add in Step 3, as shown in Figure 1-2.

Figure 1-2: `"Hello World!"` appears on the form's label.

Book III Chapter 1

Getting Smart about Smart Clients

Taking Command from Control Central

A Windows Form is a blank canvas: It doesn't do much on its own. To bring your Windows Form to life, you must add controls to it. *Controls* are UI elements, such as buttons and text boxes, designed for interacting with your Windows Form. Controls breathe life into your Windows Forms by

✦ Providing structure and navigation in the form of menus, toolbars, and status bars

✦ Allowing users to interact with your forms by using buttons, labels, and text boxes

✦ Displaying dialog boxes to provide user feedback about your application's state

Putting controls on a form is also a way of designing an application. The form with controls and no code is an adequate prototype with which you can then proceed to plan the code. By taking the time to think through the application and place the controls as they will be in the final application, you'll likely have fewer bugs, flaws, and debugging issues during the development process.

Introducing the control toolbox

Visual Studio provides a toolbox chock full of controls. The control toolbox, as shown in Figure 1-3, includes all the commonly used controls that even casual Windows users are familiar with, such as

✦ Labels, text boxes, and buttons

✦ Check boxes, list boxes, and combo boxes

✦ Calendars and date pickers

Figure 1-3:
Add
controls to
your form
from the
toolbox.

The toolbox displays controls in groups, or *tabs:*

✦ **All Windows Forms** — Contains an alphabetical list of controls.

✦ **Common Controls** — Lists frequently used controls, such as labels and text boxes.

✦ **Containers** — Used for laying out and grouping other controls on the form.

◆ **Menus & Toolbars** — Creates the menus and toolbars your application uses.

◆ **Data** — Contains controls and wizards for accessing data.

◆ **Components** — Contains controls that provide back-end services, such as connecting to an event log.

◆ **Printing** — Provides printing features.

◆ **Dialogs** — Allows you to add common dialog boxes, such as those used for saving files.

◆ **WPF Interoperability** — Provides interoperability between Windows Presentation Foundation and Windows Forms.

◆ **Crystal Reports** — Allows you to add a Crystal Report to your form. See Book VI, Chapter 4 to read more about Crystal Reports.

◆ **General** — Contains an empty group.

This chapter demonstrates how to use frequently used controls, such as labels, text boxes, and buttons. More advanced controls, such as those in the containers and on the menus and toolbox tabs, are discussed in Chapter 2 of this mini-book. To read more about using data controls on Windows Forms, see Book IV, Chapter 2.

Customizing the toolbox

You can customize the toolbox by

◆ Adding and removing tab groups

◆ Moving tab groups up or down

◆ Adding and removing controls to and from the tab groups

To customize the toolbox, follow these steps:

1. **Right-click an item, such as a specific control or tab, in the toolbox you want to customize.**

A contextual menu appears, as shown in Figure 1-4.

2. **From the shortcut menu, choose the action you want to take.**

To add new controls to the toolbox, choose Choose Items from the contextual menu.

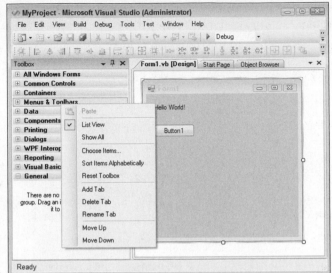

Figure 1-4:
Right-click a tab header to customize the tab.

Adding controls to your form

The easiest way to add a control to a form is to drag and drop it from the toolbox onto the Windows Form. You can also draw a control to specify its exact size. To draw a text box on a Windows Form, follow these steps:

1. **Click the text box control in the toolbox.**

If the toolbox is closed, press Ctrl+Alt+X to display it.

2. **Move your mouse pointer to the Windows Form.**

Note: It isn't necessary to drag the text box.

The pointer changes to a plus sign (+).

If you change your mind about drawing the control, click a different control or click the pointer in the toolbox to reset your mouse pointer without adding a control to the form.

3. **In the upper-left corner, click the mouse pointer wherever you want to start drawing the text box.**

To draw a default-size text box, click and release your mouse button without dragging.

4. Drag the mouse pointer to the upper-left corner where you want the text box to end, as shown in Figure 1-5, and release the mouse button.

The text box is drawn on the form. When you're done placing controls, the next step is typically to format them and set how you want them to behave. See the next section "Manipulating Controls" for details.

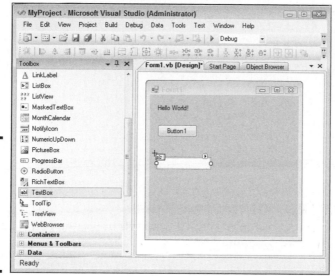

Figure 1-5: Release the mouse pointer in the lower-left corner of the toolbox.

Using more controls

Whenever possible, you should use the controls provided in Visual Studio. Using them creates a consistent user experience because Windows users are generally familiar with most Windows controls. Sometimes, however, you might need a control that isn't available in the Visual Studio toolbox. You have several options:

✔ **Build your own.** Because .NET is an object-oriented language, you can extend an existing control or build your own.

✔ **Use ActiveX controls.** Windows Forms can host ActiveX controls, which are built by using the Component Object Model (COM) technology.

You add controls to the Visual Studio toolbox by choosing the Choose Toolbox Items command from the Tools menu.

✔ **Buy the control.** Many third-party vendors sell controls. You could also sell a control that you build.

✔ **Download the control.** Sometimes, you can find controls available for free or as shareware on the Internet. Be sure to read the license before you redistribute controls you find there.

You can search for controls online by using the Community Search feature. See Book II, Chapter 3 for more information.

Manipulating Controls

Creating a UI with controls involves more than dragging and dropping. To get the most from controls, you need to know how to position them on your form. This section covers some common tools for putting controls exactly where you want them.

Formatting controls

Even the simplest Windows Form can have dozens of controls. Developers often want to align controls in a way that's visually appealing to users. Although you can work with each control individually — drag, drop, resize, and align — using the Visual Studio Format menu is much easier. After selecting two or more controls, use the Format menu to perform the following actions:

✦ **Align** — Position controls into alignment with one another.

✦ **Make Same Size** — Make controls the same width or height.

✦ **Horizontal Spacing** — Set the side-by-side spacing between controls.

✦ **Vertical Spacing** — Set the spacing above and below controls in a row.

✦ **Center in Form** — Position a control or group of controls in the center of the Windows Form.

✦ **Order** — Set controls to appear in front of other controls.

✦ **Lock Controls** — Lock the position of a single control or group of controls so that the position can't be changed.

Visual Studio displays a Layout toolbar with many of the common formatting commands. To display the Layout toolbar if it's not already open, follow these steps:

1. **Choose View⇨Toolbars.**

A submenu displays a list of all Visual Studio toolbars, and check marks indicate all visible toolbars.

2. **Select the Layout option.**

The Layout toolbar appears, as shown in Figure 1-6. You can use this toolbar to access common formatting commands.

Figure 1-6:
The Layout
toolbar.

Here's how to create a form with aligned labels and buttons for accepting user input:

1. **Draw three labels on the form. Stack the labels vertically and try not to align them.**

2. **Draw three text buttons on the form — again, without aligning them.**

3. **Hold down the Shift key and then click the three buttons to select them.**

You have three options for selecting formatting controls:

- *Shift+click* — Format all controls to conform with the first control selected.

- *Ctrl+click* — Format all controls to conform with the last control selected.

- *Click and drag* — Click the form and then drag a selection rectangle around all the controls you want to select.

4. **Click the Make Same Size icon on the Layout toolbar, as shown in Figure 1-7.**

The buttons are made the same size.

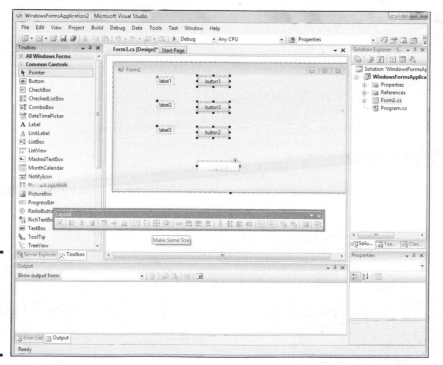

Figure 1-7:
Click the
Make Same
Size icon on
the Layout
toolbar.

5. **Click the Align Lefts icon on the Layout toolbar.**

   Align Lefts is the second icon on the toolbar. The buttons are aligned to the left.

6. **Position the mouse pointer over the right side of the buttons. When the pointer turns to an arrow, drag your mouse to the right and left.**

   The buttons widen and narrow with the mouse movement.

7. **Click the form to deselect the buttons.**

8. **Hold down the Shift key while you select the three label controls.**

9. **Choose Format⇨Align⇨Rights.**

   The labels are aligned to the right.

10. **Position the pointer over the labels until it turns into a four-way arrow. Drag the labels to the left to create space between the labels and buttons.**

   You can use the arrow keys on your keyboard to move the labels around on the form.

Seeing the snaplines

When you add a control to a form, Visual Studio provides visual cues, or *snaplines,* for positioning the control. Snaplines recommend the best position for the controls in accordance with spacing recommendations set in the official Microsoft UI guidelines. The snaplines appear while you drag controls around the form to let you know when the controls are at appropriate positions.

To see snaplines in action, follow these steps:

1. **Drag a button control from the Visual Studio toolbox to the form design surface and don't release the button.**

2. **Move the mouse pointer to the lower-right corner of the form.**

   As you approach the corner, blue snaplines appear, as shown in Figure 1-8.

3. **Drop the button on the form.**

4. **Drag a text box control to the form and don't release the text box.**

5. **Position the text box above the button. When the snapline appears between the text box and the button, release the text box.**

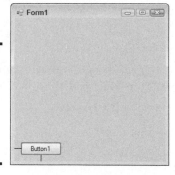

Figure 1-8:
Snaplines
provide
visual
cues for
positioning
controls.

Snaplines are visible any time you move controls on the design surface. The space between the button control and the edge of the form is the sum of the button's margin property and the form's padding property. Margins define the exterior space between controls, and padding designates space between a control's interior border and its contents. You can set these properties yourself or use snaplines to do it for you. See the section "Using the Properties Window," later in this chapter, for more information on setting control properties.

Locking controls

Getting the layout just right on a form can be a chore. You can keep your controls positioned where you want them by locking them in place. You have two options for locking controls:

✦ **To lock all your controls and the form itself,** choose Lock Controls from the Format menu.

✦ **To lock an individual control,** set the control's Locked property to True.

Setting the tab order

Nothing's worse than when you press the Tab key in a Windows application, and the cursor jumps to an unexpected field. The tab order determines the order in which the Tab button moves from field to field on your form. To set the tab order, follow these steps:

1. **Choose View⇨Tab Order.**

The controls on the page display numbers representing their tab order.

2. **Click to select the controls in sequential order to set the tab order, as shown in Figure 1-9.**

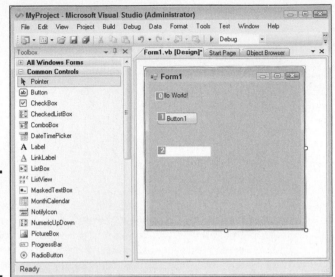

Figure 1-9:
Select the
controls
sequentially
to set the
tab order.

3. **Repeat Step 1 to take the form out of tab-order selection mode.**

To designate that a control shouldn't be tabbed to, set the control's
`TabStop` property to `False`. Controls with the `TabStop` property set to
`False` are skipped when the user presses Tab. Controls that aren't visible or
enabled are also skipped when the user presses Tab.

To set a control as invisible or disabled, set the control's `Visible` and
`Enabled` properties to `False`.

You can set a control's tab order by using the `TabIndex` property. (See the
section "Using the Properties Window," later in this chapter, to see how to
set a control's properties.)

Access a control's tasks with smart tags

Some of the controls you add to your form can walk you through simple task
wizards by using smart tags. Smart tag-enabled controls have a little arrow
in the upper-right corner of the control. When you click the arrow, a list of
common tasks associated with the control appears. To see a smart tag-
enabled control in action

1. **Drag and drop a `CheckedListBox` control onto the forms designer.**

2. **Click the smart tag arrow to display a list of common tasks, as shown
in Figure 1-10.**

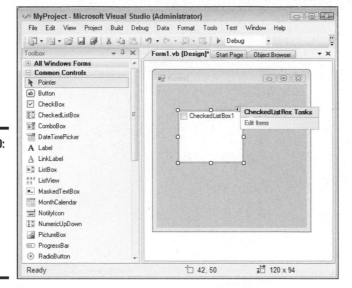

Book III
Chapter 1

Getting Smart
about Smart Clients

Figure 1-10:
Click the
control's
smart tag
arrow to
display a
list of
common
tasks.

3. **In the `CheckedListBox` Tasks window, click Edit Items.**

   From the String Collection Editor that appears, you can add items to the
   `CheckedListBox` control.

The smart tags display a subset of tasks for the control. Use the control's
Properties window to see all the tasks and properties available for the control.

Using the Properties Window

Every control has a set of properties and events that define how the control
acts when your application runs. For example, the button control's `Text`
property specifies the text that's displayed on the button. The button control has a `Click` event that's executed each time a user clicks the button.

The Visual Studio Properties window displays a control's properties and
events in a grid, as shown in Figure 1-11.

The Properties window is open by default. If you close the Properties
window at some point, you have two options for opening it again:

✦ Choose View➪Properties Window.

✦ Press F4.

Figure 1-11:
Setting a
control's
properties
and events.

The Properties window has the following elements:

✦ **A drop-down list at the top displays the selected control.** Use the list to select a control to view.

✦ **A toolbar changes the view settings.** Your view-setting choices are, from left to right

   • *Categorized* — Properties appear in groups.

   • *Alphabetical* — Properties are sorted in alphabetical order.

   • *Properties* — The control's properties are displayed.

   • *Events* — The control's events are displayed.

✦ **Two columns display the name-value pairs of the control's properties or events, depending on the view setting.**

✦ **A brief description of the selected property or event appears at the bottom of the window.**

The Properties window is a visual tool that organizes and categorizes the thousands of properties and events available for manipulating controls. You use the Properties window for two tasks:

✦ Set a control's properties.

✦ Create event handlers for a control.

When you use the Properties window, Visual Studio generates the code to set the control's properties and create event handlers. You can do all this by using code, although it's much easier to use Visual Studio. To read about how to set properties and work with events in code, see Book V, Chapter 4.

You can access thousands of properties and events by using the Properties window. Visual Studio groups properties and events into categories so that they're easier to manage. The following list describes the properties and events categories:

✦ Action — Creates handlers for events, such as Click and Scroll.

✦ Accessibility — Sets properties that make controls accessible to people with disabilities.

✦ Appearance — Contains properties related to font, color, border, and cursor style. The Text property and text-formatting properties are in this group.

✦ Behavior — Contains properties and events related to how a control acts. Examples include Sorted, TabStop, and SelectedIndexChanged.

✦ Data — Sets a control's data source, gets items selected in a control, and responds to changes in the data.

✦ Design — Contains design-time properties, such as whether controls are locked. The Name property is here, too.

✦ DragDrop — Responds to events related to dragging and dropping controls.

✦ Focus — Captures events related to how the control gains and loses focus.

✦ Key — Responds to keyboard-related events.

✦ Layout — Sets layout properties, such as anchor, margin, and size.

✦ Mouse — Responds to mouse events, such as MouseUp.

✦ WindowStyle — Sets properties that define the Windows Form itself.

Within each control are properties that you can set. Here are some common properties that many controls share:

✦ Name — Sets the identifier used to reference the control in code.

✦ Text — Sets the text displayed in the control.

To set the access key for a control, add an ampersand (&) in front of the letter to use as the access key in the Text property. For example, to set the letter *P* in Print as the access key, set the Text property for the control equal to &Print. A user can then press the Alt key in combination with the access key to execute the control.

Windows Forms are controls. You access the properties of a Windows Forms control the same way you access the properties for any control. Here are the common properties for Windows Forms:

+ `Text` — Sets the text displayed on the form's title bar

+ `DefaultButton` — Sets the button that responds to the Enter key by default

+ `CancelButton` — Sets the button that responds to the Esc key by default

+ `MainMenuStrip` — Sets the primary menu control for the form

In addition to the controls you use to customize your forms, you have events to consider. *Events* are actions that your application might handle or respond to. Examples of common events include

+ `Click`

+ `KeyDown`

+ `Load`

+ `ValueChanged`

You can get context-sensitive help for any property or event you see in the Properties window by positioning your cursor in the value field for the property or event, and pressing F1.

Setting properties

Properties are expressed as name-value pairs. A property's value isn't always as simple as `color=black`. Values can be complex. You can use the selectors, wizards, and ellipses on the Visual Studio Properties page to dynamically build complex property values.

Examples of complex properties include properties related to

+ Setting data sources

+ Editing collections of items

+ Applying fonts and formatting

+ Selecting images and files

To set properties for a control on a Windows Form, follow these steps:

1. **Click the control in the forms designer.**

2. **Press F4 to display the Properties window.**

The control's name and type appear on the drop-down list at the top of the Properties window.

3. Click the Properties button on the Properties window's toolbar to display a list of the control's properties.

The Properties button is the third toolbar button from the left.

4. Scroll down the properties list and enter property values.

You can type simple property values or select them from a drop-down list. Click the ellipsis button for more complex properties, such as collections to display a dialog box that builds the property, as shown in Figure 1-12. Click the plus sign (+) next to compound properties to set individual properties.

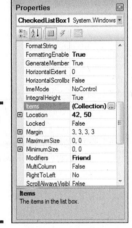

Figure 1-12:
Click the ellipsis button to build complex properties.

Responding to events

The Visual Studio Properties window displays a control's events. For example, when a user clicks a button, the button's Click event occurs. You can use event handlers to write code that fires each time the event fires.

To set an event handler by using the Properties window, follow these steps:

1. Select a form's control by clicking the control.

2. In the Properties window, click the Events button to display the control's events.

To create an event handler by using a default name, either press Enter without typing a name or double-click the field for the name.

Double-click a control on the Windows Forms Designer to create the control's default event handler.

3. Type a name for the event handler next to the event and press Enter.

Visual Studio creates the event handler and opens the code editor to the event handler.

See Book V, Chapter 4 for more details about responding to events.

Chapter 2: Building Smart Client User Interfaces

In This Chapter

✔ Customizing Windows interfaces

✔ Using dialog boxes

✔ Adding menus and toolbars

✔ Inheriting from a base Windows Form

✔ Laying out controls in a Windows Form

*U*sing Visual Studio to build Windows applications gives you a head start in your race against project deadlines. This chapter offers tools and techniques you can use to transform Visual Studio's out-of-the-box Windows projects into Windows applications that could make Bill Gates proud. In this chapter, you'll see most examples in VB and C#.

Building the Windows Container

As the container that holds your controls, the Windows Form is one of the most important elements in building Windows applications. The Windows Form is your application's foundation, and it's highly customizable.

This section explores some properties and controls that you can use to modify how your Windows Forms look and behave.

Setting common form properties

You can probably spot a typical Windows Form from ten paces:

✦ It usually has the familiar little red Close button in its upper-right corner.

✦ If it's like most windows, it has menus and toolbars.

✦ It's displayed on the taskbar along the bottom of the screen.

All these features of a typical window are determined by properties. Simply turning a property on or off can give a Windows Form a complete makeover. The default Windows Form that Visual Studio creates in all new Windows projects has most of these typical properties. Some properties, such as menus, you have to set on your own.

Table 2-1 describes some common Windows Forms properties, sorted by property group.

Table 2-1	Common Windows Forms Properties
Property	*What It Does*
FormBorderStyle	Determines whether the window is resizable
Text	Sets the caption that appears on the form's title bar
ContextMenuStrip	Sets the shortcut menu that's displayed when a user right-clicks the form
Name	Sets the identifier used to access the form in code
StartPosition	Determines where the form appears when it's first opened
AcceptButton	Sets the default Enter button
CancelButton	Sets the default Esc button
ControlBox	Toggles the form's minimize, maximize, and close controls on and off
IsMdiContainer	Determines whether the form is a parent container in a Multiple Document Interface (MDI) application
Icon	Sets the icon displayed on the title bar and the taskbar when the form is minimized
ShowInTaskBar	Shows the form on the Windows taskbar
MainMenuStrip	Sets the form's menu control

You set these properties by using the Properties window. For more information on how to set a control's properties, see Chapter 1 in this mini-book.

Creating dialog boxes

A dialog box is a Windows Form with attitude. The dialog box pops up on top of forms that are already open and refuses to leave until the user responds. Many Windows applications use dialog boxes to get a user's attention.

Most dialog boxes are *modal,* which means that they must be closed or hidden before users can continue working with other windows. *Modeless* forms can remain open alongside other windows. Modeless dialog boxes are harder to manage because you have to keep track of the different windows a user works with. Visual Studio provides a modal dialog form that you can add to your application.

To add a modal dialog box to an existing Windows project, follow these steps:

1. **Press Ctrl+Shift+A to open the Add New Item window.**

2. **Select the Dialog template.**

3. **Enter a name for the dialog box, such as MyDialog.**

4. **Click Add.**

   Visual Studio adds the dialog box to your project.

The difference between a modal and a modeless dialog box is the method with which you invoke it. For modal dialog boxes, you use the `ShowDialog` method after the dialog object has been created. For modeless dialogs, you use the `Show` method after the dialog object has been created.

The dialog box is just a regular Windows Form with the modified properties shown in the following table:

Property	*Sets To*
`AcceptButton`	The form's OK button
`CancelButton`	The form's Cancel button
`FormBorderStyle`	`FixedDialog`
`MinimizeBox`	`False`
`MaximizeBox`	`False`
`ShowInTaskbar`	`False`
`StartPosition`	`CenterParent`

The dialog box also has an OK button and a Cancel button. The Cancel button's `DialogResult` property is set to `Cancel`. The `DialogResult` property returns the selected value to the parent form of the dialog box when the button is clicked.

To use the dialog box, follow these steps:

1. **Add a label and a text box to the dialog box you create in the preceding set of steps.**

2. **Set the OK button's `DialogResult` property to `OK`.**

   When the user clicks the OK button in the dialog box, the value set in the `DialogResult` property is sent to the parent form.

3. **Add a label, text box, and button to the project's parent form. If no other forms exist in the project, press Ctrl+Shift+A to open the Add New Items window and add a Windows Form.**

4. Double-click the button to access the button's `Click` event.

The Code Editor appears.

5. In the button's `Click` event, type this code:

- *VB*

```
Dim dlgMyDialog As New MyDialog()
If dlgMyDialog.ShowDialog = Windows.Forms.DialogResult.OK Then
    txtTextFromDialog.Text = dlgMyDialog.txtEnteredText.Text
End If
```

- *C#*

```
MyDialog dlgMyDialog = new MyDialog();
if( dlgMyDialog.ShowDialog() == DialogResults.OK )
{
    txtTextFromDialog.Text = dlgMyDialog.txtEnteredText.Text;
}
```

The first two lines of code open the dialog box you create in the preceding set of steps. The remaining four lines test the `DialogResult` property of the dialog box and set the `Text` property on the text box of the parent form.

6. Press Ctrl+F5 to run the application.

To test the application, follow these steps:

1. On the parent form, click the button that launches the dialog box.

The dialog box appears.

2. In the dialog box, type Hello! in the text box and then click OK.

The dialog box closes.

3. The word *Hello!* appears in the text box in the parent form.

Figure 2-1 shows you the parent form with the dialog box open.

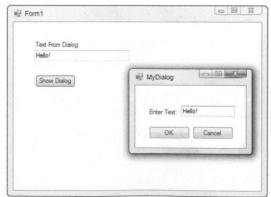

Figure 2-1: Text typed in the dialog box appears in the parent form.

The complete program (both C# and VB versions) for this example can be downloaded from this book's companion Web site. See the Introduction for details about the Web site.

Visual Studio has a number of preconfigured dialog-box components that you can use in your applications. You work with the dialog-box components in the Visual Studio toolbox by using code (unlike working with the dialog box you create in this section). The preconfigured dialog boxes create a consistent way for you to provide access to common features, such as printing and opening files. Table 2-2 lists the preconfigured dialog boxes.

Table 2-2	Preconfigured Dialog Boxes	
Toolbox Tab	*Dialog Box*	*What It Does*
Dialogs	`ColorDialog`	Displays a color palette and controls for selecting a color
	`FolderBrowserDialog`	Prompts the user to select a folder
	`FontDialog`	Prompts the user to select a font
	`OpenFileDialog`	Prompts the user to open a file
	`SaveFileDialog`	Prompts the user to save a file
Printing	`PrintDialog`	Prompts user to select a printer and configure settings
	`PageSetupDialog`	Prompts user to change page-related settings
	`PrintPreviewDialog`	Previews the document to be printed

Use the preconfigured dialog boxes, rather than create your own. The steps for using a preconfigured dialog box vary slightly because each dialog box has its own set of properties you must set.

To use the `ColorDialog` dialog box, follow these steps:

1. **Create a new Windows Form.**

2. **Drag and drop a text box and button onto the form.**

3. **Drag and drop a `ColorDialog` control onto the form from the Dialogs tab of the toolbox.**

    The `ColorDialog` appears at the bottom of the Windows Forms Designer, rather than on the Windows Form.

4. **Set the `ColorDialog` control's `Name` property to `MyColorDialog`.**

5. **Double-click the button on the Windows Form.**

    The Code Editor appears.

6. **Type the following code in the Code Editor:**

- *VB*

```
If MyColorDialog.ShowDialog() = Windows.Forms.DialogResult.OK Then
    txtSelectedColor.BackColor = MyColorDialog.Color
End If
```

- *C#*

```
If( MyColorDialog.ShowDialog() == DialogResult.OK )
{
    txtSelectedColor.BackColor = MyColorDialog.Color;
}
```

Use the `ShowDialog()` method to display preconfigured dialog boxes.

7. **Press Ctrl+F5 to run the application.**

8. **Click the button on the form to launch the `ColorDialog` control.**

The `ColorDialog` appears, as shown in Figure 2-2.

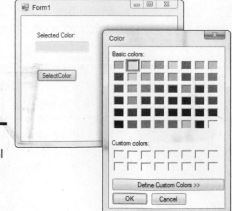

Figure 2-2:
This control
is a pre-
configured
dialog box.

9. **Select a color and then click OK.**

The background color of the text box changes.

The complete program (both C# and VB versions) for this example can be downloaded from this book's companion Web site. See the Introduction for details.

Adding menus and toolbars

Most Windows applications have menus and toolbars that give users access to commands. Visual Studio provides these two menu controls and three toolbar controls:

+ `ContextMenuStrip` — The shortcut menu that appears when a user right-clicks

+ `MenuStrip` — A standard menu that usually appears at the top of a form

+ `StatusStrip` — A band that usually appears along the bottom of a form that displays status feedback information

+ `ToolStrip` — A control that creates toolbars

+ `ToolStripContainer` — A container for hosting menu and toolbar controls

The `ToolStrip` control, the granddaddy of all the menu and toolbars controls, has these features:

+ Items that you can add to the menu and toolbar controls, such as `ToolStripMenuItem`

+ Container controls that allow menus and toolbars to coexist in the same container

+ Properties that allow you to set the look and feel of menus and toolbars

Because all menu and toolbar controls are related, they share the `ToolStrip` control's features. The procedure for adding items, working with containers, and setting properties is consistent across all menu and toolbar controls.

To add a menu to a form and configure the menu, follow these steps:

1. **Drag a `MenuStrip` control to a form and drop it.**

   The menu docks itself to the top of the form.

2. **Click the arrow in the upper-right corner of the `MenuStrip` control to display a list of tasks.**

3. **In the MenuStrip Tasks dialog box, click Insert Standard Items.**

   The `MenuStrip` control adds menu items for File, Edit, Tools, and Help, as shown in Figure 2-3.

4. **Repeat Steps 1–3 to add a `ToolStrip` control to the form and insert standard items on the toolbar.**

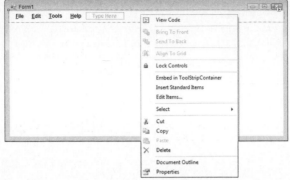

Figure 2-3:
Click Insert
Standard
Items to add
standard
menu items
to the
`MenuStrip`
control.

All the menu and toolbar controls are smart tag-enabled. A smart tag-enabled control has a little arrow in its upper-right corner. Click this arrow to access a task dialog box that displays common tasks for each control. The `MenuStrip` and `ToolStrip` controls display the same task dialog box. (Figure 2-3 shows the MenuStrip Tasks dialog box.) The available `MenuStrip` and `ToolStrip` tasks are shown in this list:

+ **Embed in ToolStripContainer** — Moves the control inside a `ToolStripContainer` control

+ **Insert Standard Items** — Adds standard command items to the control

+ **RenderMode** — Sets a specific style for the control

+ **Dock** — Sets the control's location to the top or bottom, or the left or right side, of the form

+ **GripStyle** — Makes the control's move handle hidden or visible

+ **Edit Items** — Opens the Items Collection Editor, which you use to edit the control's items

Menus and toolbars display commands that users can execute. Each command is an item on the menu or toolbar control. A control's entire set of commands is the control's *items collection*. You can edit a control's items collection by using the Windows Forms Designer or the Items Collection Editor.

To edit items by using the Windows Forms Designer, follow these steps:

1. **Drag and drop a `StatusStrip` control on the form.**

The control docks itself to the bottom of the form by default.

2. **Click the drop-down arrow in the control.**

A list of available `StatusStrip` items appears, as shown in Figure 2-4.

Figure 2-4:
Select
an item
from the
drop-down
list to add
to the
`Status`
`Strip`
control.

3. Select a `StatusLabel` control from the list.

The `StatusLabel` control is added to the `StatusStrip` control.

4. Repeat Step 3 to add a progress bar.

To add items to a `MenuStrip` control by using the Windows Forms Designer, follow these steps:

1. Click the `MenuStrip` control in the form.

A command placeholder named `MenuItem`, with the prompt Type Here, appears; see Figure 2-5.

Book III
Chapter 2

Building Smart
Client User
Interfaces

Figure 2-5:
Type a
command
in the
`MenuItem`
placeholder.

To insert a command between existing commands, right-click a command and choose Insert from the shortcut menu. Choose an item to insert from the list of available items.

2. Type a command name, such as View, and then press Enter.

The placeholder expands for you to add more commands.

Table 2-3 lists the items you can add to the menu and toolbar controls.

Table 2-3	Items You Can Add to the ToolStrip Controls
Control Name	*Item You Can Add*
MenuStrip	MenuItem
	ComboBox
	Separator
	TextBox
ToolStrip	Button
	Label
	SplitButton
ToolStrip	DropDownButton
	Separator
	ComboBox
	TextBox
	ProgressBar
StatusStrip	StatusLabel
	ProgressBar
	DropDownButton
	SplitButton

You can start a control's Items Collection Editor in one of three ways:

✦ From the control's Tasks dialog box

✦ By using the control's Properties window

✦ From the control's shortcut menu

To use the Items Collection Editor from the control's shortcut menu:

1. **Right-click the form's StatusStrip control.**

The control's shortcut menu appears.

2. **Choose Edit Items.**

The Items Collection Editor appears.

3. **Click the drop-down list at the top of the editor to display a list of available items for the control.**

4. **Select DropDownButton from the list.**

5. **Click Add.**

   A `DropDownButton` control is added to the members list, as shown in Figure 2-6.

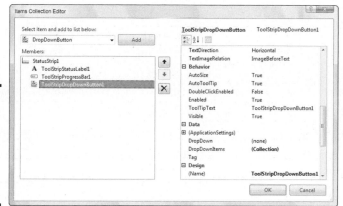

Figure 2-6:
Click Add to add an item to the control's items collection.

6. **Click the up arrow to move the `DropDownButton` control to the top of the list.**

7. **Select the progress bar control from the Members list.**

   The progress bar control is named `ToolStripProgressBar1`.

8. **Click the button with the X on it to delete the progress bar.**

9. **Click OK.**

   The Items Collection Editor closes.

The properties of individual items on menu and toolbar controls are easier to manage if you use the Items Collection Editor instead of the Properties window.

Using a ToolStripContainer

The `ToolStripContainer` control makes it easy to host multiple menu and toolbar controls on a single form. The `ToolStripContainer` control has panels, as shown in Figure 2-7, where you place your menu and toolbar controls. The advantage of using `ToolStripContainer` is that your controls automatically stack horizontally and vertically in the panel.

Book III
Chapter 2

Building Smart
Client User
Interfaces

Figure 2-7:
Place menu and toolbar controls in this control's panels.

To use a ToolStripContainer control in a Windows Form, follow these steps:

1. **Drag and drop a ToolStripContainer control on a Windows Form.**

2. **Click Dock Fill in Form in the ToolStripContainer control's Tasks dialog box.**

   The control expands to fill the form. The control's top panel is visible by default.

3. **Drag and drop a MenuStrip control on the top panel.**

4. **Click the arrow tab on the ToolStripContainer control's top pane.**

   The pane expands to accommodate another menu or toolbar.

5. **Drag and drop a ToolStrip control on the top panel, positioned below the MenuStrip control.**

6. **Click the tab on the bottom panel to make the panel visible.**

7. **Add a StatusStrip control to the bottom panel.**

Users can use the ToolStripContainer control to customize their work environments by moving toolbars and menus around within the panels of the ToolStripContainer control. Figure 2-8 shows you an example of a toolbar being moved.

Controlling styles

You can style the menu and toolbar controls by using the RenderMode property. You can use it to specify how you want the menu or toolbar rendered. The .NET built-in styles render your menus and toolbars to look like Office or Windows. You can set the RenderMode property to one of these four values:

✦ `Custom` — Sets the style to a custom renderer

✦ `ManagerRenderMode` — Uses the renderer specified in the `ToolStripManager`

✦ `Professional` — Uses a style that looks like Office 2003 and Windows XP

✦ `System` — Uses a flat Windows style

ToolStrip

ToolStrip container   MenuStrip

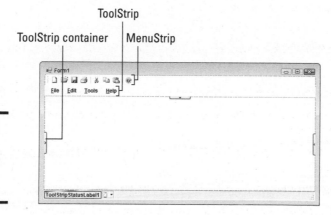

Figure 2-8:
Using a
control to
move
toolboxes.

Figure 2-9 shows the same form with two different rendered styles. The form on the left uses system styling, and the form on the right uses professional styling. The professionally styled menus and toolbars are rounded and more elegant. You can set these styles by using the Tasks dialog box for each of the controls. The most obvious difference is the use of hot keys.

Figure 2-9:
The System
menu style
is "flatter"
than the
Professional
style.

You use `ToolStripManager` to set a single style for all `ToolStrip` controls. For example, to set all the menus and toolbars to Professional, follow these steps:

1. **Set the `RenderMode` property for each menu and toolbar control to `ManagerRenderMode`.**

2. **Set the `RenderMode` property on `ToolStripManager` in the form's `Load` event by using this code:**

   - *VB*

     ```
     ToolStripManager.RenderMode = ToolStripManagerRenderMode.Professional
     ```

   - *C#*

     ```
     ToolStripManager.RenderMode = ToolStripManagerRenderMode.Professional;
     ```

You access `ToolStripManager` in code. It's not a control that you can access from the toolbox, like on other menus and toolbars.

Creating a Multiple Document Interface

You might have used a Windows application where all the application windows are contained within a parent window. An application in which all child windows are contained within a parent window is a *Multiple Document Interface (MDI)*.

Creating an MDI application involves these high-level steps:

1. Create the parent container form.
2. Create child forms.
3. Write code that opens the child forms in the container.

To create the parent MDI form, follow these steps:

1. **Create a new Windows application in Visual Basic.**

   Visual Studio creates a new Windows project with an empty Windows Form named Form1.

   See Chapter 1 in this mini-book for more information about creating Windows applications.

2. **Set the Form1 `IsMdiContainer` property to `True`.**
3. **Add a `MenuStrip` control to the form.**
4. **Add the menu items Select and Window.**
5. **Add the menu items Open Form 2 and Open Form to the Select menu.**

After you have the parent form, create these child forms to open in the parent MDI form:

1. **Add a new form named Form2.**

2. **Add a label and a text box to the form.**

3. **Add a new form named Form3.**

4. **Add a `MonthCalendar` control to the form.**

In the parent MDI container Form1, follow these steps:

1. **Double-click the form to access the form's `Load` event.**

2. **In the Load event, type this line:**

- *VB*

```
MenuStrip1.MdiWindowListItem = WindowsToolStripMenuItem
```

- *C#*

```
MenuStrip1.MdiWindowListItem = WindowsToolStripMenuItem;
```

This line sets the Windows menu item as the `MdiWindowListItem` control for the menu strip. As child windows are opened, the Windows menu displays the windows, along with a check mark, next to the active window.

3. **Below the `Load` event, type these lines:**

- *VB*

```
Private Sub GetChild(ByRef frmChild As Form)
    frmChild.MdiParent = Me
    frmChild.Show()
End Sub
```

- *C#*

```
private void GetChild(ref Form frmChild)
{
    frmChild.MdiParent = this;
    frmChild.Show();
}
```

This code sample creates a procedure named `GetChild` that accepts a child form as a parameter. When the child form is passed to `GetChild`, the procedure sets the child form's MDI parent container as the displayed form and displays the child form in the container.

4. **In the Windows Forms Designer, double-click the Open Form 2 menu item.**

The `Click` event is created.

5. **Type this line in the `Click` event:**

```
GetChild(New Form2)
```

This line passes Form2 to the `GetChild` procedure.

6. **Repeat Steps 4 and 5 for the Form 3 menu item and substitute Form3 for Form2 in the code.**

The entire code sample (minus the hidden code that Visual Studio creates) for Form1 is shown in Listing 2-1.

Listing 2-1: Code That Services the Multiple Document Interface

```
Public Class Form1
    Private Sub Window1ToolStripMenuItem_Click(ByVal sender As System.Object,
    ByVal e As System.EventArgs) Handles Window1ToolStripMenuItem.Click
        GetChild(New Form2)
    End Sub
    Private Sub Form1_Load(ByVal sender As System.Object, ByVal e As
    System.EventArgs) Handles MyBase.Load
        Me.MenuStrip1.MdiWindowListItem = Me.WindowsToolStripMenuItem
    End Sub
    Private Sub Window2ToolStripMenuItem_Click(ByVal sender As System.Object,
    ByVal e As System.EventArgs) Handles Window2ToolStripMenuItem.Click
        GetChild(New Form3)
    End Sub
    Private Sub GetChild(ByRef frmChild As Form)
        frmChild.MdiParent = Me
        frmChild.Show()
    End Sub
End Class
```

To test the MDI application, follow these steps:

1. **Press Ctrl+F5 to run the application.**

2. **Choose the Select menu item.**

3. **Choose Open Form 2 from the Select menu.**

Form2 opens and is contained within the parent form.

4. **Repeat Steps 1–3 to open Form3.**

5. **Click the Windows menu.**

The Windows menu displays the open windows. A check mark appears next to the active window, as shown in Figure 2-10.

Figure 2-10:
Use the
Windows
menu to
manage
child
windows.

Taking advantage of visual inheritance

Sometimes, you want to reuse forms. You can inherit from an existing form rather than create forms from scratch. You need two forms: the base form and one to inherit from the base form.

To create the base form, follow these steps:

1. **Press Ctrl+Shift+A to open the Add New Item window. Add a new Windows Form to the project.**

2. **Add a label and a text box to the form.**

3. **Choose Build⇨Build Solution.**

   You must build the base form in order to inherit from it.

To inherit from the base form, follow these steps:

1. **Choose Project⇨Add New Item.**

   The Add New Item window appears.

2. **Click the Inherited Form template.**

3. **Enter a name for the form.**

4. **Click Add.**

   The Inheritance Picker appears.

5. **Click the base form in the Inheritance Picker, as shown in Figure 2-11.**

**Book III
Chapter 2**

**Building Smart
Client User
Interfaces**

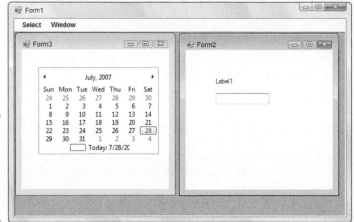

Figure 2-11:
Use the
Inheritance
Picker to
inherit from
a base form.

6. **Click OK.**

The inherited form displays the base form's controls.

You must build your solution whenever you make changes to the base form in order to make changes appear in the inherited form.

Laying Out Your Controls

As UI design becomes more sophisticated, users expect to have more control over the user experience. This means being able, at minimum, to resize windows. Resizing can wreak havoc on the controls that you spend lots of time nudging into their proper positions. Windows Forms provide several options for managing controls for resizing, including containers for grouping controls and properties for locking controls in place.

Grouping controls

The Visual Studio toolbox has a group of container controls. Use container controls whenever you need to

✦ Easily manipulate groups of controls in the Windows Forms Designer

✦ Create visible groupings of controls

✦ Make it easier to resize a form

The container controls are shown in this list:

✦ FlowLayoutPanel — Arranges controls in a horizontal or vertical flow

✦ GroupBox — Creates a visible grouping of controls with a caption

✦ `Panel` — Creates a scrollable grouping of controls

✦ `SplitContainer` — Arranges controls on two separate panels separated by a movable bar

✦ `TabControl` — Arranges controls on multiple tabs or pages, similar to a file folder

✦ `TableLayoutPanel` — Arranges controls in a tabular grid

You can position container controls inside other controls. The `FlowLayoutPanel` and `TableLayoutPanel` controls can dynamically reposition the child controls placed inside them when the Windows Form is resized. To see `FlowLayoutPanel` in action, follow these steps:

1. **Add a `FlowLayoutPanel` control to a form.**

2. **Click the arrow in the upper-right corner of the control.**

The control's task dialog box appears.

3. **Click Dock in the parent container.**

The `FlowLayoutPanel` control expands to fill the form.

4. **Add two text boxes to the form.**

5. **Grab the second text box with your mouse and try to move the box below the first one.**

The text box "jumps" back because the controls placed in a `FlowLayoutPanel` flow either horizontally or vertically.

6. **Add a `GroupBox` control to the form.**

7. **Place a label and a text box inside the `GroupBox` control.**

As you add the controls, notice that snaplines appear inside the `GroupBox` control.

Although all the controls placed inside the `GroupBox` can be positioned exactly where you want them, `GroupBox` flows with the rest of the controls in the `FlowLayoutPanel` control.

8. **Add a `MonthCalendar` control to the form.**

9. **Press Ctrl+F5 to run the form.**

10. **Resize the form and notice that the controls move.**

Figure 2-12 shows the form in its default size and again resized. Notice that the controls are stacked in the form on the left because the form is narrow. As the form is resized, the controls move to fill the form.

Figure 2-12:
Resizing the window causes the controls to move.

You have some options for controlling the flow in a `FlowLayoutPanel` control:

✦ **To force a control to move to the next line** — Set the control's `FlowBreak` property to `True`.

✦ **To change the direction of the `FlowLayoutPanel` control** — Set the `FlowDirection` property.

✦ **To set `FlowLayoutPanel` so that child controls are clipped rather than wrapped to the next line** — Set the `WrapContents` property to `False`. Figure 2-13 shows a form that has `FlowLayoutPanel` with a clipped `MonthCalendar` control.

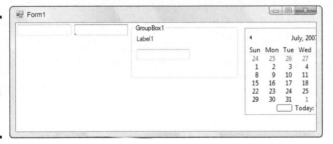

Figure 2-13:
Set a property to `False` to clip controls rather than wrap them.

Setting layout properties

You might want to position controls in a way that they stay in place in the face of resizing. You can set many properties for controlling a control's layout:

✦ `Anchor` — Specifies an anchor position that the control maintains when the form is resized

✦ `Dock` — Positions the control so that one edge of the control is always touching the parent control's edge

✦ `AutoSize` — Allows a control to grow or shrink automatically

✦ `Margin` — Sets spacing outside a control's borders

✦ `Padding` — Adds spacing between a control's borders and its interior contents

The best way to picture these properties in action is to see them at work. The following sections walk you through using these properties.

Anchoring and docking

Anchoring and docking are two properties you can use to position a control when a form is resized. When you set a control's `Anchor` and `Dock` properties, you specify the edges of a form — top, bottom, left, right — to which you want to position your control. The `Dock` property accepts a `Fill` value, which forces the control to expand to touch all four sides of a form.

The primary difference between `Anchor` and `Dock` is that anchoring allows you to maintain a set distance between the edge of the control and the edge of the form. With docking, the control always maintains constant contact with the form's edge. There's no space between the control and the edge. Figure 2-14 shows a button that's anchored to the lower-left corner of the form and a status strip that's docked to the bottom.

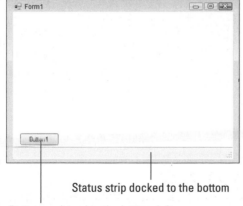

Figure 2-14:
`Anchor`
and `Dock`
properties
let you
position a
control.

Status strip docked to the bottom

Button anchored to the bottom left

Menus, toolbars, and status strips are always docked by default.

To anchor a Submit button to the lower-left corner of a form, follow these steps:

1. **Add a button to a form.**

For more information on adding a button to a form, see the section in Chapter 1 of this mini-book about adding controls to your form.

2. **Click the button and press F4 to open the Properties window.**

3. **Scroll to the Anchor property.**

The Anchor property is in the Layout category.

4. **Click the arrow on the drop-down list for the Anchor property.**

A visual positioning tool appears.

5. **Click the left and bottom bars to set the anchor.**

6. **Click the top bar to clear the anchor.**

Figure 2-15 shows you an example.

7. **Press Enter to set the property.**

8. **Press Ctrl+F5 to run the form.**

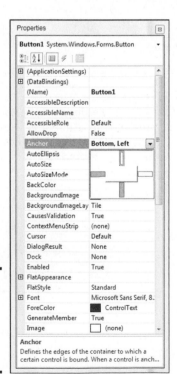

Figure 2-15:
Click the bars to set and clear the anchor positions.

9. **Resize the form from the bottom, top, left, and right.**

Notice that the button maintains its distance from the bottom and the left.

You can use the Anchor property to expand a control as the form expands. To set a text box to grow as the sides of a form expand, follow these steps:

1. **Add a text box to the center of the form.**

2. **Set the text box's Anchor property to Left, Right.**

3. **Press Ctrl+F5 to run the form.**

4. **Resize the form to the left and the right.**

Figure 2-16 shows the form in its default size and resized. Notice how the text isn't completely displayed in the text box. After the form is resized, the text box expands and maintains equal distance from the left and right sides.

 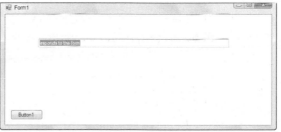

Figure 2-16:
The text box expands as its anchor sides expand.

Setting a control's Dock property is similar to setting the Anchor property. With the Dock property, you specify the edges to which you want to dock the control. The control always maintains contact with the edge you specify. Figure 2-17 shows a form with a StatusStrip control docked on the bottom of the form. As the form is resized, the StatusStrip control remains at the bottom.

Figure 2-17:
The control remains docked to the form's bottom edge as the form is resized.

Using automatic sizing

Two properties are related to setting automatic sizing:

✦ AutoSize — Specifies, by using a True/False value, whether the control should be automatically sized

✦ AutoSizeMode — Sets a control to GrowAndShrink or GrowOnly

The AutoSizeMode property works only if AutoSize is set to True. Although not all controls have an AutoSizeMode property, it provides more control than AutoSize when it's available. The size of a control grows rightward and downward.

To set the automatic sizing properties for a button, follow these steps:

1. **Add a button to a form.**

2. **Use the Properties window to set the button's Text property to Please click this button.**

Notice that the button displays only part of the text.

3. **Set the button's AutoSize property to True.**

The button expands to display the text, as shown in Figure 2-18.

Figure 2-18: The button expands to display the text when the AutoSize property is set to True.

The AutoSize and AutoSizeMode properties honor the MinimumSize and MaximumSize property settings.

Setting margins and padding

Margins and padding set the space outside and within a control's borders, respectively. Because a control's border has four sides, the margins and padding properties comprise a set of properties. When you set the margins and padding properties, you can specify values for top, left, right, bottom, or all.

To set a control's margins and padding, follow these steps:

1. **Add a button to a form.**

   For more information about adding a button to a form, see the section in Chapter 1 of this mini-book about adding controls to your form.

2. **Click the new button and press F4 to open the Properties window.**

3. **Scroll to the Margin property.**

4. **Click the plus (+) sign next to the Margin property to expand the property.**

5. **In the All property, type** 20.

   All the button's margins are now set to 20.

6. **Drag another button to the form.**

   As you approach the first button, notice that the snaplines are farther apart than usual because the first button's margin is higher.

   The space between the two buttons when the snaplines are present is 23. The snapline's distance between controls is a sum of the two control's margins. The default margin for a button control is 3.

7. **Allow the second button to snap to the first button and drop the second button.**

8. **Change the padding property on the second button to** `All = 10`.

9. **Resize the second button so that you can see the button's text.**

   Notice the padding that appears around the text now. Figure 2-19 shows you an example.

Book III
Chapter 2

Building Smart
Client User
Interfaces

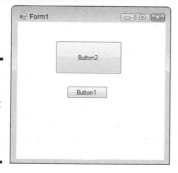

Figure 2-19:
The second button's text is padded in all directions.

Chapter 3: Building Visual C++ Applications

In This Chapter

✔ Taking a fresh look at C++

✔ Peeking at the Visual C++ application wizards

✔ Creating managed and unmanaged applications

*V*isual C++ has been with us for quite some time, and C++, the core language on which Visual C++ is based, is even older! Rick remembers how excited he was when he started learning C++ in 1985. Just because Visual C++ is, shall we say, *mature* doesn't mean that it can't hold its own against more modern programming languages. Many folks still use Visual C++ when they need to perform tasks outside the managed box. Or, they also use Visual C++ to take advantage of the huge pile of C++ code they've developed over the years. This chapter gives you the scoop on Visual C++ and shows you how to create Visual C++ applications by using Visual Studio 2008. Microsoft has big plans for updating Visual C++ in the future.

Getting to Know Visual C++

Visual C++ is one language in the suite of .NET languages. Unlike the other .NET languages, the core syntax libraries in Visual C++ and its primary helper libraries aren't necessarily part of the .NET Framework. You can write managed Visual C++ applications, but most developers who write in C++ want to output native code. As a result, most applications written in Visual C++ don't require the .NET Framework.

Creating a full-blown Windows application by using just C++ syntax can be quite challenging. If you're guessing that this is where Visual C++ comes in, you're right. Visual C++ is different from plain old C++ because it provides additional libraries, tools, and widgets that you can use to build sophisticated applications for Windows and the Web.

Visual C++ includes these elements:

✦ **Standard libraries for building C++ applications** — The C++ object-oriented language was created to extend the popular C language. The downside of using a low-level language like C++ is that you have to write more code to get something done than you do when you're using a higher-level language, such as Visual Basic or C#.

The result is that C++ programs are smaller and faster than higher-level languages because they can

• Run without the .NET common language runtime

• Interact directly with the operating system (OS)

• Manage their own memory and resources

C++ compilers exist for almost every OS. If you write your application by using only C++ syntax, you may be able to compile your program to run in Unix, even if you wrote it on a Windows computer.

✦ **Microsoft Foundation Classes (MFC), a library for building Windows applications** — The MFC library of classes wraps the Windows application programming interface (API). The MFC library was written in C++ to provide object-oriented access to the features and commands of the Windows API. Before MFC was created, developers used the procedural language C to access the Windows API.

✦ **The Active Template Library (ATL) for building small, lightweight components** — The ATL library of C++ classes is designed for building components such as ActiveX controls. Components built with ATL are usually consumed by another application. ATL Server is an extension of ATL for building powerful, high-performance Web applications and Web services.

ATL creates components known as COM objects. The *COM (Component Object Model) standard* defines how components talk with each other. Components created with ATL conform to the COM standard and can use the COM services provided by Windows to communicate.

✦ **Support for accessing the services of the .NET Framework** — Wait a minute! Earlier in this section, you can read that C++ applications don't require .NET. That's right: Although they don't require .NET, they *can* access the services of .NET when they want. As a result, code written in Visual C++ is either

• *Managed* — A Visual C++ program that uses the services of the .NET Framework. Any code that's executed in the .NET Common Language Runtime (CLR) is *managed*. Programs written in Visual Basic and C# are always managed because they can't be executed without the services of .NET, such as the CLR. You can read more about CLR and .NET in Book I, Chapter 2.

- *Native code* — An application that doesn't require .NET. You create unmanaged Visual C++ applications by using the MFC library, the ATL library, or any of the standard C++ libraries. Even unmanaged Visual C++ applications can access some managed components through a mechanism that this chapter discusses next.

The ability of managed and unmanaged code to coexist peacefully in Visual C++ is *interoperability,* or Interop. To read more about Interop, search the Visual Studio Help index for *Interop.*

You can use Visual C++ to create all kinds of applications and components:

✦ Console applications

✦ Controls

✦ Dynamic link libraries (DLLs)

✦ Web services

✦ Internet Server Application Programming Interface (ISAPI) Filters

✦ Windows applications

✦ Windows services

Introducing Visual C++ Templates and Wizards

Because Visual C++ is a low-level language, you have to write more lines of code to do even simple tasks. Lots of code is involved in wiring up all the Visual C++ libraries in just the right way so that you can start building software. Thankfully, Visual Studio provides many templates and application wizards for building Visual C++ applications.

Visual Studio provides project templates for managed C++ applications. Because unmanaged applications require more code, Visual Studio uses application wizards to walk you through the process of setting up your application. Table 3-1 lists the project templates for managed applications, and Table 3-2 lists the Visual C++ application wizards.

Table 3-1	Visual Studio Project Templates for Creating Managed Visual C++ Applications
Project Template	*What It Does*
ASP.NET Web Service	Creates XML Web services by using ASP.NET
Class Library	Creates reusable class libraries and components that you can use in other projects

(continued)

Table 3-1 *(continued)*

Project Template	What It Does
CLR Console Application	Creates a command line application without a graphical user interface (UI)
CLR Empty Project	Creates an empty project to which you must add files manually
SQL Server Project	Creates a data access class library that you can deploy to SQL Server
Smart Device Project	Creates a project aimed at smart devices, such as a BlackBerry
Windows Forms Application	Creates a Windows application
Windows Forms Control Library	Creates custom controls for use in Windows Forms
Windows Service	Creates an application that runs as a Windows service

Table 3-2   Visual Studio Application Wizards for Creating Unmanaged Visual C++ Applications

Project Template	Application Wizard	What the Application Creates
ATL Project	ATL Project Wizard	DLLs, applications, and services for creating components using ATL libraries
ATL Server Project	ATL Server Project Wizard	A Web application and ISAPI extension DLLs for responding to HyperText Transfer Protocol (HTTP) requests
ATL Server Web Service	ATL Server Project Wizard	An ATL server application configured to run as a Web service
ATL Smart Device Project	ATL Smart Device Project Wizard	A DLL or an application created by using ATL and designed to run on a smart device
Custom Wizard	Custom Application Wizard	A custom wizard
Makefile Project	Makefile Application Wizard	A project that sets build settings for a project built by using the command line
MFC ActiveX Control	MFC ActiveX Control Wizard	An ActiveX control using the MFC library
MFC Application	MFC Application Wizard	A Windows application using the MFC library

Project Template	Application Wizard	What the Application Creates
MFC DLL	MFC DLL Wizard	A DLL using the MFC library
Win32 Console Application	Win32 Application Wizard	A command line application with or without MFC and ATL libraries
Win32 Project	Win32 Application Wizard	A Windows or console application, DLL, or class library with or without MFC and ATL libraries

The ATL, MFC, and Win32 application wizards include some support for smart devices, but more specific support is available if you create a Smart Device Project.

Visual C++ projects are organized into three folders:

✦ **Header Files** — Holds source files that reference entities in the C++ libraries

✦ **Resource Files** — Holds resources, such as bitmap files and cursors, as well as the files that manage an application's resources

✦ **Source Files** — Holds source code files, including the main C++ source files that have the extension .cpp

The Visual Studio project templates and application wizards generate the header, source, and resource files for the kind of application you create. For more information, search for *file types* in the Visual Studio Help index.

Saying "Hello, Visual C++"

The Visual Studio project templates and application wizards make it easy to build managed and unmanaged Visual C++ applications. The steps for creating managed Visual C++ applications with project templates are virtually the same for building C# or Visual Basic applications. Whether you're using a project template or an application wizard, creating a Visual C++ project is similar to creating any other project in Visual Studio:

1. **Choose File⇨New⇨Project.**

The New Project dialog box appears.

2. **In the Project Types tree, click the plus sign (+) next to Visual C++ to expand the list of available project types.**

A list of available project types appears, as shown in Figure 3-1.

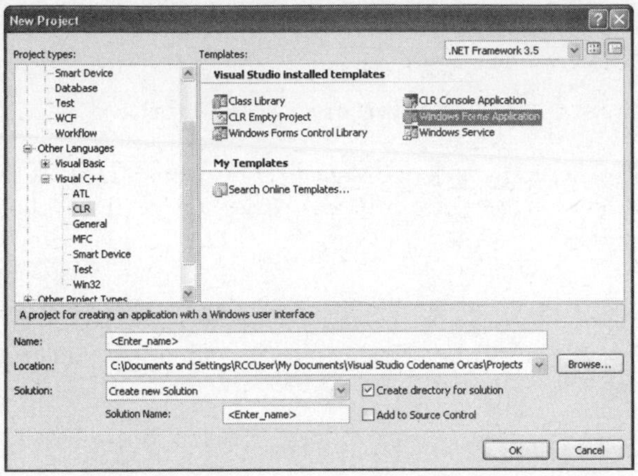

Figure 3-1:
Click a
project type
to see a list
of available
Visual C++
project
templates.

Figure 3-1 shows the New Project window using the C++ development
environment settings. You don't have to use the C++ development environment settings to create C++ projects. See Book II, Chapter 1 for more
information on changing your development environment settings.

3. **Click the project type you want to create.**

   A list of available project templates for that project type appears in the
   Templates area of the screen.

4. **Click a project template.**

5. **Enter a name for your project in the Name text box.**

6. **Click OK to create your project.**

   For unmanaged applications, Visual Studio starts the appropriate
   wizard. For managed applications, Visual Studio creates the project and
   adds header, resource, and source files.

Creating managed applications

Creating a managed Windows Forms application in Visual Studio is the same
as creating a Windows Forms application in any other .NET language. To
create a new managed Windows application by using the Visual C++ language, follow these steps:

1. **Open the New Project window, as described in the preceding section.**

2. **In the Project Types tree, click the plus sign (+) next to Visual C++.**

3. **Click the CLR project type.**

   A list of project templates available for creating a CLR application
   appears.

4. **Click the Windows Forms Application template.**

5. **Enter a name for the application.**

6. **Click OK to create the project.**

Visual Studio creates the project and opens a blank Windows Form in the Windows Forms Designer. The project created by Visual Studio includes these elements:

✦ **References** — Give your project access to the services of the .NET Framework.

✦ **Source files** — Jump-start your project.

✦ **Header files and resource files** — Support the project's source files.

To say, "Hello world" in a managed Visual C++ Windows Form Application, follow these steps:

1. **Drag and drop a label control and a button control on the Windows Form.**

2. **Double-click the button control to access the control's `Click` event.**

The Code Editor opens.

3. **Type this code in the Code Editor:**

```
this->label1->Text = "Hello world";
```

4. **Press Ctrl+F5 to run your form.**

When you click the button on the form, the text `Hello world` appears in the label.

Working with managed Windows Forms in the Windows Forms Designer is the same, regardless of the underlying programming language. Refer to Chapters 1 and 2 of this mini-book for more information on using the Windows Forms Designer.

To say, "Hello world" in a managed Visual C++ Console Application, follow these steps:

1. **Add this code in the Code Editor:**

```
Console::WriteLine(L"Hello World");
```

2. **Press Ctrl+F5 to run your form.**

When you click the button on the form, the text `Hello World` appears in the output.

Creating unmanaged applications

The Visual Studio application wizards help you step through the creation of unmanaged Visual C++ applications. After you complete an application wizard, use Visual Studio resource editors and code wizards to complete your project.

Using a wizard to create an unmanaged application

Visual Studio has several wizards for creating Visual C++ projects. Use the Visual Studio application wizard to

✦ Generate source code to create the program's basic structure.

✦ Include resources, such as menus and toolbars.

✦ Wire all the libraries to make the project work.

To create a new Windows Forms application by using MFC, follow these steps:

1. **Open the New Project window, as described at the beginning of this section.**

2. **Expand the list of Visual C++ project types and click MFC.**

   A list of available MFC application wizards appears.

3. **In the Templates pane, click the MFC Application icon.**

4. **Give your project a name and then click OK.**

   The MFC Application Wizard appears.

5. **Click Next to step through the wizard.**

6. **On the Application Type page, set the application type to Single Document, as shown in Figure 3-2.**

   Use the Application Type page to specify the kind of Windows Form to create.

7. **Continue stepping through the wizard to set options for database support and user interface features.**

8. **On the Generated Classes page, open the Base Class drop-down list. Select CFormView, as shown in Figure 3-3.**

   The base class determines the kind of Windows Form that the application creates.

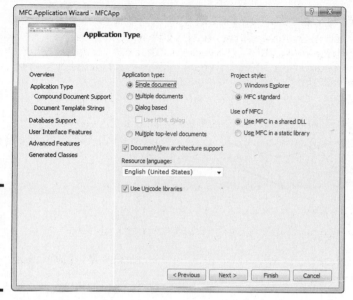

Figure 3-2:
Set the
application
type to
Single
Document.

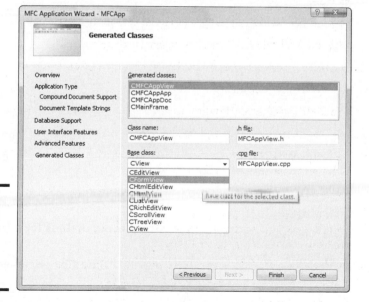

Figure 3-3:
Select this
class to
set the
Windows
Form.

9. Click Finish.

Visual Studio adds the source, header, and resource files that are necessary to build the options you specify in the wizard.

The wizard generates a fully functioning Windows application. Press Ctrl+F5 to run it. You should see a window similar to the one shown in Figure 3-4.

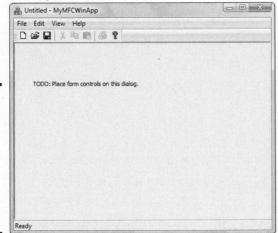

Figure 3-4:
The application wizard generates a fully functioning Windows application.

If your goal is to use C++ syntax, application wizards probably aren't the route you want to take. Pick up a copy of *C++ For Dummies,* 5th Edition, by Stephen Randy Davis (Wiley), if you need to know about C++ syntax.

Managing resources

Visual Studio provides resource editors for working with a Visual C++ project's resources. Here are a few resource editors:

✦ **Dialog Editor** — Manages dialog boxes

✦ **Menu Editor** — Manages menus

✦ **String Editor** — Manages all your project's strings

To access a project's resources, follow these steps:

1. Choose View➪Resource View or press Ctrl+Shift+E.

A tree view of the project's resources appears.

2. **Expand the resource folders until you see the Menu folder.**

3. **Click the Menu folder to expand it.**

4. **Double-click the Menu resource IDR_MAINFRAME.**

   The Menu Editor opens, as shown in Figure 3-5.

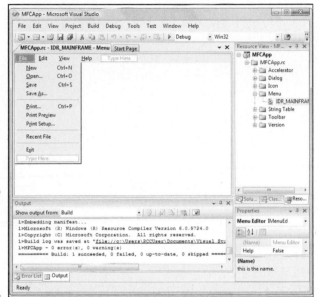

Figure 3-5:
Use the
Menu Editor
to edit the
project's
menus.

Book III
Chapter 3

Building Visual C++
Applications

To add controls to your Windows Form, follow these steps:

1. **Click the plus sign (+) next to the Dialog folder in your project's Resource View pane.**

   A list of your project's forms appears.

2. **Double-click the form IDD_MYMFCWINAPP_FORM to open it.**

   The form opens in the Dialog Editor, as shown in Figure 3-6. Note that the name of the form is generated by using the project name you specify. If you used a project name other than MyMFCWinApp, insert your project's name between IDD_ and _FORM.

3. **Drag and drop controls from the toolbox onto the Dialog Editor.**

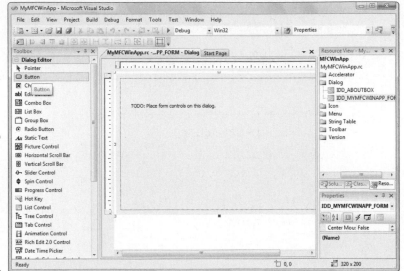

Figure 3-6:
Use the
Dialog
Editor to add
controls to
your
project's
forms.

You can build event handlers for controls by choosing Add Event Handler from the control's shortcut menu.

To add a resource to a project, follow these steps:

1. **Click the Resource View pane.**

2. **Choose Project⇨Add Resource.**

   The Add Resource dialog box appears.

3. **Choose a resource from the list of resource types.**

4. **Click the New button, as shown in Figure 3-7, to add the resource.**

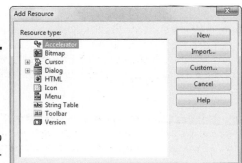

Figure 3-7:
Use the Add
Resource
window
to add
resources to
your project.

Chapter 4: Building Web Applications

In This Chapter

✔ Using Visual Web Developer

✔ Creating your first Web site

✔ Understanding server controls

✔ Getting comfortable with ASP.NET syntax

✔ Creating user controls

*T*o help you build Web applications, Microsoft offers a wide array of products. Among them are ASP.NET and Visual Studio, which are used to create enterprise Web sites featuring e-commerce and full-blown Web-based applications. ASP.NET Web sites use server-side code to do many things, from rendering dynamic content to accessing databases.

In addition to these high-end tools, Microsoft offers Web design and development tools for a range of sites and skill levels, all of which support Web design standards, such as Cascading Style Sheets (CSS), to work together seamlessly. The bigger picture of Microsoft tools looks something like this:

✦ **Visual Web Developer** — The premiere Microsoft toolset for building ASP.NET Web sites is part of Visual Studio 2008.

✦ **Microsoft Expressions** — This set of three products (Graphic Designer, Interactive Designer, and Web Designer) targets professionals who design Web sites.

✦ **SharePoint Designer** — Because this tool for designing SharePoint sites is built on *FrontPage* (a program for creating HTML-based sites, which Microsoft is phasing out), SharePoint Designer can create the file-based sites of FrontPage. SharePoint Designer supports the limited development of ASP.NET Web sites.

The Microsoft Web design and development products recognize that building Web sites requires specialized skills. The person designing Web site graphics isn't usually the same person who's writing the site's data access procedures.

Because the specialized tools "talk" to each other, Web designers, graphics designers, and developers can all work on different facets of the Web site without interfering with other areas or having to translate each other's work.

You can read more in Book VII about Microsoft Expression products and SharePoint Designer, as well as how they work with Visual Studio. This chapter focuses on *Visual Web Developer,* which is the Web development tool that comes with Visual Studio 2008.

Getting to Know the Visual Web Developer

This section helps you get acquainted with Visual Web Developer, which you can use for any of the following tasks:

✦ Create and edit Web sites by using ASP.NET.

✦ Design Web pages by using visual design tools.

✦ Test your Web sites on your choice of Web servers, including the light-weight ASP.NET Development Server.

✦ Use server-side ASP.NET controls for creating dynamic content.

✦ Publish your Web site to a host server.

✦ Use syntax-aware editors for HTML and server-side code.

✦ Access data by using server-based controls and wizards.

✦ Create a consistent "look and feel" for your Web sites by using themes and master pages.

✦ Build Web sites that have sophisticated features, such as personalization, membership, and site navigation.

Building better Web applications with ASP.NET

The *ASP* in ASP.NET stands for Active Server Pages. After people started realizing that using HTML to write Web pages by hand was a long and laborious chore, they started figuring out that they could replace static HTML content with server-side programs. For example, rather than write the same page header repeatedly, you can call a program on a server that magically spits out the page banner every time it's called. The ASP.NET code still generates HTML, but the developer doesn't have to write that common HTML in all the files.

Web Forms

ASP.NET Web pages are also called *Web Forms* because they use the HTML form element. The programming style for Web Forms is similar to Windows Forms, which may be another reason that the term *Web Forms* is used. Microsoft has mostly stopped using this term in favor of *Web page.* Interestingly, applications created to target the Aero interface in Windows Vista employ a user interface (UI) control called a *page,* not *Windows Forms.*

An ASP.NET Web site uses its own kind of Web pages. ASP.NET Web pages are different from plain old Web pages in the following ways:

✦ Files end in .aspx rather than the usual .htm or .html for Web pages.

✦ Directives in the form of

```
<@ Page attribute="value">
```

set configuration attributes used by the compiler.

✦ A form element in the following syntax

```
<form id="formname" runat="server">
```

is required on every ASP.NET Web page. The form control is responsible for intercepting a user's interaction with your Web page and sending it to the server for processing. But it does so differently than the standard HTML <form> tag that it uses and its code-behind to add much more functionality.

Microsoft didn't invent the form tag. Rather, the form tag is part of the HTML syntax and is often called a *server form.* Many server-side scripting languages, such as Perl and PHP, are used with the form tag to respond to actions taken by someone using an HTML form. Microsoft invented the runat="server" attribute, which ASP.NET uses to build the form so that it can be sent to the browser.

✦ You can use Web server controls to invoke server-side programs. These special elements are discussed later in this chapter.

You use the visual design tools in Visual Web Developer to drag and drop Web server controls on an ASP.NET Web page. Visual Studio then generates the code to make the controls work, and you write your own, custom code that processes the controls when users interact with them in their browsers. Visual Studio packages all this code and creates a compiled computer program that's executed whenever a user requests the page.

Understanding how ASP.NET pages are served

ASP.NET Web sites are hosted on the Microsoft Internet Information Services (IIS) Web server. The server intercepts all ASP.NET requests and passes the requests to ASP.NET for processing. The IIS Web server identifies an ASP.NET request from a plain old HTML request because ASP.NET Web pages use the `.aspx` file extension.

When you use Visual Studio to run an ASP.NET Web site, Visual Studio compiles the pages. When you deploy your Web site to an IIS Web server, the files are copied as-is, and ASP.NET takes over the process of compiling the code for you. You can force Visual Studio to compile the code before you deploy it to IIS. See Book VI, Chapter 2 for more information about deploying ASP.NET Web sites.

Any time a user requests an ASP.NET Web page in her browser, a program runs on the Web server to deliver the page. When the user performs an action on the page, such as clicking a button to submit information, the page sends a request back to the server. The process of sending data back to the server is a *postback*.

The postback calls the same ASP.NET Web page that the user interacted with. The data the user entered into the browser is passed to the ASP.NET Web page's server-side code for processing. The server-side code customarily sends back a confirmation message to the user indicating whether the data was successfully processed.

A postback is also referred to as a *round trip* because data flows from the browser to the server and back to the browser each time the user performs an action on the page. For more information about writing the server-side code that responds to a postback in an ASP.NET Web page, see Book V, Chapter 4.

You can avoid postbacks in many cases. You can use validation controls, which inject script into the HTML to perform the validation tasks without a postback. AJAX adds even more functionality on the client side, thus avoiding even more postbacks.

Creating Web sites

You can use the Visual Web Developer in Visual Studio to create different kinds of Web sites, depending on where you want to work with the site's content and the kind of Web server you want to use for testing. Here are the four kinds of sites you can create with Visual Studio:

✦ **File system** — Store your Web site's files in a folder on your local hard drive and use the Visual Studio built-in Web server for testing.

✦ **Local IIS** — Create a Web site on your local machine by using IIS as your Web server. Visual Studio creates the Web site in IIS for you.

✦ **Remote server** — Access an IIS Web server on a different computer by using the HTTP protocol.

✦ **FTP** — Access a Web server on a different computer by using the File Transfer Protocol (FTP). You typically use FTP when you access a site hosted on a third-party server.

Note that the kind of Web site you create doesn't determine how you choose to deploy it. That is, you can create a file system Web site and then later deploy it to an IIS server by using FTP. For more information on deployment options, see Book VI, Chapter 2.

Working with a file system Web site is generally much easier than working with any of the other configurations. If more than one developer is working on a single Web site, you might need to use one of the other approaches. For more information about team development and source code control, see Book VI, Chapter 3.

Saying "Hello, World Wide Web"

Creating a Web site in Visual Studio is the easy part of building a Web application. Choosing the content that goes into your Web application is a little trickier. When you create a Web site, Visual Studio does all the work for you. Visual Studio creates the folder structure and configuration files necessary to run the Web site. Here's what ASP.NET does when it creates a Web site:

✦ Creates a folder structure on your local computer for managing the Web site's files

✦ Provisions the project to the specified Web server

✦ Creates a new Web Forms page named `default.aspx`

✦ Creates a *code-behind file* (the code that provides the functionality to the presentation layer) for writing server-side code for the forms page named `default.aspx.vb`

✦ Adds an App_Data folder for storing data-related files

✦ Creates a `web.config` file for storing Web site configuration information

This book describes folder-based systems exclusively because they're easy to work with.

Goodbye, IIS; hello, ASP.NET Development Server

Because previous versions of Visual Studio didn't include a Web server, most developers used a local copy of IIS installed on their computers. Although IIS is no longer required for testing ASP.NET Web sites, it's still required for running ASP.NET Web sites in a production environment.

IIS adds a layer of complexity that you might not want to deal with. However, because IIS is the production Web server, you need to test your site with it, anyway.

Because file-based Web sites use the ASP.NET Development Server, you don't need to do any configuration.

To create a new folder-based Web site, follow these steps:

1. **Choose File⇨New Web Site.**

The New Web Site dialog box appears.

2. **Click the ASP.NET Web Site template.**

3. **The default location for a new Web site is the file system. Accept this location and enter a name, such as** MyWebSite, **after the pathname, as shown in Figure 4-1.**

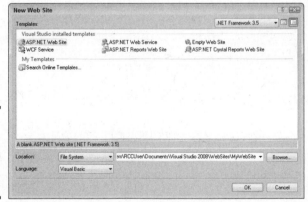

Figure 4-1: Append the name of the Web site to the file path.

Leave the language set to Visual Basic.

4. **Click OK to create the ASP.NET Web site.**

The default.aspx page opens in Design view.

Viewing ASP.NET syntax

An ASP.NET Web page is a combination of HTML markup elements and ASP.NET syntax. The `runat="server"` attribute is an example of ASP.NET syntax that tells the ASP.NET compiler to process tags differently. Any plain-text or HTML tags are rendered to the browser exactly as they appear on the Web page. You use the Source view of an ASP.NET page to view its syntax. To view the `default.aspx` page in Source view, click the Source tab at the bottom of the Document Explorer, as shown in Figure 4-2.

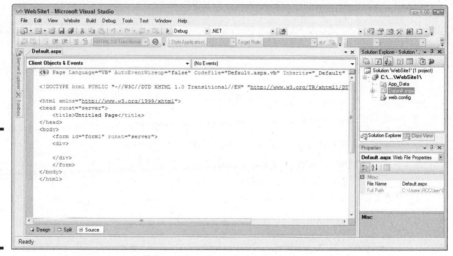

Figure 4-2: Click the Source tab to display the page in Source view.

**Book III
Chapter 4**

**Building Web
Applications**

Notice the markup elements displayed in Source view:

✦ The `<%@ Page . . . %>` directive at the top of the page provides additional configuration information for the ASP.NET compiler.

✦ The `<!DOCTYPE . . . >` entry tells the client's Internet browser that the page complies with the XHTML standard.

   If you don't care about this standard, you can safely delete this line.

✦ Familiar HTML tags, such as `<html>` and `<head>`, are used.

✦ The `runat="server"` attribute is used on the `<head>` and `<form>` tags.

The syntax you see displayed in Figure 4-2 appears in every Web page you add to your project. You drag and drop controls from the toolbox onto the

Web page's Design view, as described in the next section. As you add controls to the page, ASP.NET syntax appears in the page's Source view.

You can use the View menu to access the Web page's Source and Design views.

Adding content

The Web page that's added to a newly created ASP.NET Web site is blank. To make the page meaningful, you must fill it with content, such as

✦ Text boxes, labels, and buttons

✦ Plain text in paragraphs or lists

✦ Images and animations

✦ Tables displaying data and forms that allow users to enter and interact with data

You have several options for adding content to your Web page. If you know the ASP.NET syntax for building ASP.NET Web pages, you can just open any text editor and start adding content. But most people prefer to use Design view in Visual Studio to add content, so they can see how the content they're adding appears on the page as they go.

Using the Visual Designer to add content in Visual Studio 2008 involves these three steps:

1. Drag and drop the controls on the visual design surface.

2. Set the properties that determine attributes, such as appearance and function.

3. Specify what happens (if anything) when a user interacts with a control by either using a wizard to build the code or writing the code manually.

Suppose that you want to create a simple Web form page that displays the text Hello world! when a user clicks a button. To add the content to the default.aspx Web page that you can see how to create in the preceding section, follow these steps:

1. **In Design view of the default.aspx page, drag and drop a Label control from the Toolbox task pane.**

If the toolbox isn't visible, press Ctrl+Alt+X.

2. **Drag and drop a Button control on the designer surface.**

A button appears on the page.

3. **Press Ctrl+F5 to run the Web page.**

The Web page that appears has a label and a button. If you click the button, however, it doesn't do anything. To display `Hello world!`, you have to finish setting the controls' properties and configuring the button to work.

To set the controls' properties, follow these steps:

1. **In Design view, press F4 to open the Properties window.**

2. **Click the `Label` control in the designer to display the label's properties in the Properties window.**

    The Properties window lists properties on the left and their corresponding values on the right.

3. **Locate the `Text` property and then set the value to `Blank` by deleting the contents.**

4. **Locate the `ID` property and name it `lblMessage`.**

Repeat these steps to set the button's `Text` property to `Show Message`, and its `ID` to `btnDoIt`. The `Text` property specifies the text that appears on the page.

Adding the code to make the button work requires you to work in Code view on the page. Although you can type the code directly in the Code Editor, it's easier to start in Design view and let Visual Studio write some of the hookup code for you. Follow these steps:

1. **In Design view, double-click the button you placed on the designer.**

    The Code Editor appears. Double-clicking any control in the designer creates a block of code that's linked to the default event handler for that control. In the case of a button, the default event handler is the `Click` event. The code that's typed in the code block is executed every time the button is clicked. For more information on event handlers, see Book V, Chapter 4.

2. **In the Code Editor, type this line:**

    • *VB*

    ```
    lblMessage.Text = "Hello World!"
    ```

    • *C#*

    ```
    lblMessage.Text = "Hello World!";
    ```

3. **Press Ctrl+F5 to run the Web page.**

4. **When the Web page appears, click the button.**

    The statement `Hello World!` appears on the page, as shown in Figure 4-3.

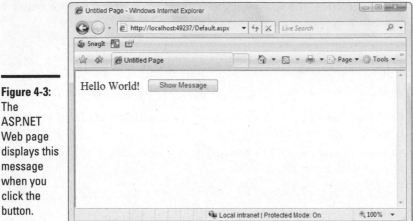

Figure 4-3:
The
ASP.NET
Web page
displays this
message
when you
click the
button.

The complete program (both C# and VB versions) for this example can be downloaded from the companion Web site for this book, which you can read about in the book's Introduction.

Some of you might be thinking that something mysterious happens with ASP.NET applications. If you choose View Source from the browser's contextual menu, though, you'll see that the output of the ASP.NET application is common HTML. Yes, you write your code in a combination of HTM and C# or VB, but the output is simple HTML.

Working with Web Sites

As described earlier in this chapter, creating a Web site using Visual Studio is easy. The hard part is figuring out what content to add. Luckily for you, Visual Studio lets you add all kinds of content to your Web pages and Web site, and you have a ton of different ways to view and edit your Web pages.

Adding new pages

Adding new pages involves more than just adding Web pages. You can use Visual Studio to add these elements:

✦ **Web pages** — ASP.NET Web forms, Web services, mobile Web forms, user controls, and plain old HTML files, for example

✦ **Web pages for mobile Web sites** — Mobile Web forms and user controls, for example

✦ **Files to control the look and feel of your Web site** — Master pages, site maps, skin files, and CSS, for example

✦ **Files for managing data** — XML files, class files, and datasets, for example

Use the Add New Item dialog box to add new content to your Web site. You can open this dialog box in two ways:

✦ Right-click the project folder in Solution Explorer and choose Add New Item.

✦ Choose Web Site⇨Add New Item.

You can add items that you already created by choosing the Add Existing Items option. Many of these items, such as the datasets, are displayed in their own designers. You don't have to write everything from scratch.

To add a new Web page to an existing Web site, follow these steps:

1. **Choose Website⇨Add New Item.**

The Add New Item dialog box appears.

2. **Click the Web Form template.**

3. **Enter the name About.aspx and leave the language as Visual Basic.**

Leave the Place Code in Separate File check box selected and the Select Master Page check box deselected.

The Place Code in Separate File option places all your program code in a separate, code-behind file. Master pages are used to control the look and feel of your Web pages. See Chapter 6 in this mini-book for more information about using master pages.

4. **Click Add; see Figure 4-4.**

Book III
Chapter 4

Building Web
Applications

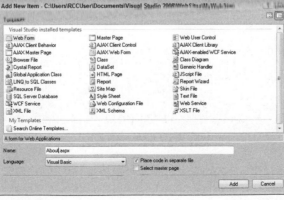

Figure 4-4:
Add a new
Web page
to your
Web site.

A new ASP.NET Web page is added to your Web site. The page opens in Design view so that you can add content. See Chapter 6 in this mini-book for more information on site navigation and linking to Web pages.

You can add empty folders for organizing your content. ASP.NET Web sites use several reserved folders, which you can add to your site at any time:

+ App_Browsers — Stores browser definition files, which are used to tell ASP.NET how to render markup for certain kinds of browsers, such as on mobile devices

+ App_Code — Contains source code for class libraries, helper utilities, and business objects

+ App_Data — Stores data files, including a local database for managing Web site membership and roles

+ App_GlobalResources and App_LocalResources — Contains resource files used for translating page content into other languages

+ App_Themes — Stores all your skins, CSS, images, and other "look and feel" files

+ App_WebReferences — Contains files for Web services

+ Bin — Stores compiled assemblies that you want to use in your Web site

You can add any of these folders by either choosing Website⇨Add ASP.NET Folder or right-clicking the project folder and then choosing Add ASP.NET Folder. You can also right-click any of these folders in Solution Explorer and then choose Add New Item to display an abbreviated list of items you can add in that folder.

Benefiting from the battle of the server controls

ASP.NET provides several different kinds of controls you can use on your Web pages. You use *controls* to display dynamic content on your Web page. ASP.NET writes all the plumbing code that renders your content and passes a user's response back to the server for you to process.

ASP.NET provides these kinds of server controls:

+ **Web server** — Simple controls (such as a label or text box) and complex controls (such as calendars and menus)

+ **HTML server** — Simple HTML elements that you expose for server-side coding

✦ **Validation** — A special kind of Web server control that validates the input of other Web server controls

✦ **User** — A custom control you create by using ASP.NET markup elements that can be embedded in a Web page

Server controls have many similarities. All of them

✦ Have the `runat="server"` attribute in their markup code.

✦ Must be placed inside an ASP.NET Web page in order to execute.

✦ Are accessible from server-side code, which means that you can write a program to manipulate the controls.

✦ Have events.

✦ Have properties that set their behavior at run-time.

✦ Must reside within the form control. (Each page can have only one.)

✦ Are rendered on the browser as a combination of plain HTML and JavaScript.

All these server controls, except user controls, are accessible from the toolbox. You add user controls by using Solution Explorer. You can place other kinds of controls in a user control to create a composite control.

The syntax

The ASP.NET syntax for Web server controls looks similar to HTML markup syntax. Like with HTML, ASP.NET syntax uses tags with attribute/value pairs. The markup for a Web server button control looks like this:

```
<asp:Button ID="Button1" runat="server" Text="Button" />
```

You can add attributes to the markup code by either typing them directly in Source view of the Web page or by using the Properties window. The attributes specified in the markup code are properties of the Web server control, not HTML attributes. Some properties are mapped to HTML attributes. ASP.NET uses the collection of properties to determine how best to render the markup in a browser.

The markup code for an HTML server control looks like this:

```
<input id="Button2" type="button" value="button" runat="server" />
```

All server-side controls have these markup elements:

✦ `ID` attribute — Tells the server-side code how to access the control

✦ `Runat` attribute — Flags the control as a server-side control

Notice that the tags are a little different for Web server controls and HTML server controls. Web server control tags start with `asp:` and then the name of the control — for example, `asp:button` and `asp:textbox`. HTML server controls use HTML syntax, such as `<input>` and `<div>`. You can convert any HTML element to a server control by simply adding the `runat` attribute to the markup.

Server controls provided by ASP.NET use the tag prefix `asp`. Custom server controls created by you or a third party use the tag prefix defined for the custom server control. The tag prefix maps the control to the control's namespace. The namespace tells ASP.NET where to find the code that defines how the control works. Tag prefixes are defined by using a Register directive at the top of each Web page that uses the control. Alternatively, you can place the prefix information in the Web site's configuration file so that all pages in the site can use the custom server control.

All server controls must be contained within the `<form>` element on the Web page.

Web server controls versus HTML server controls

At first blush, HTML server controls and Web server controls look similar. They have some differences, however, as Table 4-1 illustrates.

Table 4-1	Comparison of HTML Server Controls and Web Server Controls	
HTML Server Controls	*Web Server Controls*
Map almost one-to-one to HTML elements	Render to a single HTML element or a combination of elements
Are client-side by default	Server-side only
Properties mapped to HTML attributes	Properties aren't mapped directly to HTML attributes
Customized using CSS	Customized using CSS or templates
Don't support themes	Support themes

Here are some examples of Web server controls:

✦ `Label`, `TextBox`, and `Button`

✦ `LinkButton`, `ImageButton`, and `HyperLink`

✦ `TreeView` and `SiteMapPath`

To add an HTML control to a Web page and convert it to a server control, follow these steps:

1. **Click the plus sign (+) next to the HTML tab in the toolbox to expand the list of HTML controls.**

   If the toolbox isn't displayed, press Ctrl+Alt+X to open it.

2. **Drag an Input (Button) control to the design surface and drop it.**

   The image of a button appears.

3. **Right-click the button's image and choose Run As Server Control from the contextual menu.**

   The button image is updated to show a little arrow in its upper-left corner.

The markup code for the button is changed to include this `runat` property:

```
<input id="Button2" runat="server" type="button" value="button" />
```

All the events captured for this control are now server-side. Double-click the button's image to display a server-side code block, where you can enter server-side code for the button's `Click` event.

To convert the HTML control back to a regular control, you can either

✦ Right-click the button's image and choose Run as Server Control.

✦ Remove the `runat` property from the control's markup in Source view.

Unless you plan to use server-side resources, you should always use plain HTML elements. Server-side controls use more resources than client-side controls. You should also consider whether you can deliver functionality in a client-side script rather than use server-side code. By using a client-side script, you eliminate a round trip back to the server. (For a little background on round trips and postbacks, see the earlier section "Understanding how ASP.NET pages are served.")

For example, you can easily create a `Hello World!` example by using a client-side script. Follow these steps:

1. **Add a paragraph element to your Web page by typing the following code in Source view on the Web page:**

   ```
   <p id="output" style="color: Red; font-weight: bold"></p>
   ```

2. **Drag and drop an Input (Button) control in Design view on the page by using the HTML tab in the toolbox.**

Book III
Chapter 4

Building Web
Applications

3. Enter Show Message **in the Value property on the Properties window.**

If the Properties window isn't displayed, press F4.

4. Double-click the image of the Input button.

A JavaScript code block appears in Source view on the page. (*JavaScript* is a client-side scripting language.)

5. Type this code in the JavaScript code block:

```
document.getElementById("output").innerHTML = "Hello world!";
```

6. Press Ctrl+F5 to run the Web site.

The Web site appears in your browser.

7. Press the button.

The phrase Hello World! appears on the page.

A simple page demonstrating the JavaScript for this can be found as a link at the companion Web site for this book, which you can read about in the book's Introduction.

This code sample uses the innerHTML property of the paragraph element. (This property was used for brevity.) The appropriate way to modify page content dynamically is to access the node and modify it by using the Document Object Model (DOM). The benefit of using innerHTML is that you can easily understand what this code is doing. The downside is that because the property isn't universal and doesn't provide a reference to the node in question, accessing the node again by using client-side code is impossible.

Earlier, this chapter uses a Web server button control. How do you know when to choose an HTML input button and when to choose a Web server button control? Here are a couple of reasons to choose HTML input button controls instead of Web server button controls:

✦ **HTML server controls provide more control over the HTML markup that's rendered in the browser.** You can also control the markup of Web server controls by using a template, but it requires more work than using HTML server controls.

✦ **HTML server controls are easier for non-Visual Studio users to understand.** This information is especially valuable if you're working with Web designers who provide you with CSS because the designers might not understand how to provide styles for Web server controls.

On the other hand, here are some reasons why you might choose Web server button controls instead of HTML input button controls:

✦ **You want access to more properties than are available with a typical HTML element.**

✦ **You don't want to take the extra step of converting the controls to server-side, like you do with HTML server controls.** By default, Web server controls are server-side.

✦ **You want to take advantage of device filters and browser definition files.**

Visual Studio provides more visual design support for Web server controls than for HTML server controls. If you want to rely on HTML server controls, why use ASP.NET? Rick uses Web server controls almost exclusively, except for the two generic HTML tags `div` and `span`. Any time he wants to add dynamic text content to a page, such as a warning message, he uses a server-side `div` or `span` tag to display the message programmatically.

You can also use a Label Web server control to display messages. Label controls are rendered as HTML `span` tags. The `span` tag is a generic inline container for use inside block-level containers, such as `div` tags and paragraph `<p>` tags. Because messages are usually rendered at the block level, some folks prefer to use `div` tags. If you plan to display a message inside a block tag, such as a paragraph tag, you can choose a `Label` control. In reality, most browsers aren't affected if your `div` and `span` tags are improperly nested. It matters only if you're a purist.

For an in-depth discussion of additional Web server controls, see Chapter 6 in this mini-book. It describes site navigation controls and hyperlinking mechanisms for transitioning between Web pages.

Login controls are covered in Chapter 6 of this mini-book, and data controls are covered in Book IV, Chapter 2.

User controls and custom controls

Sometimes, you want to create a reusable control that doesn't already exist in the Visual Studio toolbox. You can choose from two types:

✦ **User** — Create this type of control with the same tools you use to build Web pages. Like other controls, user controls are contained within an ASP.NET Web page.

✦ **Custom** — Build your own, custom control and add it to the Visual Studio toolbox. Writing a custom control requires some programming expertise.

**Book III
Chapter 4**

**Building Web
Applications**

User controls are similar to ASP.NET Web pages because you can include HTML and server-side code in a single file. Unlike Web pages, user controls

✦ End in the file extension `.ascx`

✦ Use the `@ Control` directive, rather than `@ Page`

✦ Must be hosted as part of an ASP.NET Web page

✦ Don't include host page elements, such as `html`, `body`, and `form`

In previous versions of Visual Studio, user controls were used extensively as a means of providing page templates. For example, you would create header and footer user controls on each of your Web pages. That's no longer necessary with master pages.

This doesn't imply that user controls are no longer valuable. You can use a user control any time you want to encapsulate a group of controls and make them reusable. For example, you could create a user control for displaying calendar controls.

To create this user control in an existing Web site, follow these steps:

1. **Right-click the Web site's project folder in Solution Explorer and then choose Add New Item from the contextual menu.**

   The Add New Item dialog box appears.

2. **Click the Web User Control icon.**

3. **Give the user control the name `calendar.ascx` and then choose Visual Basic as the language.**

4. **Click the Add button to add the user control to your Web site.**

   Visual Studio opens the user control in Design view.

To add your user control to an existing Web page, drag the `calendar.ascx` file from Solution Explorer and drop it on Design view of the Web page. Visual Studio adds the following markup to your Web page:

✦ At the top of the page:

```
<%@ Register Src="~/calendar.ascx" TagName="calendar" TagPrefix="uc1" %>
```

✦ In the page content:

```
<uc1:calendar ID="Calendar1" runat="server" />
```

This example shows a tag prefix being used for a custom control, as described in the earlier section "The syntax." The `Register` directive specifies the name of the control (`calendar`, in this case) and the tag prefix. To use the control on the page, the syntax references the custom control's tag prefix, `uc1`, and places the control's name after the colon. In this example, the control isn't mapped to a namespace. Instead, the control is mapped to the user control file using the attribute `Src="calendar.ascx"`. That's how ASP.NET knows where to find the control when it processes the control on the page.

In Design view of the Web page, the user control is displayed with a placeholder box until content is added to the user control. To open the user control for editing, follow these steps:

1. **In Design view of the Web page, click the smart tag arrow on the user control.**

The UserControl Tasks list appears.

2. **Click the Edit UserControl link, as shown in Figure 4-5.**

The user control opens for editing.

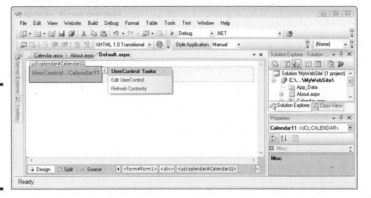

Figure 4-5: Click Edit UserControl to open the control for editing.

Book III
Chapter 4

Building Web Applications

A user control is blank when you first create it. You add controls to newly created controls. Adding controls to a user control is similar to adding controls to a Web page. You simply drag and drop controls from the toolbox onto the design surface.

Because user controls are made up of other controls, they're often called *composite* controls.

One control that you can't use on a user control is the `<form>` server control. You might recall that user controls, like all server controls, are hosted in Web forms. You can't call a user control as a normal HTML element. Web forms can have only one `<form>` server control. You place your user control inside the `<form>` server control on the page where you want to display your user control.

If you happen to place a <form> server control in a user control, you don't receive an error message until you execute the page where the user control is hosted.

The following example demonstrates how to create a user control — specifically, a specialized calendar control that displays the preceding, current, and following months. This user control encapsulates the controls and code that make the calendars work, so you can reuse the control without having to customize the code each time.

Follow these steps to create the calendar user control:

1. **Drag and drop a calendar control from the toolbox to Design view of the user control. Press Ctrl+Alt+X to display the toolbox.**

2. **Add two more calendar controls by repeating Step 1 or copying and pasting the markup code in Source view.**

You should have three calendar controls: Calendar1, Calendar2, and Calendar3.

3. **Position your controls so that Calendar2 is between Calendar1 and Calendar3.**

4. **On Calendar1 and Calendar3, use the Properties window to set the ShowNextPrevMonth property to false. Set the SelectionMode property to None.**

Press F4 to open the Properties window if it's closed.

5. **With the user control displayed in Design view, double-click a blank area of the designer.**

Visual Studio opens the Code Editor and positions your cursor inside a code block for the Page_Load event.

The Page_Load event is called when the user control is loaded.

6. **In the Page_Load code block, enter this code:**

- *VB*

```
If (Not Page.IsPostBack = True) Then
    Me.Calendar2.VisibleDate = System.DateTime.Today
    Me.Calendar1.VisibleDate =    Me.Calendar1.TodaysDate.AddMonths(-1)
    Me.Calendar3.VisibleDate =    Me.Calendar1.TodaysDate.AddMonths(1)
End If
```

- *C#*

```
if( !IsPostBack )
{
    Calendar2.VisibleDate = System.DateTime.Today;
    Calendar1.VisibleDate = Calendar1.TodaysDate.AddMonths(-1);
    Calendar3.VisibleDate = Calendar1.TodaysDate.AddMonths(1);
}
```

TIP

If you want to test whether your code is working, press Ctrl+F5 to run your Web site.

7. In Design view of the user control, click `Calendar2` and then press F4 to display the Properties window for that control.

8. Click the Events button on the Properties window toolbar.

The Events button looks like a lightning bolt.

9. Double-click the `VisibleMonthChanged` event.

Visual Studio creates an event handler and opens the Code Editor for you.

10. Type these two lines of code:

```
Me.Calendar1.VisibleDate = Me.Calendar2.VisibleDate.AddMonths(-1)
Me.Calendar3.VisibleDate = Me.Calendar2.VisibleDate.AddMonths(1)
```

11. Press Ctrl+F5 to run your Web site.

Your Web page displays the user control with three calendars, as shown in Figure 4-6. As you navigate with the middle control, the other controls are updated, too.

Figure 4-6: Click the middle calendar to update all three calendars.

Changing your view

You can use one of several views to edit ASP.NET Web pages in Visual Studio 2005:

✦ **Design view** — The `default.aspx` page is opened in Design view by default. Design view is a WYSIWYG visual designer in which you can build your Web page by typing content or dragging and dropping controls on the design surface.

✦ **Source view** — You can view and edit the underlying HTML markup that's used to build the Web page.

✦ **Code view** — Display the programming language editor associated with that Web page.

✦ **Component Designer view** — Create a visual design surface for non-visual components.

Straight to the Source (view)

Source view in Visual Web Developer displays the HTML markup and ASP.NET syntax used to create the Web page or user control. You use Source view to edit HTML markup and ASP.NET syntax.

You can display Source view of a Web page in one of three ways:

✦ Click the Source tab at the bottom of the Document Explorer on the Web page.

✦ Choose View⇨Markup.

✦ Right-click the Web page in Solution Explorer and choose View Markup from the contextual menu.

Source view automatically displays the HTML Source Editing toolbar. It has several commands for formatting the markup and has these two additional validator commands:

✦ **Target Schema for Validation** — Use this drop-down list to specify whether Visual Studio should use XHTML 1.x, HTML 1.0, or a version of Internet Explorer in validating the Web page's markup.

✦ **Check Page for Accessibility** — The accessibility validator uses a number of accessibility standards to determine whether people with disabilities can use assistive technologies with your page.

Run the validator commands if you want to ensure that your page conforms to industry standards.

When you run your ASP.NET Web page, the content that's sent to the browser isn't what you see in Source view in Visual Studio. Rather, the ASP.NET syntax is converted to HTML.

Figure 4-7 shows, on the top, Source view for the `default.aspx` page (created in the section "Saying 'Hello, World Wide Web,'" earlier in this chapter). The HTML that's rendered to the browser by ASP.NET is shown on the bottom.

**Book III
Chapter 4**

**Building Web
Applications**

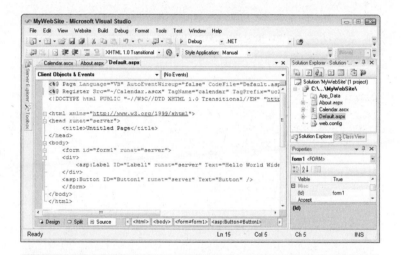

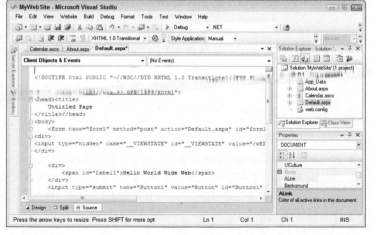

Figure 4-7: Check out this comparison of ASP.NET markup (top) and the HTML rendered by ASP.NET (bottom).

In this example, the ASP.NET syntax is cleaner than the HTML. Part of the reason is the view state values you see in the HTML. The view state values are shown in the long sequence of characters and represent data stored on the page. View state is added by ASP.NET. In the case of simple HTML elements, such as labels and text boxes, ASP.NET syntax isn't much simpler than HTML. The real difference between HTML and ASP.NET shows up when you use more complex display structures, such as tables. For example, the GridView control requires a few lines of ASP.NET syntax and is rendered as a table created by using numerous lines of HTML.

See Chapter 7 in this mini-book for information about the view state.

Notice a couple of characteristics about the comparison:

✦ ASP.NET directives, such as @Page, aren't present in the output.

✦ Any HTML markup with the runat="server" attribute is converted to HTML.

For example, this line

```
<form id="form1" runat="server">
```

is converted to this one:

```
<form name="form1" method="post" action="default.aspx" id="form1">
```

The <form> tag is special because it designates which controls the users of your Web page can interact with. When you add controls to your Web page by using Design view, the markup necessary to build those controls is placed inside the <form> tag.

Source view is a syntax-aware editor that you can use to write or edit HTML and ASP.NET syntax. For example, to add a new hyperlink to your Web page, follow these steps:

1. **Type an opening tag bracket (<).**

A list of valid HTML and ASP tags appears.

2. **Press the down-arrow key to highlight the a tag, and then press Tab.**

3. **Press the spacebar to display a drop-down list of valid attributes.**

4. **Select the href attribute by pressing either the down-arrow key or the letter *h*. When the href attribute is displayed, press Tab to select it.**

5. **Type an equal sign (=).**

6. **When the list of available Web pages appears, type**
   "http://www.cnn.com" **(with the double quotation marks).**

   You can also use the Pick URL option to pick a URL.

7. **Type the closing tag bracket (>).**

   Visual Studio fills in the closing tag for you.

You can also add new attribute/value pairs to existing HTML and ASP.NET tags by pressing the spacebar inside any of the tags.

Code editing

Visual Studio takes care of much of the task of writing code for you. ASP.NET has two coding styles:

✦ **Inline** — Code is written in Source view by using script tags.

✦ **Code-behind** — All code is maintained in a separate file.

The default approach uses the code-behind style. The code-behind file is divided into two files:

✦ One file, generated automatically by Visual Studio, contains all the code generated by Visual Studio to handle the controls you place on the screen and wires up the events you write code for.

✦ You view the other file when you click in Code view. This file contains all the code you write.

When you run your Web site, the code from these two files is combined.

Earlier versions of ASP.NET had only one code-behind file. This single code-behind file contained all the code generated by Visual Studio and the code written by the developer. Microsoft changed this model into two separate files to keep the code clean and prevent developers from being confused by the generated code. The feature that enables the code to be split into two files is *partial classes.* Together, the files create a class, which is a unit of a program. Partial classes make it possible to split a single class across two files. Partial classes are intended for use with code-generation tools. As a rule, you shouldn't create your own partial classes. You can read more about using classes to organize your code in Book V, Chapter 3.

You shouldn't change the code generated by Visual Studio. Any changes you make will likely be overwritten when the file is regenerated. It's okay to open the generated file from Solution Explorer and view its contents. But you shouldn't add or edit the code.

**Book III
Chapter 4**

Building Web
Applications

Running your Web site

You need to run your Web site from time to time while you're developing to make sure that it's working properly. If you're working mostly with the visual Design view, you shouldn't have many problems. You can run your Web site in one of two modes:

✦ **Debug mode** — Provides detailed information about errors you might encounter in running your Web site. Most developers execute their Web sites in Debug mode while they're actively developing their sites.

✦ **Release mode** — After a site is ready to be deployed, its developer usually switches it from Debug mode to Release mode because the site runs faster in Release mode. However, the process halts when an error is encountered, and you don't get much useful feedback.

Most of the sample code in this book uses Release mode because it has less overhead. The downside is that you don't get good feedback when errors occur.

To start your Web site without debugging, press Ctrl+F5. To start it with debugging turned on, press F5. You can also use Debug menu commands for starting your Web site.

Debugging a Web site can be overwhelming — even professionals get hung up. For more information about using and configuring the debugger, see Book V, Chapter 7.

Using Starter Kits

A *starter kit* is a fully functional Web site that you can open and customize to suit your needs. Visual Studio 2005 includes a Personal Web Site starter kit. Starter kits are listed alongside other project templates in the New Web Site dialog box.

You can download additional starter kits from the Downloads page from the ASP.NET site, www.asp.net.

Microsoft adds starter kits regularly. Here are some available starter kits:

✦ **Club Site** — A Web site for a club or organization

✦ **Time Tracker** — A Web site for tracking hours spent on a project

✦ **PayPal-enabled eCommerce** — A site for getting started with PayPal

✦ **DotNetNuke** — A good way to get started with *DotNetNuke,* which is a Web application framework for creating and deploying Web sites

Chapter 5: Using AJAX For Rich Web Pages

In This Chapter

✔ Discovering what AJAX does and why you should consider using it

✔ Using AJAX extensions to create rich Web Applications

✔ Extending ASP.NET controls with AJAX for smooth page response

✔ Creating custom AJAX controls for additional functionality

Creating Web pages with rich content while also creating Web pages with nimble response is the Holy Grail of Web development. For years, desktop applications have performed user interface (UI) operations with almost no perceptible delay, but Web applications are at the mercy of the Internet connection speed. Even with a fast Internet connection, though, many Web applications with rich content are sluggish, taking as long as several seconds to load.

This chapter offers a solution: the addition of Asynchronous JavaScript And XML (AJAX) extensions. These extensions go beyond the traditional ASP.NET controls and give you the ability to make your Web pages respond almost as well as desktop applications, even if the content is relatively rich.

AJAX Explained: What It Does and Why You Should Consider Using It

AJAX is a relatively new technology that relies on JavaScript. The JavaScript code that AJAX employs allows it to perform to the point where very little perceptible delay is seen with the UI because AJAX reduces the amount of data that must be transferred from the server to the client. This means that the user experience is far more enjoyable because users don't wait for page updates and refreshes.

ASP.NET postback architecture

Start with a little background on the ASP.NET postback architecture. Say that you create an ASP.NET Web application that has two text fields: a button and a label. Here's what happens:

1. The text fields allow users to enter the width and a height of a rectangle.

2. The button calculates the area of the rectangle.

3. The area is placed into the label showing the result of the calculation.

If this Web application were a desktop application, the architecture would be trivial. The program code would simply get the values, do the calculation, and then display the result. However, ASP.NET controls execute on the server and not on the client machine. This means that the page needs to present its data to the server so that the server can do the calculation, populate the label with the result, and serve up the new page.

When Microsoft introduced this technology in 2000, developers weren't crazy about it. It puts more load on servers because the calculation and result display require a round trip to the server. Developers soon realized, though, how easy it made Web application development, so the postback architecture won the day.

Unfortunately, though, the round trip to the server causes a delay. Although a desktop application does this with no real delay, a Web application might give a noticeable delay during heavy traffic. So, although the ASP.NET post-back architecture is brilliant for easy and robust Web development, AJAX, a way to get rid of the page roundtrip delays, was developed.

Partial page updates

You can just about solve the postback delay issue if your applications can simply update the portion of the page that needs to be updated. Easy, right? People have been trying to solve that for years with IFrames and other technologies. None, though, have worked nearly as well as AJAX, which is built on JavaScript technology.

AJAX allows Web applications to perform partial page updates. Only the page elements that need to be updated are, thus providing a far more responsive page refresh mechanism. And if a Web application developer is judicious in how pages are designed, almost no perceptible refresh delay is noticed.

AJAX uses JavaScript to perform partial page updates. This section gives a short description of the mechanism.

How JavaScript interacts in HTML documents

First, make sure you know that JavaScript is not Java. *Java* is compiled binary code that can reside on the Internet as applets. These applets are loaded and executed via the Java Virtual Machine (JVM).

Comparatively, *JavaScript* can be part of an HTML page. It can technically be a separate file that's referenced in an HTML page, but the browser treats it as if the referenced code is part of the HTML where it's referenced.

The browser interprets JavaScript code. Interpreted code isn't as fast as compiled code, but modern-day browsers and fast machines easily handle the interpretation so that users don't notice.

JavaScript has been used for many years in a technique known as *Dynamic HTML* (DHTML), which is a way of making HTML more dynamic by allowing the client machine to act on HTML elements. For instance, DHTML code can cause a test string to turn green when the mouse hovers over it and then back to black when the mouse leaves its area.

Here's a simple JavaScript page that changes the color of a text string when the mouse hovers over it:

```
<html>
<body>
<h1>This page demonstrates DHTML.</h1>
<span id="Test"
  onMouseOver="this.style.color='green'"
  onMouseOut="this.style.color='black'">
    Hi there, hover over me.</span>
</body>
</html>
```

If you're unsure how to work with JavaScript, you can check out this tutorial:

www.w3schools.com/js/default.asp

Using the JavaScript HttpRequest mechanism

DHTML isn't enough to do partial page updates. You still need a way to make a request from the server. The mechanism that's used for this is an HTTP request, performed by the JavaScript XMLHttpRequest object.

With an HTTP request, a Web page can make a request to — and get a response from — a Web server without reloading the page. The user will stay on the same page, not noticing that scripts might request pages or send data to a server in the background.

Listing 5-1 performs a simple fetch of a document via an HTTP request that relies on the XMLHttpRequest object.

Listing 5-1: Simple Document Fetch Using XMLHttpRequest

```
<script language="JavaScript">

var XMLHttp;

function LoadData(url)
{

    XMLHttp = null;

    // code for Firefoxetc.
    if( window.XMLHttpRequest )
    {
        XMLHttp= new XMLHttpRequest();
    }

    // code for Internet Explorer
    else if( window.ActiveXObject )
    {
        XMLHttp= new ActiveXObject( "Microsoft.XMLHTTP" );
    }

    if( xmlhttp != null )
    {
        XMLHttp.onreadystatechange = state_Change;
        XMLHttp.open( "GET", url, true );
        XMLHttp.send( null );
    }
    else
    {
        alert( "Your browser does not support XMLHTTP." );
    }

}
</script>
```

Fortunately, you never need to do this kind of JavaScript coding. The AJAX extensions do it all for you. The AJAX controls inject the appropriate JavaScript code into the HTML output stream without you needing to code any JavaScript yourself.

Using the XML Data that is returned

The data that's returned is in XML format. XML is simply a way of representing data. It's done with tags, the same way that HTML is done, except that XML allows you to create your own tags that best describe and represent your data.

Here again, you might be worried about handling the XML. Converting simple XML to non-XML data isn't hard, but it's an extra step that can complicate things. Fortunately, the AJAX controls handle all this for you. Instead of actually getting XML, your controls give you simple data types, such as strings and integers.

Using AJAX Extensions

AJAX extensions are included in Visual Studio 2008. In Visual Studio 2005, you had to download and install them, but these extensions are part of the Visual Studio 2008 installation. You can find the AJAX extensions in the toolbox, in the section labeled AJAX Extensions, as shown in Figure 5-1.

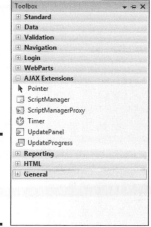

Figure 5-1:
The AJAX extensions are in the toolbox.

Book III
Chapter 5

Using AJAX
For Rich Web Pages

Creating your first AJAX Web application

Get started with AJAX by creating your first AJAX Web site. To create a new AJAX-enabled Web site, follow these steps:

1. Choose File⇨New Web Site.

The New Web Site dialog box appears.

2. **Click the ASP.NET Web Site template.**

3. **Select the language from the Language drop-down list.**

4. **Choose HTTP for the location for the new Web site. Enter a name, such as FirstAJAXWebSite, after the pathname, as shown in Figure 5-2.**

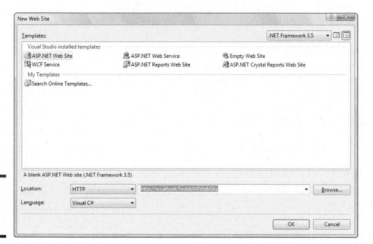

Figure 5-2:
Name the
Web site.

5. **Click OK to create the ASP.NET Web site.**

   The `default.aspx` page opens in Split view.

6. **From the AJAX Extensions tab of the toolbox, place one — and only one — `ScriptManager` object into the form in the Design view.**

That's all you need to do to create an AJAX-enabled Web site. Continue to explore how Ajax sites work by adapting and modifying this basic application in the sections that follow.

Adding traditional ASP.NET controls to the form

Controls in a Web site are similar to controls in applications that you create in Visual Studio — the buttons, boxes, and so on that users interact with on-screen. The easiest way to figure out how they work is to experiment with them. Using the site you created in the preceding section, you can start by adding three labels and a button to the site. These are traditional ASP.NET controls. Get these working and take a look at this simple application first, though, before going on to implement a partial page update pattern.

To add the ASP.NET controls, follow these steps:

1. **Add three labels and a button to the form.**

2. **Double-click the button to create an event that causes a postback.**

3. **Double-click the page and create a `Page_Load` event handler.**

4. **Add this code to the Page_Load method:**

   - *VB*

   ```
   Label1.Text = Date.Now
   Label2.Text = Date.Now
   Label3.Text = Date.Now
   ```

   - *C#*

   ```
   Label1.Text = DateTime.Now.ToString();
   Label2.Text = DateTime.Now.ToString();
   Label3.Text = DateTime.Now.ToString();
   ```

5. **Run the program by pressing Ctrl+F5.**

   You see the labels reflect the time of the last postback, as shown in Figure 5-3. The button causes postbacks and subsequent time changes.

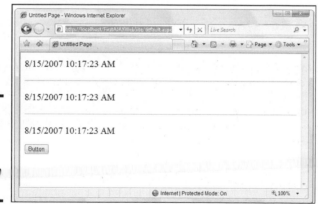

Figure 5-3: The labels on the form show the current date and time.

**Book III
Chapter 5**

**Using AJAX
For Rich Web Pages**

Using AJAX to implement a partial page update pattern

After you have an ASP.NET application working, use AJAX to implement a partial page-update pattern. Working from the site created in the preceding section, the end result is that the button causes an update for the second label only.

To implement the partial page update pattern, follow these steps:

1. From the AJAX Extensions tab of the toolbox, add an `UpdatePanel` control above the second label.

2. Drag the second label into the `UpdatePanel` control.

3. Drag the button into the `UpdatePanel` control.

4. Run the program by pressing Ctrl+F5.

You see the labels reflect the time of the first page load. Then, only the second label is updated in response to a button click, as shown in Figure 5-4.

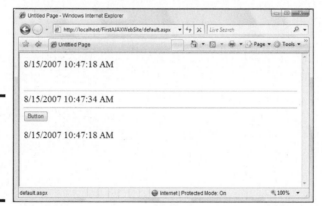

Figure 5-4: The button causes an update in the second label only.

Updating controls outside UpdatePanel

Sometimes, you need to do partial page updates when the control that fires off the update can't be inside `UpdatePanel`. Modify your application from preceding sections once again and take the button out of `UpdatePanel`. Then, add a `Triggers` collection to `UpdatePanel`. A `Triggers` collection manages the AJAX events that fire off in response to UI events. In the `Triggers` collection, specify that the second label should be updated by the button, even though the button is outside `UpdatePanel`.

To implement the `Triggers` collection and have a button outside `UpdatePanel` cause an update, follow these steps:

1. **From the FirstAJAXWebSite that you're working with, move the button from inside UpdatePanel to the bottom of the page so that it's no longer inside UpdatePanel.**

2. **Open the Properties window for UpdatePanel.**

3. **Click the ellipsis button beside the Triggers property.**

   The Collection Editor dialog box appears, as shown in Figure 5-5.

Figure 5-5: The Collection Editor allows you to add a trigger.

4. **Click the Add button.**

   An AsynPostBack member is added.

5. **In the right side of the editor, set the controlID to Button1 and the EventName to Click.**

   This wires up the buttons Click event to the UpdatePanel update so that the Click even fires off an event trigger that connects it to UpdatePanel.

6. **Click Add.**

   An AsynPostBack member is added.

7. **Run the program by pressing Ctrl+F5.**

   The labels reflect the time of the first page load. Then, only the second label is updated in response to a button click, even though it's no longer in UpdatePanel, as shown in Figure 5-6.

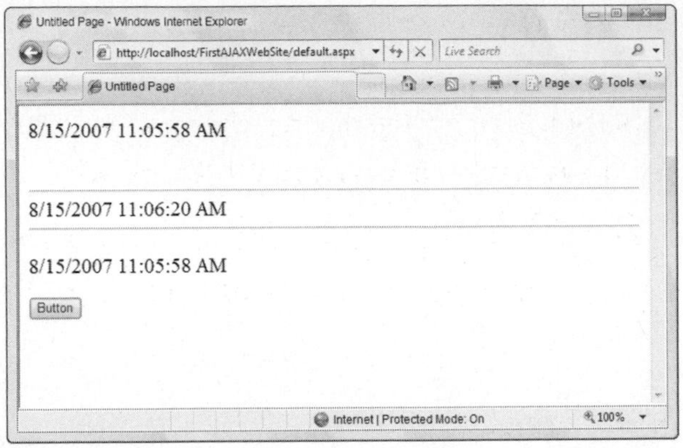

Figure 5-6:
The button
causes an
update only
in the
second
label.

Using the AJAX Controls

There's more to AJAX than the extensions. A rich set of controls is provided in the AJAX Control Toolkit. It can be downloaded from www.asp.net. At this Web site, click the AJAX button, click the Download button, and then follow the links to download the latest AJAX Control Toolkit. The URL can be found at

```
http://asp.net/ajax/downloads
```

The Toolkit is contained inside a Zip archive, so extract it to your hard drive. For this explanation, use the extraction path

```
C:\Users\RCCUser\Documents\Visual Studio 2008\AJAX Toolkit
```

Please note that the authors created the AJAX Toolkit directory. The actual AJAX Control DLL (dynamic link library) file can be found at

```
C:\Users\RCCUser\Documents\Visual Studio 2008\
    AJAX Toolkit\SampleWebSite\bin\AjaxControlToolkit.dll
```

Adding the AJAX Control Toolkit to the Visual Studio toolbox

Before using the AJAX Control Toolkit, you need to add a reference to the Visual Studio toolbox. This makes it easy to drag controls to the Web application's form.

To add the AJAX Control Toolkit to the Visual Studio toolbox, follow these steps:

1. **Open the Visual Studio toolbox.**

2. **Right-click and choose Add Tab.**

3. **Open the Properties window for** `UpdatePanel`.

4. **Name the tab** AJAX Toolkit.

5. **Right-click the newly created tab and choose Choose Items.**

6. **Click the Browse button and navigate to the file at**

```
C:\Users\RCCUser\Documents\Visual Studio 2008\
     AJAX Toolkit\SampleWebSite\bin\AjaxControlToolkit.dll
```

You see many controls appear in the AJAX Toolkit tab, as shown in Figure 5-7.

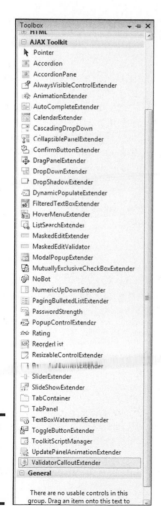

Figure 5-7:
The AJAX Toolkit has many controls.

Using AJAX controls from the Toolkit

After you have the AJAX Toolkit installed and set up, as explained in the preceding section, get started using the controls. Begin by using a `ConfirmButtonExtender`. The control gives you the ability to confirm actions in response to user button clicks.

To use a `ConfirmButtonExtender`, follow these steps:

1. **Drag a `ConfirmButtonExtender` control from the AJAX Toolkit tab area of the toolbox onto the form right above the button.**

2. **Open the `ConfirmButtonExtender` properties.**

3. **Choose `Button1` as the `TargetControlID`.**

4. **Enter some text into the `ConfirmText` property.**

   For example, enter **Do you want to update the second label?**.

5. **Run the program by pressing Ctrl+F5.**

   When you click the button, you get a confirmation alert, as shown in Figure 5-8.

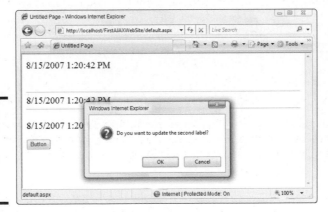

Figure 5-8:
This AJAX control confirms a button action.

Chapter 6: Laying Out Your Site

In This Chapter

✔ **Validating user input**

✔ **Adding navigation controls to your site**

✔ **Using themes and master pages**

✔ **Laying out Web pages with Cascading Style Sheets (CSS)**

*L*ook at any Web site, and you're likely to see common elements, such as form-validation feedback, navigational aids, and consistent headers and footers. In previous versions of Visual Studio, you had to be conversant in technologies as varied as JavaScript and XML to provide these features. Thanks to many of the new features in Visual Studio and ASP.NET, you can create high-quality Web sites while writing a minimal amount of code.

This chapter gets you acquainted with themes, skins, and master pages and introduces you to the benefits of using CSS to lay out your Web pages. You can also see how to use the ASP.NET validation controls to test user input and provide feedback to users.

Keeping Track of Input with Validation Controls

After you create only a few Web forms, you'll realize that you need some way to make sure that all your check boxes are checked and your text boxes are filled with the right information. ASP.NET has a collection of validation controls to help you do just that.

Validation controls provide validation services for the controls you place on a Web page, ensuring that the data that's entered is in the correct format. The validation controls also enable you to give users feedback about the correct data. For example, a Web page can include text boxes to capture these input types from users:

✦ E-mail address

✦ Phone number

✦ Date of birth

How can you be sure that the values that are entered are in the proper formats? Further, how can you ensure that values are even entered?

You have three options:

+ **Do nothing and hope for the best.**

+ **Write server-side code that validates your text boxes after visitors click the Submit button.** This process requires a round trip to the server. You can read more about these round trips, usually called *postbacks,* in Chapter 4 of this mini-book.

+ **Write client-side script that validates your text boxes as users enter their data.**

Whenever possible, using client-side script for form validation is the preferred approach because it eliminates a trip to the server and provides immediate feedback to visitors. You can write all this client-side script yourself, or you can let the ASP.NET validation controls write it for you.

You can use multiple validation controls for form fields. For instance, you might need to check a form field to make sure that it has data in it, and at the same time check to make sure that it's identical to another form field. In a case such as this, you could use two validation controls for one form field. ASP.NET provides these validation controls:

+ `RequiredFieldValidator` — Ensures that required fields contain a value

+ `RangeValidator` — Checks whether entries fall within a specified range, such as between start and end dates

+ `RegularExpressionValidator` — Tests whether entries match a certain pattern, such as ZIP + 4 or a telephone number

+ `CompareValidator` — Compares an entry with a value

+ `CustomValidator` — Lets you write your own control when none of the other controls provides the level of validation you need

+ `ValidationSummary` — Displays a summary of all validation errors

Adding a validation control

Using validation controls is straightforward. For example, to require that a user fill in a text box on an existing Web page, follow these steps:

1. **Open the Web page to which you want to add validation controls. Or, create a new Web page.**

See Chapter 4 in this mini-book for more information about creating Web pages.

2. **Drag and drop a `Label` control and a `TextBox` control onto the Web page. Set the `Text` property on the label to `Enter Name` and set the text box `ID` property to `txtEnterName`.**

3. **Drag and drop a `RequiredFieldValidator` control from the Validation section of the toolbox.**

4. **Set the following properties for the `RequiredFieldValidator` control from the Properties window:**

   - `ID` — Type this: **EnterNameRequired**.

   - `ControlToValidate` — Select txtEnterName from the drop-down list. It's the text box control you create in Step 2.

   - `Text` — Type this: **Name is a required field**.

5. **Add a `Button` control and a `Label` control to the page. Set the label's `ID` property to `lblConfirmation` and its `Text` property to `Confirmation Message`. Set the button control's `Text` property to `Submit`.**

6. **Double-click the button.**

   The button's `Click` event appears in the Code Editor.

7. **Type this code in the button's `Click` event:**

   - *VB*

     ```
     If Page.IsValid Then
         lblConfirmation.Text = "Page is valid! "
     End If
     ```

   - *C#*

     ```
     if( Page.IsValid )
     {
         lblConfirmation.Text = "Page is valid!";
     }
     ```

   This code snippet displays the message `Page is valid!` on the Confirmation label when the user clicks the button.

 See Book V, Chapter 4 to read more about using events.

Testing a validation control

To test your validation control, follow these steps:

1. **Press Ctrl+F5 to run your site.**

2. **Click the Submit button on the page.**

   The page displays `Name is a required field` next to the text box, as shown in Figure 6-1.

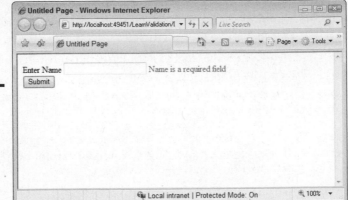

Figure 6-1:
This error message is displayed next to the required text box.

The RequiredFieldValidator control uses client-side scripting to test the contents of the text box. When you click the Submit button, the browser doesn't call the server. Instead, a client-side script validates the control. If the control passes the validation, data is sent to the server. Using client-side scripting is more efficient because you don't make wasted trips back to the server just to see whether the user has filled in a text box.

You should make a trip to the server whenever you need to validate sensitive information, such as a password. Using a validation control with client-side scripting isn't appropriate because you have to store the password in the client-side script. Client-side scripts are visible to users, so you would compromise your password. See Chapter 6 in this mini-book to see how to use the new ASP.NET Login controls to validate passwords.

3. **Type a name in the text box, and then press Tab.**

   The error message goes away.

4. **Delete the name from the text box, and then press Tab.**

   The message appears again.

5. **Type a name in the text box again and click the Submit button on the page.**

   The button's Click event is sent to the server for processing because the text box has a value in it, as required by the RequiredFieldValidator control.

6. **The page displays** Page is valid! **next to the button.**

   You might wonder why the Page is valid! message wasn't displayed earlier, when you typed a name in the text box in Step 3 and the error message disappeared. For the message to appear, the data must be sent to the server. The data can be sent only if the validation control confirms that the data is valid when the button is clicked.

A project for the preceding example can be downloaded from the companion Web site for this book. You can find out more in the book's Introduction.

Handling multiple validation controls

You can also mix and match validators. Often, multiple validations must be performed on a single control. For example, you may want to test whether a control has a value and whether the value conforms to a certain pattern, such as a phone number. In this case, you use a RequiredFieldValidator and a RegularExpressionValidator. The following example walks you through using the comparison and pattern validators to validate the same control:

1. **Drag and drop a label control and text box control to your Web page. Set the label's Text property to Enter e-mail address and set the text box ID to txtEmail1.**

2. **Drag and drop another label control and text box control onto your Web page. Set the label's Text property to Re-enter e-mail address, and set the text box ID to txtEmail2.**

3. **Add RequiredFieldValidator controls for each of the text boxes. Set the properties for the controls as described earlier in this section.**

4. **Add a RegularExpressionValidator control to the page.**

5. **Set the control's properties as follows:**

   - ValidationExpression — Click the ellipsis and choose Internet E-mail Address.

   - Text — Enter **Must match e-mail address above**.

   - ControlToValidate — Select txtEmail1 from the drop-down list.

6. **Add a CompareValidator control to the page.**

7. **Set the control's properties:**

   - ControlToCompare — Select txtEmail1.

   - ControlToValidate — Select txtEmail2.

   - Text — Type **Must match e-mail address above**.

8. **Add a button control, setting the Text property to Submit.**

9. **Press Ctrl+F5 to run your site and test the validators.**

   Your page should look similar to the one shown in Figure 6-2.

A project for the preceding example can be downloaded from the companion Web site for this book, which you can read about in the book's Introduction.

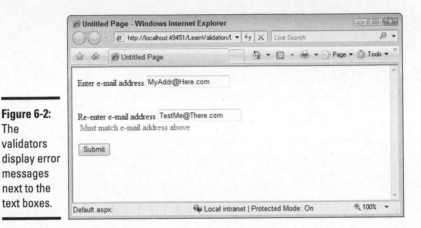

Figure 6-2:
The
validators
display error
messages
next to the
text boxes.

Notice how the error message for the RegularExpressionValidator doesn't align next to the text box. That's because a placeholder for RequiredFieldValidator is sitting between the text box and the RegularExpressionValidator error message, as in this abbreviated code:

```
<asp:TextBox ID="email1" runat="server"></asp:TextBox>
<asp:RequiredFieldValidator>E-mail address is required.
    </asp:RequiredFieldValidator>
<asp:RegularExpressionValidator>Email address must be in the form
    user@company.com.</asp:RegularExpressionValidator>
```

To eliminate the placeholder, change the Display property on RequiredFieldValidator from Static to Dynamic. Now, your error message flows with the page layout.

Instead of displaying your messages next to text boxes, you can display them in a message box on the page. Follow these steps:

1. **Add a ValidationSummary control to the top of your page.**

2. **Type** Please correct these errors: **in the HeaderText property.**

3. **Set the ErrorMessage property on each of your validation controls to the message you want to display in the ValidationSummary control.**

4. **Put an asterisk in the Text property of each of your validation controls.**

5. **Press Ctrl+F5 to run your site and test it.**

The ValidationSummary control displays all error messages at the top of the page, as shown in Figure 6-3.

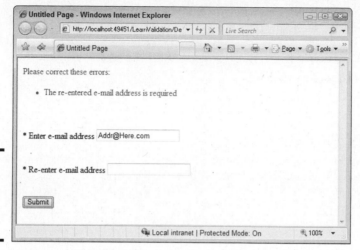

Figure 6-3:
Your site should look similar to this one.

Now, the user receives all error messages at the top of the screen after clicking the Submit button. An asterisk is displayed next to the text boxes, which makes an interesting demonstration of the ErrorMessage and Text properties:

**Book III
Chapter 6**

Laying Out Your Site

✦ Use the ErrorMessage property, along with the ValidationSummary control, when you want to display all feedback in a single place on the screen at one time.

✦ Use the Text property to display immediate feedback next to the control being validated.

Combining these approaches allows the user to see a visual cue next to the text box in question. These properties can accept text, HTML, or images.

You can group validation controls by using the ValidationGroup property. You can then use, for example, two ValidationSummary controls on a single page.

Mapping Out Your Site Navigation

ASP.NET provides built-in support for Web site navigation by using a combination of a site map and a set of navigation controls driven by the site map.

A *site map* is a logical description of the layout of a Web site. Visual Studio includes the following navigation controls:

✦ Menu

✦ SiteMapPath

✦ TreeView

Adding a site map

ASP.NET supports an XML-file-based site map by default. You can use a database-driven site map, if you choose. The syntax for the site map uses these two nodes:

✦ <sitemap> — The root node of the sitemap document contains all the <sitemapnode> nodes.

✦ <sitemapnode> — Each node represents a page on your Web site. Nodes can be nested.

The <sitemapnode> node has these attributes:

✦ Description — The page description

✦ Title — The page title

✦ URL — The URL for accessing the page

You can also specify a collection of roles that can access <sitemapnode> and a collection of custom attributes. These roles are likely to be used with a custom site map provider.

To create a new site map for an existing Web site, follow these steps:

1. Right-click the Web site's project folder in Solution Explorer and choose Add New Item from the contextual menu.

The Add New Item dialog box appears.

2. Click the Site Map icon.

Don't change the name of the site map.

3. Click the Add button to add the site map to your Web site.

Visual Studio opens a new site map file in Document Explorer.

4. Type the URL, title, and description in the siteMapNode tags for each page in your Web site, as shown in Figure 6-4.

You can add as many siteMapNode tags as required. siteMapNodes can be nested to create a tree of nodes.

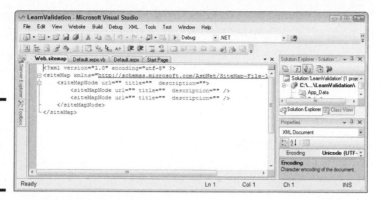

Figure 6-4:
Type your
information
in the site
map file.

Suppose that you have a Web site with the following four pages:

✦ `default.aspx`

✦ `about.aspx`

✦ `blogs.aspx`

✦ `bookmarks.aspx`

The following bit of code creates a site map you can use to describe access
to the four pages:

```
<siteMapNode url="~/default.aspx" title="Home">
   <siteMapNode url="~/about.aspx" title="About the site" />
   <siteMapNode url="" title="My Research Page">
     <siteMapNode url="~/blogs.aspx" title="Blogs I Read" />
     <siteMapNode url="~/bookmarks.aspx" title="Sites I Visit" />
   </siteMapNode>
</siteMapNode>
```

Adding navigation controls

To do something meaningful with the site map, you must include it with one
of the navigation controls to display its contents. To add a `TreeView` control to the `default.aspx` page, for example, follow these steps:

1. **Drag and drop the `TreeView` control from the Navigation tab of the
toolbox into Design view of the `default.aspx` page.**

An image of the `TreeView` control appears, along with a list of tasks.

If the list of tasks isn't displayed, click the glyph in the upper-right
corner of the `TreeView` control.

2. **In the TreeView Tasks list, click the drop-down arrow for Choose Data Source. Then select <New Data Source> from the drop-down list.**

3. **In the Data Source Configuration Wizard, click the Site Map icon.**

4. **Click OK.**

   The tree view is updated to reflect your site map, as shown in Figure 6-5.

Figure 6-5:
The
`TreeView`
control gets
is data from
the site
map.

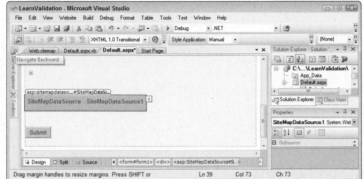

5. **Run your Web site by pressing Ctrl+F5 and test the hyperlinks in your `TreeView` control.**

Managing Your Site's Appearance with Themes and Master Pages

Visual Studio and ASP.NET provide two tools for managing the look and feel of your Web sites:

✦ **Themes and skins:** Easily separate the appearance attributes of controls from the controls themselves.

✦ **Master pages:** Create a single page template to use with all your content pages.

Themes and master pages make administering your Web site easier. When you use themes and master pages, visitors can personalize their user experience on your Web site. For more information on personalization, see Chapter 7 of this mini-book.

Cascading styles

A *CSS style* is a set of attributes that defines the appearance and layout of an HTML element. For example, you can create a CSS style that sets a paragraph to use a specific font and font size. Think of a Web page as a container that holds containers of HTML elements. Paragraphs and `div` tags are examples of containers that hold content and other HTML elements.

You can define styles for each container (such as a Web page or a paragraph). As you define styles, the styles closest to the content are applied. For example, you may define a style

that sets the font color to black and the font family to Arial at the Web-page level. If you define another style at the paragraph level that sets the font color to red, the content inside the paragraph is red. The font family is Arial, as defined for the Web page, unless you define a different font family for the paragraph.

In this way, styles *cascade* — like a waterfall — from higher-level containers to lower-level containers. The style elements defined closest to the content win over style elements defined in higher containers.

Using themes and skins

A *theme* defines the look and feel of your Web site. Themes include these elements:

✦ **Skins** — A set of properties that define a control's appearance

✦ **CSS** — A standard for defining the appearance and layout attributes of HTML elements

   See the upcoming section "Laying Out Web Pages with CSS" for more information about creating Cascading Style Sheets.

✦ **Images** — Files that define the site's appearance, such as a company logo

A theme has, at minimum, a skin file. Some overlap occurs between skins and CSS because both are used to control appearance. They have some crucial differences, however:

✦ **Skins don't cascade.** Unlike with CSS, where you can create a hierarchy of styles, you define one skin for each type of control you use on your site. See the sidebar "Cascading styles" for more details on how CSS styles cascade.

✦ **Skins define properties for ASP.NET Web server controls.** CSS styles apply to HTML elements.

✦ **Skins apply to a single Web server control.** Styles can apply to a single HTML element or to collections of elements.

✦ **Styles can be used to control the positioning of elements on a page.**

Here are some guidelines for choosing between skins and styles.

✦ **Use skins when**

• You're setting properties specific to Web server controls.

• You want to provide personalization features for your visitors. For instance, you might want to display images specific to users or provide color themes.

✦ **Use styles to**

• Set site-wide or page-wide properties, such as fonts.

• Control page layout.

Use skins to define general properties. If you need to define the appearance of a single element on a page, use styles.

Adding a theme to an existing site

You define themes for individual Web pages, an entire Web site, or all sites hosted on a Web server.

To add a theme to a Web site and associate the theme with the site, follow these steps:

1. **Right-click the Web site's project folder in Solution Explorer and choose Add ASP.NET Folder. Choose Theme from the submenu.**

A theme folder is added to the project.

2. **Enter a name, such as MyTheme, for the theme folder.**

You can rename themes by right-clicking and choosing Rename from the theme folder's contextual menu.

3. **Double-click the web.config file in Solution Explorer to open it.**

All your Web site configuration information is stored in the web.config file.

4. **Add the theme attribute to the page node in the web.config file so that the node looks like this:**

```
<pages theme="MyTheme">
```

5. **Close the web.config file and save the changes when you're prompted.**

All pages on your Web site now use the skins and the style sheet you add to the MyTheme folder.

Adding a theme as a style sheet

You can also apply a theme as a style sheet. A *style sheet theme* cascades like a style sheet, which means that local page settings take precedence over the theme. To set the Web site to use a style sheet theme, use this code instead of the code in Step 4 in the preceding set of steps:

```
<pages StyleSheetTheme="MyTheme">
```

To apply a theme to an individual page on your Web site, specify the proper attribute on the page's directive line, like this:

```
<%@ Page Theme="MyTheme" %>
<%@ Page StyleSheetTheme="MyTheme" %>
```

To apply a theme to all sites on a Web server, add a Themes folder to the path:

```
iisdefaultroot\aspnet_client\system_web\version\
```

Add your themes to the Themes folder. You can also add the Theme attribute to the pages element in the Web server's `machine.config` file.

Defining skins

Before you can start defining skins, think about the steps for creating your page layout and design:

1. Identify all common elements that you expect to use repeatedly throughout your site. You want to think in abstract terms about how many headings you want and how each one is different from the others. Picture your content in sections, such as sections for searches, What's New information, RSS (really simple syndication) feeds, and banner ads.

2. Decide which pages, if any, are unique. For example, a site commonly has a unique home page, and then individual pages reuse common elements.

3. Decide whether you want to use skins or styles to control the site's appearance. You can always change your mind.

4. Implement your skins and styles.

5. Test your layout frequently. Don't be afraid to change your mind.

Refactoring: Trying a new approach

Going through and changing your approach to solving a problem is *refactoring*. Although this process is often used in the context of building software libraries, it applies to any situation in which you have to make design choices. Choosing to use skins may make perfect sense today, but you may decide to implement style sheets later when you're upgrading the site. The point of refactoring is to allow yourself the freedom to make a decision now with the understanding that you can change your mind in the future.

Try not to get hung up on whether you should implement a skin or a style. Folks who have used styles for a long time sometimes lean toward using them. Remember that your goal is to have working software. Don't fret over best-practices implementation. Go with what works, and don't be afraid to change your approach later.

The following example assumes that you're creating a Web site with these elements:

✦ A header to place elements such as your site's name and logo

✦ A sidebar on the left side for navigation

✦ A footer to place elements such as copyright information

✦ A main content area

The main content area is the part of the screen that changes dynamically. To define skins for both recurring content and one-off elements, suppose you identify that you need these labels:

✦ A Web site title

✦ Sidebar content

✦ Header content

✦ A page content title

✦ Default content

The easiest way to build skins for controls is to add the control to a page, set the control's properties, copy the generated ASP.NET markup code to the skin file, and delete the ID and Text properties. To create a skin for the Web site title, follow these steps:

1. **Drag and drop a label control onto a page on your Web site.**

2. **Press F4 to display the label's properties.**

3. **Set these properties:**

   - `Bold = True`
   - `Name = Verdana`
   - `Size = X-Large`
   - `ForeColor = DarkRed`

   You can set the properties however you like. This book uses these values only as an example.

4. **Click the Source tab to display the page's source markup.**

5. **Copy the markup for the label you created and paste it in your skin file.**

   You add skin files the same way you add any new item: Right-click the App_Themes folder and choose Add New Item.

6. **Delete the `ID` and `Text` attributes from your label's markup.**

7. **Add the attribute `SkinID="siteTitle"` to the label's markup.**

8. **Add a comment above your label, like this:**

   ```
   <%-- Web site title --%>
   ```

Repeat this process to add all your labels to the skin file.

To apply a skin to an individual control, set the control's `SkinID` property to the `SkinID` that you set in the skin file. For example, to apply the skin you create in the preceding set of steps to a label, follow these steps:

1. **Add a label control to your Web page.**

2. **Set the label's `SkinID` property to `siteTitle`.**

To test whether your skin is working, add text to your label and then press Ctrl+F5 to run your Web site.

A skin that uses a `SkinID` is a *named* skin. You can also define a default skin that applies to all controls of the same type by not using a `SkinID`. For example, the following skin applies to all label controls that use the theme with this skin:

```
<asp:Label runat="server" cssclass="label" />
```

You can use skins with CSS styles. For example, the following label control uses a CSS style. Any skins defined for the page are applied, also:

```
<asp:Label runat="server" cssclass="labelstyle" />
```

Mastering master pages

In the old days of development, developers used server-side includes and user controls to create a page template feel for their Web sites. Using the new ASP.NET master page feature, you no longer have to copy and paste repetitive code into your Web pages to create a template effect.

Although you could create page templates in previous versions of ASP.NET, you needed some coding expertise. The visual designer in Visual Studio didn't support custom page templates, either. Visual Studio has visual designer support for master pages.

The master page looks and feels like any Web page, with two major differences:

✦ Master pages aren't called from the browser.

✦ The `ContentPlaceHolder` control on the master page is replaced with content from a content page.

Think of the master page as the template for your Web site. Any content that you want repeated on each of your Web sites is added to this page. For example, add the header and footer and any navigation element to your master page. After you associate your content pages with your master page, those elements appear on all your content pages.

To add a master page to an existing Web site:

1. **Right-click the Web site's project folder in Solution Explorer and choose Add New Item.**

    The Add New Item dialog box appears.

2. **Click the Master Page icon.**

3. **Click the Add button to add the master page to the Web site.**

    Visual Studio creates the master page and adds it to the Web site.

Adding content to your master page

Adding content to a master page is similar to adding content to any Web page. If you use table layout, add a table and start adding your header, footer, and other elements. If you use CSS layout, add `div` tags or other placeholders you like to use. See the upcoming section "Laying Out Web Pages with CSS" for more information on CSS layout.

You can also use ASP.NET expressions to add content to your master page. You can use expressions to add content to your page without typing the content in the page. For example, you can place information in a separate configuration file and then display that information on your master page. When you want to update the information, you only have to make a change in your configuration file.

Many people add configuration information to the AppSettings section in the `web.config` file. To add copyright information to the AppSettings section of an existing Web site, follow these steps:

1. **From the Internet Information Services (IIS) administrative Microsoft Management Console (MMC), right-click the Web application and bring up its properties.**

   The Properties dialog box appears.

2. **Click the ASP.NET tab.**

3. **Click the Edit Configuration button.**

4. **Click the Add button in the bottom section.**

5. **In the Name text box, type** copyright.

6. **In the Value text box, type** &copy 2008 MySite, **as shown in Figure 6-6.**

Figure 6-6:
Add application settings with the ASP.NET Web Site Administration tool.

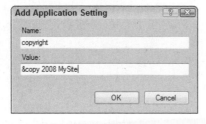

7. **Click OK.**

   The name/value pair is saved in the `<appSettings>` section of the `web.config` file.

8. **Click OK and close your browser.**

Any time you want to change the site's copyright information, use the Web Site Administration Tool.

The syntax for an ASP.NET expression is

```
<%$ expressionPrefix: expressionValue %>
```

ASP.NET expressions are often used for managing connection strings to database resources. For more information on managing connection strings, see Book IV, Chapter 5.

To use your new copyright on your Web site, follow these steps:

1. **Drag and drop a `Literal` server control from the toolbox to your master page.**

2. **Set the control's `Text` property equal to `<%$ AppSettings: copyright %>`.**

Your copyright is displayed in Design view on the master page, as shown in Figure 6-7.

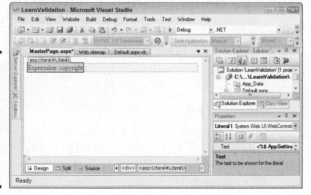

Figure 6-7: The copyright appears in Design view of the master page.

The `ContentPlaceHolder` control at the bottom of the screen, as shown in Figure 6-7, is where the content from your content pages appears. The control is added by default to the master page.

Adding new content pages

Without content from your Web pages, a master page is nothing more than a shell. You must add new Web pages to your site and associate them with the master page.

To add new content pages to use with your master page, follow these steps:

1. **Right-click the Web site's project folder in Solution Explorer. Choose Add New Item from the contextual menu.**

The Add New Item dialog box appears.

2. **Click the Web Form icon.**

3. **Enter a name for the Web form in the Name text box.**

4. **Select the Select Master Page check box.**

5. **Click Add.**

The Select a Master Page dialog box appears.

6. **Click the master page that you want to associate with the Web form.**

7. **Click OK.**

The new Web form is different from a free-standing Web form in several ways:

✦ The attribute `MasterPageFile` is added to the `@Page` directive.

✦ A `ContentPlaceHolder` server control is added to the Web form.

✦ None of the usual HTML markup is present.

A page associated with a master page can't be executed on its own. As you add content to the page by using Design view, Visual Studio adds the content to the `ContentPlaceHolder` control on the page.

You can convert existing Web pages for use with master pages. Walk through the steps in this section so that you can see the differences between a Web page that doesn't use a master page and one that does. Then you can modify your Web page to make it work with the master page.

Accessing the master page

You can make your content pages and master pages talk to each other. For example, you can store the content page's title in the content page and then display the title on the master page.

To use the best-practices guideline, display a title for each page on the browser's title bar by using the HTML element title. The problem is that when you use master pages, the title element is on the master page. You need to display the title from the content page using the title element on the master page.

To set the master page's title element by using content from the content page, follow these steps:

1. **Add this script to the master page Source view between the `<head></head>` tags:**

```
<script runat="server">
    Dim m_Title As String
    Public Property Title() As String
        Get
            Return m_Title
        End Get
        Set(ByVal value As String)
            m_Title = value
        End Set
    End Property
Sub Page_Load(ByVal sender As Object, ByVal e As EventArgs)
        If Not Page.IsPostBack Then
            Mytitle.DataBind()
        End If
End Sub
</script>
```

This Visual Basic code example creates a `Title` property for the master page. When the page loads, the master page's `DataBind` method is called on the `MyTitle` control, which tells the control to load data. For more information about data binding, see Book IV, Chapter 2.

2. **Add an `ID` attribute to the master page's title element:**

```
<title id="Mytitle">
```

The `ID` attribute makes it possible to access the title element with a script.

3. **Add the following ASP.NET expression between the opening and closing title tags:**

```
<%# me.Title %>
```

The title element appears this way:

```
<title id="Mytitle">
  <%# me.Title %>
</title>
```

The expression evaluates to the `Title` property you create in Step 1.

4. **On the content page, add this directive below the `@Page` directive:**

```
<%@ MasterType virtualpath="~/MasterPage.master" %>
```

The `@ MasterType` directive creates a link between the content page and the master page so that you can access the master page's Title property.

5. **Add this script to the content page just below the @ `MasterType` directive you added in Step 4:**

```
<script runat="server">
    Protected Sub Page_Load(ByVal sender As Object,
    ByVal e As System.EventArgs) Handles Me.Load
        Master.Title = "My Main Page"
    End Sub
</script>
```

This Visual Basic code example sets the `Title` property of the master page to `My Main Page`.

6. **Run your site by pressing Ctrl+F5.**

Your Web page displays the title on the browser's title bar, as shown in Figure 6-8.

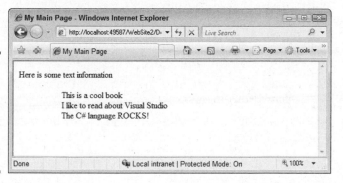

Figure 6-8:
The title from the content page appears on the title bar.

You aren't limited to using the title in the title element. You can use it with any server control. For example, to display the title in a label control, you use the following code:

```
<asp:Label ID="TitleLabel" runat="server">
  <%# me.Title %>
</asp:Label>
```

Just remember to call the control's `DataBind` method. In this case, you would call `TitleLabel.DataBind()`.

Laying Out Web Pages with CSS

You may be familiar with using CSS for setting fonts and background images. CSS also provides attributes for laying out and positioning elements on a Web page.

Regardless of whether you use master pages, you need a way to lay out your Web pages. Back when Web sites were first becoming popular, everyone used tables to lay out their Web pages. Using tables was a pain because of the markup that was involved. The World Wide Web Consortium (W3C) intended for tables to be used for displaying tabular data, not for laying out Web pages. Without an alternative, many designers used tables to lay out their Web pages, too.

Microsoft Web-design products have included visual designers for CSS layout for a few years now, and Microsoft is committed to supporting CSS layout and positioning in its Internet Explorer Web browser.

Laying out a Web page by using table-based layout requires tables and some-times nested tables. The large amount of HTML markup required to create tables obscures your content. CSS layout eliminates the table markup tags in your content pages. Using CSS, you can store all your layout information in a file separately from your content. If you decide to change your layout or your content, you can look at each one in isolation. CSS is also a great way to address the accessibility issues. For example, you could replace the small font used on a Web site with a very large one to make it readable.

Introducing CSS basics

Visual Studio provides a style builder you can use for building CSS style rules. It helps if you're a little conversant in CSS syntax first. In a nutshell, CSS syntax is composed of these elements:

✦ **A selector** — An HTML element or custom-defined element that gets styled

✦ **A declaration** — A set of attribute/value pairs.

Here are some examples of selectors:

✦ **HTML elements** — Examples are h1, a, and input.

✦ **Classes that can be applied to any element** — Classes use the syntax .class.

✦ **IDs that can be applied to any element** — Only one style ID can be used per page. IDs use the syntax #id.

Here are a couple of examples of declarations:

✦ Single-value declarations, such as color: black;

✦ Multiple-value declarations, such as border: solid thick black;

Put together a selector and some declarations, and you have a style rule that looks like this:

✦ Applies to instances of the HTML element p:

```
p
{
    color: Black;
    font: arial;
}
```

✦ Applies to all HTML elements with the attribute class="container":

```
.container
{
    clear: both;
    border: solid thin red;
}
```

✦ Applies to the single HTML element on the page, using the attribute id="header":

```
#header
{
    position: relative;
    width: 798px;
}
```

Here are some of the layout and positioning elements you should know about:

✦ **Top, Bottom** — Sets the top or bottom position of an element

✦ **Left, Right** — Sets the left or right position of an element

✦ **Height, Width** — Sets the height or width of an element

✦ **Z-index** — Sets the layer of an element where higher-order elements appear on top of lower-order elements

✦ **Position absolute** — Designates that an element is positioned according to the exact settings of the top, bottom, left, and right positions and the z-index

✦ **Position relative** — Designates that an element flows with the page layout and that any positioning attributes are relative to the flow of the page

Adding and creating CSS styles

You add CSS style rules to a style sheet. To add a style sheet to an existing Web site's theme folder, follow these steps:

1. **Right-click the Web site's App_Themes folder in Solution Explorer and then choose Add New Item from the contextual menu.**

   The Add New Item dialog box appears.

2. **Click the Style Sheet icon.**

3. **Click the Add button.**

A style sheet is added to the folder.

Using Visual Studio to create styles is a two-step process:

1. **Add a style by choosing Styles⇨Add Style Rule.**

2. **Build the style by choosing Styles⇨Build Style.**

To create a style for all paragraphs on your Web site, follow these steps:

1. **Choose Styles⇨Add Style Rule.**

The Add Style Rule dialog box appears.

2. **From the Element drop-down list, select the HTML element for paragraph, P.**

3. **Click the arrow button in the center of the dialog box to move the P element into the Style Rule Hierarchy box on the right.**

Use the style rule hierarchy to create styles that select elements nested within elements, classes, or element IDs.

4. **Click OK to add the style to the style sheet.**

To build a style for the paragraph style, follow these steps:

1. **Choose Styles⇨Build Style.**

The Style Builder window appears.

2. **On the Font tab, click the Family ellipsis button. Use the Font Picker to select a font family, such as Arial.**

3. **Set additional attributes, such as font size and effects.**

4. **Click OK to build the style.**

The style builder builds the style declaration in the style sheet for you.

Creating a page template with CSS

You can use the style builder to build the CSS layout for your Web page. To create a page template with a header, a left-side sidebar for navigation, a content placeholder, and a footer, use the style builder to create the styles. Follow these steps:

1. **Add style rules for each of these classes:**

- wrapper
- header
- leftnav
- content
- footer

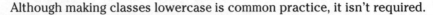

Although making classes lowercase is common practice, it isn't required.

2. **Using the style builder, set the styles for each of the rules created in Step 1 so that they look like this:**

```
#wrapper
{
    width: 798px;
    height: 100%;
    text-align: left;
    margin: 0 auto 0 auto;
    border-left: solid thin black;
    border-right: solid thin black;
    border-bottom: solid thin black;
    background-color: White;
}
#header
{
    width: 100%;
    position: relative;
    height: 100px;
    border-bottom: solid thin black;
    background-color: #66CC33;
    vertical-align: middle;
}
#leftnav
{
    position: relative;
    float: left;
    width: 200px;
    border-right: groove thick #66CC33;
}
#content
{
    float: left;
    width: 70%;
    position: relative;
    margin-left: 25px;
}
#footer
{
```

```
clear: both;
width: 100%;
background-color: #66CC33;
border-top: solid thin black;
font-size: smaller;
padding-bottom: 10px;
}
```

3. **Add the following style to the Body element:**

```
text-align: center;
margin: 0;
background-color: #CCFF99;
font-family: Arial;
```

Use div tags to apply your layout classes to the master page Source view, as shown here:

```
<body>
    <form id="form1" runat="server">
        <div id="wrapper">
        <div id="header">
        </div>
        <div id="leftnav">
        </div>
        <div id="content">
            <asp:contentplaceholder id="mainContent" runat="server">
            </asp:contentplaceholder>
        </div>
        <div id="footer">
        </div>
        </div>
    </form>
</body>
```

Now, add content to your master page:

1. **Add a TreeView control in your leftnav div tags.**

2. **Add a Breadcrumb control to the content div tag before the content placeholder.**

3. **Add header information, such as your site name and site logo, in the header div tags.**

4. **Add your copyright information to the page footer.**

Learning to use CSS layout is no small feat. For more information, check out *CSS Web Design For Dummies,* by Richard Mansfield (Wiley). Microsoft provides several design template starter kits that use CSS layout. You can download starter kits for free at

```
http://msdn2.microsoft.com/en-us/asp.net/aa336613.aspx
```

To apply your style sheet to an existing Web page, follow these steps:

1. **Drag your style sheet from Solution Explorer.**

2. **Drop the style sheet on the Web page.**

Visual Studio adds a link tag to your Web page, to associate it with the style sheet.

Applying styles to controls

You have a few options for applying styles to controls. For example, you can create CSS classes to store styles. To apply a CSS class to a server control, follow these steps:

1. **Select the control on the Web page.**

2. **Press F4 to display the control's properties.**

3. **Add your CSS class to the `CssClass` property.**

You can also use the style builder to create styles for individual controls. To use the style builder with a control, follow these steps:

1. **Add a control to a Web page or select an existing control.**

2. **Right-click the control and choose Style from the contextual menu.**

The Style Builder window appears.

3. **Build your style by using the style builder.**

The style is applied to the control by using the control's `Style` property.

Chapter 7: Exploring ASP.NET Services

In This Chapter

✔ **Introducing ASP.NET 3.5 services**

✔ **Managing state in your Web site**

✔ **Creating a membership-enabled site**

✔ **Personalizing your Web site**

*I*t has never been a better time to be an ASP.NET Web developer. After all those years of building tools for constructing Web sites, Microsoft finally realized that Web developers are trying to solve the same types of problems, such as registering people, logging in registered users, creating a personalized user experience, and monitoring the status of Web applications.

The latest version of ASP.NET provides the services developers need in order to build professional-quality Web sites without having to reinvent the wheel with each new Web site. This chapter introduces you to those new ASP.NET services and shows you how to use Visual Studio to leverage ASP.NET services in your next Web site project.

What a Wonderful Provider!

ASP.NET 3.5 offers many new services that provide common Web development features. These services include

+ **Membership** — Creates and manages user accounts for providing access to a secure Web site

+ **Role Manager** — Adds role-based management to your user accounts

+ **Personalization** — Gives visitors to your site a personalized experience by storing user profile information or allowing them to create their own user experiences with Web parts

✦ **Session State** — Manages user sessions and chooses the data store that's appropriate for your situation

✦ **Site Navigation** — Shows your site visitors how to move around in your site by using site maps and navigation controls

✦ **Web Events** — Monitors and stores your Web site's health

As you can imagine, writing all the code yourself to provide these services would be time consuming. Each of these ASP.NET services provides a combination of Web server controls, public properties, and methods that implement the service, as well as access to a data store. And they all work well right out of the box.

ASP.NET services are made possible by the ASP.NET provider model. In this case, a *provider* is a type of software architecture that allows a framework, such as ASP.NET, to provide sophisticated services while hiding the implementation details of those services. The ASP.NET provider model has four layers:

✦ **Controls** — This set of Web server controls serves as the visible face of the service.

✦ **Services** — This public set of properties and methods, accessible by using Web server controls, provides the functionality of the service.

✦ **Providers** — All the implementation details that make the service "just work" happen by using these bits of code.

✦ **Data Stores** — This physical layer saves and retrieves the provider's data.

Table 7-1 shows the four layers of the ASP.NET provider model.

Table 7-1	Layers of the ASP.NET Provider Model
Layer	*Sample Technologies*
Controls	`Login`, `TreeView`
Services	Membership, site navigation
Providers	`SqlProvider`, `XMLProvider`, custom provider
Data Stores	SQL Server, XML document, custom data store

Why all these layers of abstraction? Why not just pass your data from the controls to the database? Creating distinct layers provides these benefits:

✦ You can customize any of the provider's layers without breaking the way the service works.

✦ The default implementation offers sophisticated services that work well out of the box.

Most ASP.NET services use a SQL Server database with a predefined database schema as the data store. If you decide that you want to change the data store's schema or use a completely different data store, you can create your own provider to access the data store. Any Web server controls that you use keep working because the data access implementation details are hidden away in lower layers of the service.

For example, the Membership service uses a SQL Server database by default to store membership data. To use a new data store with the service, such as an XML file, you need to create a new provider. After you implement the details of accessing the XML data store in your new provider, telling the Membership service to use the new data store is a matter of changing the `SQLProvider` entry in the configuration file to `MyCustomXMLProvider`. Your membership-enabled Web site keeps working because the login controls are hidden from the details of the data store.

Using these ASP.NET services is a matter of using the controls associated with the service or setting configuration options in the Web site's `web.config` file.

A *web.config* file is an XML file that stores configuration settings for your Web site. To add a `web.config` file if your site doesn't have one yet, press Ctrl+Shift+A to open the Add New Item dialog box and select the Web Configuration File template.

Table 7-2 lists the ASP.NET services that use the provider model, and the control or the `web.config` section that enables each service.

Table 7-2	ASP.NET Services and Their Controls
Service	*Control or Type of Configuration Setting*
Membership	Login
Role management	`<roleManager>` section in `web.config`
Personalization	Web parts and `<profile>` section in `web.config`
Session state	Session object
Site navigation	Site map and navigation controls
Web events	`<healthMonitoring>` section in `web.config`

This chapter walks you through the process of using membership, role management, personalization, and session state services. Chapter 6 in this minibook covers site navigation.

If you're itching to get under the hood of the ASP.NET provider model so that you can create your own custom providers, check out the ASP.NET Provider Toolkit:

```
http://msdn2.microsoft.com/en-us/asp.net/Aa336558.aspx
```

Managing State

Web applications are different from other kinds of applications, such as Windows applications, because Web pages use the HyperText Transfer Protocol (HTTP) for communications between the browser client and the server. HTTP is a *stateless* protocol: After a Web page is rendered to the browser, the Web server severs its connection to the client. As a result, the Web server has no memory of anything your visitor clicks on the Web page.

To get around this limitation of HTTP, Web frameworks such as ASP.NET provide many services for storing and retrieving a Web page's data after a user performs some action, such as clicking a button that requires processing on the server. Collectively, this process is *state management*.

You can use the ASP.NET state management features to develop your Web site without much consideration for how state is managed. ASP.NET takes care of all those details for you and hides their implementation. State management is one reason that frameworks such as ASP.NET are popular. Before ASP.NET, developers had to manage all state management details on their own. By using ASP.NET to handle the services of state management, you can focus on building your Web site.

The ASP.NET state-management offerings are client-side or server-side:

+ **Client-side state management** stores state information on the client.

+ **Server-side** stores state information on the server.

Generally, you should use client-side state management for storing small amounts of short-lived information. Server-side state management is more secure and can store more state information over longer time intervals than client-side options can.

Your client-side choices are described in this list:

+ **View state** — A property used by ASP.NET Web pages

+ **Hidden-field** — A standard HTML hidden field

✦ **Cookies** — Files stored on the client's computer for saving key/value pairs

✦ **Query strings** — Key/value pairs appended to the end of a Web page URL

Here are the ASP.NET server-side offerings:

✦ **Application state** — Stores global values for the entire application to access

✦ **Session state** — Stores values for a user's session

✦ **Database** — Stores state information in a custom database

Regardless of whether you choose client-side or server-side management, ASP.NET uses these state-management features by default:

✦ View state stores all values associated with the Web server controls on a page.

✦ Application and session state are stored in server memory.

Understanding view state

Every time you add a Web server control to a Web page, you're using view state to capture any data associated with that control. For example, if you add a `CheckBox` server control to a Web page, the user's check box selection is stored in view state. ASP.NET removes the user's check from view state and sets the `checked` property on the check box equal to `True`. You don't have to know anything about view state to determine the check box's state. ASP.NET manages all that for you. You just query the check box's `checked` property.

**Book III
Chapter 7**

Exploring ASP.NET
Services

You can use the view state to store your own data values independently of a Web server control. For example, here's how to add a customer's identification number to a Web page's view state:

1. **Add a text box control and a button control to a Web page.**

2. **In Design view of the page, double-click a blank area of the design surface.**

Visual Studio creates a `Page_Load` event handler and opens the Code Editor.

3. **Save the customer's identification number to the view state by using these lines of code:**

- *VB*

```
If Not Page.IsPostBack Then
    ViewState("CustID") = "123456"
End If
```

- *C#*

```
if( !Page.IsPostBack )
{
    ViewState["CustID"] = "123456";
}
```

4. **In Design view of the page, double-click the button control.**

Visual Studio creates a `Button Click` event and opens the Code Editor.

5. **To retrieve the customer's identification number from view state and display it in the text box, type this line:**

- *VB*

```
me.TextBox1.Text = ViewState("CustID").ToString()
```

- *C#*

```
TextBox1.Text = ViewState["CustID"].ToString();
```

6. **Press Ctrl+F5 to run your Web site.**

When you first run your Web site, the text box is empty. After you click the button, the value `123456` appears in the text box. Here's how it works:

1. When the page is first loaded in the browser, the Web page stores the value `123456` in its view state.

2. When you click the button, the browser sends the request to the Web server, along with the view state. The Web server passes along the request with the view state data to ASP.NET.

3. ASP.NET picks apart the view state that the browser sent and provides state information to any controls. ASP.NET holds on to the `123456` value.

4. ASP.NET calls the `Page_Load` event. ASP.NET skips the code inside the `If` statement because the request is a postback.

A *postback* occurs when a request is sent from a Web page back to the Web server. See Chapter 4 in this mini-book for more information about postbacks.

5. The `Click` event is processed next, where `123456` is retrieved from the view state and placed in the text box.

The view state is a key/value dictionary. It acts like you would expect a dictionary to work. You add a key (such as `CustID`) and then a value (such as `123456`). You retrieve the value by using the key. Application state and session state are also key/value dictionaries. You add key/value pairs to application state and session state, just as you do to view state:

VB

```
Object("Key")  = "value"
```

C#

```
Object["Key"]  = "value";
```

Here's an example:

VB

```
Application("AppStart") = Now
Session("CustID") = "123456"
```

C#

```
Application["AppStart"]; = Now;
  Session["CustID"] = "123456";
```

Use view state whenever you need to

+ **Store small amounts of data,** such as lookup keys for customer data or user identification data.

+ **Pass data** from page to page and hide it from view.

Using session state

Whenever a user visits your Web site, a new session is created. ASP.NET creates a unique session identifier and associates it with the user's browsing session. You can store a collection of key/value pairs with the user's session. A collection of key/value pairs associated with a user's session is its *session state*.

Session state is enabled by default in ASP.NET. You can use session state to store information about a user's progress through your Web site on your Web server. Session state preserves the values across the lifetime of the user session as the user moves from page to page in your Web site.

Session state is stored in a dictionary and works similarly to view state. You can use session state anywhere you would use view state. (See the preceding section for an example of how to use view state to store state information.)

Application state is similar to session state except that it stores values for the entire application, not just a single user's session.

Any time you need to store state, the view state, session state, and application state are at your disposal, with no additional configuration required.

Providing the Perks of Membership

One way to create a professional-looking Web site is to provide membership. *Membership* is the gateway to providing personalization features for your site, such as user profiles and Web parts. You can use membership to provide secure access to your Web site.

In the sections that follow, you find out how to set up and get started with membership.

Configuring the default database

Before you can configure your Web site to use membership, you need to configure the default application services provider database. You must have SQL Server Express installed on your computer to set up the default provider database. After you do that, follow these steps:

1. **Launch the `Aspnet_regsql.exe` tool.**

   You can find this at

   > *drive:*\WINDOWS\Microsoft.NET\Framework*version number*

   The ASP.NET SQL Server Setup Wizard starts.

2. **Click Next to step through the wizard.**

3. **On the Select a Setup Option page, select Configure SQL Server for Application Services and then click Next.**

4. **On the Select the Server and Database page**

   a. *Enter your database server's name and SQL Server instance.*

   Be sure to enter your SQL Server instance in the Server text box, as shown in Figure 7-1. The default instance name for SQL Server Express is SQLExpress. ***Note:*** You might have a name other than the default. The one used here is RCCUSER-PC. You can get more information about SQL Server Express in Book IV, Chapter 6.

   b. *Select the Windows Authentication radio button.*

   c. *Accept the <default> database.*

5. **Click Next.**

6. **Click Next again to create the database.**

7. **Click Finish.**

You now have a default database that you can use for all ASP.NET services, including membership.

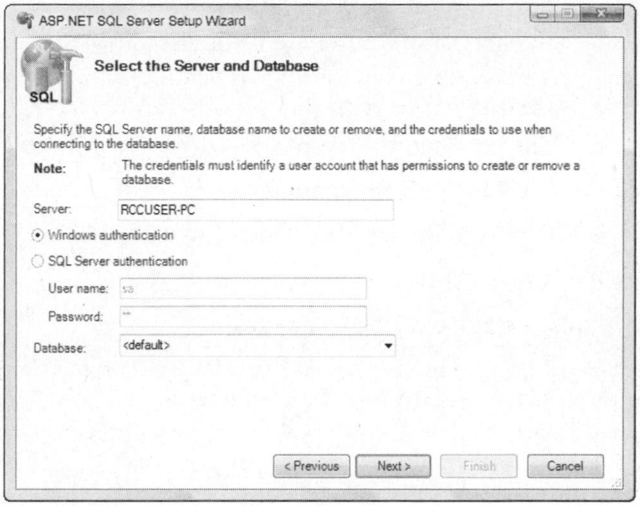

Figure 7-1:
Your
settings are
displayed on
a summary
page.

Running a site on IIS

You need to set up Internet Information Services (IIS) for the following examples to work. To do so, follow these steps:

1. **Open Control Panel.**

2. **Click the Programs applet.**

3. **Click the Turn Windows Features On or Off link.**

4. **Select Internet Information Services, as shown in Figure 7-2.**

Figure 7-2:
Select
Internet
Information
Services so
that IIS will
install.

You need a Web site running on an IIS server to use the ASP.NET membership features. To create a Web site running on IIS, follow these steps:

1. **Choose File➪New➪Web Site.**

The New Web Site dialog box appears.

2. **Click the ASP.NET Web Site template.**

3. **Choose HTTP from the Location drop-down list.**

4. **Click the Browse button.**

The Choose Location dialog box appears.

5. **Click Local IIS and then select Default Web Site from the site hierarchy, as shown in Figure 7-3, and click Open.**

Figure 7-3:
A new Web site is added to the site hierarchy.

If you haven't installed IIS, when you click the Local IIS button, you might get an error message that reads

```
To access local IIS Web sites, you must install all of
     the following Windows components
```

6. **Enter a name, such as MembershipWebSite, in the Location field; see Figure 7-4.**

7. **Click OK.**

Visual Studio opens your new IIS Web site.

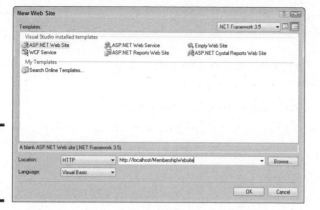

Figure 7-4:
Enter the
location
name here.

Securing membership content

The easiest way to secure content is when it's organized into folders. Add folders named Members and Administrative to the Web site.

To configure membership for the Web site, follow these steps:

1. **Choose Website⇨ASP.NET Configuration.**

The ASP.NET Web Site Administration Tool is launched in a browser.

2. **Click the Security tab.**

Use the Security tab to manage your users, roles, and access rules.

3. **On the Security tab, click the Use the Security Setup Wizard to Configure Security Step By Step link.**

The Security Setup Wizard starts.

4. **Click Next to step through the wizard.**

5. **In Step 2 of the wizard, select the From the Internet option. Then click Next.**

Step 3 of the wizard confirms that you're using the default data store.

6. **Click Next to continue.**

7. **Use Step 4 of the wizard to define roles for your members. Select the Enable Roles for This Web Site check box and then click Next.**

8. **Type a new role — Administrators — and then click the Add Role button. Repeat to add a Members role. Click Next to continue.**

9. **In Step 5 of the wizard, create a user account for yourself. Then click Next.**

10. **In Step 6 of the wizard, click the plus sign (+) next to the MembershipWebsite directory hierarchy. Select the App_Data folder; see Figure 7-5.**

11. **In the Rule Applies To section, choose Administrators from the Role drop-down list; see Figure 7-5.**

12. **Select the Allow radio button (from Permission) and then click the Add This Rule button; see Figure 7-5.**

The rule is added.

13. **Add a rule denying anonymous users access to the Members folder.**

14. **Click Next.**

The wizard is complete.

15. **Click the Finish button to close the wizard and return to the Security tab.**

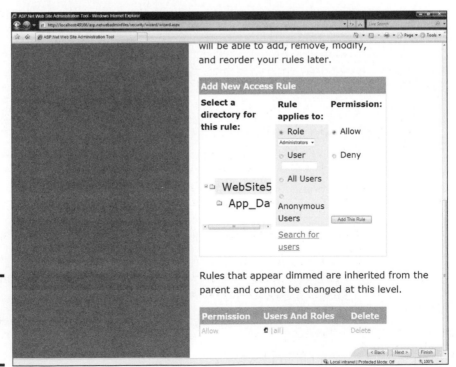

Figure 7-5:
Add an
access rule
for the
Admin role.

Setting up a login page

You need a way for people to log into your Web site now that your site is set up for membership. Before ASP.NET 2.0, you had to create your own custom login pages. ASP.NET provides all the login controls you need in order to create a professional membership experience. The `Login` controls are shown in this list:

✦ `Login` — Provide the text boxes for username and password.

✦ `LoginView` — Create separate views for logged-in and anonymous users.

✦ `LoginStatus` — Tell users whether they're logged into the site.

✦ `LoginName` — Display a user's login name.

✦ `PasswordRecovery` — Retrieve user passwords by using their e-mail addresses.

✦ `CreateUserWizard` — Provide controls for self-registration.

✦ `ChangePassword` — Allow users to change their passwords.

`Login` controls are wired to work with the membership database. You don't have to write any code to make them work. The appearance of `Login` controls is customizable using control templates.

Using `Login` controls requires you to create a few Web pages. In your Web site, add these pages:

✦ `Login.aspx` — Your Web site's main login page must be named `Login.aspx` if you want to use the `LoginStatus` control.

✦ `Registration.aspx` — On this self-registration page, site visitors create their own usernames and passwords.

✦ `Members.aspx` — Add this page to your Members folder. A user must be logged into your site in order to access the page.

After you have the membership set up, create your Web site's start page for logging in:

1. **Add a `LoginStatus` control from the Login group of the toolbox to `default.aspx`, the start page of your Web page.**

2. **Add a `LoginView` control to your start page.**

**Book III
Chapter 7**

Exploring ASP.NET Services

3. **In the LoginView control AnonymousTemplate view, add a Hyperlink control from the Standard group in the toolbox.**

   The control has two view templates: Anonymous and Logged In. Access the view templates by clicking the arrow in the upper-right corner of the control.

4. **Press F4 to display the Properties window. Set these properties for the Hyperlink control:**

   • Text: Type **I Need To Register**.

   • NavigateUrl: Click the ellipsis and browse to registration.aspx.

5. **In the LoginView control LoggedInTemplate view, type the text Welcome, .**

   Be sure to leave a space after the comma so that the user's name doesn't appear right next to the comma.

6. **Add the LoginName control to the LoginView control LoggedInTemplate immediately following the text you enter in Step 5.**

7. **Press Ctrl+F5 to run your site.**

   Your page displays Anonymous Login view, as shown in Figure 7-6.

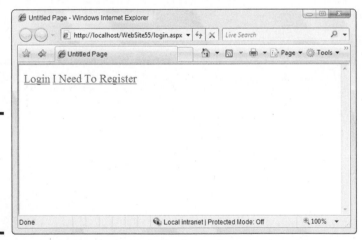

Figure 7-6:
This page displays the Login View anonymous template.

Now, you need to add login and user-registration capabilities to your site. To set up the login page, Login.aspx, follow these steps:

1. **Add a Login control from the Login group of the toolbox.**

2. **Set the control's appearance by using the Auto Format feature.**

3. **Set the control's DestinationPageUrl property to the default.aspx page in the Members folder.**

To set up the registration page, Registration.aspx, follow these steps:

1. **Add the CreateUserWizard control from the toolbox's Login group.**

2. **Set the control's ContinueDestinationPageURL property to the default.aspx page in the Members folder.**

Run your Web site and test it. You should be able to log in and create a new user account.

You can use membership and login controls in conjunction with master pages to keep the look and feel of your login page similar to the rest of your site. (Turn to Chapter 6 in this mini-book for more on master pages.) Figure 7-7 shows you a master page using login controls in the Web site you create in Chapter 6 of this mini-book. Users who aren't logged in are directed to the login page.

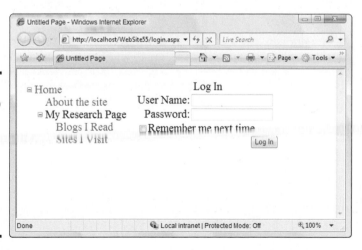

Figure 7-7: Membership and login controls go hand in hand with master pages and site navigation.

Getting Personal

Even the simplest Web site now offers personalization features that allow a visitor to create a personalized user experience. This section introduces two ASP.NET personalization features: profiles and Web parts.

Saving visitor settings with profiles

A *profile* is used to store and retrieve user settings from a data source, such as a database. Examples of profile attributes include

✦ Contact information

✦ A favorite movie

✦ Preferences, such as themes

The ASP.NET profile service is easy to configure and use. It requires the application services default data store or a custom data store of your choosing. (Read the earlier section "Providing the Perks of Membership" to see how to create the default data store.) If you already created the data store, the profile service uses it.

To enable profiles for your Web site, you must add the profile attributes to your Web site's web.config file. To add a favorite color attribute to your profile, follow these steps:

1. **Open the web.config file.**

As mentioned earlier, a *web.config* file is an XML file that stores configuration settings for your Web site. To add a web.config file if your site doesn't have one yet, press Ctrl+Shift+A to open the Add New Item dialog box and select the Web Configuration File template.

2. **Between the system.web open and closing tags, add this code:**

```
<profile>
  <properties>
    <add name="FavoriteColor"
      type="System.String"  />
  </properties>
</profile>
```

It's that easy! You can start saving the favorite colors of all your logged-in users.

By default, only logged-in users can use properties. To allow anonymous users to use properties, follow these steps:

1. **Add this line to the `web.config` file:**

```
<anonymousIdentification enabled="true" />
```

2. **Add this line to the Properties section:**

```
<name="Property" allowAnonymous="true" />
```

To use the profile in your Web site, follow these steps:

1. **Add a `profiles.aspx` page to your Web site.**

2. **Add `Label`, `Textbox`, and `Button` server controls to the page.**

3. **Set the label's `Text` property to `Favorite Color`.**

4. **Double-click the button to add code to its `Click` event.**

The Code Editor appears.

5. **Type this line to set the profile attribute:**

```
Profile.FavoriteColor = Me.TextBox1.Text
```

6. **Double-click Design view of the page to access the page's `Load` event.**

The Code Editor appears.

7. **Type this line to load the profile's property:**

```
If Not Page.IsPostBack Then
    Me.TextBox1.Text = Profile.FavoriteColor
End If
```

To test your profile, run your site and log in. Enter a favorite color and click the button to save the profile.

Letting users customize with Web parts

Web parts controls are the ultimate in personalization. What makes them powerful is that they allow users to customize their user experience. A visitor accessing a Web parts page can add and remove Web parts or change the layout of the page.

Web parts controls have three elements:

✦ **User interface (UI) controls** — These controls are the standard ASP.NET server controls, such as labels, text boxes, and buttons.

✦ **UI structure components** — Structural components provide the layout and management features of Web parts. The two main structural components are the Web parts manager and the Web part zone.

✦ **Personalization layer** — This underlying infrastructure layer allows users to change the page layout by moving controls around, or adding and removing controls from the page. Users' changes are saved permanently.

The Web parts controls are accessible from the WebParts group in the toolbox. You should be familiar with these Web parts:

✦ WebPartManager — Required by each page in order to manage the Web parts on the page.

✦ WebPartZone — Provides zones for laying out Web parts controls. A page can have multiple zones.

✦ CatalogZone — Provides a zone for creating a catalog of Web parts that a user can use to modify the page.

✦ EditorZone — Allows users to edit the Web parts on a page.

✦ ConnectionsZone — Enables you to create connections among Web parts.

Note that the zone-related controls are logical zones for working with Web parts. You're still responsible for laying out the page by using tables or Cascading Style Sheets (CSS).

The main reason for using Web parts is their personalization features. Getting personalization up and running is no small feat. Use Web parts and Web parts pages for building portals that allow visitors to customize their views. A popular portal that uses Web parts is Microsoft SharePoint Portal Server 2003. SharePoint Portal Server's underlying infrastructure, Windows SharePoint Services, also uses Web parts.

Chapter 8: Building a Mobile Application

In This Chapter

✔ **Exploring smart devices**

✔ **Creating applications for smart devices**

✔ **Building a mobile Web application**

✔ **Emulating smartphones**

O ver the years, computers have insinuated their way into everyday life. Computers are used in machines, from cars to refrigerators. All these computers need some kind of operating system to make them work. Sometimes, a company makes its own, proprietary operating system (OS) to go with a device, such as Palm personal digital assistants (PDAs). Other times, device manufacturers license their operating systems from companies, such as Microsoft.

Microsoft provides several different flavors of operating systems for these devices, such as Windows CE. These versions of Windows, known as *smart devices,* are found in everything from ATMs and automobiles to cellular phones. Sometimes, these devices are mobile, in the case of cellular phones and PDAs. Other times, they're not, like the CD player or digital video recorder you might have connected to your living room television.

You can use Visual Studio 2008 to build software applications that run on smart devices. Visual Studio 2008 provides everything you need to connect to a smart device and test your application. If you don't have a physical smart device, you can use a device emulator for testing purposes.

As operating systems and hardware have become more robust, mobile devices can now move beyond being mere cell phone and personal information managers (PIMs). More widespread adoption has users clamoring for everything from multimedia applications to business applications.

This chapter explores two ways to use Visual Studio 2008 to create applications for smart devices:

✦ Build an application that runs on the device itself.

✦ Build a mobile Web site that users can access by using the Web browser on a smart device.

Developing Applications for Smart Devices

Building an application for a smart device by using Visual Studio 2008 is as simple as dragging and dropping. Unfortunately, a lot of forethought is required before you start developing mobile applications.

Mobile everything

Before you begin building applications for mobile devices, you have to identify the devices that you intend to work with. Mobile devices are in three general categories:

✦ **Smartphones** — These devices are used primarily as cellular phones. They have additional applications, such as calculators and note-taking tools, but don't include mobile versions of Office software (such as Word and Excel).

✦ **Pocket PCs** — These devices have touch screens and use mobile versions of Office applications, such as Word and Excel. The Pocket PC Phone Edition uses cellular phone features.

✦ **Ubiquitous, embedded devices** — These devices aren't general-purpose computers, even though they have embedded microchips.

Microsoft groups its mobile strategy into these offerings:

✦ **Windows Mobile** — Includes smartphones and Pocket PCs

✦ **Windows CE Embedded** — Not device specific; embedded in everything from automobiles to industrial controllers

✦ **Tablet PC** — Uses a special version of Windows

✦ **Windows Embedded** — Used more in set-top boxes and points-of-sale where Windows security features are required

Any Windows application can run on a Tablet PC or a Windows Embedded device if the device is properly configured. The smart-device development options in Visual Studio 2008 don't apply to those devices.

Decisions, decisions

You have several options for building applications for smart devices. You have to decide whether to

✦ Target Windows Mobile, Windows CE (version 5.0 or later), or both.

✦ Build managed applications by using Visual Basic and C#, or native code with C++.

✦ Write server-side code.

✦ Provide access to data.

Some of these decisions are easier to make than others. For example, if you're not conversant in C++, writing an unmanaged application is challenging. And ASP.NET applications are likely to work on a very broad range of device types without relying on native code at all. This chapter shows you how to work through these decisions and go from there.

Pick your platform

Deciding which platforms to target is influenced by the problem you're trying to solve. For example, in a corporate environment, you probably have control over the kinds of devices employees are using, which makes the problem easier to solve. However, if you're trying to target multiple platforms, the problem is a bit trickier to solve.

Several flavors of Windows Mobile-based devices are on the market:

✦ Windows Mobile 5.0 Pocket PC

✦ Windows Mobile 5.0 Smartphone

✦ Windows Mobile 6.0 Pocket PC

✦ Windows Mobile 6.0 Smartphone

✦ Windows CE 5.0

✦ Pocket PC 2003

Book III
Chapter 8

Building a Mobile
Application

The distinction between Pocket PC and Smartphone is going away with the version of Windows Mobile known as Neo. Expect to see the Pocket PC platform merged with the Smartphone.

Windows Mobile-based devices already have the .NET Compact Framework installed on them. You can write managed applications by using Visual Basic and C# to target the .NET Compact Framework on these devices.

If your device doesn't have the .NET Compact Framework installed, you have to install it.

Devices with Windows CE embedded might not already have .NET installed. Because these devices tend to be specialized models, you should consult the manufacturers' documentation before deciding to use them.

When you're picking your platform, you must also consider these issues:

✦ **Smartphones don't have touch screens.** Your application must be menu driven (using the two soft keys on the number pad).

✦ **Pocket PCs have touch screens.** You aren't limited to developing a menu-driven application.

✦ **Windows CE devices are often embedded into all kinds of form factors.** The form factors might not use the Windows graphical user interface (GUI).

Know that the natives are restless

For the most part, smart-device development has strictly been the domain of *native code* (binary code that the CPU can directly execute) written in C++. Now that more memory and processing power can be packed into a smaller package, the arguments against using managed code are starting to fall away.

By using managed code, developers can use the rapid application development features of Visual Studio and create slicker user interfaces (UIs) in less time.

One downside is that managed code requires the device to run the .NET Compact Framework, which increases the size of the application and the resources required to run it.

On the other hand, because unmanaged code doesn't require the .NET Compact Framework, applications run faster and require fewer resources. However, developers using unmanaged code must have significantly more technical skill in order to develop applications by using C++.

Of course, some purists will always argue that unmanaged code runs faster than managed code. Although that may be true, the real question is whether it makes a difference to users. If they can't tell the difference, it becomes a matter of developer productivity. Similar arguments were made about the move from lower-level languages to higher-level languages. In most cases, developer productivity always wins out over hardware productivity.

Examples of applications created with C++ are utilities and games. You should use managed code for applications that have an intensive UI and when developer productivity is required.

You can safely assume that any Windows Mobile-based device has adequate hardware to run managed code, although you should thoroughly stress-test your application before deploying it to production.

Go server-side

If the devices you need to target aren't running on a Windows Mobile-based platform or Windows CE, consider building a mobile Web application. Make sure that

✦ The devices have regular access to the Internet.

✦ You have enough bandwidth to accommodate your Web application.

✦ The user interface is device friendly.

Access the data

Developing applications for smart devices that require data access is similar to working with data access in other kinds of Visual Studio projects. The special Microsoft database engine SQL Server Mobile is designed to work with smart-device applications. You can use SQL Server Mobile to

✦ Keep a local copy of data stored on your smart device.

✦ Synchronize the local copy with a master copy.

SQL Server Mobile is the perfect approach to providing data access for smart devices that are occasionally connected to a network. For a detailed discussion on data access, see Book IV.

TIP

As of this writing, the current version of SQL Server that is designed for mobile devices is SQL Server 2005 Everywhere Edition.

Differences in smart-device development

When you develop smart-device applications, you find that getting around in Visual Studio is similar to working with Windows applications. You can leverage everything you might already know about building applications with Visual Studio 2008. You create smart-device applications the same way that you create Windows applications, namely, by dragging and dropping controls on the form, although a few conditions are different:

✦ You must choose a device or device emulator to connect to when you debug your application.

✦ Because smart devices use the .NET Compact Framework, you don't have access to the same things as you do in the .NET Framework.

✦ Testing is done on the device or device emulator, not on the development machine.

✦ Distributing applications requires a CAB file.

A *CAB* file, or Microsoft Cabinet file, is used to compress many files into a single file. CAB files are often used with installation packages.

✦ You have to work with intermediary software, such as device emulators and ActiveSync, to connect to the device.

✦ You have to work within the constraints of the device itself (for example, the device has a small screen or lacks a touch screen).

Saying, "Hello, Smartphone!"

Visual Studio 2008 provides templates for creating device applications, class libraries, and console applications for Windows Mobile and Windows CE devices. You can also create control libraries for Pocket PC 2003 and Windows CE devices.

Getting your machine ready

Before you start building smart-device applications, you have to take a few steps to get your machine ready. Visual Studio 2008 ships with project templates and device emulators for Pocket PC 2003, Windows Mobile 5.0 Pocket PC, Windows Mobile 5.0 Smartphone, and Windows CE 5.0. The latest platform version for smart devices is Windows Mobile 5.0.

Before you start, download and install these programs from the Microsoft Download Center (www.microsoft.com/downloads):

✦ Windows Mobile 6.0 Standard SDK

✦ Windows Mobile 6.0 Professional SDK

✦ Windows Mobile Device Center

You need to download the software development kits (SDKs) for Windows Mobile 6.0 devices only if you plan to target those platforms with your application.

You can do a search to find the SDKs that you need or browse right to the single tools page on its Mobile Developers Center portal, where you can download all these tools:

```
www.microsoft.com/downloads/details.aspx?
    familyid=06111a3a-a651-4745-88ef-3d48091a390b
```

Follow the installation instructions for each tool. You should be able to accept the defaults and install these tools without incident. If you have problems, go to the Windows Mobile support options page:

```
http://msdn2.microsoft.com/en-us/windowsmobile/
     bb510377.aspx
```

Creating a smart-device application

To create a new smart-device application for a Smartphone model, you start by setting up the project in Visual Studio. To do so, follow these steps:

1. **Choose File⇨New⇨Project.**

   The New Project dialog box appears.

2. **In the Project Types tree, expand the Smart Device section.**

   A list of devices appears.

3. **Type a name for the project, such as MyVerySmartPhoneApp, as shown in Figure 8-1.**

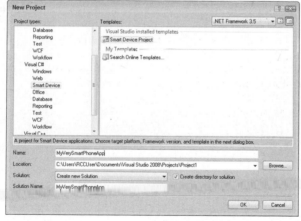

**Book III
Chapter 8**

**Building a Mobile
Application**

Figure 8-1:
Enter a
name for the
smart-
device
application.

4. **Click to select Windows Mobile 6 Standard SDK.**

   A list of available project templates for this device is displayed.

5. **Click to select Device Application.**

6. **Click OK to create the project.**

Visual Studio 2008 creates the smart-device application and displays a forms designer. Rather than see a Windows Form displayed, you see a device skin that looks like a smartphone. A main menu control is automatically added to the application because smartphone navigation is menu-driven.

To create the "Hello world!" application for the Windows Mobile 6 Device, follow these steps:

1. **Drag a label control from the toolbox and drop it on the device skin. If the toolbox isn't open, press Ctrl+Alt+X to open it.**

2. **Click the menu bar at the bottom of the device skin display. Type some menu text on the left and right menus.**

   Figure 8-2 shown **Main** on the left menu and **Hit Me!** on the right menu.

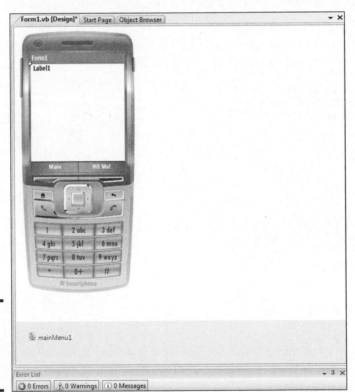

Figure 8-2:
Enter menu commands in the menu control.

On smartphone devices, the left menu (soft key 1) is used for affirmative actions (such as OK, Yes, and New); the right menu (soft key 2) is for Cancel or for choosing menu options.

3. **Double-click the right menu to enter the code that's executed whenever a user selects the menu.**

A `Click` event is created, and the Code Editor appears.

4. **Enter this line of code in the Code Editor:**

```
Label1.Text = "Hello World!"
```

5. **Press Ctrl+F5 to run your device on the device emulator.**

Visual Studio builds your application, and the Deploy dialog box appears.

6. **Choose the Windows Mobile 6 Standard Emulator from the device list and click the Deploy button.**

Your device application is executed on the emulator. Use your mouse to "press" the right soft key. The device application displays `Hello World!` on the screen, as shown in Figure 8-3.

Book III
Chapter 8

Building a Mobile
Application

Figure 8-3:
Press the
right soft
key to
execute
your
program.

You can also use the Device toolbar to select the specific device to connect to, connect to a device, and set device options. If the device toolbar isn't open, open it by choosing View⇨Toolbars⇨Device.

Changing the application's target platform

If you decide that you want your application to target a different platform, such as the Pocket PC, making changes is simple. Follow these steps:

1. **Right-click the project name and choose Change Target Platform from the contextual menu.**

The Change Target Platform dialog box appears.

2. **From the Change To drop-down list, select the platform you want to target, as shown in Figure 8-4.**

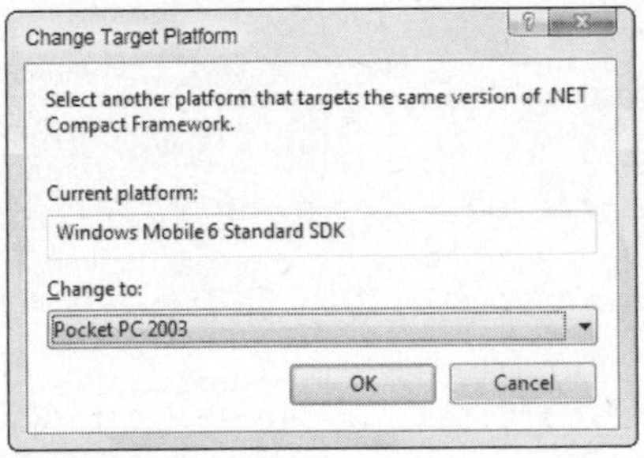

Figure 8-4:
Change the application's target platform to Pocket PC 2003.

> Change Target Platform
>
> Select another platform that targets the same version of .NET Compact Framework.
>
> Current platform:
>
> Windows Mobile 6 Standard SDK
>
> Change to:
>
> Pocket PC 2003
>
> OK   Cancel

3. **Click OK.**

A confirmation window appears.

4. **Click Yes to confirm your choice.**

Visual Studio closes and reopens the projects to reset the target platform.

Setting up a C++ smart-device application

To create a C++ smart-device application, follow these steps:

1. **Choose File⇨New⇨Project.**

2. **In the New Project dialog box, expand the C++ project types.**

3. **Select Smart Device.**

4. **Select the Microsoft Foundation Classes (MFC) Smart Device Application template.**

5. **Name the project and click OK.**

The MFC Smart Device Application Wizard appears.

6. **Click Next to advance the wizard.**

7. **In the Platforms step, select the platforms you want to target and then click Next.**

8. **Accept the defaults for the Application Type step and then click Finish to complete the wizard.**

   The MFC application is created. The `ReadMe.txt` file offers a list and an explanation of the files created by the wizard. Open the `MyMFCView.cpp` file to add your code.

Building Mobile Web Applications

You can use Visual Studio 2008 to create Web sites specially designed for smart devices. You don't need to be a Web developer to do it.

You should be able to reuse your existing Web site development skills. Keep in mind, however, that building mobile Web sites requires you to do two things:

✦ Use mobile controls that can adapt to the device on which the Web site is being displayed.

✦ Display the Web site in a Web browser on the device itself, rather than in a Web browser on your local development computer.

Visual Studio uses mobile controls and device adapters to hide the complexity of building Web sites for multiple kinds of devices. As when you're building applications that run on smart devices, bear in mind that the user interface is restricted and some devices don't have touch screens. Also, your device must have network connectivity in order to access your Web server where the mobile Web site is hosted.

Setting up the mobile Web site

To create a Web site for a mobile Web application in Visual Studio 2008, follow these steps.

1. **Choose File➪New➪Web Site.**

   The New Web Site dialog box appears.

2. **Select the ASP.NET Web Site template.**

3. **Select File System from the Location drop-down list.**

4. **Accept the default location to create the Web system. Type a name, such as** MobileWebSite, **at the end of the location.**

5. **Select Visual Basic from the Language drop-down list.**

6. **Click OK to create the Web site.**

The Web site is created, and Visual Studio opens the `default.aspx` page.

To turn the Web site into a mobile Web site, follow these steps:

1. **Delete the `default.aspx` page by right-clicking the page in Solution Explorer and choosing Delete from the contextual menu. Click OK in the confirmation window.**

   The page is deleted.

   `default.aspx` is a regular ASP.NET Web Forms page.

2. **Add a Mobile Web Form page to the project by right-clicking the project in Solution Explorer and choosing Add New Item from the contextual menu.**

   The Add New Item dialog box appears.

3. **Select the Mobile Web Form template.**

4. **Click Add.**

   The page is added to the project.

You now have a fully functioning mobile Web site. You need to add your content to the Mobile Web Form you added in the preceding set of steps. For example, to create the "Hello world!" application, follow these steps:

1. **Press Shift+F7 to display the `default.aspx` page in the Visual Forms Designer.**

   Alternatively, you can click the Design tab to display the page in Design view.

2. **In the toolbox, scroll down to the Mobile Web Forms section. Drag a label to the forms designer.**

   The Mobile Web Forms section is visible in the toolbox only when you have a Mobile Web Form open in the designer.

3. **In the Properties window, delete the word *Label* from the `Text` property.**

4. **Drag a `Command` button to the design surface and set the button's `Text` property to `Hit me`.**

5. **Double-click the `Command` button to display the command's `Click` event.**

6. **Enter this line of code:**

   ```
   Label1.Text = "Hello world!"
   ```

7. **Press Ctrl+F5 to run your Web site.**

Your mobile Web application is displayed in a Web browser. That's probably not what you want, though. Fire up your device emulator so that you can see what your mobile Web application looks like on your device.

Exploring device emulators

Before you can run your mobile Web site by using the Visual Studio Build command, you need to get your computer ready to work with the device emulator. Otherwise, your device can't communicate with the Web server on your local computer. If you're using a physical device, you should connect it now. Before you can connect to a device, either physical or emulated, you must cradle it. Before it's cradled, it has no Internet connectivity. In other words, the device emulator has no data plan from a carrier to get any such connectivity "over the air." To cradle a device emulator, follow these steps:

1. **Launch the Device Emulator Manager by choosing Tools⇨ Device Emulator Manager in Visual Studio 2008.**

2. **Right-click one of the available emulators, such as the Pocket PC 2003 SE Emulator, and choose Connect from the contextual menu.**

The emulator opens.

3. **In the Device Emulator Manager, right-click the emulator name again. Choose Cradle from the contextual menu, shown in Figure 8-5.**

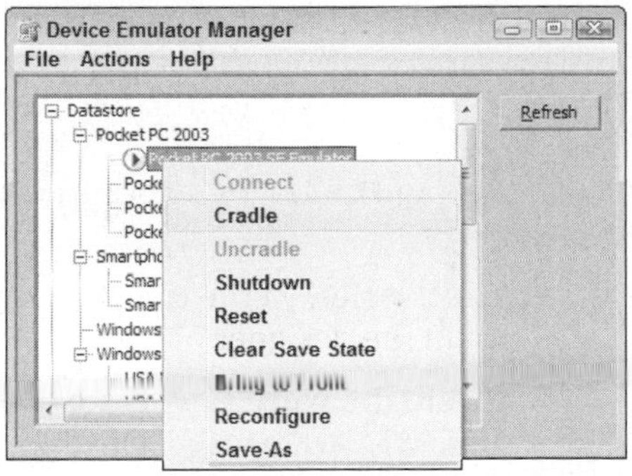

Figure 8-5:
Cradle the device emulator by using the Device Emulator Manager.

After the device is cradled, you can establish connectivity to it with ActiveSync, which automatically detects that a new device has been connected. To connect to your cradled device or device emulator, follow these steps:

1. **In the Get Connected Wizard, click Next.**

The wizard searches all available ports for a cradled device.

2. **When the device is found, the New Partnership step appears. Select the Guest Partnership option.**

   Guest partners don't synchronize data.

3. **Click Next to advance the wizard.**

   ActiveSync connects to the device.

After your device or device emulator is connected to your PC via ActiveSync, you can view your mobile Web site on the device. Follow these steps to pull up the mobile Web site in the device emulator:

1. **In the device emulator, click Start.**

   The Start menu appears.

2. **Choose Internet Explorer.**

3. **On the Internet Explorer address bar, type the URL of the Web server where your mobile Web site is hosted.**

   The Web page is displayed in the device emulator, as shown in Figure 8-6.

Figure 8-6:
Test your mobile Web site in a device emulator.

If you host your mobile Web site by using Microsoft Internet Information Services (IIS), you don't have to type the port number in the URL.

Save the state of your device emulator so that the next time you fire it up, Internet Explorer is already open. To save the state, choose File⇨Save State and Exit. The next time you open that device emulator, it opens in the same state.

Automating your connection

Here are the high-level steps for using a device emulator to view your mobile Web application:

1. Connect to the device emulator.

2. Use the Device Emulator Manager to cradle the emulator.

3. Connect to the device by using ActiveSync.

4. Browse to your mobile Web application by using Internet Explorer on the device emulator.

You can automate a few of these steps, if you want. You can use the Visual Studio 2008 Browse With command to specify which browser you want to use for your Web site. You aren't restricted to just Web browsers — you can choose any kind of executable file, including batch files. That way, you can conveniently short-circuit all the steps involved in using an emulator.

A *batch file* is a text file with a series of commands in it. The commands you use in a batch file are the same ones you use on the command line or in the Run box that appears when you choose Run from the Windows XP Start menu. A batch file ends with the file extension .bat. When you execute a batch file, the commands in the file are executed just as though you were typing them on the command line.

To short-circuit all the steps involved in viewing your mobile Web site in a device emulator, use a batch file to open the device emulator and open the Device Emulator Manager.

The device emulator and Device Emulator Manager are installed by default in the file location

```
C:\Program Files\Microsoft Device Emulator\1.0
```

The device emulator needs to know the path to the saved state of the device you want to use. By default, state files are saved at

```
C:\Users\RCCUser\Documents\My Device Emulators
```

State files have the file extension .dess.

To create a batch file that opens these tools, follow these steps:

1. **Open Notepad or your favorite text editor.**

2. **In Notepad, type the command to open the device emulator:**

```
start /d "C:\Users\RCCUser\Documents\My Device Emulators\1.0\"
    deviceemulator.exe /s "C:\Users\RCCUser\Documents\
    My Device Emulators \<GUID>.dess"
```

Your saved state filename should look something like

```
{DE425A95-FBB8-46CB-8DFD-89867130F732}.dess
```

3. **Type the command to open the Device Emulator Manager in Notepad:**

```
start /d "C:\Users\RCCUser\Documents\
    My Device Emulators \1.0\" dvcemumanager.exe
```

4. **Save your file and give it a name, such as `mydevice.bat`.**

To tell Visual Studio 2008 to use your batch file, follow these steps:

1. **Right-click the project folder in Solution Explorer and then choose Browse With from the contextual menu.**

The Browse With dialog box appears.

2. **Click Add.**

The Add Program dialog box appears.

3. **Click the ellipsis button next to Program Name and browse to your `mydevice.bat` file.**

4. **Enter a name for the program in the Friendly Name text box.**

The friendly name appears in the Browse With dialog box.

5. **Click OK.**

The Add Program dialog box closes, and your batch file is added to the Browse With dialog box.

6. **Click the Set As Default button to set your batch file as the default browser for this project.**

Figure 8-7 shows the Browse With dialog box after setting the default.

7. **Click the Browse button to launch your batch file.**

The device emulator you specified in the batch file opens. The Device Emulator Manager opens also. Use the device manager to cradle your device emulator. If the device emulator doesn't show that it's connected, press F5 to refresh the screen. After the device emulator is cradled, ActiveSync should automatically try to connect to it.

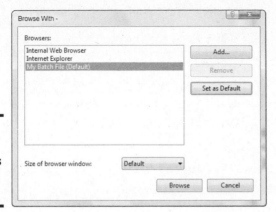

Figure 8-7:
Set your
batch file as
the default
browser.

If your batch file fails, make sure that the commands are executed on a command line. If they don't work on the command line, they don't work in a batch file, either.

You can start multiple device emulators in a single batch file or create multiple batch files for each device emulator you want to run.

You need to execute your device emulator, cradle it, and connect to it only once. Afterward, you can build your Web site by using the Build menu and then refresh the browser in your device emulator.

Accommodating Special Considerations for Smart-Device Applications

Even though Microsoft has made creating smart-device applications super easy, you must bear in mind that smart devices aren't just miniature Windows machines. Testing and deploying smart device applications is still a chore compared to testing and deploying regular Windows applications. Keep these considerations in mind as you start building smart-device applications:

✦ **A smartphone is designed to be used with one hand.** Make sure that you emulate this one-handed experience when you test your application.

✦ **ActiveSync doesn't always behave the way you expect.** Be prepared to spend some time becoming comfortable with its idiosyncrasies.

✦ **Be sure to read through the SDK for the device you're targeting.** SDKs are quite informative.

✦ **Security is a big concern with smart devices.** Refer to the SDK for your device for more information on how to create security certificates for testing and deploying your application.

✦ **In addition to the device's form factor, you must consider the battery life and memory constraints of the device you're targeting.**

Book IV

Getting Acquainted with Data Access

The 5th Wave — By Rich Tennant

"Now that we got Visual Studio, we should probably pimp our data storage system."

Contents at a Glance

Chapter 1: Accessing Data with Visual Studio..291

Chapter 2: Show Me the Data 309

Chapter 3: Working with Strongly Typed DataSets 345

Chapter 4: Working with XML 381

Chapter 5: Under the Hood with ADO.NET...399

Chapter 6: Using Visual Studio with SQL Server...437

Chapter 7: LINQ 467

Chapter 1: Accessing Data with Visual Studio

In This Chapter

✔ Taking a sneak peek at ADO.NET

✔ Getting acquainted with databases

✔ Adding data controls to Windows and Web Forms

*N*owadays, it's hard to find an application that isn't data-driven. Even if the application isn't centered around entering and viewing data, you might be surprised to find a tremendous amount of data access occurring behind the scenes — especially for Web sites. What might look like a static, boring Web site might be one that was built by using dynamic Web pages that get their content from a database.

Applications, such as Windows SharePoint Services, store all their information in databases. For example, when a user uploads an Excel document to a SharePoint document library, the file is stored in a database. Don't bother to traverse the file directory and look for the file, though, because it's not there.

Even when data isn't involved in an application, metadata might still be involved. *Metadata* is data about data, and it's showing up everywhere. For example, when you take a picture with a digital camera, the camera automatically stores the image resolution and thumb file format as metadata within the JPEG image. This information, which is the image's metadata, can be used to determine how the image appears in an application.

Yes, the world has gone data crazy. Fear not, however, because Visual Studio has everything you need for accessing data and metadata in your applications. This chapter shows you how to use Visual Studio to create data-driven applications without getting bogged down in all the technology that makes data access possible.

Accessing Data with Visual Studio and .NET

Visual Studio provides many tools for accessing and manipulating data. The underlying technology that makes the tools in Visual Studio work is ADO.NET. It provides all the commands and widgets you need in order to work with data in your application. With ADO.NET, you can

✦ Connect to data sources.

✦ Retrieve data from data sources.

✦ Display data in your application.

✦ Update data to reflect changes your users make.

Read on to see how ADO.NET works.

Meeting ADO.NET

ADO.NET is the technology in the Microsoft .NET Framework that makes it possible to work with data in your applications. You can work with ADO.NET by using wizards in Visual Studio or by writing your own code to access ADO.NET. Either way, it helps to understand conceptually how ADO.NET works.

ADO.NET is a part of the .NET Framework in the same way that ASP.NET and Windows Forms are part of the .NET Framework. The .NET Framework provides all the code that brings these technologies to life. Visual Studio 2008 provides wizards that generate code that let you use these technologies of the .NET Framework without digging into the details of how the technologies work.

Starting at the data source

Data access in ADO.NET begins with data sources. Starting with data sources makes sense: You can't display data until you know its source.

ADO.NET can access almost any data source imaginable. Using ADO.NET, you can access these data sources:

✦ **Databases, such as SQL Server and Oracle** — See Chapter 6 of this mini-book for an overview of Microsoft SQL Server.

✦ **XML files** — Chapter 4 of this mini-book shows you how to access XML files.

✦ **Objects** — Chapter 2 of this mini-book shows you how to connect to an object.

✦ **Web services** — Book V, Chapter 6 shows you how to work with Web services.

✦ **Local data stored in your project** — See Chapter 6 of this mini-book for more information on local data sources.

Visual Studio provides two tools for creating and managing data sources:

✦ The **Data Source Configuration Wizard** walks you through creating a new data source.

✦ The **Data Sources window** is a container for managing all your project's data sources. It's available only in Windows applications.

ASP.NET includes a set of data source controls for configuring data sources, and Windows has the new `BindingSource` component for wiring data sources to data-bound controls.

Retrieving data from data sources

Setting up data sources for your projects is the first step in retrieving data from the data sources. You have two options for telling ADO.NET which data to get from data sources:

✦ Write code by using ADO.NET commands.

✦ Use the Visual Studio `TableAdapter`.

Before ADO.NET, an application stayed connected to the data source while getting data. You had to manage the process of walking through data records to reach the record you wanted. ADO.NET eliminates all that by using a *disconnected model*. With ADO.NET, you download your data from your data source and then disconnect from it. If you make changes to the data that you want to send to the data source, you have to connect to the data source again.

In a *connected model,* the data always remains in the data source. You connect to the data source, read data, and then display that data as you're reading it. You make changes to data while you're connected to the data source.

In the ADO.NET disconnected model, you don't have live access to the data to execute commands. Instead, you download a copy of the data, work with it offline, and then reconnect to the data source to pass back any changes.

**Book IV
Chapter 1**

**Accessing Data
with Visual Studio**

When you work with a disconnected model, you need a place to store the data you download from your data source. ADO.NET has two methods for executing offline downloads:

✦ DataSet — Stores the data you download from your data source. The DataSet is made up of tabular sets of data, similar to a database. A DataSet is essentially an offline database. You connect to the data source and download your data to the DataSet. The DataSet includes commands for accessing the data. Many controls can work with DataSets.

ADO.NET offers a *strongly typed* DataSet, which is a special type of DataSet. A regular DataSet uses generic names for its contents — for example, Table1, column1, or column2. In a strongly typed DataSet, generic placeholder names are replaced with meaningful names from the data source, such as replacing Table1 with Customer table, and column1 or column2 with CustID or CompanyName.

You can use the Visual Studio TableAdapter Configuration Wizard to work with tables in DataSets. The wizard builds all the commands to retrieve and update the table's underlying data source.

✦ DataReader — Downloads your data but doesn't have an offline storage mechanism. When you use a DataReader, ADO.NET expects you to have a place to store the data in your application and a means of accessing the data from that store. Although a DataReader is much faster than a DataSet, a DataSet is more convenient.

The wizards and controls in Visual Studio work with DataSets. See Chapter 3 in this mini-book for information on working with DataSets and DataReaders in your code.

The Data Source Configuration Wizard creates and configures the TableAdapter for retrieving data and filling a DataSet for storing the data offline. The section "Dragging and Dropping Data," later in this chapter, walks you through using the Data Source Configuration Wizard.

Displaying data

The user interfaces for Windows applications and Web applications are built by using controls, such as labels, text boxes, and buttons. ADO.NET provides an entire set of controls just for displaying data.

Different controls are used for Web Forms and for Windows Forms, as listed in Table 1-1.

Table 1-1	Data Controls for Windows Forms and Web Forms	
Project Type	*Control*	*Description*
Windows	DataGridView	Displays data in a table
	BindingSource	Binds data to a control
	BindingNavigator	Provides navigation to records
	ReportViewer	Displays a reporting services report
Web	GridView	Displays data in a table
	DataList	Displays data using a customizable format
	DetailsView	Displays a single row of data; often used with a GridView
Project Type	Control	Description
	FormView	Displays a single record in a form
	Repeater	Displays data in a customizable list
	ReportViewer	Displays a reporting services report

ADO.NET data controls are designed to display data from a data source. *Data binding* connects a control to a data source. Any control can be data-bound, including everyday controls, such as labels, text boxes, and buttons.

Many of the Web data controls are customizable. Controls, such as the Repeater control, don't have any display properties. You define how your data appears by defining a template for the control. The template defines the HTML that is used to display the data. See Chapter 2 in this mini-book for an example.

Web controls are rendered as HTML markup. More data-specific controls are provided for Web Forms than for Windows Forms because rendering data via HTML is more challenging. Both Windows Forms and Web Forms can use any control to display data.

Chapter 2 in this mini-book demonstrates some of the ADO.NET data controls available for Windows Forms and Web Forms applications. Chapter 2 also shows you how to filter and sort by using data controls and also how to bind data to regular controls, such as labels and text boxes.

Updating data

Most applications do more than just display data. Many times, users create new data or manipulate existing data. Updating and adding data is similar to viewing data: You have to store your changed data offline in your application by using either an ADO.NET `DataSet` or your own, custom data store; connect to your data source; and then execute commands against the data source that update it to reflect the changes made in the offline data store.

Visual Studio provides the TableAdapter Configuration Wizard for updating data. Chapter 3 in this mini-book shows the wizard in action.

Exploring the Visual Studio data toolbox

Working with data in your application requires many steps. Visual Studio provides a nice set of tools that "wrap around" ADO.NET and hide from you many of the complexities of how ADO.NET works. Table 1-2 lists the tools and what they help you do.

Table 1-2	Visual Studio Tools for Using ADO.NET	
Visual Studio Tool	*ADO.NET Feature*	*Where You Can See the Tool in Action*
Data controls	Display data	Chapter 2
Data Source Configuration Wizard	Manage data sources Retrieve data Store data in `DataSets`	Next section, Chapter 2, and Chapter 3
Data Sources window Retrieve data	Manage data sources Next section and Chapter 2	
TableAdapter Configuration Wizard	Retrieve data Update data	Chapter 3

Visual Studio also includes these tools:

✦ **DataSet Designer** — Create and modify `DataSets`. See Chapter 3 in this mini-book for an extensive walkthrough.

✦ **XML Designers** — Choose from several designers for working with XML data. See Chapter 4 in this mini-book for an extensive walkthrough.

✦ **Server Explorer and Data Explorer** — Use Server Explorer and Data Explorer to manage database objects. See Chapter 6 in this mini-book for more information about working with databases.

Understanding Databases

To be able to work with data, you have to know a little something about how it's stored in a relational database, especially if you want to use `DataSets`. You often access databases, although Visual Studio can access more types of data sources than just databases. Even if data isn't stored in a database, you might decide to use a `DataSet` to store the data in your application's memory. A `DataSet` uses concepts that are similar to using a database.

A *database* is simply a place to store data. For example, you can store lists of information in a plain-text file, which is a database. Although plain-text files (often called *flat files*) might work fine for storing to-do lists, they don't work well for storing business data. That's why modern database management programs, such as Microsoft SQL Server, were created.

Introducing relational databases

Believe it or not, before relational database management systems, business data was stored in flat files, which are hard to work with. They aren't fast, and gathering data from multiple files is difficult, especially when no standard exists for determining how data is stored in the files.

Programmers, therefore, needed a means of not only storing data, but also accessing it again and associating it with other data in the database. The relational database management system was created to solve this problem. A *relational database management system,* or *RDBMS,* allows you to group common data records in a table. A table is made up of columns that represent fields in the records. Each record is a row in the table. For example, a database might have a Customer table and an Order table. Figure 1-1 shows an example of the Customer table.

Figure 1-1: The Customer table comprises rows and columns.

	CustomerID	TerritoryID	AccountNumber	CustomerType	rowguid	ModifiedDate
▶	1	1	AW00000001	S	3f5ae95e-b87d-4...	10/13/2004 11:
	2	1	AW00000002	S	e552f657-a9af-4...	10/13/2004 11:
	3	4	AW00000003	S	130774b1-db21-...	10/13/2004 11:
	4	4	AW00000004	S	ff862851-1daa-4...	10/13/2004 11:
	5	4	AW00000005	S	83905bdc-9f5e-4...	10/13/2004 11:
	6	4	AW00000006	S	1a92df88-bfa2-4...	10/13/2004 11:
	7	1	AW00000007	S	03e9273e-b193-...	10/13/2004 11:
	8	1	AW00000008	S	801368a1-4323...	10/13/2004 11:

People who work with data commonly show how a record in one table relates to another record in another table. For example, someone in sales might want to know how many customers placed orders during the preceding quarter. By using a relational database management system, you can flag columns in your table so that you can answer this kind of question.

The flagged columns are primary keys and foreign keys. When a column in a table is marked as a *primary key,* each row in the table must have a unique value in its primary key column. For example, in a Customer table, the

CustomerID column must be unique if the column is marked as the table's primary key. You use the primary key to look up values in the Customer table and know that you can find but one unique entry.

You can reference a table's primary key in another table. For example, in the Order table, you need to know who the customer is for the order. Rather than store the customer's name, which can change, you can store the customer's `CustomerID` value so that you can look up the customer's information by using the Customer table. In the Order table, `Customer ID` is a *foreign key* because it's another table's primary key (the Customer table) referenced in a different table. Figure 1-2 shows an example of primary and foreign keys.

Figure 1-2:
Use primary and foreign keys to create associations between tables.

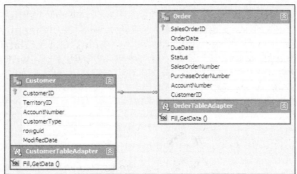

Understanding SQL

A RDBMS is a standardized set of commands for creating tables and columns and for inserting, updating, and reading data. This set of commands is *Structured Query Language (SQL)*.

You can pronounce SQL as either *es-cue-el* or *SEE-quel*. Typically, always spell the acronym (the former) when referring to the language. However, when talking about Microsoft SQL Server, use the latter. That way, you can differentiate between the standard and the product.

To see some examples of SQL, see Chapter 6 in this mini-book. You might be amazed at the number of professional developers who shun SQL, preferring instead to use graphical tools to build their queries. Although graphical tools are easy to use, you need to understand the basics of SQL.

Relational database management systems consist of more than just tables. Most RDBMSs include these elements:

✦ **Administrative tools** — Manage database objects, such as tables, queries, and users.

✦ **Wizards** — Add database objects, back up databases, and schedule administrative services.

✦ **Visual tools** — Build queries and diagrams of the database structure.

✦ **Rules** — Protect your data from being erroneously deleted.

Some popular RDBMSs are Microsoft SQL Server 2005 (see Chapter 6 in this mini-book), Oracle 10x, and Sybase SQL Anywhere.

Other kinds of database management systems exist, in addition to relational database management systems. *Object* database management systems, for example, store data as objects instead of as tables. Object databases are becoming especially popular because many programs are written using object-oriented techniques. You can find more information about object databases at www.odbms.org.

Dragging and Dropping Data

Visual Studio provides wizards you can use to add data to your Windows and Web applications. Adding data to an application is similar, whether it's a Windows Form or a Web Form. Essentially, adding data is as simple as dragging and dropping a control onto your form. After you drop the control, use the Data Source Configuration Wizard to

✦ Connect to a data source.

✦ Select tables or build a query from the data source.

✦ Store data in an offline data store.

✦ Bind data sources to a control to display the data.

Preparing your computer to work with data

The examples in this section use the Adventure Works sample database, along with Microsoft SQL Server 2005 Express Edition. SQL Server Express is installed with Visual Studio 2008 Professional. Please note that you need to install Service Pack 2 for Microsoft SQL Server Express. You also need to add the current user when the Provisioning Tool runs.

This book uses the Adventure Works sample database, rather than the usual Northwind sample database, because Microsoft recommends using Adventure Works with SQL Server 2005. The Adventure Works database has been tuned to work with SQL Server 2005 and show off some of the features of SQL Server 2005.

If you didn't install SQL Server Express with Visual Studio 2008, see Chapter 6 in this mini-book for more information on installing SQL Server Express. The examples in this section also work with SQL Server 2005 Developer Edition.

To download the Adventure Works database, go to

```
www.microsoft.com/downloads/details.aspx?FamilyID=
    e719ecf7-9f46-4312-af89-6ad8702e4e6e
```

Download and install the AdventureWorksDB.msi file. See Chapter 6 of this mini-book for more information about the SQL Server samples.

Adding data to Windows applications

To add data from the Adventure Works database to a Windows Form, follow these steps:

1. **Create a new Windows application.**

   See Book III, Chapter 1 for more information on creating Windows applications.

2. **Drag and drop a `DataGridView` control from the Data section of the toolbox to a blank Windows Form.**

   If the toolbox is closed, press Ctrl+Alt+X to open it.

3. **Click the arrow in the upper-right corner of the `DataGridView` control to display the Common GridView Tasks dialog box.**

4. **Click the Choose Data Source drop-down list.**

   A list of the project's data sources appears. The list should be blank unless you already added data sources.

Before you can select data to display, you must configure the Data Source Configuration Wizard by following these steps:

1. **Click the Database icon on the Choose a Data Source Type page of the wizard (see Figure 1-3) and then click Next to go to the Choose Your Data Connection step.**

Figure 1-3:
Select the
Database
object.

2. **Click the New Connection button to create a new database connection.**

3. **Make sure that the Data Source field is set to Microsoft SQL Server (SqlClient), as shown in Figure 1-4. Otherwise, click the Continue button and set the data source to Microsoft SQL Server.**

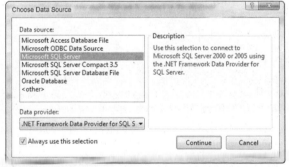

Figure 1-4:
Make sure
that the data
source is
set to
Microsoft
SQL Server.

4. **From the Server Name drop-down list, select your computer's name from the list.**

   You can also type **(local)** or a period for the server name to indicate that you're using the local server.

5. **Append \SQLExpress to the server name you entered in Step 4, as shown in Figure 1-5.**

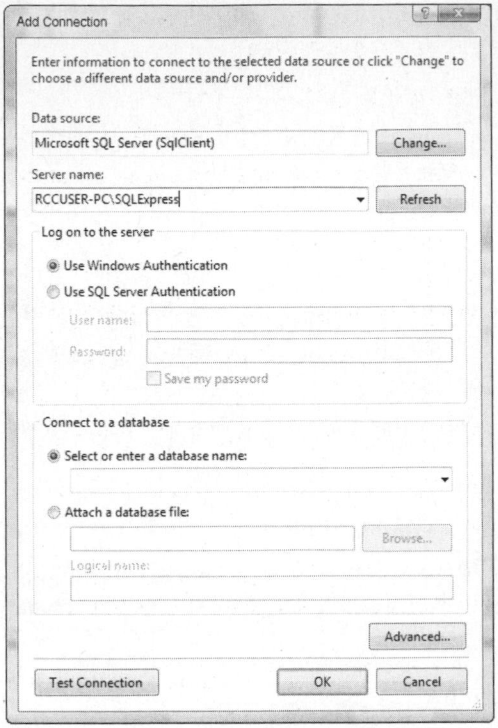

Figure 1-5:
Append the
default
name to
the server
name.

SQLExpress is the default name of the instance installed by SQL Server Express. (To read more about SQL Server instances, see Chapter 6 of this mini-book.) Even though the Visual Studio documentation says that you don't need to enter the SQL Server instance, you do. Otherwise, Visual Studio cannot connect to your database.

6. **Unless you have something other than a default installation, leave the Use Windows Authentication radio button selected (the default) in the Log On to the Server section.**

   See Chapter 6 of this mini-book to read more about Windows and SQL Server authentication.

7. **Select the Attach a Database File option in the Connect to a Database section, and then click the Browse button to attach a database file.**

   The Select SQL Server Database File dialog box opens.

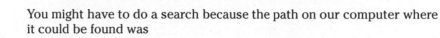

8. **Browse to the SQL Server database file directory where the Adventure Works sample is installed.**

The default location for SQL Server databases is

```
C:\Program Files\Microsoft SQL Server\MSSQL.1\MSSQL\Data
```

You might have to do a search because the path on our computer where it could be found was

```
C:\Program Files (x86)\Microsoft SQL Server\90\Tools\
   Samples\AdventureWorks OLTP
```

9. **Select the `AdventureWorks_Data.mdf` database file and click Open.**

The path to the Adventure Works database file appears in the Add Connection dialog box.

If the file isn't on your computer, you can download it from

```
www.microsoft.com/downloads/details.aspx?FamilyId=
   E719ECF7-9F46-4312-AF89-6AD8702E4E6E
```

10. **Click the Test Connection button.**

If the connection is successful, you see the message `Test Connection Succeeded`. If the connection is unsuccessful, start troubleshooting your connection.

See Chapter 6 of this mini-book for some tips on troubleshooting database connections.

11. **Click OK to close the test connection window.**

12. **Click OK to close the Add Connection dialog box.**

The connection information appears in the Data Source Configuration Wizard.

13. **Click Next.**

You're prompted to save the connection information.

14. **Leave the Save the Connection option selected and then click Next.**

The Choose Your Database Objects page appears.

15. **In the database objects pane, click the plus sign (+) next to Tables.**

The list of database tables expands.

16. **Select the Department table, as shown in Figure 1-6, and then click Finish to add the data to the form.**

Visual Studio adds to your form the components that bind the `DataGridView` control to the AdventureWorks data source.

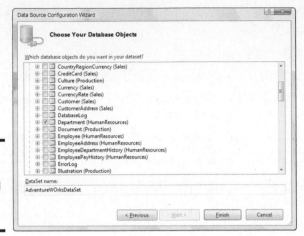

Figure 1-6:
Select a
table to add
it to your
form.

Run your form by pressing Ctrl+F5. Data from the Adventure Works
Department table appears in the DataGridView control, as shown in
Figure 1-7.

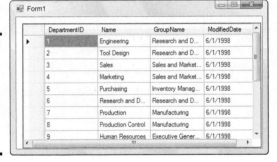

Figure 1-7:
Data from
the
Department
table
appears in
the control.

To read more details about using the Data Source Configuration Wizard,
adding data source connections, and working with other data-bound controls, see Chapter 2 in this mini-book. The following section demonstrates
how to use the Data Source Configuration Wizard to add data to a Web Form.

Adding data to Web Forms

You add data to Web Forms by using the Data Source Configuration Wizard.
You can also use the wizard to add data to Windows Forms; however, selecting database objects, such as tables, varies slightly for Web Forms.

To add data to a Web Form using the Data Source Configuration Wizard, follow these steps:

1. **Create a new Web site.**

See Book III, Chapter 4 for more information on creating Web sites.

2. **Drag and drop a `GridView` control from the Data group in the Visual Studio toolbox to the Web Form.**

3. **Right-click the arrow in the upper-right corner of the `GridView` control to view the Common GridView Tasks dialog box (see Figure 1-8).**

4. **Select New Data Source from the Choose Data Source drop-down list, as shown in Figure 1-8.**

The Data Source Configuration Wizard appears.

Figure 1-8:
Add a new data source via the Common GridView Tasks dialog box.

5. **Click the Database icon for the data source and then click OK.**

6. **On the Choose Your Data Connection page, select your data connection. If you completed the steps for the Windows section, click the drop-down arrow to reuse that connection. Otherwise, follow Steps 2 through 12 in the preceding section to create a new data connection to the Adventure Works database.**

7. **Click Next.**

You're prompted to save the connection string.

8. **Click Next again.**

The next page of the wizard, Configure the Select Statement, appears.

9. **Click the drop-down list of tables and choose Department.**

The list of columns in the Department field appears.

10. **Select the asterisk check box to select all the columns, as shown in Figure 1-9.**

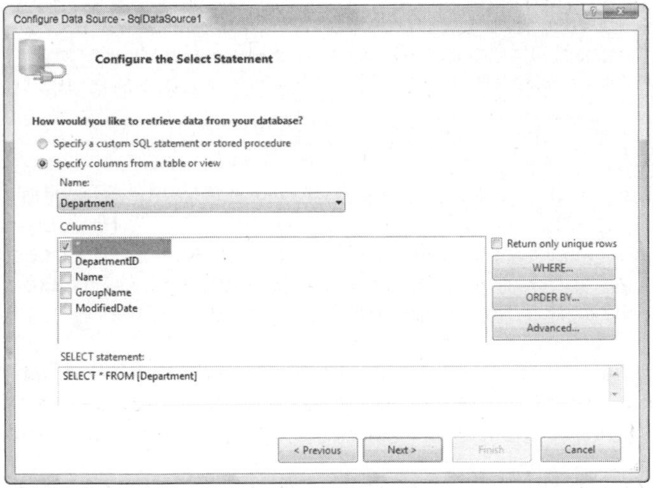

Figure 1-9:
Select the columns you want to appear in the control.

11. **Click Next.**

The Test Query page appears.

12. **Click the Test Query button to test the query.**

An error message might read that Department is an invalid object name. A bug in the Data Source Configuration Wizard makes it not work properly with databases that use schemas. To read more about configuring the Adventure Works database to work around the schemas, see Chapter 6 in this mini-book. You can work around this error after completing the wizard.

13. **Click Finish.**

The Data Source Configuration Wizard closes.

Visual Studio adds the following declarative syntax to the Web Form to make it display the data in the `GridView` control:

```
<asp:GridView ID="GridView1" runat="server" DataSourceID="SqlDataSource1">
</asp:GridView>
<asp:SqlDataSource ID="SqlDataSource1" runat="server" ConnectionString=
    "<%$ ConnectionStrings:AdventureWorksConnectionString %>"
    SelectCommand="SELECT * FROM [Department]">
</asp:SqlDataSource>
```

For the `GridView` control to access the Department table, the `SelectCommand` property must be more specific about how to reach the table. To make the `SelectCommand` property more specific, change it to

```
SelectCommand="SELECT * FROM [HumanResources].[Department]"
```

The HumanResources schema is associated with the Department table in the Adventure Works database. `[HumanResources].[Department]` is the *fully qualified* name because it makes it clear how the table is accessed. Whenever you have trouble accessing a database table, make sure that you can access it by using its fully qualified name.

If you receive invalid-object errors while working with the Data Source Configuration Wizard in ASP.NET, make sure that the object's name is fully qualified and spelled correctly (including the use of upper- and lowercase).

Alternatively, you can use the Query Builder to build the select statement in Step 10 in the preceding set of steps. The Query Builder correctly builds the select statement.

Press Ctrl+F5 to run the Web Form. The data from the Department table appears, as shown in Figure 1-10.

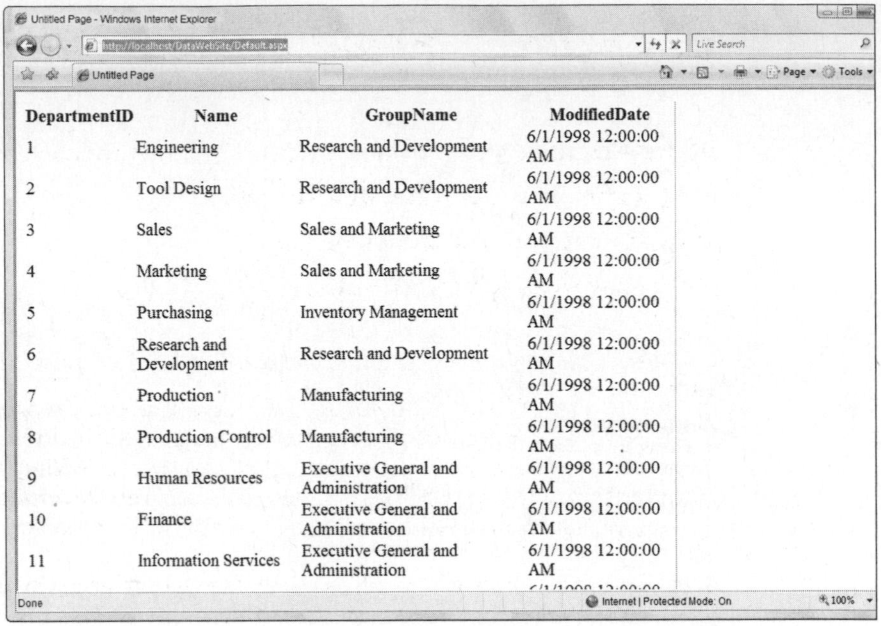

DepartmentID	Name	GroupName	ModifiedDate
1	Engineering	Research and Development	6/1/1998 12:00:00 AM
2	Tool Design	Research and Development	6/1/1998 12:00:00 AM
3	Sales	Sales and Marketing	6/1/1998 12:00:00 AM
4	Marketing	Sales and Marketing	6/1/1998 12:00:00 AM
5	Purchasing	Inventory Management	6/1/1998 12:00:00 AM
6	Research and Development	Research and Development	6/1/1998 12:00:00 AM
7	Production	Manufacturing	6/1/1998 12:00:00 AM
8	Production Control	Manufacturing	6/1/1998 12:00:00 AM
9	Human Resources	Executive General and Administration	6/1/1998 12:00:00 AM
10	Finance	Executive General and Administration	6/1/1998 12:00:00 AM
11	Information Services	Executive General and Administration	6/1/1998 12:00:00 AM

Figure 1-10: The Department data appears in the Web Form's `GridView` control.

Chapter 2: Show Me the Data

In This Chapter

✔ **Accessing data in a Windows application**

✔ **Taking a closer look at data binding**

✔ **Creating a data-centric Web site**

Data is data is data, or so you would think. When you're working with data in Visual Studio, the approach you take for Windows Forms varies slightly from the one for Web applications. Although the Windows Forms Designer sports the Data Sources window, Visual Web Developer has no such jumping-off point for managing all your project's data sources.

Both designers share some tools, such as the Data Source Configuration Wizard, but the experience in Visual Web Developer is less refined. The data tools in Windows Forms Designer integrate very well and flow seamlessly. Rest assured, whether you're building Windows applications or Web sites, Visual Studio has a data tool to get the job done. You just might have to tweak the Web tools until they mature.

This chapter walks you through the procedure for working with the set of data tools in Visual Studio. Don't be surprised to see the same tools demonstrated once for Windows applications and again for Web sites. Despite having the same names, sometimes the tools behave completely differently.

Adding Data Access in Windows Applications

Visual Studio provides plenty of ways to add access to data in a Windows application. Here are the primary ways to do so by using the Windows Forms Designer:

✦ **Drag and drop a data control onto a form.**

   You can read how to access data by using the `GridView` control in Chapter 1 of this mini-book.

✦ **Use the Data Source Configuration Wizard.**

✦ **Use the Data Sources pane.**

Data sources are any source of data you wish to access in your application. Examples of data sources include databases, Web services, objects, and XML files. There's a Visual Studio wizard you can use to access almost every form of data you can imagine.

You aren't restricted to just accessing Microsoft's data offerings, such as SQL Server and Access. You can connect to any vendor's database management system by creating a data connection, as described in the upcoming section "Connecting to databases."

All the Visual Studio data tools are intertwined in such a way that even if you start out using one tool, you often end up finishing the task by using another wizard altogether.

Regardless of which tool you use, you always start by specifying a data source. After configuring the data source, you configure a control to use with the data source. Visual Studio generates the code to take care of everything that happens between those two points.

Of course, you can always write your own code to access data. (Sigh.) If you insist on doing things the hard way, see Chapter 5 for examples of using the Code Editor to access data with ADO.NET. Sometimes, though, writing your own data access code is necessary to do things outside "normal data access."

The sections that follow focus on the maneuvers that Visual Studio makes so easy. Find out the basics of the Data Sources pane and how you use it to view, add, and connect to data sources.

Working with the Data Sources pane

The Data Sources pane is a handy tool for managing all your project's data sources. The Data Sources pane works hand in hand with the Data Source Configuration Wizard to create new data sources and configure access to the data.

You can use the Data Sources pane to work with data source objects. Open the window in one of two ways:

✦ Choose Data⇨Show Data Sources.

✦ Press Shift+Alt+D.

Use the Data Sources pane to add new data sources to your project and work with existing data sources. The Data Sources toolbar, as shown in Figure 2-1, has these commands, from left to right:

Add New Data Source

Configure DataSet with Wizard

Figure 2-1:
Use the
Data
Sources
toolbar to
work with
data
sources.

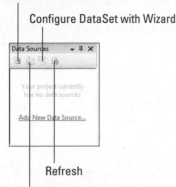

Refresh

Edit DataSet with Designer

✦ **Add New Data Source** — Start the Data Source Configuration Wizard.

✦ **Edit DataSet with Designer** — Open the DataSet Designer with the selected `DataSet` from the Data Sources tree. See Chapter 3 of this minibook for more information about using the DataSet Designer.

✦ **Configure DataSet with Wizard** — Start the Data Source Configuration Wizard so that you can select database objects to add to the `DataSet`.

✦ **Refresh** — Refresh the data sources listed in the Data Sources tree.

Datasets are used to store data retrieved from data sources.

Viewing data source objects

Data sources are listed in tree view in the Data Sources pane, as shown in Figure 2-2.

The Data Sources tree is a hierarchical view that shows these elements:

✦ **Expandable parent data sources** — A data source that uses `DataSets`, such as a database, shows the `DataSet` as the parent. Objects and Web services show a namespace.

✦ **Expandable child objects nested within the parent** — A `DataSet` expands to list the tables contained with it.

✦ **A set of child objects** — A table within a `DataSet` expands to list the table's columns.

Figure 2-2:
The Data Sources pane displays a project's data sources in tree view.

Adding data sources

The Data Sources pane uses the Data Source Configuration Wizard to add new data sources. To start the Data Source Configuration Wizard from the Data Sources pane, follow these steps:

1. **Create a new Windows project.**

See Book III, Chapter 1 for more information on creating Windows projects.

2. **Choose Data⇨Show Data Sources.**

The Data Sources pane appears.

3. **Click the Add New Data Source button on the Data Sources toolbar.**

The Data Source Configuration Wizard appears.

Alternatively, you can choose Data⇨Add New Data Source to start the Data Source Configuration Wizard. Data sources created with the wizard appear in the Data Sources pane.

To add a new data source by using the Data Source Configuration Wizard, follow these steps:

1. **On the Choose a Data Source Type page in the wizard, select a data source, as shown in Figure 2-3.**

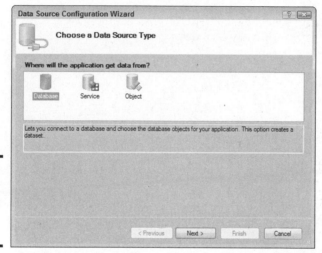

Figure 2-3: Select the data source in the wizard.

Your data source choices in the wizard are Database, Service, and Object.

2. **Click Next.**

   Depending on the data source you select in Step 1, the wizard displays one of the following pages to create your connection:

   • *Database* — The Choose Your Data Connection page appears. Select an existing database connection or select New Connection to add a new database connection. See the following section for more about managing database connections.

   • *Service* — Opens the Add Web Reference dialog box. Enter the URL for the Web service or browse for one. See Book V, Chapter 6 for more information about Web services.

- *Object* — The Select the Object You Wish to Bind To page appears. It displays a tree view of the classes in your project. Click the Add Reference button to add a reference to another project.

After you establish a connection to the data source, the wizard displays a list of the data source's objects.

> The generic term *object* refers to the contents of the data source. For example, the objects in a database are tables.

3. **Select from the data source the objects you want to use.**

4. **Click Finish.**

   The data source is added to the Data Sources pane. Figure 2-4 shows a Data Sources pane with a database and objects added to it.

Figure 2-4: The wizard adds data source objects to the Data Sources pane.

Connecting to databases

A database is a kind of data source — probably the most popular. Because databases are such popular data sources, Visual Studio provides a special dialog box for creating connections to databases.

You can access the Add Connections dialog box in several ways, including the ones listed here:

✦ Choose Tools⇨Connect to Database.

✦ Use the Choose Your Data Connection page in the Data Source Configuration Wizard.

✦ Click the Connect to Database button on the Server Explorer toolbar.

Regardless of how you access the Add Connections dialog box, use it to make connections to all your project's databases.

Database connections are reusable. You don't have to create a new database connection each time you use the database as a data source.

Figure 2-5 shows the Add Connection dialog box for accessing a Microsoft SQL Server database. The choices available in the dialog box change to suit the selected database source.

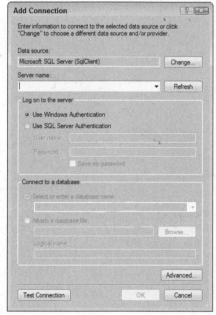

Figure 2-5:
Use the Add Connection dialog box to create database connections.

To change the database source in the Add Connection dialog box, follow these steps:

1. **Choose Tools⇨Connect to Database.**

The Add Connection dialog box appears.

2. **Click the Change button to change the data source.**

The Change Data Source dialog box appears, as shown in Figure 2-6.

Figure 2-6:
Select a
new data
source from
the Change
Data Source
dialog box.

The available data sources are

- Microsoft Access Database File

- Microsoft ODBC Data Source

- Microsoft SQL Server

- Microsoft SQL Server Compact 3.5

- Microsoft SQL Server Database File

- Oracle Database

- Other

You should pick the data source from the list that most closely matches your data source. For example, you should choose Microsoft SQL Server to connect to a SQL Server database rather than the more generic ODBC Data Source. Although you can use the Microsoft ODBC Data Source to access almost any data source imaginable, the other choices offer better performance with a specific kind of data source. Click a data source in the dialog box to view a description.

3. Choose a data source from the list.

When you click a data source, the Change Data Source dialog box displays the data source's default data provider and description.

A *data provider* is a component in *ADO.NET,* which is the data access technology in the Microsoft.NET framework. ADO.NET provides data providers for connecting to a database and executing commands against the database. The Add Connection dialog box configures the ADO.NET default data provider to work with the data source you select. For more information about data providers, see Chapter 5 in this mini-book.

If needed, open the Data Provider drop-down list to select a different ADO.NET data provider to use with your data source. The data source's default data provider is selected automatically.

4. **Click OK to close the Change Data Source dialog box.**

The Add Connection dialog box is updated to reflect the connection information required to connect to the data source.

5. **Use the Add Connection dialog box to finish configuring the connection.**

The information required from the Add Connection dialog box varies, depending on the data source selected. All the data sources have these features:

- *Advanced button* — View and modify the data source's connection information in a property grid.

- *Login information* — Specify the kind of login you want to use, as well as a username and password to use (if required).

6. **When you're done, click the Test Connection button in the Add Connection dialog box to make sure the connection works without closing the dialog box.**

Any time you're having difficulties accessing a database, use the Add Connections dialog box to test your database connection. Without a working database connection, you can't access the database.

Use the Add Connections dialog box to create your connections, even if you plan to write code to access data. You can use the Add Connections dialog box to test your connection, which saves you from having to do a lot of troubleshooting if your code isn't working properly.

The Add Connections dialog box creates a connection string that specifies how your application should access the data source. *Connection strings* store everything you type in the Add Connections dialog box, including server names, usernames, and passwords. You have to manage connection strings securely. To read more about managing connection strings, see Chapter 5 in this mini-book.

ABCs of ODBC

ODBC — *Open Database Connectivity* — is a standard that has been used for many years to access everything from Access databases to text files. ODBC is a good choice when you need to access a data source for which Visual Studio doesn't already provide a way to access.

Adding controls from the Data Sources pane

The Data Sources pane is much more than a container for storing your project's data sources. You can drag and drop data from the Data Sources pane onto the Windows Forms Designer. Visual Studio adds a databound control to your form and "wires" it to your data source so that it magically works.

A control is *databound* if it retrieves data from a data source. A control's properties can also be databound. See the section "Binding by using the Binding property," later in this chapter, to see how to bind data to a control's property.

To add a databound control from the Data Sources pane, follow these steps:

1. **Use the Data Source Configuration Wizard to add the Department table from the Adventure Works database by following the steps described in the "Adding data sources" section, earlier in this chapter.**

   This example uses the Adventure Works sample database from Microsoft. See Chapter 1 in this mini-book for information about downloading and installing the sample.

2. **Choose Data⇨Show Data Sources to display the Data Sources pane.**

3. **In the Data Sources pane, expand the AdventureWorks data source by clicking the plus sign (+) next to the data source.**

4. **Drag and drop the Department table on the Windows Form.**

   Visual Studio adds a `DataGridView` control and a `BindingNavigator` component to the form, as shown in Figure 2-7.

   Alternatively, you can expand the Department table in the Data Sources pane and add columns individually to the form.

5. **Press Ctrl+F5 to run the form.**

You will see the data populating the control. In addition to the `DataGridView` control, the Data Sources pane automatically adds several components to the Windows Form:

✦ `BindingSource` — Connects data sources to databound controls.

✦ `BindingNavigator` — Provides built-in record navigation, including buttons to add and delete records.

✦ `TableAdapter` — Builds the commands for retrieving and updating data from the data source.

DataGridView control   BindingNavigator

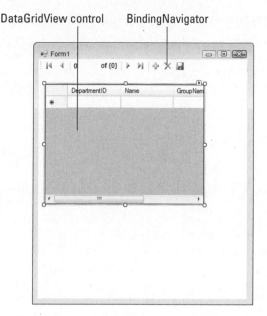

Figure 2-7:
Drag and
drop data
objects from
the Data
Sources
pane to
create
databound
controls.

These components are responsible for wiring your data source to your controls so that they "just work." You don't have to write any code to retrieve your data or update it. Simply drag and drop the data objects from the Data Sources pane onto the Windows Forms Designer. Visual Studio takes care of all the details, and you get all the credit!

You can view these components in the lower part of the designer screen.

Visual Studio adds a `DataGridView` control by default when you drop data from the Data Sources pane. You can specify the control you want to add to the Windows Form. To set controls for items in the Data Sources pane, follow these steps:

1. **Click the drop-down arrow for the data source in the Data Sources pane.**

A list of available controls appears.

You can work with a parent container, such as a database table, or you can set controls for individual columns in the table.

2. **Select a control from the drop-down list, as shown in Figure 2-8.**

Select a control from the drop-down list.

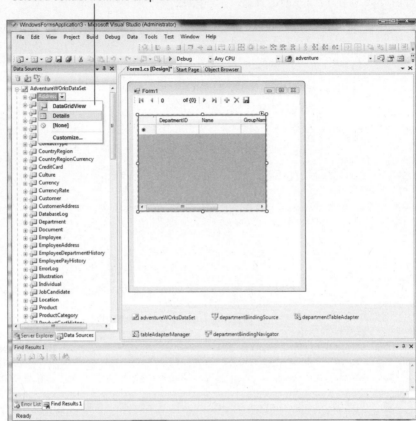

Figure 2-8:
Click the
drop-down
arrow to
change the
default
control
that's added
to the
Windows
Form.

When you drag the data object onto the form, the selected control appears.

3. **Set the parent container's control to Details to drop the parent's child controls on the form.**

The kinds of controls that are listed depend on the type of data in the data source. For example, a column that stores date-and-time data lists the `DateTimePicker` control. To use the shortcut menu to select a different control, right-click the data item in the Data Sources pane and then either

✦ **Choose None** to display no control for the data.

✦ **Choose Customize** to add a control to the list.

Getting Your Data in a Bind

Binding is the process of "wiring" a data source to a data control. Visual Studio provides several tools that make quick work of binding data sources to data controls, thus making it possible to perform the following actions:

✦ Navigate

✦ Update

✦ Delete

✦ Sort

✦ Filter

ADO.NET provides two components dedicated to providing binding services that make databound controls come alive with little or no coding:

✦ BindingSource — Links the data source and the databound control to make it possible to access and manipulate data

✦ BindingNavigator — Provides navigation to the data source linked to the BindingSource component

Visual Studio creates the BindingSource and BindingNavigator components any time you drag and drop data from the Data Sources pane.

Using BindingSource is the recommended method for binding data in Windows applications, regardless of the data source. No similar component exists for Web applications.

Using BindingSource to connect to other data

The BindingSource component, which is new to Visual Studio 2008, sits between your data source and the databound controls. The BindingSource component wires your data source to a control that displays the data. You can use BindingSource to

✦ Bind data to your controls without writing code.

✦ Change the data source without breaking the databound controls.

✦ Sort, filter, and add new data.

The BindingSource component simplifies working with data by exposing properties for common data-manipulation tasks, such as sorting and filtering data.

BindingSource is called a component instead of a control because no on-screen display is associated with it. A control is a specific kind of component — one that you use to build your user interface.

The easiest way to work with the BindingSource component is to drag and drop data from the Data Sources window. The following examples show you how to use BindingSource to sort and filter properties:

1. **Display the properties of a BindingSource component by selecting the component in the designer and then pressing F4.**

   The Properties window appears.

   For example, to use the BindingSource component, you could create a departmentBindingSource in the earlier section "Adding controls from the Data Sources pane," click the component, and then press F4.

2. **In the Filter property, type a value to use to filter the data source.**

   For example, to filter the GroupName column in the DepartmentBindingSource, enter a GroupName like

   ```
   Executive%
   ```

   The *like operator* (such as =) checks whether a value matches a pattern.

3. **In the Sort property, type the name of a column to sort by.**

   For example, enter **Name asc** to sort the Name column in ascending order.

   asc is short for ascending, and desc is short for descending.

4. **Press Ctrl+F5 to run your form.**

   The list of departments is filtered on the GroupName column and sorted in ascending order by name, as shown in Figure 2-9.

Figure 2-9:
The data is filtered and sorted based on properties set in the BindingSource component.

	DepartmentID	Name	GroupName	Modifie
▶	12	Document Control	Quality Assurance	6/1/199
	1	Engineering	Research and D...	6/1/199
	16	Executive	Executive Gener...	6/1/199
	14	Facilities and Mai...	Executive Gener...	6/1/199
	10	Finance	Executive Gener...	6/1/199
	9	Human Resources	Executive Gener...	6/1/199
	11	Information Servi...	Executive Gener...	6/1/199
	4	Marketing	Sales and Market...	6/1/199
	7	Production	Manufacturing	6/1/199
	8	Production Control	Manufacturing	6/1/199
	5	Purchasing	Inventory Manag...	6/1/199
	13	Quality Assurance	Quality Assurance	6/1/199
	6	Research and D...	Research and D...	6/1/199

Two other important properties for the `BindingSource` component are

✦ `DataSource` — Specifies the data source used by BindingSource

✦ `DataMember` — Specifies which table or object within the `DataSource` to use to get the data

In the preceding example, `DataSource` is set to `AdventureWorksDataSet`. The `DataMember` property is `Department`. You can add another table to the `DataSet` and specify the `DataMember` property for the table.

You can use `BindingSource` features to step forward and backward through a set of records and add, update, and delete data. When a `BindingNavigator` component is used with `BindingSource`, its data-navigation and -manipulation features are automatically mapped to the `BindingNavigator` toolbar buttons.

Using BindingNavigator

The `BindingNavigator` component is a built-in menu control for navigating data. You can find the `BindingNavigator` control in the Data tab of the Visual Studio toolbox. The control, as shown in Figure 2-10, includes the following buttons (from left to right) for navigating and manipulating data:

Figure 2-10:
Use this control to navigate and manipulate data.

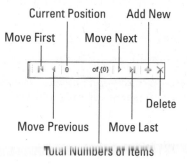

Current Position   Add New
Move First   Move Next

Move Previous   Move Last

Delete

Total Numbers of Items

✦ Move First

✦ Move Previous

✦ Current Position

✦ Total Number of Items

✦ Move Next

✦ Move Last

✦ Add New

✦ Delete

The `BindingNavigator` component is used in conjunction with `BindingSource`. The component has a `BindingSource` property that, when set to a `BindingSource` component, allows you to navigate and manipulate data.

Clicking a button on `BindingNavigator` triggers events in `BindingSource`. For example, when a user clicks the Add New button on `BindingNavigator`, the `AddNew` method in `BindingSource` is called. You don't have to worry about making it work. Just setting the `BindingSource` property for `BindingNavigator` wires the two components together. Better yet, just dragging and dropping objects from the Data Sources pane makes Visual Studio create and configure these two components for you.

To prevent users from adding data to the underlying data source, set the `AllowNew` property of `BindingSource` to False. The Add New button is automatically disabled in `BindingNavigator`.

Binding by using the Binding property

Any control's property can be bound to data. You don't always have to use special data controls to work with data. In the example in this section, you can see how to bind a department's name to a label control's `Text` property:

1. **Drag and drop a label control onto a Windows Form.**

2. **Open the label control's properties by pressing F4.**

   The Properties window appears.

3. **Click the plus sign (+) to expand the `DataBindings` property.**

4. **Click the down arrow for the `Text` property in the DataBindings section.**

   A list of data sources appears.

   To access additional properties you can create data binding for, click the ellipsis button for the `Advanced` property.

5. **Select a data source from the drop-down list or click the Add Project Data Source link to add a new data source.**

   If you add a new data source, the Data Source Configuration Wizard appears. You step through the wizard and add your data.

6. **Expand the data source and select the column you wish to bind the property to.**

   For example, select the Name column in the Department table to bind the `Text` property to it, as shown in Figure 2-11.

Figure 2-11: Select the Name column from the data source.

The text `DepartmentBindingSource — Name` is added to the property's value.

7. Press Ctrl+F5 to run the form.

The value of the first record in the data source appears in the label control's `Text` property.

TIP

Using a `BindingSource` component as the data source in Step 5 enables you to step through the records on your control with a `BindingNavigator`. By using the `BindingSource` as your data source for multiple controls, you can synchronize the data displayed by the controls. For example, if you add a `DataGridView` control to your form, you could use a `DepartmentBindingSource` from the Data Sources pane. Then the `DataGridView` and the label control both display the same record. As you navigate through the records, subsequent records are shown after clicking the Navigate button as shown in, as shown in Figure 2-12.

Figure 2-12:
Both controls display data for the current record.

Data binding to properties is useful any time you want to dynamically populate properties.

Creating Web Forms That Access Data

Developing Web applications is challenging because you have to send information across a network. Of course, this isn't just any network. Your Web pages are sent out by way of the world's network, the Internet.

Processing a Web page involves these stages:

1. A client's browser sends a request to a server for the Web page.

2. The server responds to the client and sends the contents of the Web page.

3. The client's browser receives the Web page and displays its content.

Repeat this process 100 bazillion times per day, and you have some idea of the amount of requests and responses bouncing around on the Internet.

The requests and responses of clients and servers are controlled by a set of rules named *HyperText Transfer Protocol* (HTTP). One characteristic of HTTP is that it's *stateless,* which means that after a request or response is processed, HTTP forgets that the response or request ever existed. If clients and servers on the Web suffer from amnesia with every click of the mouse, how is it possible to get data from servers to clients and back again?

When you want to make data work on the Web, three players do the heavy-duty lifting of making data-centric Web applications work:

✦ ASP.NET provides features that overcome HTTP's inability to maintain state.

✦ ADO.NET provides lots of widgets and commands for getting data from data sources, such as databases and XML files.

✦ Visual Studio provides the designer tools that make light work of using the high-tech gadgetry that makes Web applications work.

In this section, you can read how to use Visual Studio to access data on your Web pages. You can sleep better at night knowing that Visual Studio is protecting you from dealing with ASP.NET, ADO.NET, and HTTP; or, you can have your own case of amnesia and happily get on with building data-centric Web applications with Visual Studio.

Meet the controls

The Visual Studio toolbox includes many data controls for displaying data and creating data sources. All the data controls are grouped on the toolbox's Data tab, as shown in Figure 2-13. To open the toolbox, choose View➪Toolbox or press Ctrl+Alt+X.

Figure 2-13: Data controls are grouped on the Data tab of this Visual Studio toolbox.

Five controls display data on a Web page. They're often called *databound* controls because data is bound to them:

+ `GridView` — Displays a tabular view of data.

+ `DataList` — Displays data in a list with a customizable format.

+ `DetailsView` — Displays a single record at a time in a table row. This control is often used with `GridView` to create master/detail views.

+ `FormView` — Displays a single record without specifying how the data is displayed. The display can be customized.

+ `Repeater` — Displays data in a list that can be customized.

Each of these controls uses HTML markup to render your data to the client's Web browser. By default, the text is rendered by using table markup. All these controls can be customized, so you can specify the exact HTML markup that you want ASP.NET to use when it sends the page to the browser.

Visual Studio provides a data source control for each kind of data source you can access in ASP.NET. The five controls for creating data sources are

+ `SqlDataSource` — Accesses a database, such as Microsoft SQL Server or Oracle

+ `AccessDataSource` — Accesses a Microsoft Access database

+ `LinqDataSource` — Accesses data from a LINQ query

+ `ObjectDataSource` — Accesses data in a business object

+ `XmlDataSource` — Accesses data in an XML file

+ `SiteMapDataSource` — Creates a data source to access a site map

The data source controls are comparable to the `BindingSource` component used with Windows Forms. The obvious difference, of course, is that `BindingSource` works with multiple data sources, whereas the ASP.NET data source controls are specialized to work with specific data sources.

Going to the source

You use data source controls to configure access to a particular type of data source. Each control, except for the `SiteMapDataSource` control, has a configuration wizard that you use to configure the data source control. The `SiteMapDataSource` control doesn't need a wizard because it magically works with the site's site map. See Book III, Chapter 6 for more about site maps.

To launch the configuration wizard for any of the data source controls, follow these steps:

1. **Drag and drop one of the data source controls onto a Web Form.**

2. **Click the arrow in the upper-right corner of the control to display a context menu.**

3. **Click the Configure Data Source link in the context menu, as shown in Figure 2-14.**

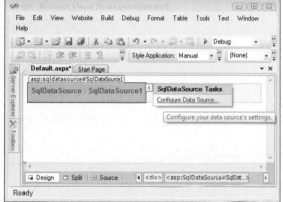

Figure 2-14: Click the Configure Data Source link to launch a configuration wizard.

4. **Step through the wizard to configure the data source.**

Data source controls often store their results in `DataSets`. By using `DataSets`, you can easily sort and filter the data. You can also use parameters with data sources to specify criteria for which data should be retrieved, deleted, or updated. See the section "Updating data with the DataSet Designer," later in this chapter, for an introduction to working with `DataSets`.

You can configure data sources by using the databound controls.

Using databound Web server controls

The ASP.NET databound controls are bound to a data source control. Visual Studio provides built-in designer support for configuring data sources to work with databound controls.

The steps for adding databound controls are similar for all the controls:

1. **Drag and drop a databound control, such as DataList, onto the Web Form.**

    Databound controls are grouped on the Data tab of the toolbox.

2. **Right-click the arrow in the upper-right corner of the control to display the control's Tasks dialog box.**

3. **Select New Data Source from the Choose Data Source drop-down list, as shown in Figure 2-15.**

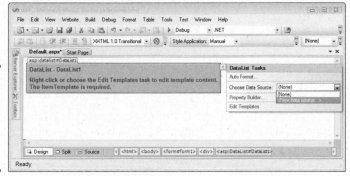

Figure 2-15:
Select New
Data Source
to add a
new data
source.

The Data Source Configuration Wizard appears.

Alternatively, you can select an existing data source control. See the earlier section "Going to the source" for more information on creating data source controls.

You associate an existing data source control with a databound control using the databound control DataSourceID property.

4. **Click the data source icon on the Choose a Data Source Type page.**

5. **Click Next.**

    Depending on the data source you choose, the wizard displays a dialog box for configuring the data source.

    This step displays the same wizard you see after completing Step 3.

    After you configure the data source, Visual Studio adds a data source control to match the type of data source you select on the first page of the Data Source Configuration Wizard.

6. **Step through the wizard to configure the data source.**

Customizing layout with templates

All Web server controls are converted to HTML markup so they can be displayed in a Web browser. Some controls, such as the GridView control and DetailsView control, are configured by default to render as HTML tables. Other controls, such as FormView and Repeater, allow you to specify the HTML markup you wish to use to display the control's contents.

You specify the HTML markup that determines how a control is displayed by setting the control's template properties. (The content you define in a template property comprises a *template*.) You can define several template properties for a control, such as

✦ HeaderTemplate — Defines the HTML markup used to create the control's header.

✦ ItemTemplate — Defines the HTML markup used to display data items. Several variations of the ItemTemplate allow you to specify different HTML markup for alternating item rows or rows being edited. By specifying different markup, you provide visual cues to your user.

✦ PagerTemplate — Defines the HTML markup used for navigating between pages as data. For example, you might specify to use Next and Previous.

✦ FooterTemplate — Defines the HTML markup used to create the control's footer.

Data controls aren't the only controls that use template properties. Many Web server controls allow you to define their layouts by using templates. See the topic "ASP.NET Web Server Controls Templates" in the Visual Studio documentation for more information.

By using templates, you can explicitly define the HTML markup used to display your data in the Web browser. You can display data from a data source using controls, such as labels and text boxes, that are databound to the data source. The following example shows you how to create an AlternatingItemTemplate property for a DataList control:

1. **Drag and drop a data source control, such as a SqlDataSource control, on a Web Forms page**.

2. **Configure the data source control to access a data source, such as the Department table in the Adventure Works sample database.**

   See the earlier section "Going to the source" for more information about adding data sources to your Web pages.

3. **Drag and drop a DataList control on a Web Forms page.**

4. **Choose the data source you create in Steps 1 and 2 from the Choose Data Source drop-down list.**

   The DataList `ItemTemplate` property updates with the fields from the data source.

5. **Click the EditTemplates link in the Common DataList Tasks window.**

   The control appears in Template Editing Mode, as shown in Figure 2-16.

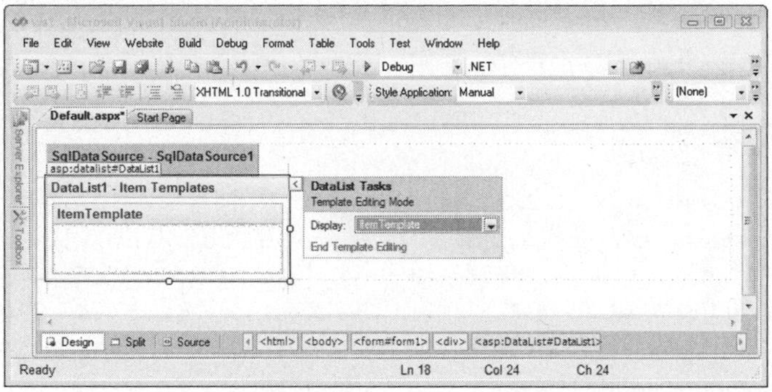

Figure 2-16: Customize the template using Template Editing Mode.

6. **Choose AlternatingItemTemplate from the Display drop-down list in the Common DataList Tasks window.**

   The `AlternatingItemTemplate` appears in the control.

7. **Drag and drop a `Label` control inside the `AlternatingItemTemplate` and then click the EditDataBindings link in the Label Tasks window.**

   The DataBindings dialog box appears.

8. **Select the Field Binding radio button and then choose a field from the Bound To drop-down list, as shown in Figure 2-17. Then click OK.**

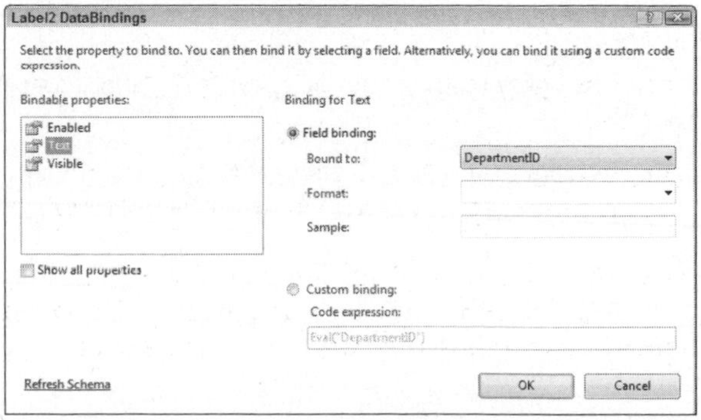

Figure 2-17: Bind your data to the control.

If the Field Binding option isn't available, click the Refresh Schema link (lower left). After the schema is refreshed, you should be able to select the option. If the option doesn't become available, you have a problem with your data source.

The `Label` control `Text` property is bound to the field you select. You can choose to bind the data to a different property in the DataBindings dialog box. When you run the page, data from the field appears in the `Label`.

An alternative approach to manually adding content to the `AlternativeItemTemplate` property is to copy and paste the content from the `ItemTemplate` property.

9. **Repeat Steps 7 and 8 to add all the data you wish to display from your data source.**

You now have a `DataList` control that has templates defined for the `ItemTemplate` and `AlternatingItemTemplate` properties. In order to provide a visual cue to the user for the alternating rows, you must define the style properties for the template. Each template has its own set of style properties. You use the style properties to create a custom look for displaying your data.

To set the style for a template in a Web server control:

1. **Click the control in the Web Forms Designer to select it.**

For example, click the `DataList` control used in the preceding example.

2. **Press F4 to open the Properties window.**

3. **Scroll to the Styles properties.**

If you have properties grouped using the Categorized button in the Properties window, all the style properties are grouped together in the Styles category. All the style properties end in the word *style,* such as `HeaderStyle` or `ItemStyle`. Each style corresponds to a template.

4. **Expand the style property you wish to set.**

For example, expand the `AlternatingItemStyle` property.

5. **Set the individual property items or specify a `CssClass` you wish to use from a CSS.**

For example, select a `BackColor` for the `AlternatingItemStyle` property to set a different background color for alternating items.

Figure 2-18 shows the `DataList` control with the `BackColor` property set for the `AlternatingItemStyle` property. The data displayed in the alternating rows uses the `AlternatingItemTemplate` property defined earlier in this section.

**Book IV
Chapter 2**

Show Me the Data

Figure 2-18:
Use styles to control the appearance of your data.

Working with tasks and properties

Databound Web server controls share many common tasks and properties. Table 2-1 lists some common tasks and properties. Tasks are accessed by using the control's Tasks dialog box, and properties are accessed by way of the Properties window.

Table 2-1	Common Data Web Server Control Tasks and Properties	
Feature	*How to Access It*	*Controls*
Choose Data Source	Tasks	All data Web server controls
Auto Format	Tasks	`DataList`, `GridView`, `DetailsView`, `FormView`
Edit Templates	Tasks	`DataList`, `GridView`, `DetailsView`, `FormView`
Edit Columns, Edit Fields	Tasks	`GridView`, `DetailsView`
Gridlines	Property	`DataList`, `GridView`, `DetailsView`
ShowHeader, ShowFooter	Property	`DataList`, `GridView`
Paging	Property	`GridView`, `DetailsView`, `FormView`

Use tasks and properties to specify style qualities, such as formatting and pagination. You can also determine whether a control allows data manipulation if the data source supports it.

Staying on the same page

Paging is a common property that wires a data display so that users can page through it. To change the paging properties for a `FormView` control, follow these steps:

1. **Add a `FormView` control to a Web page and configure it to access a data source, such as the Department table in the Adventure Works database.**

   See Chapter 1 in this mini-book for information about installing the Adventure Works sample database from Microsoft.

2. **In the FormView Tasks dialog box, set the `AllowPaging` property to `True`.**

3. **In the Properties window, click the plus sign (+) next to PagerSettings.**

   The pager properties appear.

4. **Set these properties:**

   - `Mode` — Select NextPrevious.

   - `NextPageText` — Type **Next**.

   - `PreviousPageText` — Type **Previous**.

5. **Press Ctrl+F5 to run your site.**

   The pager displays the words `Previous` and `Next`, as shown in Figure 2-19.

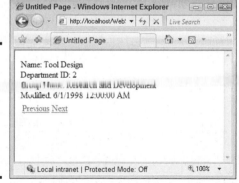

Figure 2-19:
Use the
Pager
Settings
property to
set custom
data paging
settings.

AutoFormatting

All the databound Web controls can be customized. The AutoFormat feature is an easy way to apply a custom style to databound controls. To apply AutoFormatting to a control, follow these steps.

1. **In the FormView Tasks dialog box, select the Auto Format option.**

The Auto Format dialog box appears.

2. **Select a format from the list of schemes.**

The selected format is previewed in the Preview pane.

3. **Click OK.**

The format is applied to the control.

To customize the Auto Format style, edit the control's `Style` properties in the Properties window or in the page's Source view, as shown in Figure 2-20.

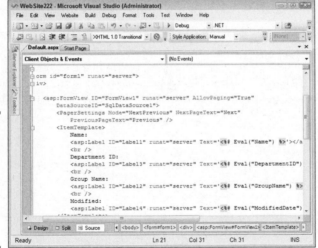

Figure 2-20: Customize the Auto Format style by using the page's Source view.

Updating data with the DataSet Designer

Visual Studio provides the DataSet Designer as a means to add data to your Web site quickly and easily. The DataSet Designer makes light work of these tasks:

✦ Creating data sources

✦ Retrieving data from data sources

✦ Creating commands to update data in data sources

The `DataSet` stores an offline copy of the data retrieved from a data source.

To create a new `DataSet`, follow these steps:

1. **Click the Web site's project folder in Solution Explorer and then choose Website⇨Add New Item.**

The Add New Item dialog box appears.

2. **Click the DataSet icon and enter a name, such as** AdventureWorks.xsd, **in the Name text box. Then click Add.**

Visual Studio prompts you to add a new App_Code folder.

3. **Click Yes.**

4. **Drag a `TableAdapter` from the toolbox onto the AdventureWorks.xsd page.**

The TableAdapter Configuration Wizard appears.

5. **Select an existing database connection or create a new connection on the Choose Your Data Connection page in the wizard.**

If you already created a connection to the Adventure Works database by following earlier examples, you can reuse that connection by choosing it from the drop-down list of connections. Figure 2-21 shows the wizard reusing an existing connection.

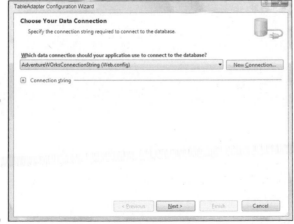

Figure 2-21:
Select an existing database connection or create a new one.

Book IV Chapter 2

Show Me the Data

Click the New Connection button to create a new connection to the Adventure Works database. See the earlier section "Connecting to databases" to see how to configure a new database connection.

6. **Click Next.**

   The Choose a Command Type page appears.

7. **Accept the default command choice, Use SQL Statements. Then click Next.**

   You may use this page in the wizard to choose new or existing stored procedures instead of SQL statements.

8. **On the Enter a SQL Statement page, click the Query Builder button.**

   The Query Builder appears with the Add Table dialog box open.

9. **Select a table, such as the Department table, and click the Add button to add the table to the Query Builder.**

10. **Click the Close button to close the Add Table window.**

11. **Select each column in the Department table to add the columns to the query's output, as shown in Figure 2-22.**

    You can select the asterisk-symbol (All Columns) check box to select all columns in the table, but selecting columns individually is usually considered best practice. If you use the All Columns option, you run the risk of displaying additional columns if a new column is added to the table in the database.

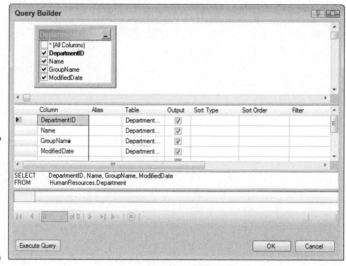

Figure 2-22: Select all the columns in the Department table for your query.

12. **Click the Execute Query button to test your query and then click OK to close the Query Builder.**

Your SQL statement appears in the TableAdapter Configuration Wizard.

13. **Click Next.**

The Choose Methods to Generate page appears.

14. **Accept the defaults and click Next.**

The Wizard Results page appears.

15. **Click Finish.**

Visual Studio creates the `DataSet` and a `TableAdapter` for accessing and updating the Department table. See Chapter 3 in this mini-book for more information about `DataSets` and `TableAdapters`.

To use the `DataSet` as a data source for a data source Web control, follow these steps:

1. **Drag and drop an `ObjectDataSource` control on the Web Form.**

2. **Right-click the arrow in the upper-right corner to display the control's Tasks dialog box.**

3. **Click the Configure Data Source link.**

The Configure Data Source Wizard appears.

4. **Select the `TableAdapter` from the Business Object drop-down list.**

If you used the Department table from the Adventure Works database, the name of the `TableAdapter` is `DepartmentTableAdapter`.

5. **Click Next.**

The Define Data Methods page appears. The methods created by the DataSet Designer appear on the SELECT, UPDATE, INSERT, and DELETE tabs. You may use the default methods or select different methods.

To create new methods, right-click the `TableAdapter` in the DataSet Designer and then choose Configure. The TableAdapter Configuration Wizard starts, and you can specify methods to generate.

6. **Click Finish.**

You have a `DataSource` control that you can use as the data source for a databound control.

`DataSets` are reusable. To add an existing `DataSet` from another project to your project, right-click the project's folder and choose Add Existing Item.

Getting the view right with the GridView control

By far, the easiest data Web server controls to use are GridView and DetailsView. They have built-in support for sorting, paging, selecting, editing, and deleting.

Sorting and paging

To enable sorting and paging on a GridView control, follow these steps:

1. **Right-click the upper-right corner of the control to display the control's Tasks dialog box.**

2. **Select the Enable Paging and Enable Sorting options.**

3. **Press Ctrl+F5 to run your site.**

   The data appears in a table.

4. **To sort the table by the column — such as GroupName — click the column name hyperlink.**

5. **To page forward, click the numeral 2 in the table's footer (the little underlined 2 shown in Figure 2-23).**

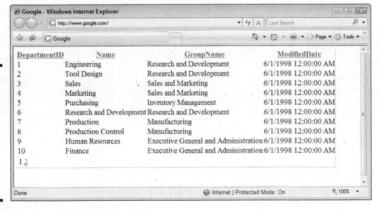

Figure 2-23: Click the hyperlink to the table's footer to advance to the table's next page.

Editing and deleting

When GridView uses an updatable data source, such as a DataSet, you can use the built-in functionality of GridView for editing and deleting records. To enable editing and updating in a GridView control, follow these steps:

1. **Drag and drop a `GridView` control on the form.**

2. **Set the GridView data source to an updatable data source, such as the `ObjectDataSource` control you create in the section "Updating data with the DataSet Designer," earlier in this chapter.**

The list of available tasks expands.

3. **Select the Enable Editing and the Enable Deleting options, as shown in Figure 2-24.**

The Edit and Delete commands are added to the `GridView` control.

4. **Press Ctrl+F5 to run the site.**

5. **Click the Edit button on one of the rows.**

The row is placed in Edit mode, as shown in Figure 2-25.

6. **Modify the record and then click Update (on the far left of the row).**

The record is updated.

7. **Click the Delete button.**

You see an error message. The Delete button tries to delete the record, but the database doesn't let it. This example shows why you have to make sure that the data source can execute the commands that Visual Studio builds.

Select these options.

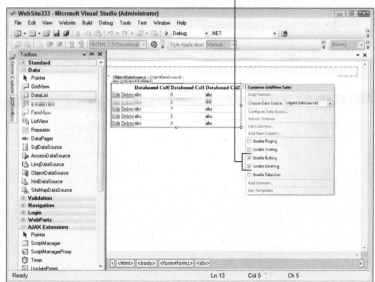

Figure 2-24:
Select
Enable
Editing and
Enable
Deleting.

	DepartmentID	Name	GroupName	ModifiedDate
Edit Delete	1	Engineering	Research and Development	6/1/1998 12:00:00 AM
Edit Delete	2	Tool Design	Research and Development	6/1/1998 12:00:00 AM
Edit Delete	3	Sales	Sales and Marketing	6/1/1998 12:00:00 AM
Update Cancel	4	Marketing	Sales and Marketing	6/1/1998 12:00:00 AM
Edit Delete	5	Purchasing	Inventory Management	6/1/1998 12:00:00 AM
Edit Delete	6	Research and Development	Research and Development	6/1/1998 12:00:00 AM
Edit Delete	7	Production	Manufacturing	6/1/1998 12:00:00 AM
Edit Delete	8	Production Control	Manufacturing	6/1/1998 12:00:00 AM
Edit Delete	9	Human Resources	Executive General and Administration	6/1/1998 12:00:00 AM
Edit Delete	10	Finance	Executive General and Administration	6/1/1998 12:00:00 AM
Edit Delete	11	Information Services	Executive General and Administration	6/1/1998 12:00:00 AM
Edit Delete	12	Document Control	Quality Assurance	6/1/1998 12:00:00 AM

Figure 2-25:
Click the
Edit button
to place the
row in Edit
mode.

Generally speaking, *delete* is a bad word when you're working with data. You should mark records as inactive rather than delete them. This strategy preserves the integrity of the data.

Binding to expressions

Visual Studio allows you to bind a control's property to an expression. You can bind a property to these kinds of expressions:

✦ `AppSettings`

✦ `ConnectionStrings`

✦ `Resources`

`AppSettings` and `ConnectionStrings` expressions are stored in the `web.config` file. *Resources* are resource files that store user interface information. To bind a control's property to an expression, you must first create something to which to bind. Book III, Chapter 6 walks you through how to add a name-value pair to the `AppSettings` section of the `web.config` file.

To bind to an `AppSetting` key named `AppName`, follow these steps:

1. **Select a data control and view the control's properties by right-clicking and choosing Properties from the contextual menu.**

2. **In the Properties window, click the ellipsis button for the `Expressions` property.**

The Expressions dialog box appears.

3. **Select a property from the list of bindable properties.**

4. **Select AppSettings from the Expressions Type drop-down list.**

5. **Type** AppSettings **in the Expressions Properties box, as shown in Figure 2-26.**

Figure 2-26:
Type an
App
Settings
key in the
properties
box.

6. **Click OK.**

When you run the site, the property's value is replaced with the value that the AppSettings expression evaluates to.

Chapter 3: Working with Strongly Typed DataSets

In This Chapter

✔ Creating `DataSets` in a class library

✔ Using the DataSet Designer

✔ Accessing data with `TableAdapters`

✔ Digging into the code of a typed `DataSet`

✔ Consuming typed `DataSets`

Programmers have always needed a way to work with data in their applications. Accessing data from files or databases every time you need data is impractical. To accommodate the need to have programs access data quickly, programmers store data in memory, using everything from arrays to integers to custom data structures.

Instead of making you spend lots of time thinking about how to store data in memory, Microsoft created the `DataSet` to provide a standardized means of storing data in memory for quick access.

A `DataSet` works like an in-memory database. The `DataSet` has tables with columns and rows, and you create relations between tables. You can load data into a `DataSet` from a database, or you can enter new data into the `DataSet`. You can insert, delete, and update records. After you make all the changes to records in your `DataSet`, you commit those changes to the actual database.

Visual Studio provides the DataSet Designer for creating and manipulating `DataSets`. This chapter explains what a `DataSet` is and shows you how to use the DataSet Designer to create a special kind of `DataSet`, the strongly typed `DataSet`.

Understanding the DataSet

A `DataSet` is a resource provided by the Microsoft .NET Framework for storing data in memory. `DataSets` store data in tables, and you can create relations between tables, similar to how you create them in a database.

You use a `DataSet` to

✦ **Store an in-memory copy of data from a database or other data source.**

Data stored in a `DataSet` is disconnected from its original data source. The `DataSet` stores data in the computer's memory, where it can be quickly accessed by your program.

✦ **Store data modified by your program.**

As data stored in the `DataSet` is modified by your program or people using your program, the `DataSet` maintains copies of the original and modified records. You can specify constraints that prevent records from being modified or deleted in the `DataSet`. Because `DataSet`s don't remain connected to the data source, you can provide feedback to your users without modifying the original data source.

✦ **Execute commands that retrieve data from the data source and send modified data back to the data source.**

`DataSet`s accept a set of SQL statements specified by the programmer to select, insert, update, and delete records in the data source.

✦ **Act as a data source for databound controls, such as `GridView`. For more about this, you can check out Chapter 2 of this mini-book.**

`DataSet`s are a natural data source for databound controls. You assign your `DataSet` and a table in the `DataSet` to the control's `DataSource` and `DataMember` properties, and the control displays the data from the `DataSet`.

The .NET `DataSet` acts as an intermediary between your data source and a databound control, as shown in Figure 3-1.

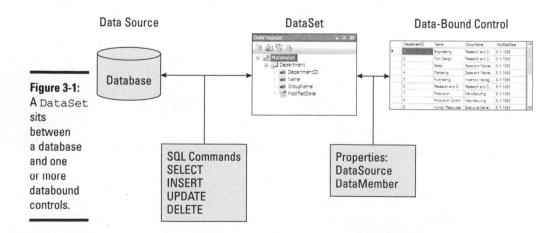

Figure 3-1: A `DataSet` sits between a database and one or more databound controls.

The .NET `DataSet`, which provides a basic structure for storing data, is composed of a set of these objects:

✦ `DataTable` — Contains a set of `DataColumn` and `DataRow` objects that represent a tabular set of data

✦ `DataColumn` — Represents a column in a `DataTable` object

✦ `Constraint` — Identifies `DataColumn` objects as unique or foreign keys

✦ `DataRelation` — Creates a parent-child relationship between two `DataTable` objects

✦ `DataRow` — Represents a row in a `DataTable` object

A `DataSet` can contain one or more `DataTables`. A `DataTable` contains one or more `DataColumn` and `DataRow` objects. Figure 3-2 illustrates the relationship between the objects in a `DataSet`.

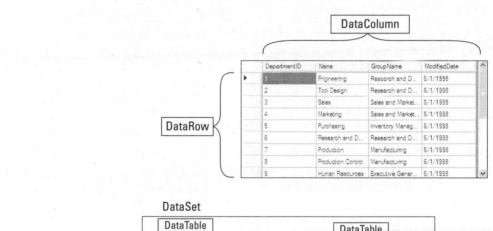

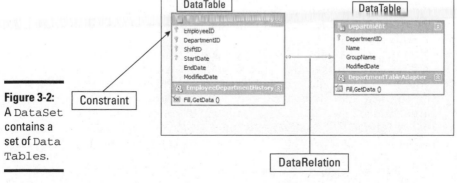

Figure 3-2: A `DataSet` contains a set of `Data Tables`.

What's your type?

Typed and untyped DataSets are nothing new to .NET and Visual Studio. In early versions of .NET, hardly anyone used typed DataSets. The code generated for typed DataSets by previous versions of Visual Studio had some quirks. People who saw how easy it was to use typed DataSets figured out ways to work around the flaws. With this release of Visual Studio 2008 and .NET, the bugs are worked out. Microsoft is again singing the praises of typed DataSets, although most articles you'll see about typed DataSets refer to them as *strongly typed DataSets*. Whether you choose to call them *typed* or *strongly typed*, using them makes your coding go a lot faster.

Discerning typed versus untyped DataSets

You can create two kinds of DataSets in .NET:

+ **Typed** — This kind uses a schema from an existing data source to define the tables, columns, and constraints in the DataSet.

+ **Untyped** — No schema is defined when the DataSet is created.

Because no schema is defined for untyped DataSets, you must create each DataTable you need, along with the DataColumn objects. A typed DataSet is an intelligent DataSet because it's "aware" of an existing schema. Visual Studio provides the DataSet Designer visual tool for creating typed DataSets.

Typed DataSets force you to use the types defined in the DataSet schema. For example, a typed DataSet that uses a schema to store customer data can't be used to store order data. You must modify the DataSet schema so that the DataSet knows how to store order data. An untyped DataSet, however, has no such restriction. You can store customer and order data in an untyped DataSet without explicitly defining how the data is stored.

Although it might be tempting to think that using a DataSet is easier if you didn't have to explicitly define a schema, using untyped DataSets allows you to get sloppy and can make your code difficult to read and follow. Using typed DataSets eliminates the ambiguity of not knowing for sure what data is stored in the DataSet. By referring to the DataSet schema, you have no doubts about the typed DataSet purpose in your code. The DataSet Designer makes it very simple to create typed DataSets.

Typed DataSets are often called *strongly typed,* and untyped DataSets are usually just referred to as DataSets.

Working with untyped DataSets

You create untyped `DataSet`s by using the `DataSet` control on the Data tab of the control toolbox.

To create an untyped `DataSet`, follow these steps:

1. **Create a new Windows application.**

2. **Drag and drop a `DataSet` control from the Data tab of the toolbox onto the Windows Forms Designer.**

The Add DataSet window appears.

3. **Select the Untyped Dataset option.**

4. **Click OK.**

Visual Studio adds the `DataSet` to your form.

You can create a `DataSet` in code. (See Chapter 5 of this mini-book.)

An untyped `DataSet` has no schema. A schema defines the structure of the `DataSet`. You must add the tables and columns to define the schema. To add tables and columns to your untyped `DataSet`, follow these steps:

1. **Click the `DataSet` you added to your form in the preceding set of steps.**

2. **Press F4 to display the Properties window.**

3. **Click the ellipsis button for the `Tables` property.**

The Tables Collection Editor appears.

4. **Click Add to add a new table.**

The table's properties appear on the right side of the editor.

5. **Type a name for your table in the `TableName` property, such as Customer.**

The table's default name is Table1.

6. **Click the ellipsis button for the `Columns` property.**

The Columns Collection Editor appears.

7. **Click Add to add a new column.**

8. **Type a name for the column in the `ColumnName` property, such as CustomerName.**

You can set the column's properties, such as its default value and maximum length, in the Columns Collection Editor (see Figure 3-3).

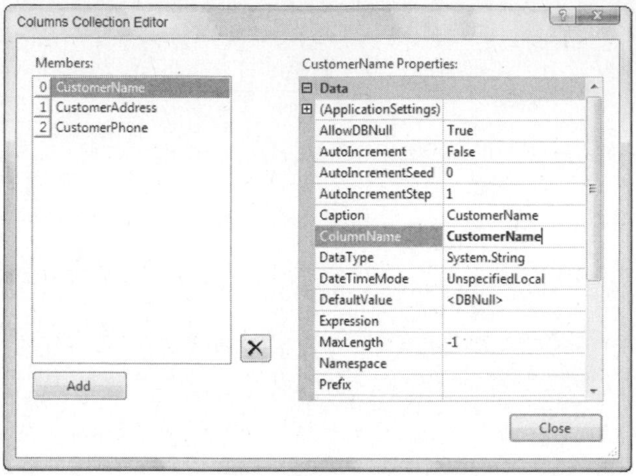

Figure 3-3:
Use the Columns Collection Editor to access the `DataSet` properties and collections.

9. **Repeat Steps 3 through 8 to add more tables and columns.**

You can use the `DataSet` Properties window to access collection editors for relations between tables and constraints within a table.

Using the Properties window to add tables and columns doesn't change your `DataSet` from untyped to typed. In order to be a typed `DataSet`, the `DataSet` must have a schema file.

Flexing your strongly typed DataSets

Data types are used in programming languages to set the rules for how data is expected to behave. Examples of data types are integers and characters. When you declare a new variable, you specify the data type of the variable so that your program knows what to expect. A strongly typed `DataSet` creates a new data type for your application to use.

Strongly typed programming languages require you to specify a data type at the time you declare a variable. *Weakly typed* languages also use data types, but they aren't as strict about their usage. For example, a weakly typed language allows you to treat a string as an integer. Strongly typed languages are stricter about how type rules are enforced. Because strongly typed languages allow you to bend fewer rules, the language's compiler has more opportunities to prevent you from using types incorrectly. Many scripting languages, such as JavaScript and Perl, are weakly typed. Visual Basic and C# are strongly typed languages. The computer doesn't actually care about data typing: All it sees is a series of bits. The use of data typing helps the developer work with the data correctly.

For example, if you create the typed `DataSet CustomerDataSet` to store customer data, you create a new data type. Your new customer `DataSet` might include tables to store your customer's identity and contact data. You can declare a new `MyCustomer` variable that uses your customer `DataSet` type, like this:

VB

```
Dim MyCustomer As New CustomerDataSet()
```

C#

```
CustomerDataSet MyCustomer = new CustomerDataSet();
```

When you access your `MyCustomer` variable, it already knows how you want to define your customer's identity and contact data because it's of the type `CustomerDataSet`. For example, to add a new customer and set the caption for the account number column, you type

VB

```
MyCustomer.Customer.AddCustomerRow("123456", "John", "Smith")
MyCustomer.Customer.AccountNumberColumn.Caption = "Account Number"
```

C#

```
MyCustomer.Customer.AddCustomerRow("123456", "John", "Smith");
MyCustomer.Customer.AddCustomerRow("123456", "John", "Smith");
```

Using typed `DataSet`s saves you from doing a lot of coding because Visual Studio generates the code for you. All you have to do is drag and drop tables from your database onto the DataSet Designer. To read more about the DataSet Designer, see the upcoming section "Creating Typed DataSets."

Take another look at `DataSet`s if you wrote them off in the past. In previous versions of Visual Studio, the code that was generated for typed `DataSet`s was buggy and difficult to extend.

DataSets and XML, together at last

`DataSet`s can use XML as their data source *and* be converted to XML. The XML language is used to create self-describing data files. For example, you can read an XML file into a `DataSet`, modify the data in the `DataSet`, and then produce the modified data as XML output. Or, you can open data from a database in a `DataSet` and produce the data as XML output.

You have to be able to write code to read and write XML to `DataSet`s. No wizards are available to do it for you. See Chapter 5 in this mini-book to read more.

Typed `DataSet`s use an XML schema to define their tables, columns, relations, and constraints. See the section "Viewing the source," later in this chapter, for more about viewing a typed `DataSet` XML schema.

Book IV
Chapter 3

Working
with Strongly
Typed DataSets

Creating Typed DataSets

Visual Studio provides the DataSet Designer for creating and working with strongly typed `DataSets`. A `DataSet` is *strongly typed* if it's generated from an existing data source schema that outlines the `DataSet` structure. You don't have to create this schema yourself — you can drag and drop items from a database onto the DataSet Designer. The DataSet Designer builds the schema for you.

Whether you're using the DataSet Designer in a Windows application, Web site project, or smart-device project, the DataSet Designer looks and acts the same.

Creating a DataSet in a class library

When you work with data, use the best practice of isolating your data code into separate projects so that you can reuse your data with other presentation layers. For example, if you create a data project that can be accessed by a Windows project and a Web site project, isolate your data in its own project so that you don't have to define it twice.

To use an existing `DataSet` in a Windows or Web project, see the upcoming section "Using a Typed DataSet."

You create a data project by using a class library. To create a new class library, follow these steps:

1. **Choose File⇨New.**

2. **Choose Project from the submenu.**

The New Project dialog box appears.

3. **Expand the Visual Basic project type.**

You can create class libraries in other project types, such as C#, J#, and C++.

4. **Click the Class Library icon.**

5. **Type a name, such as** DataLibrary, **in the Name text box.**

6. **Click OK.**

Visual Studio creates a new class library project.

The class library project template creates an empty class file named `class1.vb`. You can safely delete this file for this example. To delete the file, right-click the file in Solution Explorer and then choose Delete from the contextual menu.

Visual Studio includes a project item named `DataSet` that you use to add a typed `DataSet` to your project.

To add a typed `DataSet` to your class library, follow these steps:

1. **Click the class library's project folder in Solution Explorer.**

The project folder is under the solution.

2. **Choose Project➪Add New Item.**

The Add New Item dialog box appears.

3. **Click the DataSet icon.**

4. **Type a name, such as** MyDataSet.

Typed `DataSets` end with the file extension `.xsd`, which is the extension for XML schemas. To read more about XML schemas, see Chapter 4 in this mini-book.

5. **Click Add.**

Visual Studio opens the typed `DataSet` in the DataSet Designer, as shown in Figure 3-4.

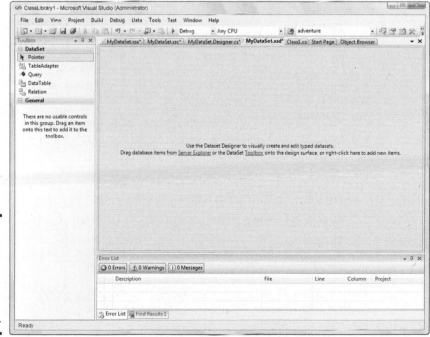

Figure 3-4:
Use the DataSet Designer to created typed DataSets.

Book IV
Chapter 3

Working with Strongly Typed DataSets

Adding typed DataSets to existing projects

To access the DataSet Designer, you must create a new `DataSet` or open an existing one. The steps for these two tasks differ slightly, depending on whether you're opening a `DataSet` in a Web site project or a Windows project.

Follow these steps to add a strongly typed `DataSet` to a Web project:

1. **Right-click the Web site's project folder in Solution Explorer.**

2. **Choose Add New Item from the contextual menu.**

The Add New Item dialog box appears.

3. **Click the DataSet icon.**

4. **Type a name for the `DataSet` in the Name text box.**

5. **Click Add.**

Visual Studio prompts you to add the `DataSet` to the App_Code folder.

The App_Code folder is part of the new Web site folder structure in ASP.NET 3.5. You can read more about the App_Code folder in Book III, Chapter 4.

6. **Click Yes to add the `DataSet` to the Web site's App_Code folder.**

The `DataSet` appears in the DataSet Designer.

Visual Studio launches the TableAdapter Configuration Wizard. The wizard allows you to create a connection to a database and configure SQL statements for selecting and updating data. To see the TableAdapter Configuration Wizard in action, see the section in Chapter 2 of this mini-book about updating data with the DataSet Designer.

To add a `DataSet` to a Windows project, follow these steps:

1. **Choose Project⇨Add New Item.**

The Add New Item dialog box appears.

2. **Click the DataSet icon.**

3. **Type a name for the `DataSet` and then click Add.**

The `DataSet` appears in the DataSet Designer.

To read more about the different ways to add `DataSets` to Windows applications, see Chapter 2 in this mini-book.

Exploring the DataSet Designer

Anytime you add a typed `DataSet` to your application, you use the DataSet Designer to create and modify its schema. A typed `DataSet` schema is stored in an XML Schema file with the file extension `.xsd`. The DataSet Designer is essentially a visual schema designer where you define the tables and relations in the typed `DataSet`. Visual Studio uses the schema to generate the code to create your typed `DataSet`.

The DataSet Designer provides two features for creating typed `DataSet`s:

+ **A toolbox** — Use the toolbox to build tables and relations.

+ **A design surface** — Drag and drop items from the toolbox or an existing database connection to the design surface.

Meet the players

The DataSet Designer uses a distinctive set of toolbox items for building typed `DataSet`s. When you drag and drop database objects (such as tables) from an existing database connection, Visual Studio populates items from the DataSet Designer toolbox by using the schema information from your database connection.

This list describes the toolbox items used by DataSet Designer:

+ **TableAdapter** — Retrieves data from the database and sends updates back for an associated `DataTable`

+ **Query** — Retrieves data from the database, not associated with a specific `DataTable`

+ **DataTable** — Provides a representation of a database table

+ **Relation** — Creates links and constraints between `DataTables`

The DataSet Designer toolbox items are visual representations of technologies used in *ADO.NET,* which is the data access technology in the Microsoft .NET Framework. To read more about ADO.NET, see Chapter 5 in this mini-book.

You use DataSet Designer to work with representations of your data visually. Behind the scenes, DataSet Designer

+ Creates an XML schema that defines the tables and columns in your `DataSet`. The `DataSet` file itself is an XML schema file. DataSet Designer adds annotations to the XML schema files to extend the XML schema syntax.

+ Generates the ADO.NET code that allows your program to access the data source.

**Book IV
Chapter 3**

**Working
with Strongly
Typed DataSets**

See the section "Looking under the Hood of a Strongly Typed DataSet," later in this chapter, to read more about viewing the code and XML markup generated by DataSet Designer.

Building a DataSet of your own

You can use the tools in the DataSet Designer toolbox to manually create a typed `DataSet`.

Here are the steps you follow to add a new table to a typed `DataSet`:

1. **Create a new typed `DataSet` by following the steps in the earlier section "Creating Typed DataSets."**

2. **Drag and drop a `DataTable` from the toolbox onto DataSet Designer.**

   A `DataTable` with the name `DataTable1` appears in the DataSet Designer.

   Press Ctrl+Alt+X to open the toolbox if it's closed.

3. **Click the `DataTable` name and type a name, such as** Customer.

The `DataTable` needs columns. Add them by following these steps:

1. **Right-click the Customer `DataTable`.**

2. **From the contextual menu that appears, choose Add⇨Column.**

   A new column appears in the `DataTable`.

3. **Type a name for the column, such as** CustID.

4. **Repeat Steps 1 through 3 to add FirstName and LastName columns to the `DataTable`.**

You can set properties for the `DataTable` columns by using the Properties window. Examples of properties you can set are the column's `DataType` and `DefaultValue` properties. See the section "Going beyond database tables," later in this chapter, for an example of setting a column's property.

You add constraints to your `Customer DataTable` to specify whether a column is unique. To set the CustID column as the table's primary key, follow these steps:

1. **Right-click the Customer `DataTable`.**

2. **From the contextual menu that appears, choose Add⇨Key.**

   The Unique Constraint dialog box appears.

3. **Select the CustID column by placing a check mark next to it.**

4. **Select the primary key option.**

5. **Click OK.**

    A little key icon appears next to the CustID column name, as shown in Figure 3-5.

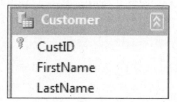

You use the `Relation` item from the DataSet Designer toolbox to create a parent-child relationship between two tables. The `Relation` item creates a relation that represents the relationship.

You can create a relationship between a table and itself. When a table is related to itself, the relationship is *reflexive*. See the next section for an example of a reflexive relationship.

You can create three kinds of relations by using the `Relation` item:

✦ **Both Relation and Foreign Key Constraint** — Creates a parent-child relationship between two tables by using the columns selected in the Columns grid. A foreign key constraint is created that allows you to set rules for what happens when records are updated or deleted.

✦ **Foreign Key Constraint Only** — Identifies columns in the child table as foreign keys and allows you to set constraints for what happens when records are updated or deleted. You cannot access child records via their parent records because no parent-child relationship is established.

✦ **Relation Only** — Creates a parent-child relationship between the tables but doesn't implement rules for what happens when records are updated or deleted.

Select the Relation Only option whenever you want to access a child table's records via its parent's records. Create a foreign key constraint whenever you want to specify rules for when parent or child records are updated or deleted. Generally, set up both relation and foreign key constraints because this affords the highest amount of data integrity.

Follow these steps to create a relation between two tables:

1. **Follow the first two step lists in this section to create a `DataTable` and columns. Then create a `DataTable` named CustomerAddress and add these columns:**

   - CustID
   - Address1
   - Address2
   - City
   - State
   - Zip

2. **Drag and drop a `Relation` item from the toolbox onto the designer.**

   The Relation dialog box appears, which you use to specify a parent and child table, and select the columns in each table that link the tables.

3. **Type a name for the Relation in the Name field.**

   Relation names are usually some combination of the two tables' names, such as Customer_CustomerAddress.

4. **Select Customer as the parent table and CustomerAddress as the child table.**

   When your `DataSet` has only two tables, the DataSet Designer selects the parent-child tables for you.

5. **In the Columns grid, select the CustID column from each table.**

   The CustID column is the column that both columns share.

   Be sure to create columns before adding the relation. You can't add new columns by using the Columns grid.

6. **Select the Both Relation and Foreign Key Constraint options.**

   Choosing the Both Relation and Foreign Key Constraint option or the Foreign Key Constraint Only option enables the constraint rule selectors, as shown in Figure 3-6.

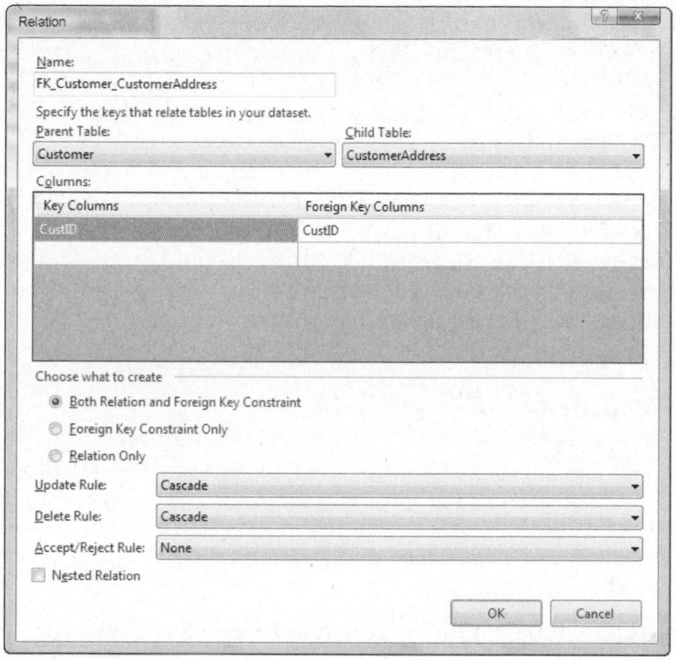

Figure 3-6:
Choosing to create foreign key constraints enables the constraint rule selectors.

7. **Use these constraint rule selectors to set the foreign key constraints:**

   - *Update Rule* — Cascade
   - *Delete Rule* — Cascade
   - *Accept/Reject Rule* — Cascade

   Constraint rules specify the action taken on a child record by the database when its parent record is updated or deleted. Your choices for Update Rule and Delete Rule are the following:

   - *None* — Nothing happens to the child rows when a parent is updated or deleted.
   - *Cascade* — The child rows are deleted or updated.
   - *SetNull* — The values in the child rows are set to null.
   - *SetDefault* — The values in the child row are set to the default values.

   The *Accept/Reject Rule option* specifies what happens to the child rows when a parent row either accepts or rejects changes. Your choices for Accept/Reject Rule are

   - *None*
   - *Cascade*

8. **Leave the Nested Relation check box cleared.**

Nesting the relation causes the child table to be nested inside the parent table.

9. **Click OK.**

You use the `TableAdapter` and `Query` items from the DataSet Designer toolbox to fill your `DataSet` with data. Using the `TableAdapter` item opens the TableAdapter Configuration Wizard, and the `Query` item opens the TableAdapter Query Configuration Wizard. To see both wizards in action, see the section "Shepherding Data," later in this chapter.

Adding database objects

The easiest way to build a typed `DataSet` is to build it from an existing database. You use Server Explorer to drag and drop database objects onto the DataSet Designer surface. The designer presents a visual representation of the `DataSet` and creates a basic set of queries to select and update data. You then use a wizard to modify those queries or create new ones.

You use the set of Visual Database Tools, including Server Explorer, for manipulating database objects. See Chapter 6 in this mini-book for more information about the Visual Database Tools.

To connect to a database by using Server Explorer, follow these steps:

1. **Open Server Explorer by choosing View⇨Server Explorer.**

You can open Server Explorer by clicking the Server Explorer link from the DataSet Designer.

2. **Click the Connect to Database button on the Server Explorer toolbar.**

The Add Connection dialog box appears.

Alternatively, you can right-click the Data Connection icon and choose Add Connection from the contextual menu.

3. **Create a new connection to the Adventure Works database.**

The connection appears in Server Explorer. (Chapter 2 in this mini-book walks you through using the Add Connection dialog box.)

Adding database objects to the `DataSet` is a matter of dragging them from Server Explorer and dropping them on the design surface. Follow these steps to add new tables to DataSet Designer:

1. **Click the plus sign (+) next to the data connection you created in the preceding set of steps.**

   The data connection expands.

   Server Explorer displays data connections as a hierarchical display of database objects. You view an object's contents by clicking the plus sign (+) to expand the container.

2. **Click the plus sign (+) next to the Tables folder.**

   A list of the data connection's tables appears.

3. **Drag the Department table to the design surface and drop the table.**

   A representation of the table and a `TableAdapter` appear on the DataSet Designer. The `TableAdapter` is responsible for creating commands to retrieve and update the data for the table with which it's associated.

4. **Drag and drop the EmployeeDepartmentHistory table onto the DataSet Designer.**

   The table and a `TableAdapter` appear on the designer. Visual Studio creates links between the tables, as shown in Figure 3-7.

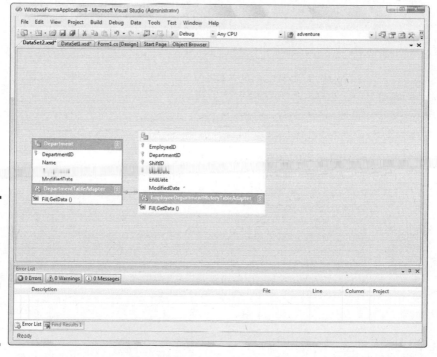

Figure 3-7:
The database tables appear on the designer with links between them.

5. **Drag and drop the Employee table onto DataSet Designer.**

The designer creates a link between the Employee table and the EmployeeDepartmentHistory table.

6. **Press Ctrl+S to save the DataSet.**

Notice the link at the top of the Employee table that points back to itself, as shown in Figure 3-8. The Employee table has a record for each employee. Employees have a manager, but managers are employees, too. Instead of creating a separate Manager table that duplicates information in the Employee table, the Employee table has a ManagerID column. The source of the ManagerID column is the Employee table, which creates a link. A column in a table using that table as its source is an example of a reflexive relationship.

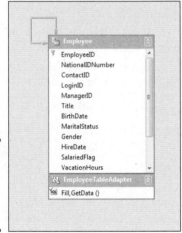

Figure 3-8:
The Employee table has a link to itself.

Going beyond database tables

Tables aren't the only database objects you can add to your strongly typed DataSet. You can also add other kinds of database objects, such as stored procedures and views.

You access views and stored procedures by using Server Explorer. See the preceding section, "Adding database objects," for an example of using Server Explorer to access database objects.

To add a view from the Adventure Works sample database to your `DataSet`, follow these steps:

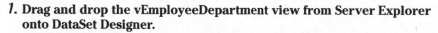

1. **Drag and drop the vEmployeeDepartment view from Server Explorer onto DataSet Designer.**

   The view appears on DataSet Designer. Views often start with the letter *v*.

2. **Click the vEmployeeDepartment DataTable name and change it to EmployeeDepartment.**

3. **Right-click the FirstName column.**

4. **Choose Properties from the contextual menu that appears.**

   The Properties window appears.

5. **Set the FirstName column's `Caption` property to FirstName, as shown in Figure 3-9.**

   Set the `Caption` property for a column to specify the text you want displayed in the column's header.

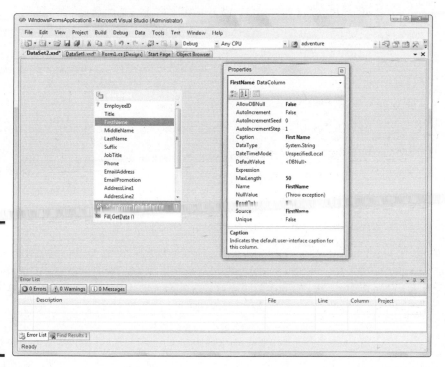

Figure 3-9:
Set the column `Caption` property via the Properties window.

DataSet Designer cannot generate SQL commands to update your data when you use a view or stored procedure. You have to use the TableAdapter Configuration Wizard to write your own SQL statements or select stored procedures. (See the next section for more information about the wizard.)

Shepherding Data

You need some way to move data in and out of your `DataSet`. The new Microsoft .NET Framework technology, the `TableAdapter`, shepherds data between your data source and `DataSet`. Each table in your `DataSet` requires its own `TableAdapter`. The `TableAdapter`, located between your database and `DataSet`, performs these functions:

✦ Connects to your database

✦ Sends SQL statements to the database to retrieve and update data

When you add a database object from Server Explorer to a `DataSet` by using DataSet Designer, the designer automatically creates a `TableAdapter`. The `TableAdapter` connects to the data source and generates a SQL statement to retrieve data to fill the table in the `DataSet`.

A single table in a `DataSet` doesn't have to correlate directly to a database table. A table in a `DataSet` can be filled with data from a view, a stored procedure, or an SQL statement you specify. See the preceding section, about going beyond database tables, for more information on adding views and stored procedures to a `DataSet`.

The DataSet Designer provides two wizards for creating `TableAdapters`:

✦ **TableAdapter Configuration Wizard** — Walks you through connecting to a database and creating SQL statements or stored procedures for accessing data

✦ **TableAdapter Query Configuration Wizard** — Allows you to add queries for accessing data

The TableAdapter wizards generate the code to make database connections and execute SQL commands by using ADO.NET to access the database. To read more about connections and SQL commands in ADO.NET, see Chapter 5 in this mini-book.

The TableAdapter wizards can generate SQL statements to retrieve and update data when the table's data source is a single table in a database.

If you use multiple tables in a database to fill a single table in a `DataSet`, you need to supply your own SQL statements or stored procedures to update the original data source.

Using the TableAdapter Configuration Wizard

`TableAdapter`, the workhorse of the `DataSet`, is responsible for shepherding your data in and out of the database. DataSet Designer configures a `TableAdapter` for each table you drop on the DataSet Designer.

You use the TableAdapter Configuration Wizard to

✦ Generate stored procedures for a single table.

✦ Specify the exact SQL statements you want the wizard to use.

✦ Bind the `TableAdapter` to existing stored procedures.

Common practice in data access is to use stored procedures to retrieve and update data. A *stored procedure* is a program that's saved with your database and is normally written by using T-SQL. You can use SQL statements to write stored procedures to do anything you want to do to your data.

For example, you can write a stored procedure to retrieve data from your database. The SQL statement to retrieve an employee looks like this:

```
SELECT EmployeeID,FirstName, LastName
FROM Employee
WHERE EmployeeID = @EmployeeID
```

Rather than execute the preceding SQL statement every time you need to get an employee's data, you create a stored procedure named `GetEmployee`, which has the SQL statement inside it. To execute the `GetEmployee` stored procedure, you type

```
EXEC GetEmployee @EmployeeID = 4
```

See the sidebar "The anatomy of a stored procedure" for more information on how to write a stored procedure.

You should use stored procedures over SQL statements because stored procedures are

✦ Stored centrally on the database server

✦ More secure than using SQL statements

✦ Reusable

✦ Easier to execute

The anatomy of a stored procedure

A *stored procedure* is a set of saved SQL statements. Stored procedures can

✔ Accept input parameters and return values as output parameters.

✔ Return a status value to indicate whether the procedure succeeded or failed.

When you create a new stored procedure, you have to do a few things, such as

✔ Use the CREATE PROCEDURE statement.

✔ Specify parameters.

✔ Use the SET statement to send information to the database about how you want the query executed.

✔ Type SQL statements that operate on data, such as SELECT, INSERT, UPDATE, or DELETE.

For example, to create a new stored procedure named GetEmployees with one input parameter, type the following lines:

```
CREATE PROCEDURE GetEmployee
    @EmployeeID int = 0
AS
BEGIN
    SET NOCOUNT ON;
    SELECT EmployeeID,FirstName, LastName
    FROM Employee
    WHERE EmployeeID = @EmployeeID
END
GO
```

After executing this block of SQL statements, SQL Server adds the stored procedure to the database. SQL Server changes the CREATE PROCEDURE statement to ALTER PROCEDURE after the procedure is created. The remaining lines in the procedure stay the same unless you modify them.

The most commonly used stored procedures in data access are CRUD (Create, Read, Update, and Delete) procedures. The four letters in CRUD relate to each of the four SQL commands you use to retrieve and update data:

✦ INSERT

Although the *C* in *CRUD* stands for create, the SQL command is INSERT. (After all, CRUD is easier to remember than ISUD.)

✦ SELECT

✦ UPDATE

✦ DELETE

Generating stored procedures

You can use the TableAdapter Configuration Wizard to create new stored procedures for a single table. By default, the wizard creates SQL statements and uses them to access data.

Stored procedures are preferred because they provide a performance advantage over regular SQL statements.

Naming stored procedures

You need a standard system for naming database objects, such as stored procedures. Most developers try to create a system that groups like procedures by using a combination of prefixes, table names, SQL commands, and clauses, such as:

✔ prefixTableNameCommand

✔ prefixCommandTableName

✔ prefixTableNameCommandWhere

✔ prefixCommandTableNameWhereSortby

You can argue for and against each standard. When you're dreaming up your standard, remember that your database can easily contain thousands of stored procedures. Chances are that your scheme will break down as the quantity of stored procedures increases.

Changing your naming standard after the fact is almost impossible, so pick something and stay consistent. Naming conventions may not help you actually find something. No matter what you dream up, you will struggle to find one stored procedure in a sea of stored procedures. Instead, your naming conventions should take the guesswork out of naming. It's one less issue you have to think about. When you're creating a stored procedure or using an existing one, the naming standard helps you know what to expect.

When you want to find stored procedures, get into the habit of using the SQL Server Management Studio to view table dependencies. (See Chapter 6 in this mini-book.)

Whatever your standard system for naming stored procedures, never use the prefix sp (short for *system procedure*). Using that prefix on your own stored procedures creates a slight performance hit because SQL Server expects sp-prefixed stored procedures to reside in the master database. Microsoft uses the usp prefix (short for *user stored procedure*), in its Adventure Works database.

Book IV
Chapter 3

Working
with Strongly
Typed DataSets

To generate new stored procedures for the Department table, follow these steps:

1. **Right-click the Department table in DataSet Designer.**

2. **Choose Configure from the contextual menu.**

   The TableAdapter Configuration Wizard opens with the Enter a SQL Statement page displayed.

   Alternatively, you can choose Data⇨Configure.

3. **Click the Previous button to step back to the preceding page in the wizard.**

   The Choose a Command Type page appears.

4. **Select the Create New Stored Procedures radio button, as shown in Figure 3-10.**

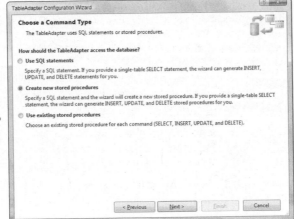

Figure 3-10: Select the options to create new stored procedures.

5. **Click Next twice to advance to the Create the Stored Procedures page.**

6. **Type a name for each stored procedure in the appropriate text box, as shown in Figure 3-11.**

   See the sidebar "Naming stored procedures" for more information on naming stored procedures.

7. **Click the Preview SQL Script button to view the SQL script that Visual Studio uses to create the stored procedures.**

   You can save the script and modify it to use with other tables.

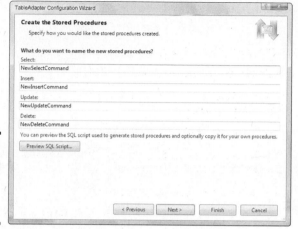

Figure 3-11:
Type a name
for each
stored
procedure.

8. Click Finish.

Visual Studio creates the four stored procedures in the database.

`TableAdapter` uses the new stored procedures, rather than regular SQL statements, to access your data.

Expand the Stored Procedures folder in Server Explorer to view the new stored procedures, as shown in Figure 3-12.

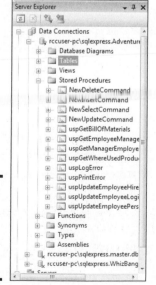

Figure 3-12:
View the
new stored
procedures
in Server
Explorer.

Binding to existing stored procedures

You can tell the DataSet Designer to use an existing stored procedure to access data, usually whenever you already have stored procedures created. You're likely to use this feature often because `DataSets` rarely are simple enough to use only one table.

Follow these steps to bind a `TableAdapter` to an existing stored procedure:

1. **Follow Steps 1 through 3 in the preceding section, "Generating stored procedures," to open the TableAdapter Configuration Wizard.**

2. **Select the Use Existing Stored Procedure option on the Choose a Command Type page.**

3. **Click Next.**

   The Bind Commands to Existing Stored Procedures page appears.

4. **Click the drop-down arrow for each of the commands and select the stored procedure to use, as shown in Figure 3-13.**

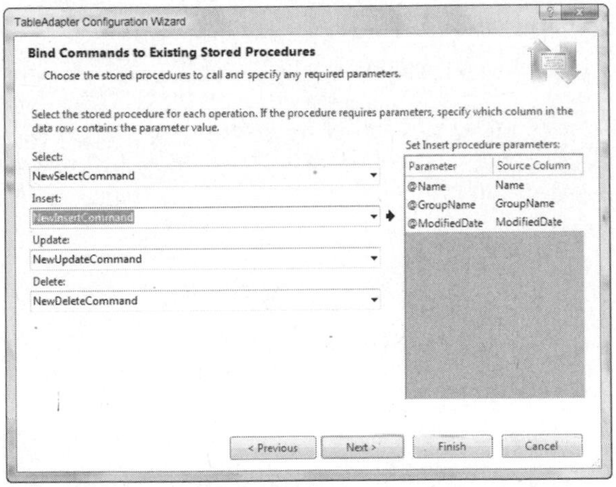

Figure 3-13: Select existing stored procedures from the drop-down list for each command.

5. **Verify that the source column matches the stored procedure's input parameters.**

   DataSet Designer displays the stored procedure's input parameters and their corresponding source columns from the `DataSet` table. To select a different source column, click the Source Column drop-down list and select a different column, as shown in Figure 3-14.

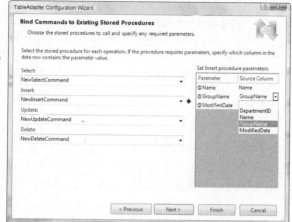

Figure 3-14:
Select a
different
source
column to
use as the
stored
procedure's
input
parameter.

6. **Click Finish.**

Visual Studio generates the code to use the stored procedures.

Using the TableAdapter Query Configuration Wizard

You aren't stuck with the select statements that DataSet Designer creates for you. You can specify additional statements for retrieving and updating data.

You use the TableAdapter Query Wizard to create additional queries. To start the wizard, follow these steps:

1. **Right-click the table in the DataSet Designer.**

2. **Choose Add from the shortcut menu.**

A submenu appears.

3. **Click Query.**

The TableAdapter Query Configuration Wizard appears.

Alternatively, you can access the Add submenu from the Data menu.

You can use the TableAdapter Query Wizard to create CRUD statements in the following ways:

✦ **Use SQL statements to access data.** The wizard automatically generates the SQL statements for single-table data sources. Otherwise, you can use the Query Builder to build your statement.

✦ **Create new stored procedures.** For single-table data sources, the DataSet Designer generates the SQL statements for you. You can copy and paste your SQL statement into the wizard or use the Query Builder to build the SQL statement.

✦ **Use existing stored procedures.** The wizard displays input parameters and results columns for the stored procedure you select.

To create an additional query to sort your output, follow these steps:

1. **Open the TableAdapter Query Wizard by following the preceding set of steps in this section.**

2. **Accept the default to use SQL statements.**

Or, you can choose the option to create new stored procedures. Either way, DataSet Designer generates the SQL statements for you.

3. **Click Next.**

The Choose a Query Type page appears.

4. **Accept the** SELECT **default type, which returns rows.**

5. **Click Next.**

The Specify a SQL SELECT statement page appears.

DataSet Designer generates the following SQL statement, which appears in the wizard:

```
SELECT DepartmentID, Name, GroupName, ModifiedDate FROM
    HumanResources.Department
```

6. **Click the Query Builder button.**

The Query Builder appears.

7. **Click the Sort Type drop-down list on the column grid.**

8. **Select Ascending from the Sort Type drop-down list, as shown in Figure 3-15.**

9. **Press Enter.**

The Query Builder adds the following clause to the SQL statement:

```
ORDER BY Name
```

10. **Click OK.**

The updated SQL statement appears in the wizard.

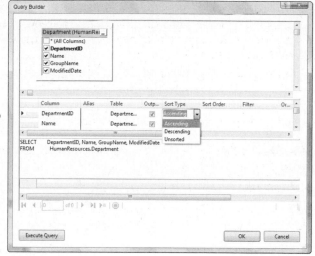

Figure 3-15:
Select
Ascending
from the
Sort Type
drop-down
list in the
column grid.

11. **Click Next.**

The Choose Methods to Generate page appears.

12. **Type names that you want the wizard to use in generating methods, as shown in Figure 3-16.**

Figure 3-16:
Type names
you want
the wizard
to use in
generating
methods.

- • *For the Fill a DataTable method,* type **FillBySortByName**.

- • *For the Return a DataTable method,* type **GetDataBySortByName**.

13. **Click Finish.**

DataSet Designer generates the code using the SQL statement you enter in the wizard. The designer updates the `TableAdapter` to show the new query, as shown in Figure 3-17.

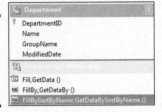

Figure 3-17:
The `Table Adapter` displays the new query.

Looking under the Hood of a Strongly Typed DataSet

DataSet Designer generates an XML schema and some ADO.NET code while you're creating a strongly typed `DataSet`. Creating a `DataSet` with only a few tables can generate thousands of lines of code. You may want to view that code so that you can understand how to build XML schemas or work with ADO.NET.

Viewing code

When you drop database objects on the design surface, Visual Studio generates code "behind the scenes." To view the code that Visual Studio generates, follow these steps:

1. **Click the Show All Files button on the Solution Explorer toolbar.**

2. **Click the plus sign (+) next to your XSD file.**

3. **Double-click the file with the extension `.Designer.vb` file.**

Visual Studio opens the file in the Code Editor.

Don't change the code generated by Visual Studio. You can't be sure that the program won't overwrite your changes.

Using partial classes

You can add your own code to extend the typed `DataSet`. The typed `DataSet` takes advantage of partial classes. A *class* is a unit of code. In previous versions of .NET, all the code for a class had to be in a single file. Partial classes can span multiple files. As long as each partial class shares the same name and use the keyword `Partial`, Visual Studio smooshes them together when it compiles the class.

Partial classes are intended to separate Visual Studio–generated code from the code you write. As a rule, you don't need to create new partial classes.

For example, you can use a partial class to set the default value of a column or to set validation. Follow these steps to set a column's default value in a partial class for the Department table from the earlier section "Adding database objects":

1. **Open the typed `DataSet` you can read how to create in the earlier section "Adding database objects".**

   The typed `DataSet` contains a partial class generated by Visual Studio called `DepartmentDataTable`.

   When Visual Studio generates code for typed `DataSet`s, it names the class by appending `DataTable` to the end of the table's name.

2. **Right-click the DataSet Designer.**

3. **Choose View Code from the contextual menu.**

   The Code Editor appears.

4. **Position your cursor between the start and end statements for the `Partial` class in the Code Editor.**

5. **Type the following line:**

   ```
   Partial Class DepartmentDataTable
   ```

   As you type, IntelliSense lists the available partial classes from the generated typed `DataSet` code. IntelliSense is a feature of the Code Editor that helps you write code.

6. **Select or type DepartmentDataTable.**

7. **Press Enter.**

   Visual Studio generates the closing `End Class` statement.

8. **Select DepartmentDataTable Events from the Class drop-down list in the upper-left corner of the Code Editor, as shown in Figure 3-18.**

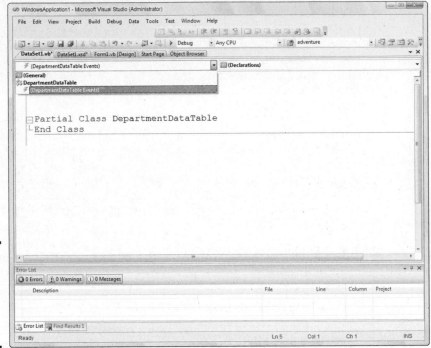

Figure 3-18:
Select the
events from
the Class
drop-down
list.

9. **Choose Initialized from the Methods drop-down list in the upper-right corner of the Code Editor.**

   Visual Studio inserts the following event handler for the `Initialized` event in `DepartmentDataTable`:

   ```
   Private Sub DepartmentDataTable_Initialized(ByVal sender As Object, ByVal e As System.EventArgs) Handles Me.Initialized
   End Sub
   ```

   The `Initialized` event is called after the data table completes its initialization. Visual Studio generates the code for initializing the data table, and this code is responsible for creating all the columns in the table.

10. **Type the following line to set the ModifiedDate column's default value to the current date and time:**

    ```
    Me.columnModifiedDate.DefaultValue = System.DateTime.Now
    ```

    The ModifiedDate column displays the current date and time when a new row is created.

Updating a ModifiedDate column when rows are inserted or updated in a table is a common practice. You can return the ModifiedDate value in the rows to test for optimistic concurrency violations, which assumes you won't have any data concurrency issues. With optimistic concurrency, you don't lock rows when they're read from a table. DataSets use optimistic concurrency.

Using the debugger to step through the code generated by Visual Studio is a valuable way to learn new coding techniques. See Book V, Chapter 7 for more information on debugging.

Viewing the source

You can view the XML Schema of a DataSet. To view the XML schema of a typed DataSet, follow these steps:

1. **Right-click a DataSet in Solution Explorer.**

   For more information on adding DataSets to a project, see the section "Creating Typed DataSets," earlier in this chapter.

2. **Choose Open With from the contextual menu.**

3. **In the Open With dialog box, select the editor you want to use, as shown in Figure 3-19.**

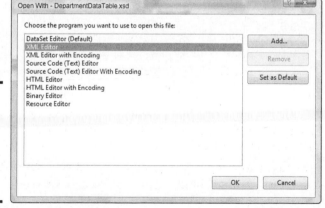

Figure 3-19: Choose the editor you want to use to view the DataSet schema.

Book IV
Chapter 3

Working with Strongly Typed DataSets

- *Open the DataSet in a visual XML schema designer.*
- *Choose XML Editor to view the XML source for the DataSet.*

4. **Click OK.**

The schema opens in the editor of your choice.

You can open any XML schema file with DataSet Designer. In the preceding steps, substitute your XML schema file in Step 1 and choose the DataSet Designer in Step 3. To read more about creating XML schemas, see Chapter 4 in this mini-book.

DataSet Designer marks up the standard syntax of an XML schema so that the schema can be used to generate ADO.NET code. By default, the attribute designating that an XML schema should open in the DataSet Designer is

```
msdata:IsDataSet="true"
```

Using a Typed DataSet

Merely creating a `DataSet` is not enough. You must configure your application to use the `DataSet` in some way. Earlier in this chapter, you can read how to create a typed `DataSet` in a class library (in the section "Creating Typed DataSets"). This section, however, shows you how to use a class library in a Windows project.

Typed `DataSets` are reusable. After you create a `DataSet` for one application, you can reuse the `DataSet` in another project. You might think that this refers to copying the `DataSet` file from one project to another. Although the copy-and-paste method is one means of "reusing," a more elegant approach is to create your `DataSet` in a class library, as described in the earlier section "Creating a DataSet in a class library," and use that library in other projects.

You can use any .NET programming language you wish when you create your class library in Visual Studio. The programming language of the class library and the project that uses the class library can be different.

To use a class library in a Windows Form, follow these steps:

1. **Open or create your Windows project and Form wherever you want to display the `DataSet`.**

2. **Choose Data⇨Add New Data Source.**

The Data Source Configuration Wizard appears.

3. **Click the Object icon on the Choose a Data Source Type page.**

4. **Click Next.**

5. **On the Select the Object You Wish to Bind to page, click the Add Reference button.**

The Add Reference dialog box appears.

By adding a reference to the class library in your Windows project, you can access the class library.

6. **Click the Browse tab and browse to the folder where your class library is saved.**

7. **Select the DLL file that was generated when you built your class file.**

The class library appears in the wizard, and the DLL file is stored in the project's Bin folder.

8. **Select DataSet1, as shown in Figure 3-20.**

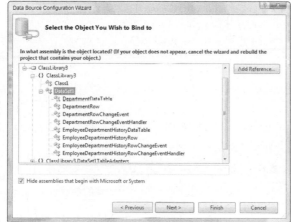

Figure 3-20: Select the DataSet after adding a reference to the class library.

9. **Click Finish.**

The wizard adds the class library as a data source.

To use the data source with a databound control, follow these steps:

1. **Drag and drop the table from the DataSet in the Data Sources window onto the Windows Form.**

The Windows Form Designer adds a DataGridView control that's bound to the DataSet on the form.

2. **Double-click the Windows Form.**

   The designer creates an event handler for the form's `Load` event and displays the handler in the Code Editor.

3. **Below the event handler, create a new variable to hold the table's `TableAdapter` by typing the following code:**

   ```
   Friend WithEvents MyTableAdapter As DataLibrary.
       MyDataSetTableAdapters.DepartmentTableAdapter
   ```

   When you add the `DataSet` to the form, the Windows Form Designer generates the code to display the `DataSet` in the `DataGridView` control. Unfortunately, because the designer doesn't wire up the table adapter to automatically load data, the `DataSet` doesn't have any data.

4. **In the form's `Load` event handler, type the following lines:**

   ```
   MyTableAdapter = New DataLibrary.
       MyDataSetTableAdapters.DepartmentTableAdapter
   Me.MyTableAdapter.Fill(Me.MyDataSet.Department)
   ```

   This code uses the `TableAdapter` you create in Step 3 to fill the `DataSet`.

Follow these steps to enable `DataGridView` to edit and update data:

1. **On the Form, click the Save Item button on the `BindingNavigator` component.**

2. **Press F4 to display the button's properties.**

3. **Set the button's `Enabled` property to true.**

4. **Double-click the Save Item button.**

   The Windows Form Designer creates an event handler for the Save Item button `Click` event.

5. **Type the following code in the Save Item button `Click` event:**

   ```
   Me.Validate()
   Me.DepartmentBindingSource.EndEdit()
   Me.MyTableAdapter.Update(Me.MyDataSet.Department)
   ```

6. **Press Ctrl+F5 to run your Windows application.**

   The Windows Form displays the data from the `DataSet` in the `DataGridView` control. As you use `DataGridView` to modify the data, the updates are saved in the `DataSet`.

7. **Click the Save Item button to save the data to the database.**

Use the `ObjectDataSource` control in ASP.NET to connect a typed `DataSet` to databound controls in a Web site. See Chapter 2 in this minibook for a walkthrough of using the `ObjectDataSource` control.

Chapter 4: Working with XML

In This Chapter

✔ Creating and storing XML files in Visual Studio

✔ Using XML Designer to create an XML Schema

✔ Transforming XML with style sheets

✔ Using XML with the .NET Framework

XML is the gold standard for working with data in modern software application development. XML, short for *eXtensible Markup Language,* is a markup language like HTML, which is the language used to create Web pages. In HTML, you use a set of predefined markup tags, such as `<html>` and `<body>`. The tags use attributes to further define the markup, such as `<body background="white">`.

XML uses tags and attributes like HTML does. However, unlike in HTML, you define what tags and attributes to use. XML is used to describe data, so you make up your own tags and attributes to define the data. For example, an XML file could use these tags to describe data about a book collection:

```
<Books>
<Book>
<Author></Author>
<Title></Title>
<Book>
</Books>
```

The XML file might use these tags because no predefined rules specify the tags you use. You decide which ones to use. As long as you declare which tags you want to use and then use them consistently, anyone can understand how to read your XML file. As you can see, XML is a powerful language for describing data because XML files

✦ Are plain-text files that you can edit and read in any text editor

✦ Include a schema definition that identifies all the elements and attributes to use to describe data

✦ Can transform into other languages, such as HTML

Microsoft has wholeheartedly embraced XML, and Visual Studio has several intelligent editors for creating and manipulating XML files. The .NET Framework has an entire namespace for reading and writing XML files, and Microsoft SQL Server supports XML, as well. If you're a .NET developer, you have all the support you need for creating and consuming XML.

With Visual Studio, you can use XML without writing any code whatsoever. This chapter shows you how to use the tools that Visual Studio provides for generating XML, including

+ XML Editor with IntelliSense and validation

+ XSLT Debugger

+ XML Schema Designer

+ XML snippets

DataSet Designer generates an XML Schema to support the creation of strongly typed DataSets. (See Chapter 3 in this mini-book to read more about DataSet Designer.)

Having some understanding of XML technologies is helpful as you work with the Visual Studio Tools. Don't worry: You don't have to be a whiz. This chapter has everything you need to know to get started using XML in Visual Studio. You can fill in the gaps in your XML knowledge as you go along. You can find some great tutorials at

www.w3schools.com

Storing Data the XML Way

More than a decade ago, developers had few options for transmitting data between disparate systems or storing configuration data. Everybody used comma- or tab-delimited, plain-text files. Although XML is stored in a plain-text file, the power of XML lies in its ability to describe itself. Walk through the following scenario to see how XML has transformed data transmission.

Imagine that you need to send purchase order data to a supplier. Here's what the transaction might look like without XML:

1. You export the data from your database to a plain-text file, either comma- or tab-delimited.

2. You prepare a document that explains each of the columns in the output file, such as the data type and whether the data is required.

3. You send the file and the document to your supplier.

4. Your supplier tells you that the file doesn't meet the specifications for his system and sends you the specifications.

5. You realize that you have to hire a programmer to transform your data to meet the supplier's specifications.

6. You decide that it's too much trouble and keep faxing your order forms.

This scenario has played itself out in many variations over the years. Somebody gets the bright idea to submit data electronically. However, without agreed-upon standards, the idea quickly gets abandoned because too much custom programming is usually required.

This scenario uses XML instead:

1. You create an XML Schema file that describes all the fields and attributes in your XML file.

2. You export your data to an XML file that conforms to the XML Schema.

3. You send your XML file, along with the schema, to your suppliers.

4. Each supplier uses the schema to validate that your XML file contains all the required fields and attributes.

5. Each supplier uses a style sheet that transforms your XML file into the XML file that conforms to the schema for their corporate databases.

Here's another scenario that might hit close to home for you. You use Word or another Office application to provide the form on-screen. The user fills in the data but saves the output as XML, rather than as a DOC or a DOCX file. Even though the user sees a form, the system sees XML. You can provide some great automation for this kind of setup by using Visual Studio Tools for Office (VSTO). You can actually use this kind of setup to convert invoice letters to XML. You can print the invoice letter as a letter or send it to someone as a DOC file yet keep your personal storage as an XML file, which takes considerably less space than a DOC file and is easier to manipulate for other uses (such as accounting or statistics).

Of course, not everybody plays nice all the time. A handful of suppliers might reject your file and tell you that they don't use XML, or they might want to use a comma-delimited file. It's no big deal — just create a style sheet (known as Extensible Stylesheet Language, or XSLT) that transforms your XML file into a comma-delimited file that meets their requirements.

This example shows you the beauty of XML. You can accommodate the input and output requirements of multiple systems without having to write a new program every single time. As long as your program knows how to work with the XML, you can make all the changes you need.

Using XML to define your data is fairly straightforward, especially when you harness the power of Visual Studio. A little knowledge of XML, combined with the Visual Studio tools, goes a long way toward creating XML.

Use XML to describe data any time you need to

+ Transmit data between disparate systems.

+ Store configuration data for your application.

+ Avoid the overhead of a relational database management system, such as SQL Server.

XML files can get really bulky when used to store large quantities of data, which doesn't make them appropriate for all data transmission scenarios. You should try to send the minimal amount of data required to complete a transaction when using XML.

Creating a new XML file

The first step in using the XML editors in Visual Studio is to create a new XML file. For example, Visual Studio supports creating these types of XML files:

+ **XML document** — Stores self-describing data

+ **XML Schema** — Defines the elements and attributes used in an XML document to describe data

+ **XSLT style sheet** — Transforms an XML document into another format, such as XML or HTML

XML documents, XML Schemas, and XSLT style sheets — they're all XML files. XML files use XML markup tags. XML Schemas and XSLT style sheets use a set of predefined XML tags.

To create an XML file in Visual Studio, follow these steps:

1. **Choose File⇨New.**

2. **Choose File from the contextual menu that appears.**

The New File dialog box appears.

Alternatively, you can press Ctrl+N on your keyboard to open the New File dialog box.

3. **Click the icon for the type of XML file to create: XML File, XML Schema, or XSLT File.**

Clicking the XML File icon creates an XML document file.

4. **Click Open.**

Visual Studio displays the XML file in the appropriate editor. Figure 4-1 shows an XML document in the XML Editor.

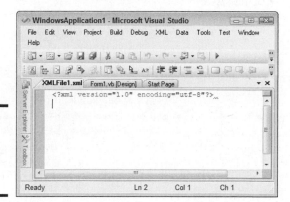

Figure 4-1: A blank XML file appears in the editor.

All XML files require a declaration on the file's first line. This declaration is a processing instruction that is important when reading the XML data. Visual Studio adds the following XML declaration for you:

```
<?xml version="1.0" encoding="utf-8"?>
```

The declaration specifies which version of XML you're using and in which language the content is encoded. You don't need to change the declaration.

Describing data in an XML document

Suppose that you want to create a Web site to display your large set of recipes. You can easily store those recipes in an XML document and then transform them to HTML so that they can be displayed in a browser.

For each recipe, you need to store the following information:

✦ The recipe name

✦ A list of ingredients, including quantities

✦ A list of step-by-step instructions

You can use the Visual Studio XML Editor to create an XML document that describes a set of recipes.

XML files contain markup tags to describe the data they store.

All's well (and valid) that's formed well

When you create an XML document, you want your document to be well-formed and valid. An XML file is considered well-formed if all tags

✔ Are contained within a single document root tag, such as `<recipes>`

✔ Are properly nested so that inner tags are closed

✔ Are opened and closed properly

✔ Possess all the proper punctuation, such as quotation marks around attribute values

An XML file is valid if the document is

✔ Well-formed

✔ Consistent with the data schema defined for the document

You know whether your document is well-formed because the XML Editor displays squiggly lines under any incorrect syntax. In this chapter, you can read how to validate an XML document by using an XML Schema.

To create an XML document for storing data, such as the recipes in this example, follow these steps:

1. **Create a new XML document file by following the steps in the preceding section.**

2. **In a blank XML document file, type an opening root tag, such as** `<recipes>`.

Visual Studio inserts the closing tag `</recipes>` for you, and then the XML Editor displays `<recipes></recipes>` in the XML document.

XML uses opening and closing tags to describe data. The `<recipes>` tag is the XML document's root tag; in this case, it encloses a collection of recipes. A *root tag* is the outermost tag in an XML document.

3. **Between the recipes' tags, type** `<recipe></recipe>`. **Use the `<recipe>` tags to enclose a single recipe.**

4. **Inside the first `<recipe>` tag, type** `name=""`.

The tags appear as `<recipe name=""></recipe>`.

`name` is an attribute of recipe. XML tags use attributes similar to HTML tags. *Attributes* allow you to describe properties for the tag.

5. **Between the `<recipe>` tags, type** `<ingredients>`.

The `<ingredients>` tag stores a collection of individual `<ingredient>` elements.

6. **Between the `<ingredients>` tags, type** `<ingredient>`.

7. **Inside the `<ingredient>` tag, add tags for quantity and item.**

Figure 4-2 shows an example of the XML file.

Figure 4-2:
Create an XML document file to describe your data.

A blank XML file appears in the editor.

8. **Save your file as `recipe.xml`.**

Creating an XML Schema

The value of XML lies in its self-describing documents. One technology that makes it possible for XML data to describe itself is the XML Schema. If you ever work with databases, you probably recognize the word *schema*. A *schema* describes all the tables, columns, and data types in a database. An XML Schema does the same thing.

A schema is used to verify an XML document's validity. XML files are opened by using a processor. A schema allows an XML file to respond to the processor's query, "Tell me about yourself." The processor uses the schema's response about the XML document to determine whether the XML document is valid.

An XML file must be well-formed in order to be valid. The properties of a well-formed XML file are described in the sidebar "All's well (and valid) that's formed well."

Building an XML Schema

The syntax for creating an XML Schema is straightforward to understand but somewhat tedious to write. Never fear: Visual Studio provides a tool for generating an XML Schema. Visual Studio generates the schema by inferring the schema from an existing XML document. Inferring a schema from an existing document and then tweaking it is much easier than building the schema from scratch.

Generating an XML Schema from an existing XML document is more accurate when the document contains data. Having data in the file allows Visual Studio to make intelligent guesses about how the data is structured in the file. For more information on creating XML Schemas from scratch, see the W3 Schools tutorial at

www.w3schools.com/schema

To infer the schema for an existing XML document, follow these steps:

1. **Open the XML document in Visual Studio.**

2. **Choose XML⇨Create Schema.**

    Visual Studio generates the schema file and displays it in the Code Editor.

    Figure 4-3 shows the schema that's inferred for the `recipe.xml` file you can read how to create in the earlier section "Describing data in an XML document." See the next section for more information on understanding the XML Schema syntax.

3. **Save the schema file.**

    XML Schema files use the `.xsd` file extension.

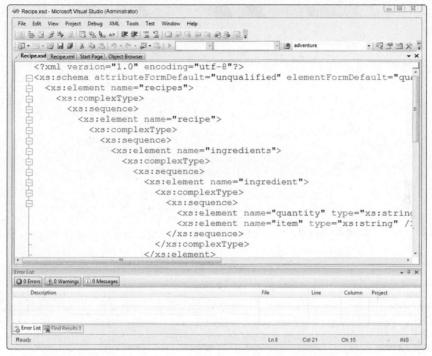

Figure 4-3:
Visual
Studio infers
the schema
from an
existing
XML file.

Visual Studio associates the schema file with the XML file by using the XML document file's `Schema` property. Press F4 to display the XML document's properties.

Associating the schema with your XML document does two things:

✦ Validates your XML document against the XML Schema

✦ Allows you to use IntelliSense in the XML Editor

Using XML snippets

The XML Editor uses XML snippets to insert commonly used XML tags. In this context, a *snippet* is a block of XML tags. You can create your own snippets, or you can quickly insert a snippet if your XML document is associated with a schema.

**Book IV
Chapter 4**

Working with XML

TECHNICAL STUFF

XML snippets are a kind of code snippet, which is an IntelliSense feature. You use code snippets to insert commonly used C# and Visual Basic code. See Book V, Chapter 5 for more details on using code snippets.

To use an XML snippet with the `recipe.xml` file described in the earlier section "Describing data in an XML document," follow these steps:

1. **Position your cursor after the guacamole recipe.**

2. **Type an opening tag: <.**

IntelliSense displays a list of available elements based on the document's schema.

3. **Press your down-arrow key to select the recipe element from the drop-down list and then press Enter.**

4. **Press the Tab key.**

Visual Studio inserts an XML snippet from the schema, as shown in Figure 4-4. The recipe tags and everything in between are inserted.

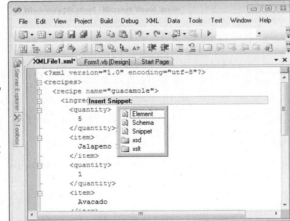

Figure 4-4: Press Tab to insert an XML snippet based on the document's schema.

The areas that need to have text entered are highlighted in the Code Editor. Use the Tab key to move between the highlighted areas.

To create your own XML snippets from scratch, follow these steps:

1. **Right-click the XML document and choose Insert Snippets from the contextual menu.**

2. **Choose Snippet from the IntelliSense menu.**

Visual Studio inserts a boilerplate template for creating XML snippets.

3. **Replace the boilerplate content with your own XML tags.**

   See the Visual Studio help system for more information.

4. **Save your file with the filename extension .snippet.**

Transforming XML with Extensible Stylesheet Language Transformations

The role of XML is to store self-describing data documents. At some point, that data needs to be displayed. You use a special kind of style sheet that uses XSLT to convert XML to another language, such as HTML, that you can use to display the file's contents.

You can use XSLT to transform XML documents into

+ XML documents.

+ HTML documents.

+ XHTML (Extensible Hypertext Makeup Language) documents.

+ Plain text documents.

+ Programming languages, such as C# or SQL.

+ Other kinds of data documents: The uses are nearly unlimited.

Visual Studio provides a file template and a Code Editor for creating XSLT files. Like all the Code Editors in Visual Studio, the XSLT Editor includes support for IntelliSense and code snippets.

Visual Studio can apply a style sheet to your XML file and display the output. An XSLT debugger is available to help you track down errors in your style sheet.

To create a new XSLT style sheet in Visual Studio, follow these steps:

1. **Press Ctrl+N to open the New File dialog box.**

2. **Click the XSLT File icon.**

3. **Click Open.**

   An XSLT file appears in the Code Editor, as shown in Figure 4-5.

Unfortunately, no visual designer or code-generation tool in Visual Studio creates XSLT style sheets. Another glaring oversight is a lack of support for building the expressions you need for selecting nodes from your XML file.

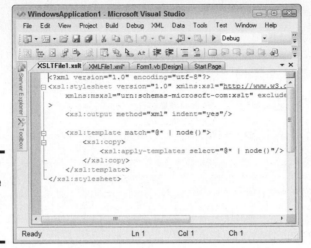

Figure 4-5:
An XSLT file appears in the Code Editor.

The technology for selecting nodes from an XML document is XPath. You can read more about it later in this section.

If you're having trouble building expressions, use InfoPath to dynamically build XPath expressions. InfoPath 2003 provides a visual tool for building XPath expressions. You can copy and paste the expressions from InfoPath into your style sheet. You can also use XML Notepad 2007, which you can download from

```
www.microsoft.com/downloads/details.aspx?
    familyid=72D6AA49-787D-4118-BA5F-4F30FE913628
```

Writing an XSLT style sheet

XSLT is written in XML. A style sheet consists of the following elements:

✦ **Declaration** — Identifies the file as an XSLT style sheet

✦ **Templates** — Define the style sheet's output

✦ **Supplementary content** — HTML tags, for example, that you want to present in the output

The "meat and potatoes" of an XSLT style sheet consists of the template (or templates) that defines the style sheet's output. The following example of an XSLT template uses the recipe.xml file that you can read how to create earlier in this chapter. Notice that the template combines XSLT syntax with HTML:

```
<xsl:template match="/">
  <html>
    <body>
      <xsl:for-each select="recipes/recipe">
        <ul>
          <xsl:for-each select="ingredients/ingredient">
            <li>
              <xsl:value-of select="quantity" />
              <xsl:text> </xsl:text>
              <xsl:value-of select="item" />
            </li>
          </xsl:for-each>
        </ul>
      </xsl:for-each>
    </body>
  </html>
</xsl:template>
```

The output from this template looks like this:

```
<html>
  <body>
    <ul>
      <li>1 avocado</li>
      <li>1 onion</li>
      <li>2 tomatoes</li>
      <li>3 pepper</li>
    </ul>
    <ul>
      <li>2 tomatoes</li>
      <li>3 pepper</li>
    </ul>
    <ul></ul>
  </body>
</html>
```

The HTML tags are composed of output from the style sheet. The ingredients data is pulled from the recipe.xml document by using XPath expressions.

An XSLT template includes these items:

✦ Elements, such as for-each and value-of, that are used to operate on the data from the XML document

✦ XPath expressions used in the select attribute of a template's elements to navigate the XML document

✦ Functions, such as last() and position(), for evaluating whether to select a node or include text in the output

✦ Text, such as HTML markup tags, for inclusion in the output

Figure 4-6 shows an example of an XSLT style sheet used to transform the `recipe.xml` file from the earlier "Describing data in an XML document" section into HTML.

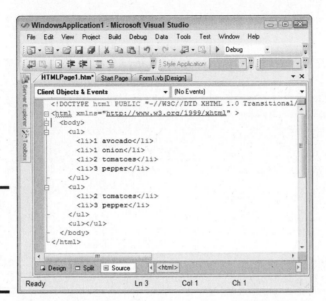

Figure 4-6:
XSLT
templates
transform
XML into
HTML.

Linking an XSLT file to another document

After you create your XSLT style sheet, you must associate it with your XML document. Linking the XSLT file to the XML document makes it possible for you to view the output created by the XSLT style sheet.

To associate an XSLT file with an existing XML document in Visual Studio, follow these steps:

1. **Open the XSLT style sheet in Visual Studio.**

2. **Press F4 to display the Properties window.**

3. **Click the ellipsis button for the `Input` property.**

4. **Browse to the XML document that you want to transform and then select it.**

   The file's path appears in the `Input` property.

5. **Choose XML⇨Show XSLT Output.**

   The output appears in a separate window.

You can place, at the top of your XML document, a directive that links the style sheet to your document. When your XML document is displayed in an XML-aware browser, the output of the style sheet appears. To add a link for the `recipe.xml` document, type the following line at the top of the `recipe.xml` file:

```
<?xml-stylesheet type="text/xsl" href="recipe.xslt"?>
```

Figure 4-7 shows the XML document displayed in Internet Explorer.

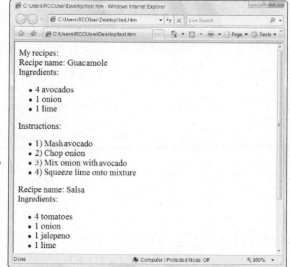

Figure 4-7:
The XSLT output appears in the browser window.

Staying on the path with XPath

XPath is an important technology for XSLT templates. You use XPath to navigate an XML document and find the nodes, or sets of nodes, that you want to display in your output. Suppose that you have an XML document for storing recipes with a structure like this:

```
<recipes>
<recipe name="string">
    <ingredients>
      <ingredient>
        <qty>unsignedByte</qty>
        <item>string</item>
      </ingredient>
    </ingredients>
```

```
      <instructions>
        <steps ordinal="string">
          <text>string</text>
        </steps>
      </instructions>
    </recipe>
</recipes>
```

You can use an XPath expression, such as `/recipes/recipe`, to navigate to the recipe node in the XML document. Table 4-1 describes the XPath syntax.

Table 4-1	XPath Syntax	
XPath Expression	*Syntax*	*What It Selects*
Nodename	`instructions`	The child nodes of the `instructions` node
/	`/recipes`	An absolute path to the root node
	`/recipes/recipe`	The child `recipe` nodes of the `recipes` node
//	`//steps`	All `steps` nodes, regardless of their recipe
.	`/recipes/recipe/ingredients/.`	The current node; the `qty` and `item` nodes in the example
..	`/recipes/recipe/..`	The parent node; all the nodes in the `recipes` node in the example
@	`/recipes/recipe/@name`	The `name` attribute of the recipe node

The easiest way to understand XPath is to use the `value-of` element in an XSLT style sheet and experiment with different expressions, like this:

```
<xsl:value-of select="recipes/recipe/@name" />
```

XML and .NET

The Microsoft .NET Framework provides many resources for working with XML in code. The XML-related classes in the .NET Framework have names that are similar to the XML technologies. For example, you use

XPathNavigator in .NET to write code that navigates an XML document. The XML-related classes are in the System.XML namespace in .NET. Table 4-2 describes some of its common resources.

Table 4-2	System.XML Namespace in .NET
.NET Class	*What It Does*
XMLReader	Reads XML documents
XMLWriter	Writes to XML documents
XMLDocument	Represents an XML document
XPathNavigator	Navigates and edits XML documents
XMLSchema	Represents an XML Schema

Each of the classes in the table includes numerous properties, methods, and additional classes for working with XML documents. For more information on using XML in code, see Chapter 5 in this mini-book.

Chapter 5: Under the Hood with ADO.NET

In This Chapter

✔ Using the .NET Framework Data Providers

✔ Connecting to data sources

✔ Managing connection strings

✔ Executing commands

✔ Accessing data with `DataReaders`

✔ Filling `DataSets` with `DataAdapters`

✔ Converting `DataSets` to XML

✔ Using ADO.NET in the real world

*V*isual Studio provides many controls, designers, editors, and wizards for accessing data in Windows and Web applications. These tools are made possible by *ADO.NET,* the data access technology of the .NET Framework.

ADO.NET provides a common coding structure for accessing data, regardless of the data source. The Visual Studio data access tools, such as DataSet Designer, generate ADO.NET code behind the scenes for you. This chapter shows you how to "get under the hood" with ADO.NET and write your own ADO.NET code to access your data.

ADO is short for *ActiveX Data Objects,* the previous version of the data access technologies, before the .NET Framework was introduced.

Meet the Players

The purpose of ADO.NET is to provide a simplified model for data access, regardless of the underlying data source. By using a model like ADO.NET, developers can improve their productivity because they use one data access model — ADO.NET — to access many different kinds of data sources.

ADO.NET provides a set of common components for accessing data:

✦ **.NET Framework Data Provider** — Acts as a bridge between your application and a data source. Providers are available for many popular databases, including SQL Server and Oracle. When a native provider is unavailable for your data source, you use an Open Database Connectivity (ODBC) or Open Database Connectivity database (OLE DB) provider to access your data source.

Each .NET Framework Data Provider offers a set of services for accessing data. See the following section for details on using data providers.

✦ `DataReader` — Provides forward-only access to a data source one row at a time by using one of the .NET Framework Data Providers. See the section "Reading Data with DataReaders," later in this chapter.

`DataReaders` are a service of the .NET Framework Data Providers. `DataReader` is listed separately here because it represents an important model for data access. `DataSets` are populated with `DataReaders`.

✦ `DataSet` — Provides an in-memory cache of data that's retrieved from a data source by way of one of the .NET Framework Data Providers. See the section "Caching Data with DataSets," later in this chapter.

Figure 5-1 shows the interplay of the .NET Framework Data Providers, `DataReaders`, and `DataSets` in ADO.NET.

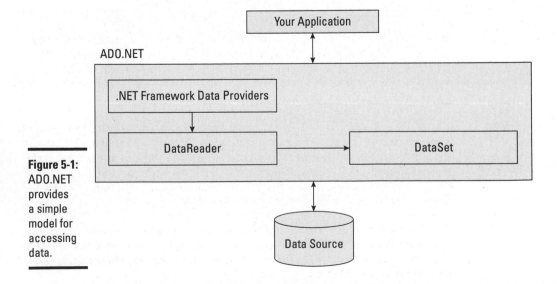

Figure 5-1: ADO.NET provides a simple model for accessing data.

You access the components of ADO.NET through the `System.Data` namespace in .NET.

The services of the .NET framework are organized into groups, or namespaces. To read more about namespaces, see Book V, Chapter 1.

Picking a Provider

ADO.NET uses data providers to provide access to many different kinds of data sources, such as SQL Server and Oracle databases. Table 5-1 summarizes the data providers available in the .NET Framework.

Table 5-1	.NET Framework Data Providers	
Data Source	*.NET Namespace*	*What It Accesses*
SQL Server	`System.Data.SqlClient`	SQL Server 7.0 databases and later
OLE DB	`System.Data.OleDB`	SQL Server 6.5, Oracle, and Microsoft Access databases by using OLE DB
ODBC	`System.Data.Odbc`	SQL Server, Oracle, and Microsoft Access databases by using ODBC
Oracle	`System.Data.OracleClient`	Oracle databases by using the Oracle client connectivity software

You should always use the provider that's tuned for your data source. For example, always use the SQL Server provider to access SQL Server 7.0 databases and later, and use the Oracle provider to access Oracle databases. Microsoft recommends the OLE DB provider for accessing Microsoft Access databases.

Never use a Microsoft Access database in a multi-tiered application. (A *multi-tiered application* is one in which there are several layers that each perform different functions in the process, such as data access, business rules, and presentation.) Access isn't an enterprise-quality database and doesn't always perform well across a network. Consider using SQL Server Express Edition if you need a lightweight database.

The SQL Server provider uses its own communication channel for transmitting commands to SQL Server. As a result, the SQL Server provider is faster than the OLE DB and ODBC providers, both of which add their own layers of communication channels.

Always use the .NET Data Framework Provider for SQL Server to access SQL Server 7.0, SQL Server 2000, SQL Server 2005, and SQL Server 2008 databases.

Accessing providers

You access the .NET Framework Data Providers through their .NET namespaces. (Table 5-1 in the preceding section lists the namespaces for each of the .NET Framework Data Providers.) For example, to access the features of the SQL Server provider, type the following namespace in the Code Editor:

```
System.Data.SqlClient
```

Because of how ADO.NET is constructed, you can access data without choosing a specific data provider. For example, you can write code that retrieves data from a data source without knowing in advance whether you want to use the SQL Server provider or the Oracle provider. Not choosing a data provider is useful when you need code to be flexible enough to choose your data source at runtime.

When you access data without using a data provider, you write *provider-independent* code. When you write it, you use the System.Data.Common namespace rather than one of the data provider namespaces listed in Table 5-1.

Writing provider-independent data access code isn't for the faint of heart. To read more about what's involved in writing provider-independent code, look for the topic **provider independent code** in the index of the Visual Studio 2008 documentation. A good resource for the topic can be found online at

```
http://msdn2.microsoft.com/
    en-us/library/t9f29wbk(VS.80).aspx.
```

Objectifying the providers

Each .NET Framework Data Provider provides access to a common set of data access features and services. You use the following features and services of the providers to connect to your data source and retrieve data:

✦ Connection — Connects your application to a data source

✦ Command — Executes a SQL statement against a data source

✦ DataReader — Reads a forward-only stream of data one row at a time

✦ DataAdapter — Retrieves data for a DataSet and sends updates to the data source

Each .NET Framework Data Provider has its own flavor of the features and services in the preceding list. For example, the `DataAdapter` for the SQL Server data provider is the `SqlDataAdapter`.

Figure 5-2 illustrates the relationship among the data providers' features and services.

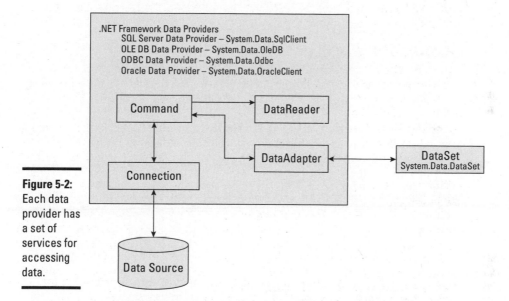

Figure 5-2: Each data provider has a set of services for accessing data.

You access the features and services of the data providers through the provider's namespace. For example, you access the Oracle data provider's `DataReader`, `OracleDataReader`, at `System.Data.OracleClient`. Table 5-1 lists the namespaces for each of the data providers.

The features and services in the preceding list are *objects* of the .NET Framework Data Providers. Before you can use any of these features, you must create a new *instance* of the object you want to use. To read more about creating object instances, see Book V, Chapter 3.

Making Connections

Each of the .NET Framework Data Providers has a connection object for establishing a connection to a data source. The *connection object* is the communication pipeline from the .NET Framework Data Providers and the underlying data source to your application. Table 5-2 lists the connection objects for each data provider.

Table 5-2	.NET Framework Data Provider Connection Objects
Provider	*Connection Object*
SQL Server	SqlConnection OleDbConnection
ODBC	OdbcConnection
Oracle	OracleConnection

Connecting to a database

You use the connection object for your data provider to connect to your data source. As you can imagine, connecting to a data source is a prerequisite for retrieving data from the data source. You use a connection object to

✦ **Pass a connection string to the connection object.** A connection string includes your username and password for accessing the data source. The connection object sends the connection string to the data source for validation.

✦ **Open the connection.** Opening a connection allows you to communicate with the data source.

✦ **Send commands by using the connection.** Send queries to retrieve and update the data source. See the section "Using Commands," later in this chapter.

✦ **Close the connection.** Each connection to the data source consumes resources on the server. Always close the connection as soon as you execute your commands.

ADO.NET uses a feature called *connection pooling* that groups multiple database requests into a single connection. Connections that are exactly the same — same server, same database, same user credentials — are pooled by default with ADO.NET. Pooling connections together so they can be reused reduces the overhead required to open and close connections.

You should leave connection pooling enabled. You can disable connection pooling if you are trying to achieve optimized performance for a specific application by using `pooling='false'` in your connection strings.

You follow the same sequence of events each time you want to access a data source. For example, to use a connection object to access a SQL Server 2005 database, follow these steps:

1. **Pick your .NET Framework Data Provider.**

You should always use the .NET Framework Data Provider for SQL Server to access SQL Server 7.0 databases and later. You access the SQL Server data provider by using the `System.Data.SqlClient` namespace.

2. **Create a new `SqlConnection` connection object.**

To create the new `SqlConnection` object `MyConnection`, type the following lines of code in the Code Editor:

- *VB*

```
Dim MyConnection As New System.Data.SqlClient.SqlConnection
```

- *C#*

```
System.Data.SqlClient.SqlConnection MyConnection =
    new System.Data.SqlClient.SqlConnection();
```

3. **Create a new connection string to connect to a SQL Server 2005 database.**

The connection string to connect to the Adventure Works sample database installed on a local instance of SQL Server 2005 Express Edition using integrated security is

```
Data Source=(local)\sqlexpress;Initial Catalog=
    AdventureWorks;Integrated Security=True
```

Visual Studio provides many tools for building connection strings. See the later section "Stringing up connections" for more information on creating and managing connection strings.

4. **Assign the connection string you create in Step 3 to the `ConnectionString` property of the `MyConnection SqlConnection` object, as shown in the following example:**

- *VB*

```
MyConnection.ConnectionString = ("Data Source=(local)\sqlexpress;
    Initial Catalog=AdventureWorks;Integrated Security=True")
```

- *C#*

```
MyConnection.ConnectionString = "Data Source=(local)\"+"sqlexpress;
    Initial Catalog=AdventureWorks;"+"Integrated Security=True";
```

5. **Call the Open method in `MyConnection` to open the database connection with the following line:**

- *VB*

```
MyConnection.Open()
```

- *C#*

```
MyConnection.Open();
```

The data provider connects to the data source by using the connection string specified in Step 4.

6. **Send commands to the database to retrieve or update data.**

See the upcoming section "Using Commands" to see how to send commands to a data source.

7. **Call the `Close` method in `MyConnection` to close the database con-nection with the following line:**

- *VB*

```
MyConnection.Close()
```

- *C#*

```
MyConnection.Close();
```

Here's the entire code listing for the preceding code example:

VB

```
Dim MyConnection As New System.Data.SqlClient.SqlConnection
MyConnection.ConnectionString = ("Data Source=(local)\
    sqlexpress;Initial Catalog=AdventureWorks;
    Integrated Security=True")
MyConnection.Open()
'send commands
MyConnection.Close()
```

C#

```
        System.Data.SqlClient.SqlConnection MyConnection =
    new System.Data.SqlClient.SqlConnection();
MyConnection.ConnectionString = "Data Source=(local)\"+
        "sqlexpress;Initial Catalog=AdventureWorks;"+
        "Integrated Security=True";
MyConnection.Open();
// Send Commands
MyConnection.Close();
```

To use the connection object for any .NET Framework Data Providers, sub-stitute the name of the provider's connection object listed in Table 5-2 where you see `SqlConnection` in the preceding code example.

For example, to work with an ODBC connection, type this line:

VB

```
Dim MyConnection As New System.Data.Odbc.OdbcConnection
```

C#

```
System.Data.Odbc.OdbcConnection MyConnection =
    new System.Data.Odbc.OdbcConnection();
```

Always use structured exception handling every time you open a connec-tion. (See Book V, Chapter 7.)

Closing your connection

You should always explicitly close your connection to your data source. Closing the connection releases resources.

Opening your connections with a Using block is a good way to remember to always close your connections. A Using *block* consists of starting and ending statements that create and dispose of the resource, respectively. The following code shows a Using block:

VB

```
Using resource as New resourceType
.
.
.
End Using
```

C#

```
using( resource = new resourcetype )
{
}
```

You place, between the Using ... End Using statements, statements that access the resource. A database connection is an example of a resource you can use with a Using block, as shown in the following code sample:

VB

```
Using MySqlConnection As New
    System.Data.SqlClient.SqlConnection()
  MySqlConnection.ConnectionString = ("Data
    Source=(local)\sqlexpress;Initial Catalog=
    AdventureWorks;Integrated Security=True")
  MySqlConnection.Open()
  'send commands
End Using
```

C#

```
using( MySqlConnection = new System.Data.SqlClient.SqlConnection() )
{
    MySqlConnection.ConnectionString =
    "Data Source=(local)\sqlexpress;Initial Catalog="+
        "AdventureWorks;Integrated Security=True";
    MySqlConnection.Open();
    // Send Commands
}
```

There's no need to explicitly call the connection object's `Close` method with the `Using` block. The `End Using` statement automatically closes the connection for you.

Instead of creating a new, identical connection to a data source each time, ADO.NET reuses existing connections, in a process known as *connection pooling*. When you explicitly close your connection, the connection is returned to the connection pool, where it can be reused.

Stringing up connections

Nothing stops you in your tracks faster than an incorrect connection string. Without a valid connection string, your code can't establish a connection to the data source. If you're lucky enough to connect to the same data sources over and over, you have to build a working connection string only once. As long as the data source doesn't change, you can reuse your connection string.

Whether you work with the same data sources day in and day out, or are always using different data sources, Visual Studio and .NET provide many tools to help you build and manage your connection strings. See the next section for more information.

A data provider's connection object uses the connection string to establish a connection to a data source when the connection object's `Open` method is called. A *connection string* is a set of name/value pairs *(keywords)* separated by semicolons, as shown in the following example:

```
Data Source=(local)\sqlexpress;Initial Catalog=
    AdventureWorks;Integrated Security=True
```

The set of keywords used to create a connection string are determined by the data source. Common name/value pairs used to connect to the SQL Server database are described in Table 5-3.

Table 5-3	Common SQL Server Connection-String Keywords	
Keyword	*What It Does*	*Usage*
`Data Source` or `Server`	Serves as name or network address of server	`server=myserver, data source=myserver\server instance, server=(local)`
`Encrypt`	Uses SSL encryption	`encrypt=true`
`Initial Catalog` or `Database`	Sets the name of the database to access	`Initial Catalog= AdventureWorks`

Keyword	What It Does	Usage
Integrated Security	Determines whether to use Windows security	`integrated security=true`
Password or Pwd	Sets the password to use when not using integrated security	`password=mypassword`
User ID	Sets the user ID to use when not using integrated security	`user id=myuserid`

Always use integrated security to access your data sources.

See the topic **Securing connection strings** in the Visual Studio 2008 documentation for more information. See the **Impersonation** topic in the Visual Studio 2008 documentation to read more about using integrated security with ASP.NET.

You set a connection string by using the `ConnectionString` property of the connection object.

ADO.NET uses the `ConnectionString` property to set the connection object's `DataSource` and `DataBase` properties.

Building connection strings

Visual Studio has many ways to help you build connection strings, including

✦ Application settings in Windows applications

✦ ASP.NET configuration settings

✦ The Add Connection dialog box

✦ .NET Framework Data Provider connection string builders

The .NET Framework makes extensive use of configuration setting files, such as application settings in Windows applications and configuration settings in ASP.NET, to store all kinds of information related to your application. Visual Studio provides tools for adding settings, such as connection strings, to .NET configuration files. For example, the ASP.NET Web Site Administration Tool can be used to add several predefined and custom settings to your Web site. See Book III, Chapter 6 for more information on using the Web Site Administration Tool.

Don't store connection strings in your source code. Your connection strings can be extracted from compiled code, in essence enabling anyone to bypass security measures you put into place.

Adding connection strings to Windows projects

Windows projects store application settings, such as connection strings, in an XML configuration file named `app.config`.

To add connection strings to the application settings of a Windows project, follow these steps:

1. **Right-click the My Project folder in an existing Windows project to access the project's properties.**

2. **Click the Settings tab.**

   A grid appears where you enter application settings.

3. **Type MyDbString in the Name cell of the grid.**

4. **Select Connection String as the settings type.**

5. **Click the ellipsis button in the Value cell.**

   The Connection Properties dialog box appears.

6. **Connect to your data source by using the Connection Properties dialog box.**

   The dialog box returns a connection string to the Value cell from the Connection Properties dialog box, as shown in Figure 5-3.

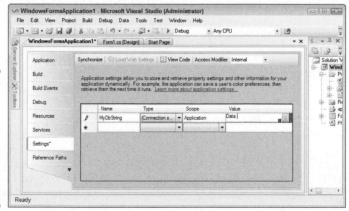

Figure 5-3: Use the Connection Properties dialog box to build your connection string.

See the section in Chapter 2 of this mini-book about connecting to databases for more information on creating a connection string.

7. **Save the settings.**

   Visual Studio creates a new `app.config` file with your connection string.

You access the connection string by using the `My.Settings` expression when writing code in VB. (Use `Properties.Settings` when writing code in C#.) See the upcoming section "Using Commands" to see an example of accessing a connection string from application settings.

Adding connection strings to Web projects

Web projects use the `web.config` file to store configuration settings, such as connection strings. The easiest way to add new connection strings to the `web.config` file is with the Data Source Configuration Wizard. (Chapter 1 of this mini-book walks you through using the wizard in the section about adding data to Web Forms).

You can use the Data Source Configuration Wizard to configure many different kinds of data sources. Configuring a database with the wizard prompts you to select an existing data connection or configure a new connection. After creating the configuration string, the wizard saves the connection string in the `web.config` file, as shown in Figure 5-4.

Figure 5-4:
Use the Data Source Configuration Wizard to save connection strings in the file.

The wizard writes the connection string to the `web.config` file. Alternatively, you can add the connection string manually to the `web.config` file. For example, a connection string for the Adventure Works database might look like this:

```
<connectionStrings>
   <add name="AdventureWorksConnectionString" connectionString=
   "Data Source=(local)\sqlexpress;Initial Catalog=
   AdventureWorks;Integrated Security=True"
          providerName="System.Data.SqlClient" />
</connectionStrings>
```

Add your connection string between the `<connectionStrings>` `</connectionStrings>` tags.

Building connection strings manually

A common theme in building connection strings is the use of the Add Connection dialog box. It's used in both the application settings for Windows and the configuration settings for Web applications.

You access the Add Connection dialog box by choosing Tools⇨Connect to Database. The Add Connection dialog box creates a new connection in Server Explorer. Use Server Explorer to manage your connections to servers in your project.

You can grab the connection string from Server Explorer and reuse it elsewhere, in either code or a configuration-settings file. To copy a connection string from a data connection in Server Explorer, follow these steps:

1. **Create a new data connection by choosing Tools⇨Connect to Database.**

   The Add Connection dialog box appears.

2. **Use the Add Connection dialog box to create a connection string.**

   A new data connection appears in Server Explorer, as shown in Figure 5-5.

3. **Right-click the data connection in Server Explorer.**

   You can open Server Explorer by choosing View⇨Server Explorer. The keyboard shortcut for Server Explorer is Ctrl+Alt+S.

4. **Choose Properties from the shortcut menu.**

   The Properties window appears.

5. **Highlight the `ConnectionString` property.**

6. **Copy and paste the property.**

Figure 5-5: Copy and paste the property from Server Explorer.

Using the ADO.NET connection string builders

Each of the .NET Framework Data Providers includes a service for building and managing connection strings. The connection string builders provide the properties needed to build a connection string. The builder outputs a properly formatted connection string that you pass to the data provider's connection object. Table 5-4 lists the connection string builders for each data provider.

Table 5-4	Connection String Builders
Data Provider	*Object*
SQL Server	SqlConnectionStringBuilder
OLE DB	OleDbConnectionStringBuilder
ODBC	OdbcConnectionStringBuilder
Oracle	OracleConnectionStringBuilder

The following code uses the SQL Server data provider's connection string builder, SqlConnectionStringBuilder, to build a connection string for the Adventure Works sample database:

VB

```
Dim builder As New System.Data.SqlClient.SqlConnectionStringBuilder
builder.DataSource = "(local)\sqlexpress"
builder.InitialCatalog = "AdventureWorks"
builder.IntegratedSecurity = True
```

C#

```
System.Data.SqlClient.SqlConnectionStringBuilder builder =
    new System.Data.SqlClient.SqlConnectionStringBuilder();
builder.DataSource = "(local)\sqlexpress";
builder.InitialCatalog = "AdventureWorks";
  builder.IntegratedSecurity = True;
```

You pass the connection string from SqlConnectionStringBuilder to the connection object's ConnectionString property like this:

VB

```
Dim MyConnection As New System.Data.SqlClient.SqlConnection
MyConnection.ConnectionString = builder.ConnectionString
```

C#

```
System.Data.SqlClient.SqlConnection MyConnection =
    new System.Data.SqlClient.SqlConnection();
MyConnection.ConnectionString - builder.ConnectionString;
```

Using Commands

You use a .NET Framework Data Provider's `Command` object to execute queries after connecting to a data source. Each of the data providers has a `Command` object. To use a `Command` object, follow these steps:

1. **Associate the `Command` object with a connection object. Use the `Connection` property to make the association, like this:**

- *VB*

```
MySqlCommand.Connection = MySqlConnection
```

- *C#*

```
MySqlCommand.Connection = MySqlConnection;
```

The `Connection` object is the communication pipeline between the command and the data source.

2. **Specify a SQL statement. Use the `Command` object `CommandText` property to set the SQL statement.**

For example, to set the SQL statement for an ODBC data provider `Command` object, type

- *VB*

```
MyOdbcCommand.CommandText = "SELECT * FROM CUSTOMER"
```

- *C#*

```
MyOdbcCommand.CommandText = "SELECT * FROM CUSTOMER";
```

3. **Call one of the `Command` object's `Execute` methods.**

The `Execute` method runs the SQL statement specified in the `Command` object `CommandText` property. The `Command` object has three `Execute` methods:

- `ExecuteReader` — Returns a `DataReader` object. Use `ExecuteReader` any time you want fast access to a forward-only stream of data.

- `ExecuteScalar` — Returns a single value. Use `ExecuteScalar` when you know that your query will return only one value, such as a `SELECT Count(*)` query.

- `ExecuteNonQuery` — Doesn't return any rows. Use `ExecuteNonQuery` any time you need to execute a query, such as a `CreateTable` statement, that doesn't return any rows.

You must call the `Open` method of the data provider's connection object before you call the `Command` object `Execute` method.

Most data-centric applications make extensive use of stored procedures for data access. To use a stored procedure with a Command object, you must

✦ Set the Command object CommandType property to StoredProcedure.

✦ Use the Command object Parameters collection to define the stored procedure's input and output parameters.

To use the following stored procedure to access a SQL Server database by using the SQL Server data provider, follow these steps:

1. **Create the SqlConnection object and set the object's ConnectionString property, as shown in the following example:**

   • *VB*

   ```
   Dim MySqlConnection As New System.Data.SqlClient.SqlConnection
   MySqlConnection.ConnectionString = My.Settings.MyDbString
   ```

   • *C#*

   ```
   System.Data.SqlClient.SqlConnection MySqlConnection =
        new System.Data.SqlClient.SqlConnection();
   MySqlConnection.ConnectionString =
        Properties.Settings.MyDbString;
   ```

   The ConnectionString property accesses the MyDbString connection string from the project's app.config file. See the earlier section "Adding connection strings to Windows projects" for more information about the app.config file.

2. **Create the SqlCommand object by entering the following lines:**

   • *VB*

   ```
   Dim MySqlCommand As New System.Data.SqlClient.SqlCommand
   ```

   • *C#*

   ```
   System.Data.SqlClient.SqlCommand MySqlCommand =
        new System.Data.SqlClient.SqlCommand();
   ```

3. **To set the SqlCommand object Connection property, enter this line:**

   • *VB*

   ```
   MySqlCommand.Connection = MySqlConnection
   ```

   • *C#*

   ```
   MySqlCommand.Connection = MySqlConnection;
   ```

4. Set the `CommandText` property of the `SqlCommand` object to the name of the stored procedure you wish to execute, as the following lines show:

- *VB*

```
MySqlCommand.CommandText = "uspGetEmployeeManagers"
```

- *C#*

```
MySqlCommand.CommandText = "uspGetEmployeeManagers";
```

5. Set the `CommandType` property to `StoredProcedure` by entering the following line:

- *VB*

```
MySqlCommand.CommandType = CommandType.StoredProcedure
```

- *C#*

```
MySqlCommand.CommandType = CommandType.StoredProcedure;
```

6. Create a new `SqlParameter` object, like this:

- *VB*

```
Dim MyParameter As New System.Data.SqlClient.SqlParameter
```

- *C#*

```
System.Data.SqlClient.SqlParameter My Parameter =
    new System.Data.SqlClient.SqlParameter();
```

7. To set the `ParameterName` and `Value` properties for the `SqlParameter`, assign values to the properties as shown below:

- *VB*

```
MyParameter.ParameterName = "@EmployeeID"
MyParameter.Value = "6"
```

- *C#*

```
MyParameter.ParameterName = "@EmployeeID";
MyParameter.Value = "6";
```

8. Add the `SqlParameter` object to the `SqlCommand Parameters` collection, like this:

- *VB*

```
MySqlCommand.Parameters.Add(MyParameter)
```

- *C#*

```
MySqlCommand.Parameters.Add(MyParameter);
```

9. **Call the Open method of the SqlConnection object:**

   - *VB*

     ```
     MySqlConnection.Open()
     ```

   - *C#*

     ```
     MySqlConnection.Open();
     ```

10. **Call the Command object's Execute method with the following statement:**

    - *VB*

      ```
      MySqlDataReader = MySqlCommand.ExecuteReader()
      ```

    - *C#*

      ```
      MySqlDataReader = MySqlCommand.ExecuteReader();
      ```

    The Execute method passes the stored procedure from the Command object to the database by using the connection object.

The Command object has a CommandBuilder you can use to automatically generate Command objects for single-table data access. See the topic **CommandBuilder object** in the Visual Studio 2008 documentation.

Reading Data with DataReaders

ADO.NET DataReaders are old-school data-access services. You use a DataReader any time you need fast, forward-only access to your data. Unlike a DataSet, which retrieves your data into an in-memory database model, there's no storage mechanism with a DataReader. When you retrieve data by using a DataReader, you had better have your "catcher's mitt" open to store the data.

A DataReader is often called a *firehose cursor.*

Each of the .NET Framework Data Providers provides a DataReader. Table 5-5 lists the DataReader objects for each provider.

Table 5-5	DataReader Objects
Provider	*DataReader Object*
SQL Server	SqlDataReader
OLE DB	OleDbDataReader
ODBC	OdbcDataReader
Oracle	OracleDataReader

You use the ExecuteReader method of the Command object to retrieve data for a DataReader.

Using a DataReader to retrieve data from a data source involves these steps:

1. **Call the Command object's ExecuteReader method.**

   ExecuteReader builds the DataReader.

2. **Call the DataReader Read method to advance to the next record.**

   The first time you call Read, the next record is the first record because the DataReader is positioned in front of the first record.

3. **Use the DataReader Get accessors to retrieve data from the row of data.**

   The DataReader retrieves one row at a time.

   See the section "Retrieving data with the Get accessors," later in this chapter, to see the DataReader Get accessors in action.

4. **Advance to the next record by using the Read method.**

   Because the DataReader retrieves one row at a time from the data source, use common practice to execute the Read method by using a loop.

   See the following section to see the DataReader used with a while loop.

Even though you need only two methods to use the DataReader — ExecuteReader and Read — a lot of setup work is involved. The following steps walk you through using a DataReader to retrieve records:

1. **Select a .NET Framework Data Provider, as described in the section "Picking a Provider," earlier in this chapter.**

2. **Create a new connection object for the data provider, as described in the earlier section "Making Connections."**

3. **Declare a new variable of the DataReader object type for your data provider.**

   For example, to declare a new DataReader variable for the ODBC data provider, you would type the following:

   • *VB*

   ```
   Dim odbcReader As System.Data.Odbc.OdbcDataReader
   ```

- *C#*

```
System.Data.Odbc.OdbcDataReader odbcReader =

    new System.Data.Odbc.OdbcDataReader();
```

Notice that you aren't using the New keyword to create a new instance of the DataReader object. There are no constructors for DataReaders. Calling the Command object ExecuteReader method builds the DataReader.

4. **Create a new Command object for your data provider to retrieve data for the object, as described in the preceding section.**

5. **Call the Open method of the connection object to establish a connection to the data source.**

6. **Call the ExecuteReader method of the Command object you create in Step 4 and pass the results to the DataReader object you create in Step 2.**

   For example, to call the ExecuteReader method on an OdbcCommand object and pass the results to an OdbcDataReader object you create in Step 3, type the following:

   - *VB*

   ```
   odbcReader = odbcCommand.ExecuteReader()
   ```

   - *C#*

   ```
   odbcReader = odbcCommand.ExecuteReader();
   ```

   The OdbcCommand object executes the query against the OdbcConnection object when ExecuteReader is called and builds the OdbcDataReader object.

7. **Call the Read method of the DataReader object to retrieve one record from the data source. For example, to call the Read method for the OdbcDataReader you create in Step 3, type the following:**

   - *VB*

   ```
   odbcReader.Read()
   ```

   - *C#*

   ```
   odbcReader.Read();
   ```

   The OdbcDataReader object advances to the next record.

   The default position of the DataReader is before the first row in the result set. The Reader method advances the DataReader to the next record.

8. Retrieve values from the DataReader.

See the section "Retrieving data with the Get accessors," later in this chapter, for more information about using the DataReader Get accessors to retrieve data.

9. Close your connection object, as described in the section "Closing your connection," earlier in this chapter.

Close the Connection object by calling the Close method of the connection object or using a Using block.

Here's the entire code listing:

VB

```
Dim odbcConnection As New System.Data.Odbc.OdbcConnection
Dim odbcReader As System.Data.Odbc.OdbcDataReader
Dim odbcCommand As New System.Data.Odbc.OdbcCommand
odbcConnection.ConnectionString = My.Settings.MyOdbcConnectionString
odbcCommand.Connection = odbcConnection
odbcCommand.CommandText = "SELECT * FROM CUSTOMER"
odbcConnection.Open()
odbcReader = odbcCommand.ExecuteReader()
odbcReader.Read()
'do something here with the data in the row
odbcConnection.Close()
```

C#

```
System.Data.Odbc.OdbcConnection odbcConnection =
     new System.Data.Odbc.OdbcConnection();
System.Data.Odbc.OdbcDataReader odbcReader =
     new System.Data.Odbc.OdbcDataReader();
System.Data.Odbc.OdbcCommand idbcCommand =
     new System.Data.Odbc.OdbcCommand();
odbcConnection.ConnectionString =
     Properites.Settings.MyOdbcConnectionString;
odbcCommand.Connection = odbcConnection;
odbcCommand.CommandText = "SELECT * FROM CUSTOMER";
odbcConnection.Open();
odbcReader = odbcCommand.ExecuteReader();
odbcReader.Read();
//do something here with the data in the row
odbcConnection.Close();
```

Stepping through data

The DataReader Read method advances the DataReader to the next row in the result set. As long as more rows are present, the Read method returns the value True. The Read method is typically used to test the Read method's return value in a while loop.

A while loop loops through a set of statements as long as a test condition remains True. You can use a while loop to iterate through each row in a DataReader's result set and perform the same action on each row. For example, to use a while loop to step through a SqlDataReader object named MySqlDataReader, type the following lines:

VB

```
While (MySqlDataReader.Read() = True)
   Me.lstDepartments.Items.Add(MySqlDataReader("Name"))
End While
```

C#

```
while( MySqlDataReader.Read() )
{
    lstDepartments.Items.Add(
       Convert.ToString(MySqlDataReader["Name"]));
}
```

The preceding example gets the value in column Name of the MySqlDataReader result set and adds the value to the items collection of a lstDepartments list box. The while loop performs the statement inside the loop as long as the Read method returns True. You end up with a list box full of items from the SqlDataReader. See the next section, about how to get data from a row.

Use the HasRows property of the DataReader to test whether the DataReader has more rows. The HasRows property returns the value True if more rows are present.

Retrieving data with the Get accessors

The DataReader object provides access to a forward-only result set which presents one row at a time. When you're deciding how to work with the data in a row, you have to consider whether you want to work with the data

✦ In its native format or by using a typed accessor

✦ In a single column in the row or all the columns in the row

DataReader provides several Get accessors for retrieving data. You should retrieve the data by using a typed accessor, such as GetDateTime.

The data types used in the underlying data source aren't the same as the data types used in the .NET Framework. The typed accessors convert the value from its native database type to a .NET Framework type.

DataReader provides several options for retrieving data by using typed accessors. Each DataReader provides a set of common typed Get accessors, such as

✦ GetChar — Retrieves data as a char data type

✦ GetDateTime — Retrieves data as a DateTime data type

✦ GetInt16 — Retrieves data as an Int16 data type

✦ GetString — Retrieves data as a string data type

SqlDataReader provides special types that work exclusively with SQL Server database types. Examples include

✦ GetSqlChars

✦ GetSqlDateTime

✦ GetSqlInt16

✦ GetSqlString

Use GetSql typed accessors when you're using the SqlDataReader. GetSql typed accessors are more precise than the .NET data types.

If you're unsure of the column's native data type, query the data source. DataReaders provide the GetFieldType and GetDataTypeName methods you can use.

Of course, you can also retrieve data in its native format. DataReader provides several methods, such as

✦ GetValue and GetValues

✦ Item

When you access the data in its native format, you must ensure that the data is converted to the appropriate .NET Framework data type. For example, the following statement retrieves a column by using the Item method and uses the ToString method to convert it to a string:

VB

```
myString = MySqlDataReader.Item("Name").ToString()
```

C#

```
myString = MySqlDataReader.Item["Name"].ToString();
```

To read more about converting data types, see Book V, Chapter 2. Additionally, see the topic **mapping data types** in the Visual Studio 2008 help documentation to see how native data types are mapped to .NET Framework data types.

Most `Get` accessors use a zero-based column index to retrieve a column. A zero-based index starts counting elements at zero instead of at one. For example, in a table with the columns CustID, FirstName, and LastName, the FirstName column might have the column index of one. To access the FirstName column by using the `GetSqlString` accessor, you type the following line:

VB

```
MySqlDataReader.GetSqlString(1)
```

C#

```
MySqlDataReader.GetSqlString(1);
```

Using column indexes to retrieve values may be fast for the `DataReader`, but it's slow and confusing to a programmer. Fortunately, `DataReaders` have two methods for accessing columns by name:

✦ `Item` — Returns the column's value in its native format

✦ `GetOrdinal` — Returns the index number of the column

Each of these approaches has its drawbacks. If you use the `Item` method, you must explicitly convert the column to a .NET data type. Using `GetOrdinal` hits the data source twice — once to get the ordinal and again to retrieve the data by using the ordinal.

Here's an example of using `GetOrdinal` to access data:

VB

```
Dim nameCol, groupNameCol As Integer
nameCol = MySqlDataReader.GetOrdinal("Name")
groupNameCol = MySqlDataReader.GetOrdinal("GroupName")
While (MySqlDataReader.Read() = True)
  myString = String.Format("{0} {1}",
    MySqlDataReader.GetString(nameCol),
    MySqlDataReader.GetString(groupNameCol))
  Me.lstDepartments.Items.Add(myString)
End While
```

**Book IV
Chapter 5**

**Under the Hood
with ADO.NET**

C#

```
int nameCol, groupNameCol;
nameCol = MySqlDataReader.GetOrdinal("Name");
groupNameCol = MySqlDataReader.GetOrdinal("GroupName");
while( MySqlDataReader.Read())
{
  myString = String.Format("{0} {1}",
    MySqlDataReader.GetString(nameCol),
    MySqlDataReader.GetString(groupNameCol));
  lstDepartments.Items.Add(myString)
}
```

Use the `GetValues` method to retrieve all the columns in a row at one time. The `GetValues` method requires you to pass in an array that the method fills with the columns from the row.

Here's an example of using the `GetValues` method:

VB

```
Dim MyArray(MySqlDataReader.FieldCount - 1) As Object
MySqlDataReader.GetValues(MyArray)
```

C#

```
Object[] MyArray = new Object[MySqlDataReader.FieldCount-1];
MySqlDataReader.GetValues(MyArray);
```

In the first line of this example, you use the `DataReader FieldCount` property to set the size of the array. In the second line, you pass the array to the `GetValues` method. The array is filled with the values for the entire row.

The `GetValues` method retrieves values in their native data formats. The values must be converted to .NET data types.

With the values in the array, you can access them by using the properties and methods of arrays. To read more about using arrays, see Book V, Chapter 2.

The `GetValues` method, which is a fast way to grab an entire row, is typically used by `GetValues` to pass the array to the `ItemArray` method of the `DataRow` object.

`DataRows` are rows in a `DataTable`. You specify ahead of time which columns and data types exist in the `DataTable`. When you add a new row by using `ItemArray`, the data is plugged into the columns and converted to the column's data type. The following code fills an array and passes the array to a new `DataRow` in the `myTable DataTable`:

VB

```
MySqlDataReader.GetValues(array)
row = myTable.NewRow()
row.ItemArray = array
```

C#

```
MySqlDataReader.GetValues(array);
row = myTable.NewRow();
  row.ItemArray = array;
```

The values in the array are converted to the appropriate data type for each column in the DataRow.

Retrieving schema info

The DataReader includes a GetSchemaTable method that you can use to retrieve the schema information about the result set. The GetSchemaTable method returns a DataTable, as shown in the following code:

VB

```
Dim table As New DataTable
table = MySqlDataReader.GetSchemaTable()
```

C#

```
DataTable table = new DataTable():
  table = MySqlDataReader.GetSchemaTable();
```

You can use the DataRow's ItemArray method, as described in the preceding section, to add new rows to a table built with GetSchemaTable.

Caching Data with DataSets

DataSets are an important element in data access. ADO.NET provides the DataSet as a built-in memory cache for storing data retrieved from a data source. See the section about understanding DataSets in Chapter 3 of this mini-book.

The workhorse behind the DataSet is the DataAdapter. It provides the following services to the DataSet:

✦ Populates the DataSet with data from a data source by using the Fill method

✦ Updates a data source with changes made in the DataSet by using the Update method

Each of the .NET Framework Data Providers has a DataAdapter object. Table 5-6 lists the DataAdapter object for each data provider.

Table 5-6	DataAdapter Objects
Data Provider	*DataAdapter Object*
SQL Server	SqlDataAdapter
Ole DB	OleDbDataAdapter
ODBC	OdbcDataAdapter
Oracle	OracleDataAdapter

The DataAdapter object uses a set of Command objects to send SQL statements to a data source. The DataAdapter object exposes the Command objects by using the following set of properties:

+ SelectCommand

  You must specify a SelectCommand before you can call the DataAdapter Fill method.

+ InsertCommand

+ UpdateCommand

+ DeleteCommand

See the earlier section "Using Commands" to read more about the properties of Command objects.

Filling a DataSet

A DataAdapter acts as a bridge between the DataSet and the data source. Filling a DataSet involves these tasks:

+ Create a DataAdapter and a DataSet.
+ Create a Command object that holds the SELECT statement or stored procedure to retrieve data from the data source.
+ Set the DataAdapter SelectCommand property to the Command object.
+ Call the DataAdapter Fill method and pass in the DataSet.

As is the case with all the data access features of ADO.NET, filling a DataSet isn't as simple as creating a few objects and then calling the Fill method. You have to complete a number of prerequisite steps, such as creating a connection object.

The following example walks you through using a DataAdapter to fill a DataSet:

1. **Pick the .NET Framework Data Provider best suited for your data source, as described in the earlier section "Picking a Provider."**

   This example uses the SQL Server data provider to fill a DataSet by using data from the Adventure Works sample database in SQL Server 2005.

2. **Create a new connection and connection string, as described earlier in this chapter, in the section "Making Connections." Enter the following lines of code:**

   - *VB*

   ```
   Dim MySqlConnection As New System.Data.SqlClient.SqlConnection
   MySqlConnection.ConnectionString = My.Settings.MyDbString
   ```

   - *C#*

   ```
   System.Data.SqlClient.SqlConnection MySqlConnection =
       new System.Data.SqlClient.SqlConnection();
     MySqlConnection.ConnectionString =
   Properties.Settings.MyDbString;
   ```

3. **Create a new DataAdapter and DataSet, as shown in the following example:**

   - *VB*

   ```
   Dim MySqlDataAdapter As New System.Data.SqlClient.SqlDataAdapter()
   Dim MyDataSet As New System.Data.DataSet
   ```

   - *C#*

   ```
   System.Data.SqlClient.SqlDataAdapter MySqlDataAdapter =
       new System.Data.SqlClient.SqlDataAdapter();
   System.Data.DataSet MyDataSet =
       new System.Data.DataSet();
   ```

4. **Create a new Command object, associate the Command object with your connection object, and set the CommandText property, as described in the earlier section "Using Commands."**

   For example, the following code sample creates a new SqlCommand object, associates the object with a SqlConnection object, and sets the SqlCommand object to a SQL statement:

   - *VB*

   ```
   Dim MySelectCommand As New System.Data.SqlClient.SqlCommand
   MySelectCommand.Connection = MySqlConnection
   MySelectCommand.CommandText = "SELECT * FROM HumanResources.Department"
   ```

- *C#*

```
System.Data.SqlClient.SqlCommand MySelectCommand =
    new System.Data.SqlClient.SqlCommand();
MySelectCommand.Connection = MySqlConnection;
    MySelectCommand.CommandText =
        "SELECT * FROM HumanResources.Department";
```

5. **Set the DataAdapter's SelectCommand property to the Command object you create in Step 4, as shown in the following:**

   - *VB*

   ```
   MySqlDataAdapter.SelectCommand = MySelectCommand
   ```

   - *C#*

   ```
   MySqlDataAdapter.SelectCommand = MySelectCommand;
   ```

6. **Call the DataAdapter Fill method and pass in the DataSet as a parameter:**

   - *VB*

   ```
   MySqlDataAdapter.Fill(MyDataSet)
   ```

   - *C#*

   ```
   MySqlDataAdapter.Fill(MyDataSet);
   ```

Behind the scenes, the Fill method does the following:

✦ Retrieves data from the data source by passing the SQL statement specified in the SelectCommand to a DataReader.

✦ Creates a DataTable by using the column information from the data source and adds the rows to the DataTable.

✦ Adds the DataTable to the specified DataSet.

Figure 5-6 shows the relationship among the objects of the SQL Server data provider used in the preceding example. The relationships are similar for other .NET Framework data providers.

Updating data with the Update method

You call the DataAdapter Update method to send data updates from the DataSet to the data source. The Update method uses InsertCommand, UpdateCommand, and DeleteCommand to update the data source.

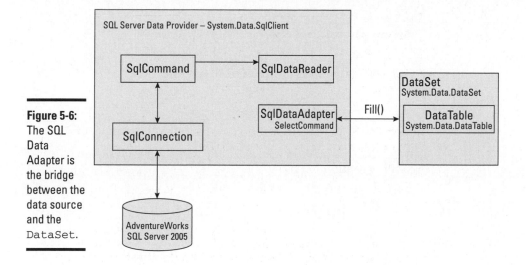

Figure 5-6:
The SQL
Data
Adapter is
the bridge
between the
data source
and the
`DataSet`.

The `Update` method requires you to pass in a `DataSet`, a `DataTable`, or an array of `DataRows`, as shown in the following example:

VB

```
MySqlDataAdapter.Update(MyDataSet)
```

C#

```
MySqlDataAdapter.Update(MyDataSet);
```

The `DataAdapter` uses the `Command` objects specified in its properties to execute SQL statements against the data source.

Each of the .NET Framework Data Providers has a `CommandBuilder` object that you can use to automatically generate commands against a single-table data source. `CommandBuilder` automatically builds the commands for a `DataAdapter` to use.

To use `SqlCommandBuilder` with the example from the preceding section, follow these steps:

1. **Create a new `SqlCommandBuilder` object after Step 5 in the preceding section.**

- *VB*

```
Dim builder As New System.Data.SqlClient.SqlCommandBuilder()
```

- *C#*

```
System.Data.SqlClient.SqlCommandBuilder builder =
    new System.Data.SqlClient.SqlCommandBuilder();
```

2. **Set the `SqlCommandBuilder` `DataAdapter` property:**

```
builder.DataAdapter = MySqlDataAdapter
```

The `SqlCommandBuilder` uses the `DataAdapter` `SelectCommand` property to build the `Insert`, `Update`, and `Delete` commands.

3. **Call the `Update` method instead of the `Fill` method in Step 6 in the preceding section.**

Using TableAdapters

`TableAdapter`, a new data access feature in ADO.NET, encapsulates all the retrieve and update commands and a connection object for a single table. Visual Studio provides extensive support for creating `TableAdapters` by using the TableAdapter Configuration Wizard in DataSet Designer.

You can call the commands of a generated `TableAdapter` by using the standard "dot" notation of IntelliSense in the Code Editor. To access the properties and methods of a generated `TableAdapter`, follow these steps:

1. **Use DataSet Designer to create a new `DataSet` with the Department table from the Adventure Works database.**

   See the section about exploring DataSet Designer in Chapter 3 of this mini-book for more information on creating `DataSets`.

2. **Open a Windows Form, and then drag and drop the Department table from the Data Sources window.**

   A `DepartmentTableAdapter` is created.

3. **Double-click the form to access the form's `Load` event.**

   The Code Editor appears.

4. **Type the following code in the Code Editor:**

   - *VB*

   ```
   Me.DepartmentTableAdapter.
   ```

   - *C#*

   ```
   DepartmentTableAdapter.
   ```

   The Code Editor displays a list of properties and methods available for `DepartmentTableAdapter`, as shown in Figure 5-7.

Figure 5-7:
Use
IntelliSense
to access
the methods
and
properties
of Table
Adapters
generated
by the
designers in
Visual
Studio.

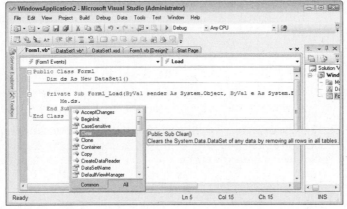

5. **Select a property or method from the list.**

Use the TableAdapter Configuration Wizard to generate TableAdapters.

Using transactions

SQL statements are executed by databases in transactions. A *transaction* is a group of statements executed against a database. You use statements such as BEGIN TRANSACTION and COMMIT WORK to mark the start and end of a transaction. Between the start and end are SQL statements that retrieve and modify data. The ROLLBACK WORK statement rolls back, or undoes, the statements executed in the transaction.

The .NET Framework provides a new model for transaction processing with the System.Transactions namespace. You use it to create two kinds of database transactions:

✦ **Implicit transactions** — Use the TransactionScope object to encapsulate a block of ADO.NET code in a transaction, as shown in this code:

- *VB*

```
Using scope As New System.Transactions.TransactionScope()

    .

    .

    .

End Using
```

**Book IV
Chapter 5**

**Under the Hood
with ADO.NET**

- *C#*

```
using(scope = new System.Transactions.TransactionScope())
{
.
.
.
}
```

✦ **Explicit transaction** — Create a `CommittableTransaction` object where you specifically call the object's `Commit` and `Rollback` methods. The following code creates a new `CommittableTransaction` object:

- *VB*

```
Dim tx As New System.Transactions.CommittableTransaction
```

- *C#*

```
System.Transactions.CommittableTransaction txt =
    new System.Transactions.CommittableTransaction();
```

You must add a reference to `System.Transactions` before you can access the objects in the namespace.

The `System.Transactions` namespace is the model for all kinds of transactions in .NET, not just database transactions. (See the Visual Studio 2008 documentation.)

Supporting XML with ADO.NET

ADO.NET provides extensive support for XML. You can use ADO.NET to do the following:

✦ **Fill a `DataSet` by using an XML document.**

Call the `DataSet ReadXml` method to populate a `DataSet` with an XML document.

✦ **Create or infer a `DataSet` schema from an XML Schema definition.**

Call a `DataSet ReadXmlSchema` or `InferXmlSchema` methods to create the `DataSet` schema.

✦ **Create an XML document or XML Schema from a `DataSet`.**

Call the `DataSet GetXml` method to write the `DataSet` content as an XML document. Call `GetXmlSchema` to write an XML Schema file from the `DataSet` schema.

✦ **Synchronize a `DataSet` contents with an XML document.**

Use the `XmlDataDocument` object to create an XML document with the data from a `DataSet`.

The following sample code creates a `DataSet` and populates it with data from an XML document with the name `recipe.xml`:

VB

```
Dim ds As New System.Data.DataSet
ds.ReadXml("recipe.xml", XmlReadMode.InferSchema)
```

C#

```
System.Data.DataSet ds = new System.Data.DataSet();
  ds.ReadXml("recipe.xml", XmlReadMode.InferSchema);
```

Using the `DataSet` from the preceding code example, write an XML Schema to the `recipe.xsd` file with this code:

VB

```
ds.WriteXmlSchema("recipe.xsd")
```

C#

```
ds.WriteXmlSchema("recipe.xsd");
```

You can combine the extensive ADO.NET support for XML with SQL Server 2005 support for XML. Using SQL Server 2005, you can

✦ Use the `xml` data type to store entire XML documents or fragments.

✦ Associate XML Schemas with `xml` data types to create typed XML.

✦ Retrieve data stored in relational tables as XML markup using the FOR XML clause.

✦ Retrieve XML data as relational data by using the OPENXML function.

The Adventure Works sample database provides several examples of using the `xml` data type. To read more about using XML with SQL Server 2005, see the topic **Using XML in SQL Server** in the SQL Server 2005 Books Online documentation.

Using ADO.NET in Your Applications

Using the features described in this chapter, you can use ADO.NET to access data seven ways from Sunday. Couple these features with all the designers in

Visual Studio, and you have even more choices. Here are some recommendations for accessing data with ADO.NET:

✦ **Populate custom data entities with `DataReaders`.**

Many developers create their own custom data types for storing the data entities their application uses. For example, you can create a `Customer` data type and a `CustomerAddress` data type. Use a `DataReader` to populate your `Customer` and `CustomerAddress` data types. You can use this approach to separate the application from its underlying data source. (See Book V, Chapter 2.)

✦ **Use typed `DataSets` for prototyping or in conjunction with other data storage.**

Although typed `DataSets` are very fast to build, they perform slower than custom data entities in your application. They can be especially slow in Web applications. You don't have to use a typed `DataSet` for all your data access — you can use a combination of approaches. Typed `DataSets` are a good way to quickly build prototype applications.

✦ **Create data access class libraries.**

Whatever approach you use, usually you should encapsulate your data access methods in a separate class file or class library. You create public methods or properties that return `DataSets`, `DataTables`, hashtables, arrays, or custom data entities that your data controls consume. See Book V, Chapter 2 for more information on hashtables and arrays.

For example, here's a method signature that returns a `DataTable` from the class `DataAccess`:

• *VB*

```
Public Function GetDepartments() As System.Data.DataTable
```

• *C#*

```
public System.Data.DataTable GetDepartments()

{

}
```

The `GetDepartments` method encapsulates all the data access code populating the `DataTable`.

To use the `DataTable` as a data source for a `BindingSource` component, enter these lines:

• *VB*

```
Dim data As New DataAccess

Me.MyBindingSource.DataSource = data.GetDepartments
```

- *C#*

```
DataAccess data = new DataAccess();

MyBindingSource.DataSource = data.GetDepartments();
```

Use the `BindingSource` component as the data source for a databound control.

✦ **Evaluate whether to use stored procedures or ad hoc SQL queries.**

People are on both sides of the camp on this issue. Ad hoc queries don't automatically make the sky fall.

✦ **Extend generated typed `DataSets`.**

Use partial classes to add features to typed `DataSets`. For example, you may decide to use a `DataReader` to populate a simple lookup table.

✦ **Create your own helper classes.**

A great deal of repetition occurs in building data access code. You can create your own helper classes, though, to cut down on all the repetition.

✦ **Use the Enterprise Library.**

Another way to deal with all the repetition involved in coding data access is to use the Enterprise Library. It has all the best practices of using ADO.NET baked right in.

Chapter 6: Using Visual Studio with SQL Server

In This Chapter

✔ Installing SQL Server 2005 Developer Edition

✔ Configuring the Adventure Works sample database

✔ Creating scripts in database projects

✔ Creating stored procedures in SQL Server projects

✔ Using Visual Database Tools

M̲ost useful programs require some kind of data storage. Often, that's a database program like Microsoft SQL Server. While SQL Server 2008 is the latest release of the popular database program, SQL Server 2005 is what ships with Visual Studio 2008. This will probably change in future releases of Visual Studio 2008. SQL Server 2005 works better than ever with Visual Studio 2008.

This chapter shows you how to install SQL Server 2005 and how to use Visual Studio to create and manage database objects.

Getting Acquainted with SQL Server 2005

SQL Server 2008 is the latest version of the popular Microsoft database management system, but this chapter covers SQL Server 2005 because it ships with Visual Studio 2008. Each edition of Visual Studio includes a license for one of the editions of SQL Server 2005. Table 6-1 lists the editions of SQL Server and describes how to get the program.

Table 6-1	SQL Server Editions	
SQL Server Version	*When to Use It*	*How to Get It*
Enterprise Edition	In large companies	Purchase separately; retail price $24,999
Standard Edition	In small- and medium-size businesses	Purchase separately; retail price $5,999

(continued)

Table 6-1 *(continued)*

SQL Server Version	When to Use It	How to Get It
Workgroup Edition	In departments or branch offices	Purchase separately; retail price $3,899
Express Edition	For prototypes or local development	Free download from Microsoft Web site; included with all Visual Studio Express Editions and Visual Studio Standard Editions
Developer Edition	For prototypes or local development	Included with Professional, Tools for Office, and Team Editions of Visual Studio
Mobile Edition	In a database for mobile devices	Free download from Microsoft Web site

Get more information about each of the SQL Server 2005 editions, including pricing and product comparisons, on Microsoft's SQL Server portal at

`www.microsoft.com/sql/prodinfo/default.mspx`

You can download SQL Server Express Edition and Mobile Edition from the portal. The URL can be found at `http://www.microsoft.com/downloads/details.aspx?FamilyID=220549b5-0b07-4448-8848-dcc397514b41`.

Most developers use one of these two editions of SQL Server:

✦ **Express Edition** is free to use and redistribute. Express Edition replaces Microsoft SQL Server 2000 Desktop Engine (MSDE), the lightweight SQL Server 2000 database. You can include a local copy of a database in your application and freely distribute Express Edition with your application. You can easily use Express Edition as the database for a small Web site, for example. The size of Express Edition databases is limited to 4GB. Express Edition is also a good choice for developers who don't want or need the overhead of Developer Edition.

✦ **Developer Edition** is a fully functioning version of SQL Server 2005 Enterprise Edition. A Developer Edition license restricts you to using the product only in development and testing environments. Developer Edition is a good choice for consultants and corporate developers who may need to access complex databases.

Unless you know that you need the features of Developer Edition, start out with Express Edition and then upgrade if you need it.

The examples in this book use SQL Server Express Edition; many developers always install Developer Edition. Why use SQL Server 2005 Express Edition when Visual Studio 2008 Professional includes SQL Server 2005 Developer Edition? Express Edition is free! SQL Server 2005 Express Edition is installed by default with Visual Studio 2008.

Installing SQL Server Developer Edition

SQL Server 2005 Developer Edition is installed separately from Visual Studio 2005.

Install Visual Studio 2008 first and then install SQL Server 2005 Developer Edition. Developer Edition requires version 2.0 of the .NET Framework, which is installed as part of the SQL Server 2005 installation. Although Visual Studio 2008 installs SQL Server 2005 Express Edition, installing the Developer Edition *upgrades* SQL Server.

Preparing your machine to install SQL Server requires many steps. Your installation steps depend on the services and components you choose to install.

Follow these steps to install SQL Server Developer Edition:

1. **Install Visual Studio 2008 or version 2.0 of the .NET Framework.**

See Book II, Chapter 1 for more information about installing Visual Studio 2008 Professional.

2. **Launch the SQL Server Developer Edition setup by inserting the CD.**

The Start page appears.

If setup doesn't start when you place the disc in the drive, double-click the setup.hta file.

3. **Click the hyperlink for your operating system type.**

The Start page for your operating system appears.

4. **Before installing SQL Server, review the hardware and software requirements and read the release notes.**

The hardware and software requirements include instructions for accessing the Books Online documentation, where you can find complete installation instructions.

5. **After reviewing the installation documentation, click the link to install the server.**

The pre-setup wizard opens, and the end user license agreement appears.

6. **Read the license agreement and select the option if you agree to the terms and conditions of the license. Click Next.**

The wizard installs any prerequisites.

7. Click Next again.

The wizard scans your system's configuration and starts the installation wizard.

8. Click Next one more time.

The results of the system configuration check appear.

9. Review the results and address any of the warnings or error messages, as shown in Figure 6-1. You can find out how to fix the errors by clicking on the Messages links. Click Next.

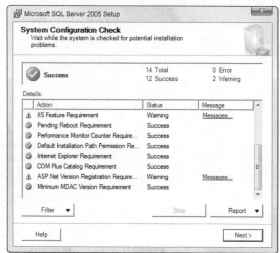

Figure 6-1:
Review the
results of
the system
configuration
check.

The installation wizard prepares the installation files.

10. Enter your registration information and then click Next.

11. On the Components to Install page, select the components you want to install.

The components you can choose to install include:

- *Database Services* — Installs the database engine which allows you to create and use databases

- *Analysis Services* — Installs tools to support data analysis and mining

- *Notification Services* — Installs services that enable users to subscribe to events and receive messages when those events occur

- *Integration Services* — Installs services that make it possible to merge data from multiple data sources

- *Workstation components, Books Online, and Development Tools* — Installs the client tools and documentation you need to administer SQL Server 2005 and develop database applications

At a minimum, you should choose to install Database Services and Workstation components, Books Online, and Development Tools. The remaining services allow you to create specialized database applications. You should install them as you need them.

Unless you need the more advanced features of Developer Edition, you may find that Express Edition works fine. You can download SQL Server 2005 Express Edition with Advanced Services SP1 at

> http://msdn2.microsoft.com/en-us/express/bb410792.aspx

12. **Click the Advanced button.**

The Feature Selection dialog box appears.

13. **Click the plus sign (+) next to Documentation, Samples, and Sample Databases.**

14. **Select the Sample Databases, and Sample Code and Applications options for installation, as shown in Figure 6-2, and then click Next.**

Figure 6-2: Install the sample databases.

15. **Complete the steps to configure the services you selected to install in Step 11.**

The wizard displays a summary page before installation.

Refer to the SQL Server Books Online documentation for specific details on configuring services.

16. **Click the Install button, as shown in Figure 6-3, to start the installation.**

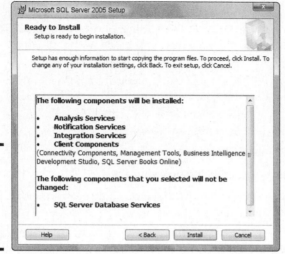

Figure 6-3:
Click the Install button to start the installation.

Use the Add or Remove Programs utility in Windows Control Panel to add components to, or remove them from, your SQL Server installation.

For the Vista operating system, you'll need to make sure you install Service Pack 2 (SP2) for SQL Server 2005. When the SP2 installation is complete, you'll need to run the Provisioning Tool. This allows you to select users that will have adequate rights and permissions to administer SQL Server. Figure 6-4 shows the Provisioning Tool.

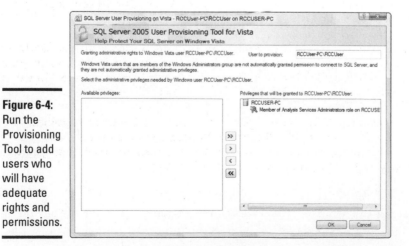

Figure 6-4:
Run the Provisioning Tool to add users who will have adequate rights and permissions.

Working with the SQL Server tools

SQL Server 2005 includes many helpful tools for working with databases. These tools include

✦ **SQL Server Management Studio** — Create and manage database objects.

✦ **Books Online** — Browse the comprehensive SQL Server documentation.

✦ **Sample databases and code** — Use samples to figure out how things are supposed to work.

If you decide to use SQL Server 2005 Express Edition, you need to install some additional tools to make your life easier. You should install the following tools:

✦ Adventure Works sample database

✦ Books Online

✦ Management Studio Express

You can download these tools at the Microsoft TechCenter download page for SQL Server 2005 at

```
https://www.microsoft.com/downloads/details.aspx?familyid=e719ecf7-9f46-4312-
    af89-6ad8702e4e6e
```

Run the SQL Server Surface Area Configuration Tool after installation. The tool helps you disable unused services and features of SQL Server so that you can minimize your security exposure.

You're likely to use the SQL Server Management Studio frequently for administering your databases. You can launch the Management Studio by choosing Start⇨All Programs⇨Microsoft SQL Server 2005. Figure 6-5 shows a Management Studio pane.

The Management Studio features Object Explorer, which is similar to Server Explorer in Visual Studio. Like in Server Explorer, you right-click an object in Object Explorer to display a list of commands you can execute, as shown in Figure 6-6.

The Management Studio uses many of the same designers and explorers as Visual Studio. For example, Query and View Designer is the same. See the section "Managing Your Database with Visual Database Tools," later in this chapter, to see Query and View Designer in action.

**Book IV
Chapter 6**

**Using Visual Studio
with SQL Server**

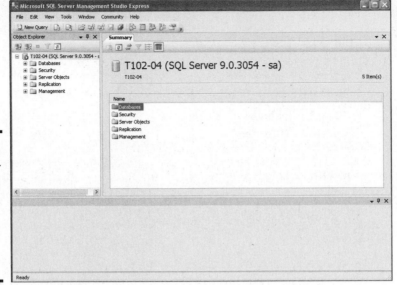

Figure 6-5:
Use the SQL Server Management Studio to administer your databases.

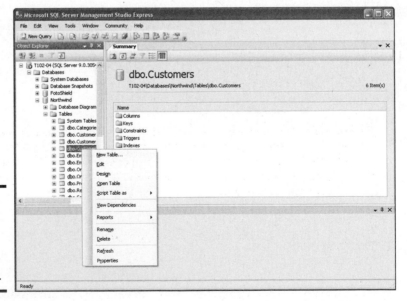

Figure 6-6:
Right-click an object to display a list of commands.

One cool feature of the Management Studio is the `Script As` command: Right-click a table in Object Explorer and choose Script As from the contextual menu. Select the kind of script you want to create, such as `CREATE`, and Management Studio generates the script.

Use the Management Studio or Visual Studio for creating queries. SQL Server 2005 doesn't include a separate query tool, such as the SQL Server 2000 Query Analyzer.

The Management Studio for SQL Server Developer Edition includes support for solutions and projects. You use Solution Explorer similarly to how you use Visual Studio to work with database projects that store script items and database connections.

Using the Adventure Works sample

The Adventure Works sample database showcases many of the new features of SQL Server 2005. One feature that Adventure Works uses extensively is *schemas,* which allow database objects to be grouped together. For example, the Adventure Works database uses a schema named HumanResources. The tables Employee and Department are associated with the HumanResources schema.

One drawback of using schemas is that more typing is required when you use SQL statements to access data. For example, to access the Employee table, you must type **HumanResources.Employee**.

The code samples you install with SQL Server 2005 provide a set of scripts you can use to either remove the schemas or create synonyms for the schemas. The scripts are

+ `AlterSchemaToDbo.sql`
+ `CreateSynonymsDbo.sql`

Both of these scripts have the same net effect: You can access the tables without specifying a schema first. The main difference is that if you use the first script, `AlterSchemaToDbo.sql`, the code samples included with SQL Server don't work. If you don't care about using code samples, use whichever script you want.

You can reverse either script by using the scripts `AlterSchemaFromDbo.sql` or `DropSynonymsDbo.sql`.

The scripts are installed at

```
C:\Program Files\Microsoft SQL Server\90\Samples\Engine\
    Administration\AdventureWorks\Scripts
```

Work around this problem by executing one of the scripts in this section. You can work around the problem by manually editing the SQL statements; see the section about adding data to Web Forms in Chapter 1 of this mini-book.

Creating Database Projects

You can create two kinds of database projects in Visual Studio, and they are vastly different:

✦ **Database Project** — Create and manage scripts by using SQL.

✦ **SQL Server Project** — Create database objects and retrieve and update data from databases by using .NET programming languages such as Visual Basic and C#.

In a SQL Server Project, you use Visual Basic or C# to write complex data access procedures that take advantage of the features of the .NET Framework. Database projects are containers for storing SQL scripts.

Managing scripts with database projects

Visual Studio provides a project template for database projects. You use database projects to

✦ Create SQL scripts.

✦ Store database references.

✦ Place scripts under source control.

✦ Run and test scripts.

Storing scripts in a project keeps them together in a single container and allows you to place those scripts under source control. You can use the Visual Studio Visual Database Tools to generate scripts.

For more information about these tools, see the section "Managing Your Database with Visual Database Tools," later in this chapter. To read more about source control, see Book VI, Chapter 3.

You can add any kind of SQL script to a database project. Visual Studio provides templates and tools for generating certain kinds of scripts, such as

✦ Change and Create scripts

✦ Stored procedures

✦ Triggers

✦ Tables

✦ Views

✦ Database queries

To create a database project, follow these steps:

1. Press Ctrl+Shift+N to open the New Project dialog box.

2. Click the plus sign (+) to expand the Other Project Types line.

3. Click the Database project type.

A list of project templates appears.

4. Click the Database Project icon.

5. Type a name and location for the project.

6. Click OK.

Visual Studio prompts you to select a database reference.

The Add Database Reference dialog box appears if Visual Studio finds existing database connections in Server Explorer. The New Database Reference dialog box appears if no existing database connections are in Server Explorer.

7. Select an existing database reference or create a new one.

Visual Studio creates the database project and adds the database reference to Solution Explorer. Figure 6-7 shows a reference to the Adventure Works database.

Figure 6-7:
Visual Studio adds the database reference to the database project.

Adding a new database reference is similar to creating a new database connection. See the section about connecting to databases in Chapter 2 of this mini-book for more information.

See the next section for more information about working with database references.

Referencing databases

Database projects use database references to know which database to execute a SQL script against. Database references appear in Solution Explorer and are saved with the database project.

A SQL Server project uses a single database reference for the entire project. Other projects, such as Windows and Web projects, use database *connections* rather than database *references.* See the section about connecting to databases in Chapter 2 in this mini-book.

A database reference uses a database connection to know how to connect to the database. Database connections are visible in Server Explorer. You use Server Explorer to browse a database connection and view database objects, such as tables and views. You can't browse database objects by using a database reference in Solution Explorer. However, you can use Server Explorer to browse the database connection to which a database reference points.

When you add a new database reference to a database project, Visual Studio checks to see whether any existing database connections are in Server Explorer. If so, it prompts you to select those connections.

Otherwise, Visual Studio prompts you to add a new database reference. Adding a new one creates a new data connection in Server Explorer. The New Database Reference dialog box functions exactly the same as the Add Connection dialog box, which you use to add new data connections in Server Explorer.

See the section about connecting to databases in Chapter 2 of this mini-book for more information on creating database connections in Server Explorer.

A database project can have multiple database references. To add a database reference to an existing database project, follow these steps:

1. **Right-click Database References in Solution Explorer.**

2. **Choose New Database Reference from the contextual menu.**

The Add References dialog box appears, or the New Database Reference dialog box appears if no database connections exist in Server Explorer for the project.

3. **Select an existing reference or create a new one.**

The Add References dialog box displays a list of all existing data connections in Server Explorer, as shown in Figure 6-8. If there are no existing data connections, the Add References dialog box doesn't appear.

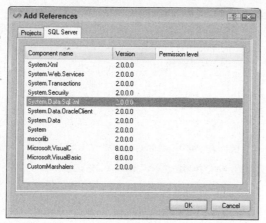

Figure 6-8:
The Add
References
dialog box
displays a
list of
existing
data
connections
from Server
Explorer.

4. **Click the Add New Reference button if you don't see the data connection you need.**

5. **Click OK.**

Visual Studio adds the database reference to the Solution Explorer.

Database references allow you to store references to multiple databases. For example, use a reference to a local database when you're working with a test database. Use another reference to a production database when you're ready to execute your scripts in a live environment.

Set your test database as the default database reference. All your scripts are executed against the default database reference. To run your scripts against another database, you must explicitly select the database each time you execute the script. To set a database as the default database, right-click the database reference in Solution Explorer and then choose Set As Project Default from the contextual menu.

Creating scripts

Database projects include five project templates for creating SQL scripts. The available templates are

- ✦ Stored Procedure Script
- ✦ SQL Script
- ✦ Table Script
- ✦ Trigger Script
- ✦ View Script

The templates provide boilerplate SQL statements for creating scripts. For example, the Table Script template has a CREATE TABLE statement. The SQL Script template is a blank template.

Create your own SQL Script templates and save them as project item templates.

To create a new script in a database project, follow these steps:

1. **Right-click the database project folder in Solution Explorer.**

2. **Choose Add SQL Script from the contextual menu.**

   The Add New Item dialog box appears.

   Alternatively, choose Add Existing Item from the contextual menu to add an existing SQL script.

3. **Click the icon for the kind of SQL script you want to create.**

4. **Type a name for the script.**

5. **Click the Add button.**

   Visual Studio adds the script to the database project. The script appears in the Script Editor.

You can use the Visual Studio Visual Database Tools to generate scripts and queries. Scripts that you can generate include

✦ Change scripts

✦ Create scripts

✦ Database queries

See the upcoming section "Managing Your Database with Visual Database Tools" to read more about using the Visual Database Tools to generate scripts.

Scripts created with Visual Studio use the file extension .sql. Because there are so many naming conventions for SQL scripts, Visual Studio recognizes more than just the .sql extension. An abbreviated list of file extensions appears in Table 6-2.

Table 6-2	File Extensions
File Extension	*File Type*
.tab	Table definition
.prc	Stored procedure

File Extension	File Type
.viw	View
.trg	Trigger
.udt	User-defined data type

Using the script editor

Visual Studio includes a script editor for creating SQL scripts. The editor doesn't feature IntelliSense, like other Visual Studio editors such as the Code Editor, do. However, you can use the Query Builder to generate SQL statements in the script editor.

To use the Query Builder with the script editor, follow these steps:

1. **Create a new script file by following the steps in the preceding section.**

2. **Right-click the area in the editor where you want to add a new SQL statement.**

   The Query Builder returns the SQL statement to the location where your cursor is positioned in the script editor.

3. **Choose Insert SQL from the contextual menu.**

   The Query Builder appears.

4. **Use the Query Builder to build an SQL statement.**

   Visual Studio returns the SQL statement to the script editor.

   See the section "Managing Your Database with Visual Database Tools," later in this chapter, for more information on using the Query Builder.

The script editor places a blue line around SQL statements. You can invoke the Query Builder to edit the SQL statement inside that blue box. To edit an existing SQL statement, follow these steps:

1. **Create a script with at least one SQL statement, as the preceding set of steps describes.**

2. **Right-click the SQL statement inside the blue box, as shown in Figure 6-9.**

3. **From the contextual menu that appears, choose Design SQL Block.**

4. **When the Query Builder appears, use it to modify the SQL statement.**

**Book IV
Chapter 6**

**Using Visual Studio
with SQL Server**

Figure 6-9:
Right-click
the SQL
statement
inside the
blue box.

Executing scripts

You can execute an entire script or portions of a script, depending on what you want to accomplish. SQL scripts are often quite lengthy. If you don't need to run the whole script, you can simply highlight the portion of the syntax you need to run. Of course, you can always let the whole script run from start to finish.

To execute a script from a contextual menu, follow these steps:

1. **Right-click the script in the script editor or Solution Explorer.**

2. **Choose Run from the contextual menu.**

   The SQL script executes against the default database. The output appears in the Database Output window.

Follow these steps to run a portion of a SQL script that's open in the script editor:

1. **Highlight the SQL statement you want to execute in the script editor.**

2. **Right-click the selected text.**

3. **Choose Run Selection from the contextual menu.**

To execute a script against a specific database reference, follow these steps:

1. **Right-click the script file in Solution Explorer.**

2. **Choose Run On from the contextual menu.**

   The Run On window appears.

3. Select the database reference you want to use.

The script executes against the database reference.

The Run On dialog box gives you the option to create a temporary database reference. The reference is deleted after the script executes.

Drag and drop a script file onto the database reference that you want to execute against in Solution Explorer.

Handling data with SQL Server projects

Previous versions of Visual Studio featured integration between the Visual Studio toolset and SQL Server. Integration was limited to using wizards and visual designers for manipulating database objects. Although that level of integration still exists, the Visual Studio SQL Server projects allow you to access SQL Server 2005 in a way that wasn't possible until now.

SQL Server projects are a new project type in Visual Studio designed to take advantage of integration between SQL Server 2005 and the .NET Framework. With SQL Server projects, you can do any of the following tasks:

✦ Write and debug .NET code that performs complex data operations by using the Code Editor.

✦ Deploy .NET assemblies as database objects to SQL Server 2005 databases.

✦ Execute .NET assemblies in SQL Server 2005.

Code written using the languages of .NET, such as C# and Visual Basic, is compiled into .NET assemblies. Code that takes advantage of the services of the Common Language Runtime (CLR) is *managed* code.

Using SQL Server projects, you write stored procedures, views, triggers, and other database objects by using .NET code. You execute your code using SQL statements to call the database objects.

Managed code that executes in SQL Server 2005 is a *CLR routine.* CLR routines are sometimes also described using the word *managed,* such as managed stored procedure or managed trigger.

To create and execute a managed stored procedure named GetEmployees, follow these steps:

1. Use .NET code to create a data access method named GetEmployees.

Assume that the method uses the namespace

```
MyDataProcedures.GetEmployeesProc.GetEmployees
```

It doesn't matter what the code inside `GetEmployees` actually does. Presumably, the code accesses data, but it could just as easily add 2 + 2.

2. Compile the code into the .NET assembly `GetEmployees.dll`.

Because .NET assemblies use the file extension `.dll`, they're often referred to as DLL files.

3. Deploy the `GetEmployees.dll` to a SQL Server 2005 database.

You can choose Build⇨Deploy Solution in Visual Studio to deploy assemblies to SQL Server 2005 databases in SQL Server projects.

Alternatively, connect to your SQL Server 2005 database by using the Management Studio and execute the following SQL statement in a new query:

```
CREATE ASSEMBLY GetEmployees from 'GetEmployee.dll'
    WITH PERMISSION_SET = SAFE
```

4. Create a stored procedure with the following SQL statement to execute the .NET assembly:

```
CREATE PROCEDURE uspGetEmployees

AS

EXTERNAL NAME MyDataProcedures.GetEmployeesProc.GetEmployees
```

Visual Studio performs this step for you when you use the `Deploy Solution` command.

5. Type the following SQL statement in a new query in SQL Server Management Studio to execute the stored procedure:

```
EXEC uspGetEmployees;
```

SQL Server 2005 executes the code in the .NET assembly `GetEmployees`.

You use a SQL Server project to create .NET assemblies that you can deploy to SQL Server 2005. To create a new SQL Server project, follow these steps:

1. Press Ctrl+Shift+N to open the New Project dialog box.

2. Click the plus sign (+) next to the Visual Basic project type.

3. Click the Database project type.

A list of database project templates appears.

4. Click the SQL Server Project icon.

5. Type a name and location for the project.

6. **Click OK.**

The Add Database Reference dialog box appears, or the New Database Reference dialog box appears if no data connections exist.

7. **Select an existing database reference or create a new reference.**

Visual Studio creates the new SQL Server project.

Unlike a database project, a SQL Server project can reference only a single database. See the earlier section "Managing scripts with database projects" for more information on creating database references.

To change the database that a SQL Server project references, follow these steps:

1. **Double-click My Project in Solution Explorer.**

The project's settings appear in the document window.

2. **Click the Database tab.**

The database reference appears.

3. **Click the Browse button.**

The Add Database Reference dialog box appears.

4. **Select an existing database reference or create a new reference.**

Enabling integration with SQL Server 2005

At the heart of SQL Server projects lies the integration of SQL Server 2005 with the CLR of the .NET Framework. SQL CLR integration allows you to deploy and execute .NET code to your SQL Server.

Before you can execute .NET code on your SQL Server, you must enable integration between SQL Server and the Common Language Runtime. To enable SQL CLR integration, execute the following SQL statement using the SQL Server Management Studio:

```
sp_configure 'clr enabled', 1
GO
RECONFIGURE
GO
```

Create a script file in a database project to execute the preceding statement or use the SQL Server Management Studio.

Saying, "Hello, SQL Server"

SQL Server projects provide templates for creating common database objects, such as

✦ Stored procedures

✦ Triggers

✦ User-defined functions

✦ User-defined types

✦ Aggregates

You add new items to the project by using the Add New Item dialog box. To create a stored procedure that outputs `Hello SQL Server!`, follow these steps:

1. **Right-click the project in Solution Explorer.**

2. **Choose Add⇨Stored Procedure from the contextual menu.**

 The Add New Item dialog box appears.

3. **Type the name** hellosqlserver.vb.

4. **Click the Add button.**

 The stored procedure appears in the Code Editor.

5. **Replace the line Add your code here with the following line:**

```
SqlContext.Pipe.Send("Hello SQL Server!")
```

 Figure 6-10 shows you the code. Notice that you don't have to write any SQL statements to create the stored procedure. Visual Studio creates the stored procedure to access your .NET code when you deploy the project.

6. **Choose Build⇨Build Solution.**

 Visual Studio compiles the project.

7. **Choose Build⇨Deploy Solution.**

 Visual Studio deploys the stored procedure to the Adventure Works database.

 Deploying the stored procedure creates the stored procedure in SQL Server.

You can use Server Explorer in Visual Studio or the SQL Server in Management Studio to execute the stored procedure.

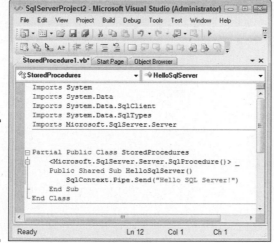

Figure 6-10:
Create a
stored
procedure
in the Visual
Studio Code
Editor.

Executing CLR routines

You execute your managed CLR routines by using SQL statements. For example, to execute a managed stored procedure, type the following line:

```
EXEC mystoredprocedure
```

To use Server Explorer to execute the `hellosqlserver` stored procedure from the preceding section, follow these steps:

1. **Expand the Stored Procedures folder in Server Explorer.**

   Press Ctrl+Alt+S to open the Server Explorer window if it's closed.

2. **Right-click the `hellosqlserver` stored procedure.**

   You may need to refresh Server Explorer if you don't see the stored procedure. To refresh the Server Explorer contents, right-click the Stored Procedures folder and choose Refresh from the contextual menu.

3. **Choose Execute from the contextual menu.**

   The output from the stored procedure appears in the Output window, as shown in Figure 6-11.

   If an error message tells you to enable CLR integration, see the earlier section "Enabling integration with SQL Server 2005."

**Book IV
Chapter 6**

**Using Visual Studio
with SQL Server**

Figure 6-11:
The stored procedure's output appears in the output window.

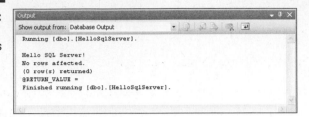

Debugging SQL Server projects

Visual Studio provides support for debugging SQL Server projects. You must enable debugging before you can use the debugger. To enable debugging, right-click the database connection in Server Explorer and choose Allow SQL/CLR Debugging.

To debug the `hellosqlserver` stored procedure, follow these steps:

1. **Right-click the Test Scripts folder in Solution Explorer.**

2. **Choose Add Test Script from the contextual menu.**

A new test script appears in the Code Editor.

3. **Type** exec hellosqlserver **in the script.**

4. **Insert a breakpoint by clicking the gray border to the right of the statement you type in Step 3.**

A red dot appears next to the statement.

5. **Right-click the test script in Solution Explorer and choose Set As Default Debug Script from the contextual menu.**

6. **Press F5 to start debugging.**

The debugger stops at your breakpoint.

7. **Press F11 to step through each line in your stored procedure.**

To read more about using the debugger, see Book V, Chapter 7.

You can also start the debugger by right-clicking the stored procedure in Server Explorer and choosing Step into Stored Procedure.

Managing Your Database with Visual Database Tools

Visual Studio provides an extensive set of tools for creating and managing database objects. Almost any time you work with database objects or SQL

Server projects, you're using one of the Visual Database Tools. Although the tools work with many kinds of databases, they're tightly integrated with SQL Server.

Visual Studio includes these tools for manipulating databases:

✦ **Server Explorer** — Connects to databases and accesses database objects

✦ **Database Diagram Designer** — Views or modifies a database's structure using a visual designer

✦ **Table Designer** — Creates and modifies tables

✦ **Query and View Designer** — Creates views and queries

Server Explorer is the key to accessing Visual Database Tools. Database objects appear in a hierarchical tree view in Server Explorer. You invoke most tools by right-clicking a database object in Server Explorer and choosing a tool from the contextual menu.

Change the hierarchical view of Server Explorer by right-clicking a data connection and choosing Change View from the contextual menu.

Before you can work with a database in Server Explorer, you must create a connection to a database. For more information, see the section about connecting to a database in Chapter 2 of this mini-book.

You can use Server Explorer to create a new database in SQL Server. To create a new database, follow these steps:

1. **Choose View⇨Server Explorer to open Server Explorer.**

2. **Right-click the Data Connections folder.**

3. **Choose Create New SQL Server Database from the contextual menu.**

The Create New SQL Server Database dialog box appears.

4. **Type your server's name or select a server from the Server Name drop-down list.**

Be sure to include the instance name. The default instance name for SQL Server 2005 Express is SQLExpress. The default instance name for SQL Server 2005 Developer Edition is MSSQLSERVER.

5. **Select the appropriate authentication type and enter your login credentials, if required.**

6. **Type a name for the database, such as** MyNewDatabase, **in the New Database Name field, as shown in Figure 6-12.**

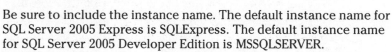

Figure 6-12:
Type a name
for the new
database.

> **Create New SQL Server Database**
>
> Enter information to connect to a SQL Server, then specify the name of a database to create.
>
> Server name:
> T102-04   Refresh
>
> Log on to the server
>
> ⦿ Use Windows Authentication
> ○ Use SQL Server Authentication
>
> User name:
> Password:
> ☐ Save my password
>
> New database name:
> MyNewDatabase
>
> OK   Cancel

7. Click OK.

A connection to the new database appears in Server Explorer.

Using a local database

In most cases, you create a database on a database server running SQL Server. Sometimes, however, you may wish to run the database on the local computer. A database that you deploy with your application is called a *local database*. You may choose to store your application's data in a local database rather than an XML file or a plain text file. Visual Studio supports using SQL Server and SQL Server Express `.mdf` database files and Access `.mdb` database files as local databases. All the Visual Database Tools work with local databases.

Here how to create a new local database:

1. Create a new Windows application.

See Book III, Chapter 1 for more information on creating a Windows application.

2. Right-click the project folder in Solution Explorer.

3. Choose Add⇨New Item from the contextual menu.

The Add New Item window appears.

4. Click the SQL Database icon.

5. **Type a name for the database in the Name text box and then click the Add button.**

   The database file is added to Solution Explorer. A data connection to the local database file appears in Server Explorer. The Data Source Configuration Wizard starts.

6. **Click Finish to exit the wizard.**

The Data Source Configuration Wizard creates a strongly typed `DataSet`. You use the Visual Database Tools to add tables, queries, and views to your local database, as described in the next two sections. You access local databases using ADO.NET the same way you access remote databases.

You may also add an existing SQL Server or Access database to your project. To add an existing database file, right-click the project folder and choose Add⇨Existing Item. You need to create a database connection to your local file in order to access the database. See Book IV, Chapter 2 to read about connecting to databases.

Deploying a local database

When you deploy a project that uses a local database, Visual Studio automatically includes SQL Server 2005 Express Edition. If the local client that installs your application doesn't already have SQL Server installed, it's installed with your application.

The first time you build your application, Visual Studio places a copy of the database file into your application's bin folder with all the rest of the application's output, such as executable and DLL files. You have three choices for how Visual Studio manages the database file each time you build:

✔ **Copy If Newer** — Copies the database file from your project to the bin folder if the project's file has been updated more recently than the copy in the bin folder.

✔ **Copy Always** — Copies the file from your project to the bin folder every time. This is the default action.

✔ **Do Not Copy** — Never copies the file from your project to the bin folder.

You have to decide which approach is the most appropriate for your situation. Usually, the Copy Always option works fine.

You set the copy option using the `Copy to Output Directory` property on the local database file. Access the property using the Properties window by right-clicking the local database file and choosing Properties.

Follow Steps 2 through 5 of the preceding list to add a local database to a Web site. The Data Source Configuration Wizard doesn't start. The default application services provider database used for Membership and other ASP.NET services is a local database. See Book III, Chapter 6.

Adding tables with Table Designer

Add tables to a database by using Table Designer. To add a new table to the database you create in the preceding section, follow these steps:

1. **Click the plus sign (+) to expand the data connection in Server Explorer.**

2. **Right-click the Tables folder.**

3. **Choose Add New Table from the contextual menu.**

   Table Designer displays a grid that you use to add new columns.

4. **Add these columns to the table by using the grid:**

   • CustID, data type `uniqueidentifier`

   • FirstName, data type `varchar`

   • LastName, data type `varchar`

5. **Right-click the CustID column.**

6. **Choose Set Primary Key from the contextual menu.**

   A key appears next to the column name, as shown in Figure 6-13.

7. **Press F4 to display the table's Properties window.**

8. **Set the `Name` property to Customer.**

9. **Save the table.**

   Visual Studio adds the table to the database, and it appears in Server Explorer.

Table Designer is capable of doing much more than just adding columns. Click the Table Designer menu to see a list of commands that enable you to

✦ Create foreign key relationships.

✦ Create indexes.

✦ Add check constraints.

A key appears.

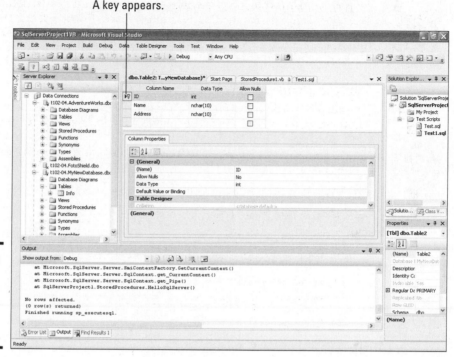

Figure 6-13:
A key
appears
near to the
column
name.

Table Designer generates change scripts that execute the changes you make in the designer in SQL Server. You can harness the power of these scripts and reuse them, modify them, or execute them later.

To generate change scripts, follow these steps:

1. **Create a new table or modify an existing table in Table Designer.**

Double-click an existing table object in Server Explorer to open it in Table Designer.

2. **Choose Table Designer⇨Generate Change Script.**

The Save Change Script dialog box appears.

3. **Click Yes to save the script.**

To generate create scripts in database projects, right-click the table in Server Explorer and choose Generate Create Script to Project from the contextual menu. In a database project, you can generate create scripts for any table in Server Explorer. Create scripts are most often used to add tables or fields to a database, and on rare occasions to add databases themselves.

Adding queries and views

Query and View Designer is a visual tool for creating queries and views. The tool is known as Query Designer when it's used for creating queries and View Designer when used to create views.

Query Designer is also known as *Query Builder*.

Use a query any time you need to execute a SQL statement against the database. Create a view when you want to save your query in the database.

You can save queries in a database project.

Examples of queries you can create with Query and View Designer include

✦ **Select** — Retrieves rows by using a SELECT statement

✦ **Insert Results** — Copies rows from one table to another by using an INSERT INTO ... SELECT statement

✦ **Insert Values** — Inserts a new row by using the INSERT INTO ... VALUES statement

✦ **Update** — Updates rows by using an UPDATE statement

✦ **Delete** — Deletes rows by using the DELETE statement

✦ **Make Table** — Copies results of a query into a new table by using the SELECT ... INTO statement

To start Query Designer, follow these steps:

1. **Right-click an existing data connection in Server Explorer.**

2. **Choose New Query from the contextual menu.**

   The Query Designer opens.

To start View Designer, follow these steps:

1. **Right-click the Views folder in an existing data connection in Server Explorer.**

2. **Choose Add New View from the contextual menu.**

   The View Designer opens.

Query and View Designer has three panes that help you build SQL statements. Figure 6-14 shows Query Designer.

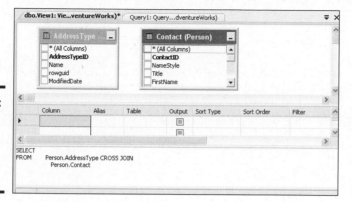

Figure 6-14: Query and View Designer has three panes.

The three panes, from top to bottom, are

✦ **Grid** — Specifies which columns to display and how to sort, group by, and filter

✦ **SQL** — Displays the SQL created by the Designer

✦ **Results** — Displays the query's output

To see the Query Designer in action, check out the section about updating data with the data designer in Chapter 2 of this mini-book.

Chapter 7: LINQ

In This Chapter

✔ Seeing how LINQ differs from SQL

✔ Creating a simple program to query integers

✔ Finding active processes

✔ Creating new object queries

*E*arlier chapters of this book use SQL Server as a data store and then use the objects that Visual Studio makes available to access the data in the databases. And although that's a large portion of data access techniques, there's more to managing data than database storage. The new kid on the block is Language Integrated Query (LINQ). Seemingly, every Web site on.NET technologies is talking about it.

LINQ, which is integrated into the newest versions of C# and VB.NET, helps you organize your data structures in a manner similar to how databases organize data. Similar to SQL, you can query program data. For instance, say you have a list of data structures, and you want to find the one that has an ID of 26. You can use LINQ to query the data and find the structure you're looking for.

LINQ is not just an enhancement to the collection classes. Instead, it's built right into the language. Yup, the querying capabilities are built right into the language. You can run queries against pretty much any kind of data — not just collections. This is one of those language features that you'll wonder how you got along without. LINQ is a set of extensions to the .NET Framework that encompasses language-integrated query, set, and transform operations. It extends C# and Visual Basic with native language syntax for queries and provides class libraries to take advantage of these capabilities.

Using LINQ to Query Integers

LINQ is so simple that the best way to see how to use it is to dive in and get going. The first program shown here illustrates how to create an array of integers that you'll initialize in a loop. Then you can see how to use LINQ to query the array for integers greater than 55.

First, write the code that initializes an integer array from which you'll obtain the query results. The VB and C# code follows:

VB

```
Dim nValues(50) As Integer
For i = 0 To 49
    nValues(i) = 1 + i * 2
Next
```

C#

```
int[] nValues = new int[50];
for (int i = 0; i < 50; i++)
{
    nValues[i] = 1 + i * 2;
}
```

The next thing to do is perform the query. LINQ queries resemble SQL queries. They have a `from` clause, a `where` clause, and a `select` clause. LINQ queries are structured slightly differently than SQL queries, though. The following is a LINQ query that obtains all numbers greater than 55 from the integer array created from the previous code snippet:

VB

```
Dim Results = From n In nValues Where n > 55 Select n
```

C#

```
var Results = from n in nValues where n > 55 select n;
```

Figure 7-1 shows the relationship of a SQL query to the equivalent LINQ query.

Figure 7-1:
The LINQ query has many of the same elements of a SQL query, but they are structured slightly differently.

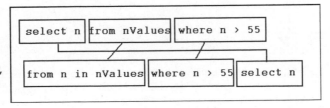

You can see the results of the running program in Figure 7-2.

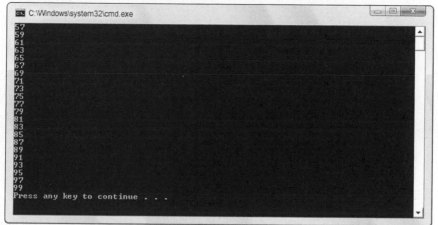

Figure 7-2:
This console application shows all numbers, from the list, which are greater than 55.

The complete program in VB and C# follows:

VB

```
Sub Main()
    Dim nValues(50) As Integer
    For i = 0 To 49
        nValues(i) = 1 + i * 2
    Next

    Dim Results = From n In nValues Where n > 55 Select n

    For Each Result In Results
        Console.WriteLine(Result)
    Next

End Sub
```

C#

```
static void Main(string[] args)
{
    int[] nValues = new int[50];
    for (int i = 0; i < 50; i++)
    {
        nValues[i] = 1 + i * 2;
    }

    var Results = from n in nValues where n > 55 select n;

    foreach (var Result in Results)
    {
        Console.WriteLine(Result);
    }

}
```

**Book IV
Chapter 7**

LINQ

The complete program (both C# and VB versions) for this example can be downloaded from this book's companion Web site. (See the book's Introduction for details about the site.)

In the `Linq1` program in the preceding example, notice the data type of the `Results` variable: There isn't one. Instead, note the datatype called `var`, which means the compiler will figure out (at compile time) what type to make for the variable. When programming with LINQ, this helps simplify matters.

Finding Active Processes

In this example, you can see how to create another console application that finds the current active processes.

You need the `System.Diagnostics` namespace for this program.

The query for this is as follows:

VB

```
Dim Processes = From p In Process.GetProcesses() Select p
```

C#

```
var Processes = from p in Process.GetProcesses() select p;
```

There is no `where` clause. Like with SQL queries, `where` clauses are optional.

You could add a `where` clause that will find only process names that contain the letter *x,* as follows:

VB

```
Dim Processes = From p In Process.GetProcesses() _
          Where p.ProcessName.Contains("x") Select p
```

C#

```
var Processes = from p in Process.GetProcesses()
    where p.ProcessName.Contains("x") select p;
```

The complete program (both C# and VB versions) for this example can be downloaded from this book's companion Web site. (See the Introduction for details about the site.)

Notice how the query is set up: A `from` clause specifies the collection of process names returned by `Process.GetProcesses`. Then, a `where` clause gives the criteria. Concluding is the `select` clause.

Visual Studio's IntelliSense (that thing that pops up and shows you the members of your variables, for example) is incredibly smart. When you start typing a `where` clause, IntelliSense kicks in. But look closely: IntelliSense knows the type of the `var` in the expression (p, in the preceding example). In order to determine the type of p, IntelliSense had to

1. Parse the second half of the `from` clause.

2. Determine that `Process.GetProcesses` returns a collection of `Process` types.

3. Knowing that `p` is an individual element in the collection, determine that p's type is `Process`.

Whew!

To finish off this section, Rick created a program with a graphical user interface (GUI). You can enter a search string, and it will match your search string to process names that are active. You can see the program running in Figure 7-3.

Figure 7-3: This program has a GUI and allows users to enter a search string.

The complete program (both C# and VB versions) for this example can be downloaded from this book's companion Web site. (See the Introduction for details about the site.)

Creating New Objects in the Query

The `select` clause might seem unnecessary at first. In the previous examples, the `select p` business would probably seem obvious. Seemingly, the code

```
from n in numbers where n > 25
```

should be all you need. However, the `select` clause does serve a purpose; in it, you can create new objects based on those objects that fit the criteria in the `where` clause.

Have a look at this code, which is a slightly modified version of the previous:

```
static void Main(string[] args)
{
    var Processes = from p in Process.GetProcesses()
        where p.ProcessName.Contains("x")
        select new { p.ProcessName, p.Id};

    foreach( var Proc in Processes )
    {
        Console.WriteLine( Proc.ProcessName );
        Console.WriteLine( Proc.Id );
    }
}
```

Look carefully at the `select` clause. It creates a set of new objects, each with a `ProcessName` member and an `Id` member. These new objects don't have a class name; you're creating an anonymous type. The new statement is called for each item in the resulting set, and the members of the anonymous object are initialized with the values in `p.ProcessName` and `p.Id`. (The names of the members of the anonymous class are inherited from the original object; thus, the names are `ProcessName` and `Id`.)

Now, look at the `foreach` statement. The members of the collection are no longer instances of `Process`, so you can't declare the loop variable as `Process`. Instead, just use `var` to let the compiler figure it out for you.

The type is anonymous, so it doesn't have a direct name.

The anonymous types you create actually have kind of a cool feature: They automatically get a `ToString()` method. You could code your `foreach` statement like so:

```
foreach (var x in processes)
{
    Console.WriteLine(x.ToString());
}
```

Book V

Coding

The 5th Wave   By Rich Tennant

"So should I look under handling, catching, or throwing exceptions? Throwing, right?"

Contents at a Glance

Chapter 1: Programming with Visual Studio 2008 475

Chapter 2: Understanding Data Types...493

Chapter 3: Get Some Class 525

Chapter 4: Wiring Up Events in the User Interface...551

Chapter 5: Getting Productive with Visual Studio 2008....................................569

Chapter 6: Exploring Web Services 595

Chapter 7: Handling Exceptions and Debugging 617

Chapter 8: Testing Code with Visual Studio 639

Chapter 1: Programming with Visual Studio 2008

In This Chapter

✔ Performing common tasks in the Code Editor

✔ Organizing code in C# and Visual Basic

✔ Getting started with the basics of C# and Visual Basic

Do you ever get the feeling that sometimes you're not alone? If you've ever written a program with one of the Visual Studio Code Editors, you know what I mean. Writing code in Visual Studio is like having a word processor that knows what you want to say next.

When you start to type code in Visual Studio, helpers appear magically out of nowhere. Like the host at your favorite restaurant, they share with you a list of today's specials: "Might I suggest an `Integer`, or how about a `DataSet`, sir?"

Even if you have no clue about all the choices that Visual Studio offers in the convenient pop-up list, just hover your mouse over one of them, and a description appears. Like a museum tour guide, Visual Studio shares with you the intimate details of the programming artifacts you're inspecting.

This chapter shows you some of the magical helpers and guides that Visual Studio uses to help you write better code. There's also a quick overview of how to write programs using two popular .NET languages: C# and Visual Basic.

Using the Code Editor

Although Visual Studio provides a great number of visual designers that allow you to generate code by dragging and dropping controls and components onto visual designers, at some point, you have to write some code. Visual Studio really helps you write code by providing you with many editors for editing all kinds of files. The Source Code Editor is especially feature rich, offering a number of productivity boosting features.

Here are some of the ways to open source code files in the Code Editor:

+ Double-click a source code file in Solution Explorer.

+ Press F7 while viewing a form in the Windows or Web Forms designers.

+ Add a new source code file via the Add New Items window.

The Code Editor is more than just a plain text editor like Notepad. You can use the Code Editor to do many things, such as

+ Enter code in the main Code Pane area.

+ Set breakpoints in the gray Indicator Margin along the left of the editor.

+ Select lines of code by clicking the space between the Code Pane and the Indicator Margin.

  You can optionally display line numbers in the Selection Margin.

+ Collapse code by using the outline lines along the left margin of the Code Editor.

+ Jump to code via the Navigation bar along the top of the Code Editor.

Figure 1-1 shows an example of the Code Editor.

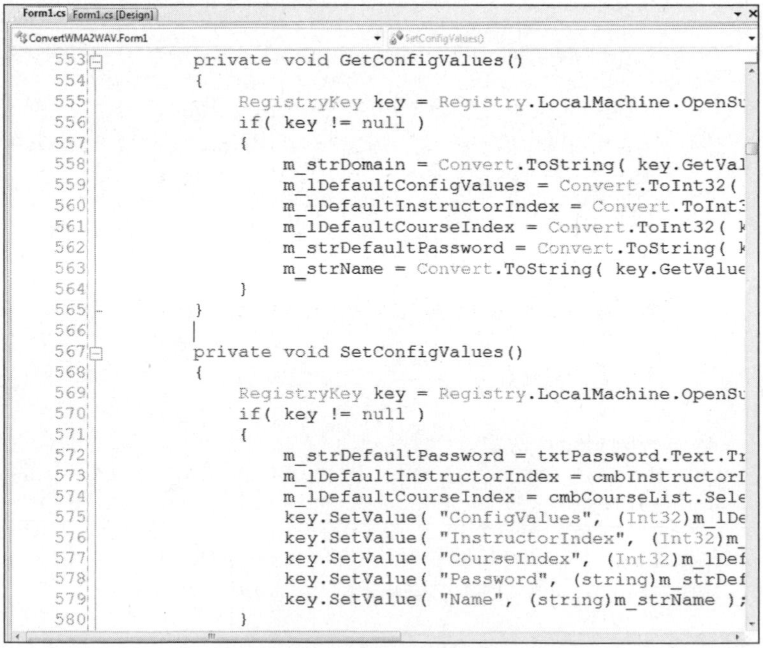

Figure 1-1:
Use the
Code Editor
to write
source
code.

Simplifying your common tasks

The Code Editor has many features similar to what you'd expect to find in a word processor. Some features, such as formatting, however, are slightly different. For example, you can't bold your code in the Code Editor, but you can use familiar features, such as copy and paste.

Managing indents

An important aspect of writing code is handling indentation. When you properly indent, you make it easier to read on-screen. The Visual Studio Code Editor provides three indentation styles:

✦ **None** — No indentation is applied to code.

✦ **Block** — Indentation matches the preceding line of code.

✦ **Smart** — Lines are automatically indented according to the standards of the programming language.

By default, the Code Editor indents each code line based on the standards for the programming language: *smart indenting.* When you're typing your code, the Editor automatically indents the line. When smart indentation is enabled, you can't manually increase indentation by pressing the Tab key.

To change the indentation style used by the Code Editor, follow these steps:

1. **Choose Options from the Tools menu.**

2. **Expand the Text Editor folder.**

3. **Expand a language to configure, or click the All Languages folder to apply the setting to all programming languages.**

4. **Click Tabs.**

A list of tab settings appears.

5. **Set the Indenting style, as shown in Figure 1-2.**

Accessing formatting commands

You can access formatting features to indent your code by choosing
Edit⇨Advanced. Table 1-1 lists the Code Editor's formatting commands and
what they do. Note that not all commands are available for all languages.

Table 1-1	Code Editor Formatting Commands
Menu Item	*Description*
Format Document	Applies indentation style to the entire document
Format Selection	Applies indentation style to the selected text
Tabify Selected Lines	Converts indentations to tab characters
Untabify Selected Lines	Converts indentations to white space
Make Uppercase	Changes the code of the selected text to uppercase
Make Lowercase	Changes the code of the selected text to lowercase
Delete Horizontal White Space	Deletes all white space on the line
View White Space	Displays character marks in the editor
Word Wrap	Toggles line wrapping on and off
Incremental Search	Activates a search of your document, letter by letter, as you type
Comment Selection	Places comment characters in front of the selected text
Uncomment Selection	Removes comment characters from selected text
Increase Line Indent	Increases indentation
Decrease Line Indent	Decreases indentation

Some indentation and comment commands are available on the Text Editor toolbar, as Figure 1-3 shows.

Figure 1-3:
Use the Text Editor toolbar to increase indentation or comment out a selection.

Decrease Indent   Comment out

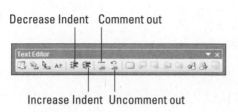

Increase Indent   Uncomment out

Most of these commands are useless if you're using smart indentation. As mentioned earlier, smart indentation automatically manages indentation for you. You might choose to turn off smart indentation if your company uses a different indentation standard. Also, you might want to use your own indentation standard, such as using white spaces instead of tabs.

Searching with Find and Replace

Visual Studio provides extensive Find and Replace capabilities that go way beyond what you find in a standard text editor. Table 1-2 lists the Find and Replace options. You access the Find and Replace commands by choosing Edit⇨Find and Replace or by using keyboard shortcuts.

Table 1-2	Find and Replace Commands	
Command	*Keyboard Shortcut*	*Purpose*
Quick Find	Ctrl+F	Searches for text
Quick Replace	Ctrl+H	Replaces text
Find in Files	Ctrl+Shift+F	Includes options for searching for text in a set of files
Replace in Files	Ctrl+Shift+H	Includes options for replacing text in a set of files
Find Symbol	Alt+F12	Restricts search scope to symbols only

The Find and Replace commands all use the same dialog box, and most of the commands use the same options. As Figure 1-4 shows, your Find and Replace options are the following.

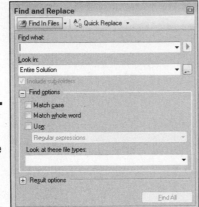

Figure 1-4:
Use Find
and Replace
commands
to search
your code.

✦ **Find What** — In this text box, enter text for which to search.

✦ **Replace With** — In this text box, enter text to replace the found text. (Note that Figure 1-4 doesn't show Replace options.)

✦ **Look In** — From this drop-down list, specify the scope of the search, such as Current Document or Entire Solution.

✦ **Find Options** — Use these checkboxes to specify options, such as whether to match case or the whole word.

✦ **Find Next** — Click this button to find the next text match. The button toggles to **Replace Next** when you are in Replace mode.

✦ **Replace All** — Clicking this button replaces all matches. The button toggles to **Find All** when you are in Find mode.

To select a different kind of Find and Replace command, open the drop-down lists displayed at the top of the Find and Replace dialog box.

Before you use Find and Replace, ask yourself whether one of the Visual Studio new refactoring features might work better. See Chapter 5 of this minibook for an overview of refactoring in Visual Studio.

The Find Symbols command restricts your search to only symbols. *Symbols* are the methods and type definitions declared in source code. You can use the Find Symbols command to search your own code or external libraries for which you don't have source code. The results of the Find Symbols code appear in the Find Symbol Results window. Figure 1-5 shows the results from a search for SayHello in a set of source code. The results show exactly where SayHello is used in source code. Double-click any of the results to go to the source code.

Figure 1-5:
The Find
Symbol
Results
window
displays
all the
instances
where the
text appears
in symbols.

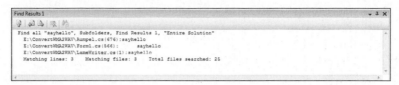

```
Find Results 1                                                              ⌄ ₊ ×
Find all "sayhello", Subfolders, Find Results 1, "Entire Solution"
    E:\ConvertWMA2WAV\Aumpel.cs(676):sayhello
    E:\ConvertWMA2WAV\Form1.cs(566):        sayhello
    E:\ConvertWMA2WAV\LameWriter.cs(1):sayhello
    Matching lines: 3    Matching files: 3    Total files searched: 25
```

Getting on task

Use the Visual Studio Task List to keep track of a simple list of to-do items.
The Task List window displays two kinds of tasks:

✦ **User tasks** — Tasks entered directly into the Task List window

✦ **Task comments** — Comments placed in your source code using special
tags

The Task List provides a consolidated list of tasks you enter directly into the
Task List window and tagged comments you place inside your source code.
The default set of tags you use to mark your comments comprises TODO,
HACK, or UNDONE.

You can create your own custom tags.

To tag a comment within your source code, use the standard comment mark
for your programming language, followed by one of the task comment tags.
For example, to add a task comment in Visual Basic or C#, you type the
following:

VB

```
'todo Add method body
```

C#

```
// todo Add method body
```

Tags may be entered in upper- or lowercase. By default, tags are in
uppercase.

The Task List window consolidates all your task comments in a single view. You can double-click a comment in the Task List to jump to the location in the source code where the comment appears. To open the Task List window, click Task List on the View window. Figure 1-6 shows an example of the Task List window.

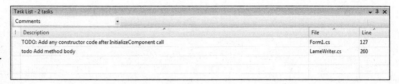

Always check the Task List for code samples you download from Microsoft and other third parties. The samples usually include a list of tasks you need to complete in order to use the sample.

You can add your own task comment tags. Figure 1-6 uses a comment tag called TODO. To add your own task comment tags, do the following:

1. **Choose Tools⇨Options.**

2. **Expand the Environment folder.**

3. **Click Task List.**

4. **Type a name for the comment tag in the Name text box.**

5. **Click the Add button.**

Your new comment tag appears in the list.

6. **Click OK.**

Collapsing code

The Code Editor includes outlining features you can use to expand and collapse your source code. Use the Edit⇨Outlining menu to access options for toggling outlining options.

The .NET programming languages provide syntax to create a named section of code you can collapse and expand, known as a *region directive*. To use a region directive, sandwich your code block between a start and end region directive. The syntax for the directive varies, depending on the language you're using.

In Visual Basic, the directive looks like this:

```
#Region "Description of code block"
'source code here
#End Region
```

In C#, the directive appears as follows:

```
#region Description of code block
//source code here
#endregion
```

Note that C# doesn't require double quotes around the description. Figure 1-7 shows an example of a class using regions to organize the source code.

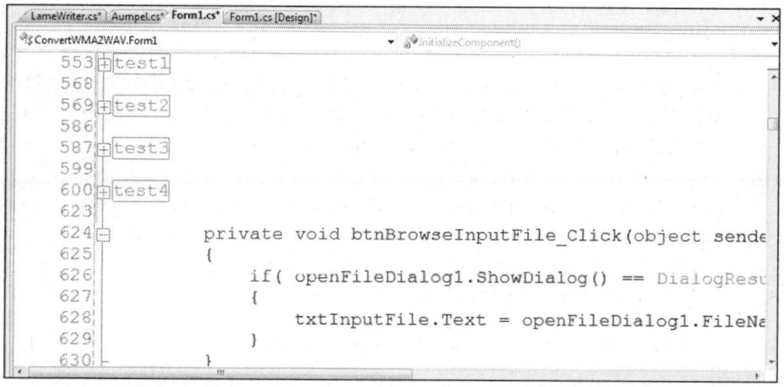

Figure 1-7:
Use a region directive to create collapsible blocks of code.

Using IntelliSense

The Visual Studio Code Editor has a special feature — IntelliSense — that helps you complete syntax while you type. You might recognize IntelliSense on the feature that brings your dot notation to life. When you type a variable's name and then type a period or dot, you get a list of properties and methods that you can use for that variable. The context-aware list of properties and methods is brought to you courtesy of IntelliSense.

IntelliSense is capable of more than listing methods and properties. You can see IntelliSense in action when you

✦ Hover your mouse over a property or method to view its signature.

✦ Open the parentheses on a method and receive feedback about acceptable parameter values.

The new IntelliSense features in Visual Studio 2008 take point-and-click code generation to a whole new level. See Chapter 5 in this mini-book for a demonstration.

Using visual cues

The Visual Studio Code Editor provides several visual cues that you can use while writing code, such as these:

✦ **Colors are used to identify different kinds of code.** For example, strings are red, and commented text is green.

✦ **Bookmark and breakpoint symbols appear in the far-left margin.**

✦ **Coding errors have colored squigglies beneath them to indicate the kind of error.** For example, syntax errors appear with red squigglies beneath them, whereas warnings use green squigglies beneath them.

Figure 1-8 shows an example of a squiggly underline on an undeclared variable.

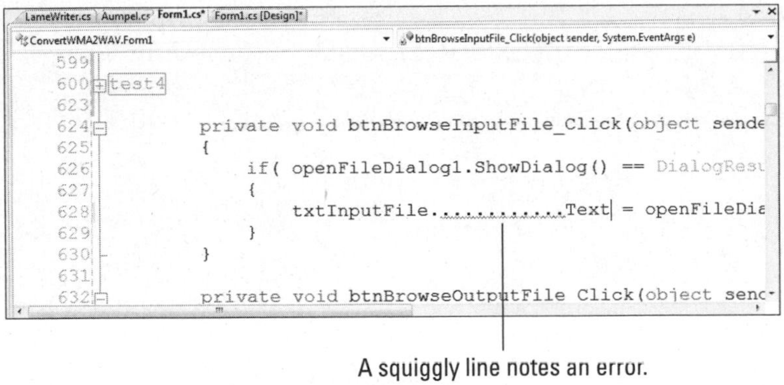

Figure 1-8:
The Code Editor uses visual cues, such as squiggly lines, for errors. You can also turn line numbers on.

A squiggly line notes an error.

You can optionally turn on line numbers to help you with your code. To turn on line numbers, follow these steps:

1. **Choose Tools⇨Options.**

2. **Expand Text Editor.**

3. **Click All Languages.**

4. **Select the Line Numbers check box.**

Use the options in the Text Editor section to customize the Code Editor. You may wish to disable certain features in the Code Editor, such as word wrap, if you're working with especially large source code files. Disabling features when you're editing large files can make the editor less sluggish.

Browsing and navigating code

Often, you need to browse your own code or try to navigate your way through code that someone else has written. Visual Studio provides two basic kinds of tools for browsing code:

✦ When you have the source code

✦ When you have a compiled assembly

The Code Editor has the following tools for browsing your own source code:

✦ **Navigation bar** — Allows you to jump to the classes and methods defined in a source code file

✦ **Bookmarks** — Allow you to place a bookmark in your code

The Navigation bar appears at the top of a source code file in the Code Editor. The left drop-down box lists types or classes that you can find in the source code file. After selecting a type, you can view the type's members in the right drop-down list. Selecting a member takes you to its declaration in source code. Figure 1-9 shows an example of selecting a type's member from the Navigation bar.

Figure 1-9:
Use the
Navigation
bar to select
the types
and
members
declared in
source
code.

A *bookmark* sets a place in code where you can jump to via the Bookmark window. To set a bookmark in source code, do the following:

1. **Position your cursor on the line where you want to set the bookmark.**

2. **Choose View⇨Bookmark Window to open the Bookmark window.**

3. **Click the Toggle button on the far left of the Bookmark window to set the bookmark.**

4. **Type a descriptive name for the bookmark.**

After you set a bookmark, double-click the bookmark in the Bookmark window to jump to that place in the code.

Visual Studio provides the Object Browser, Class View, and Code Definition for viewing assemblies. See the section on browsing types in Chapter 2 of this mini-book for more information.

Exploring Visual Basic and C#

Visual Studio supports many programming languages. Visual Basic and C# are two popular .NET programming languages. This section shows you the highlights of using Visual Basic and C# with Visual Studio 2008.

Mastering the basic syntax of programming languages, such as Visual Basic and C#, is not the same as learning how to program. When you discover how to program, you also discover basic programming constructs, such as conditionals and iterators. By grasping the concepts of programming constructs, you can easily and quickly pick up any language syntax.

Organizing programs

An important element of using a new programming language is figuring out how you should organize your program. You might already know that you use a `Dim` statement to declare variables in Visual Basic and that you use a `using` statement in C# to reference a namespace. That's all well and good, but if you don't know how to organize those statements in your source code file so they're in the proper order and nested, your program won't compile.

Both Visual Basic and C# have similar approaches to program organization that use these elements:

✦ **Non-executable statements** — Lines of source code that provide setup and wrapper statements for grouping executable statements, including

   • `Imports` *(Visual Basic)* or `using` *(C#) statements* — `Imports` and `using` statements allow you to use code elements from resources external to your project without fully qualifying the element's namespace each time you use it. These statements create a shortcut, in essence, to the namespace.

- *Namespace and type declarations* — These statements create wrappers that organize your code.

  Namespace declarations create unique identifiers for the types you declare within the namespace.

  Data type declarations contain executable code. Examples of data types include classes and structures. See Chapter 2 in this mini-book for more details on types. Visual Basic includes a `Module` statement that allows you to write code without using types.

Visual Basic uses the `Options` statement to specify how and when syntax checking occurs. `Options` statements are set by default on the project's property pages, so you don't need to include `Options` statements in your source code.

✦ **Executable statements** — Lines of source code that provide the functionality of your program are *executable statements*. Executable statements are nested inside data type declarations and organized into members. Examples of members include

- *Methods*
- *Fields*
- *Properties*
- *Events*

In C# programming, a *member* is defined as a method, field, property, or event based on the style of programming you use and how you intend to use the member. For example, a class could implement its color as a property member, in which case you would access it as

```
MyClass.Color
```

Implemented as a method, it might look like this:

```
MyClass.GetColor()
```

Coding standards dictate that using the property is preferred over using the method; however, both approaches work and can return the same value.

Visual Basic includes additional executable statements — *procedures* — that can be used as class members or as part of a module. Examples of procedures in Visual Basic include

- `Function` — A set of statements that returns a value
- `Sub` — A set of statements that doesn't return a value
- `Property` — Declares a property with `Get` and `Set` procedures

The long and short of these organizing differences between Visual Basic and C# is that everything must be a data type in C#. In Visual Basic, you don't have to use types to organize your code, but it's recommended.

The most common data type used is a class. Classes are the fundamental building blocks of object-oriented programming (OOP). You don't have to follow the principles of OOP to use classes in C# or Visual Basic. Some would have you believe that you always write object-oriented code in C#, and that it's easier to write old-style procedural code with Visual Basic. That simply isn't true. Yes, C# forces you to *use* classes and objects, but that's not the same thing as writing object-oriented code. You can write procedural code by using objects. See Chapter 3 in this mini-book to read more about classes and OOP.

Figure 1-10 shows two functions where you can see the differences between the coding styles in Visual Basic and C#. Notice, for example, that Visual Basic uses `Namespace...End Namespace`, and C# uses `namespace {}`. Note also that because C# is case sensitive, all its keywords are in lowercase (bottom of Figure 1-10). Comparatively, Visual Basic keywords are in proper case with initial letters capitalized (top of Figure 1-10).

Figure 1-10: The coding styles in Visual Basic and C# are similar, but their syntax differs slightly.

Most development professionals adhere to a set of capitalization standards when it comes to naming variables, classes, and other units of code. The casing standards are consistent, regardless of the programming language used. Chapter 5 in this mini-book covers these standards.

Lots of folks say that one or the other language is better, but you can write good code in Visual Basic, and you can write horrible code in C#, and vice versa. What matters is how well you learn how to code, not which language you choose.

Getting started

The following sections provide a few syntax details for C# and Visual Basic. Refer to the Visual Studio documentation for more specifics on programming with either language.

Beginning at the beginning: The Main procedure

Every executable program requires a procedure called `Main`. The `Main` procedure is the entry point into your application. In Visual Basic Windows applications, the Visual Basic compiler creates a `Main` function for you when the Enable Application Framework check box is selected on the Application tab of the project's property pages.

Only executable programs, such as Windows applications, require a `Main` procedure. Class libraries don't require a `Main` procedure.

The Movie Collection Starter Kit for C# has a good example of a `Main` procedure. In the `Program.cs` source file, you'll find the following `Main` procedure:

```
static void Main()
{
  Application.EnableVisualStyles();
  Application.SetCompatibleTextRenderingDefault(false);
  Application.Run(new MainForm());
}
```

Declaring variables and assignment

You must declare variables you wish to use and specify their data type. You can assign a value to the variable when you create it or assign a value in a separate assignment statement.

Visual Basic uses the keyword `Dim` to declare variables, like this:

```
Dim variablename as DataType
```

For example, to declare the variable i as the data type integer in Visual Basic, you type

```
Dim i As Integer
```

Comparatively, C# doesn't require any special keywords when declaring variables. You declare variables in C# with the following syntax:

```
DataType variablename;
int i;
```

You assign values to variables using the equal (=) operator. For example, to assign the value 7 to the variable i, you'd type this:

```
i = 7  "(VB)
i = 7; //(C#)
```

When you read an assignment statement, you say i "gets" 7, not i "equals" 7. In the case of variable assignment, the equal operator is not the same as equality.

You can declare a variable and assign a value in one statement. To combine declaration and assignment in Visual Basic, you type

```
Dim i As Integer = 7
```

And in C#:

```
int i = 7;
```

See Chapter 2 in this mini-book for more details on declaring variables and assigning values.

Creating classes and working with objects

The primary means of organizing code in Visual Basic and C# is class declarations. Your executable code is nested within a class declaration. The code below is an example of a class declaration in Visual Basic:

```
Public Class Customer
"executable code here
End Class
```

You use a class using the new keyword, which creates an instance of the class, called an *object*. You use the object to access the executable code inside the class. For example, to create an object called newCust from the class Customer in Visual Basic, you'd type

```
Dim newCust As New Customer()
```

Here's the equivalent statement in C#:

```
Customer newCust = new Customer();
```

To call an executable procedure on the newCust object, you use dot notation, as shown here:

```
newCust.ValidateAddress()
```

You can consume objects in either language, regardless of what language the object is written in. For example, you can consume a Customer object written in Visual Basic using C#, and vice versa.

See Chapter 3 in this mini-book for more details on declaring classes and creating objects.

Creating executable code

A single line of code is a *statement*. Both Visual Basic and C# provide syntax that allows you to write multiple statements as a block of code.

Examples where you need to use code blocks include If...Then statements and Try...Catch statements.

C# uses curly braces to encapsulate multiple statements. Visual Basic uses the syntax Procedure...End Procedure. Compare these two If statements for clarification:

```
"Visual Basic
If flag = True Then
   j = j + 1
   flag = False
End If

//C#
if (flag = true)
 {
    j = j + 1;
    flag = false;
 }
```

Members and procedures

Executable code is implemented as members of a data type, usually a class. Basically, everything inside a class is a member of the class. A procedure that adds two integers and returns a value is a *method*. Variables declared for use within the class are *fields*.

Visual Basic also uses classes and members, but it uses keywords such as `Function` and `Sub` to declare a procedure.

See Chapter 3 in this mini-book for more details on creating members and procedures in classes.

My Visual Basic

Visual Basic includes a object called `My`, which you can use to access features related to your application and the .NET Framework. For example, you can use `My.Settings` to access your application's configuration settings.

You don't have to declare variables or create an instance to use `My`. You simply type **My** and a dot in the Visual Basic Code Editor, and a list of available objects appears. Three commonly used `My` objects are

✦ `My.Application` — Sets properties of the current application, such as setting a startup splash screen

✦ `My.Computer` — Provides access to computer resources, such as the Clipboard and the file system

✦ `My.User` — Provides information about the user account using the application

Chapter 2: Understanding Data Types

In This Chapter

✓ Declaring variables

✓ Seeing the differences between value types and reference types

✓ Understanding how data types are used in the .NET Framework

✓ Handling more than one variable

✓ Finding data types and using them in your code

Data types are the fundamental organizing blocks of code in .NET. Your program can do very little without using data types. If you've never programmed with .NET, you might be thinking of data types in terms of integers and characters. Those are one kind of data type, but other data types are more flexible, sophisticated, and powerful than integers and characters. Examples include classes, structures, and enumerations.

Variables are used to access data that you place in your computer's memory. When you declare a variable, you specify its data type. This is how your computer program knows how to assign meaning to the ones and zeroes that you store in your computer's memory.

The data type you specify for the variable declaration determines everything about how that variable is treated throughout its entire life cycle. This chapter shows the data types available in the .NET Framework and how to create your own data types.

The Rules of Data Types

From the perspective of the computer, all data is just a set of ones and zeroes. Computer programs apply meaning to those ones and zeroes by using data types. A *data type* tells your computer how your program can interact with the data and what operations are legal.

Examples of data types are integers and characters. By telling your computer program that a given variable holds an `integer` data type, the computer knows that you can add and subtract the value. The same data type law tells your computer that you can't add and subtract characters. When you use data types, you tell the computer the rules for interacting with your data.

These rules are to your benefit. The compiler for your program uses the rules for your data type to tell you in advance whether your program will break when you run it. Data types allow the compiler and Visual Studio to give you feedback about your code before you even execute it. Giving you feedback early in the process allows you to correct errors before your end users find them.

The many kinds of data types include simple data types (such as integers and characters) as well as complex data types (such as those provided by the .NET Framework). You can create your own data types by combining simple and complex data types.

Making a Declaration

Any time you want to use data in your program, you must first declare a variable to hold the value in memory. When you declare a variable, you do two things:

✦ **Name your variable.** You create an identifier that allows you to access the variable's value in memory and pass it around in your program.

✦ **Specify a data type.** You tell the computer how to allocate memory for the variable.

You'll most frequently declare variables in your programs, but you aren't limited to declaring only variables. You can declare constants, enumerations, functions, namespaces, and new data types.

Not all programming languages require you to specify a data type when you declare a variable. Languages (such as the languages of the .NET Framework) that require you to specify a data type are *strongly typed* languages. Specifying a data type at the time of variable declaration

✦ Enables the Code Editor to use features, such as IntelliSense

✦ Allows the compiler to provide you feedback if you try to use data types improperly

Declaring a variable is a straightforward process. For example, here's how you declare a variable in Visual Basic and C#:

VB

```
Dim myVariable as DataType
```

C#

```
DataType myVariable;
```

After you declare a variable, you might assign a value to it. The first value assigned to a variable is its *initial value.* Assigning a value to a variable for the first time is *initializing* the variable.

You don't have to initialize variables. The .NET Framework provides default initial values for you, depending on the data type; however, the initial values might not be what you expect. Certain kinds of data types are initialized to `null`, for example. You can't work with `null` in your program. You want to make sure that you assign a value to your variables before you start taking actions on those variables in your program.

You can initialize a variable when you declare it. For example, the following statement declares a variable of type `integer` and sets the variable's initial value to 7.

VB

```
Dim i As Integer = 7
```

C#

```
int i = 7;
```

Alternatively, you can assign an initial or subsequent value by using the equal (=) operator, as shown in the following snippets:

VB

```
i = 6
```

C#

```
i = 6;
```

Complex data types called *classes* require you to use the `new` operator when you assign a value. For example, the following code declares a variable of the data type `System.Data.DataSet`. The second line of code uses the `new` operator to assign a value to the variable.

VB

```
Dim ds as System.Data.DataSet
ds = new System.Data.DataSet
```

C#

```
System.Data.DataSet ds;
ds = new System.Data.DataSet();
```

Using the new operator creates an *instance* of the class. The class is like a template that defines what values can be stored. When you assign an instance of a class to a variable, the variable is like a blank entry form based on the class template.

You can declare and initialize a class in one line, as shown here:

```
Dim ds as new System.Data.DataSet
```

The .NET Framework's Common Type System

One of the services provided by the .NET Framework is data type management in the form of the Common Type System (CTS). The CTS defines all the rules for how the programming language you use

+ Declares types
+ Creates new types
+ Uses types in your source code

The CTS ensures data type consistency among the programming languages of the .NET Framework.

Understanding the type hierarchy

The CTS has a type hierarchy that provides a base set of data types used by all the .NET programming languages. The root data type for all data types in the .NET Framework is System.Object.

The most common use of data types is declaring variables, as shown in the preceding section. When you initialize a variable, either through assignment or the new operator, the computer uses the variable's data type to know how to allocate the memory for the variable. You can use two basic kinds of data types in .NET:

✦ **Value types** — Simple data types that are built into most programming languages, such as `integer` and `Boolean`.

The .NET Framework has a set of built-in value types that derive from the data type `System.ValueType`.

✦ **Reference types** — Complex data types that hold a memory address that points to data stored elsewhere in memory. Examples of reference types include classes, interfaces, strings, arrays, and delegates.

The easiest way to know the difference between value types and reference types is to look at how you declare and initialize variables of either type. Reference types use the `new` operator, whereas value types don't.

For example, the following code declares a variable of the value type `integer` by using the C# keyword `int`:

```
int i = 1;
```

When you create a variable with a reference data type, you use the `new` operator. The code that follows creates a new variable o of the data type `System.Object`. Recall that `System.Object` is the root data type in the CTS:

```
System.Object o = new System.Object();
```

Throwing it on the stack or the heap

Value types and reference types are stored differently in memory, which contributes to why they're used differently. Value types are stored on the stack, and reference types are stored on the managed heap. The *stack* — more specifically, the *call stack* — is an area of memory set aside for managing the execution of your program. You can visualize the stack as one memory address stacked on top of another. The *heap,* however, is a large pool of memory where objects that require longer life spans can live. (*Longer life span means that the object needs to live beyond the execution of a single* function on the call stack.)

The stack is more efficient to access than the heap because the stack discards a variable stored in memory as soon as your program stops using the variable.

Variables stored in the heap, however, are managed by the .NET garbage collector. The `new` operator requests storage to be allocated on the heap for the variable. The garbage collector clears the variable out of memory when it determines that the variable is no longer being used by your program, which might not correspond to the point in time when your program stops using the variable.

By being stored on the stack, value types are directly accessible. Reference type variables, however, return a reference to an address on the heap where the variable's value is actually stored. Figure 2-1 shows an example of value types and reference types in memory. The reference to a reference type is stored on the stack, which is how your program knows how to access the variable.

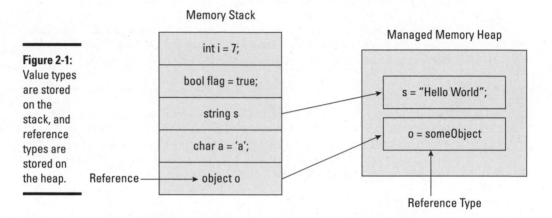

Figure 2-1: Value types are stored on the stack, and reference types are stored on the heap.

Completing your assignments

Another key difference between value types and reference types is how they're handled by assignments. When you assign a variable of a value type, the contents of the value type are copied. When you assign a reference type, only the reference is passed along.

The difference in how value types and reference types are assigned is attributable to how they're stored in memory. A reference type stores only a memory address that points to the actual value. When you copy a reference type, you copy the memory address stored on the stack.

The following code sample uses value types, and the value for variable i is copied to the variable j:

```
private void TestValueTypes()
{
  int i;
  int j;
  i = 8;
  j = i;
  i = 5;
}
```

When this code executes, j has the value 8, and i has the value 5. j and i are independent variables. The value from i is copied to j.

Now, look at how code using reference types does this. Note that the variables start out pointing to two separate values but wind up pointing to the same value:

```
private void TestReferenceTypes()
{
  System.Data.DataSet ds1 = new DataSet("DataSet 1");
  System.Data.DataSet ds2 = new DataSet("DataSet 2");
  ds2 = ds1;
  ds1.DataSetName = "My DataSet";
}
```

The statement ds2 = ds1; assigns the value referenced in the variable ds1 to the variable ds2. What happens to the value originally referenced by ds2? It's still there, but it can no longer be accessed because ds2 let go of it, as you can see in Figure 2-2. Eventually, the garbage collector recognizes that the object is no longer in use and destroys it.

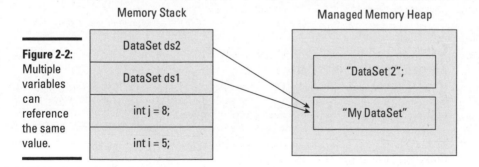

Figure 2-2:
Multiple variables can reference the same value.

You might think it's silly that someone would create two variables and then assign one to the other. After you start creating an application, you'd be surprised how easy it is to pass a variable by reference and not understand why your data isn't what you expected.

You need to understand the differences between value types and reference types. Table 2-1 compares value types and reference types.

Table 2-1	Comparison of Value Types and Reference Types	
Category	*Value Types*	*Reference Types*
Data accessibility	Directly accessible	Accessed through a reference to the data
Memory allocation	Stack	Managed heap
When is memory freed?	When variable is destroyed	When garbage collection determines no longer in use
Garbage collection	Doesn't use	Uses garbage collection
Initialization	No special initialization required	Must use `new` operator
Default value	Initialized as zero	Initialized as `null`
Null values	Can never be `null`	Throws an exception when you try to use a `null` reference
Assignment	Assignment copies the value	Assignment passes a reference to the value
Base class	Derives from `System.ValueType`	Derives from `System.Object`
Conversion	Can be converted to reference type	Can be converted to value type in some cases

Popular value types

If you've done any programming at all, you're probably familiar with data types, such as `char` and `integer`. These are *value types* in the .NET Framework. The CTS provides a set of built-in value types.

Your programming language provides a set of primitive data types that map to the built-in value type in the CTS. Table 2-2 lists the value types in .NET and their respective keywords in Visual Basic and C#. When you use one of these keywords as a data type in your program, it's compiled as the underlying .NET data type listed.

A *primitive data type* is a type that the programming language's compiler natively understands.

Table 2-2	Built-In Value Types and Their Language Keywords		
.NET Data Type	*Visual Basic Keyword*	*C# Keyword*	*Description*
`System.Boolean`	`Boolean`	`bool`	True or false
`System.Byte`	`Byte`	`byte`	Unsigned integer with values ranging from 0 to 255

.NET Data Type	Visual Basic Keyword	C# Keyword	Description
System.Char	Char	char	Represents characters in the Unicode Standard, such as the letter *a*
System.Decimal	Decimal	decimal	Decimal numbers ranging from −79,228,162,514,264,337,593,543, 950,335 to +79,228,162,514,264,337,593,543, 950,335
System.Double	Double	double	Fifteen decimal points of precision for binary floating-point arithmetic
System.Int16	Short	short	Signed integer with values ranging from −32,768 to +32,767
System.Int32	Integer	int	Signed integer with values ranging from −2,147,483,648 through +2,147,483,647
System.Int64	Long	long	Signed integer with values ranging from −9,223,372,036,854,775, 808 through +9,223,372,036,854, 775,807
System.SByte	Sbyte	sbyte	Signed integer with values ranging from −127 to +127
System.Single	Single	float	Seven decimal points of precision for binary floating-point arithmetic
System.UInt16	Ushort	ushort	Unsigned integer values ranging from 0 to 65,535
System.UInt32	UInteger	uint	Unsigned integer values ranging from 0 to 4,294,967,295
System.UInt64	Ulong	ulong	Unsigned integer values ranging from 0 to 18,446,744,073,709,551,615

You might notice that many data types represent numbers. The amount of memory used by each of these data types corresponds to the range of values that the data type can store.

Use the System.Decimal data type for financial calculations where rounding errors can't be tolerated.

Most of the .NET programming languages have a keyword for a data type that represents strings. Strings are not value types: They are reference types. See the next section, "Popular reference types," to read more about strings.

In addition to the value types listed previously, the .NET Framework includes two other programming elements that define value types:

✦ **Structures** — A *structure* is a data type comprising other data types. You use a structure to consolidate other data types into a single, named data type. Examples of two commonly used structures provided by the .NET Framework are `System.DateTime` and `System.Guid`.

The Visual Basic keyword that corresponds to `System.DateTime` is `Date`. C# doesn't have a keyword. `guid` (rhymes with *squid*) is short for *globally unique identifier*. You use a `guid` any time you need a unique identifier.

You use structures to create your own data types. See the section "Creating Your Own Types" for examples of using structures.

✦ **Enumerations** — An *enumeration* defines a set of constants that can be accessed by the name applied. `System.DayOfWeek` is an example of an enumeration that enumerates the days of the week, as shown in Figure 2-3. Enumerations derive from `System.Enum`.

Figure 2-3: Enumerations define a set of constants.

```
FakeWebService.cs | GetUploadInformation.cs [Design] | MyMath.cs | LameWriter.cs | Aumpel.cs | Form1.cs* | Form1.cs [Design]* | Start Page       ▼ ✕
%s ConvertWMA2WAV.Form1                                     ▼  %f DoConvert(string strSrcFilePath, string strDestFilePath, bool bShowMessage ▼
630         }
631
632    private void btnBrowseOutputFile_Click(object send
633    {
634        if( saveFileDialog1.ShowDialog() == DialogResu
635        {
636            txtOutputFile.Text = saveFileDialog1.FileN
637        }
638    }
639
640    void DoConvert( string strSrcFilePath, string strD
641    {
642
643        AudioWriter writer = null;
644
645        System.DayOfWeek.
646                             ┌──────────────┐
647        try                  │ ⚹ Friday     │
648        {                    │ ⚹ Monday     │
649            DateTime dt      │ ⚹ Saturday   │ etCreationTime( strSrc
650            StoreFileN       │ ⚹ Sunday     │ stFilePath, dt.ToShort
651                             │ ⚹ Thursday   │
                               │ ⚹ Tuesday    │
                               │ ⚹ Wednesday  │
                               └──────────────┘
```

Popular reference types

All the classes in the .NET Framework are reference types, so-called because the variable holds a reference to the value — not the actual value itself.

All classes in the CTS derive from `System.Object`. You could say that makes `System.Object` the most popular reference type. Hopefully, however, you aren't actually declaring your variables by using the `System.Object` type. Although doing so isn't incorrect, try to use the most specific data type possible.

C# provides the `keyword` object, and Visual Basic uses `Object` to map to the `System.Object` type in CTS.

One of the most popular reference types is `System.String`. Many people think that `System.String` is a value type, but it's actually an array of characters. That's probably because you don't have to use the `new` operator when you create a new string. You declare and use a string variable similarly to how you use value types, such as `integer` and `Boolean`.

Visual Basic and C# both provide a keyword to represent `System.String`. The following code declares and initializes a string variable:

VB

```
Dim s As String = "Hello"
```

C#

```
string s = "Hello";
```

Another popular reference type is `System.Exception`. Any time your program throws an exception, the exception you see is a reference type derived from `System.Exception`.

See the section "Browsing Types," later in this chapter, to see how you can find more reference types in the .NET Framework.

Creating Your Own Types

Developers long ago figured out that describing a business domain strictly in terms of `int`s and `char`s isn't easy. You can't bend the business to fit the limitations of a programming language. No, instead, you must use a programming language that allows you to model whatever real-world problem you're trying to solve.

The .NET Framework allows you to create your own data types. You can use your own data types to

✦ Model your business in your software.

✦ Provide utility features.

✦ Customize existing types that don't quite fit your needs.

You can use the following kinds of data types to create your own data types:

✦ **Classes** — *Classes* are reference types that derive from `System.Object`. Class types define the data and behavior of a variable. In other words, classes define the data that a variable can store and provide procedures that act on that data. For example, a `Customer` class may store a customer's name and unique identifier. It may include an `AccountBalance()` procedure that returns the customer's current balance.

Visual Basic and C# provide the `Class` statement and `class` keyword, respectively, for creating your own class data types. See the next chapter for more information on creating classes.

✦ **Structures** — *Structures* are value types that derive from `System.ValueType`. Structures can store virtually all the same data and behaviors as a class.

You use the `Structure` statement in Visual Basic to create a structure. C# provides the `struct` keyword:

- *To create a Customer structure in Visual Basic, type the following code:*

```
Structure Customer
   Dim m_firstName As String
   Dim m_lastName As String
   ReadOnly Property Name() As String
     Get
       Return m_firstName + " " + m_lastName
     End Get
   End Property
   WriteOnly Property FirstName()
     Set(ByVal value)
        m_firstName = value
     End Set
   End Property
   WriteOnly Property LastName()
     Set(ByVal value)
        m_lastName = value
     End Set
   End Property
End Structure
```

- *To create a variable by using the Customer data type, type the following code:*

```
Dim cust As New Customer
```

- *To assign values to a variable, type the following code:*

```
cust.FirstName = "John"
cust.LastName = "Smith"
```

The following line of code assigns the variable's `Name` property to a text box:

```
txtCustomerName.Text = cust.Name
```

Notice that the `cust` variable accesses only the structure's properties, and not the variables declared at the beginning of the structure. The structure's properties, in turn, access the variable declared at the top of the structure. The variables and properties of the structure are the *members* of the structure. See the next chapter to read more about a data type's members.

✦ **Enumerations** — *Enumerations* are value types that derive from `System.ValueType`. You define a set of constants, such as the days of the week, in an enumeration. You can use the `System.Enum` data type to access additional features of enumerations.

Visual Basic provides the `Enum` statement, and C# uses the `enum` keyword for declaring enumerations. The following code shows an enumeration in C#:

```
enum Fiber
{
  Angora,
  Mohair,
  Wool
}
```

With object-oriented programming (OOP) techniques, you can extend virtually all the types provided in the .NET Framework to meet your specific needs. See Chapter 3 in this mini-book for more information about OOP.

You often create user-defined types in a class library project. You can reference the class library in a Windows project or Web application when you need to use your user-defined types.

You can use your class and structure data types just like you do any other data type. You can declare them as variables, pass them as parameters, and return them from procedures. Use enumerations any time you need to reuse a set of values throughout your application.

At first blush, you might think there isn't much difference between structures and classes. Recall, however, that structures are value types and classes are reference types. As a result, structures often use less memory than classes. Each time a value type like a structure is passed around in a program, a copy of the structure is made. So, what starts out using less memory could end up consuming quite a bit. For this reason, you'll often find that classes are used more than structures. Even though classes are initially more expensive to create because there is both memory allocation and startup code to execute, their memory usage is often more economical throughout their lifetime.

In general, you should create structures when the data type you're creating is small in size, like an integer, and you expect it to be short-lived.

When There's More than One

Quite often, you need to handle more than just one of something. Rarely does your business have just one customer or one product. You're usually dealing with sets of things. The .NET Framework provides many data types for dealing with situations when you have more than one item.

Data types that can handle sets of data are often referred to as *data structures* or *collections*.

The collection-related data types provided by the .NET Framework often allow you to

✦ Add, remove, and modify individual elements.

✦ Copy elements to another collection.

✦ Sort and index elements.

✦ Iterate through a set of elements.

The .NET Framework provides several data types you can use to manage collections. The two biggies are

✦ Array **class** — An *array* is a set of data of all the same data type. You set the size of the array when you declare it. Arrays have been the staple data structure for a long time.

Picture an array as an Excel spreadsheet. A one-dimensional array is like a single row in the spreadsheet. A multidimensional array has more than one row.

✦ System.Collections **namespace** — Other kinds of collections, such as lists and hashtables, are found in the System.Collections namespace.

A namespace references a set of data types. A namespace isn't a data type itself. No System.Collections data type exists in the .NET Framework. Rather, you use the System.Collections namespace to access data types used to manage collections.

Another kind of data structure provided by the .NET Framework is the ADO.NET, which is an in-memory representation of a database with tables, columns, and rows. For more on DataSets, turn to Book IV, Chapter 3.

Using arrays

The .NET Framework provides the `System.Array` class for creating arrays. An *array* defines a set of data that all have the same data type. You can define an array to use any kind of data type, such as a set of integers or a set of strings. You can even define an array by using your own custom data types.

All items in an array must be of the same data type.

An array has the following properties:

✦ **Elements** — Each item that you add to an array is an element of the array. The data type of the element is the *element type*.

✦ **Index** — The *index* is the position of each element in the array. Arrays use zero-based indexes, so the first value in an array has an index of zero.

✦ **Length** — This is the total number of elements in the array.

✦ **Rank** — This is the number of dimensions in the array. A one-dimensional array has one row of data. A two-dimensional array has multiple rows.

✦ **Bounds** — These are the lower and upper bounds of an array that define the starting and ending index for an array's elements. For example, an array with four elements has a lower bound of zero and an upper bound of three.

Declaring arrays is similar to declaring other types of data. In Visual Basic, you append parentheses to the variable's identifier, as shown in the following:

```
Dim dailyWeights() As Integer
```

To declare a multidimensional array in Visual Basic, you place a comma inside the parentheses for each additional dimension, such as

```
Dim dailyWeights(,) As Integer
```

In C#, you append brackets to the element's data type when you declare an array, as shown here:

```
int[] dailyWeights;
```

Similar to Visual Basic, you use commas to create multidimensional arrays, as shown in the following:

```
int[,] dailyWeights;
```

You can also create arrays of arrays, which are called *jagged arrays*. You add extra sets of parentheses or brackets for each nested array. A declaration for a jagged array in Visual Basic looks like this:

```
Dim dailyWeights()() As Integer.
```

Declaring an array doesn't actually create the array. Because arrays are reference types, you use the `new` operator to create the array and assign it to the variable you declare. For example, to create an array with five elements and assign it to the one-dimensional dailyWeights array using Visual Basic, you'd type

```
dailyWeights = New Integer(4) {}
```

Recall that arrays have a zero-based index. Inside the parentheses, you place the array's upper bound, which is 4 in this example. The array's length is 5 because you start counting at zero.

Use the curly braces to place values into the array, as the following Visual Basic code shows:

```
dailyWeights = New Integer(4) { 155, 153, 154, 152, 150 }
```

Here's the equivalent statement in C#:

```
dailyWeights = new int[5] { 155, 153, 154, 152, 150 };
```

You might have noticed some subtle differences in syntax between Visual Basic and C#. Most notably, in the Visual Basic statement, you use the upper bound; in C#, you use the array's length. If you switch back and forth a lot between the two languages, maybe you can get a tattoo so you can keep it straight.

You don't need to size an array when you're initializing the array in the same statement. Supplying five values automatically creates an array of `length = 5`. For example, the following statements are equivalent:

```
dailyWeights = new int[5] { 155, 153, 154, 152, 150 };
dailyWeights = new int[] { 155, 153, 154, 152, 150 };
```

Here are three steps to using arrays:

1. Declare the array variable.

2. Create the array.

3. Initialize the array with values.

You can perform each step discretely or combine all three steps into one statement, as shown in the following C# statement:

```
int[] dailyWeights = new int[5] { 155, 153, 154, 152, 150 };
```

The equivalent statement in Visual Basic is

```
Dim dailyWeights() As Integer = New Integer(4) {155, 153, 154, 152, 150}
```

You supply three pieces of information to declare and create an array:

✦ The element's data type

✦ Its rank

✦ The upper bound or the size of the array

To access the elements in an array, use an indexer to specify the position of the element you wish to access. For example, the following C# code accesses the third element in an array of integers:

```
dailyWeights[2] = 175;
```

Arrays use a zero-based index, which means that you start counting from zero.

Using System.Collections

The .NET Framework provides many kinds of collections that you can use when you need to handle more than one of something at a time. Table 2-3 lists the specialized collection types you can find in the System.Collections namespace.

Collection data types in the System.Collections namespace can be grouped based on the mechanism used to access elements in the collection:

✦ **Indexed** — These access elements by using their position in the list of elements.

✦ **Keyed** — These access elements by using the key in a key/value pair.

✦ **Neither indexed nor keyed** — Data types provide access methods other than an indexer or a key.

Collections that use indexes are *lists*. Keyed collections are *dictionaries*.

Table 2-3		Data Types in the System.Collections Namespace		
Accessor	*Collection Type*	*Data Type*	*Description*	*Example*
Both	Dictionary	`SortedList`	A set of key/value pairs sorted by the key	A glossary of terms
Indexed	Collection	`BitArray`	An array of Boolean values	Whether your dog responds to the Come command given successively at the bark park
Indexed	List	`ArrayList`	An array of variable size	The number of debits to your bank account in the next 30 days
Keyed	Dictionary	`Hashtable`	A set of key/value pairs sorted by the key's hash number	The movies being shown at a theater
Neither	Collection	`Stack`	Last-in, first-out (LIFO) list	A pile of football players on a quarterback
Neither	Collection	`Queue`	First-in, first-out (FIFO) list	Line at the grocery store

The `System.Collections` namespace defines the `DictionaryEntry` structure, which represents a key/value pair in a dictionary collection type. See the upcoming section "Iterating through arrays and collections" to see a code sample that uses the `DictionaryEntry` structure.

The collection data types found in the `System.Collection` namespace are all classes. You use the `new` operator to create a new instance of a collection. The following code shows a `Hashtable`:

```
Dim ht As New Hashtable
```

Important actions you take on collections, such as a `Hashtable`, include adding and removing elements. A `Hashtable` is a key-based collection, so you add elements by using a key/value pair. The following code sample shows how to add elements to a `Hashtable`:

```
ht.Add("Screen 1", "Shane")
ht.Add("Screen 2", "My Friend Flicka")
```

Use the `Remove` method to remove an element from the hashtable:

```
ht.Remove("Screen 1")
```

You supply the key when you want to remove the element.

Of course, you aren't limited to using just primitive types and strings in your collections. You can use any data type, including your user-defined data types. For example, instead of placing a movie title in the hashtable, you could place a value created from a `Movie` class. The `Movie` class might store a movie's title, actors, release date, and show times. See the earlier section on creating your own types for more information.

The .NET Framework provides two other namespaces for using collection data types:

✦ `System.Collections.Generic` — Provides data types that allow you to create type-specific collections. In a type-specific or strongly typed collection, you specify in advance the type of data that can be placed into the collection.

Type-specific collections are *generic collections.* All the collections listed in Table 2-3 have generic counterparts.

For example, the `Dictionary` data type is the generic version of the `Hashtable` data type. To create a keyed collection that accepts only the `Customer` data type, you use the `Dictionary` data type, as shown here:

```
Dim invoiceCustomers As New Dictionary(Of String, Customer)
```

You add objects of the type `Customer` with a string key that represents their customer ID by using the `Add` method, as shown in the following code:

```
invoiceCustomers.Add("1234", cust)
```

✦ `System.Collections.Specialized` — Contains a set of strongly typed or specialized collections. For example, `StringDictionary` is a generic hashtable that works only with the data type string. If you try to put some other data type (such as an integer) into a `StringDictionary`, you receive an exception.

Collections are used extensively throughout the .NET Framework. For example, Windows Forms and Web Forms have a set of control collections. You can iterate through a form's collection of controls to add controls or find a specific control you wish to use.

Iterating through arrays and collections

An important task when working with collections is to be able to step through the elements within the collection. C# and Visual Basic provide the `foreach` and `For Each` statements, respectively, for iterating through a collection.

For example, the following code shows iterating through an `ArrayList` using `For Each` in Visual Basic:

```
Dim list As New ArrayList
list.Add(1)
list.Add(2)
list.Add(3)
For Each i as Integer In list
  Dim j As Integer
  j = j + i
Next
```

The `For Each` statement in the preceding sample executes once for each element in the `ArrayList` for a total of three times. On third execution, `j = 6` because 1 + 2 + 3 = 6.

The variable `j` is in scope only while execution is inside the `For Each` statement. After execution moves off the `Next` statement the third time, you can no longer access `j`. If you want to use the variable `j` outside the `For Each` statement, you need to declare it outside the `For Each` statement.

Keyed collections use the `DictionaryEntry` structure for iterating through values, as the following C# code sample shows:

```
Hashtable ht = new Hashtable();
ht.Add("Screen 1", "Shane");
ht.Add("Screen 2", "My Friend Flicka");
foreach (DictionaryEntry de in ht)
{
    lstMovies.Items.Add(de.Key + ":" + de.Value);
}
```

Figure 2-4 shows an example of the key/value pair from the hashtable in a list box.

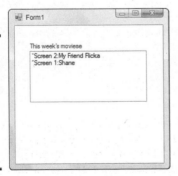

Figure 2-4:
Iterate through the hashtable to display key/value pairs in a list box.

Collections in the real world

You have many choices for working with collections. Here are some guidelines to help you decide:

✦ **Choose arrays over collections** when the number of elements is known and not expected to grow.

✦ **Choose collections over arrays** any time you find yourself looking for methods, such as `Add`, `Remove`, `Item`, or `Count`.

✦ **Choose generic collections** when you know in advance the data type you want to store in the collection. Generic collections perform better than nongeneric collections because their code doesn't have special cases to consider.

Besides selecting the best type of collection for the job, you must also consider how you'll actually use the collection in your code. If you're creating your own data types, you need to consider how to manage multiples of your data types. You have a few options:

✦ Extend the collections classes provided by .NET.

✦ Wrap an existing collection by creating a class to manage it.

In most cases, you'll probably wrap an existing collection when you want to provide your own custom collections. You have two approaches to wrapping an existing collection:

✦ **Create a new data type that wraps the collection.**

For example, you can create a data type called `MovieCollection` that allows you to handle a collection of movies without thinking about the underlying collection actually used.

✦ **Use a collection in an existing data type.**

An alternative approach to creating a separate wrapper collection is to include the collection in your data type. For example, you could create a generic collection of `Movie` types that you access from within your `Movie` type.

Converting Types

An important task when working with variables is converting a variable of one data type to another data type. For example, a variable with the Boolean value `True` is not the same as a variable with the string value `true`. They might look the same, but the language sees the Boolean variable as either on or off, and the string variable as an array of characters.

A variable's data type determines how much memory is allocated for the variable. When you convert from one data type to another, you're essentially asking the computer to give you more or less memory. Here are the two kinds of conversions that you can perform:

✦ **Widening** — Going from a smaller data type to a larger data type

✦ **Narrowing** — Going from a larger data type to a smaller data type

You risk data loss with narrowing conversions.

The syntax that you use to widen or narrow depends on whether the conversion is

✦ **Implicit** — Implicit conversions don't require any special syntax in order for the conversion to occur. For example, the following code implicitly converts a `Boolean` value to a `string` value:

```
Dim b As Boolean = True
Dim s As String = b
```

✦ **Explicit** — Any time you have to use special syntax to convert a variable, you make an *explicit conversion*. Explicit conversions are often necessary when you perform a narrowing conversion.

The .NET Framework provides the `System.Convert` class, which you can use to explicitly convert from one type to another. For example, the following code converts a `string` to an `integer` in C#:

```
string s = "1000";
int i = System.Convert.ToInt32(s);
```

C# provides the `cast` operator for performing explicit conversions. The following code converts from an `integer` value to a `byte`, which is a narrowing conversion:

```
int i = 255;
byte b = (byte)i;
```

Narrowing conversions can cause loss of data. For example, take a look at the following code sample:

```
int i = int.MaxValue;
byte b = (byte)i;
```

The maximum value of an `integer` data type is north of two million. So what's the value in the variable `b` after the conversion of integer `i`? It's `255`. A byte holds values from only 0 to 255.

Visual Basic provides the CType function, which you can use for explicit conversions. You pass an expression to convert and the data type to convert to the CType function, as shown here:

```
Dim s As String = "255"
Dim b As Byte = CType(s, Byte)
```

Visual Basic has type conversion functions for each primitive data type and a function each for converting reference types and strings. For example, the following code is equivalent to using CType in the preceding sample:

```
Dim s As String = "255"
Dim b As Byte = CByte(s)
```

Any implicit conversion can be explicitly stated. The following code explicitly converts a Boolean value to a string value:

```
Dim b As Boolean = True
Dim s As String = Convert.ToString(b)
```

There's no harm in using an explicit conversion in place of an implicit conversion. You should use explicit conversion any time you want to make it clear to readers of your code that a conversion is occurring.

You aren't restricted to converting between primitive types and strings. You can convert any data type in the .NET Framework, your programming language, or your user-defined data types. System.Convert, CType, and the cast operator all allow any kind of data type for making conversions. The catch, of course, is that the data types you're converting must be compatible.

In order for a conversion to be successful, a conversion operator must be defined for the type you wish to go from to. See the Visual Studio documentation for a list of available conversions for your language.

Converting value types (such as integers and Booleans) to reference types (such as strings and objects) is *boxing*. Boxing and its converse — unboxing — occur any time you use a value type when a reference type is expected. Passing value types as parameters when a reference type is expected is one example of when a value type is boxed.

All data types derive from System.Object; therefore, you can convert a variable of any data type to System.Object.

You can use the System.Type class to find out more information about a data type, such as the data type from which the data type is derived, as well as whether the data type is a value type or a reference type.

Meet the Nullable Types

Often, when working with values from databases, you encounter null values, which are undefined values. A null value can make your program blow up when the program is expecting to see an integer or a Boolean or a string. To help you process and anticipate null values, the .NET Framework includes a data type called System.Nullable.

You use System.Nullable to tell your program to accept a null value in your variable. System.Nullable provides the following properties:

✦ HasValue — Returns a true or false value indicating whether the variable has a value or is null.

✦ Value — Retrieves the variable's value. You use the HasValue property to test that the variable contains a value before using the Value property.

System.Nullable works with value types. *Values types* are primitive data types, such as integer and char. By definition, value types can't store null values. Reference types, such as strings, can store null values. As a result, it's not necessary for System.Nullable to work with reference types.

That's not to say that null reference types can't wreak the same kind of havoc in your program as trying to assign a null value to a value type. You should test your reference types for null values before you try to access the value.

When you declare a nullable value type, you tell System.Nullable which value type you wish to use. The following Visual Basic code sample creates a nullable integer:

```
Dim i As System.Nullable(Of Integer)
```

The equivalent declaration in C# is

```
System.Nullable<int> i;
```

C# provides the question mark (?) shortcut operator you can use when declaring nullables. The following statement is equivalent to the preceding statement:

```
int? i;
```

By declaring a variable as nullable, you can use the HasValue property to test for a null value. In the following code sample, if a nullable integer i has a value, the value is returned. Otherwise, the procedure returns 0 (zero).

```
int checkValue(int? i)
{
  if (i.HasValue == true)
     return i.Value;
  else
     return 0;
}
```

Browsing Types

The .NET Framework has hundreds of data types. Your own code base might have dozens — possibly even hundreds — of data types. Visual Studio provides Object Browser for perusing the vast libraries of data types available to you.

You use Object Browser any time you need to

+ Find a data type.

+ View the members of a data type, such as properties and methods.

+ View a description and get help for a data type.

You open Object Browser using the View menu or the key combination Ctrl+Alt+J. You don't need to have a project open to use Object Browser. Your open projects appear in Object Browser.

Setting the scope

You'd be quickly overwhelmed if you had to look at all the data types in Object Browser at once. Instead, Object Browser allows you to limit the scope of the types you view at any one time to the following:

+ .NET Framework

+ Third-party components

+ Your own projects and components

To view only the components in the .NET Framework, follow these steps:

1. **Press Ctrl+Alt+J to open Object Browser.**

2. **Click the Browse drop-down list on the Object Browser toolbar.**

A list of browsing scopes appears.

Object Browser displays data types from these browsing scopes:

• *All Components* — Displays the data types from the other options

• *.NET Framework* — Displays data types found in the .NET Framework

- *My Solution* — Displays data types created and referenced in the open solution

- *Custom Component Set* — Displays data types from a third-party component.

3. **Select .NET Framework from the drop-down list.**

   The assemblies in the .NET Framework appear in the Objects pane on the left, as shown in Figure 2-5.

Figure 2-5: The assemblies from the selected browsing scope appear in the Objects pane.

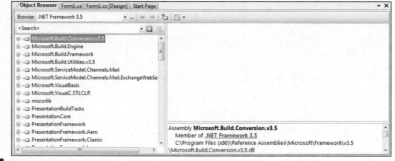

Use the My Solution browsing scope to view the assemblies referenced by your project.

Alternatively, you can use the Object Browser Search drop-down list to search for a word. Search is limited to the browsing scope selected in the Browse drop-down list. See Chapter 7 of this mini-book for an example of using Search in Object Browser.

Setting the view

Object Browser displays data types of all kinds, including classes, enumerations, and interfaces. By default, data types appear in assembly containers; however, there are many different views, such as

✦ **Assemblies** — The physical files in which the data type is defined. *Assemblies* are the DLL files that are output when your source code is built.

✦ **Namespaces** — The logical namespace in which the data type is defined

✦ **Object types** — The kind of data type, such as class, enumerator, or structure

To view the data types by namespaces

1. **Right-click inside the Objects pane.**

A shortcut menu appears.

2. **Choose View Namespaces.**

The data types are grouped by their namespaces.

To group the data types by assembly, repeat Step 1 and choose View Containers from the shortcut menu.

Choose Group by Object Type from the shortcut menu to group the data types by the type of data type.

To view the physical assembly file where data is defined

1. **Group the data types by assembly, as described in the preceding set of steps.**

2. **Click the assembly you wish to view.**

The assembly's name, path, and attributes appear in the Description pane. Figure 2-6 shows the assembly information for the System assembly.

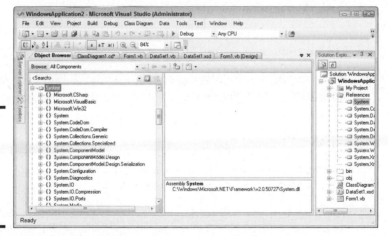

Figure 2-6:
Click an assembly to view information about the assembly.

Viewing data types

You can use Object Browser to view all kinds of information about data types, including the following data types.

✦ Assembly and namespace

✦ Members, such as properties and methods

✦ Base data type and derived data types

Here's how to view a data type in Object Browser:

1. **Set your browsing scope and view.**

2. **Click the plus sign (+) next to the container of data types.**

Depending on how you set up your view, you might also have to expand the Namespaces and Object Type folders to access the actual data types.

3. **Click the data type to view its members and description.**

For example, to access the System.Enum data type with the data types grouped by assemblies and object types, follow these steps:

1. **Click the plus sign (+) next to the mscorlib assembly.**

The Namespaces folder appears.

The mscorlib assembly contains the core namespaces of the .NET Framework.

2. **Click the plus sign (+) next to the Namespaces folder.**

A list of namespaces found in the mscorlib assembly appears.

3. **Click the plus sign (+) next to the System Namespace folder.**

A list of Object Type folders appears.

Note that the .NET Framework has a System assembly and a System namespace. The System namespace spans across both the mscorlib and System assemblies.

4. **Click the Structures folder.**

A list of structure data types appears.

5. **Click the Enum data type.**

The members and description appear in the browser.

To view a member's description, click the member, as shown in Figure 2-7.

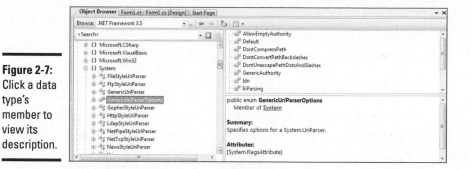

Figure 2-7:
Click a data
type's
member to
view its
description.

A data type's base data type can give you clues about whether the type is a
value type or reference type. Viewing the type's derived data types shows
you more specific implementations of the data type that might be more
appropriate for you to use.

You can view a data type's base type and any derived types by expanding
the data type. In the case of the System.Enum data type, its base type is
System.ValueType. Many types are derived from System.Enum, as shown
in Figure 2-8.

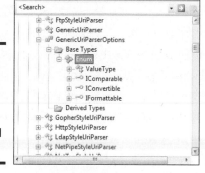

Figure 2-8:
Expand a
data type
to view its
base types
and derived
types.

You might have noticed that the data types, members, and other items in
Object Browser have icons next to them. A different icon is used to represent each kind of data type, such as classes or structures. Search for the
topic "Class View and Object Browser Icons" in the Visual Studio Help documentation for a summary of the icons used.

Viewing source code

Visual Studio provides several tools for browsing and navigating source code, including

✦ **Class View** — Use Class View to display a hierarchical view of the solution you're developing.

✦ **Code Definition** — This displays a read-only view of the source code for the selected object.

You use the Code Definition window in conjunction with the Class View or Object Browser to view an object's source code. When viewing objects from outside your project, the Code Definition window displays only the source code's type and method declarations and comments. You can't actually view the source code that implements the object.

The Code Definition window doesn't work in Visual Basic.

To use the Code Definition window with Class View, follow these steps:

1. **Open a C# project in Visual Studio.**

If you don't have an existing C# project, you can open one of the C# Starter Kits, such as the Movie Collection Starter Kit, from the New Project window.

2. **Press Ctrl+Shift+C to open Class View.**

The project appears in the Class View window.

3. **Choose Code Definition Window from the View menu.**

The Code Definition window appears.

4. **Expand the classes in Class View and click one of the objects.**

The object's methods appear in the bottom pane of Class View.

Class View and Object Browser use a number of icons to represent different kinds of objects. For example, the open and closing curly braces { } represent a namespace. See the topic "Class View and Object Browser Icons" in the Visual Studio documentation for a complete list of the icons used.

5. **Click one of the public methods.**

The method's source code appears in the Code Definition window, as Figure 2-9 shows.

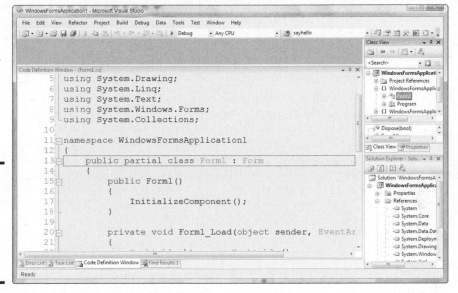

Figure 2-9:
Source
code
appears in
the Code
Definition
window.

The Code Definition window is a read-only view of the source code. To open
the source code file in the Code Editor, right-click the item in the Class View
window and choose Go to Definition from the contextual menu.

To view the object in Object Browser, right-click the object in the Class View
window and choose Browse Definition from the contextual menu.

Accessing Types in Your Source Code

Data types are logically organized into namespaces but physically organized
into assemblies. In order to consume types in your source code, you need to
know how to access the physical and logical paths to data types.

✦ **References** provide access to the physical assembly files where the
types can be found.

✦ **Namespaces** provide access to the logical path of the type within the
referenced assembly.

You access the physical file where types are stored by adding a reference to
the type. Visual Studio provides the ability to add new references and
manage existing references in your project.

When you create a new project, Visual Studio automatically adds a number
of references to common, physical DLL files you might need to use in your
project. You might remove any reference that you aren't using.

After you add a reference to the physical assembly where the type resides, you must also supply the logical namespace to access the type and its members. You can type the namespace in source code. If you have properly referenced the assembly, IntelliSense pops up to help you find the namespaces you need.

You can also include namespace directives — at the top of your source code — to provide a shortcut to namespaces you wish to use in your source code. The namespace directive in C# is `using`, and it's `Include` in Visual Basic. These directives allow you to access types within a namespace without fully qualifying the namespace every time.

For example, say you want to create a new `DataSet` in your source code. The `DataSet` type is found in the `System.Data` namespace. Using the fully qualified namespace looks like this in C#:

```
System.Data.DataSet ds = new System.Data.DataSet();
```

However, if you add the following using directive at the top of your source code file

```
using System.Data;
```

you can create a new `DataSet` like this:

```
DataSet ds = new DataSet();
```

Using namespace directives often saves space in your code and makes your code easier to read.

Another approach is to create an alias for the namespace so that it quickly identifies that the type is being referenced from another namespace. To create an alias in C#, type the following:

```
using data = System.Data;
```

Now, you can qualify the type by using the alias, as shown in the following code:

```
data.DataSet ds = new data.DataSet();
```

The same code in Visual Basic appears as

```
Imports data = System.Data
Dim ds as new data.DataSet
```

Chapter 3: Get Some Class

In This Chapter

✔ **Using objects and classes**

✔ **Declaring classes and members**

✔ **Designing classes with Class Designer**

When Rick first learned how to program computers, the flow of programming was sequential. You wrote one line of code after another. Each line of code was numbered, and you thought about your program in terms of what happens first and what happens next.

When he went to college, he was taught a more sophisticated approach to programming that uses functions to group statements of code. Functions are great because you can easily organize your code into reusable blocks.

When he started working as a programmer, he encountered yet a third programming paradigm that organizes code into classes. He found this curious because even though a program's basic building block is classes, the style of programming is called object-oriented programming (OOP).

Visual Studio provides many tools that support the activities of object-oriented design (OOD) and programming. This chapter covers some of the basics of working with objects and classes, and shows you how to use Class Designer to visually design and inspect classes and objects.

Bringing Programs to Life the Object-Oriented Way

Most programmers take awhile to figure out the relationship between objects and classes when they first encounter OOP. If you think of software as a means of modeling a real-world scenario, the following points are worth remembering:

✦ *Objects* **represent the people, places, and things in your program.** For example, think about a business that sends an invoice to a customer. Invoice #100984 and Customer #60093 are objects that your program needs to manipulate. The business, ABC Graphics, sending invoice #100984 to customer #60093 is an object, too.

✦ *Classes* **are the units of code you write to make objects come to life in your program.** For example, your program defines `Invoice` and `Customer` classes. Each class encapsulates the data and behaviors required to create objects that represent real-world invoices and customers.

You *write* classes, but you *think* in terms of objects, which is why programming with objects is called *object-oriented programming*. Table 3-1 compares OOP with procedural and sequential programming styles.

Table 3-1	Comparison of Programming Styles	
Programming Style	*Programmers' Approach*	*Basic Building Blocks*
Object-oriented	What objects am I modeling in my program?	Objects
Procedural	What functions do I need to tackle this problem?	Functions
Sequential	What's the next line of code to write?	Statements

Thinking in objects isn't limited to programmers. Objects are often found in the planning and design stages of a project, where object-oriented thinking is formally known as both of the following:

✦ **Object-oriented analysis** — Requirements analysts use objects to model problems in the business domain.

✦ **Object-oriented design (OOD)** — Designers use analysis objects to model classes that programmers will write to create objects.

Programmers use object-oriented programming languages (OOPLs) — such as Visual Basic, C#, C++, and Java — to implement classes.

Even if you've never written an object-oriented program or know nothing about objects, chances are you're familiar with several of the characteristics of OOP:

✦ Using the familiar dot notation to access the members of an object

✦ Using the new operator to initialize a reference type

✦ Setting an object's properties

What's with Objects?

Classes and objects are the bedrock of OOP. *Classes* are special kinds of data types that you use to create objects in your code. Objects are placeholders in your code for the real people, places, and things upon which your program acts.

Classes are a complex data type. Simple data types store values, such as integers and Booleans. Composite data types, such as structures that are capable of storing more than one value, aren't more sophisticated than integers and Booleans. The values that you can store by using classes, however, are beyond mere integers or sets of integers.

You might recognize simple data types as value types and complex data types as reference types. See Chapter 2 in this mini-book for a thorough discussion of the differences between value types and reference types.

A *class* is a data type that's capable of storing data and actions. When you declare and initialize a variable by using a class data type, you create an object that stores data and action values defined by the class data type. Objects are used to accommodate the potential complexity of values stored for class data types. An object is often referred to as an *instance* of the class data type.

The term *object* is often interchanged for the term *class.* People often use the term *object* in a generic sense to mean "the class that defines the object." People seldom use *class* when they mean *object.* You must consider the context in which the term is used to determine whether the author or speaker means class or object. (Ask whether the author is writing about a data type or the value represented by the data type. If it's the former, it's a *class.* Otherwise, it's an *object.)*

Classes act as a template for defining the data and actions of an object. You create objects by using the class as a template. Each object created from the class is like a blank form into which you can place data. The source of that data may be a database, data typed on a screen by a user, or another object.

Some people find it helpful to think of classes as the blueprints for objects — or to think that classes are abstract and that objects are concrete.

Think of classes as a template for creating an object.

You're familiar with the concept of data, but you might not immediately understand what the potential actions of a class data type may be. Consider a class data type called `Customer`. You expect a `Customer` data type to store a customer's name and account number. If you need to tell someone a customer's 30-days aging of their account, how might you approach solving this problem?

Given that an account's aging is based on the current date, you need to be able to calculate the value in real time. You can't query a database for the answer. Your `Customer` class needs a procedure that returns the account's aging.

Storing calculated values in a database is usually considered bad form. There are a number of reasons that you don't want to store calculated values, but the two most important reasons are that the calculated values consume additional space and they can become outdated when the values that support them change. Classes often return calculated values for an object. For example, an `Employee` class may have a procedure that returns the employee's age.

Another way to think of actions is that they are sometimes things that an object can do. For instance, a student registers for courses. Registering for courses is an action that a student object is capable of doing.

Classes are important to software development because they

+ Are a basic building block of programs

+ Group related code in a unit

+ Control visibility and accessibility of your code

+ Encourage reuse

+ Are easy to extend

+ Can model real-world scenarios

+ Map code to the real world

Code created with objects and classes, adhering to the principles of OOP, display these characteristics:

+ **Abstraction** — Models a real-life thing by using only the attributes relevant to solving the problem at hand

   Creating user-defined classes is an example of an abstraction. When you approach a problem you're trying to solve, you identify the objects that are relevant to the problem. For example, you need a `Customer` object and an `Invoice` object to prepare invoices. You determine the level of detail required in your `Customer` and `Invoice` classes to adequately solve the problem of printing invoices.

+ **Encapsulation** — Wraps the data and actions of an entity into a single unit

   Encapsulation isn't unique to OOP. Functions and subroutines are example of encapsulation, as are classes.

✦ **Inheritance** — Builds a hierarchy of related code by creating parent-child relationships between units of code

   Inheritance allows you to create a supertype/subtype relationship between types. A simple example of inheritance is having a `Dog` class and a `Cat` class that inherits from an `Animal` class. The `Animal` class has all the data and actions common to both dogs and cats. However, unique behaviors — such as a cat's purr — appear in the appropriate derived class.

✦ **Polymorphism** — Allows child types to provide their own code to implement actions performed by their parent or sibling

   Polymorphism makes it possible for a class hierarchy to share a common set of behaviors while each has its own implementation. For example, the `Animal` class has a reproductive cycle. The `Dog` and `Cat` classes each require their own implementation of a reproductive cycle. Polymorphism allows you to refer to the generic concept of a reproductive cycle in your code, regardless of whether you mean a dog or a cat.

Another important characteristic of OOD is information hiding. You should design your classes so that important design decisions are hidden. In other words, one should have to think about only initializing and accessing your classes, not understanding how you've written them. The classes in the .NET Framework are a good example of information hiding. You must explicitly think about information hiding as you design your application. It's possible to abstract, encapsulate, inherit, and polymorph without hiding information. Simply using object-oriented techniques doesn't ensure that you're hiding information.

You use an OOPL (such as Visual Basic, C#, or C++) to write object-oriented programs. The .NET Framework is an object-oriented library of classes.

In addition to the OOP languages, Visual Studio provides several tools to support OOP, including

✦ Class Designer

✦ Class View

✦ Object Browser

✦ Object Test Bench (OTB)

The only way to learn OOD and programming is to do OOD and programming. Memorizing terms and definitions can help your vocabulary, but by themselves, they do very little to increase your understanding of OOD and OOP. So, instead of getting hung up on terminology, just start coding.

Anatomy of a Class in .NET

Classes and OOP have terminology with which you might not be familiar and which might seem overwhelming at first. At its heart, classes are just ways to organize code similar to the modules, functions, and subroutines with which you might be familiar. Like modules, functions, and subroutines, you declare variables and procedures similarly to how you do in modules.

Classes are templates that define an object's

+ **Data** — Data is sometimes referred to as the object's *state,* which is the set of values an object holds at a given point in time.

+ **Behavior** — Behaviors are the actions that the object takes.

The code that creates a new class is a *class declaration.* A class declaration consists of the class header and body. The class header defines the following:

+ **Attributes** — Optional keywords used by the compiler

    The .NET Framework provides several attributes for use in your class and method declarations.

    Chapter 6 of this mini-book shows you how to use the `WebService` and `WebMethod` attributes to turn ordinary classes and methods into Web services.

+ **Modifiers** — Keywords that define how the class may be used

    For example, classes and members use access modifiers, such as `public` and `private`, to determine whether the class or member may be accessed by code outside the class or namespace.

+ **Name** — Identity of the class

+ **Base class** — Data type from which the class is inheriting.

    All classes implicitly inherit from `System.Object`.

+ **Interfaces** — Comma-separated list of interfaces implemented by the class

    An *interface* is a set of member declarations with no source code to implement them. Interfaces make it possible to define a publicly con-sumable contract without writing the source code. Other developers can target the interface without fear of the interface changing. See Chapter 4 of this mini-book for more information on interfaces.

A class' *body* defines the class' data and behavior. The items declared inside a class are its *members*. The members you can create inside a class body include

+ **Constants** — Values in the class that don't change

+ **Constructors** — Special procedures that are called to create an object using the class

   An object is often referred to as an *instance* of the class.

+ **Destructors** — Special procedures that are called before an object is discarded by your program

+ **Events** — Procedures that raise a notification when a certain action occurs

+ **Fields** — Variables declared for use within the class, often for storing data

+ **Indexers** — Procedures that index individual instances of the class

+ **Methods** — Procedures that provide the behaviors of the class

+ **Operators** — Procedures that define conversions for the class and extend built-in operators

+ **Properties** — Procedures that provide access to the class' data structure

+ **Types** — Nested data types, such as classes or structures, created within the class

The combination of a class header and its body is its *definition*.

You might have noticed that a class' body is made up of procedures and variables. If you've done any programming at all, you should be familiar with the concept of using variables and procedures to create your program.

In C#, a class' body is wrapped in opening and closing curly braces. Listed here is a class definition in C#:

```
public class Message
{
  private string m_message;
  public string Contents
  {
    get { return m_message; }
    set { m_message = value; }
  }
  public Message(string message)
  {
```

```
        this.m_message = message;
    }
    public string ReverseContents()
    {
        char[] c = this.m_message.ToCharArray();
        StringBuilder sb = new StringBuilder();
        for (int i = 1; i <= c.Length; i++)
        {
            sb.Append(c, c.Length - i, 1);
        }
        return sb.ToString();
    }
}
```

Can you tell which elements in this class are fields, properties, and methods? It's not immediately obvious just by looking at the code. To someone not familiar with OOP, this code looks like variable and procedure declarations. Table 3-2 summarizes the members in this class.

Table 3-2		Members Found in the Message Class
Member Type	*Quantity*	*Example*
Field	1	`m_message`
Property	1	`Contents`
Constructor	1	`Message(string message)`
Method	1	`ReverseContents()`

Take a look at the equivalent code sample in Visual Basic. Notice how the Visual Basic keywords `Property` and `New` provide clues as to the member's purpose:

```
Public Class Message
    Private m_message As String
    Public Property Contents() As String
        Get
            Return Me.m_message
        End Get
        Set(ByVal value As String)
            Me.m_message = value
        End Set
    End Property
    Public Sub New(ByVal message As String)
        Me.m_message = message
    End Sub
    Public Function ReverseContents() As String
        Dim c As Char() = Me.m_message.ToCharArray()
```

```
      Dim sb As New StringBuilder
      For i As Integer = 1 To c.Length
        sb.Append(c, c.Length - i, 1)
      Next
      Return sb.ToString()
    End Function
End Class
```

Classes are logically organized within namespaces. Your class code is stored in a physical file called an *assembly*. A single namespace can span multiple assembly files, but a single class can reside in only one assembly. To access classes, you must reference the assembly and the namespace within your project. See Chapter 2 of this mini-book for more information.

The C# keyword this and Visual Basic keyword me are used to reference the current instance of an object in your code.

Inheriting the services of System.Object

All classes inherit from the .NET class System.Object. Inheriting from System.Object provides all the basic services your classes need to function as objects and get along with other objects.

System.Object is the base class of your class, and your class is a derived class of System.Object.

Any time your classes derive from a base class, you should check the documentation of the base class to determine if there are any methods you should override. When you *override* a member, you write your own code to implement the member.

For example, the System.Object class has a method called ToString that you should override. By overriding ToString in the classes you define, you can get a string representation of objects created from your class. See Chapter 5 of this mini-book for more information on overriding.

Several overridden methods are available for System.Object. Table 3-3 lists all the methods your class inherits from System.Object and identifies those that you should override.

Overriding a base class' methods when recommended is considered good form. Overriding ensures that your derived class works as expected. Look for the "Note to Implementers" section in the base class' type for information on overriding.

Table 3-3	Methods of System.Object	
Method	*Description*	*Override*
New	Constructor	Not required
Finalize	Destructor	Not recommended
Equals	Determines whether two object instances are equivalent	Yes
GetHashCode	Generates a hash code for use in hashtables	Not required
GetType	Returns the data type of the object instance	No
MemberwiseClone	Copies a value or an object reference	No
ReferenceEquals	Determines whether two object instances are the same object	Not required
ToString	Returns a human-readable representation of the object instance	Recommended

Using classes in your code

Recall that classes are data types. Therefore, you use them like you use any data type. They're reference types, so you use the new operator to create a new instance of a class.

The new operator calls the class's constructor method. A class may have more than one constructor. If no constructor method is defined in the class, the object is initialized by using the default constructor. The default constructor is the New() method defined in the System.Object class. Recall that all classes derive from System.Object.

Classes are reference types, so everything in Chapter 2 of this mini-book about how memory is allocated for reference types applies to classes. When you initialize a new instance of a class, the object itself is allocated on the heap. The reference to the object is allocated on the stack.

To create a new instance of the Message class created in the preceding section, you type the following:

```
Message m = new Message("Hello");
```

You use dot notation to access the members of the class. The member's visibility is determined by the modifier set on the member's declaration. You can always see public members, but not private members. To call the ReverseContents member, type the following:

```
string s = m.ReverseContents();
```

Here's the equivalent code, using Visual Basic syntax:

```
Dim m As New Message("Hello")
Dim s As String = m.ReverseContents()
```

There's no need to declare the `Message` class using Visual Basic and C# syntax. You can just as easily create the class in C# and then reference and instantiate it in Visual Basic.

Hopefully, this syntax looks familiar to you. If you've used any features in the .NET Framework, you've encountered this syntax.

You can use any of the classes in the .NET Framework or any third-party library just by knowing the rules for declaring variables based on a class data type and creating instances of objects.

Using Class Designer

Visual Studio provides a visual design tool — Class Designer — that you can use to create class diagrams. Some common uses of Class Designer are

+ Designing new classes

+ Visualizing existing classes

+ Refactoring classes

Another use of Class Designer that might not be immediately evident is as a training aid. You can use Class Designer to familiarize yourself with the concepts of OOP. You can also use it to learn syntax.

Use Class Designer as an aid, and not a crutch. If you rely too heavily on the tool, you risk being dependent on the tool. This is definitely not where you want to be if your company decides to migrate some projects to another object-oriented language, such as Java.

Like most of the visual designers in Visual Studio, Class Designer generates diagrams from code and code from diagrams. The diagrams and code are synchronized. The class diagram is a visual representation of source code.

The class diagrams created by Class Designer are design diagrams — not analysis diagrams. Design diagrams usually show more implementation details than analysis diagrams. If you want a tool better suited to creating analysis diagrams, try Visio for Enterprise Architects. You can easily generate classes from your Visio diagrams and then view those classes in Class Designer. You can learn more about Visio by reading *Visio 2007 For Dummies* by John Mueller and Debbie Walkowski (Wiley).

Common tasks you can do in Class Designer include the following:

✦ Create new classes and members.

✦ Define relationships among classes.

✦ View classes and relationships.

✦ Refactor code.

Exploring Class Designer

Class Designer is capable of designing more than just classes. You can use Class Designer to design or view any kind of data type, including

✦ Classes

✦ Delegates

✦ Enumerations

✦ Interfaces

✦ Structures

Class Designer can also create Visual Basic modules, which are used to encapsulate your code. See the Visual Basic documentation for more information on the differences between classes and modules.

You add a new class diagram to your project using the Add New Item window. A project may have multiple class diagrams. To add a new class diagram

1. **Right-click your project's folder in Solution Explorer.**

2. **From the contextual menu that appears, choose Add⇨New Item.**

   The Add New Item window appears.

3. **Click the Class Diagram icon.**

4. **Type a name for the class diagram in the Name field.**

   The example uses ClassDiagram1 as the class diagram name.

5. **Click the Add button.**

   Visual Studio adds the class diagram file to Solution Explorer and opens it in Class Designer.

Class diagrams use the .cd filename extensions. Like most files in Visual Studio, the class diagram file is an XML file.

Class diagrams are visual representations of classes in a project. The diagrams are similar to diagrams created using the Unified Modeling Language (UML) specification.

UML is a modeling language that identifies 13 diagrams used for designing software. Many tools available on the market are capable of creating UML diagrams, including Microsoft Visio for Enterprise Architects. Visual Studio class diagrams won't replace UML diagrams you're already using. Consider them another tool to add to your modeling arsenal.

Class Designer consists of the

✦ Toolbox

✦ Designer surface

✦ Class Details pane

The Designer provides a toolbar and shortcut menus to access additional features. The Designer works with Solution Explorer, Class View, and OTB.

Class Designer provides several commands you can use for working with your diagram. The commands that you can use depend on what you have selected in the diagram. You have three levels of commands for working with class diagrams:

✦ **Diagram** — To work with the entire diagram, click a blank area of the diagram.

✦ **Type** — Click a shape to access commands that act on the data type.

✦ **Member** — Click a member within the type to view commands.

Figure 3-1 shows the Class Designer toolbar. The first column of Table 3-4 lists the commands of the Class Designer toolbar, as they appear on the toolbar from left to right.

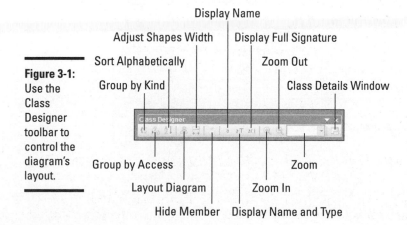

Figure 3-1:
Use the Class Designer toolbar to control the diagram's layout.

Table 3-4	Class Designer Toolbar Commands	
Command Type	*Command*	*Description*
Arrangements of shapes	Group by Kind	Groups by kind of data type
	Group by Access	Groups by data type's access modifier
	Sort Alphabetically	Sorts by data type's names
Layout	Layout Diagram	Organizes diagram
	Adjust Shapes Width	Widens shapes
Member display options	Display Name	Displays members' names only
	Display Name and Type	Displays names and type
	Display Full Signature	Displays full declaration
Visual	Zoom In	Zooms in on diagram
	Zoom Out	Zooms out on diagram
	Zoom Percentage	Sets a zoom percentage
	Class Details Window	Opens the Class Details window

The Class Designer menu provides you the opportunity to act upon the shapes that represent data types on the diagram. Table 3-5 lists the options available for data types you click in the class diagram.

Table 3-5	Class Designer Menu Type-Level Commands
Command	*Description*
Add	Selects a member to add to the type
Refactor	Accesses refactoring options for the type
IntelliSense	Generates code using IntelliSense
Show Base Class	Displays the type's base type on the diagram
Show Derived Class	Displays types derived from the type on the diagram
Collapse	Collapses members
Expand	Expands members
Show All Members	Displays any hidden members
Create Instance	Creates an object using the OTB
Invoke Static Method	Calls a static method using the OTB

You can access most of these commands from a shortcut menu when you right-click a shape in a class diagram. The shape's shortcut menu includes commands to delete the shape from the diagram and view the type's underlying source code.

Designing classes

One of the more exciting features of Class Designer is the ability to design classes. You can drag and drop data types on the class diagram; in the background, Visual Studio is generating the code to create the data type.

Creating a new class

Class Designer can create all kinds of data types. The Toolbox includes all the shapes you need to create data types and show relationships between data types.

To create a new class with Class Designer, follow these steps:

1. **Add a new class diagram, following the steps in the previous section.**

2. **Press Ctrl+Alt+X to open the Toolbox.**

The Toolbox pane displays icons representing items you can add to the Class Designer. Open the Class Designer tab, if necessary, to see the controls you can use.

3. **Drag and drop a Class icon from the Toolbox onto Class Designer.**

The New Class dialog box appears.

4. **Type a name for the class in the Name text box.**

The example uses Message as the name.

5. **Select an access modifier from the Access drop-down list.**

The `public` access modifier is accepted by default. The example uses `public` as the access modifier.

6. **Type a new filename for the class or select an existing file to add the class.**

The example uses the Create New File option and `Message.cs` as the filename.

7. **Click OK.**

The Class shape appears on Class Designer.

Visual Studio generates the class declaration and places it in the file you created or selected in Step 6.

Figure 3-2 shows Class Designer with a class called `Message`. You can see the `Message.cs` source code that Visual Studio created in the pane next to the class diagram.

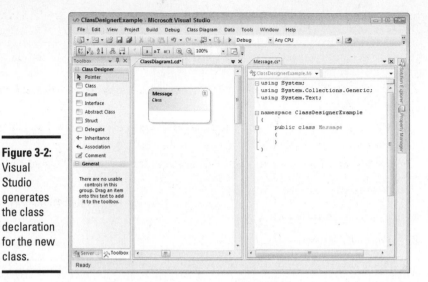

Figure 3-2:
Visual
Studio
generates
the class
declaration
for the new
class.

To add more types to the class diagram, drag the type from the Toolbox onto the design surface. A dialog box appears, similar to the one in Step 3.

Adding members to a class

You use Class Designer to add members to your class. When you add a member using the designer, you specify the following information about a member:

+ Name
+ Data type
+ Access modifier

You can, optionally, supply a descriptive comment and mark whether to hide the member on the class diagram.

Visual Studio uses the information you supply to create a member declaration in your source code. You have two options for adding members to your class with Class Designer:

+ **Type the members in the Class Details pane.** The Class Details pane shows the class's members grouped by methods, properties, fields, and events.
+ **Add the members to the class in the class diagram.**

The class diagram and the source code are synchronized. Any members you declare directly in source code appear in the class diagram.

To add a new member via the Class Details pane

1. **Click the section of the Class Details pane for the type of member you wish to add.**

   If the Class Details pane is closed, choose View➪Other Windows➪Class Details to open the pane.

2. **Type the member's name in the line immediately below the section's header.**

   For example, to add a new field, click the line below the Fields section where you see <add field>.

3. **Press the Tab key.**

   The cursor stops in the Type cell.

4. **Type the member's data type.**

   IntelliSense works in the Class Details pane.

5. **Press Tab and select the member's access modifier.**

6. **Press Tab and add a optional descriptive comment.**

7. **Click to place a check mark in the Hide column if you don't want the member to appear on the class diagram.**

   Figure 3-3 shows a field (m_strMessage) and a property (Content) in the Class Details pane.

Figure 3-3:
Use the Class Details pane to add new members.

Visual Studio generates the member declarations for you in the class's source code file.

The Class Details pane features a toolbar button with shortcuts for adding members. To access the shortcut button, click the arrow on the button, as shown in Figure 3-4.

Figure 3-4:
Use the
Class
Details
toolbar
to add
members.

A method's declaration is a little more complex than a field or property declaration because a method may accept parameters. In addition, multiple kinds of methods are available, such as constructors and destructors. The Class Details pane has no problems adding methods to your class. To add a new constructor method, follow these simple steps:

1. **Click the shortcut button on the Class Details toolbar.**

2. **Chose New Constructor.**

A new constructor method appears in the Methods section of the Class Details pane.

Constructors use the same name as the class in C#. In Visual Basic, constructors are named New.

3. **Type the constructor's parameters in the lines below the constructor's declaration, as shown in Figure 3-5.**

Figure 3-5:
Add
parameters
to the
constructor
method.

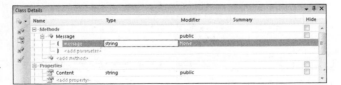

Visual Studio generates the member declarations and stubs out the member's bodies (the members don't perform any useful task — they simply provide a placeholder for code you add later). Exceptions are placed inside the generated members to remind you that you need to add your code if you try to use the members. For example, the following code is the constructor generated for the preceding sample:

```
public Message(string message)
{
  throw new System.NotImplementedException();
}
```

Class Designer is a good tool to use for designing a class domain. Designers can lay out the classes and then pass off their implementation to a programmer.

You can also create members by using the class diagram. To create a member in the class diagram, do the following:

1. **Right-click the class in the class diagram.**

2. **From the contextual menu that appears, choose Add.**

A list of members appears, which you can add to the class.

3. **Select the type of member you wish to add.**

The member appears in the diagram.

4. **Type the member's name in the diagram, as shown in Figure 3-6.**

Use the Class Details pane to complete the member's declaration.

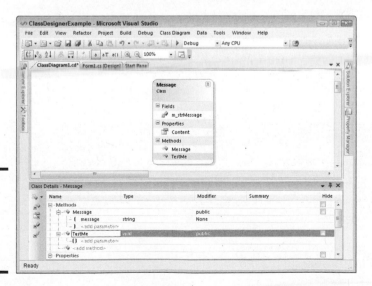

Figure 3-6:
Type the member's name in the class diagram.

Creating associations

The nature of OOP is that classes interact. You create an interaction between classes when you create member declarations in your class. For example, if you declare a field of the string type, you create an association between your class and the string class.

In Class Designer, you show associations between only classes that are relevant to the model you're creating. You could show every association, but then your diagrams would be too crowded for people to understand. Instead, you should show only the associations that you want to draw attention to.

Here's how to create an association between two types:

1. **Create both types on the class diagram.**

2. **Click the Association icon in the Toolbox.**

3. **Click the type where you want to draw the association.**

   The cursor appears as a line, as shown in Figure 3-7.

4. **Drag the line to the class.**

   An association between the classes appears. Visual Studio adds the association as a property.

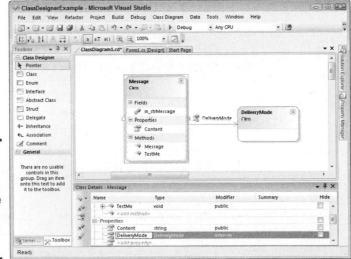

Figure 3-7: Drag the cursor between the two classes to create an association.

You can show associations between classes and collections. To show an association between a class and a strongly typed collection, follow these steps:

1. **Add the member to your class that uses the strongly typed collection.**

For example, add a field that uses a generic collection based on another data type in your diagram. The example uses a field named m_Collection, which is of type Int32[] (an array).

2. **Right-click the member on the class diagram.**

3. **From the contextual menu that appears, choose Show as Collection Association.**

An association between the classes appears, as shown in Figure 3-8.

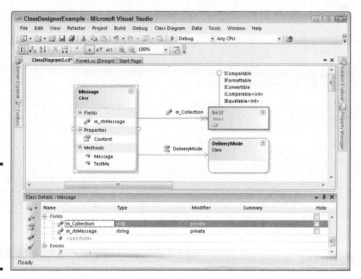

Figure 3-8:
Create an association between a class and a collection.

Generating code

Class Designer takes advantage of the Visual Studio code generation features. While using Class Designer, you can access

✦ **Advanced IntelliSense features,** such as overriding type members and implementing abstract base classes

✦ **Refactoring commands,** such as extracting interfaces from a type and renaming members

Refactoring commands aren't available while designing classes using Visual Basic.

See Chapter 5 in this mini-book for more information on using IntelliSense and refactoring features of Visual Studio.

Viewing existing classes

Class Designer is an excellent tool for viewing information about data types. You can view data types within your own project, as well as any types referenced by your project. This means that you can view types from the .NET Framework or a third party.

To view a type in your project, simply drag and drop the source code file from Solution Explorer to the class diagram.

You use Class View to drag referenced types from your project to the class diagram. For example, to add the type NullReferenceException to a class diagram, follow these steps:

1. **Add a new class diagram to your project.**

2. **Press Ctrl+Shift+C to open Class View.**

3. **Type** System.NullReferenceException **in the Search box.**

   Alternatively, expand the Project Reference folders and navigate to the NullReferenceException type.

   The NullReferenceException type is in the System namespace in the mscorlib assembly. Your project references the mscorlib assembly by default.

4. **Press Enter.**

   The System.NullReferenceException appears in the search results.

5. **Drag and drop System.NullReferenceException on the class diagram.**

Admittedly, viewing a single type on a class diagram isn't very exciting. You can use the Class Details pane to view the type's members. You can also view a type's inheritance hierarchy. To view a type's base type, follow these steps:

1. **Right-click the type and choose Show Base Class from the shortcut menu.**

   The base type appears on the class diagram.

2. **Repeat Step 1 for each base type you display.**

Show Base Class appears dimmed when you reach the top of the inheritance hierarchy.

Figure 3-9 shows the class diagram for the `NullReferenceException` type. Notice that `System.Object` is at the top of the hierarchy.

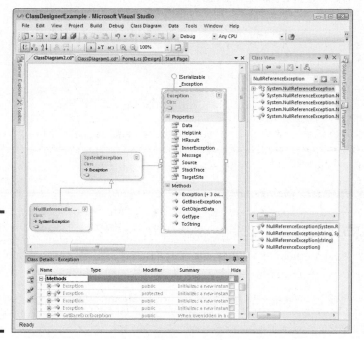

Figure 3-9:
Use Class
Designer
to view
a type's
inheritance
hierarchy.

To view the class diagram for an entire project, follow these steps:

1. **Right-click the project folder in Solution Explorer.**

2. **From the contextual menu that appears, choose View Class Diagram.**

A class diagram of the project appears. Figure 3-10 shows the class diagram for this example (which started out as a Windows Form application).

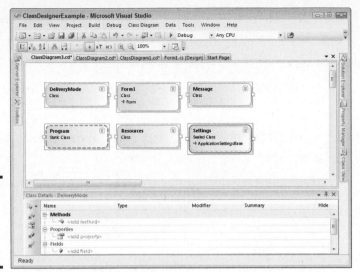

Figure 3-10:
Create
a class
diagram for
a project.

Working with objects

Earlier, this chapter describes how objects are the basis of everything programmers do in software. Programmers create classes to define the data and actions of objects in the real world, such as invoices and customers. Visual Studio provides the OTB as a means to create an object from a class in a visual environment.

The OTB is a separate tool from Class Designer, but you can access OTB from the designer. Class Designer provides two commands for creating objects from the types on your class diagram:

✦ **Create Instance** — Calls the constructor method that you select

✦ **Invoke Static Method** — Calls a static method that you select

Static is a modifier that can be used on classes and methods. When a method or class is declared as static, you can use the class or method without first creating an instance of the class. In other words, you don't use the new operator when you use a static method or class.

See Chapter 8 of this mini-book to read more about the uses of OTB.

To create an instance of an object in the OTB with Class Designer:

1. **Right-click the class that you want to use on the class diagram.**

The type can't be a static class.

2. From the contextual menu that appears, choose Create Instance.

A list of the class's available constructors appears in a submenu.

3. Choose the constructor you wish to use.

The Create Instance window appears, in which you supply input parameters to the constructor and specify a name to use as the object's identifier.

4. Type a variable name. Supply parameter values, if required.

5. Click OK.

The object appears in the OTB.

Invoking a static method is similar to creating an object instance. For example, to invoke a static method on a static class, such as `System.Environment`, do the following:

1. Drag and drop the static class onto the class diagram.

The `System.Environment` type is in the `mscorlib` assembly. Drag the type from Class View, as described in the preceding section "Viewing existing classes."

2. Right-click the static class.

A shortcut menu appears.

3. Choose Invoke Static Method.

A list of static methods appears.

4. Select a static method from the list.

The example uses the `GetLogicalDrives()` static method. The Invoke Method window appears.

5. Enter parameter values, if required.

6. Click OK.

The Method Call Result window appears.

If the method doesn't return a value, the method executes but no results appear.

The Method Call Result window displays the return value.

7. Type an identifier for the return value.

The identifier appears in the object's shape in the OTB.

8. **Click OK.**

The return value appears in the OTB. Figure 3-11 shows the return value for the `GetLogicalDrives()` static method on the `System.Environment` static class. Hover your mouse over the object to view the return value.

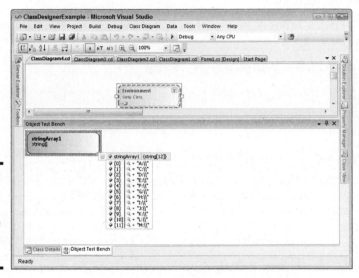

Figure 3-11: The static method's return value appears in the OTB.

Chapter 4: Wiring Up Events in the User Interface

In This Chapter

✔ Understanding events and event handlers

✔ Using Visual Studio to discover events

✔ Creating event handlers with Visual Studio

✔ Getting a grip on Windows and Web applications life cycles

S ay that you create a Windows Form that requires a user to enter her username and password. Maybe you create a Web page with a drop-down list of state names that you want populated when the user browses to the page. Or, you add a Print command to a menu that you want to execute the command to print a report. What do all these scenarios have in common?

All these scenarios require some action to occur before your code can execute. A user must submit his credentials; a Web page loads; a user clicks a menu command. All these actions are *events*.

You can probably think of several events off the top of your head: click, double-click, hover, and exit. You probably associate events with direct actions that a user takes to interact with your program. In reality, events go way beyond mere button clicking and mouse hovering. Events allow your entire application, as well as each form and control within the application, to have its own life cycle. From the moment your application fires up until the moment it shuts down, events are firing along the way.

As you already likely know, code fires in response to events, such as button clicks. Taking advantage of the events in an application and control life cycles allows you to run code at a precise moment in an application's or a control's life cycle. Instead of waiting for a user to click a button, you can run code as soon as your application starts — or even when a user's cursor leaves a text box.

In Visual Studio, responding to events is as simple as a double click, in many cases. Visual Studio generates codes behind the scenes that wire up your code to the event that fires it.

Handling Events

In most modern applications, an application responds to actions that a user takes. Your application sits in a waiting state until a user comes along and clicks a button, a menu, or a drop-down list. When a user clicks a button, an action (the *event*) occurs. The code that executes when an event fires is an *event handler.*

Procedures that run when an event occurs — *event handlers* — um, handle events. Still, they're just procedures, just like any procedure you write. You're responsible for writing event handlers to handle any events to which you wish to respond.

For instance, say you want a message box to pop up when a user clicks OK on your Windows Form. The following code sample uses Visual Basic syntax to make a message box appear:

```
MessageBox.Show("You clicked the OK button", "Handling
    Events", MessageBoxButtons.OK)
```

Now, the question is where to put that code. You know that you want the message box to appear when the user clicks a button. You need to write an event handler for the button's `Click` event.

Right here is where you should stop. How do you know that the code belongs in the button's `Click` event? Is it as simple as pulling the verb out of a sentence and calling it an *event?* Not quite.

Discovering events

Most documentation and articles that you can read about events and event handling assume that readers somehow magically know for what events they're supposed to write code. Most people intuitively get the concepts of *click* or *double-click,* but what about *hover* or *paint?*

In order for a button or some other component to have an event, someone must have written an event method for the component. The event method is the other side of the event-handling story.

For example, a button that you add to a Windows Form is actually the `Button` class in the `System.Windows.Forms` namespace. The button's `Click` event is the `Button` class' `Click` event method. An *event method* is a procedure in the same way that an event handler is a procedure. The difference is that the event method creates the event, whereas the event handler responds to the event.

The class with the event method is the *sender,* and the class with the event handler is the *receiver.* When an event fires, the sender *raises* the event. The receiver *consumes* the event with an event handler.

By reducing events to methods in a class, all you have to do is refer to the class' documentation to figure out the set of events available to you. Of course, Visual Studio has a few tools you can use to help you in your quest:

✦ **The Properties window** — View the Properties window of a component and click the lightning bolt icon to see a list of the component's events.

✦ **The Code Editor Navigation bar** — Use the Navigation bar at the top of the Code Editor to select an event.

✦ **Help documentation** — Use the index or the Class Library Reference in the .NET Framework software development kit (SDK) to locate documentation on a specific class.

The easiest way to discover events is to add a component to Windows Forms Designer or Web Forms Designer and view its properties. Here's how:

1. **Create a new Windows or Web project or open an existing project.**

2. **Drag and drop a control or component from the toolbox onto the form designer.**

The control or component appears in the designer.

Press Ctrl+Alt+X to open the toolbox if it's closed.

3. **Click the control or component to select it.**

4. **Press F4 to open the Properties window.**

The control or component's properties appear in the Properties window.

5. **Click the Events button on the Properties window toolbar to display a list of events available for the control or component.**

The Events button is the button with the lightning bolt.

The lightning bolt is the icon used to represent events in Visual Studio. You'll see the lightning bolt used in Object Browser, Class View, and the Code Editor Navigation bar.

Figure 4-1 shows an example of a button's properties in a Web site project. Notice that the button's class name appears in the drop-down list at the top of the Properties window. In this figure, the fully qualified class name for a Web button is `System.Windows.Form.Button`.

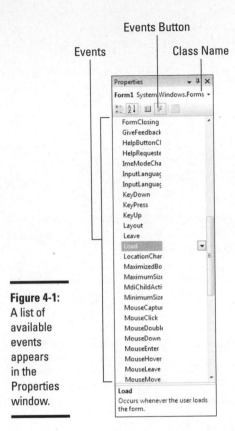

Events

Events Button

Class Name

Figure 4-1:
A list of available events appears in the Properties window.

The class name is `Button`, and `System.Windows.Form` is the name-space used to access the `Button` class. You can use this information to look up the class documentation in the Visual Studio documentation.

Web projects and Windows projects use different controls. They might go by the same name — in the case of a button, for example — but they're actually different classes. The fully qualified name for a Windows button is `System.Windows.Forms.Button`. You can read more about fully qualified namespaces in Chapter 2 of this mini-book.

You can view a list of events in the Visual Basic Code Editor Navigation bar. To view a list of events via the Navigation bar, follow these steps:

1. **Repeat Steps 1 and 2 from the preceding step list.**

2. **Press F7 to open the Code Editor.**

3. **Click the Class Name drop-down list on the Navigation bar.**

You can find the Navigation bar is at the top of the Code Editor.

4. **Select the control for which you wish to view events.**

5. **Click the Method Name drop-down list of the Navigation bar.**

A list of events appears, as shown in Figure 4-2. Notice the lightning bolt icons next to the event names.

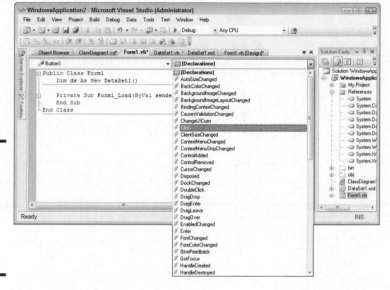

Figure 4-2:
A list of events appears in the Code Editor Navigator bar.

Having a list of event names is helpful, but it doesn't really tell you what the events do. You need to use the Visual Studio documentation to look up the class that creates the event. Before you can look up the event, you need to know the name of the class that creates the event. You can use the Properties window to get the fully qualified class name; refer to Figure 4-1.

Here's how to look up event information in the Visual Studio Help documentation:

1. **Choose Help➪Index in Visual Studio.**

The index to the Visual Studio Help documentation appears.

2. **Select .NET Framework from the Filtered By drop-down list.**

3. **Type the fully qualified class name in the Look For text box.**

The index jumps to the topic while you're typing.

4. **Click the index entry that corresponds to the class.**

The documentation appears in the Documents pane.

A list of hyperlinks to topics within the Help documentation appears across the top of the pane.

5. Click the Events link.

A list of events for the class appears, as shown in Figure 4-3.

A description appears for each event. Click an event to view details documentation about the event method. You'll often find examples of how to write event handlers for the event method.

Your Help documentation might look different if you have Visual Studio configured to view Help integrated inside Visual Studio. Figure 4-3 shows the external Help viewer. You can change your help settings by choosing Tools⇨ Options.

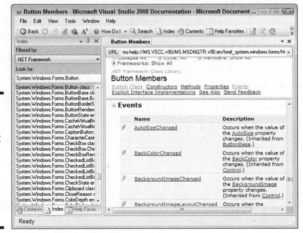

Figure 4-3:
View a class' event details in the Visual Studio documentation.

Wiring up events and event handlers

For your code to execute when an event fires, the event must have some way to know your event handler exists. You create a link between the event and the event handler that essentially says, "When this event occurs, call me."

You have several ways to create a link between an event and an event handler. Well, really, only one way: You have to register your event handler with the event method, which means writing code. But hardly anyone bothers to register their own event handlers because you can use Visual Studio to generate the code for you.

Creating a link between an event and an event handler is *wiring up the event handler.*

Here are the two steps to registering an event handler:

1. Create the event handler.

You place the code that you want to execute when the event fires inside the event handler.

2. Wire up the event handler to the event.

Visual Studio takes care of both of these steps for you. Here are two approaches that you can take to register an event handler, depending on whether you're accessing default or nondefault events.

Every control or component designates a default event. The default event is usually the event most frequently fired for the control. For example, the `Click` event is the default event for a button on a Windows Form. And that makes sense when you consider that for buttons, the `Click` event is the most common event that is needed.

Visual Studio makes it really easy to register an event handler for a default event. All you have to do is double-click a control in the Windows or Web Forms Designers. For example, if you double-click a button control in the Windows Forms Designer using C#, Visual Studio generates the following code:

✦ **Event handler:**

```
private void button1_Click(object sender, EventArgs e)
{
}
```

The code block for the event handler appears in the code file for the Windows or Web Form.

Event handlers accept two arguments: a reference to the sender object that raised the event and any data associated with the event in the form of event arguments. Events that don't have any data use the `EventArgs` event data class provided by the .NET Framework. Any time you see a custom event data class, such as `MouseEventArgs e`, you know there's probably data available that your event handler can use. Otherwise, you can safely assume that the event doesn't have any data.

✦ **Wiring up the event handler to the event:**

```
this.button1.Click += new System.EventHandler(this.button1_Click);
```

The preceding code isn't readily visible to the programmer. In the case of Windows applications, the code appears in the partial class with the file extension `designer.cs` or `designer.vb`. In Web sites, the code is generated when the page is run.

System.EventHandler is a delegate data type provided by the .NET Framework for wiring up event handlers to events. System.EventHandler is not actually an event handler. Rather, System.EventHandler acts as the go-between for the event handler and the event. The event has no knowledge of the event handlers sitting out there waiting to handle the event. The event does have knowledge of the System.EventHandler delegate. System. EventHandler holds a reference to your event handler, which it passes along to the event.

You can use Visual Studio to generate event handlers and wire them to events for nondefault events, too. To create event handlers for nondefault events, follow these steps:

1. **Open the Properties window for the control or component for which you wish to handle an event.**

See the preceding sections for an example of using the Properties window to view events.

2. **Locate the event for which you wish to create an event handler.**

3. **In the property grid, type the name of the event handler you want to create, as shown in Figure 4-4.**

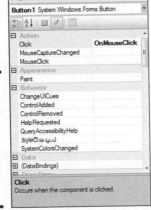

Figure 4-4:
Use the Properties window to add event handlers for nondefault events.

Alternatively, you can select an existing event handler from the drop-down list. You can also double-click the grid to create an event handler with a default name.

The default name used by Visual Studio for event handlers is variableName_Event. For example, the Click event for button1 is button1_Click.

Of course, an alternative approach to using the Properties window or a forms designer is to write your own event handler and wire the handler to the event. Earlier in this chapter, you can see the syntax for C#. What follows is the syntax for Visual Basic:

```
Friend WithEvents Button1 As System.Windows.Forms.Button
Private Sub Button1_Click(ByVal sender As System.Object,
    ByVal e As System.EventArgs) Handles Button1.Click
End Sub
```

Getting a Life Cycle

If you've already started developing ASP.NET applications, perhaps you've been overwhelmed by the number and order of events that fired every time a user browsed to a Web page. However, after you take the time to understand the life cycle of ASP.NET applications and their resources — such as Web pages and Web services — figuring out when you want your code to execute can be a snap.

Each kind of application has its own life cycle events with which you should be familiar. ASP.NET applications, Windows applications, and mobile applications all have their own sets of controls and application life cycles. If you specialize in one of these kinds of applications, you need to understand what happens when a user fires up your application.

Understanding life cycles in Windows applications

Sometimes, waiting for an end user to click a button before your code executes is too late. For example, it's common to want to retrieve data from a database to populate a drop-down list. If you want the drop-down list populated before the user clicks a button, you need to find a different event to handle.

When your application starts up, a series of events fire off. These events call the main form in your application, which in turn adds controls, such as the text boxes, menus, and buttons you dragged onto the form. Each control fires its own series of events as it goes about the business of drawing itself on-screen. The events of the application, main form, and controls describe a life cycle that you can use to insert your own code via event handlers.

When your application starts, the main form and controls in your application go through the following events:

+ `HandleCreated` — Provisions resources from Windows for the control

+ `Load` — Occurs before the form or control appears for the first time

✦ `Layout` — Occurs when child controls are added

✦ `Activated` — Occurs when the form is active

✦ `Shown` — Occurs the first time a form is displayed

The events just listed do not include every event that fires. Even more events exist. As you can see, you have a lot of opportunities to control what happens while forms and controls are appearing. For example, using the `Load` event to provision resources for controls on the form is fairly common. You might hit a database and populate a drop-down list during a form's `Load` event.

Events aren't limited just to startup. Several events occur during shutdown, such as

✦ `FormClosing` — Occurs as the form is closing

✦ `FormClosed` — Occurs once the form has closed

✦ `Deactivate` — Occurs when the form loses focus and is no longer active

Events don't occur sequentially for parent and child controls. That is, you don't step through the form's events and then through the controls on the form. Rather, the events are nested. For example, imagine a form with a button and a text box. The `HandleCreated` event occurs three times, once for each control. The form's `HandleCreated` event occurs first, then the button's, and then the text box's. The form goes through its load, layout, activated, and shown events.

Forms are derived from the control class, so forms are controls like buttons and text boxes. Forms share a lot of events with other kinds of controls.

One final event, `ApplicationExit`, occurs before your application shuts down. You can use the `ApplicationExit` of the `Application` class to perform any cleanup tasks before your application shuts down.

Visual Basic provides its own set of language-specific events for application startup and shutdown — `MyApplication`. To use `MyApplication`, follow these steps:

1. **Right-click your project in Solution Explorer.**

2. **Choose Properties from the shortcut menu.**

The Project Designer appears.

3. **Click View Application Events on the Application tab.**

The Visual Basic `MyApplication` class appears in the Code Editor.

4. **Add an event by using the Code Editor Navigation bar.**

Between startup and shutdown, any number of events might occur on forms and controls. Examples include `Paint`, `Lostfocus`, and `Leave`. Many seemingly simple activities have several events that make it happen. For example, consider a button click. Before the button's `Click` event occurs, the `MouseEnter`, `MouseDown`, and `MouseClick` events occur. After the click happens, the `MouseUp` event fires.

As you can see, you have plenty of opportunities to jump in and execute code without waiting on an end user to come along and interact with your program.

You might be asking yourself which events to use and in which order they should occur. Sometimes, you can figure it out just by reading a class' documentation, as described in the earlier section "Discovering events." Other options are to

✦ **Add event handlers for the events you're trying to discover.** You can use the debugger to step through the event handlers while code executes, write output to a file when the handler fires, or display text on a form.

✦ **Use reflection to discover events.** *Reflection* is a feature of the .NET Framework that essentially asks your code to look in a mirror and describe itself.

Sample code on the GotDotNet Web site uses reflection to write event information to a file. The code sample is called `EventSpy`, and you can find it at

www.gotdotnet.com/community/usersamples/Default.aspx?query=eventspy

Understanding Web page life cycles

Say you're sitting at your home in Denver, Colorado, where you browse to a Web page created with ASP.NET. Your request for a Web page must travel from your browser to a Web server in Kansas. The challenge in ASP.NET Web pages is getting the event from the client in Colorado to the server in Kansas. Thankfully, ASP.NET handles most of the details of making this work for you.

Nevertheless, you need to understand some concepts related to events in ASP.NET. At first blush, the event model seems similar to Windows applications. You double-click a control in the Web Forms Designer, and Visual Studio creates an event handler in your source code. In reality, it's more complicated than that. Many people get confused when their code doesn't execute as they expect it to.

Web pages are *stateless,* which means that ASP.NET forgets what it processes from page to page. Each request for a Web page is independent from previous requests. Of course, this isn't the experience that you have as an end user. You must understand a few concepts as a developer to keep this process transparent to your end users:

+ **View state** — This is a hidden field in your Web page that stores data associated with a Web page's controls, such as the value in a text box.

   ASP.NET 2.0 introduced a view state feature called *control state,* which stores a limited set of a control's property data.

+ **Postback** — *Postback* refers to an action that occurs when a Web page sends data back to the server for processing. Clicking a submit button on a form is an example of a postback.

   Read more about postbacks in the later section "Handling postback events."

+ **Render** — Web browsers don't understand the declarative syntax of ASP.NET or server-side code written with C# or Visual Basic. As a result, Web pages must be converted to — *rendered* as — HTML.

The ASP.NET life cycle starts when someone uses a Web browser to request a Web page. The ASP.NET life cycle includes three players:

+ **Application** — The Web page request is sandwiched in a set of `Application` events that set up and tear down an environment to host and fulfill the client's request.

+ **Page** — The Web page has its own life cycle where it builds itself and prepares the HTML that makes its way to the browser.

+ **Controls** — Each server control has a life cycle that creates the control on the page.

Unlike Windows applications, Web pages live and die in one sitting. That is, the life cycles for the application, page, and controls last a matter of seconds. Each time a page is requested, the application, page, and controls are built, sent to the browser, and then discarded.

Examine these life cycles a little more closely to see what's going on. The very first request for a resource, such as a Web page for an ASP.NET Web site, results in the `ApplicationManager` being created for the entire Web site. The `ApplicationManager` sets up a hosting environment in which all subsequent requests are processed. This hosting environment is an *application domain.* Each ASP.NET Web site operates in its own exclusive application domain.

Each request is handled within its own application inside the application domain. The application steps through a number of events that set up the execution environment to process the request, such as

✦ `BeginRequest` — Occurs before any other event during the processing of a request

✦ `AuthenticateRequest` — Establishes the identity of the user

✦ `AuthorizeRequest` — Ensures that the user has permission to process the request

✦ `PreRequestHandlerExecute` — Occurs before an event handler is called to process the request

At this point, the request is processed. For example, a request to a Web page calls the Web page's constructor, or a request to a Web service calls the Web service's constructor.

If the page has already been called, it might be stored in the ASP.NET cache. As a result, the request might be fulfilled from the cache rather than calling the resource each and every time a request is made.

An ASP.NET Web page has its own life cycle that it uses to fulfill the request. Here it is:

✦ `Page_PreInit` — This determines whether this is a new request or a postback request.

✦ `Page_Init` — Controls are available and accessible via each control's `UniqueID` property.

✦ `Page_Load` — Control properties are populated from view state and control state if the request is a postback.

✦ **Execute control events** — If the request is a postback, this controls which postback events, such as a button click, are fired.

✦ `Page_PreRender` — This is the last chance to make final changes to the page before its view state is saved.

✦ `Page_Render` — A view state is added to the page, and each control renders itself to HTML.

✦ `Page_Unload` — The page has been sent to the Web browser and is ready to be discarded.

After the page is discarded, the application wraps up the request processing by saving state data if required and updating the cache. The final event is the `EndRequest` event.

You'll interact with three kinds of events the most:

✦ **Postback events** — When users interact with your Web page by selecting items from drop-down lists and clicking buttons, it causes your Web page to post back to the server.

✦ **Page setup events** — You use page setup events, such as `Page_Load`, to perform tasks such as populate controls with data from databases respond to postbacks.

✦ **Application events** — You use application-level events to perform initial startup and shutdown tasks and handle errors.

Handling postback events

A postback occurs when a user interacts with your Web page and sends data back to the server. Postback events fire after the Web page's `Page_Load` event. Handling postback events is similar to handling events in Windows Forms.

Postback events, such as a button click, occur after the Web page's `Page_Load` event.

To create an event handler for a default event, double-click the control in the Web Forms Designer. You use the Properties window to set event handlers for nondefault events. See the section "Wiring up events and event handlers" for more details on creating event handlers with Visual Studio.

One thing that Visual Studio does that's different for ASP.NET Web page event handlers is that it adds the event handler to the Web server control's declaration in the ASP.NET page. For example, assume that you double-click a button in the Web Forms Designer. Visual Studio creates an event handler called `Button1_Click`. Visual Studio ties the event handler to the Web server's declaration by using the `OnClick` attribute, as shown in the following snippet:

```
<asp:Button ID="Button1" runat="server"
    OnClick="Button1_Click" Text="Button" />
```

You don't need to designate an event handler for a button's `Click` event. The default behavior of a button that is clicked is to post back to the server. If you want code to execute in response to the `Click` event, you place it inside the button's `Click` event handler. Other postback events fire after the button's `Click` event handler.

You aren't restricted to processing just button clicks. You can respond to other events, such as when an item is selected from a drop-down list. The default event for a drop-down list is `SelectedIndexChanged`. This event allows you to capture the value a user selects from a drop-down list. For example, the following code uses the `SelectedValue` property of a drop-down list to place the selected value in a text box:

```
protected void DropDownList1_SelectedIndexChanged
    (object sender, EventArgs e)
{

    this.TextBox1.Text = this.DropDownList1.
    SelectedValue;
}
```

When the user selects a value from the drop-down list, it appears in the text box, as shown in Figure 4-5. The user must click the Submit button first in order to cause the page to post back.

Figure 4-5:
This event
fires when
the page
posts back
to the
server.

An important concept in handling postbacks and postback events is to query the Web page's `IsPostback` property. The property returns `true` if the request is the result of a postback. It's common to check the `IsPostBack` property during the `Page_Load` event.

For example, assume you need to load items into a drop-down list. You create a procedure called `LoadItems`, as shown in the following code.

```
private void LoadItems()
{
  this.DropDownList1.Items.Add("Hello World");
  this.DropDownList1.Items.Add("Goodbye");
}
```

You assume you can call `LoadItems()` in the `Page_Load` event. Unfortunately, when you do that, your `LoadItems()` procedure is called every time the page posts back. This results in your drop-down list being loaded every time. The `IsPostBack` property allows you to test whether the page is posting back. The `IsPostBack` is a Boolean property, which means that it returns one of two values.

✦ True — If you want your code to execute every time after the page's first load, use this statement.

- *C#*

```
If (Page.IsPostback == true)
```

- *Visual Basic*

```
If Page.IsPostBack = True Then
End If
```

✦ False — If you want your code to run only the first time the user accesses it, you test the IsPostBack property for false.

- *Alternatively, you can use the C# not operator !, as shown here:*

```
If(!Page.IsPostBack)
```

- *Using the Visual Basic keyword Not looks like this:*

```
If Not Page.IsPostBack Then
End If
```

You just include your code inside the If clause, as the following code shows:

```
protected void Page_Load(object sender, EventArgs e)
{
  if (Page.IsPostBack == false)
    LoadItems();
}
```

Many controls have an AutoPostBack property that you can enable. When this property is enabled, the control causes a postback without requiring the user to click a button.

Handling application events

Sometimes, you need to capture an event that's related to the application. For example, you might want to log the first time when an application starts or when errors occur. ASP.NET provides application-level events for which you can write event handlers.

You write event handlers in the global application class file. The global application class file is named global.asax. To add the global.asax file to your Web site, do the following:

1. **Right-click your Web site folder in Solution Explorer.**

2. **Choose Add New Item from the shortcut menu.**

The Add New Item window appears.

3. **Click the Global Application Class icon.**

Leave the name of the file as `global.asax`.

4. **Click Add.**

The file opens in the Documents pane, as shown in Figure 4-6.

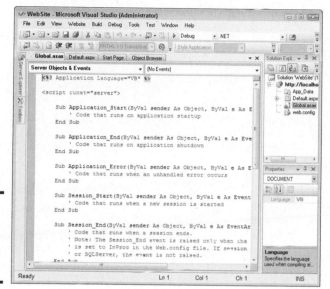

Figure 4-6:
Place
application-
level events
in this file.

You can add several application-level events to the `global.asax` file, including the following:

✦ `Application_Start` — Fires only the very first time a Web site is accessed

✦ `Application_End` — Fires only once before the entire Web site is shut down

✦ `Application_Error` — Fires any time an unhandled exception occurs

`Global.asax` derives from the `HttpApplication` class. As a result, `Global.asax` supports all the events of the `HttpApplication` class. `Application_Start` and `Application_End` are special events that aren't part of the `HttpApplication` class. ASP.NET knows to fire these two events at the very beginning and the very end of a Web site's life cycle.

`Application_Error` is your last opportunity to catch unhandled exceptions in your ASP.NET applications. It's common practice to use `Application_Error` as the event handler to place code that you want executed every single time an execution is thrown.

For example, assume that you have a `Try/Catch` block in your Web page. In your `Catch` clause, you simply use the `throw` statement, as shown here:

```
Try
  'some code here
Catch ex As Exception
  'attempt to handle the exception
  Throw
End Try
```

The `throw` statement passes the exception to `Application_Error` event handler where you have the chance to log the exception. `Application_Error` allows you to pass your user to a friendly error-message page, if appropriate.

Be sure to use `Server.ClearError()` to clear the exception before you pass the caller from `Application_Error` to another page in your application.

`Global.asax` allows you to place code in the `Session_Start` and `Session_End` event handlers. `Session_Start` is a very reliable event that you can use to log that a new session has started. You can use `Session_End` to clean up resources.

Many additional events are available to you in the application life cycle. Unfortunately, not all these events fire consistently. The only event that's guaranteed to fire, besides the three application events mentioned earlier, is `Application_EndRequest`.

Chapter 5: Getting Productive with Visual Studio 2008

In This Chapter

✔ Analyzing your code with FxCop

✔ Digging into the new IntelliSense features

✔ Creating XML documentation from code comments

✔ Refactoring C# code

The promise of the latest suite of Visual Studio products is personal productivity coupled with extended functionality. Features (such as Language Integrated Query [LINQ]) make writing code substantially faster, and other features (such as Asynchronous JavaScript and XML [AJAX]) make your code substantially more efficient and flexible. However, the most important productivity aids are the ones you use every day and in every project, such as IntelliSense. The features covered in this chapter show you how to take your productivity with Visual Studio 2008 to the next level.

This chapter shows you how to use Visual Studio 2008 Professional to analyze your code with FxCop. You can also read about the code snippets and refactoring features. If you're new to object-oriented programming (OOP), Visual Studio 2008 has several IntelliSense features that make light work of turning your code into objects.

Sending Your Code to Boot Camp

Have you ever wondered how some developers know what to name their variables and custom data types? Does some secret society exist in which all the in-the-know developers get memos on when to use a field instead of a property? Actually, there is — sort of.

Attending the naming convention

The .NET Framework software development kit (SDK) contains the Design Guidelines for Class Library Developers. Even though these design guidelines are indeed meant for class library developers, you can take advantage of the recommendations in the guidelines when writing your own code. Some of the topics covered in the guidelines include

✦ Naming conventions

✦ Using data types and class members

✦ Handling errors and raising exceptions

If nothing else, the naming conventions outlined in the design guidelines are very helpful. Using naming conventions makes it very easy to quickly identify the purpose of a block of code just by looking at how it's named. It also reinforces the concepts in OOP because you associate certain naming conventions with specific OOP constructs.

The following two case standards are used the most in naming conventions:

✦ **Camel casing** — In a concatenated word, the first letter is lowercase, and the first letter of the second half is uppercase, as in dogBark. If you have more than two words, all the following words also initial capped: for example, dogBarkLoud.

✦ **Pascal casing** — In a concatenated word, both the first letter as well as the first letter of the second word are uppercase, as in DogBark.

Table 5-1 shows some of the naming guidelines that use camel and Pascal casing.

Table 5-1	Naming Guidelines	
Case	*Identifier*	*Example*
Camel	Fields	`customerName`
	Local variables	`employeeID`
	Parameters	`updateSql`
Pascal	Class	`Customer`
	Method	`ValidateAddress()`
	Property	`CompanyName`

Other examples of conventions include prefixing the letter `I` to interfaces, such as `IEnumerable`; and appending the word `Exception` to derived exceptions, such as `NullReferenceException`.

You should use the keywords `Me` (in Visual Basic) and `this` (in C#) to distinguish between fields and local variables. For example, the following code uses a local string variable named `text` and a field named `greetingName` in a method, as shown here:

```
Public Function DisplayMessage() As String
  Dim text As String
  If String.IsNullOrEmpty(Me.greetingName) Then
     text = SayHello()
  Else
     text = SayHelloName()
  End If
    Return text
  End Function
```

One convention not covered in the design guidelines is how to name controls. Many developers still use Hungarian notation-style prefixes in front of their controls — such as `txt` for *text box* or `btn` for *button*. For details on Hungarian notation, see these references:

`www.fmsinc.com/dotnet/Analyzer/Rules/Hungarian.htm`

`www.byteshift.de/msg/hungarian-notation-doug-klunder`

If you want to do that, you can, as long as you're consistent. Some developers like to use a single prefix for all controls, such as `UI` for *user interface*. Some developers have started to use `UX` for *user experience*. Either way, all your controls are grouped, as shown in Figure 5-1.

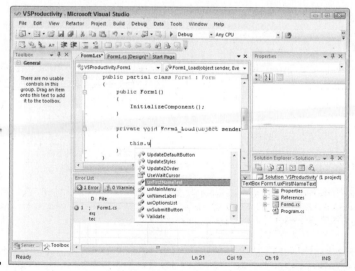

Figure 5-1:
Using a single prefix on all user interface controls groups them.

Charles Simonyi created the concept of using prefixes to identify variables. He's originally from Hungary, which is why this style of notation is called Hungarian notation. You can find a list of Hungarian naming conventions for Visual Basic in Microsoft's knowledge base at

`http://support.microsoft.com/kb/q173738`

Search for the topic "Class Library Design Guidelines" in the Visual Studio documentation to access the complete guidelines.

Calling all cars! FxCop to the rescue!

You're likely thinking that you don't have time to read a bunch of rules. You have deadlines. You get paid to bang out code, not read rulebooks. And you certainly don't have the discipline it takes to review your code for compliance to rules.

What you need is a *cop* — someone who (or something that) can police your code and tell you when you violate the rules. *FxCop* is a code analysis tool that analyzes your code for conformance to the .NET Design Guidelines for Class Library Developers.

You can download the software for free from the GotDotNet Web site at `www.gotdotnet.com/team/fxcop`. Or, check the MSDN Web site at

`http://msdn2.microsoft.com/en-us/library/bb429476(VS.80).aspx`

The latest version targets version 2.0 of the .NET Framework, but it will do an analysis of any version of the Framework — it just needs version 2.0 of the Framework to operate.

For those of you working with Vista, you might notice that you can't even download FxCop. The first step is to set the Web site as one of your trusted Web sites, using the following steps.

1. **Double click the Internet icon at the bottom of Internet Explorer.**

   You see the Internet Security dialog box.

2. **Highlight the Trusted Zones entry.**

3. **Click Sites.**

   You see the Trusted Sites dialog box. The URL of the site appears in the Add This Web Site to the Zone field.

4. **Clear the Require Server Verification (https:) For All the Sites in This Zone option.**

5. **Click Add.**

   Internet Explorer adds the Web site to the list of trusted Web sites.

6. Click Close and then click OK.

You see the Internet icon change to a Trusted Sites icon (with a green check mark).

After you enable the download, you'll probably notice that Vista prevents you from saving the file. To overcome this problem, you must perform this set of unlikely steps:

1. Choose Start➪Programs➪Windows Mail to open Windows Mail.

You see an initial display that might include a wizard for configuring Windows Mail. If you see the wizard, click Cancel and then click Yes to cancel the wizard.

2. Choose Tools➪Options to display the Options dialog box. Choose the security tab.

You see a list of security options.

3. Clear the Do Not Allow Attachments to be Saved or Opened that Could Potentially Be a Virus option.

4. Click OK.

5. Close Windows Mail.

At this point, you can finally download and save the file. Log out of Vista and then back in to make the changes permanent. To download the file, right-click the link and choose Save Target As from the context menu. You'll see a dialog box for saving the file on your system.

Visual Studio Team System (VSTS) has integrated support for code analysis using FxCop. For more on Visual Studio Team System, turn to Book VII, Chapter 2.

FxCop analyzes compiled assemblies. You need to build your project at least once before FxCop can analyze your code. You can build your project by using the Build menu. See Book VI, Chapter 1 for an in-depth discussion of builds. To use FxCop to analyze an assembly, follow these steps:

1. Open FxCop.

Access FxCop from the All Programs menu from your Start button.

2. From the Project menu, choose Add Targets.

The Open window appears.

The assemblies you want to analyze are called *targets* in FxCop.

3. Browse to the location of your assemblies.

Note that assemblies are located in the bin folder in your solution's directory.

4. **Select the assembly you wish to analyze and then click the Open button.**

   Note: You may need to locate `System.Core.dll` for version 3.5 of the .NET Framework. If this is the case, navigate to

   ```
   C:\Windows\assembly\GAC_MSIL\System.Core\3.5.0.0__b77a5c561934e089
   ```

   and load `System.Core.dll`.

   The assembly appears in FxCop. (Press the Shift key to select multiple assemblies.)

5. **Choose Analyze from the Project menu.**

   The FxCop engine analyzes your assemblies. The results appear in FxCop.

6. **Browse through the list of warnings and select one to view its details.**

The first time you use FxCop, you'll likely be overwhelmed by the volume of messages. You might like to sort the list by the Rules column while you step through and examine the messages.

When you click a message in FxCop, a description of the message appears. The description provides you with

✦ Member under inspection

✦ A link to the source code

✦ Problem description and suggestion resolutions

✦ A link to an online help description of the problem and resolution

Figure 5-2 shows a warning triggered by a violation of the Test for Empty Strings Using String Length Rule in the Movie Collection Starter Kit.

When you click the source code hyperlink, the offending code opens in Visual Studio. (Vista might show one or more error messages, depending on how you set the User Access Control [UAC] feature.) Sure enough, the code tests for an empty string instead of using `String.IsNullOrEmpty`, as shown in the following code:

```
if (singleString == "")
{
  singleString = part;
}
```

Figure 5-2:
FxCop
provides
detailed
descriptions
of the
problems
discovered
and
suggests
resolutions.

By changing the code to the following, the warning goes away:

```
if (string.IsNullOrEmpty(singleString))
{
    singleString = part;
}
```

If you come across a certain rule that you don't care about enforcing, you can choose to exclude the rule. To exclude the rule, right-click the message and choose Exclude, as shown in Figure 5-3.

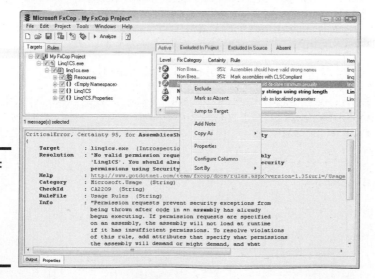

Figure 5-3:
Exclude
rules that
aren't
relevant
for your
situation.

If you don't like the rules included with FxCop, you can create your own. See the documentation for FxCop for more information.

Setting up FxCop as an external tool

FxCop features a command line version that you can include in build scripts or integrate into Visual Studio as an external tool. To integrate FxCop as an external tool in Visual Studio, just follow these steps:

1. **Choose External Tools from the Tools menu.**

The External Tools window appears.

2. **Click the Add button if this isn't the first tool added to the menu.**

3. **Type** Run FxCop **in the Title field.**

4. **Browse to the FxCop command line executable for the Command field.**

The default value for Windows XP is

```
C:\Program Files\Microsoft FxCop 1.35\FxCopCmd.exe
```

The default value for Windows Vista (64-bit) is

```
C:\Program Files (x86)\Microsoft FxCop 1.35\
    FxCopCmd.exe for Windows Vista
```

5. **Type arguments that you normally use on the command line.**

For example, to analyze files using the solution's build directory, use the argument variable $ (TargetDir). You can click the arrow next to the Arguments field to select an argument variable, as shown in Figure 5-4.

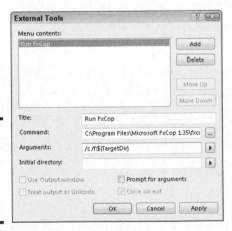

Figure 5-4: Add FxCop as an internal tool in Visual Studio.

6. **Enable the Use Output Window and Prompt for Arguments check boxes.**

7. **Click OK.**

   A new menu entry, Run FxCop, appears on the Tools menu.

It's Not Your Father's IntelliSense Anymore

For years, developers have been using homegrown tools and utilities, such as CodeSmith, to generate repetitive code. The IntelliSense features in Visual Studio 2008 do way more than generate repetitive code. IntelliSense supports coding styles such as test-driven development (TDD) and OOP. If your style is copy and paste, IntelliSense has a tool for you, too.

Using code snippets

A major goal for almost all development projects is to increase code reuse. IntelliSense code snippets are a perfect example of reuse in its simplest form.

Code snippets are like copy and paste on steroids. When using shortcut keywords or a menu, you can browse a library containing hundreds of code samples that you can insert into your code. Best of all, the code samples work like templates that highlight the fields where you need to insert code specific to your application.

For example, if you always forget the syntax for `Select` statements, you can use a code snippet to refresh your memory. To insert a `Select` code snippet in Visual Basic, simply follow these steps:

1. **Position your cursor where you want the code inserted.**

2. **Type** select **and press the Tab key.**

   A code snippet appears in the Code Editor, as shown in Figure 5-5.

   The blocks highlighted in green indicate where you place your values.

3. **Type your values.**

   Press Tab to maneuver between the highlighted blocks.

In the preceding example, you use the code snippet's shortcut to access the snippet. If you don't know the shortcut, you can select a snippet using the following options:

✦ Choose Edit⇨IntelliSense⇨Insert Snippet.

✦ Right-click the Code Editor and choose Insert Snippet from the shortcut menu that appears.

✦ In Visual Basic, type a question mark (**?**) and then press the Tab key.

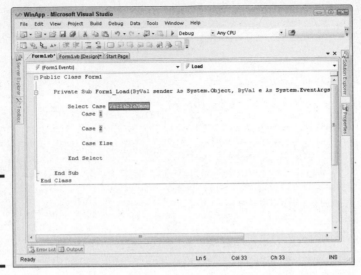

Figure 5-5:
The code
snippet
appears as
a template.

Position your cursor where you want the snippet to appear in the Code
Editor. If you just want to browse snippets without selecting a snippet, use
the Code Snippets Manager. You access the manager by choosing Code
Snippets Manager from the Tools menu.

The Code Snippets Manager allows you to access snippets for many programming languages in one screen. The manager displays a snippet's location, description, and shortcut. *Snippet files* use XML syntax and end in the
file extension `.snippet`. You can add snippet files you create or download
from the Web via the Code Snippets Manager, as shown in Figure 5-6.

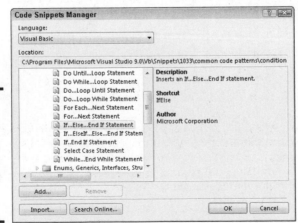

Figure 5-6:
Use the
Code
Snippets
Manager to
browse and
add code
snippets.

When you access code snippets via a menu, you use the Code Snippets Picker. Snippets are organized into folders in Visual Basic. C# provides a list of snippets. To access a snippet via the Code Snippets Picker, do the following:

1. **Position your cursor where you want to insert the code snippet.**

2. **Right-click the Code Editor.**

3. **From the shortcut menu that appears, choose Insert Snippets.**

4. **From the Code Snippet Picker that appears, select a snippet from its list.**

The snippet appears in the Code Editor.

In Visual Basic, use the Tab key to navigate the folders until you find the snippet you need.

Hover your mouse over the snippet to see the snippet's shortcut, for future reference, as shown in Figure 5-7.

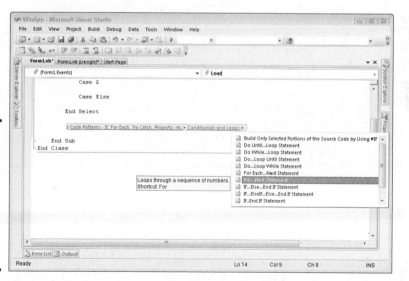

Figure 5-7: Use the Code Snippet Picker to find a snippet and view its shortcut.

Visual Basic provides a broader range of snippets for everything from basic language constructs to accessing resources in Windows. C# snippets are limited to flow control, as well as data type and member declaration snippets. C# has a folder of refactoring snippets that you can see demonstrated in the upcoming section "Factoring in the Refactoring."

Stub it out with method stubs

One of the complaints about development environments like Visual Studio is that they require you to define everything from the bottom up. Some people complain that this style requires you to dig into the minutiae before you have a chance to see the big picture of how your program should be laid out. An IntelliSense feature that allows you to generate method stubs from a method call makes it easy to stay focused.

A *code stub* is a placeholder for an unimplemented piece of code.

Generating method stubs is common in TDD. Adherents to TDD believe you should write tests first. You can use IntelliSense to generate method stubs from unit tests.

In essence, the Generate Method Stub feature allows you to use a method call before you write it. You invoke the Generate Method Stub feature to generate the method's declaration from the method call.

To create a new method stub from a method call, perform the following steps:

1. Create a method call in your code.

Be sure to specify any parameters. If you want the method stub to return a value, assign the method call to a variable of the correct data type.

For example, the following method call accepts a `string` parameter and returns a string:

```
string s = DisplayWelcomeMessage("John");
```

2. Right-click the method call and choose Generate Method Stub from the shortcut menu.

IntelliSense generates the method stub, as shown in Figure 5-8.

Note that the method body throws an exception if the method is called.

Figure 5-8:
IntelliSense can generate a method stub from a method call.

Adding using statements

If you're like some developers, you just start typing away in the Code Editor and forget to reference all the namespaces you need with a `using` statement.

IntelliSense has a feature that adds `using` statements for data types that aren't fully qualified. This can be helpful when you access a type without adding the `using` statement or when you copy code from another resource, such as a sample on the Web.

To add a `using` statement, do the following:

1. **Add an unbound data type (one that is not directly bound to a data source) to your code.**

   For example, the following code uses the `SqlCommand` without fully qualifying the namespace:

   ```
   SqlCommand cmd = new SqlCommand();
   ```

2. **Position your cursor on the last letter of the data type.**

3. **Hover your mouse over the last letter of the data type.**

   A Smart Tag appears.

4. **Click the Smart Tag and select the `using` statement, as shown in Figure 5-9.**

   Visual Studio adds the `using` statement to the top of the source code file.

   For example, the following statement is added for the `SqlCommand` type:

   ```
   using System.Data.SqlClient;
   ```

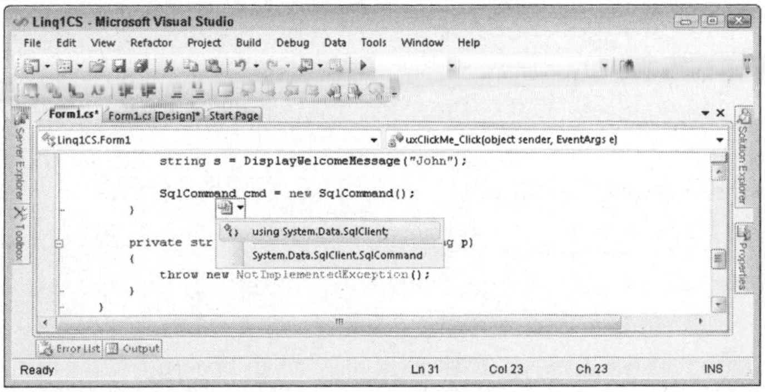

Figure 5-9:
Add a
`using`
statement
for an
unbound
data type.

This feature works for only C# using statements. You can't use it with Visual Basic Imports statements.

Objectifying your code

IntelliSense provides several features that make quick work of common, object-oriented tasks. In OOP, a number of abstract elements are defined. Developers are responsible for writing the code that implements the abstract elements. The concrete implementations are said to *inherit,* or *implement,* the abstract elements.

Abstract classes and interfaces are two abstract elements used in OOP. You inherit from an abstract class and implement an interface.

The process of inheriting or implementing from abstract elements requires a lot of typing. For example, assume you want to inherit from an abstract class that has ten members. You have to re-create all ten members in your derived class.

IntelliSense provides features that copy abstract methods to your concrete classes. You can access these features from a shortcut menu in the Code Editor or Class Designer.

Implementing abstract classes

An *abstract class* defines a class that is used for inheritance only. You can't create an instance of an abstract class. Rather, you must create a new class that inherits from or implements the abstract class. The class you implement is a *concrete class* because you can create an instance of the class.

IntelliSense provides a feature that makes quick work of inheriting from an abstract base class. Here's how to inherit from an abstract class:

1. **Create a new concrete class.**

2. **Type a colon (:) after the class name declaration.**

   For example, assume you want to create a new class called RssReader that inherits from the abstract class XmlReader. Type the following:

   ```
   public class RssReader: System.Xml.XmlReader
   ```

3. **Right-click the abstract class and choose Implement Abstract Class from the shortcut menu.**

   IntelliSense creates method stubs for all the members of the abstract class.

Figure 5-10 shows the concrete class `RssReader` in Object Browser. The class inherits from `XmlReader` and has all the same methods.

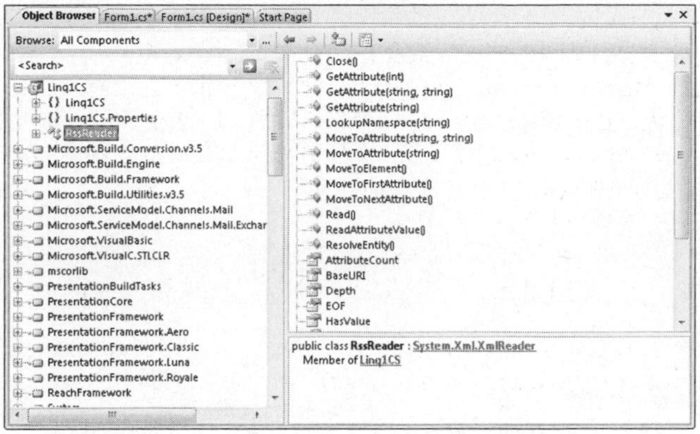

Figure 5-10:
IntelliSense
adds the
methods
from the
abstract
class to the
concrete
class.

Implementing interfaces

An *interface* is a data type that lists a set of methods. The interface doesn't actually provide the code for the methods. The implementation of the interface occurs within a class you create. Many classes can implement a single interface, and any class can implement multiple interfaces. The interface creates a contract that defines what the methods look like in a class.

To implement interfaces using IntelliSense, follow these steps:

1. **Create a new class.**

2. **Type a colon (:) after the class name declaration.**

3. **Type the name of the interfaces you wish to implement.**

For example, the following class header implements the `IFormatProvider` and `ICustomFormatter` interfaces:

```
public class RssReader: IFormatProvider, ICustomFormatter
```

4. **Right-click the interface name in the header.**

A shortcut menu appears.

5. **Choose Implement Interface from the shortcut menu.**

IntelliSense adds stubs for the methods from the interface.

Figure 5-11 shows a class that implements the `IFormatProvider` and `ICustomFormatter` interfaces.

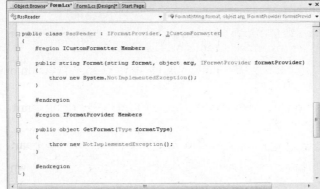

Figure 5-11:
IntelliSense
stubs out
methods
when you
implement
an interface.

Overriding members

At times, you want to provide a different implementation of a method in your new class than what's provided in the base class. For example, assume you create a new class `Dog` that inherits from the base class `Animal`. `Animal` class provides a `Vocalize` method that defines what it means for an animal to "speak." You want to change the implementation of `Vocalize` in your `Dog` class so that you can make the dog bark.

Providing another implementation of a method requires two elements:

✦ **In the base class,** the method must use the keyword `virtual`.

For example, the following code creates a `virtual` method in the `Animal` class:

```
public virtual void Vocalize()
{
  //some code here
}
```

✦ **In the derived class,** the method must use the keyword `override`.

The following code creates a new implementation of the base class's `virtual` method created in the derived class `Dog`:

```
public override void Vocalize()
{
  base.Vocalize();
}
```

You can use IntelliSense to display a list of methods that can be overridden and create method stubs for you. To use IntelliSense to override methods, follow these steps:

REMEMBER

1. **Create a new class.**

   All classes implicitly derive from System.Object. As a result, your class can override methods of System.Object.

   See Chapter 3 in this mini-book for recommendations on overriding System.Object.

2. **Position your cursor in the Code Editor where you want to insert the new method.**

3. **Type the keyword** override **and then press the spacebar.**

   A list of methods that can be overridden appears, as shown in Figure 5-12.

4. **Select a method to override.**

   The method stub appears in the Code Editor.

Figure 5-12:
Use
IntelliSense
to select a
virtual
method to
override.

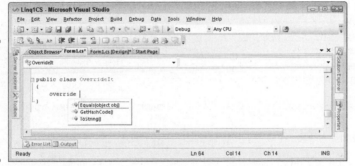

Creating XML Documentation

You probably know that you're supposed to comment and document your code. If you're like most developers, you probably don't take the time to actually do it. IntelliSense and the .NET language compilers make it easy for you to turn your lowly code comments into documentation.

Creating documentation for your code requires you to use the following:

✦ **Comment markers** — Each language has its own comment marker for creating documentation. The comment marker in Visual Basic is three, single-quotation marks (' ' '). The C# comment marker is three forward slashes (///).

✦ **XML tags** — Each language defines a set of recommended XML tags that you should use to define your comments, but you can use any well-formed XML tag you wish. Table 5-2 lists some of the recommended XML tags for Visual Basic and C#.

Table 5-2	Code Documentation XML Tags
XML Tag	*Description*
`<c>`	Marks comment as code
`<code>`	Marks multiple lines of comments as code
`<example>`	Identifies comment as an example of how to use the documented code
`<exception>`	Shows exceptions that can be thrown
`<include>`	Refers to another file containing documentation
`<list>`	Creates a bulleted or numbered list or table in your documentation
`<para>`	Denotes a paragraph
`<param>`	Describes a parameter used in a method declaration
`<paramref>`	Creates a reference in your documentation to a parameter
`<permission>`	Grants document access permissions to a member
`<remarks>`	Adds supplementation information
`<returns>`	Describes a return value
`<see>`	Creates a hyperlink to another type or member
`<seealso>`	Specifies text to appear in a See Also section
`<summary>`	Provides a brief description of the type or member
`<typeparam>`	Describes a type parameter for a generic type
`<typeparamref>`	Refers to a type parameter for a generic type
`<value>`	Describes the value a property represents

Like all XML tags, you place your text inside opening and closing tags. For example, the code that follows shows a code comment in Visual Basic and the class header it describes:

```
''' <summary>
''' This class provides a Hello World greeting.
''' </summary>
''' <remarks>Created as an example.</remarks>
Public Class HelloWorld
```

The Code Editor provides a documentation template when you add comment markers. To add documentation comments to your source code, do the following:

1. **Position your cursor above the type or member you wish to document.**

2. **Type the comment marker for your programming language.**

A documentation template appears in your source code, as shown in Figure 5-13.

3. **Type your comments in between the opening and closing XML tags.**

Figure 5-13:
The Code
Editor adds
a document
template
when you
type code
comment
markers.

The documentation template provided depends on whether you're documenting a type or a member. For example, Visual Basic supplies the following template for a method:

```
'''  <summary>
'''
'''  </summary>
'''  <returns></returns>
'''  <remarks></remarks>
```

The code comments you add appear in IntelliSense, or you can output the comments as XML documentation. Figure 5-14 shows an example of a code comment in the IntelliSense List Members feature.

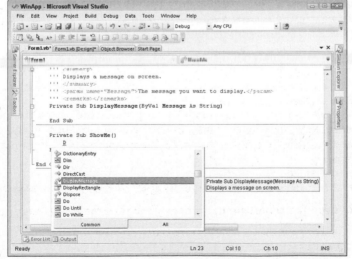

Figure 5-14:
Code
comments
appear
in the
IntelliSense
List
Members
feature.

Outputting your code comments as XML documentation is a feature of your language's compiler. You can turn on XML documentation in the Visual Studio Project Designer. To enable XML documentation using Project Designer, do the following:

1. **Right-click your project in Solution Explorer.**

   A shortcut menu appears.

2. **Choose Properties.**

   Project Designer appears.

3. **Click the Compile tab in a Visual Basic project. In a C# project, click the Build tab.**

4. **In Visual Basic, enable the Generate XML Documentation File check box. In C#, enable the XML Documentation File and the Specify a Filename check boxes.**

   By default, the XML documentation file is saved to the bin folder for the build configuration selected.

5. **Click the X in the upper-right corner of Project Designer to close the window.**

The preceding set of steps tells the compiler to use the /doc switch. You can add the /doc switch to any batch files or build scripts you use to automatically generate output.

The preceding set of steps doesn't work for ASP.NET Web sites because Web sites don't use the project model. You have a few options, which include

✦ **Precompile your site.** ASP.NET Web sites are compiled as resources on the site and accessed by users. You can, however, precompile the site, which would allow you to the /doc option on the compiler.

✦ **Use Web Application Projects.** Microsoft has released an extension to Visual Studio 2008 that allows you to use projects with your ASP.NET Web sites.

To create XML documentation for your project, build your project. Any code decorated with comment markers is output to an XML file. Figure 5-15 shows a sample of XML documentation.

Because the documentation files use XML output, you can use Extensible Stylesheet Language Transformation (XSLT) style sheets to transform your XML into any format you want, including HTML or plain text.

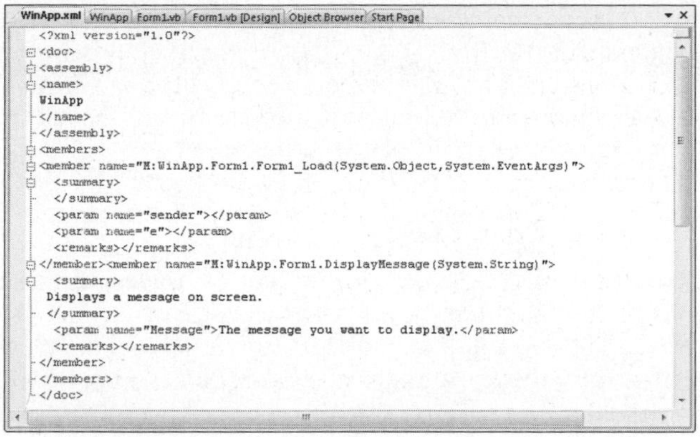

Figure 5-15:
The
compiler
creates
an XML
documen-
tation file
based on
your code
comments.

You can create MSDN-style documentation from the XML documentation files created by your language's compiler. NDoc is a tool that creates documentation for C# projects. You can download NDoc for free at

```
http://ndoc.sourceforge.net
```

VBCommenter creates documents for Visual Basic projects. Download VBCommenter from GotDotNet at

```
www.gotdotnet.com/workspaces/workspace.
    aspx?id=112b5449-f702-46e2-87fa-86bdf39a17dd
```

Read the associated article at

```
http://msdn2.microsoft.com/en-us/library/aa289191(VS.71).aspx
```

Factoring in the Refactoring

Refactoring is changing source code from its current form to another. Even if you think you've never refactored code, chances are that you have. You refactor any time you make a decision about how to implement something. Assume you need to write a program that processes data from a file. You start jotting down some ideas for procedures and variables you know you need. As you commit your ideas to code, you invariably break your code into smaller, reusable bits of code. That's refactoring.

Refactoring is often necessary when you must add a feature or fix a bug in an existing code base. You refactor code any time you ask yourself whether you should

✦ Copy and paste code or extract common code to a reusable procedure.

✦ Use a lengthy conditional statement or create separate procedures.

✦ Write a single procedure that performs three tasks or write one procedure that calls three other procedures.

Refactoring is quite common in object-oriented programming. Before OOP, programs were often *brittle*. That is, it was difficult for a developer to make a change to an existing code base without fear of triggering a cascade of bugs throughout the rest of the program. OOP provides many constructs that make it easier to break units of code into smaller, reusable pieces that are loosely coupled to one another, which makes refactoring possible.

Of course, this describes the goal of OOP techniques. In reality, most of us don't start out implementing our perfect, object-oriented designs using OOP. Nor should we strive to do so. The beauty of refactoring using OOP is that it gives you permission to let go of perfection. Letting go of your visions of building the perfect system allows you to get busy building the best system you can in the here and now. You can always refactor your code later when you have more knowledge.

In the past, refactoring often meant using a combination of Copy, Paste, and Find and Replace to rename parameters or change return values. Visual Studio 2008 provides support for many kinds of refactorings. Table 5-3 provides a list of common refactoring techniques and where you can find them.

Table 5-3	Refactoring Options in Visual Studio 2008		
Technique	*Description*	*Tool*	*Language*
Encapsulate field	Creates a property from a public field	Refactor menu	C#
Extract interface	Creates a new interface from an existing method	Refactor menu, Class Designer	C#
Extract method	Creates a new method from a code fragment	Refactor menu	C#
Implement an abstract	Creates a derived class from an abstract class	Class Designer, IntelliSense	C#, VB
Implement an interface	Creates method stubs in a class that inherits from an interface	Class Designer, IntelliSense	C#, VB
Move a type member	Moves a type member from one type to another type	Class Designer	C#, VB

Technique	Description	Tool	Language
Override	Creates a method stub for a member being overridden	Class Designer, IntelliSense	C#, VB
Promote local variable	Changes a local variable to a method parameter	Refactor menu	C#
Remove parameters	Removes parameters from a method's declaration	Refactor menu	C#
Rename identifiers	Renames a type or a member of a type	Class Designer	C#, VB
Reorder parameters	Changes the order of a method's parameters	Class Designer, Refactor menu	C#

Visual Studio 2008 updates all the places in source code where the refactored code is called. There's no need to use Find and Replace to update method calls.

The refactoring techniques implement abstract classes, implement an interface, and override features of IntelliSense. See the earlier section "It's Not Your Father's IntelliSense Any More" for examples of how to use it.

C# provides more refactoring opportunities than Visual Basic. Your choices for Visual Basic are mostly limited to those features available in IntelliSense and Class Designer.

Refactoring with Class Designer

Class Designer provides access to the IntelliSense refactoring features via the Class Designer menu. The Class Designer menu adds a Refactoring menu that you can use to access refactoring features specific to C#.

You aren't restricted to using the menu items to refactor in Class Designer. For example, to implement an interface, follow these steps:

1. **Add a class that you want to implement the interface.**

2. **Add the interface you want to implement.**

3. **Click the Inheritance icon in the toolbox.**

4. **Drag the line from the class to the interface.**

   The interface's members are stubbed out in the class, as Figure 5-16 shows.

Figure 5-16:
Drag an inheritance line to implement an interface in Class Designer.

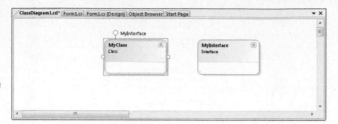

Moving a type member to another type in Class Designer is as simple as cut and paste. For example, assume that you create a Customer class. While you're adding the properties FirstName, LastName, and CompanyName, you realize that none of your customers have a CompanyName and a FirstName and LastName. You decide to create two new classes that inherit from the Customer class. You want to move the FirstName and LastName properties to a ResidentialCustomer class and the CompanyName property to a CommercialCustomer class. To move the types, you do the following:

1. **Right-click the property in the class you want to move.**

A shortcut menu appears.

2. **Choose Cut, as shown in Figure 5-17.**

The property disappears from the class.

3. **Right-click the class where you want to move the property.**

A shortcut menu appears.

4. **Choose Paste.**

The property appears in the class.

Refactoring C#

Visual Studio provides extensive support for refactoring in the C# programming language. You can access all the C# refactoring commands by clicking the Refactor menu while in the Code Editor. A limited set of commands is available in Class Designer.

In most cases, the C# refactoring commands work like this:

1. **Position your cursor on the source code that you wish to refactor.**

On commands that change methods, such as Remove Parameters, you can place your cursor on the method declaration or the method call.

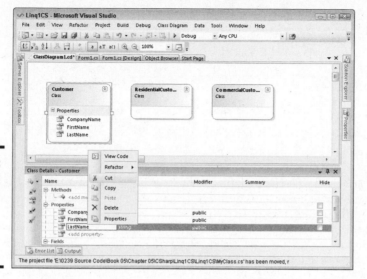

Figure 5-17:
Choose Cut
to move a
property
from one
type to
another.

2. Choose the refactoring command you wish to execute from the Refactor menu.

A dialog box appears.

3. Complete the dialog box for the refactoring command.

Some commands, such as the Reorder Parameters command, display a preview dialog box where you can review changes before you commit.

For example, to reorder a method's parameters:

1. Position your cursor on the method declaration or the method call.

2. Choose Reorder Parameters from the Refactor menu.

The Reorder Parameters dialog box appears.

3. Click the arrows to reorder the parameters.

A preview of the new method signature appears in the dialog box.

4. Enable the Preview Reference Changes check box.

5. Click OK.

The Preview Changes window appears, as shown in Figure 5-18.

The Preview Changes window displays the method signature and each method call. The changed code appears in the lower pane.

6. **Click the method's references to review code changes.**

7. **Click Apply to save the refactored code.**

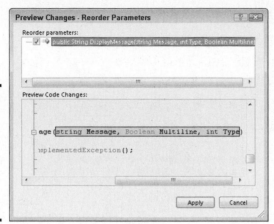

Figure 5-18:
Preview
your
refactored
code in the
Preview
Changes
window.

Chapter 6: Exploring Web Services

In This Chapter

- ✔ Creating a new Web service
- ✔ Testing Web services with GET, POST, and SOAP
- ✔ Using WSDL and UDDI to find Web services
- ✔ Consuming Web services in server-side code
- ✔ Accessing Web services with client-side code

Web service is a kind of Web application. Unlike regular Web applications, however, a Web service has no user interface. Generally, Web services aren't intended to be accessed by end users directly. Rather, Web services are consumed by other applications. For example, a Web service that returns the current temperature for a given city could be called by — or consumed by — a town's Web page.

Web services have two basic uses:

- ✦ **Interface between systems** — Many different kinds of systems run on different hardware and platforms. Trying to write software that allows all these disparate systems to talk to each other has been challenging. Many of the interfaces quickly become brittle: That is, any small change in the interface makes communication difficult, unreliable, or impossible. Web services use standards that overcome the difficulties of creating system interfaces.

- ✦ **Reusable components** — Rather than copy and paste code, or deal with distributing components, you can make the features of your code available as a Web service.

Don't be fooled by the term *Web service*. It's so called because it uses the technologies of the Web: namely, HyperText Transfer Protocol (HTTP) and eXtensible Markup Language (XML). However, you aren't restricted to publishing your Web services over the Internet. Many companies use Web services within their companies. For example, your public relations department can publish its press releases via a Web service method called `GetPressReleases(date)`. Your Web site development staff can consume those services and display them on a public Web site, a corporate portal, or a really simple syndication (RSS) feed.

Never created a Web service before? Never fear. This chapter shows you how to use Visual Studio 2008 to create a Web service, test it, and call it from another application.

Saying Hello to Web Services

Web services make extensive use of Web-based technologies, such as HTTP and XML. Thankfully, you don't need to dig into how Web services use these technologies because Visual Studio and ASP.NET take care of all that for you.

To create a new Web service, follow these steps:

1. From the File menu, choose New⇨Web Site.

The New Web Site window appears.

2. Click the ASP.NET Web Service template.

3. Type a name for your Web service.

Give your Web service a meaningful name.

4. Click OK.

Visual Studio creates the Web service project.

The Web service created by Visual Studio is fully functional. To run the Web service, press Ctrl+F5. Visual Studio launches the service in your Web browser.

Web services don't have user interfaces. ASP.NET uses a template to generate the `service.asmx` page. The page lists a single method, `HelloWorld`, created by Visual Studio.

To test the `HelloWorld` method, do the following:

1. Click the HelloWorld hyperlink on the `service.asmx` page.

A test page appears, as shown in Figure 6-1.

The page includes a button to invoke the test method. It also shows the sample Simple Object Access Protocol (SOAP) headers that ASP.NET uses to communicate with the Web service using SOAP. You don't need to know SOAP to perform basic tasks with Web services because Visual Studio and ASP.NET take care of all that for you. However, a knowledge of SOAP is very helpful when you want to perform advanced tasks and need to debug your application. SOAP is explained in more detail in the upcoming section "Testing Web services."

Figure 6-1:
ASP.NET
generates a
page to test
the Web
service's
methods.

2. Click the Invoke button.

An XML file appears with the value `Hello World` in a single string node.

To stop testing the Web service, right-click the ASP.NET Development Server icon in the Notification and choose Stop from the context menu. The Web service becomes unavailable at this point.

Understanding ASP.NET Web services

A Web service project comprises two main components: an entry point to access the service and a class that contains the code for the Web service. Because Web services don't have user interfaces like Web sites, Web services in ASP.NET are accessed via an `.asmx` page, which serves as the entry point to the Web service. An `.asmx` page has a `WebService` processing directive at the top of the page that defines the programming language of the Web service, the code-behind file, and the class name that provides the Web service's functionality. The features of a Web service are implemented in a class. The class uses attributes to identify which methods are publicly accessible via the Web service. Using attributes allows you to use private methods in your class.

Although most Web services aren't accessed via `.asmx` pages, ASP.NET Web sites are typically accessed via `.aspx` pages.

Figure 6-2 shows an example of a simple `HelloWorld` Web service created with Visual Studio.

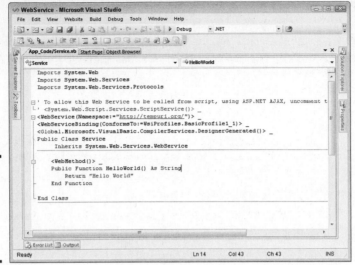

Figure 6-2:
A Web
service
includes an
entry point
and a class.

Visual Studio automatically wires up the Web service's class with the attributes that it needs to function as a Web service. The class that Visual Studio creates for the Web service uses two attributes:

✦ `WebService` — A Web service has one `WebService` attribute that identifies the Web service's namespace. The attribute can also include a description.

✦ `WebMethod` — Each method that's accessible from the Web service must have the `WebMethod` attribute above it.

To change the name of the service and the class created by Visual Studio, follow these steps:

1. Right-click the `.asmx` file in Solution Explorer.

2. Choose Rename from the shortcut menu.

3. Type a new name for the `.asmx` file, such as HelloWebService.asmx.

The name you use for the `.asmx` file is the name you use to access the Web service via its URL.

4. Repeat Steps 1 through 3 to rename the `Service.vb` or `Service.cs` class created by Visual Studio.

The class is located in the App_Code folder.

The file extension depends on whether you're using Visual Basic (`.vb`) or C# (`.cs`) as the programming language.

5. **Open the class file and change the class' name from Service to its new name, such as `HelloWebService`.**

6. **Open the `.asmx` file and change the `WebService` processing directive so that it points to the new class file and name, as shown in the following code:**

```
<%@ WebService Language="vb"
    CodeBehind="~/App_Code/HelloWebService.vb"
    Class="HelloWebService" %>
```

An `.asmx` file can point to more than just a class file. It can also point to a precompiled assembly, or you can include your code inside the `.asmx` file.

7. **Press Ctrl+F5 to run the Web service.**

   Notice that the Web service's name and URL are updated, as shown in Figure 6-3.

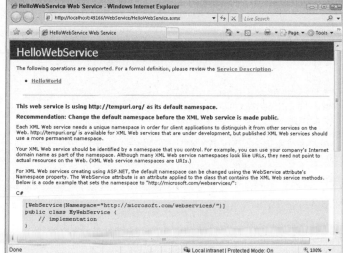

Figure 6-3:
Change the name of the Web service to make it more descriptive.

Each Web service must have a unique namespace. The namespace qualifies the Web service's methods so that each method is unique. Visual Studio automatically assigns the namespace `http://tempuri.org/` to Web services. You should change the namespace. The namespace doesn't have to point to an actual working URL. Rather, it should be unique. However, some Web services do use an URL that points to a Web site with useful information about the Web service.

The default namespace `http://tempuri.org/` is pronounced *TEMP-you-are-eye,* which is short for *temporary URI.* A URI — Uniform Resource Identifier — is used to provide a name or location for a resource.

To change the namespace and add a description to the Web service, follow these steps:

1. **Open the class file used by your service.**

The class file is in the App_Code folder.

2. **Type a new namespace in place of the default namespace and add a description for the Web service, as shown in the following:**

```
[WebService(Namespace="http://mycompany.com/webservices", Description= "A
    web service that returns a Hello World message")]
```

The `WebMethod` attribute supports the `Description` property. Use it to add a description to the methods exposed by your Web service.

3. **Press Ctrl+F5 to run the Web service.**

The Web service's description appears on the ASP.NET-generated page, as shown in Figure 6-4. Notice also that a description for the `HelloWorld` method appears.

Figure 6-4:
Use the Description property to add descriptions to your Web service and methods.

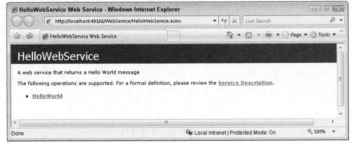

Adding a method

The methods that you add to your Web service class aren't automatically accessible via your Web service. You must explicitly mark them as Web service methods.

You mark Web service methods with a `WebMethod` attribute. Figure 6-5 shows a code sample with a single `public` method that uses two `private` methods. The `public` method is marked with the `WebMethod` attribute. Note that the `private` methods aren't accessible.

Figure 6-5:
Use the
`WebMethod`
attribute to
make a
`public`
method
accessible
via a Web
service.

Testing Web services

Short of building a full-blown application, you have several ways to test your Web services. The easiest way to test your Web services is to press F5 while in Visual Studio. You can also access your Web services via its URL or by using an HTTP form. In most cases, you communicate with Web services via HTTP (the communication protocol of the Internet).

Whichever method you choose, you must be aware of your three communication choices when working with Web services:

✦ `GET` — Uses HTTP with an encoded URL to call the Web service. This method is very much like the Representative State Transfer (REST) technique used by many public Web services — it has the advantage of being incredibly easy to use and test. The basic syntax for accessing a Web service with `GET` is to use a URL like the following:

```
http://<servername>/<projectname>/service.asmx/
    methodname?parameter1=value&parameter2=value
```

✦ `POST` — Uses HTTP to pass the method's parameters without displaying them in the URL. The `POST` approach is more secure.

✦ `SOAP` — Uses an XML dialect called SOAP to enclose the request to and response from the Web service. `SOAP` is often used in conjunction with HTTP, although it isn't required. `SOAP` is the standard for Web services message encapsulation.

The testing services provided by ASP.NET use `POST` by default. The following section shows you how to enable testing with `GET`. ASP.NET doesn't provide a facility for testing `SOAP` messages. You must create your own. To read more about using SOAP, see the section "Communicating with a Web service," later in this chapter.

Sending a GET request

To see a GET request at work, you must modify the default code provided with the Web service. The following code shows the modified version:

```
<WebMethod()> _
Public Function HelloWorld(ByVal name As String) _
   As String

    ' Supply a default value if the value is blank.
    If name.Length = 0 Then
        name = "World"
    End If

    ' Return a hello string.
    Return "Hello " & name
End Function
```

Visual Studio doesn't initially provide HTTP GET, so you need to enable the GET protocol in your project's web.config file. To add the protocol, paste the following code between the opening and closing <system.web> tags in web.config:

```
<webServices>
   <protocols>
      <add name="HttpGet"/>
   </protocols>
</webServices>
```

A GET request passes the Web services parameters with the URL. For example, the following URL calls the HelloWorld method on the HelloWebService and passes the value John to the name parameter:

```
http://localhost:49166/WebService/HelloWebService.asmx/
   HelloWorld?name=John
```

The port that your ASP.NET Development Server uses will vary from these because Visual Studio generates a random number for each project. To see the port number for your setup, hover the mouse cursor over the ASP.NET Development Server icon in the Notification area and use that port number in the GET URL you create. The Web service returns an XML document with the value Hello John, as shown in Figure 6-6.

Passing in parameters at the end of a URL is *encoding*. Any time you see a URL with parameters appended, your browser sends an HTTP GET request to the Web server. GET requests are considered more risky than POST requests because the parameter values are in plain sight. The alternative is to use an HTTP POST request, which sends the parameter values in the message body.

Figure 6-6:
The Web
service
returns
an XML
document.

Sending a POST request

You can use an HTML form to test your Web service by using a POST request. With a POST request, the Web service's parameters aren't visible in the URL.

To test a Web service with a HTTP form, follow these steps:

1. **Click the Web service in Solution Explorer.**

   Press Ctrl+Alt+L to open Solution Explorer if it's closed.

2. **From the Website menu, choose Add New Item.**

   The Add New Item window appears.

3. **Click the HTML Page icon.**

4. **Type a name for the HTML page and then click Add.**

   The HTML page appears in the Code Editor.

5. **Type the following HTML to create a form:**

   ```
   <form method="POST" action='http://<servername>/
       <projectname>/Service.asmx/HelloWorld'>
   </form>
   ```

   The action attribute specifies where the form should post. Type the URL of your Web service. Append a forward slash and the name of the method to execute. In the preceding example, the form executes the HelloWorld method on the Web service.

6. **Drag and drop input elements for text from the toolbox onto the HTML page.**

7. **Drag and drop a Submit button (note that the button type is Submit, even though the caption reads button).**

   Make sure that the elements appear between the form tags.

8. **Set the name attribute for your input elements to the parameter for your method.**

For example, the following HTML form posts to the `HelloWorld` method of the `HelloWebService` (note that the `action` attribute appears on a single line in your code):

```
<form method="POST"
    action='http://localhost:49166/WebService/
        HelloWebService.asmx/HelloWorld'>

    Enter Your Name:
    <input id="Text1" type="text" name="name"/>
    <input id="Button1" type="submit" value="button" />
</form>
```

9. **Press Ctrl+F5 to run your Web page.**

    The page appears.

    Make sure that you have the HTML page open when you press Ctrl+F5 or set the HTML page as the startup page for the site. Otherwise, you'll see the Web service test page open, rather than the HTML page. If you make a mistake, simply select the HTML page and press Ctrl+F5.

10. **Type the parameter values in the page, as shown in Figure 6-7.**

11. **Click button.**

Figure 6-7: Type the parameter values in to the test page.

When you click the Submit button, the HTML page sends the parameters in the form `parameter=value` to the Web service method. Using the example in Figure 6-7, the browser submits `name=John` to the Web service.

The Web service responds with an XML document containing the value Hello John, as shown in Figure 6-6.

See the upcoming section "Consuming a Web Service" for more information on what to do with the XML document returned by the Web service.

Testing with SOAP

You might also want to test the SOAP messages generated by your Web service. The test page generated for your Web service shows a sample SOAP message that ASP.NET generates, as shown in Figure 6-8.

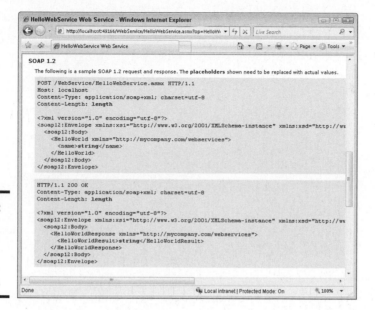

Figure 6-8:
ASP.NET
generates
sample
SOAP
messages.

Because SOAP messages are XML-based, you can use standard Web technologies to test the messages. You'll find an excellent SOAP tutorial at www.w3schools.com/soap/default.asp. The following example uses JScript and Microsoft eXtensible Markup Language (MSXML) Core Services to submit a SOAP request and display the response. *MSXML* is the Microsoft XML parser. You use it to process the XML you send and receive. *JScript* is a client-side scripting language that you use to display values on the Web page. The following example shows you how to use MSXML and JScript to test SOAP messages without assuming that you have any knowledge of these technologies.

Here's how to create a test for SOAP:

1. **Add a new HTML page to your project.**

2. **Add a `script` tag to the page between the `head` tags, as shown in the following:**

```
<head>
<script type="text\jscript">
</script>
</head>
```

3. **Create a new object to hold an XML document:**

```
var xmlDoc = new ActiveXObject("Msxml2.DOMDocument");
```

4. **Create a new object to communicate with a Web server:**

```
var xmlHTTP = new ActiveXObject("Msxml2.XMLHTTP");
```

5. **Create a new function that creates the SOAP message and loads it into the XML document that you create in Step 3:**

```
function createXmlDoc(name)
{
    var soapXml  = "<?xml version=\"1.0\" ?>" ;
    soapXml += "<soap12:Envelope ";
    soapXml += "xmlns:xsi=\"http://www.w3.org/2001/
    XMLSchema-instance\" " ;
    soapXml += "xmlns:xsd=\"http://www.w3.org/2001/
    XMLSchema\" " ;
    soapXml += "xmlns:soap12=\
    "http://www.w3.org/2003/05/soap-envelope\">" ;
    soapXml += "<soap12:Body>" ;
    soapXml += "<HelloWorld xmlns=\
    "http://mycompany.com/webservices\">" ;
            soapXml = soapXml + "<name>" + name.value  +
    "</name>" ;
    soapXml += "</HelloWorld>";
    soapXml += "</soap12:Body></soap12:Envelope>"

    xmlDoc.loadXML(soapXml) ;
}
```

You can find an example of the SOAP request on the Web service's test page. Be sure to pass any parameter values to the request. For example, here's the SOAP request generated by ASP.NET for the Web service shown in Figure 6-5:

```
<?xml version="1.0" encoding="utf-8"?>
<soap12:Envelope xmlns:xsi="
    http://www.w3.org/2001/XMLSchema-instance"
    xmlns:xsd="http://www.w3.org/2001/XMLSchema"
    xmlns:soap12="http://www.w3.org/2003/05/
    soap-envelope">
  <soap12:Body>
    <HelloWorld xmlns=
    "http://mycompany.com/webservices">
       <name>string</name>
    </HelloWorld>
  </soap12:Body>
</soap12:Envelope>
```

6. **Create a function that sends the SOAP request to the Web server.**

The following is an example of how to create a function:

```
function sendXml()
{
    xmlHTTP.Open ( "Post", "http://localhost:4251/
    HelloWebService/HelloWebService.asmx", false);
```

```
xmlHTTP.setRequestHeader("Content-Type",
 "application/soap+xml; charset=utf-8" );
xmlHTTP.setRequestHeader("Content-Length",
 xmlDoc.xml.length);
xmlHTTP.Send(xmlDoc.xml);
}
```

The `sendXML` function uses the `XMLHTTP` object to send the SOAP request to the Web service. You can find the header information for the request on the Web service's test page. Here's the SOAP request generated for the Web service shown in Figure 6-5:

```
POST /HelloWebService/HelloWebService.
    asmx HTTP/1.1
Host: localhost
Content-Type: application/soap+xml; charset=utf-8
Content-Length: length
```

7. **Create a function that outputs the SOAP request and response to the Web page:**

```
function writeResponses()
{
    SoapRequest.innerText =  xmlDoc.xml;
    SoapResponse.innerText =  xmlHTTP.responseText;
}
```

8. **Create a function that calls all three functions:**

```
function getSoap(name)
{
  createXmlDoc(name);
  sendXml();
  writeResponses();
}
```

9. **Add an HTML form that wires everything up:**

```
<form>
    <p>Enter name:<input id="inputName">
        </input></p>
    <p><input type="button" id="btn"  value="Enter"
                onclick="getSoap(inputName)"></input>
    </p>
    <p>Request:</p>
    <div id="SoapRequest"></div>
    <p>Response:</p>
    <div id="SoapResponse"></div>
</form>
```

10. **Display the page in the browser.**

Figure 6-9 shows an example.

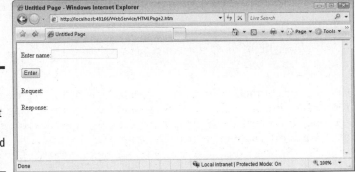

Figure 6-9:
Use a Web
page to test
your SOAP
requests and
responses.

This script is modified from the script at

`www.codeproject.com/webservices/aspwebsvr.asp`

You can also use the testing facilities in Visual Studio Team System (VSTS) to create a Web test to test your Web services. See the topic "How to: Create a Web Service Test," in the Visual Studio documentation, for more information.

You can test SOAP requests online at

`www.perfectxml.com/SOAPTestClient.asp`

Consuming a Web Service

Web services return XML documents. An XML document is just a string, so you can use any programming language to modify an XML document. In fact, people use all kinds of languages — from Python and PHP to JavaScript — to work with XML.

Of course, the .NET Framework provides extensive support for consuming XML and Web services, including the following:

+ Visual Studio generates proxy classes that allow you to use any Web service, like a local class.

+ ASP.NET generates the communication infrastructure necessary for accessing Web services.

Communicating with a Web service

Web services typically use a special message format — SOAP — that allows you to send and receive Web service requests over HTTP (the protocol of the Internet). Using SOAP is important because it's independent of both language and platform.

TIP

You aren't limited to sending SOAP messages over HTTP. You can use SOAP with any transport protocol.

SOAP encapsulates the messages that you send to and get from your Web service in a SOAP envelope. The SOAP request and response travels via a transport protocol, such as HTTP. As long as you have access to HTTP, you can use Web services. Think of SOAP as a delivery truck and HTTP as the highway. The contents of the SOAP delivery truck is your XML document.

The SOAP platform and language independence makes Web services great choices for creating interfaces between disparate systems. For example, a Linux-based application can offer data access via a Web service that's consumed by an ASP.NET Web application.

ASP.NET takes care of writing SOAP requests and responses and creating the XML messages for you when working with simple requests. Complex requests will require that you know how to work with SOAP. You don't need to learn any new technical skills to start using Web services right away. To see an example of the SOAP responses and requests generated by ASP.NET, just run your Web service. Figure 6-8 shows an example of the SOAP messages generated for the HelloWorld method of the HelloWebService.

Web services aren't limited to using just SOAP messages. They can also use GET and POST requests, as explained in the earlier section "Testing Web services." GET and POST requests are part of the HTTP protocol. ASP.NET uses POST or SOAP, depending on which protocol it thinks works best. To ensure that your messages are always sent by using SOAP, add the following code to your Web service's web.config file:

```
<webservices>
    <protocols>
        <remove name="HttpPost" />
        <remove name="HttpGet" />
    </protocols>
</webservices>
```

Finding Web services

You might not always be consuming your own Web services. On the Web, you can find plenty of Web services. Web services, including the ones you create with ASP.NET, use two technologies to announce themselves to the world:

✦ **WSDL** — Web Services Description Language

✦ **UDDI** — Universal Discovery Description and Integration

WSDL is an XML document that describes the Web service, whereas UDDI is like the Web services yellow pages. You don't have to list your Web service with a UDDI directory, but you can if you want.

The WSDL tells the world (or another developer, at least) what's needed to know to use your Web service. Among other things, the WSDL provides information about the following elements:

✦ **Namespaces** — List the services available in the namespace. The namespace encapsulates the Web service's details by using the tags shown in the following:

```
<wsdl:definitions targetNamespace=
    "http://mycompany.com/webservices">
<wsdl:documentation>A web service that returns a Hello
    World message</wsdl:documentation>
</wsdl:definitions>
```

✦ **Operations** — Use the `<portType>` element to define the Web methods available in the service. The `<message>` element defines the Web methods parameters:

```
<wsdl:portType name="HelloWebServiceHttpGet">
    <wsdl:operation name="HelloWorld">
    <wsdl:documentation>
Returns a Hello message using the name supplied,
    otherwise Hello World if name is null.
</wsdl:documentation>
<wsdl:input message="tns:HelloWorldHttpGetIn"/>
<wsdl:output message="tns:HelloWorldHttpGetOut"/>
</wsdl:operation>
</wsdl:portType>
<wsdl:message name="HelloWorldHttpGetIn">
<wsdl:part name="name" type="s:string"/>
</wsdl:message>
    <wsdl:message name="HelloWorldHttpGetOut">
<wsdl:part name="Body" element="tns:string"/>
</wsdl:message>
```

✦ **Types** — Identify the data types used by the Web service with the `<types>` element, as shown in the following:

```
<wsdl:types>
    <s:schema elementFormDefault=
    "qualified" targetNamespace="http://mycompany.
    com/webservices">
    <s:element name="HelloWorld">
    <s:complexType>
    <s:sequence>
<s:element minOccurs="0" maxOccurs="1" name="name"
    type="s:string"/>
</s:sequence>
</s:complexType>
```

```
</s:element>
    <s:element name="HelloWorldResponse">
    <s:complexType>
    <s:sequence>
<s:element minOccurs="0" maxOccurs="1"
    name="HelloWorldResult" type="s:string"/>
</s:sequence>
</s:complexType>
</s:element>
<s:element name="string" nillable="true" type=
    "s:string"/>
</s:schema>
</wsdl:types>
```

✦ **Protocols** — Use the `<binding>` element to define the message format, such as SOAP, and to set details for the port:

```
<wsdl:binding name="HelloWebServiceHttpGet"
    type="tns:HelloWebServiceHttpGet">
<http:binding verb="GET"/>
    <wsdl:operation name="HelloWorld">
<http:operation location="/HelloWorld"/>
    <wsdl:input>
<http:urlEncoded/>
</wsdl:input>
    <wsdl:output>
<mime:mimeXml part="Body"/>
</wsdl:output>
</wsdl:operation>
</wsdl:binding>
```

✦ **Services** — Identify the collection of protocols available for use with the service:

```
<wsdl:service name="HelloWebService">
<wsdl:documentation>A web service that returns a Hello
    World message</wsdl:documentation>
    <wsdl:port name="HelloWebServiceSoap"
    binding="tns:HelloWebServiceSoap">
<soap:address location="http://localhost:
    4251/HelloWebService/HelloWebService.asmx"/>
</wsdl:port>
    <wsdl:port name="HelloWebServiceSoap12"
    binding="tns:HelloWebServiceSoap12">
<soap12:address location="http://localhost:4251/
    HelloWebService/HelloWebService.asmx"/>
</wsdl:port>
    <wsdl:port name="HelloWebServiceHttpGet"
    binding="tns:HelloWebServiceHttpGet">
<http:address location="http://localhost:4251/
    HelloWebService/HelloWebService.asmx"/>
</wsdl:port>
</wsdl:service>
```

ASP.NET automatically creates a WSDL document for your Web service. To view the WSDL for your Web service, as shown in Figure 6-10, click Service Description on your Web service's test page.

Figure 6-10:
Click
Service
Description
to view the
WSDL
document
for your
Web
service.

UDDI provides a directory listing for your Web service. These are the three UDDI directories:

✦ **Green Pages** — Lists services offered by the registrant

✦ **White Pages** — Lists basic address information

✦ **Yellow Pages** — Categorizes businesses based on standard industrial classifications

Many companies set up UDDI directories within their organizations for internal consumption only. This allows developers and other consumers of Web services to easily see what services are available. Using Web services within your organization is a great way to reuse code.

You can access a public UDDI directory at

```
http://soapclient.com/uddisearch.html
```

Using a Web service in your application

Visual Studio provides excellent support for using a Web service in your application. It doesn't matter what language was used to create the Web service. When you reference the Web service in your application, Visual Studio places a wrapper around the Web service that allows you to access the Web service like it was your own code.

Adding a Web reference

To access a Web service in your projects, you must add a Web reference. When you add a Web reference, Visual Studio generates code — a *proxy class* — that you can use to access the Web reference.

To add a Web reference to a Web service, follow these steps:

1. **Right-click the project and choose Add Web Reference.**

   The Add Web Reference window appears.

2. **Type or paste the URL for a Web service in the URL text box.**

3. **Click the Go button.**

   The Web service appears in the window, as shown in Figure 6-11.

4. **Click the Add Reference button.**

   The reference appears in Solution Explorer.

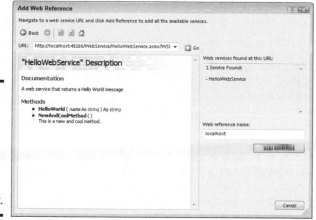

Figure 6-11:
Use the Add Web Reference window to add a Web service to your project.

Binding with BindingSource

The `BindingSource` component is the preferred way to data-bind in Windows applications. You can use a Web service as a data source for a `BindingSource` component.

Here's how to use a Web service with a `BindingSource`:

1. **Add a Web Reference to your Web service in your Windows project.**

   If you're working with a Windows Form application, add the Web reference as a Service Reference by right-clicking the solution and choosing Add Service Reference. The process works precisely the same as the Web reference discussed earlier.

2. **Create a new instance of your Web service.**

   For example, to create a new instance of the `HelloWebService`, use the following in a Web application:

   ```
   Dim ws As New localhost.HelloWebService
   ```

   When working with a desktop application, use this following code instead:

   ```
   Public ws As New HelloWebServiceSoapClient
   ```

3. **Drag and drop a `BindingSource` component from the Data tab of the Toolbox onto your Windows Form.**

4. **Add your Web service as a data source for the `BindingSource` component by using the component's `Add` method.**

   For example, the following code adds `HelloWebService` to a `BindingSource` component:

   ```
   BindingSource1.Add(ws.HelloWorld(Me.txtEnterName.Text))
   ```

5. **Set the `BindingSource` component as the source for a control's data binding.**

   For example, the following code data binds the `BindingSource` component to a `label` control's `text` property:

   ```
   Me.lblDisplayMessage.DataBindings.Add
       ("Text", Me.BindingSource1, "")
   ```

You can use the preceding code in a button's `Click` event to call the Web service. Listing 6-1 shows the entire code sample in a button's `Click` event.

Listing 6-1: Calling a Web Service in a Button's Click Event

```
Private Sub Button1_Click(ByVal sender As System.Object, ByVal e As
    System.EventArgs) Handles Button1.Click
  Dim ws As New localhost.HelloWebService

  BindingSource1.Add(ws.HelloWorld(Me.txtEnterName.Text))
  Me.lblDisplayMessage.DataBindings.Add("Text", Me.BindingSource1, "")
End Sub
```

When a user clicks the button, the code calls the `HelloWorld` method of the `HelloWebService`. The `name` parameter is passed by using the value entered by a user in the `txtEnterName` text box. The return value appears in a `label` control called `lblDisplayMessage`.

Putting your Web service in a Web application

You can use Web services in a Web application. Because ASP.NET creates a proxy class, you can call your Web service just like you'd call any other bit of code.

To use a Web service in a Web application, follow these steps:

1. **Add a Web reference to the Web service you wish to consume.**

2. **Create an instance of your Web service:**

   ```
   Dim ws As New localhost.HelloWebService
   ```

3. **Call your Web service.**

   For example, the following code calls the `HelloWebService` and returns the results to a text box:

   ```
   Me.TextBox1.Text = ws.HelloWorld("John")
   ```

Getting on the client side

You aren't limited to just accessing Web services via server-side code. You can also use client-side scripting languages, such as JScript, to call Web services.

Web services return an XML document, for which JScript provides excellent support. Listing 6-2 is a simple script and HTML page that tests the `HelloWebService`.

Listing 6-2: Simple Script and HTML Page That Tests the HelloWebService

```
<html>
<head>
    <title>Test Web Service</title>
    <script type="text/jscript">
    function callService()
    {
        var xmlDoc;
        var url;

        xmlDoc = new ActiveXObject
    ("Msxml2.DOMDocument");
```

(continued)

Listing 6-2 *(continued)*

```
        xmlDoc.onreadystatechange = function ()
           {
               if (xmlDoc.readyState == 4)
                 {
                     displayText(xmlDoc);
                 }
           }

    url =
        "http://<servername>/HelloWebService/" +
        "HelloWebService.asmx/HelloWorld?name=" +
        document.getElementById("text1").value;

    xmlDoc.load(url);

   }

   function displayText(xmlDoc)
   {

       var currentNode;
       currentNode = xmlDoc.selectSingleNode("string");

       document.getElementById("displayMessage").
   innerHTML = currentNode.text;

   }

    </script>
</head>
<body>
    <form>
       Enter your name:
       <input id="Text1" type="text" name="name" />
       <input id="Button1" type="button" value="button"
   onclick="callService()" />
       <div id="displayMessage"></div>
    </form>
</body>
</html>
```

The script works only in Internet Explorer because it uses an ActiveX control, which other browsers don't support. You can find lots of scripts on the Web for manipulating XML with JScript.

You should definitely take a closer look at the XMLHTTPRequest object. This object allows you to send GET and POST requests to a Web server. Best of all, it works without causing the browser to refresh. The XMLHTTPRequest object is at the heart of the Web development methodology called AJAX.

Chapter 7: Handling Exceptions and Debugging

In This Chapter

✔ Using `Try...Catch...Finally` **blocks**

✔ **Throwing exceptions**

✔ **Viewing exceptions in Exception Assistant**

✔ **Setting breakpoints and stepping through code**

✔ **Using the Watch window to view data**

✔ **Debugging code generated by Visual Studio**

Anyone who has done even a little coding has been deflated by seeing the Visual Studio Debugger open instead of a beautiful masterpiece — because of an error that occurs in the program code. Sometimes, you spend more time with the Visual Studio Debugger than you do writing code. Of course, you might see less of the Debugger if you start using structured exception handling to capture exceptions when they do occur. And this chapter shows you how to do just that.

This chapter provides you with a full view of the Debugger. For example, you discover the wonders of using breakpoints to control when Visual Studio pauses your code and lets you debug it. You can also read how the Watch window works. All these tools can make your debugging significantly easier.

Structured Exception Handling to the Rescue

Whether you're writing code as a professional or a hobbyist, you want your code to perform as advertised. For example, when a user clicks a button to load information from a file, you want to make sure that file is there. If the file isn't there, you need to have some way to deal with the error.

In object-oriented programming (OOP), errors are often called *exceptions*. An exception is just what it sounds like — anything that occurs in your code that's exceptional or out of the ordinary. For example, if your code opens a file and the file server goes down while you're accessing the file, that's an exception. Comparatively, not being able to access the file server or find a file in the first place isn't an exception because your code can test to see whether the file exists before it tries to open the file.

Code you write to address an exception is an *exception handler.* Exceptions that occur for which you haven't written code are *unhandled exceptions,* which can be fatal and cause your application to fail. Not good.

Visual Studio doesn't provide exception-handling features. In many cases, you'll use the built-in exception handlers supplied with the .NET Framework. In some cases, you deal with exceptions by writing exception handlers in the language of your choice. You can use Visual Studio to do the following:

+ Step through error-producing code in the Visual Studio Debugger.

+ Use Exception Assistant to view details about an exception.

+ Use code snippets to add exception handlers to your code.

The .NET Framework provides a model for managing exceptions that includes

+ Structured exception handling

+ A common-exception framework

+ The ability to create your own custom exceptions

Handling exceptions

In the good old days (say, more than six years ago), it was every man for himself when it came to handling exceptions. You could return a value when an exception occurred or do nothing at all. Although plenty of ways are available with which you *can* handle exceptions, you *should* handle exceptions by using structured exception handling. Structured exception handling makes it possible to handle exceptions in a predictable manner. Structured exception handling also reduces the learning curve for novice developers who must learn exception handling techniques and makes your code easier to read. Consequently, everyone wins when you use structured exception handling techniques.

Structured exception handling involves using the `Try`, `Catch`, and `Finally` statements to create code blocks:

+ `Try` — Executes statements that might cause an exception, such as opening database connections

+ `Catch` — Specifies the exception to catch and executes code to deal with the exception

+ `Finally` — Executes every time, whether exceptions generate or not

Another important feature of structured exception handling is the `throw` statement, which you use to create a new exception or to pass an existing exception to the calling function.

Here's an example of a `Try...Catch...Finally` block for opening and closing a database connection with ADO.NET:

```
Private Sub AccessData()
  Dim MyConnection As New System.Data.SqlClient.SqlConnection
  MyConnection.ConnectionString = My.Settings.MyDbString
  Try
     MyConnection.Open()
     'send commands
  Catch ex As Exception
     'handle exception
  Finally
     MyConnection.Close()
  End Try
End Sub
```

The statements executed in the `Try` block are wired to the `Catch` block. If any statement in the `Try` block throws an exception, the `Catch` block gives you a chance to

✦ Attempt to recover from the exception.

✦ Log the exception.

✦ Provide feedback to the user.

Any code in the optional `Finally` block executes, regardless of whether an exception occurred. Place your cleanup code, such as closing database connections, in the `Finally` block.

Catching exceptions

The .NET Framework provides an extensive catalog of exceptions that starts with the generic `System.Exception`. All exceptions inherit from `System.Exception`. You use a `Catch` block to capture exceptions and handle them. Table 7-1 lists examples of exceptions found in the .NET Framework.

Table 7-1	Example Exceptions Found in the .NET Framework
Exception	*Usage*
`System.Exception`	A generic exception
`System.NullReferenceException`	Occurs when you attempt to access the value of an object that doesn't exist

(continued)

Table 7-1 *(continued)*

Exception	Usage
System.ArgumentNullReferenceException	Occurs when an unexpected nullreference is passed as an argument
System.Data.SqlClient.SqlException	An exception thrown when SQL Server returns a warning or error
System.IndexOutofRangeException	Thrown when you attempt to access beyond an array's index
System.InvalidCastException	Thrown when an attempt to cast from one data type to another is invalid

You can handle any of the exceptions listed in Table 7-1 by using a Catch block.

Catch blocks use the following syntax:

✦ The keyword Catch

✦ An optional argument that specifies the kind of exception to catch

Here is a Catch block that catches an SQLException:

```
Catch ex As System.Data.SqlClient.SqlException
```

You can use multiple Catch blocks to catch different kinds of exceptions. Depending on your application, you may want to catch the most specific exception first. The least specific exception is System.Exception.

For example, here are two Catch blocks:

```
Catch ex As System.Data.SqlClient.SqlException
    'do something with the exception

Catch ex As System.Exception
    'do something with the exception
```

Only one of these Catch blocks executes. Always list your Catch blocks in order of most-specific to least-specific. While your code executes, it starts at the first Catch block and steps through each until it finds a match. If System.Exception is the first Catch block, no other Catch blocks execute.

Figuring out which exceptions you should use can be difficult. One option is to add the exception to the Watch window while debugging. That allows you to see the specific exception captured. Figure 7-1 shows an example of a System. Exception caught in the Watch window. See the section "Understanding Debugging," later in this chapter, for more information about using Watch windows.

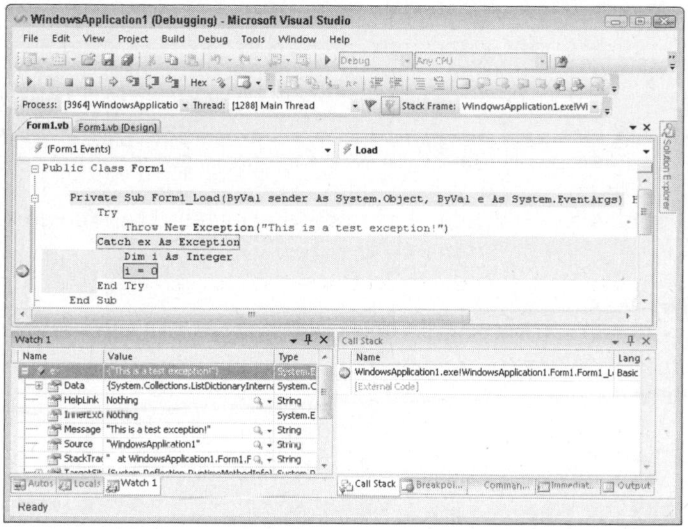

Figure 7-1:
Use the
Watch
window to
puzzle out
information
about
exceptions.

As Figure 7-1 shows, exceptions provide a lot of information. Some useful properties of exceptions include

✦ Data — Gets a set of key/value pairs that provides optional, additional information about the exception

✦ GetBaseException — Gets the root exception — the *base exception* — that causes a chain of exceptions to start

✦ InnerException — Gets the exception that causes the current exception

  The base exception's InnerException is null because the base exception is the first exception in the chain.

✦ Message — Gets the exception's description

✦ Source — Is used to get or set the name of the application or object that causes the exception

You can set the `Source` property before you pass an exception to another method to process.

✦ `StackTrace` — Provides a list of all the methods called before the exception occurs

✦ `TargetSite` — Gets the method that causes the exception

The method provided by the `TargetSite` is the same method listed at the top of the `StackTrace`.

Always capture information about exceptions. Exceptions don't always occur while you're sitting in front of your laptop with a cup o' Joe and Debugger fired up. Exceptions occur when you're two weeks past your deadline on a new project and the last thing you have time for is something you haven't thought about in six months to start malfunctioning. You can use an exception's properties to puzzle out what caused the exception.

Throwing exceptions

When an exception occurs, the exception is *thrown*. The source of this term is the keyword `throw`, which is used to raise an exception when an error occurs.

Here are the two uses of the `throw` statement:

✦ **To raise an exception in your program** — The syntax to throw an exception is `throw someException`.

For example, to throw an exception when a `null` value is passed to a method, use `System.ArgumentNullException`, as the following code demonstrates:

```
Private Function SayHello(ByVal name As String) As String
 If name = Nothing Then
   Throw New System.ArgumentNullException
 End If
 Return "Hello world, " + name
End Function
```

✦ **To pass an exception to a calling function** — You use the `throw` statement within a `Catch` block to pass an existing exception to a calling function, as the following code shows:

```
Try
    'do something that causes an exception
Catch ex as System.Exception
    Throw
End Try
```

The `Catch` block captures the exception, and the `throw` statement passes the captured exception to the calling function. Figure 7-2 shows an example of the `throw` statement in action.

Figure 7-2:
Use a
`throw`
statement to
pass an
exception
message to
a calling
function.

Note the following in the code sample shown in Figure 7-2:

✦ The subroutine `DisplayMessage()` calls the function `SayHello()` on line 15.

✦ On line 27, `SayHello()` throws an exception of the type `System.ArgumentNullException` because a `null` value was passed in as a parameter.

✦ Code execution jumps to line 31, where the `Catch` block captures the exception.

✦ Line 32 throws the exception to the caller, `DisplayMessage()`.

✦ Execution returns to line 16, the `Catch` block in `DisplayMessage()`, which captures the exception thrown to it by line 24.

✦ Line 17 displays a message box that displays the exception's `Message` property, which is `Value cannot be null`.

Other times when you might want to use the `throw` statement include

✦ **To test your exception handlers** — You might find it helpful to have your unit test or other testing harness throw exceptions to test your exception handlers and logging utilities.

✦ **When you use an exception-handling framework** — You should handle exceptions for many patterns. For example, in ASP.NET Web sites, common exception handlers are typically placed in the `Globals.aspx` page. All your code's exception handlers simply use the `throw` statement. Any exceptions are automatically handled by an application-wide handler in `Globals.aspx`.

Using a centralized exception handler makes it easier to ensure that all your exceptions are logged properly. You can also make sure your users are sent to a consistent error page.

Using Visual Studio to manage exceptions

The Microsoft .NET Framework provides an extensive set of exceptions that you can catch and throw. Although you can create your own exceptions, that isn't necessary in most cases. Instead, use Object Browser to view the list of exceptions available in the .NET Framework.

To use Object Browser, follow these steps:

1. **Press Ctrl+Alt+J to open Object Browser.**

2. **From the Browse drop-down list, choose .NET Framework 3.5.**

3. **Type** exception **in the Search box and then press Enter.**

A list of objects with the word *exception* in their names appears.

The .NET Framework uses a naming standard whereby all exceptions end with the word exception, such as System.FormatException.

4. **Right-click one of the entries listed in Object Browser and choose Group by Object Type from the shortcut menu that appears.**

The objects are grouped by type. That way, you see all the exception objects grouped in the Classes folder.

By default, the list of objects is sorted alphabetically.

To view more information about an exception, click the plus sign (+) to expand the exception. Click an exception's name to view its properties and methods. A summary pane lists summary information about the exception. Figure 7-3 shows the exceptions derived from the System.ArgumentException object.

To read more about an exception, click the exception in Object Browser and then press F1 to display help about the exception.

In most cases, you should use the most specific exception type available. For example, System.DivideByZeroException is more specific than System.ArithmeticException. In most cases, you can tell which exception is more specific by looking at the name. An arithmetic exception will include divide-by-zero errors. You can also look at the Derived Types list, as shown in Figure 7-3. Exceptions that appear in this list are based on a more generic exception.

All exceptions inherit from `System.Exception`. As a result, all exceptions have the same properties of `System.Exception`.

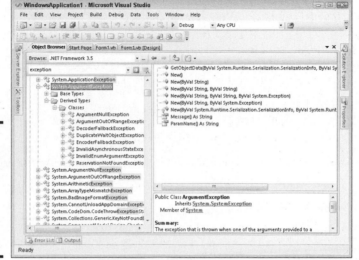

Figure 7-3:
Use Object Browser to explore the exceptions available in the .NET Framework.

Visual Studio provides Exception Assistant for viewing information about exceptions while using Visual Studio Debugger. Visual Studio displays Exception Assistant any time exceptions are either of the following conditions:

✦ **Unhandled** — Any time Visual Studio encounters an exception while executing your code, Exception Assistant appears.

✦ **Caught** — While using the Visual Studio Debugger, you can open Exception Assistant if the Debugger breaks at the point where the exception is caught. Press Shift+Alt+F10 to open Exception Assistant.

Figure 7-4 shows an example of Exception Assistant for an unhandled exception. Exception Assistant provides you with

✦ **The exception's message**

✦ **Tips for troubleshooting the exception message**

✦ **The exception's properties**

Click the View Detail link in the Actions portion of the Exception Assistant dialog box, as shown in Figure 7-4, to view the exception's properties.

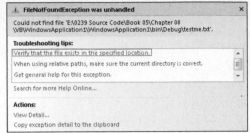

Figure 7-4:
Exception
Assistant
appears
when an
unhandled
exception is
encountered.

Understanding Debugging

When you use debugging, you can stop your code during execution and inspect it. Visual Studio provides a sophisticated Debugger that allows you to

✦ Control the execution of your code so you can peek inside your code while it's running.

✦ Test your code while you're designing it.

✦ View the data used by your code.

✦ Get detailed information about exceptions that occur.

Enabling debugging

To use the Visual Studio Debugger with your code, you must build your code by using the Debug build configuration. The Debug build configuration tells the compiler to create a program database (PDB) file for your code. The PDB file stores the data about your source code, such as

✦ Source code line numbers

✦ Variable names

✦ Method names

The Visual Studio Debugger uses the PDB file to know how to access your source code while it's being executed.

The data stored in the PDB are *symbols*.

You should generate PDB files for all builds, including release builds, so that you can debug the build, even if you didn't build it as a debug build.

To set your application to use the Debug build configuration, choose Debug from the Solution Configurations drop-down list on the Standard toolbar. To create or modify build configurations, see Book VI, Chapter 1.

Firing up the Debugger

Your application has two modes in the Debugger: executing or breaking. While your application is executing, everything's A-okay. After your application stops executing, or breaks, then you get busy with the Debugger.

Your application executes until it encounters either of the following:

✦ **Breakpoint** — A marker you set in the code that tells the Debugger to stop execution

✦ **Exception** — An unhandled error generated by your code that causes program execution to stop

While your code is in break mode, you have the features of the Debugger at your disposal for examining your code.

Controlling execution

One of the primary features of the Visual Studio Debugger is the ability to control your program's execution. Controlling execution allows you to walk through your code, as well as check the values of variables and data.

The Debugger provides the following code execution options:

✦ **Starting** — This starts your code. You must use the Debug build configuration for the Debugger to fire up.

✦ **Stepping** — This allows you to step through your code.

✦ **Breaking** — You can break the code's execution by setting a breakpoint or by manually breaking. Your code breaks automatically when an unhandled exception occurs.

✦ **Stopping** — Execution stops when your program completes execution or you manually stop it.

You have several ways to start the Debugger:

✦ **Debug menu** — From here, choose Start Debug, Step Into, or Step Over to execute your code.

✦ **Run to Cursor** — Right-click an executable line of code and choose Run to Cursor from the shortcut menu. The Debugger starts your code and breaks at the line where your cursor sits.

✦ **Keyboard shortcuts** — Table 7-2 lists common keyboard shortcuts you can use to control the Debugger.

You can use the keyboard shortcuts almost exclusively to step through code.

✦ **Debug toolbar** — The Debug toolbar acts like standard VCR buttons for controlling your code's execution. Figure 7-5 shows the Debug toolbar.

Figure 7-5:
Use the Debug toolbar to control your code's execution.

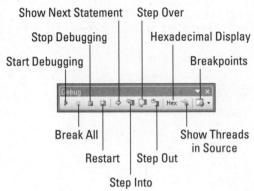

Table 7-2	Common Debugging Keyboard Shortcuts
Keyboard Shortcut	*Command*
F5	Start Debugging
Ctrl+F5	Start without Debugging
F11	Step Into
F10	Step Over
Shift+F11	Step Out

Breaking execution

The first step in using the Debugger is breaking your code during execution. To break your code during execution, you can do any one of the following:

✦ Click the Break All button on the Debug toolbar.

✦ Choose Break All from the Debug menu.

✦ Press Ctrl+Alt+Break.

In most cases, you'll likely set a breakpoint in your code before you start execution. By setting a breakpoint, your code stops executing at the line of code where the breakpoint is set. You can then step through the code and watch your variables while the code executes.

Here's how to set a breakpoint:

1. Go to the line of source code in the Code Editor where you want code execution to break.

2. From the Debug menu, choose Toggle Breakpoint.

A solid glyph (red circle) appears in the Code Editor's left gutter. The breakpoint appears in the Breakpoints window. Figure 7-6 shows the breakpoint.

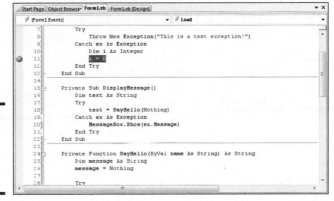

Figure 7-6:
Set a
breakpoint
in the Code
Editor.

You can use alternative ways to set breakpoints, such as the following:

✦ Click the left gutter in the Code Editor to toggle a breakpoint for an executable line of code.

✦ Right click a line of code and choose Breakpoint from the shortcut menu.

✦ Press F9.

You can use the Breakpoints window to manage your breakpoints. From here, you can

✦ Create new breakpoints.

✦ Enable or disable breakpoints.

✦ Set conditions on when the breakpoint occurs.

✦ Filter the breakpoint for specific machines, processes, and threads.

✦ Specify how many times the code should execute before execution breaks.

Here's how to create a new breakpoint via the Breakpoints window:

1. **Press Ctrl+Alt+B to display the Breakpoints window.**

2. **Choose New⇨Break at Function.**

   The New Breakpoint window appears.

3. **In the Function text box, type the name of the function where you want to create the breakpoint.**

   For example, type **SayHello()** to create a breakpoint at a function called `SayHello()`.

4. **Click OK.**

   The function appears in the Breakpoints window, as shown in Figure 7-7.

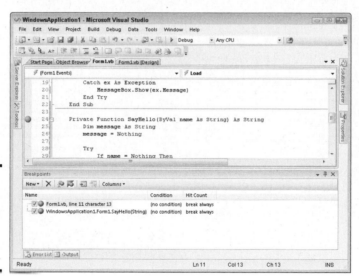

Figure 7-7:
Use the Breakpoints window to add new breakpoints.

Stepping through code

Visual Studio provides several options for controlling the execution of your code. Besides just starting, pausing, and stopping code execution, you can step through your code one statement at a time. The three step options are

✦ **Step Into** — Breaks on each line of code

✦ **Step Over** — Breaks on each line of code except functions

   The function executes, and code execution breaks at the first line outside the function.

✦ **Step Out** — Resumes execution on a function and then breaks at the first line of code outside the function

Step Into and Step Over start the Debugger at the next line of code. Step Out allows you to stop debugging a function but then break execution as soon as the function exits.

To step through your code, follow these steps:

1. **Set breakpoints in your code.**

   For example, create a form with a button and add a Click event for the button. Set the breakpoint on the button's Click event to break the code's execution when you click the button.

2. **Press F5 to start the Debugger.**

   Visual Studio builds your code and starts execution. The code executes until it encounters a breakpoint. Figure 7-8 shows an example of the Debugger hitting a breakpoint. The Code Editor highlights the code in yellow.

Figure 7-8:
The Debugger highlights the code statement when it hits a breakpoint.

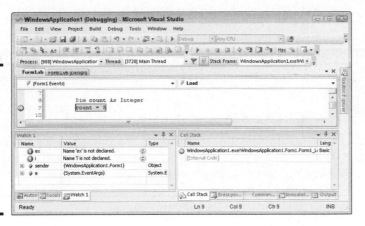

3. **Press F11 to step into the next line of execution.**

4. **Continue to press F11 until you encounter a function.**

   - *Step into:* To follow the execution into the function, press F11 to step into the function.

   - *Step over:* To execute the function without stepping through it, press F10 to step over the function.

   - *Step out:* To step out of the function after you enter it, press Shift+F11.

Figure 7-9 shows an example of the Debugger stepping into a function. The Debugger hit the breakpoint in line 52 in Figure 7-9. Press F11 to step through each line. At line 57 is the function `SayHello()`. Step into the function, and the Debugger jumps to line 21 (see Figure 7-2), where the function starts. The arrow in the Code Editor's left gutter shows the current line being executed.

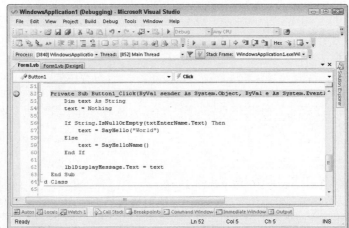

Figure 7-9:
Use the
Debugger to
step through
your code.

5. **Press Shift+F11 to step out of the function.**

   The Debugger executes the function and returns to the calling line of code.

   In the case of the code in Figure 7-9, pressing F11 returns you to line 57 and breaks execution.

6. **Resume stepping through the code by pressing F11.**

   F5 is the shortcut key for the Continue command. Press F5 at any time to resume execution until the code terminates or hits another breakpoint.

The Debug toolbar has three buttons that correspond to the Step Into, Step Over, and Step Out commands, respectively. Refer to Figure 7-5.

You can use the Run to Cursor command to execute your code to the cursor. Just right-click a line of code in the Code Editor and then choose Run to Cursor from the shortcut menu. Code execution breaks at the line where your cursor is positioned.

To know whether your code is running or debugging, look for `Running` or `Debugging`, respectively, in the title bar. Figure 7-10 shows an example.

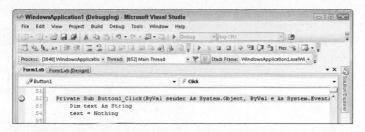

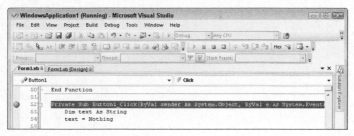

Figure 7-10:
The title bar
displays the
execution
status
of your
program.

Viewing data with the Debugger

The Visual Studio Debugger provides several windows for managing debugging. By default, these windows automatically appear in the bottom of the screen while you're debugging. You can access and open debugging windows by choosing the Debug⇨Windows menu selection. Table 7-3 lists the debugging windows and their functions.

Table 7-3	Debugging Windows and Their Functions			
Window	**Type**	**Access**	**Shortcut Key**	**Function**
Breakpoints	Execution control	Debug menu	Ctrl+Alt+B	Creates a new breakpoint or edits an existing breakpoint
Output	Feedback	Debug menu	N/A	Displays results or feedback
Script	N/A	Debug menu	Ctrl+Alt+N	Lists scripts used by your Explorer program
Watch	Variable	Debug menu	Ctrl+Alt+W, 1	Displays variables and expressions you add to the window
Autos	Variable	Debug menu	Ctrl+Alt+V, A	Displays variables used in the current and preceding lines of code

(continued)

Table 7-3 *(continued)*

Window	Type	Access	Shortcut Key	Function
Locals	Variable	Debug menu	Ctrl+Alt+V, L	Displays all variables in scope
Immediate	Variable	Debug menu	Ctrl+Alt+I	Executes commands and sets variable values
Call Stack	Memory	Debug menu	Ctrl+Alt+C	Displays functions in memory
Threads	CPU	Debug menu	Ctrl+Alt+H	Displays a set of instructions being executed by your program
Modules	Memory	Debug menu	Ctrl+Alt+U	Lists the software modules used by your program
Processes	Memory	Debug menu	Ctrl+Alt+Z	Displays processes which your program has launched or attached to
Memory	Memory	Debug menu	Ctrl+Alt+M, 1	Displays contents of memory
Disassembly	CPU	Debug menu	Ctrl+Alt+D	Displays assembly code of your program
Registers	CPU	Debug menu	Ctrl+Alt+G	Displays registers' contents
QuickWatch	Variable	Debug menu	Ctrl+Alt+Q	Displays values of current in break mode value or expression
Exception	Feedback	N/A	N/A	Displays information about an Assistant exception when an exception occurs
DataTips	Variable	Hover mouse over variable	N/A	Displays value of variable in scope

Figure 7-11 shows the tabs of the debugging windows at the bottom of a screen. Click a tab to access the window.

Many of the debugging windows allow you to observe the contents of your variables and data structures.

Figure 7-11:
Use the
debugging
windows
(bottom of
the screen)
to debug
your code.

Visual Studio offers the DataTips feature that allows you to view the contents of a variable. Simply hover your mouse over a variable that's active, and a DataTip appears that displays the variable's value. Figure 7-12 shows a DataTip. Notice that you can click the down arrow next to a DataTip and choose a different visualizer. *Visualizers* display data in different forms to make it easier to read and interpret.

Figure 7-12:
Hover your
mouse over
a variable to
display its
value in a
DataTip.

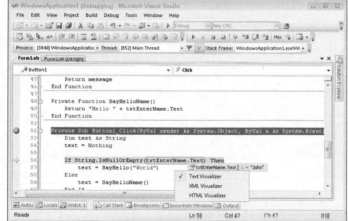

The variable in Figure 7-12 is a `string` variable. You can use DataTips to display complex variables, such as `DataSets`.

Visual Studio also provides the Autos, Locals, and Watch windows for viewing variable values. The Autos and Locals windows populate automatically. You use the Watch window to identify a specific variable that you want to monitor.

To use the Watch window to monitor a `DataSet`, follow these steps:

1. **Set a breakpoint in your code where you wish to monitor a variable.**

2. **Press F5 to start the Debugger.**

3. **When code execution breaks, choose Debug⇨Windows⇨Watch 1.**

The Watch window appears.

The Debugger must be in break mode to open the Watch window. Four Watch windows are available, and each window has a number from 1 to 4 appended to its Watch name.

4. **Right-click the object that you wish to add to the Watch window.**

5. **Choose Add Watch from the shortcut menu.**

The object appears in the Watch window.

Be sure to click the object — not a property of the object.

6. **Press F5 to resume execution.**

The code executes until it hits a breakpoint.

When the variable or object is *in scope* (part of the currently executing code), its values appear in the Watch window, as you can see in Figure 7-13.

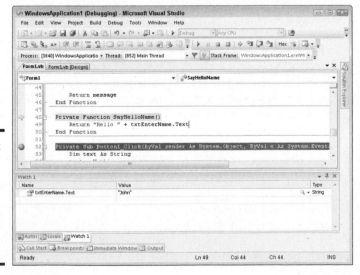

Figure 7-13: Use the Watch window to view the values of a variable or object.

You can add objects to the Watch window by typing their names in the Name field. For example, to add a Watch using a `DataSet` with the name `ds`

1. **Open the Watch window (using the preceding steps).**

2. **Type** ds **in the Name field.**

IntelliSense lists the properties and methods that you can select.

3. **Select a member of the** `DataSet` **to watch.**

Figure 7-14 shows the Watch window with `DataSet` members added.

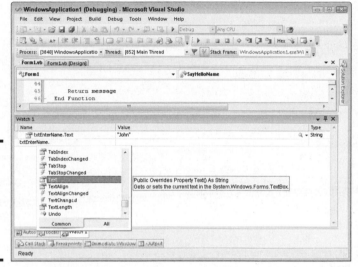

Figure 7-14:
Use
IntelliSense
to add
members to
the Watch
window.

Debugging for those special circumstances

The Visual Studio Debugger is sophisticated, and you can use it to debug very complex scenarios. Using the Debugger in a single-tier Windows application is about as easy as it gets. In the real world, however, applications aren't quite that simple.

You can use the Visual Studio Debugger to debug any of these items:

✦ ASP.NET Web sites

✦ Managed stored procedures

✦ Scripts

✦ Code on remote servers

Going through the setup processes for each of these is beyond the scope of this book. See the Visual Studio documentation for more information.

After you get the Debugger set up to work in your scenario, controlling execution and watching variables are basically the same.

Debugging generated code

Visual Studio generates a lot of code for you. Sometimes, you'll want to step through that code with the Debugger so you can see how the code works. To step into code that is not yours, however, you must disable the Debugger's Just My Code feature.

To disable the feature, follow these steps:

1. **Choose Tools⇨Options.**

The Options window appears.

2. **Click Debugging.**

3. **Clear the Enable Just My Code check box.**

4. **Click OK.**

Now, you can hit breakpoints inside generated code. To see generated code, click the Show All Files button on the Solution Explorer toolbar.

Chapter 8: Testing Code with Visual Studio

In This Chapter

✔ Understanding different kinds of software testing

✔ Creating and running unit tests

✔ Introducing stubs and mocks

✔ Using the Object Test Bench

✔ Exploring unit-testing frameworks

So you're plugging along coding like crazy. You'll have this set of requirements knocked out in no time. But how do you know when you're done? If you're unit testing your code while you go, the answer is when your code passes all your tests. If you're not unit testing while you go, you'll probably code until you feel like you're done and then pass the code off for somebody else to test.

Testing is an important part of the software development life cycle. Many kinds of tests are performed to ensure an application fulfills its requirements. Developers are usually responsible for writing tests called *unit tests* (see the next section for more these) to test the code they write. In Visual Studio 2008 Professional Edition, testing is more of a coding practice than a feature. Microsoft provides upgraded editions of Visual Studio that provide extensive support for all kinds of testing.

This chapter discusses the importance of testing, shows you how to write simple unit tests, and introduces you to some of the Visual Studio tools you can use to support your testing efforts.

Defining Unit Testing

Testing means different things, depending on the context in which it's used. Developers are usually responsible for testing the code they write — *unit testing*. After code passes unit tests, it's usually checked into a source code control repository. At some point, the entire system under development is compiled, and quality assurance testers perform even more testing.

The kinds of tests you might encounter include

✦ **Unit tests** — These programs are written by developers to test the code they write.

✦ **Integration tests** — These test units of code after they're integrated with each other.

✦ **System tests** — During *system tests,* the entire integrated system is tested. Depending on the kind of software being tested, system tests might include user interface testing, regression testing, and load testing.

✦ **Acceptance tests** — During *acceptance tests,* any or all of the system's stakeholders might participate in testing the software in a lab.

When software progresses through testing, tests become less focused on the inner workings of the code. As a result, testing becomes less automated and requires more user interaction. In the case of acceptance testing, a test lab is often set up where end users come in and bang away at the system for weeks at a time, uncovering bugs and functional shortcomings.

As a developer, you're actively involved in writing and running unit tests. Your interaction with the testing process beyond unit testing depends on several factors, including the extent to which your code provides any of the system's core functionality.

Of course, use of unit testing doesn't mean that no bugs exist. Rather, the implicit understanding is that when you "check in" your code, you're telling other developers that the code works at some basic level of functionality. Code that breaks every time that it's called by another developer shows a pretty good indication that you're either not unit testing at all or not doing enough unit testing.

If you've worked as a tester, you can likely spot those developers who never run unit tests. Not only does their code usually not conform to the requirements, but it usually blows up as soon you try to test it. Other developers, however, are very conscientious about unit testing their code. As a result, you won't need to interact with those developers as much. In other words, if you don't want quality assurance and your fellow developers on your back, unit test your code.

By definition, unit testing is about writing code. When you write a unit test, you're writing code to test code. You write a unit test to test a single unit of your code. For example, assume that your project includes code for a `Customer` object and an `Address` object. You should have one unit test for each object. The unit test contains multiple tests to test the various methods and properties of your object. Figure 8-1 shows an example.

Figure 8-1:
Write at
least one
unit test for
each object
in your
code.

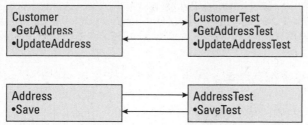

You'll find tons of rules about how you should write your tests. However, they're not really rules: They're more like opinions. And everybody has an opinion on what it means to unit test. Some of these opinions are that

✦ All tests should be automated and run as part of a suite.

✦ All your code should be tested.

✦ You should write your tests before you write your code.

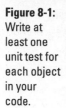

Getting started with unit testing can be quite overwhelming. Although these approaches are valid and ones to which you should aspire, it's better to

✦ Write imperfect tests than to write no tests at all.

✦ Run tests manually before you check in your code than run no tests at all. Test the riskiest parts of your code first until you get the hang of unit testing.

Unit Testing in Visual Studio

Unit testing is an important good coding practice. While you're coding, you should write tests that make sure your code works as you expect. Unit tests aren't supposed to test every aspect of the system. Rather, unit tests are sanity checks you use to make sure that your code works. For example, if your requirement states that the function should return an integer, you might create a unit test to test that the value returned by your function is indeed an integer.

When used properly, unit tests help you achieve the following important goals:

✦ Write better code.

✦ Have a starting point for testing code.

✦ Keep the development process flowing.

✦ Increase your confidence in your code.

Lots of patterns and frameworks are available for writing unit tests. At its simplest, a unit test simply tests that your code does what it says it does. Unit tests either pass or fail. There's no in-between.

Creating unit tests

Before you can write a unit test, you need code to test. This section uses a very simple Hello World example with the following methods:

✦ DisplayMessage() — Displays a Hello World message, depending on whether the user supplies a name

✦ SayHello() — Returns the message Hello World

✦ SayHelloName(*name*) — Returns the message Hello plus the name provided as an argument

These methods are used in a Windows Form that displays a Hello World message. If the user enters a name in a text box on the form, the user's name appears in the message.

Listing 8-1 shows the code to be unit tested. Notice the three methods to test.

Listing 8-1: Sample Unit Test Code

```
Public Sub DisplayMessage()
    Dim text, name As String
    name = Me.txtEnterName.Text
    If String.IsNullOrEmpty(name) Then
        text = SayHello()
    Else
        text = SayHelloName(name)
    End If
    Me.lblDisplayMessage.Text = text
End Sub
Private Function SayHello() As String
    Dim message As String
    message = "Hello World"
    Return message
End Function
Private Function SayHelloName(ByVal name As String) As String
    Dim message As String
    message = "Hello " + name
    Return message
End Function
```

To test this code, you write a set of tests that makes sure the output is as expected. For example, the `SayHello()` method is supposed to return `Hello World`. The unit test should test the return value. Listed here is a function that tests `SayHello()`:

```
Dim message As String
Dim results As New Hashtable
message = SayHello()
If Not message = "Hello World" Then
  results.Add("Form1.SayHello", "Failed")
End If
```

The test uses a hashtable to store a key/value pair that consists of the name of the test case and the case's result. You can add the results of all your tests to a hashtable and then output the hashtable to a file or screen.

Each test you create is a *test case*. Some functions might require multiple test cases. For example, `DisplayMessage` can return two different messages, so two test cases are appropriate. Listing 8-2 shows the entire code sample that tests the set of code. The code in this example requires multiple tests because multiple messages can occur.

Listing 8-2: Code to Test the Set of Code

```
Public Function SmokeTest() As Hashtable
   Dim message As String
   Dim results As New Hashtable
   'test sayhello
   message = SayHello()
   If Not message = "Hello World" Then
      results.Add("Form1.SayHello", "Failed")
   End If
   'reset variable
   message = Nothing
   'test sayhelloname
   message = SayHelloName("John")
   If Not message = "Hello Tim"" Then
      results.Add("Form1.SayHelloName", "Failed")
   End If
   'test displaymessage
   Me.txtEnterName.Text = Nothing
   Me.lblDisplayMessage.Text = Nothing
   DisplayMessage()
   If Not Me.lblDisplayMessage.Text = "Hello World" Then
      results.Add("Form1.DisplayMessageNoName", "Failed"")
   End If
   'test displaymessage
```

(continued)

Listing 8-2 *(continued)*

```
    Me.txtEnterName.Text = "John"
    Me.lblDisplayMessage.Text = Nothing
    DisplayMessage()
    If Not Me.lblDisplayMessage.Text = "Hello John" Then
        results.Add("Form1.DisplayMessageWithName", "Failed")
    End If
    Return results
End Function
```

Before you start criticizing too much repetitious code or doing too many things in one procedure in Listing 8-2, take into consideration the point of this demonstration. The point is that you don't have to write fancy code to unit test. Sure, you can find several ways to improve this code. As a developer, you might choose to improve the code or leave it a little rough around the edges. Either way, it gets the job done. At the end of the day, you know exactly whether your procedures work or don't.

The procedure in Listing 8-2 is intentionally named SmokeTest to indicate that this is a first test just to make sure the code works. In electronics, a new circuit will smoke when it's powered up if it's wired incorrectly. Attaching power to a circuit for the first time is often called a *smoke test*. If no smoke appears, presumably, the circuit is wired properly. In software development, the term *smoke test* is often applied to any initial tests that are run to ensure that a component has basic functionality. Smoke tests aren't usually comprehensive unto themselves but rather usually refined into more-comprehensive unit tests.

Running a battery of tests

You should be able to run your tests with the click of a mouse or by entering a single command. This section shows you how to create a simple Windows Form that runs your unit tests and outputs the results to the screen.

To create a Windows Form to display the results of your unit tests, follow these steps:

1. **Create a new Windows Form.**

   See Book III, Chapter 1 for how to add a Windows Form to a project.

2. **Drag a button and a list box onto the form.**

3. **Use the Properties window to set the button name to btnRunTests and the list box name to lstResults.**

4. **Double-click the button to access the button's Click event handler.**

   The Code Editor appears.

5. **Create a new instance of the class where the unit test is.**

Typically, unit tests are created as separate units of code. For example, you might create a test for a Customer object called CustomerTest. To create a new instance of the CustomerTest object so that you can access the object's tests, type the following:

```
Dim myTest as New CustomerTest
```

The unit test from the preceding example isn't in a separate unit of code. Rather, the test itself is embedded in a Windows Form called DisplayHelloWorld. You might choose to embed your tests in your forms when you first start unit testing, although it isn't considered a best practice to do so because the context is different.

Type the following code to create a new instance of DisplayHelloWorld:

```
Dim myTest As New DisplayHelloWorld
```

This code allows you to access the unit test in the Windows Form.

6. **Create a new instance of a Hashtable and a key/value pair to represent each entry in the Hashtable.**

```
Dim htResults As New System.Collections.Hashtable
Dim testcase As System.Collections.DictionaryEntry
```

This code assumes that the results of your unit tests are stored in a Hashtable.

7. **Call the unit test and pass the results to the local Hashtable.**

For example, type the following code to access a test method called SmokeTest() and pass the results to the local Hashtable.

```
htResults = myTest.SmokeTest()
```

Simple tests that are run to make sure code works are often called *smoke tests*. The method name SmokeTest() is used here to signify that this is an informal test. For example, it might be a first attempt at creating a set of tests for a unit of code.

8. **Use a For Each statement to loop through each entry in the Hashtable and display the results in the list box.**

```
For Each testcase In htResults
   Me.lstResults.Items.Add
     (testcase.Key + ": " + testcase.Value)
Next
```

9. **Press F5 to run your test form.**

10. **Click the button to run your tests.**

The results appear in the list box, as shown in Figure 8-2.

Figure 8-2:
Display the
results of
your failed
unit tests.

You might wonder why the results of the successful unit tests weren't
output. The whole point of unit tests is that they should be fast. If they aren't
fast, you won't run them. You don't care about the tests that pass: You care
only about the ones that don't. In Figure 8-2, you can immediately see that
one of the tests failed. Rats. You need to go take care of that.

Writing better code

One of the positive side effects of unit tests is that you write better code. For
example, while writing the test for `DisplayMessage()`, you can see that
the subroutine is tightly coupled to the Windows Form, which makes the
unit test harder to write. So, you can rewrite the `DisplayMessage` subroutine as a function to make it easier to test. The new function looks like
Listing 8-3.

Listing 8-3: Rewriting the DisplayMessage Subroutine as a Function

```
Private Function DisplayMessage(ByVal name As String) As String
    Dim text As String
    If String.IsNullOrEmpty(name) Then
        text = SayHello()
    Else
        text = SayHelloName(name)
    End If
    Return text
End Function
```

The unit test for `DisplayMessage` changes (Listing 8-4) so that it's more
consistent with the other unit tests.

Listing 8-4: New Unit Test for DisplayMessage

```
'test displaymessage
message = Nothing
message = DisplayMessage(Nothing)
If Not message = "Hello World" Then
  results.Add("DisplayHelloWorld.DisplayMessageNoName", "Failed")
End If
'test displaymessage
message = Nothing
message = DisplayMessage("John")
If Not message = "Hello John" Then
  results.Add("DisplayHelloWorld.DisplayMessageWithName", "Failed")
End If
```

Rewriting code is *refactoring*. See Book V, Chapter 5 for more information on refactoring.

Approaches to Unit Testing

Within the past few years, unit testing has taken on a life of its own. It's not cool not to unit test. One of the hardest choices when creating unit tests is deciding what to test. When you examine code that you want to test, you'll find the following issues to consider:

+ **Public methods** — *Public methods* are those features of your code that are exposed to the outside world. Pretty much everyone agrees you should unit test your public methods. After all, a public method is sitting there saying, "Call me."

+ **Private and protected methods** — *Private and protected methods* in your code do the work of your public methods. As a result, some people believe that testing private and protected methods is wasteful. They believe that unit testing public methods implicitly tests private and protected methods. Plus, testing private and protected methods is harder. By their nature, private and protected methods are, well, private and protected. Unlike public methods, they aren't saying, "Call me." Just the opposite is true, so you need to go out of your way to test them.

+ **Interactions with other code** — Unless you're writing all your application's features in a single function, chances are high your code needs to interact with other code. The very nature of unit testing, however, is that you want to test only a single unit of code. How can you do that if you have to interact with other code?

Public methods are easily tested because, by definition, you can call a public method from anywhere in your code. You can use the Visual Studio Object Test Bench (OTB) to call public methods in your code. See the section "Using the Object Test Bench," later in this chapter.

People take all kinds of approaches to solve the problems of testing private methods or code that interacts with other code. One popular approach is to use software that specializes in unit testing, usually called *unit testing frameworks.* See the section "Automating Tests with Testing Frameworks," later in this chapter.

The two approaches to testing code that interacts with other code are stubs and mocks. Keep reading for information on those approaches.

Letting stubs do the tough testing

By definition, a unit test is supposed to test only one unit of code. No unit of code lives in isolation, however. Most developers work around this pesky paradox by using *code stubs,* which act as placeholders for units of code that the unit being tested needs to interact with. The code stub placeholder is better than interacting with the actual units of code because each unit of code introduces a new set of variables. Instead, the code stub can be programmed to return a consistent set of values against which the unit can interact. Returning a consistent set of values creates predictability, which makes it easier to create tests that you can repeat.

In reality, developers who use stubs usually go ahead and test the real units of code that interact with the unit their testing — that is, as long as it's simple to do so. For example, say you create a `Customer` object with a public method called `GetAddress`. `GetAddress` returns an `Address` object. The `Customer` and `Address` objects are each units of code that have their own set of unit tests. Many developers will create a test that allows their `Customer` object to interact with the `Address` object even though the test extends beyond the unit they wish to test.

When the developer encounters a set of code that would be too complicated or messy with which to interact in a simple unit test, the developer usually creates a stub. The stub returns a set of canned values that the developer expects to get from the code.

For example, say your `Customer` object has a method called `UpdateAddress`. `UpdateAddress` accepts a new address for a customer and passes that data off to an `Address` object. The `Address` object calls a service that validates the address against a valid ZIP code database. You don't want to have to deal with all that when you're testing your `Customer` object.

Instead of using the `Address` object, you create a stub that returns two possible values. If you pass a valid address, it returns the value `ValidAddress`. If you pass an invalid address, it returns the value `InvalidAddress`. So, how does the stub know what's a valid address and what's an invalid address? You specify in the stub that 123 Main Street, for example, is a valid address. Everything else is invalid. Figure 8-3 shows an example of a stub.

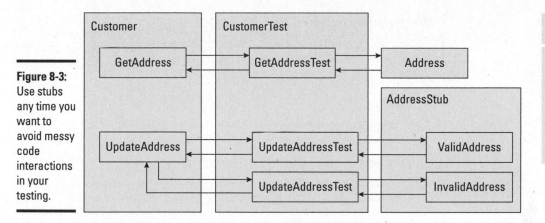

Figure 8-3:
Use stubs
any time you
want to
avoid messy
code
interactions
in your
testing.

Simplifying testing with mocking objects

Other developers believe that creating a bunch of objects and stubs is too
much work. These developers use a special library to create mock objects.
With mock objects — *mocks* — you tell the object which methods you
expect it to run, how many times the methods will run, and what values to
return.

For example, assume you use a mock Address object to interact with your
Customer address. For your UpdateAddress test, you tell the mock
Address object to call the Address object's Save method. Your test tells
the mock object that you're going to send a value of 123 Main Street to
the Save method and that you expect it to return a value of true. Your test
also tells the mock object that you're going to send the value 123 Nowhere
Boulevard and that you expect the Save method to return the value
false. Figure 8-4 shows an example of a mock object.

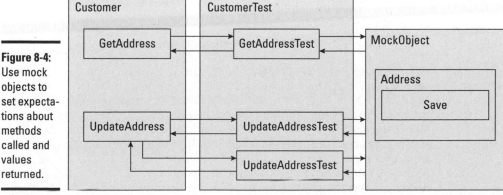

Figure 8-4:
Use mock
objects to
set expecta-
tions about
methods
called and
values
returned.

The stubbies versus the mockers

Deciding which method to use can be a little difficult at first glance, but several key differences exist between using mocks and stubs, based on what you want to test for. Here are some of them:

✦ **Mocks**

- You tell your mock objects which methods to call, how many times they'll be called by your test, and what return values you expect.

- You create mocks for all objects with which your code interacts.

- Mocks require a library of code to create the mock objects.

✦ **Stubs**

- Stubs usually return only values.

- You create stubs only when necessary.

Rick calls those who use stubs "stubbies" and those who use mock objects "mockers." Stubbies and mockers usually have totally different approaches to unit testing that go beyond the mere use of stubs and mocks.

Stubbies tend to test clusters of interacting objects together. For example, stubbies might test all the code related to customers and orders together because those units of code interact.

Mockers, on the other hand, are more likely to take a top-down approach. They might start testing at the user interface level first and then use mock objects to mimic the behavior of business rules or data access code. Mockers are likely to test first and code second. In other words, they use testing as a way to discover what code they still need to write to make their system work.

Using mock objects is very popular in the test-driven development (TDD) style. With TDD, you test first and code second. For more information, see the Test Driven Web site at www.testdriven.com.

Using the Object Test Bench

In the Microsoft .NET Framework, everything's an object. When you write code, you're writing code to create your own objects. For example, a Windows Form is an object. When you add a new Windows Form to a project, you're creating a new object. The functions you add to your form are the object's methods.

Objects must be created before you can use them. Visual Studio provides the Object Test Bench (OTB) as a test environment where you can interact with your objects.

To read more about objects, see Chapter 3 of this mini-book.

You use the OTB to perform the following tasks:

✦ Create a new instance of an object.

✦ Create multiple instances of the same object.

✦ Call an object's public methods.

✦ Evaluate the results of the method.

Using the OTB is a good way to explore your own code, somebody else's code, or the .NET Framework.

Access the OTB from Class Designer, Class View, or Object Browser. To create a new instance of an object by using Class View, follow these steps:

1. **Open a solution where you want to use the OTB.**

2. **Press Ctrl+Shift+C to open the Class View window.**

The namespace for your projects appears in Class View.

3. **Expand the namespace until you find the object you want to view in the Object Test Bench, as shown in Figure 8-5.**

Figure 8-5:
Use Class View to create a new instance of an object in the OTB.

The project displayed in Figure 8-5 is a refactored version of the `HelloWorld` example used in the preceding section.

4. Right-click the object.

A shortcut menu appears.

5. Choose Create Instance.

A submenu appears with a list of the constructors you can use to create the object.

A *constructor* is a special kind of method that creates instances of objects.

6. Choose the constructor from the menu.

The Create Instance window appears.

7. Type the name you want to use for the instance in the OTB.

A default name is provided.

For example, to create an instance of the `HelloWorld` class, open the Create Instance window and type the name **helloWorld** in the Create Instance window, as shown in Figure 8-6.

Figure 8-6:
Type a name for the object instance in the Create Instance form.

Using the Create Instance window is the same thing as typing the following code:

```
Dim helloWorld as New HelloWorld()
```

8. Click OK.

The object appears in the OTB.

Visual Studio builds your project before it creates an instance of your object. You must resolve any build errors before you can use the OTB.

You can call an object's public methods from the OTB. To call a public method, follow these steps:

1. **Right-click an object instance in the OTB.**

   A shortcut menu appears.

2. **Choose Invoke Method.**

   A submenu appears. All the object's public methods appear in the list.

3. **Click the method you wish to invoke.**

   The Invoke Method window appears.

   For example, to call the `DisplayMessage()` method on the `helloWorld` object from the preceding set of steps, choose Invoke Method⇨DisplayMessage(ByVal as String).

   The Invoke Method window displays a parameters grid where you can enter values to pass to the method, if required.

4. **(Optional) Type parameter values in the Invoke Method window, as shown in Figure 8-7.**

   For example, the `DoIt()` object accepts a string parameter. Type a value for the parameter, such as `This is a test`.

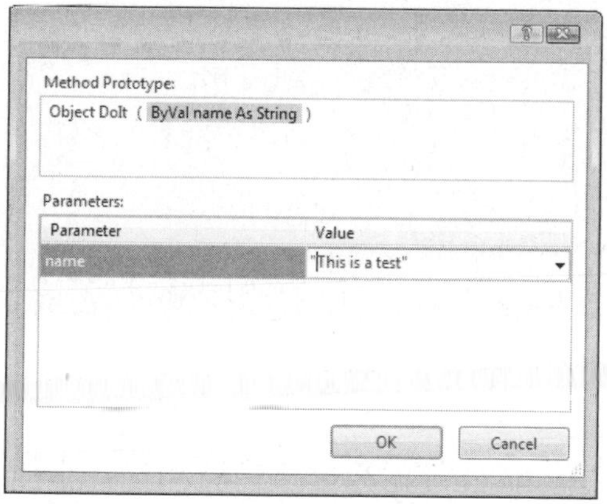

Figure 8-7:
Type parameter values in the Invoke Method window.

5. **Click OK.**

   The Method Call Result window appears, displaying the results of the method call. To save the returned value to the OTB, enable the Save Return Value check box.

6. Click OK.

An object representing the value appears in the OTB. Figure 8-8 shows the OTB with the results from two method calls.

Figure 8-8:
Use the OTB
to invoke
public
methods on
your objects
and view
the results.

Everything — *everything,* including Windows Forms — in the .NET Framework is an object. If you're struggling with getting your mind around object-oriented programming (OOP) or you want to learn more about the .NET Framework, use the OTB to explore.

Automating Tests with Testing Frameworks

Unit tests are often grouped so that they can be executed by a testing framework. A framework isn't necessary, but using a framework allows you to do these things:

+ Formalize unit testing.

+ Create consistency among unit tests.

+ Make automating testing easier.

+ Execute groups of tests at one time.

Frameworks are a necessity for most systems. Because unit tests are so small in nature, even a simple system has lots of tests. In most cases, using a framework to administer the tests makes sense. Unit testing frameworks exist for nearly every programming language under the sun. Two popular unit testing frameworks for the .NET Framework include

+ **NUnit** — By far, NUnit is the most-popular testing framework around. NUnit is an open source (free) framework. However, a drawback to NUnit is that it isn't integrated into Visual Studio. Still, many folks use NUnit to manage their unit tests. You can visit the NUnit web site at www. nunit.org.

✦ **Visual Studio Team System** — The newest edition of Visual Studio, Visual Studio Team System (VSTS), provides a unit testing framework that's integrated into Visual Studio. Using the framework is as simple as right-clicking the code you want to test and then choosing Create Tests from the shortcut menu. Your tests are stored in Test Projects. VSTS provides support for many different kinds of tests, including the ability to record Web tests. For more on VSTS, turn to Book VII, Chapter 2.

Two other popular unit-testing tools for the .NET Framework include

✦ **NMock** — Creates mock objects for use with unit tests.

✦ **TestDriven.NET** — Integrates testing frameworks, such as NUnit, into the Visual Studio development environment. TestDriven.NET gives you the ability to access testing commands from a shortcut menu in the Code Editor. You can visit the TestDrive.NET Web site at `www.testdriven.net`.

Book VI

Going the Extra Mile

The 5th Wave   By Rich Tennant

SITE MAP STRATEGY BY JERRY

" Okay, well, I think we all get the gist of where Jerry was going with the site map."

Contents at a Glance

Chapter 1: Building Solutions and Projects...659

Chapter 2: Deployment Options...675

Chapter 3: Checking Out Source Control 701

Chapter 4: Building Professional Reports with Crystal Reports......................719

Chapter 1: Building Solutions and Projects

In This Chapter

✔ Understanding the build process

✔ Creating build configurations

✔ Viewing build feedback

✔ Automating daily builds

An application comprises of many pieces — presentation code, data-access libraries, unit tests, configuration files, installation programs, and more. Visual Studio organizes these pieces into *projects,* and the entire application is a *solution.*

While you're creating the interfaces and writing the data access code for your solution, you need to stop periodically and test your application. To test your application, you need to run a compiler that converts the human-readable source code in your projects to machine-readable binary files. Visual Studio provides a set of build commands that you use to compile your projects and solutions.

By its nature, the build process is tightly coupled with deployment. In the simplest deployment case, you create a release build and distribute the output files. However, very rarely is real life so simple. Some types of applications — such as multiple-tier Windows applications, ASP.NET Web sites, and mobile applications — are inherently more difficult to deploy. You need to take many variables into consideration when creating release builds.

This chapter shows you how to build your solutions and projects for use on a local development computer. (See Chapter 2 in this mini-book to read about deploying release builds.)

Understanding Solutions and Projects

Visual Studio uses logical containers — *projects* and *solutions* — for grouping all the code and resources associated with an application.

✦ *Solutions* contain all the projects necessary to build an application.

✦ *Projects* include all the source code and support files necessary to create the application.

For example, a solution may contain one project each for the following:

✦ Windows Forms

✦ Data-access code

✦ Database code

✦ Testing code

✦ The installer

The process of converting all the code found in a set of projects to an application is *building* or *creating a build.* Builds have settings that define where the output files are located and whether debug information is included. A group of settings is a *build configuration.* Visual Studio solutions and projects include two default build configurations:

✦ **Debug** — Code compiles with information for debugging and no optimization. The nature of the build is to enable you to test your code.

✦ **Release** — Code compiles with optimizations and no debugging information. The release configuration is intended for production deployment.

Builds can target a specific hardware platform, such as the 32-bit (x86) or 64-bit (x64) architectures. The Debug and Release build configurations provided by Visual Studio target the x86 architecture.

The anatomy of a build

Building software takes a set of inputs and creates a set of outputs. The inputs include the following:

✦ Source-code files

✦ Resource files

✦ Configuration files

✦ Local database files

The build process takes these files and converts them to a set of outputs that include

+ **Tokenized files,** such as application executables and dynamic link libraries (DLLs). Binary files are *assemblies.*

+ **Debugging information,** which is stored in a program database (PDB) file. (See Book V, Chapter 7 for more information about debugging.)

+ **Feedback messages,** such as compiler warnings and errors.

The build process uses a compiler to convert your human-readable input files into machine-readable binary files. Each programming language uses its own compiler.

You use the outputs from a build to accomplish the following:

+ **Test an application you're developing.**

+ **Deploy an application to a test or production environment.**

+ **Determine whether you can check in your source code to form part of your source-code repository.**

  Inputs to the build process — the source code — are *checked in* (established as source code) after you have a successful build.

Figure 1-1 shows the build process. Note that the outputs are deployed, but usually they're not checked into source code control.

Book VI
Chapter 1

Building Solutions and Projects

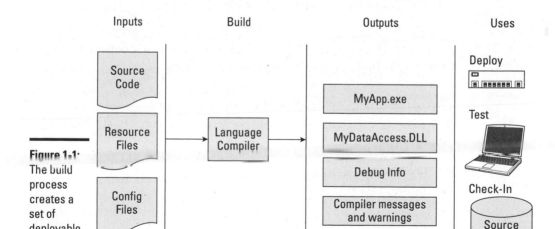

Figure 1-1: The build process creates a set of deployable outputs.

Using the Build menu

Visual Studio provides a Build menu from which you can launch different build commands for your solution or project. The options on the Build menu are

- ✦ **Build:** Compiles any source code that hasn't yet been compiled. The Build command doesn't delete any existing output files. Instead, the Build command performs an incremental build of any files not yet compiled.

- ✦ **Rebuild Solution:** Deletes, or *cleans,* any existing output files and compiles all source code into binary files.

- ✦ **Clean:** Deletes all the output files generated by previous builds.

- ✦ **Publish:** Calls the Publishing Wizard to build and deploy the solution. (See Chapter 2 in this mini-book for more information on using the Publishing Wizard.)

- ✦ **Batch Build:** Compiles multiple build configurations as a batch.

Deployable projects, such as SQL Server Reporting Projects, display the Deploy command on the Build menu. If you have the Web Deployment Project Add-In installed, you also have the option Add Web Deployment Project on the Build menu. (See Chapter 2 in this mini-book for more information about Web Deployment Projects.)

You execute build commands against solutions or individual projects. Here are some scenarios for how you may use the Build menu:

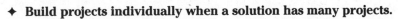

- ✦ **Build projects individually when a solution has many projects.**

    Compiling large solutions and projects is time consuming. For that reason, you may choose to build individual projects as you need them rather than building the entire solution. Using the Build command to incrementally compile source files can also save time.

- ✦ **Build each project in a solution individually when a dependent project generates compile errors.**

    When a solution has many projects that are dependent upon one another, an error in one project cascades to the dependent projects, which makes finding the original error difficult. Instead of plowing through a long list of errors and warnings, compile each project individually and deal with any errors you find.

+ **Build an entire solution.**

 If your solution builds lightning-fast, you can use either the Build or the Rebuild Solution command.

 Use the Rebuild Solution option (rather than Build) if you're getting strange errors that you don't think you should be getting. Using Rebuild Solution wipes out all the previous build's outputs.

+ **Build individual projects as changes are made to them.**

 When you have large projects and solutions, building is faster than rebuilding the entire solution.

Using the Start command from the Debug menu calls the Build command and executes your application. During development, many developers press the F5 key with the expectation that their code is going to build and execute. Only after they see that long list of compiler errors do they start using the Build menu.

The commands on the Build menu correspond to targets files used by the Microsoft Build Engine (MSBuild). To read more about MSBuild, see the upcoming section "Automating builds."

Selecting the active build and platform

When you build a solution or a project, you select a named build configuration you wish to build, such as Debug or Release. Each build configuration has specific properties that determine how the project is built. Visual Studio 2008 automatically creates the Debug and Release build configurations for each project and solution you create.

The build process creates code for a specific hardware platform (such as the Intel x86 or x64 architectures). You pick a hardware platform when you build your solution or project.

To set a build configuration and a hardware platform for a build, use the Solution Configuration and Solution Platform drop-down lists on the Standard toolbar, as shown in Figure 1-2.

Dealing with compiler errors and output

The major function of the build process is to compile your source code into binary files. The build process provides output that shows the list of commands executed, along with any feedback from those commands. If the compiler can't compile your code, error messages appear in the Error List window.

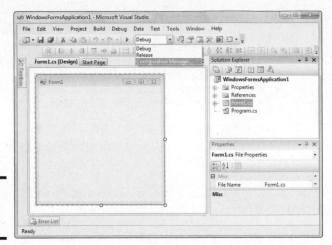

Figure 1-2:
Select the build type.

If you execute your build by using the Start command from the Debug menu, a dialog box warns you that the build was unsuccessful. If you use the Build menu, the Error List window appears. Figure 1-3 shows an error message that cropped up when trying to use a variable that hadn't yet been declared.

Each programming language uses its own compiler. The message displayed in Figure 1-3 is from the Visual Basic compiler. The C# compiler displays the following message for the same error:

```
The name 'myVariable' does not exist in the current context.
```

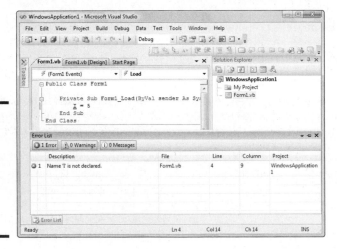

Figure 1-3:
Error and warning messages from the compiler appear here.

Among other things, you can use the Errors window to

✦ **Go to the source code where the error occurred.** When you double-click an error, Visual Studio opens the source-code file and positions the cursor where the error occurred.

✦ **Get help on an error.** Right-click an error and choose Show Error Help from the shortcut menu.

Hover your mouse pointer over an error in source code to display the error in a ToolTip, as shown in Figure 1-4.

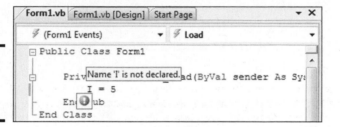

Figure 1-4:
The ToolTip
shows the
error.

Use the Output window to view the commands executed by the build process. The Output window displays the following information:

✦ Build configuration

✦ Compiler and switches used

✦ Output from the compiler

✦ Build status

Messages appear for each project compiled in the build. Figure 1-5 shows a successful build for a single project, using the Debug build configuration.

The long line that appears in Figure 1-5 between the first and last lines is a single command that executes the compiler. To create this command, the Build command pulls all the project settings, references, and properties that you set in Visual Studio.

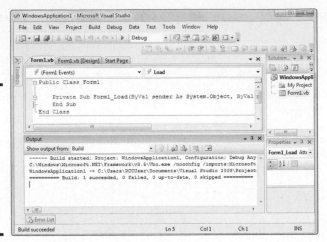

Figure 1-5:
The Output window displays the compiler command used to build your project.

You can copy and paste the compiler command from the Output window to reuse on the command line or in a batch file. Batch files are a good way to automate builds. You'll probably need to qualify the path names to your project's resources. To open a Visual Studio command prompt, choose Start⇨All Programs⇨Microsoft Visual Studio 2008⇨Visual Studio Tools⇨ Visual Studio 2008 Command Prompt.

To specify whether a file should be compiled with a project, use the Properties window to set the file's `BuildAction` property.

Using Configuration Manager

You use Configuration Manager to create new build configurations and manage existing configurations for solutions and projects. You use Project Designer to associate a project's properties with its build configuration.

To create a new build configuration by using Configuration Manager, follow these steps:

1. **Choose Configuration Manager from the Build drop-down list.**

Configuration Manager appears, displaying the configuration settings for the configuration and platform selected at the top.

2. **Choose New from the Active solution configuration drop-down list.**

The New Solution Configuration window appears.

3. **Type** Staging **in the Name field.**

4. **Choose Debug from the Copy Settings From drop-down list.**

5. **Leave the Create New Project Configurations check box selected.**

6. **Click OK.**

The new configuration appears in Configuration Manager, as shown in Figure 1-6.

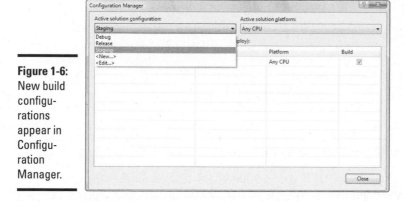

Figure 1-6:
New build configurations appear in Configuration Manager.

**Book VI
Chapter 1**

**Building Solutions
and Projects**

A solution's build configuration is composed of two main elements:

+ **Project configurations:** A set of build-and-debug properties defined for a given project.

+ **Platforms:** A setting that specifies what hardware platform the build targets

For each project in the solution, you select a project configuration and a platform, as shown in Figure 1-6. You create new project configurations and hardware platforms, if necessary. You include the project in the build by placing a check in the Build column. You use Project Designer to set the properties for each project configuration. Figure 1-7 shows an example of selecting a project configuration for a solution configuration, which you can get to by going to the project properties under the Project menu.

Visual Studio writes the build configurations you create in Configuration Manager to the appropriate solution or project file. When you build your solution or project, MSBuild uses the solution or project files as a script. For example, the following line is added to the solution file for the staging build configuration:

```
Staging|Any CPU = Staging|Any CPU
```

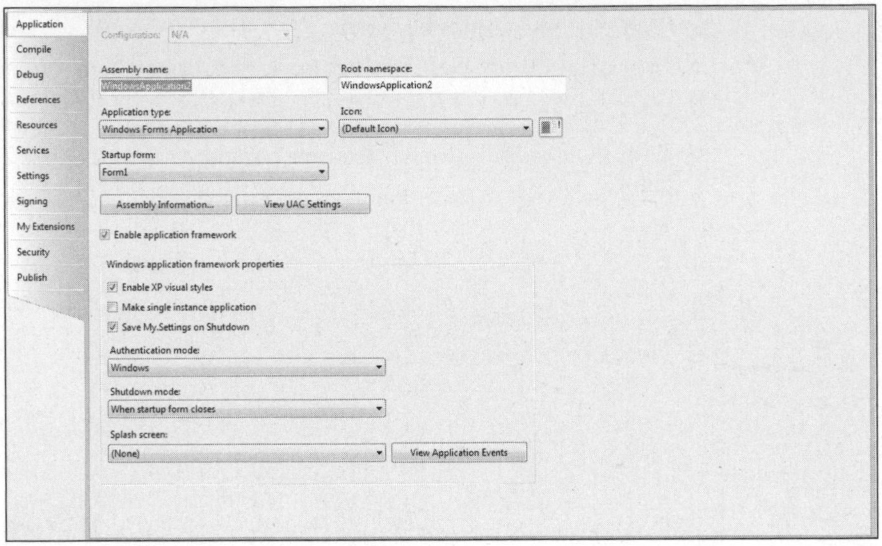

Figure 1-7:
You can set
most of the
project
configu-
ration in
Project
Designer.

Open your solution file or project file in any text editor to view the changes
made by Configuration Manager. (See the section "Automating builds," later
in this chapter, to read more about the Microsoft Build Engine.)

If you have a specific hardware platform in mind, you can use Configuration
Manager to specify that a build target that platform. For example, to create a
new Debug solution configuration that targets the x64 platform, follow these
steps:

1. **Open Configuration Manager.**

2. **Choose Debug from the Active Solution Configuration drop-down list.**

3. **Choose New from the Active Solution Platform drop-down list.**

   The New Solution Platform window appears.

4. **Select x64 as the new hardware platform.**

5. **Click OK.**

   A new Debug solution configuration for the x64 platform is created.

If you're using the MSBuild Toolkit, you can select a version of the .NET
Framework to target using the Platform. (See Book II, Chapter 4 for more
information about using the MSBuild Toolkit to target a specific version of
the .NET Framework.)

Setting project configurations

Visual Studio solutions and projects have many settings — *properties* — that define the solution or project. These properties define attributes, such as

+ Other code referenced by the project

+ Where to place the project's compiled output

+ Which debugger to use

You access the properties for a solution or project by choosing Properties from the solution's or project's shortcut menu. The two views for properties are

+ **Project Designer** — Displays properties for a project in Document Explorer. All Visual Studio projects use Project Designer to manage their properties.

+ **Property Pages** — Displays properties in a dialog box. Solutions and ASP.NET Web sites use the Property Pages window to manage their properties.

ASP.NET Web sites don't use projects, so they don't use Project Designer. Microsoft has a project type (Web Application Projects) that allows you to have ASP.NET projects.

Using Project Designer

Visual Studio 2008 includes a new feature — Project Designer — that you use to access your project's configuration settings in a single designer.

To open Project Designer, follow these steps:

1. **Right-click your project in Solution Explorer.**

A shortcut menu appears.

2. **Choose Properties.**

Project Designer appears in Document Explorer, showing a set of tabs along the left that group common properties. To access a set of properties, click its tab. Figure 1-8 shows the Project Designer for a class library project type.

You can also open Project Designer from the Project menu.

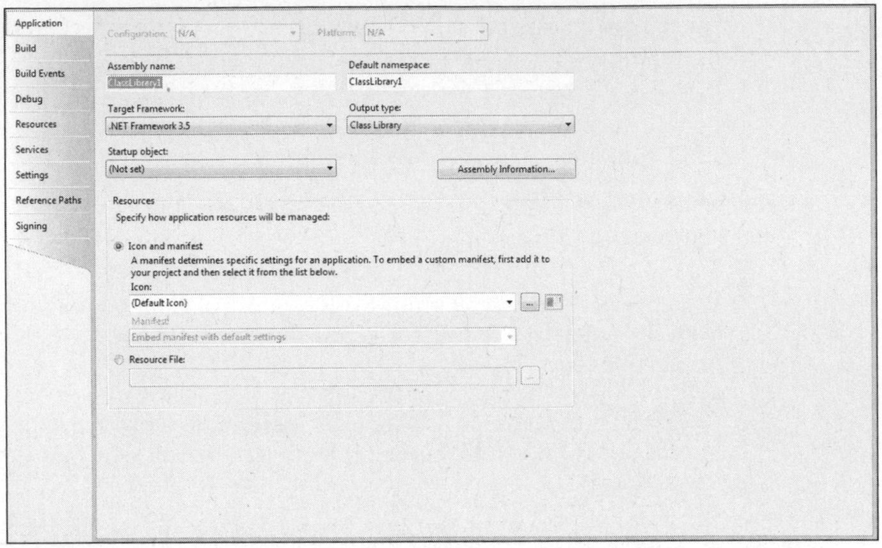

Figure 1-8:
This is
Project
Designer for
a class
library
project.

Some tabs in Project Designer feature properties that you can configure to match your build configuration type. For example, you can set build properties for a Debug build. To set the build properties for a C# or J# project type, follow these steps:

1. **Open Project Designer.**

2. **Click the Build tab.**

The project's build properties appear.

3. **Choose a build configuration from the Configuration drop-down list.**

The properties for the selected build configuration appear. If you want to manage properties for all your build configurations, you can choose All Configurations.

4. **Choose a build platform from the Platform drop-down list.**

5. **Set properties in Project Designer.**

The properties that you choose depend largely on whether you intend to debug or release the output. The properties for Visual Basic projects are slightly different because the compilers are different.

You won't find an OK or a Save button for Project Designer. The properties are saved immediately.

The Project Designer for Visual Basic project types has a Compile tab instead of a Build tab. You can access build properties from the Compile tab.

You can set unique build configuration settings for properties in the Build and Debug tabs in C# and J# project types. For Visual Basic project types, you set these items on the Build and Compile tabs.

Using property pages

Solutions and ASP.NET Web sites use the Property Pages dialog box to manage properties. Here's how to use a solution's property pages to set project dependencies:

1. **Right-click the solution in Solution Explorer.**

A shortcut menu appears.

2. **Expand Common Properties.**

A list of properties appears.

3. **Click Project Dependencies.**

4. **Choose a project from the Projects drop-down list (see Figure 1-9).**

Your project must have more than one project to set project dependencies.

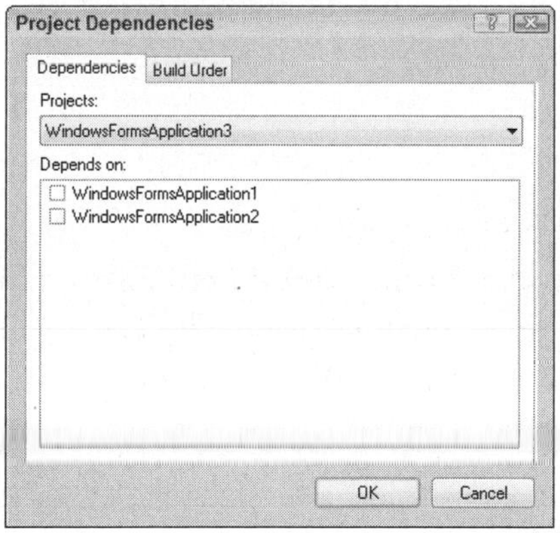

Figure 1-9:
Set project dependencies here.

5. **Check the project dependencies.**

6. **To verify that your projects build in the correct order, choose Project Build Order from the Projects menu.**

Managing Your Builds

Building software for your own use on a single computer is fairly straightforward. However, most software is developed in teams. Even if you don't plan to release the build, managing builds while a project is being developed is a challenge.

Visual Studio 2008 Professional Edition doesn't provide much support for managing team builds. However, Microsoft offers Team Foundation Server, which targets team-based development. This section discusses some of the best practices for managing builds and then highlights a few tools that can help manage your build process.

Handling Lone Ranger builds

Most builds that occur on an individual developer's workstation are part of the code/build/test cycle. You code a little. You build. You test. You code a little more.

At some point, however, the code must be integrated with the larger code base (*checking in* the new code). Many professionals use source code control software to help manage the code base. Even without source code control, the goal is the same: You need to integrate your changes without breaking your existing code.

Even hobbyists and casual developers can benefit from using source code control. (Chapter 3 in this mini-book tells you more about that process and its advantages.)

The integration process for an individual developer, whether that developer is working solo or as part of a team, should go something like this, in this order:

1. Get the latest source code from the source-code repository before starting any new task.

2. Write new code or change existing code.

3. Write unit tests for the new code.

4. Build the code on the developer's local computer.

5. Address any issues with the compiler and run unit tests.

6. Get the latest version of source code from the source code repository if other developers are adding code to the repository.

7. Build the code again using the updated code from the repository.

8. Run unit tests again.

9. If the tests pass, check the code into source code control.

At some point — ideally, daily — a master build should be made from the integrated source code. If you're working alone, you can fire up the master build any time you want. If the master build breaks, the developer who broke the build needs to figure out why — and get the code working again.

Not much time elapses between the point where a new task is started and the new code is integrated into the master source code. Code is integrated when the master source code compiles successfully and passes all unit tests.

Code kept on a developer's local workstation doesn't count for anything. Code isn't useful unless it's integrated.

Creating master builds

The build created from an integrated set of source code is the *master build*. The accepted standard is that master builds should be built daily. Tools are available that create master builds continuously so that developers have instant feedback about whether their code integrates successfully.

Master builds use the latest version of the code from source code control to create the build. Every morning, the first thing a developer does is check the status of the build. If the master build is broken, the developer can't work. Fixing the master build is the number-one priority. The developer responsible for breaking the build is usually the one responsible for fixing it.

If the master build is successful, all developers pull down the latest version of code. Each developer integrates continuously throughout the day.

It may be necessary to distribute the build's output to customers, testers, and developers. Ideally, the master build's output should be kept in a common repository; folks who need access should be able to download from there.

Automating builds

Regardless of how frequently you build your master build, your build process should be automatic and easy to execute. Ideally, you should just have to click one button or execute one command to start the process. For daily builds, you can add your build command to the server's scheduler.

If your build process requires more than just the click of a button, chances are that you won't be able to repeat your build process. Repeatable build processes make it possible to re-create a specific build when beta testers call and complain that their versions aren't working.

Daily builds are usually part of a larger process that may also involve some other tasks:

✦ Executing automated unit and regression tests

✦ Running static code analysis

✦ Creating backups of source code

✦ Logging the steps of the build

✦ Sending e-mails to all interested parties when the build is complete

The most important feature of any build is the *smoke test,* which is a thorough (and preferably automated) test of your software's major features after the build. You know that you have a good build when you pass the smoke test. If your application doesn't pass the smoke test, it's time to debug and rebuild.

Your master build process should be separate from Visual Studio, and your build process should be doable in one click. It's not a one-click process if you have to open Visual Studio, open a solution, and then choose the Build command. For master builds, you should use a *build engine,* which is a program that allows you to automate your build process. Two popular build engines are

✦ **Microsoft Build Engine (MSBuild):** When you use the Build menu in Visual Studio 2008, you're actually sending commands to the Microsoft build engine, MSBuild. MSBuild is a separate tool that specializes in building .NET projects. You can run MSBuild from the command line and build your projects without having Visual Studio installed.

MSBuild uses XML configuration files to define how projects are built. Visual Studio project files include the XML syntax that MSBuild uses to build the project. You can create your own MSBuild XML configuration files, which is helpful if you want to completely automate your build and run it on a dedicated build machine.

✦ **NAnt:** This is a popular open-source tool for creating builds from the command line. Like MSBuild, NAnt uses XML files to script the build process. NAnt build files end with the file extension `.build`.

You can download NAnt for free at

```
http://nant.sourceforge.net
```

Chapter 2: Deployment Options

In This Chapter

✔ Deploying Windows and Web applications using ClickOnce

✔ Digitally signing your code and strong naming assemblies

✔ Creating an installer

✔ Precompiling Web sites

Deploying an application can be as simple as copying a single file or as complex as installing multiple components with dependencies on each other. Deployment can be complex at times, involving multiple directories and registry entries. Deploying needs to be done not just once, but throughout the life of your application. For example, you often need to deploy the following:

✦ Prerelease versions of your application for testing

✦ Major releases

✦ Updates to your application

Even though this deployment chapter comes near the end of the book, it's one of the first things you start thinking about for your application. You should test your deployment strategy with your daily build.

Understanding Deployment Basics

For too many clients, deployment consists of 25 steps that require you to do the following (not necessarily in this order):

✦ Copy file X from this server.

✦ Copy file Y from that server.

✦ Execute file X on the client's computer.

✦ Create six ODBC connections.

✦ Register component Z on the client's computer.

✦ Create shortcuts on the desktop and on the Start menu.

Requiring your customers or internal IT staff to jump through these hoops every time a client installation is required isn't only brutal — it's unprofessional. People will invariably make mistakes when they dread installing your application. Nothing is worse than discovering that you forgot to install a required component *after* the computer is deployed 20 miles away.

Complicated installation processes can quickly overwhelm even the smallest companies. Many IT shops use ghosting software that allows them to make an image of a client computer's hard drive and copy that image onto other machines. When a technician skips a step in manual deployment, the mistake multiplies exponentially when the ghosted image is used to build new machines.

The time to think about the ease or difficulty of installing software is before the software is ever built or acquired. If you're acquiring software, ask what is required to install it. If you're building commercial software, treat simplified deployment as a competitive advantage.

Some software development houses create an opportunity for others to make a lot of extra revenue by having sloppy deployment procedures, thus creating the need for consultants and third-party technical support. This doesn't necessarily mean that you have to pay a consultant to help you configure new software, but it does mean that you have to jump through a bunch of hoops just to get the software installed.

Visual Studio provides two strategies for deploying your applications and components:

+ **ClickOnce** — Publish your application or component to a common repository, where users can download the application.

+ **Windows Installer** — Create an executable setup file that walks users through the steps in an installation wizard.

The strategy you choose depends on many factors, such as

+ The complexity of your application

+ The frequency of updates and releases

+ Whether your application needs to run locally

+ Whether users have network access

+ Whether your application is all managed code

This chapter discusses the deployment options available in Visual Studio 2008, tells you when you should use each one, and then shares some third-party alternatives you should consider.

Deploying Smart Client Applications

In the late 1990s, the development world went crazy for Web applications. Part of the draw was capturing the ease of administration that comes along with Web sites. Rather than install a single Windows application on a thousand computers, why not have a thousand computers access a single Web application? It sounds great in theory; however, many folks quickly realized that using Windows applications sometimes just makes the most sense.

Microsoft listened and created a hybrid deployment model that allows you to deploy your Windows application to a Web server. Using the new ClickOnce feature, Visual Studio 2008 copies the files needed to deploy your Windows application to a Web server. Your Windows clients then install, or even just run, the application from the Web server.

Of course, sometimes your application needs to exercise more control over the target installation machine than you can with a Web server. When you need more control over your application's installation, you may want to use *Windows Installer,* which is a component in Windows operating systems that manages software installation. Visual Studio 2008 provides several project templates you can use to target the services of Windows Installer.

From No Touch to ClickOnce

Microsoft started introducing the concept of Web-based installation in previous versions of the .NET Framework. The technology was improved, and the name changed from No Touch to ClickOnce.

You use ClickOnce to

+ Copy application files to a central Web site.
+ Deploy updates to a Web site.
+ Install applications on client machines from the Web site.

You aren't restricted to deploying to a Web site; you can also deploy to an FTP server or to CD. You can configure an application to automatically check a Web site for updates. Alternatively, you can use the `System.Deployment` namespace to write custom code that targets ClickOnce.

You can choose for your clients to run an application locally or only from the Web server. Either way, the application is downloaded to a local cache. You can find the cache at Documents and Settings\[*username*]\Local Settings\Apps.

The user is supplied with a link to the Web server or file server. For example, a user can click a link that you send by e-mail so that the application is downloaded to a local cache and executed. The user doesn't need administration privileges because the application runs in a secure mode and can't access the machine.

A ClickOnce process using Visual Studio may work like this:

1. The developer publishes a Windows application to a deployment server.

2. Visual Studio 2008 creates a Web site to act as a deployment server. All files needed to run the application are copied to the Web site.

3. The client clicks a hyperlink that deploys the Windows application on the local machine.

   The hyperlink is a link to a setup file on the deployment server. The setup file downloads the application's files to the local computer and executes the application.

You have two options for deploying the application on the client:

✦ **Online** — The user must click the hyperlink every time she wants to run the application. The application is always installed in the local cache. When the user clicks the link, the deployment server downloads any updated components before executing the application from the local cache.

✦ **Offline** — The user can choose a shortcut from the Start menu to open the application. An uninstaller is provided via Control Panel.

The good news is that you don't have to do anything special to use ClickOnce. The features are part of the .NET Framework. The bad news is that not all applications can be installed by using ClickOnce. For example, you can't access the Registry or add assemblies to the Global Assembly Cache (GAC) by using ClickOnce. Use Windows Installer instead.

ClickOnce is intended for scenarios where your applications use a rich user interface (UI) to provide access to resources, such as database servers and Web services. Many corporate applications fit into this scenario, which makes ClickOnce helpful from an administration standpoint. You don't have to physically deploy or update applications on every machine.

Visual Studio 2008 provides the Publishing Wizard for taking advantage of the .NET Framework ClickOnce technology. You have two options for accessing the Publishing Wizard:

✦ Choose Build➪Publish.

✦ Use the Publish tab in Project Designer.

Applications published via the Publishing Wizard are *ClickOnce applications*.

To publish a Windows application to a Web site by using the Publishing Wizard, follow these steps:

1. **Open the Windows application in Visual Studio.**

2. **Choose Build⇨Publish *<projectname>*.**

Your project name appears after the Publish command on the Build menu. The Publishing Wizard appears.

The default choice is to publish to a Web site (as shown in Figure 2-1), and the wizard lists a location to create the Web site. If you want to use a different URL, type the pathname in the wizard.

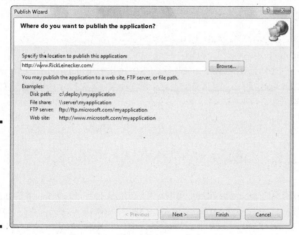

Figure 2-1:
You can specify a URL for the publish destination.

Alternatively, you can type or browse to a file share, FTP server, or disk location.

3. **Click Next.**

4. **At the prompt, choose whether to run the application online or offline.**

5. **Click Next.**

The Ready to Publish summary page appears.

6. **Verify your choices and click Finish.**

The wizard builds your project and publishes it to the Web server. If your application is published to a file, a folder directory will open, showing you the target, as shown in Figure 2-2.

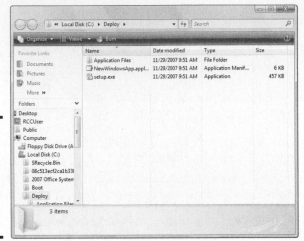

Figure 2-2:
Here you
can see the
target that
has been
saved to
disk.

Accessing the published application

When you publish the application to a Web server, ClickOnce creates a Web site with a `publish.htm` file you can use to deploy the application to the local client. Accessing a published application is often referred to as *consuming the application.*

To access the published application locally, follow these steps:

1. **Browse to the URL where the application was published.**

You can find the URL in the output window, as described in the preceding section. You can also view the Publish tab in Project Designer to determine where the application is published.

If you publish your application to a file share, use the UNC path to access the `publish.htm` file. If you publish to a CD, run the `setup.exe` file.

2. **Click the Install button on `publish.htm`.**

On machines that use Vista as the operating system, you either need the install application to be signed or you need to use administrative privileges.

ClickOnce downloads local copies of the application to a cache and launches the application. A security warning appears if the application isn't properly signed, as shown in Figure 2-3. See the later section "Signing your code" for more information on removing this security warning.

**Book VI
Chapter 2**

Deployment Options

Figure 2-3:
A security
warning
appears for
unsigned
applications.

3. **Click the Install button to complete the installation.**

The files are copied, and the application is launched.

If you chose to publish your application so that it runs offline, the installation process creates (on the Start menu) a shortcut to the cached copy of the application. Otherwise, the application can be run only by using the URL to the deployment server. The application can be removed or configured by using the Add/Remove Programs applet in Control Panel.

To remove an installed application by using Control Panel, follow these steps:

1. **Open Control Panel.**

2. **Double-click the Add or Remove Programs icon.**

3. **Navigate to the program you want to remove in the Add or Remove Programs window.**

4. **Click the Change/Remove button.**

A maintenance window appears, as shown in Figure 2-4.

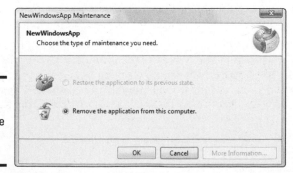

Figure 2-4:
You can
uninstall the
application
here.

5. **Select the radio button to remove the application; then click OK.**

The application is removed from the local computer.

Checking out your publishing options

Visual Studio provides several options for deploying applications with ClickOnce. You access these options from the Publish tab in Project Designer. To access the Publish tab, follow these steps:

1. **Right-click the project in Solution Explorer.**

2. **Choose Properties from the shortcut menu.**

Project Designer appears.

3. **Click the Publish tab, shown in Figure 2-5.**

You can use the Publish tab to do the following:

✦ **Set the publishing location.** Specify the path to a Web server, FTP server, network file share, or local file path where you want to publish files.

✦ **Designate the installation as online or offline.**

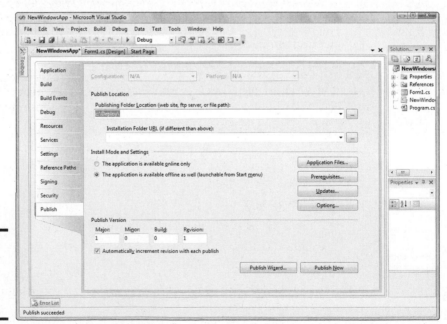

Figure 2-5:
Set the publish specifications here.

✦ **Specify which application files to include in the deployment.**

✦ **Select prerequisite components to install on the client machine.** By default, version 3.5 of the .NET Framework is required. You can choose to require your own custom components or components from third parties, such as Crystal Reports.

✦ **Schedule application updates and provide an alternative location for retrieving updated files.**

✦ **Set options, such as a URL for support, or make an application deployed to a CD automatically start when the CD is inserted.**

✦ **Specify that the Publishing Wizard automatically increments version numbers each time the application publishes.**

Signing your code

For a ClickOnce application to run on a local computer, the computer needs to know that the application is safe to run. ClickOnce accomplishes this by digitally signing the application, also known as *code signing*. Digitally signed applications bind an application's publisher to the application and ensure that the application hasn't been tampered with en route to the consumer.

A digitally signed application uses a digital certificate to store all the information required to validate an application and its publisher. When you use the Publishing Wizard, Visual Studio automatically creates a certificate you can use for testing. Common practice dictates using a separate certificate for testing and releasing software to prevent someone from obtaining test code with a release certificate.

Code signing is a fairly common requirement. You should create a single test certificate and reuse it rather than allow Visual Studio to create a new certificate every time. To sign a ClickOnce application, follow these steps:

1. **Right-click the project in Solution Explorer.**

2. **Choose Properties from the shortcut menu.**

Project Designer appears.

3. **Click the Signing tab.**

The Signing tab has two purposes:

• *Sign ClickOnce files.*

• *Sign assembly files.*

See the upcoming section "Sharing assemblies" for more information on signing assembly files.

4. **Select the Sign the ClickOnce Manifests check box.**

If you've already run the ClickOnce Wizard, Visual Studio automatically creates a test certificate. You see a check mark and the certificate's details, as shown in Figure 2-6.

5. Click Select from Store or Select from File to select a certificate to use.

If you need to create a new test certificate

   a. *Click the Create Test Certificate button.*

   You're prompted for a password to use for the certificate. Visual Studio creates the certificate and adds it to the project. The certificate is installed in your computer's personal store of certificates.

   b. *Copy the .pfx file (personal exchange file) to a central location so that you can reuse it.*

   Next time, you can choose Select from File and select the test certificate.

   Alternatively, you can use the makecert.exe command in the .NET Software Development Kit to create certificates.

6. Click the More Details button.

The Certificate window appears.

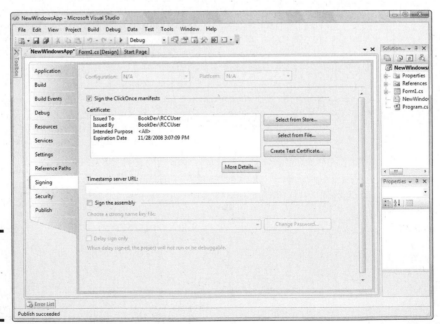

Figure 2-6:
You can digitally sign your application.

The text in the certificate states that the certificate isn't trusted. At this point, a certificate in your personal store doesn't come from a trusted certificate authority (CA). You must install the certificate in the Trusted Root Certificate Authorities store.

7. **Click the Install Certificate button, as shown in Figure 2-7.**

The Certificate Import Wizard appears.

8. **Click Next to step through the wizard.**

The Certificate Store page appears.

9. **Select the Place All Certificates in the Following Store option.**

10. **Click the Browse button.**

The Select Certificate Store window appears.

11. **Select Trusted Root Certificate Authorities and then click OK.**

The store appears in the wizard.

12. **Click Next.**

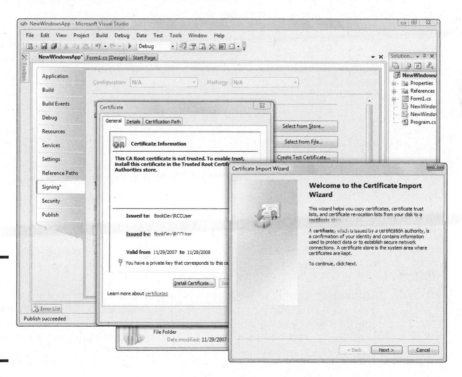

Figure 2-7:
You must invoke the Certificate Import Wizard.

13. **On the Completion page, click Finish.**

A security warning informs you that you're about to install a new trusted certificate authority. The danger is that someone can sign software with your test certificate and run the software on your computer.

14. **Click Yes to accept the security warning.**

The certificate is installed in the Trusted Root Certificate Authorities store.

15. **Repeat Steps 7 through 13 to install the certificate in the Trusted Publishers store.**

Figure 2-8 shows a certificate published in the Trusted Publishers store.

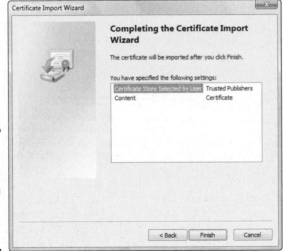

Figure 2-8:
This shows the certificate in the Trusted Publisher store.

Now, whenever you install the application, you aren't prompted to install it.

You must use Internet Explorer to sign up for its certificate. At this time, Firefox and other browsers don't appear to work.

Obviously, you don't want to deploy your test certificate into production. You need to acquire a release certificate from a CA, which is an entity whose identity has been verified and who can validate your identity. For example, VeriSign is a CA from whom you can buy a certificate. Read more about the VeriSign code-signing products on its Web site:

www.verisign.com/products-services/security-services/code-signing

If you're distributing software only within your internal organization, you may not want to purchase a certification from a third party. In that case, your organization can make itself a CA for within your organization and issue certifications.

Whichever route you take, you need some way to distribute the certificates to the Trusted Publishers store on all your clients. Additionally, if your company is issuing its own certificates, it needs to register itself on each client machine in the Trusted Root Certification Authorities store.

You probably don't want to run around to each client machine and install code-signing certificates. That defeats the purpose of using ClickOnce. Instead, use Windows Installer to create an installer package that installs the certificates. You can use other tools, too, such as the Windows certificate-management console (`certmgr.exe`).

**Book VI
Chapter 2**

Deployment Options

If you want to read more about code signing, check out the Microsoft white paper on code-signing best practices at

www.microsoft.com/whdc/winlogo/drvsign/best_practices.mspx

Updating your applications

You have several options for updating your ClickOnce applications. When you need to publish updates, you just update your software in Visual Studio and publish it again via the Publishing Wizard. Old versions of the software are retained, and new versions are pushed out.

When and how frequently a user's application checks for updates depends on how you configure the Publishing Wizard. You access update options by using the Updates button on the Publish tab of Project Designer. See the earlier section "Checking out your publishing options" for more information on using the Publish tab.

These update choices are available to you:

✦ **After the application starts** — Speeds up start time because the application checks for updates after it opens. Any new updates are downloaded and installed the next time the application runs.

✦ **Before the application starts** — Updates are installed when a user launches the application.

✦ **Scheduled updates** — Indicates how frequently the application should check for updates, as shown in Figure 2-9.

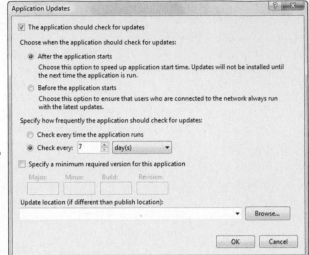

✦ **Required update to a minimum version** — Forces a client to update by requiring the use of at least a minimum version of the application.

You can use the Application Updates window to specify an update location that's different from a publish location. For example, you can publish to a CD and update to a Web server.

Each time you run the Publishing Wizard, Visual Studio automatically updates the application's version number. The version number is part of the application's digital signature, which .NET uses to ensure that the application is valid. If you haven't made any changes to the application, the build process doesn't build the application. As a result, the wizard uses a new version number when it publishes a copy of the application from the previous version. As a result, the application doesn't run on the client machine. If you want to force Visual Studio to publish an update when you haven't made any changes to the code, be sure to use the Build⇨Clean command first. The Publishing Wizard is then forced to build the application.

Making a Windows Installer

Visual Studio 2008 provides setup projects you can use to deploy your applications. Setup projects create a Windows Installer file with the extension `.msi`.

These setup projects are available in Visual Studio:

✦ **Setup projects create an installer file** that can be used to deploy a program on a target machine or to a virtual directory on a Web site. Visual Studio provides a wizard to walk you through creating setup projects.

✦ **Merge module projects create reusable setup components** for consumption by setup projects.

✦ **A Cab project creates a CAB file** from the items added to Solution Explorer. *CAB files* are often used to distribute components, such as ActiveX controls. The `.cab` file format (short for Microsoft Cabinet) is used for compressing files.

You can distribute the resulting MSI (Microsoft Installer) files by using CDs or DVDs, or a file share for installation across a network. MSI files can install an application on a target machine in a Windows application or on a Web site in a Web application.

The installation projects provided by Visual Studio take advantage of Windows Installer, which is an installation framework available on Windows operating systems. The installer takes care of how everything gets installed; you just focus on what you need to install. For example, the installer can create Registry entries, shortcuts, and Open Database Connectivity (ODBC) connections for you. You use a Visual Studio setup project to tell Windows Installer what to install. You don't have to write the code to make any of this installation happen. Windows Installer gets it installed for you.

Applications installed by using Windows Installer can

✦ Self-repair if the program is damaged.

✦ Roll back if the installation can't be completed.

Windows Installer is sophisticated, and there's nothing you can't install with it.

Creating a setup project for an existing application

Although you can create standalone setup projects, you usually add setup projects to an existing solution that you want to deploy. To create a setup project for an existing application, follow these steps:

1. **Open a solution that includes a project you want to deploy.**

2. **Right-click the solution in Solution Explorer.**

A shortcut menu appears.

3. **Choose Add⇨New Project.**

4. **In the Add New Project window, expand the Other Project Types category and select Setup and Deployment.**

A list of project templates appears.

5. **Select Setup Wizard.**

6. **Type a name for the project and then click OK.**

   The Setup Wizard appears.

7. **Click Next.**

   The Choose a Project Type page appears.

8. **Select the Create a Setup for a Windows Application option.**

   You can use the wizard to create a Web setup project, a merge module, or a CAB file.

9. **Click Next.**

   The Choose Project Outputs page appears. The project output from the other projects in the solution appears on this page. If no other projects are in the solution, this page doesn't appear. You have to add files to the setup project manually.

10. **Select the project output groups you want to deploy with your setup project.**

    You want, at a minimum, content files and the primary output, which is the assembly created by your project.

Specify that a file should be included as a content file by accessing the file's properties in Solution Explorer.

11. **Click Next.**

12. **Add any files you want to deploy with your setup project.**

13. **Click Next.**

    The Create Project page appears.

14. **Click Finish.**

    The project is created, and the content is added to Solution Explorer, as shown in Figure 2-10.

Figure 2-10:
Setup
Wizard adds
the new
setup
project in
Solution
Explorer.

Setup projects have a number of editors you can use to build your installer, including the ones in this list:

✦ **File System** — Identifies which files and shortcuts are created on the file system of the target machine

✦ **Registry** — Creates Registry entries

✦ **File Types** — Associates file extensions with applications

✦ **User Interface** — Customizes the installation wizard

✦ **Custom Actions** — Customizes the installation process

✦ **Launch Conditions** — Creates conditional installation steps

These editors are fairly straightforward to use after you realize that you're taking the perspective of the target computer. You have to start out by asking yourself what you want the target machine to look like when the installer is complete and then figure out how to make that happen by using these editors.

Putting the installer to work

To install a simple application and create shortcuts on the user's desktop and Start menu, use the File System Editor, as described here:

1. Create a new setup project, as described in the preceding set of steps.

The File System Editor opens by default.

You can open any of the editors by using the View menu or the icons on the Solution Explorer toolbar.

The File System Editor displays the file system of the target machine. You can elect to install files or shortcuts to special folders that are common to all Windows computers, such as a User's Desktop or Favorites folder.

By default, the Application Folder, User's Desktop, and User's Program Menu folders are added to the editor. Right-click the File System on Target Machine option to add more folders.

2. Select Application Folder.

The folder's contents appear in the pane on the right.

If you added your setup project to a solution with an existing project, the projects' output selected in the wizard appears. Right-click Application Folder and choose from the menu to add more files.

Use the Properties window to set an installation folder for Application Folder.

3. Right-click Primary Output in the Application folder.

A shortcut menu appears.

4. Choose Create Shortcut.

A new shortcut appears, as shown in Figure 2-11.

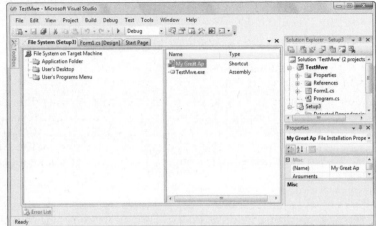

Figure 2-11:
Adding shortcuts is easy, and they show in this list.

5. Type a name for the shortcut.

You want the shortcut to appear on the target computer.

6. Right-click the shortcut and choose Cut.

7. Right-click User's Desktop and choose Paste.

The shortcut appears in the folder.

8. Right-click the User's Programs Menu folder.

9. Choose Add⇨Folder from the shortcut menu.

10. Type a name for the folder.

You want the folder to appear on the user's Program menu.

11. Repeat Steps 3 through 7 to add a shortcut to the new folder.

You now have an installer that installs your application and creates short-cuts on the user's desktop and then adds a folder with a shortcut to the Program menu.

Here's how to test the installer:

1. Right-click the setup project in Solution Explorer.

2. Choose Build from the shortcut menu.

The project builds and packages the files.

If you choose to build the entire solution, the setup project isn't included in the solution's build configuration in Configuration Manager. Either enable it to be built or build the project from the Build menu.

3. **Repeat Step 1 and choose Install from the shortcut menu.**

The installation wizard appears.

4. **Step through the wizard to install your application.**

Sharing assemblies

Most of the time, you want your assemblies to be private. Private assemblies are accessed only by your application. If you want to share your assemblies with other applications, you need to place them in the GAC. Examples of assemblies you may find in the GAC are the assemblies of the .NET Framework. When you place the assemblies in the GAC, all applications have access to them.

To publish an assembly to the GAC, it must use a strong name, which guarantees that all assemblies in the GAC have a unique name. A *strong name* comprises the assembly name, version number, public key, and digital signature. Suppose that your company creates an assembly named `OrderEntry`. Another company could feasibly create an assembly with the same name. A strongly named assembly creates a unique assembly, even if the assembly names were identical.

If you attempt to publish to the GAC an assembly that isn't strongly named, you receive an error message.

Visual Studio 2008 provides a way to strongly name assemblies and publish them to the GAC. To strongly name an assembly, follow these steps:

1. **Go to the Signing tab of Project Designer for the assembly you want to sign.**

2. **Select the Sign the Assembly option.**

3. **Open the Choose a Strong Name Key File drop-down list.**

4. **Click Browse to reuse an existing key file or click New to create a new key file.**

If you click New, the Create Strong Name Key window appears. Type a name for the key file and a password to protect the file.

The key file appears on the tab, as shown in Figure 2-12.

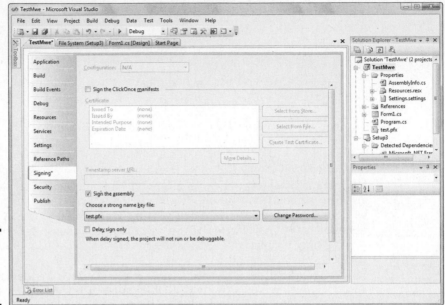

Figure 2-12:
The strong
key file has
been added.

To install the assembly in the GAC by using a setup project, follow these steps:

1. **Open the File System Editor in the setup project.**

2. **Right-click File System on Target Machine.**

   A shortcut menu appears.

3. **Choose Add Special Folder⇨Global Assembly Cache Folder.**

   A GAC folder appears in the editor.

4. **Right-click Global Assembly Cache Folder in the editor.**

5. **Choose Add⇨Project Output.**

   The Project Output Group window appears.

6. **Select the project from the Project drop-down list and then choose Primary Output, as shown in Figure 2-13.**

7. **Click OK.**

   The primary output appears in the editor.

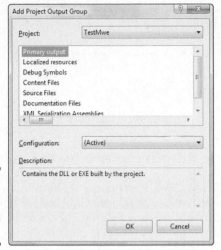

Figure 2-13:
The project
will install to
the GAC.

Build the setup project and install it on a test machine. To view the GAC to ensure that the assembly was installed, take these steps:

1. **Open Administrative Tools in Control Panel.**

2. **Double-click Microsoft .NET 3.5 Configuration.**

   The configuration management console appears.

3. **Select Manage the Assembly Cache.**

4. **Select the View List of Assemblies in the Assembly Cache option.**

   A list of assemblies appears.

Deploying Web Applications

Deploying Web applications is more complicated than deploying Windows applications. One key difference is what occurs during the build process. Windows applications are compiled into assemblies. You can distribute those assemblies by any means you want. Visual Studio provides a number of tools to assist with the distribution of Windows assemblies, as described in the preceding section.

Web sites are different. When you use the Build command with a Web site, Visual Studio compiles the page only for testing. You can't deploy the output created from the Build command — and you don't need to. Because ASP.NET Web sites are compiled on demand when users access the Web site, you can just copy and paste your Web site, if you want.

You may want to compile your Web sites before you deploy them, which is often called *precompiling*. Precompiled Web sites have these benefits:

✦ They start faster because no performance hit occurs while the requested page compiles.

✦ Source code isn't deployed to the Web server; only assemblies and static files are.

✦ You get feedback from compiler errors before the Web site is deployed.

Next, the deployment begins. Web sites often have two stages of deployment:

✦ **Test server** — When a Web site is first created, it may be initially deployed to a test server. Several developers and testers can access the test site. The test site usually remains up after the site is deployed to production. The test site provides a working copy of the production Web site, where changes can be made.

✦ **Production server** — After a site is ready to go live, it's published to a production Web server.

In reality, several versions of the Web site can run on different test servers. Developers can also have local copies of the site running on their development machines. They may deploy their local copies to the test server.

Because of the nature of Web sites, they're often changed more frequently than Windows applications. Changes are usually made to a single page or a set of pages, and then only those changes are deployed. In other cases, the entire Web site may be deployed.

Making frequent changes to the structure, layout, and design of a Web site can be disruptive to your site's visitors. As a result, more firms are starting to limit the number of changes they make to the site. Rather than change the site, firms are creating fluid sites that use content databases and configuration files to control the site's content and flow. Rather than change the Web site when you want to change content or the site flow, changes are made to content databases or configuration files.

Whether you're deploying to a test server or a production Web server, Visual Studio provides several options for deploying Web sites:

✦ **Web setup project** — Packages your Web site by using an installer that you then execute on the Web server

✦ **Copy Web Site tool** — Copies and synchronizes sites between a local store and a server

✦ **Publish Web Site** — Precompiles the Web site and copies it to the target of your choice

✦ **Web Deployment Projects** — This add-in gives you the most flexibility in precompiling your Web site

You can also just copy and paste your files from your test server to production. The major drawback of copy-and-paste strategies is that you can easily make mistakes.

Using the Publish Web Site utility

To use the Publish Web Site utility in Visual Studio, follow these steps:

1. **Open your Web site in Visual Studio.**

2. **Choose Build➪Publish Web Site.**

The Publish Web Site window appears.

3. **Specify a target location where the Web site should be copied.**

You can enter or browse to a URL, Universal Naming Convention (UNC), or local file path.

4. **Select the Allow This Precompiled Site to Be Updateable option.**

This feature copies your ASPX files as-is to the Web site. You can update these pages later without having to recompile and deploy the entire site.

5. **Click OK, as shown in Figure 2-14.**

All code-behind files are compiled into a single assembly. The assembly, ASPX files, and static files (such as images) are copied to the target location that you specify in Step 3.

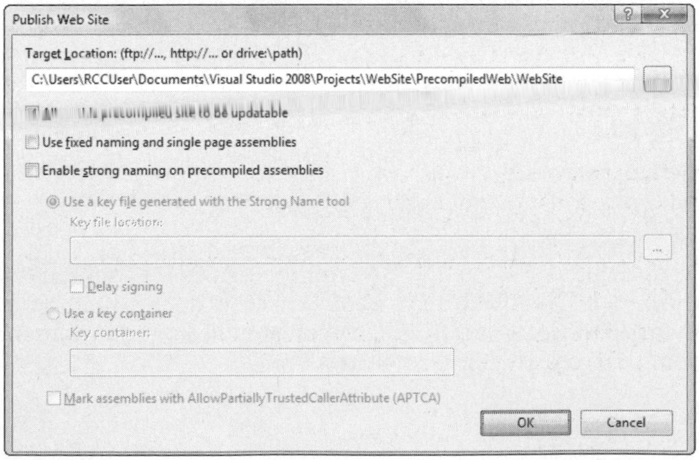

Book VI Chapter 2

Deployment Options

Figure 2-14: All necessary files will be published with your Web site.

Make a backup of your production Web site before deploying a new Web site. If the new site doesn't work, you can quickly roll back.

Handling web.config files for testing and production

A common challenge when you're deploying Web sites is not overwriting the web.config file. The web.config file on a test server usually has different settings than on a production server. For example, the test server may have connection strings that point to test databases. The Microsoft Web Deployment Projects add-in gives you more control over precompilation and web. config files.

You can download the Web Deployment Projects add-in at

http://msdn2.microsoft.com/en-us/asp.net/aa336619.aspx

The Web Deployment Projects add-in adds an Add Web Deployment Project command to the Build menu. You can't add a new project from the Add New Project window.

To add a new Web Deployment Project to a Web site, follow these steps:

1. **Download and install the Web Deployment Projects add-in.**

2. **Open an ASP.NET Web site project in Visual Studio.**

3. **Choose Build⇨Add Web Deployment Project.**

The Add Web Deployment Project window appears.

4. **Type a name for the project and then click OK.**

The Web Deployment Project appears in Solution Explorer.

You access the features of the Web Deployment Project by using its property pages. Use them to do the following:

✦ Set compilation settings.

✦ Determine how assemblies are generated.

✦ Sign assemblies.

✦ Configure how the site is deployed.

You configure a group of property page settings for each build configuration. For example, you likely don't want to use the deployment project with your debug build configuration. You can create different deployment settings for staging and release build configurations.

For example, to change the `web.config` file for deployment by using a release build, follow these steps:

1. **Right-click the deployment project in Solution Explorer and then choose Property Pages.**

2. **Choose Release from the Configuration drop-down list.**

   All settings that you create in the property pages apply only to the release build configuration.

3. **Click the Deployment tab.**

4. **Select the Enable Web.config File Section Replacement option.**

5. **In the Web.config File Section Replacements text box, type** connectionStrings=releaseconnectStrings.config.

   The `web.config` section to replace is `connectionStrings`. It's replaced by the contents of the file `releaseconnectStrings.config`, which is a text file that holds the `connectionStrings` section. You can name your `.config` file anything you like.

6. **Click OK.**

   The settings are saved.

Build your site by using the release configuration. The `web.config` file is merged with the `.config` file. And you have a release version of your Web site that you can deploy to your production server, using whatever method suits you.

Chapter 3: Checking Out Source Control

In This Chapter

✔ Setting up source control

✔ Adding and retrieving source code

✔ Performing daily integration tasks

✔ Using source control on a team project

Whether you're on a team of hundreds or a team of one, you need some way to manage your source code. You use source code control software for these tasks:

✦ Provide a central repository for storing source code.

✦ Create a new version of source code every time changes are made.

✦ Track the history of your source code.

The standard and Professional versions of Visual Studio don't provide source code control features. However, they provide menus and windows that you can use to access some third-party, source-code control products, such as Microsoft's Visual SourceSafe (VSS). Any source code control software that implements the Visual Studio Integration Protocol can provide source control services to Visual Studio.

Using Source Code Control with Visual Studio

Visual Studio provides menu commands that you can use to drive the features of your integrated source code control provider. Visual Studio acts as a gateway to third-party source control providers, which are referred to as *plug-ins* in Visual Studio.

A source code control environment includes these elements:

✦ **A centralized database** — Stores master copies of source code

✦ **Local working folders** — Holds source code that's downloaded on each developer's computer for editing

A team can use a dedicated build server that downloads source code from the database to a local working folder.

How source code control works

Any developer who needs to use source code downloads a working copy of the source code to a local folder. To edit the source code files, the developer must check out the source code files. After the editing is finished, the developer checks the files back into the source code control database.

Checking a file into source code is often referred to as *integration*. Presumably, the developer has unit-tested the code before integrating it into the master source code. Unit testing your code before checking it into source code helps maintain the integrity of the master source code. Integrated code, even when it's tested, can cause the master source code not to compile. See Book V, Chapter 8 for more information on unit testing.

Automated build processes usually download the latest version of source code and execute a build script to build the master source code. The build server may create in the database a new version of the code, labeled with the build number. The development team can then re-create the build at any time. See Chapter 1 of this mini-book for more information on build automation.

Getting ready for source control

Before you can integrate source code control with Visual Studio, you must do a couple of things first:

✦ **Set up and configure your source code control provider's server environment.** Setting up the server usually involves installing administration tools, adding users, and creating new databases.

✦ **Install your source code control provider on each client who needs access to the source control database.** Even though you access source code control via menu commands in Visual Studio, your source control provider's client software must be installed on each client computer.

After you install your source code control client, Visual Studio displays additional menus and commands that you can use to access your source code control repository. Here are some common source code controls tasks you can complete:

✦ Add a new or existing project to source control.

✦ Open an existing project from source control.

✦ Check out or check in source code.

✦ Get the latest version of source code.

✦ Remove a project from source control.

One of the first tasks you need to do before you start using source code control is setting your local working folder. The local working folder is the local repository on the client's machine where source code files are downloaded. When you edit source code files, you edit them by using files in the local working folder.

Your source-code control provider allows you to set a local working folder. If you don't set a local working folder, Visual Studio downloads files to your default projects folder. You can change the default projects folder in Visual Studio or set the local working folder in your source control provider.

To change the default projects folder in Visual Studio, follow these steps:

1. Choose Tools⇨Options.

   The Options window appears.

2. Select Projects and Solutions.

   A list of settings for projects and solutions appears.

3. Set the default folder location by using the Visual Studio Projects Location field, as shown in Figure 3-1.

4. Click OK.

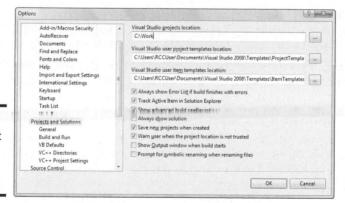

Figure 3-1:
You can set the default project location.

To set the local working folder by using VSS, follow these steps:

1. Choose File⇨Source Control in Visual Studio.

   A submenu appears.

You must have VSS installed on the client in order to use the Source Control menu in Visual Studio.

2. Choose Launch Microsoft VSS.

VSS opens.

3. Provide your login credentials, if you're prompted.

4. Click the dollar sign ($) at the top of the folder hierarchy.

5. Choose File⇨Set Working Folder.

The Browse for Folder window appears.

6. Select a folder to use as the working folder.

7. Click OK.

The working folder appears in VSS, as shown in Figure 3-2.

Figure 3-2:
You can
select the
working
folder for
Visual
SourceSafe.

If you don't set your local working folder in your source control provider, Visual Studio uses the default projects location to download source code. Use the local working folder if you want to download controlled source code to a different location than your default projects folder in Visual Studio.

Binding to a Source Control Provider

After you install your source code control provider, you can access the source code control features in Visual Studio. Promptly add your new or existing solutions and projects to your source code control database. The binding process creates a link between a local copy of source code and the source control database.

Visual Studio adds files to your source code control database in this way:

1. Creates a parent folder in your database named `<solution>.root` where `<solution>` is the solution name in Visual Studio.

2. Adds a folder to the `*.root` folder for your solution.

3. Adds folders for each project to the solution folder.

Microsoft recommends that you use solutions to organize your source code. You should add your solutions to source code control. When you add a solution, all its projects are added, too. If you add a new project to a solution, you can easily add that project to source code. Follow these rules for working with solutions and projects with source code control:

1. Create a blank solution first.

2. Always add projects to solutions.

3. Name your solutions so that they identify the system under development.

Book VI
Chapter 3

Checking Out
Source Control

The following sections explain the steps in more detail.

Adding a blank solution

To create a blank solution, follow these steps:

1. **Press Ctrl+Shift+N to open the New Project window.**

2. **Click the plus sign (+) next to Other Project Types.**

3. **Select Visual Studio Solutions.**

   A list of solution types appears in the Templates pane.

4. **Select Blank Solution.**

5. **Type a name for the solution and then click OK.**

   Select the Add to Source Control option to add the solution to source control when it's created.

Adding an existing solution

Here's how to add a solution to a VSS source code control database by using Visual Studio:

1. **Open or create the solution in Visual Studio.**

2. **Choose File⇨Source Control.**

   A submenu appears.

3. **Select Add Solution to Source Control.**

   The VSS login appears. At this step, Visual Studio passes off your request to your source code control provider.

4. **Type your login credentials to access the VSS database and then click OK.**

   The Add to SourceSafe window appears.

5. **Select a location for your solution to be added to the database and enter a name.**

   Visual Studio provides the default name `<solutionname>.root`. You should generally accept the default name, as shown in Figure 3-3.

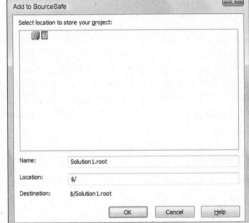

Figure 3-3: This solution is named Solution1, which Visual SourceSafe suggested.

Ideally, you want your solution's name to describe the system you're developing. If the solution name is the same as the project name, distinguishing between the solution and project folders can be confusing.

6. **Click OK.**

   VSS prompts you to create the root entry.

7. **Click Yes to create the parent folder.**

   VSS adds your solution's projects and files to the database.

Don't spend a lot of energy organizing your source control folders in your source control provider. In reality, you don't spend much time using the source control view of your solutions and projects. You mostly interact with Solution Explorer in Visual Studio. Instead, focus on using meaningful names in Solution Explorer and accept the defaults in your source control database.

Adding a project to an existing solution

Here's how to add a project to an existing solution already in the source code control database:

1. **Add the project to the source-controlled solution.**

2. **Choose File➪Source Control.**

A submenu appears.

3. **Choose Add Selected Projects to Source Control.**

A dialog box prompts you to confirm your choice.

4. **Click Yes.**

VSS adds your project to the database under the existing solution's root folder.

Breaking a binding

You might want to unbind source code from the source code control database — say, when you're working with developers (such as contractors who don't have access to VSS) or when you no longer want the file included in the project. To unbind your local copy from the database, follow these steps:

1. **Open the solution or project under source control in Visual Studio.**

2. **Choose File➪Source Control.**

A submenu appears.

3. **Choose Change Source Control.**

Use the Change Source Control window to view the binding properties, such as server name, database, and local working folder. Click the Columns button to add columns to the view.

4. **Click the solution or project to unbind, then click the Unbind button (the right-most button on the toolbar), as shown in Figure 3-4.**

Visual Studio prompts you to confirm your choice.

The binding is removed.

The source code remains in the database. Only the link between the local copy and the database is severed.

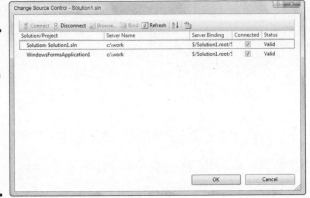

Figure 3-4:
Unbind source code from the database from the Change Source Control dialog box.

You can use the Change Source Control to connect and disconnect from the source control database. A *connection* is a live data link to the database. Disconnecting allows you to work offline from the database. You can connect to the database when you have a network connection again.

Performing Common Source Control Tasks

Source control bound to a source control database is locked. To edit a source code file that's under source code control, you need to first check it out. After you complete your edit, you check the file back into the source control database. Any time you work with source code, you should always synchronize your local copy of the source code with the master copy in the source control database.

The number of source control tasks you use daily is usually limited to three:

1. Get the latest version of source code.

2. Check the source code into the database.

3. Check the source code out of the database.

In Visual Studio, you select your source control provider by choosing File⇨ Source Control. You're likely to manage your source code in Visual Studio in these ways:

✦ **Right-click an item in Solution Explorer.**

✦ **Use the Source Control toolbar.**

Choose View⇨Toolbars⇨Source Control to open the Source Control toolbar, shown in Figure 3-5.

Figure 3-5:
The Source
Control
toolbar
makes tasks
easier.

✦ **Use the Pending Check-Ins window to manage checked-out source control.**

To get to the Pending Check-Ins window, right-click the tree node of the source module you want to check in.

Table 3-1 describes common source control commands.

Table 3-1	Common Source Control Commands
Command	*What It Does*
Check In	Checks a file into the source control database
Check Out for Edit	Checks out a file from the source control database so that it can be edited
Compare	Shows the differences between two files
Get	Creates a read-only copy of the file in the local working folder
Get Latest	Gets the latest version of the file
Undo Checkout	Discards the last checkout
View History	Displays a file's history

Visual Studio provides visual clues about a file's status — whether it's checked in or checked out, or not source controlled. A visual cue is displayed next to certain items in Solution Explorer:

✦ **Checked-in items** — A lock

✦ **Checked-out items** — A check mark

✦ **Items not in source control** — A plus sign (+)

Figure 3-6 shows the visual cues in Solution Explorer.

Figure 3-6:
Locks and
check marks
indicate
checked-out
and
checked-in
source
code.

Retrieving files from source control

The Get and Get Latest Version Visual Studio commands retrieve files from source control. You use these commands with a solution or project that's already under source control. See the earlier section "Binding to a Source Control Provider" to see how to add a solution or project to source control.

Source control providers "version" your source control files each time you perform a check-in. In most cases, you use the Get Latest Version command to retrieve the most recently checked-in version of a file. You use the Get command if you want to specify additional options, such as whether to make the file writeable when it's retrieved.

You use the View History command along with Get to access previous versions of projects and files. To open a previous version of a file, follow these steps:

1. **Right-click the file for which you want to retrieve a version.**

2. **Choose View History from the shortcut menu.**

   The History Options window appears.

3. **(Optional) Type a label or date range to filter the history.**

4. **Click OK.**

   The History window appears.

5. **Select the version you want to retrieve and then click the Get button, as shown in Figure 3-7.**

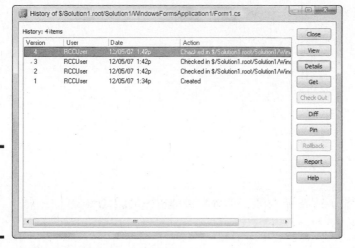

Figure 3-7:
The History
window
shows you
versions.

The Get window appears.

6. **Specify Get options, such as whether to make the file writeable.**

7. **Click OK.**

Visual Studio retrieves the file.

Editing source-controlled files

You must check out source-controlled files before you can edit them. You
can check out a single file or an entire project. Visual Studio provides a
Check Out for Edit command that instructs your source control provider to

✦ Download the latest version of the source-controlled file

✦ Mark the file as writeable

To check out a file by using the VSS plug-in, follow these steps:

1. **Right-click the file in Solution Explorer.**

2. **Choose Check Out for Edit from the shortcut menu.**

The Check Out for Edit window displays a tree view of all the files that
must be checked out. For example, the project file is automatically
checked out when you check out a code file, as shown in Figure 3-8.

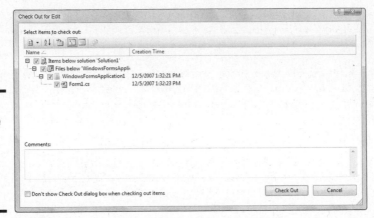

Figure 3-8:
You see the hierarchy tree when you check out source code.

3. **(Optional) Type a comment to describe the reason for the checkout.**

4. **Click the Check Out button.**

   VSS downloads the latest versions of the files to your local working folder and marks them as writeable. A check mark appears next to the filenames in Solution Explorer.

To check out a previous version of a source-controlled file, follow these steps:

1. **Download the version of the file you want from the source control database by following the steps in the preceding section.**

2. **Execute the Check Out for Edit command.**

   The Check Out for Edit window appears.

3. **Click the Options button (the first button) on the toolbar.**

4. **Select Check Out Local Version.**

   If the Check Out Local Version command is unavailable, click Advanced and then select the Don't Get Local Copy option.

5. **Click the Check Out button.**

   VSS checks out the local copy of the file.

You can undo a checkout by using the Undo Checkout command. Any changes to the local file are lost.

Depending on how VSS is deployed, it might place an exclusive lock on your file when it's checked out. This lock prevents anyone else from checking out the file from the database. If your database is configured to use multiple checkouts, other users can check out the file. As you might imagine, this is a potentially dangerous VSS configuration. All changes are merged in the database. Check with your database administrator to determine how your source control provider is configured.

Multiple checkouts are often used with ASP.NET Web sites. Multiple developers, therefore, can check out the entire Web site. Because developers aren't usually working on exactly the same source file, merge issues are infrequent.

Checking files into source control

You can check in files by using the Check In command. You can use the Pending Checkins window in Visual Studio to display a list of all files that are checked out for the open solution.

To use the Check In window, follow these steps:

1. **Right-click any file in Solution Explorer.**

2. **Choose View Pending Checkins from the shortcut menu.**

   The Check In window appears, displaying checked-out files in tree view by default. Click the Flat View button to display a flat list of files, as shown in Figure 3-9.

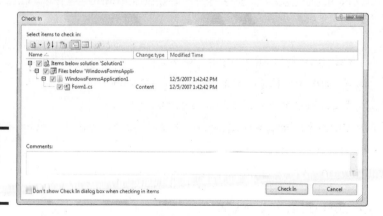

Figure 3-9:
The Check
In dialog
box.

3. **Clear the check boxes for any files you don't want to check in now.**

4. **Click the Comments button (the fifth button from the left on the toolbar) to add a check-in comment to all the files.**

5. **Click the Check In button.**

   The files are checked in to source control and marked as Read-Only in the local working folder.

Retrieving a solution or project from source control

After a new solution or project is added to source code control, you must download the solution or project from source code control before you can use it. For example, if you're working in a team environment, you might need to retrieve a solution or project that another team member creates and adds to source control.

To open a project from the source control database, follow these steps:

1. **Press Ctrl+Shift+O to open the Open Project window.**

2. **Click the icon for your source control provider along the left side of the window.**

A list of source control databases appears in the File Explorer. Figure 3-10 shows an example of accessing a VSS database.

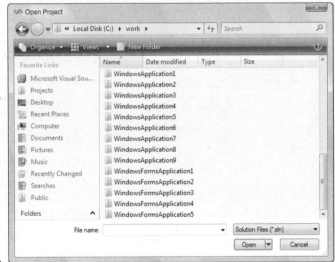

Figure 3-10: Your solutions appear when you click the Visual SourceSafe database icon.

3. **Navigate to your solution or project file and then click Open.**

Visual Studio downloads the files from the source control database to the local working folder.

See the earlier section "Getting ready for source control" for information on how to set the local working folder.

You can open a Web site from the source control database by using the Open Web Site window in Visual Studio.

Source Code Control in the Real World

Source code control is an activity that falls under a larger area of the software development life cycle known as software configuration management (SCM). SCM is often referred to as *change management* because managing the changes to software is one of SCM's primary goals.

Software configuration management encompasses many activities, such as

✦ Identifying items, such as source code, subject to change management

✦ Defining a change control process for managing changes

✦ Controlling software builds and releases

**Book VI
Chapter 3**

**Checking Out
Source Control**

In practical terms, source code control is a key element in managing changes, builds, and releases. Here are some other tools that enable SCM:

✦ Requirements-tracking software

✦ Bug-tracking software

✦ Scripts for creating builds

By using source code control software in conjunction with other SCM tools, you can

✦ Trace software features to requirements.

✦ Trace code changes to bug-fix requests.

✦ Track versions.

✦ Reproduce builds.

✦ Create a traceable history of who did what and when.

✦ Identify differences among releases.

 You can read about software configuration management in the Software Engineering Body of Knowledge (SWEBOK). The SWEBOK represents the latest thinking on how to engineer good software. Even if you don't believe that software should be engineered, you can get plenty of good information from the SWEBOK. You can download it at www.swebok.org.

A software project has many items, in addition to source code, that need to be controlled. Here are some examples, which are often referred to as *artifacts* or *work products:*

✦ Requirements specifications

✦ Architecture diagrams

✦ Build scripts

✦ Installer programs

✦ Compilers

Some people choose to place these artifacts in a source control tool, such as VSS. Because some items, such as requirements documents, aren't source-controlled, many teams use document management systems, such as Microsoft Windows SharePoint Services.

The Microsoft product Team Foundation Server (TFS) helps teams manage a project's artifacts and the SCM process. TFS works hand in hand with Visual Studio to create an integrated change-management process.

Regardless of which tools you use, be sure to follow these best practices when you use source control:

✦ Get the latest version of source code frequently.

✦ Check in your changes to source code frequently.

✦ Build your software from the master source code daily.

✦ Back up your master source code.

✦ Implement bug-tracking software that links to your source code changes.

✦ Include everything you need to reproduce a build, including build scripts, installers, and compilers.

Going Beyond Integration

The daily integration of each developer's changes to source code is only one piece of the source control puzzle. Source code control providers, such as Microsoft VSS, support additional commands related to managing version control of your software, such as

✦ Share — Shares source code between two projects without using copy and paste.

✦ Branch — Splits off a file or project as a separate file or project. For example, if you branch a file at version 3, you have two independent copies of version 3.

✦ Merge — Combines the contents of two files and creates a new, merged version. You still have two files, but the contents are merged.

✦ Diff — Compares two versions of a file. You can use the Merge command to create a new merged version.

✦ Label — Associates a lookup tag with the source-controlled item. Labels are often used at the project level for version control. For example, the daily build process may use a label to associate a build number with a project. Team members can use the build number to retrieve the source code used to create the build from the database.

✦ Rollback — Erases all successive versions after a chosen version.

✦ Pin — Marks a version of a file that can't be changed until the pin is removed.

Visual Studio 2008 has menu access to many of these commands. However, in most shops, a source control administrator performs these tasks using whichever tool is most appropriate, which is often a batch file.

Visual SourceSafe (VSS) has a command line feature that you can use to execute source control commands on the command line or in a batch file. The VSS administrator should use these commands. Your developers shouldn't use the command line for day-to-day source control activities. See the VSS help system for more information about using the SS.exe command line utility.

VSS integrates with SQL Server 2005. You can either create projects in SQL Server Management Studio or use a Visual Studio database project. Note, however, that the two project types aren't interchangeable. Therefore, you might just want to check in your script files rather than check in the entire project.

A popular tool for managing changes in SQL Server databases is DBGhost. You can read more about it at www.innovartis.co.uk.

Chapter 4: Building Professional Reports with Crystal Reports

In This Chapter

✔ **Creating new reports**

✔ **Using formulas, SQL expressions, and parameters to customize reports**

✔ **Accessing ADO.NET DataSets as report data sources**

Reports are the lifeblood of any good software. Without good reports, users abandon your software. One of the best reporting tools available is Crystal Reports, which is a product included with Visual Studio 2008. Crystal Reports isn't a Microsoft product; it's owned by a company named Business Objects (www.businessobjects.com).

This chapter shows you how to design reports using the embedded Crystal Reports Designer. You see how to connect to your data sources, including ADO.NET DataSets. Of course, creating the report is only half the battle. You need to know how to integrate the report in your application. Read here to also discover a few pointers on grouping, filtering, and creating formulas.

Choosing the Right Crystal Edition

Business Objects sells many editions of Crystal Reports. The latest version is version 2008. You can download a free trial version at

```
www.businessobjects.com/forms/default.asp?id=
    701600000009BMF&exLLmp=cr2008_product_promo_2
```

It's sold in these editions:

✦ **Developer** — Integrate reports into custom applications. This version includes a license to redistribute reporting components.

✦ **Standard Edition** — Create reports based on data stored on a local computer.

✦ **Professional Edition** — Create reports by using more than 35 data drivers, access custom in-memory data, or write custom SQL commands.

✦ **Integrated Developer Environment (IDE)** — Several editions of Crystal Reports that are created by Business Objects are embedded directly into popular IDEs, including

- Visual Studio 2008
- Visual Studio 2005
- Visual Studio .NET
- Delphi
- Borland
- Java

The official name of the edition of Crystal Reports embedded in Visual Studio is Crystal Reports for Visual Studio 2008. All editions of Crystal Reports (except for IDE) are separate, standalone software. The IDE editions are embedded within a specific IDE and can't be executed outside the hosting IDE. Developers who need advanced report design features in a separate, standalone package can upgrade to Crystal Reports Developer Edition. All editions of Crystal Reports include these features:

✦ **Report Designer** — Create professional reports with a visual designer.

Report Designer features drag-and-drop controls, guided experts, and extensive formatting options.

✦ **Data Access** — Access data from dozens of sources, including databases, such as Oracle and SQL Server.

Crystal Reports has truly impressive data access features. Rick uses Crystal Reports to access everything from Access databases to his local file system to Exchange Server databases.

✦ **Report Viewer** — View and export reports in every format imaginable.

Report Viewer provides built-in navigation and drill-down capabilities.

Business Objects offers a server product for Crystal Reports: The Crystal Reports Server includes a common, centralized repository for storing enterprise reports, a scheduler, and a framework for publishing reports to a Web server.

Creating Reports with Crystal Reports

When you create any report, the first step is deciding which information you want your report to display. Before you start using any report design tool, you should put some thought into these issues:

+ Who is your audience and how you expect the report to be used?

+ What is your data source and must it be transformed or cleansed?

+ How should records be filtered, sorted, or grouped?

+ Does the report need to prompt your users for parameters?

If you're using Crystal Reports with Visual Studio 2008, chances are that you're creating reports for a software application, such as an order-entry system. After you give some thought to how you want to build your report, follow the steps in this outline:

1. Add a Crystal Reports file to your project.

2. Select a data source for your report.

3. Design the report by using the embedded Report Designer.

4. Integrate the report with your application.

5. Deploy your application and reports.

Crystal Reports provides tools to walk you through creating your report, selecting a data source, and designing the report. You rely on a combination of tools from Crystal Reports and Visual Studio 2008 to integrate and deploy your report.

To add a new Crystal Reports file to an existing project and use the Report Wizard to create a new report, follow these steps:

1. **Use the Add New Item window to add a new Crystal Reports file.**

If this is the first time you're accessing Crystal Reports, an end-user license window appears. Read the license and choose whether to accept the terms.

The Crystal Reports Gallery appears, as shown in Figure 4-1.

2. **Select Using the Report Wizard to create a new report**

The Crystal Reports Gallery gives you three options for creating reports:

- *Using the Report Wizard*

- *As a Blank Report*

- *From an Existing Report*

Use the Report Wizard unless you have a specific need to use one of the other two options.

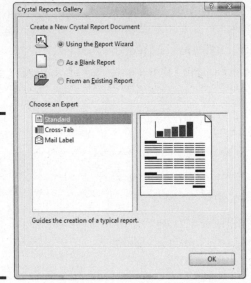

Figure 4-1:
The Crystal
Reports
Gallery
appears
after you
choose to
insert a
Crystal
Report.

3. **Select the Standard Report Expert.**

The Crystal Reports Gallery provides three experts for creating reports when you use the Report Wizard:

- *Standard* — Creates a regular report
- *Cross-Tab* — Creates a matrix report similar to an Excel pivot table
- *Mail Label* — Creates a report with multiple columns, like the kind used to print address labels

4. **Click OK.**

The Standard Report Creation Wizard appears.

5. **Create a new data source.**

To connect to the Adventure Works sample database in SQL Server 2005, use the OLE DB connection:

a. *Expand the Create New Connection folder.*

b. *Double-click the OLE DB folder.*

c. *In the OLE DB dialog box, select Microsoft OLE DB Provider for SQL Server and then click Next.*

d. *On the Connection Information page, enter your connection information and select the Adventure Works database.*

    e. *Click Finish.*

    The connection appears in the wizard.

6. Expand the AdventureWorks data source.

7. Expand the HumanResources schema and move the Department and EmployeeDepartmentHistory tables to the Selected Tables pane.

8. Click Next.

The Link page appears.

9. Confirm that the links between the two tables are correct.

The wizard automatically creates the links for you.

10. Click Next.

The Fields page appears.

11. Select the following fields for the report:

- Department.Name
- Department.GroupName
- EmployeeDepartmentHistory.EmployeeID
- EmployeeDepartmentHistory.StartDate
- EmployeeDepartmentHistory.EndDate

12. Click Next.

The Grouping page appears.

13. Select the Department.GroupName and Department.Name fields to group by, as shown in Figure 4-2.

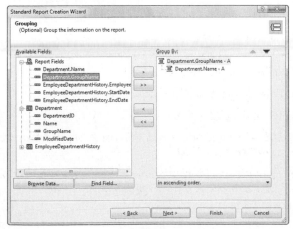

Figure 4-2:
You can group the fields according to the need.

REMEMBER

You aren't restricted to grouping by the report's fields. You can group by any field in the list of available fields.

14. **Click Next.**

   The Summaries page appears.

15. **Change the function for each of the summarized fields from Sum to Count.**

16. **Continue clicking next until you see the Report Style page.**

17. **Choose a Report Style from the list of styles and then click Finish.**

   The report appears in the Report Designer, as shown in Figure 4-3.

18. **Click the Main Report Preview button, at the bottom of the designer, to view the report's data.**

TECHNICAL STUFF

Crystal Reports files use the file extension `.rpt`. This type of file uses a proprietary file format. Visual Studio supports creating reports by using Report Definition Language (RDL).

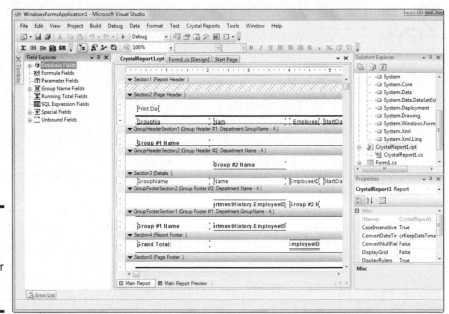

Figure 4-3:
The report appears in the designer after it's created.

Connecting to Data Sources

The most important aspect of report creation and design is the data source. All too often, developers and power users get frustrated with Crystal Reports because they aren't producing the reports they expect. The reason is usually that they don't start with the right data source. Crystal Reports provides access to almost every data source under the sun. As a .NET developer, you're likely to be most concerned with accessing these kinds of data sources:

✦ Databases, such as SQL Server and Oracle

✦ ADO.NET typed `DataSets`

✦ Custom data entities

In the preceding section, Steps 5 through 11 walk you through accessing data by using the Report Wizard. In most cases, you use the Report Wizard when you create a new report. However, you can access the Database menu and the Database Expert any time you need to manage your report's data sources.

TIP

You can use the Crystal Reports object model to pass data sources from your application, such as an ADO.NET typed `DataSet`, to a Crystal Report.

Getting to know your databases

The Crystal Reports Database menu is one of the most important menus for first creating a report. You access the menu from the Crystal Reports menu in Visual Studio or by right-clicking Database Fields in the Field Explorer and choosing one of these commands:

✦ **Database Expert** — Launches the Database Expert, which you can use to configure your report's data source

✦ **Set Database Location** — Sets the location, which is useful if you want to change from a test database to a production database

✦ **Log On or Off Server** — Lets you test to see whether the database is running

✦ **Verify Database** — Confirms the tables and columns in your data sources and synchronizes your report's fields with the data source

✦ **Verify on Every Print** — Verifies the data source's schema on every print

✦ **Show SQL Query** — Lets you view the query that Crystal Reports is using to retrieve data

Use the Show SQL Query command every time you make a modification to your report's record selection. You can then see the SQL statements generated by Crystal Reports to access your data.

Using Database Expert

Database Expert walks you through visually creating data source connections and linking tables. Note that you aren't limited to connecting to just databases. Crystal Reports supports many kinds of data sources, including the following.

✦ Microsoft SQL Server

✦ MYSQL

✦ Microsoft Access

✦ Microsoft Excel

✦ Delimited text

✦ ODBC sources

Crystal Reports uses a database metaphor to represent data sources. For example, an Excel file with three spreadsheet tabs is represented as a single database with three tables. The columns in the spreadsheet tabs are the columns in each of the tables.

Before you fire up Database Expert, decide first which data source you're using. For example, if you want to use an ADO.NET typed `DataSet` as your data source, you need to create the `DataSet` before you can select it.

You can access Database Expert in two ways:

✦ **When you create a new report with the Report Wizard** — Step 5 in the earlier section "Creating Reports with Crystal Reports" walks you through using Database Expert in the Report Wizard.

✦ **In an existing report via the Database menu** — You can access the Database menu from these menus:

   • The Crystal Reports menu

   • A shortcut menu on the report

   • A shortcut menu on Database Fields in the Field Explorer

To use Database Expert to access data, follow these steps:

 1. **Access Database Expert from the Database menu (via the Crystal Reports menu or the shortcut menus on either the Report or Database fields in the Field Explorer).**

Database Expert lists data sources in the Available Data Sources pane on the left and a list of selected tables on the right. Use the arrow buttons in the middle to move data sources between the panes.

2. **Select a data source from the list of available data sources.**

   Data sources are grouped into these folders:

   - *Project Data* — Lists sources from the current project and to which you're connected
   - *Current Connections* — Lists sources to which you're connected
   - *Favorites* — Provides a list of sources that are marked as favorites
   - *History* — Shows sources to which you were connected
   - *Create New Connection* — Shows data sources to which you can create new connections

   To connect to an existing data source, expand any folder except for Create New Connection.

   To create a new connection, follow these steps:

   a. *Click the plus sign (+) next to Create New Connection.*

      A list presents the kinds of data sources to which you can connect.

   b. *Select the type of data source you want to create.*

      For most data sources, Database Expert opens a dialog box or connection window for you to establish your connection.

   c. *In the dialog box, complete your connection to your data source.*

      The data source appears on the list of Available Data Sources in Database Expert. Figure 4-4 shows the Database Expert with a connection to the Adventure Works sample database. See the earlier section "Creating Reports with Crystal Reports" for an example of creating a connection to the Adventure Works SQL Server database.

3. **Expand your data source to reveal the resources you can access.**

   You can access more than just tables in a database. You can also access stored procedures and views. When you access resources, such as Excel files, Database Expert treats each worksheet as a table.

4. **Select the table you want to add to your report.**

5. **Click the topmost arrow button to move the table to the Selected Tables pane.**

6. **Repeat Steps 3 through 5 to add tables to your report.**

   When you add more than one table, the Links tab appears.

Figure 4-4:
Adventure
Works
appears in
the list of
database
connections.

To use the Links tab to establish links between multiple tables, follow these steps:

a. *Select the Links tab.*

If the tables share a common field, such as CustomerID, in both a Customer table and an Order table, a link appears between the tables. If not, you can create your own links. If the links are incorrect, click the Clear Links button.

b. *Drag and drop the column from one table onto the linked column on the table to create a link between the tables.*

Figure 4-5 shows two tables linked on the DepartmentName and Name columns.

To modify the kind of link between the tables, right-click the link or click the Link Options button.

7. Click OK after you add all your tables and create links between them.

If you discover that you forgot to add a table or your links are incorrect, you can always open the Database Expert again.

Figure 4-5:
You can
expand a
table and
add fields to
the report.

A good compromise between using tables and stored procedures is the virtual table. Crystal Reports has an Add Command feature, which allows you to provide your own SQL statements to execute against the data source. To use a command to create a virtual table, follow these steps:

1. **Open the Database Expert and select or create a data source, as described in the preceding steps.**

2. **Double-click Add Command.**

   The Add Command to Report window appears, as shown in Figure 4-6.

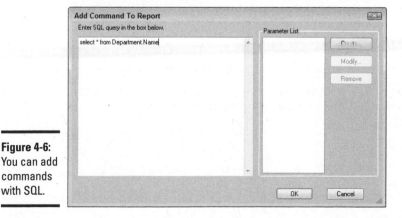

Figure 4-6:
You can add
commands
with SQL.

3. **Type your SQL statement in the query box.**

4. **Click the Create button to add parameters used by your query.**

5. **Click OK.**

The command appears in the Selected Tables pane.

To change the name of the command from the default name command to something meaningful, first click the command and then press F2.

The commands you build can be as sophisticated as stored procedures. You can't reuse commands among reports, like you can among stored procedures. However, Business Objects offers upgraded products that you can buy that allow you to store commands in a central repository.

Using the Crystal Reports Report Designer

Visual Studio 2008 includes an embedded version of the Report Designer, which you can use to visually lay out your reports. The designer includes a set of the following elements:

✦ **Experts** (similar to wizards) that walk you through building a report

✦ **Report objects,** such as report fields and charts, which you drag and drop onto the designer surface

✦ **Report sections,** to which you add report objects

To design a report, you add report objects to the section of the report where you want the object to appear. For example, you can add a title in the report's Report Header section.

Adding content to a report

Crystal Reports provides a sophisticated set of tools for adding report content. Your report's content can come from several sources, such as

✦ Plain text you enter in a text object

✦ Database fields

✦ Formulas you create

✦ Lines, boxes, and images

This section walks you through using the Report Designer to lay out a report. Follow these steps to create a report to use throughout the section:

1. **Create a new report that connects to the Adventure Works sample database.**

See the earlier section "Creating Reports with Crystal Reports" to see how to create a report that connects to the Adventure Works sample database.

2. **Add the following tables to the report:**

- Person.Contact
- Person.ContactType
- Sales.StoreContact

3. **Set the following relationships between the tables:**

- Contact.ContactID = StoreContact.ContactID
- StoreContact.ContactTypeID = ContactType.ContactTypeID

4. **Add the following data fields from the list of available fields:**

- Contact.FirstName
- Contact.LastName
- Contact.EmailAddress
- Contact.Phone

5. **Click Finish.**

6. **Click the Main Report Preview button, at the bottom of the designer, to preview the report.**

7. **Save the report as `StoreContacts.rpt`.**

Exploring Field Explorer

Field Explorer, in Report Designer, appears on the left side of the screen. You can use the objects in Field Explorer to customize your report. Field Explorer includes the following report objects:

✦ **Database Fields** — Explore the list of fields available from the data source. Right-click Database Fields to access the Database menu.

✦ **Formula Fields** — Create simple or complex calculations.

✦ **Parameter Fields** — Create parameters that prompt a user for input to run the report.

✦ **Group Name Fields** — Insert and manage groups.

✦ **Running Total Fields** — Create a running total based on a field in your report.

✦ **SQL Expression Fields** — Create a field that uses SQL expressions. SQL expression fields are executed on the SQL server.

✦ **Special Fields** — Add predefined fields, such as Print Date and Page Number.

✦ **Unbound Fields** — Create predefined formula fields based on native data types.

Figure 4-7 shows Field Explorer. Press Ctrl+Alt+T to open it.

Figure 4-7:
The Field Explorer shows information about the report.

You can mix and match fields to create sophisticated report scenarios. For example, you can create a new formula field that references a database field and a parameter field. You use fields for these tasks:

✦ Display values.

✦ Calculate values.

✦ Query users for input.

✦ Filter records.

✦ Group records.

✦ Sort records.

✦ Set formatting properties.

Reports are divided into sections, to which you add fields. A report can have all, some, or none of the following sections:

✦ Report Headers and Footers

✦ Page Headers and Footers

✦ Group Headers and Footers

✦ Details

After you add a field to a section in the report, it becomes a report field. Follow these steps to create a new report field that displays the contact's name in the format *lastname, firstname* in the StoreContacts report you create in the preceding section:

1. **Choose Insert⇨Text Object from the Crystal Reports menu.**

The mouse pointer turns into the shape of a text box.

2. **Drop the text object next to the Phone field in the report's Details section.**

The cursor blinks inside the text box.

3. **Expand Database Fields in the Field Explorer.**

4. **Drag and drop the Contact.LastName field inside the text object where the cursor is flashing.**

The text {LastName} appears.

5. **Type a comma in the text object.**

6. **Drag and drop the Contact.FirstName field inside the text object.**

7. **Click somewhere off the text object.**

8. **Use your mouse to position the report fields so that they appear in the order lastname, firstname, text object, e-mail address, and phone.**

To remove a report field, click the field and press the Delete key.

9. **Add a text object to the Page Header section above the text object you create in Step 2.**

10. **Type a column header in the text object, such as** Contact Name.

11. **Expand the e-mail address and phone fields so that they display their values without truncating data.**

Periodically click the Main Report Preview button to check your field formatting. Figure 4-8 shows a preview of the report.

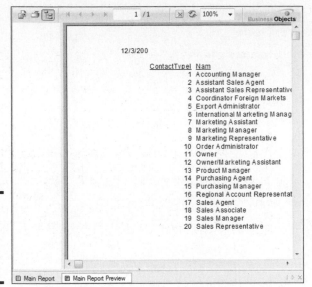

Figure 4-8:
Preview
your report
every once
in a while.

Accessing commands with toolbars

Report Designer has two toolbars that provide quick access to commonly used commands for formatting and adding content:

✦ **Insert toolbar** — Choose commands for inserting summaries, charts, and subreports.

✦ **Main toolbar** — Choose formatting commands (such as bold and font), experts, and object properties.

Formatting objects

Use the sophisticated Crystal Reports format editors and experts to completely customize the appearance and behavior of the fields and sections that appear in your reports. The formatting tools are shown in this list:

✦ **Format Editor** — To access Format Editor, right-click any field in your report and choose Format Object from the shortcut menu. The tabs visible in Format Editor depend on the type of object you're formatting. For example, a field that displays a `true/false` value has a Boolean tab. Figure 4-9 shows Format Editor for a text object; Table 4-1 describes some common uses of Format Editor.

✦ **Chart Expert** — Right-click a chart to access Chart Expert. Use it to specify the chart's type and data source and to format its axes.

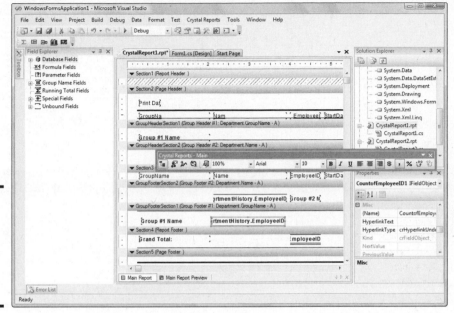

**Book VI
Chapter 4**

**Building
Professional Reports
with Crystal Reports**

Figure 4-9:
Different
report item
types have
different
items in the
toolbar.

- ✦ **Highlight Expert** — Right-click an object in a report's Details section to access Highlight Expert. Use it to apply conditional formatting to an object based on the value of the field or another field.

- ✦ **Section Expert** — Access Section Expert from the Report menu. Use Section Expert to insert, delete, and format sections.

Table 4-1	Common Uses of Format Editor	
Tab	Command	What It Does
Common	CSS Class Name	Sets the CSS class that the object should use
	Repeat on Horizontal	Repeats object on additional horizontal pages
Pages		
	Suppress	Disables the field so that it doesn't appear
	Keep Object Together	Keeps grouped objects on the same page
	Can Grow	Allows the object to expand to display values
	Suppress If Duplicated	Prevents the object from being printed multiple times if the same value is repeated
Border		Places a border around an object

(continued)

Table 4-1 *(continued)*

Tab	Command	What It Does
Date	Style	Allows you to choose a date style from a list or create your own
Font		Sets font properties
Hyperlink	Type	Allows you to choose whether the hyperlink links to a Web site, e-mail address, or file and then set the URL

Most formatting options allow you to select a discrete value or apply a formula to calculate the formatting value or determine whether the formatting should appear.

Book VII

Extending Visual Studio

"I assume everyone on your team is on board with the new system deployment."

Contents at a Glance

Chapter 1: Exploring Visual Studio Extensions...................................739

Chapter 2: Being a Team Player with Visual Studio Team System 747

Chapter 3: Using Visual Studio with Vista and Office 2007 765

Chapter 1: Exploring Visual Studio Extensions

In This Chapter

✔ **Getting the most out of Visual Studio**

✔ **Building the next generation of Web sites with AJAX**

✔ **Looking ahead to the future of Visual Studio**

The name of this chapter should be "Getting Everything You Can from Visual Studio 2008, Now and in the Future." Since the release of Visual Studio in October 2007, Microsoft has released a ton of free add-ons that you can download from the Web.

Extending Visual Studio

You have many opportunities to extend Visual Studio. Some are add-ons from Microsoft; others are cool toys created by the community. This section lists a few of both — and share some additional resources with you, including how to get hold of trial versions of development tools.

Adding administration and troubleshooting tools

One of the best things about add-ons is that all you have to do to get them is download them. Some help you administer and troubleshoot development projects; others provide new tools for programming Vista and Office 2007.

Administrative and troubleshooting downloads available from Microsoft include the following:

✦ **Team Foundation Server (TFS) Admin Tool** — As an administrator, add users to TFS through a single user interface (UI). Download the tool from

```
http://msdn2.microsoft.com/tfs2008
```

✦ **Web Application Projects** — Create ASP.NET Web sites. Originally used for Visual Studio 2005 and .NET 2.0, these projects easily load into and are converted to Visual Studio 2008 for .NET 3.5. (As this book goes to press, there is no similar page for Visual Studio 2008.) Download from

```
http://msdn2.microsoft.com/asp.net/aa336618.aspx
```

✦ **Web Deployment Projects** — Create a project to deploy your ASP.NET Web sites. Originally used for Visual Studio 2005 and .NET 2.0, these projects easily load into and are converted to Visual Studio 2008 for .NET 3.5. Download from

    http://msdn2.microsoft.com/ asp.net/aa336619.aspx

✦ **CSS Control Adapter Toolkit** — Take control of the elements rendered by Web server controls, using Cascading Style Sheets (CSS). The toolkit makes it possible to use CSS to override many server controls' default behavior of using <table> tags to render themselves to the browser. Download the toolkit from

    www.asp.net/cssadapters

If you're not that familiar with using CSS for Web-page layout, pick up a copy of *CSS Web Design For Dummies,* by Richard Mansfield (Wiley). The book goes way beyond your basic CSS styling and shows you how to create multicolumn Web pages without using HTML tables.

✦ **Developer Highway Code** — Access and use an e-book that features guidance and security checklists for .NET 1.1, 2.0, and 3.5. This PDF file covers writing secure code, brought to you by the Microsoft Patterns & Practices group. Download the e-book from

    www.microsoft.com/uk/msdn/security/dev_highway.mspx

✦ **Spec# Programming System** — Use the Spec# programming language to extend design-by-contract features to C#. Get more information at

    http://research.microsoft.com/specsharp

The Team Foundation Server Admin Tool is part of the Visual Studio Power Toys, which are released under the Microsoft Shared Source initiative. You can read more about Shared Source and find additional downloads at

www.codeplex.com/PackInstaller

CodePlex is a Web site that Microsoft dubs a "new collaborative development portal." CodePlex was formally launched in June 2006 with 30 open source projects for developers using Microsoft platforms. Be sure to check out the CodePlex Web site at www.codeplex.com.

Downloading new programming tools for Vista and Office

With the release of Windows Vista and Office, Microsoft made available a number of tools that target these newer programming models. Here are a few resources you should check out:

✦ **Extensions for Windows Workflow Foundation (WWF)** — Provide support for building applications that use WWF

✦ **WinFX Development Tools** — Support building applications that target WinFX with Extensible Application Markup Language (XAML) support and project templates

✦ **.NET Framework version 3.5** — Provides the libraries you need to target all the features of Windows Vista

✦ **Windows Software Development Kit** — Includes documentation and samples that demonstrate the features of Windows Vista

You can find the latest version of these resources on the Vista Web site at

```
http://msdn.microsoft.com/windowsvista/downloads/
    products/getthebeta
```

See Chapter 3 in this mini-book for more details on Windows Vista and the .NET 3.0 Framework.

Many resources for programming Office 2007 are available at the Office Developer Center on MSDN. Some of these resources work with Visual Studio Professional 2008, and others require Visual Studio Tools for Office. Visit the Tools and Technologies page at

```
http://msdn2.microsoft.com/office/aa905362.aspx
```

Trying out development resources and new server products

Microsoft has a Web site where you can order several resources on DVD. The resources are free, although you do pay shipping and handling. The following resources are available for order at

```
http://msdn2.microsoft.com/evalcenter/bb655864.aspx
```

✦ **Visual Studio 2008 Team Suite 180-day trial** — Includes 180-day trial of SQL Server 2008 Enterprise Edition and Team Foundation Server.

✦ **Visual Studio 2008 Professional Edition 90-day trial**

✦ **SQL Server 2008 Enterprise Edition 180-day trial**

✦ **Microsoft Developer Security Resource Kit** — Includes articles, whitepapers, Webcasts, and code samples.

- ✦ **Visual Studio 2008 Training Kit** — Includes guidance for migrating to .NET 3.5, code samples, articles, and a free e-book called *Refactor!*

- ✦ **Microsoft Patterns & Practices (January 2006 release)** — Includes several patterns and practices guides, as well as the complete January 2006 release of the Enterprise Library.

- ✦ **Windows Mobile 5.0 Developer Resource Kit** — Includes resources to get started developing applications that target Microsoft's mobile platform.

The kits are guided tours of the resources available for a given topic, conveniently available on DVD. In the meantime, you can download Software Development Kits for Windows SharePoint Services version 3.0 at

```
www.microsoft.com/downloads/details.aspx?familyid=
    05E0DD12-8394-402B-8936-A07FE8AFAFFD&displaylang=en
```

The SharePoint Server 2007 SDK can be found at

```
www.microsoft.com/downloads/details.aspx?familyid=
    6D94E307-67D9-41AC-B2D6-0074D6286FA9&displaylang=en
```

Internet Information Services (IIS) 7 — the version of IIS — has integrated support for ASP.NET. IIS7 has its own dedicated Web site at `www.iis.net`, where you'll find technical resources, articles, blogs, and other community resources. Write your own modules — using the .NET Framework to target the IIS application programming interface — or become more knowledgeable about how to configure and tweak IIS. The Downloads section features an IIS7 Managed Module Starter Kit for C# or C++.

Other fun items you might want to download from the community include

- ✦ **Spell checker for ASP.NET** — Spell-checks the text you add to your ASP.NET Web pages. This was written by one of the developers on the Microsoft Web Development Tools Team in his spare time. In other words, the tool isn't supported by Microsoft. You can download the spell checker at

  ```
  http://blogs.msdn.com/mikhailarkhipov
  ```

- ✦ **NDepend** — Code analyzer that visually displays your source code's architecture and allows you to apply many code metrics against your source code. Download for free at

  ```
  www.ndepend.com
  ```

✦ **MSBuild Community Tasks Project** — An open source project that's building a library of common MSBuild tasks. You'll find just about everything you need to automate your nightly builds. Visit the project's Web site at

```
http://msbuildtasks.tigris.org
```

✦ **RSS Toolkit** — Created by a member of the ASP.NET development team for consuming and publishing RSS feeds. Download the toolkit from

```
http://blogs.msdn.com/dmitryr/archive/2006/03/26/561200.aspx
```

Keeping up with developer blogs and other news sources

Microsoft has embraced blogging. A *blog* (short for *Web log*) is a Web site where a blogger posts entries and visitors post comments on the blog entries. Here's a short list of blogs you might want to keep tabs on:

✦ **Web Development Tools Team Blog** — These are the folks that develop Visual Web Developer. Read their blog at

```
http://blogs.msdn.com/webdevtools
```

✦ **S. "Soma" Somasegar's blog** — Soma is the corporate vice president for the Microsoft Developer Division. His blog always features the latest news about Visual Studio 2008. Find his blog on MSDN at

```
http://blogs.msdn.com/somasegar
```

✦ **Developer Division Customer Product Lifecycle Experience Team (DDCPX) Team Blog** — These are the folks responsible for bringing aftermarket solutions — such as the Visual Studio Power Toys and software development kits (SDKs) — to you. You will need a login to access this blog. Sign in at

```
http://blogs.msdn.com
```

✦ **MSBuild Team Blog** — MSBuild is the build engine for Visual Studio. Read the team blog at

```
http://blogs.msdn.com/msbuild
```

You can find more Microsoft blogs at

```
http://www.microsoft.com/communities/blogs/
    PortalHome.mspx
```

MSDN has created a number of developer centers that provide links to blogs, downloads, articles, and other resources of interest to developers. Some centers you might want to visit include

+ **Security Developer Center** — http://msdn.microsoft.com/ security

+ **Visual Studio Developer Center** — http://msdn.microsoft.com/ vstudio

+ **Smart Client Developer Center** — http://msdn.microsoft.com/ smartclient

+ **Office Developer Center** — http://msdn.microsoft.com/office

Find even more developer centers on MSDN at http://msdn.microsoft. com/developercenters.

Exploring AJAX and the Atlas Library

AJAX — Asynchronous JavaScript And XML — is a technology that allows developers to avoid traditional ASP.NET postbacks, in many cases, and provides a richer user experience with less delay. Developers use a combination of client-side JavaScript and server-side programming to create a Windows-like user experience. AJAX offers an important benefit: The browser and the server can communicate without a postback. From an end-user standpoint, that means no screen flash while the page refreshes. Popular Web sites using AJAX include

+ Google Suggest

+ Google Maps

+ Flickr

+ Gmail

+ Outlook Web Access

+ Yahoo! Mail Beta

To get a feel for some of the things you can do with AJAX, go to the demos page at http://openrico.org.

To get a feel for the underlying technologies of AJAX and what it takes to AJAX-ify your Web sites using technologies besides .NET, pick up a copy of *Ajax For Dummies,* by Steve Holzner (Wiley).

The technologies used in AJAX are nothing new. They've been around for a long time; only recently have folks applied the name AJAX to this style of programming. The technology that underlies AJAX is the object XMLHttpRequest. This one object makes it possible to send data back and forth between the client and server without a page refresh.

Atlas is Microsoft's version of AJAX. It consists of

✦ **Client-side library** — Atlas provides object-oriented access to the client-side features you would usually have to write in JavaScript. With Atlas, you can apply what you know about object-oriented programming in .NET without diving into JavaScript.

✦ **Server controls** — Server-based controls similar to existing Web server controls, such as buttons and text boxes.

Atlas makes extensive use of Web services to provide the server-side features of the client-server interaction of AJAX. It's quite common for developers to wire up the elements of their user interfaces to Web services that provide data (such as specific items for a drop-down list). Of course, you aren't limited to consuming only Web services that you create. You can also use an Atlas-enabled Web page to connect to third-party Web services.

Web sites that use content from other sources are called *mashups*. Mashups often utilize several technologies, including Web services, RSS, and AJAX. Mashups are a driving force in the *Web 2.0* movement (the term often used to refer to the next generation of Web applications).

Because the AJAX Toolkit is built into Visual Studio 2008, it no longer needs to be installed separately, like it did with Visual Studio 2005.

Looking Ahead to the Next Visual Studio

Microsoft has plans for one future version beyond Visual Studio 2008: namely, codename Hawaii. Hawaii is supposed to be a complete rebuild — from the ground up — of Visual Studio.

Keep up to date with the offerings for Visual Studio at `http://msdn.microsoft.com/vstudio/future`. You'll find previews for versions of Visual Studio, as well as extensions for the current version.

For obvious reasons, not much information is available about the next version of Visual Studio (Hawaii). It has been reported that Microsoft plans to completely redesign the product, which could be interpreted to mean a completely new approach to software development.

Rick's guess is that this next-generation approach to development will allow developers to immerse themselves in modeling their business problem — and in generating code from that model — rather than getting stuck in a "code zone." Three development resources for a closer look are

- **The Microsoft Center for Software Excellence** (www.microsoft.com/Windows/CSE) — A group in Microsoft Research focused on developer productivity at Microsoft.

- **Intentional Software** (www.intentionalsoftware.com) — The company founded by Charles Simonyi to bring to market the next generation of software development. Simonyi is the man behind Microsoft Word and Excel. He also created the Hungarian notation-naming convention.

- **Software Factories** (www.softwarefactories.com) — The idea of being able to mass-produce code from a model is being used now in Visual Studio Team System. Expect to see this concept trickle down to the individual developer in the future.

You can see how Visual Studio Team System is already using models to generate code in the next chapter of this mini-book.

Chapter 2: Being a Team Player with Visual Studio Team System

In This Chapter

✔ Figuring out the products in Visual Team System

✔ Exploring the tools of the new role-based editions

✔ Using Team Foundation Server

*I*f you've ever worked on a team project, you've probably experienced the frustrations of trying to collaborate via e-mail and folder shares. Invariably, an important document gets overwritten or an important stakeholder is left off the distribution list. Either way, the project suffers.

For most teams, the thought of implementing software to help with collaboration is about as much fun as having a root canal. Even if you decide on a vendor and manage to get the budget approved, you know the software's benefits are overshadowed by its daunting complexity.

The Microsoft approach to solving this problem is a bit different than most other vendors' approaches. Instead of creating an entire new set of tools for people to learn, Microsoft decided to create a solution that allows team members to keep using the same tools they've always used. The project managers keep using Excel and Project. The developers use Visual Studio. The architects get modeling tools that actually synchronize with code, and the testers finally get real software. The name for this make-everybody-happy approach to supporting team development is Visual Studio Team System.

Introducing the Visual Studio Team System

Visual Studio Team System (VSTS) isn't an edition of Visual Studio. Rather, it's a platform for building software in a team environment. The platform is composed of the following product offerings.

✦ **Four role-based editions of Visual Studio** — Each edition features a different set of tools tailored to a role in the software development life cycle. The current roles offered are

- Architect

- Database Professional

- Developer

- Tester

✦ **Visual Studio Team Suite** — This product suite includes all four role-based editions.

✦ **Team Foundation Server (TFS) Standard Edition** — This server product's features enable the members of a team to collaborate and manage projects. All versions of Visual Studio 2008 — except the Express Edition — can access a Team Foundation Server.

Each edition of Visual Studio in the VSTS comes with a client access license (CAL) that allows access to TFS. You must purchase a CAL separately for Visual Studio Standard or Professional editions. Each user accessing TFS must have a CAL.

You aren't required to use TFS. You can use any of the role-based editions without TFS.

✦ **Team Foundation Server Workgroup Edition** — This product provides the same features as TFS but is limited to five connections. TFS Workgroup Edition is included with any of the role-based versions of Visual Studio or the Team Suite.

If you have five or fewer members on your team, TFS Workgroup Edition is the way to go. You can upgrade to Standard Edition any time.

Each product in Visual Studio Team System comes with an MSDN Premium Subscription. Table 2-1 lists many of the tools you'll find in VSTS. (Descriptions for many of these tools appear later in the chapter.)

Table 2-1	Tools and Editions
Tool	*Edition*
Application Designer	Architect
Logical Infrastructure Designer	Architect
Deployment Designer	Architect
Class Designer	Architect, Developer
Visio and UML Modeling	Architect, Developer
Team Foundation Client	Architect, Developer

Tool	Edition
Visual Studio Professional	Architect, Developer
Dynamic Code Analyzer	Developer
Static Code Analyzer	Developer
Code Profiler	Developer
Unit Testing	Developer, Test
Code Coverage	Developer, Test
Load Testing	Test
Manual Testing	Test
Test Case Management	Test
Build Automation	Team Foundation Server
Change Management	Team Foundation Server
Work Item Tracking	Team Foundation Server
Reporting	Team Foundation Server
Project Site	Team Foundation Server
Integration Services	Team Foundation Server
Project Management	Team Foundation Server

Visual Studio Team System is more than a new suite of tools: It supports the entire application life cycle and enables processes to improve continuously.

Still, implementing VSTS is not a light-hearted undertaking. Visual Studio Team System integrates with several Microsoft server and client products. As a result, VSTS requires a *big* honkin' server with at least 15GB of storage just to get started, plus about 8GB of storage for each project. The server products required by VSTS include

✦ Windows Server 2003 or Windows Server 2008

✦ SQL Server 2005 (Standard or Enterprise Edition) or SQL Server 2008 (Standard or Enterprise Edition)

✦ Windows SharePoint Services (WSS)

Compared with other products of this type, VSTS is relatively simple to implement. A single server can support several hundred developers.

If you'd rather not deal with implementing yet another server, you can find a service provider to host a TFS for you. Developers connect to the hosted server as if it were sitting in your server room. You get all the productivity of TFS without any of the hassles of implementing and administering a server. You can find out more about hosted Team Foundation Servers on Rick's Web site at www.visualstudioallinone.com.

You can use a number of clients to access TFS. These include

✦ Visual Studio 2008

✦ Microsoft Office Excel 2003 or later

✦ Microsoft Project 2003 or later

✦ Internet Explorer

All the clients except Internet Explorer require the installation of Team Explorer (the Team Foundation client). See the section "Accessing Team Foundation Server," later in this chapter, for more about Team Explorer.

To take VSTS for a test spin, you can download a 90-day trial edition from Microsoft's Web site at

```
www.microsoft.com/downloads/details.aspx?FamilyID=
    b0155166-b0a3-436e-ac95-37d7e39a440c
```

To find out more about VSTS, check out these resources:

✦ **Team System Rocks Web site** — A Web site dedicated to VSTS that features blogs, forums, and tutorials. The site has dozens of videos on using VSTS. Visit the site at

```
http://teamsystemrocks.com
```

✦ **Visual Studio Team System Developer Center** — View the VSTS portal on MSDN at

```
http://msdn.microsoft.com/vstudio/teamsystem
```

✦ **Visual Studio Team System Virtual Labs** — Access tutorials hosted on MSDN at

```
http://msdn.microsoft.com/virtuallabs/teamsystem
```

Exploring the New Role-Based Editions

The role-based editions of Visual Studio have several tools. Some of these tools include the Application Designer in the Architect Edition. Other tools (such as static code analysis in the Developer Edition) simply integrate existing tools that many developers have used for a while. Either way, the new editions are long on features and compatibility.

Before you decide to spring for any or all of the editions, consider that you can achieve the same effect as many of these editions by using third-party tools. Depending on your situation, you may come out ahead by sticking with Visual Studio 2008 Professional and using a set of third-party tools such as these:

✦ **Unit Testing** — NUnit and NMock.

✦ **Modeling** — Visio for Enterprise Architects and Class Designer.

✦ **Build automation** — MSBuild and NAnt.

✦ **Static code analysis** — FXCop analyzes your code for compliance to standards.

✦ **Project portal** — Use WSS or create your own portal with ASP.NET 3.5 portal pages.

Windows SharePoint Services is a component in Windows Server 2003 and Windows Server 2008. You can download WSS free from Microsoft at

```
www.microsoft.com/downloads/details.aspx?FamilyId=
    B922B28D-806A-427B-A4C5-AB0F1AA0F7F9
```

✦ **Team Foundation Server** — Access TFS, using the Team Explorer add-in for Visual Studio 2008.

Visual Studio Team System for Software Architects

The Team System for Software Architects edition of Visual Studio includes a set of designers that allow architects to model their application designs. The models are more than just pretty pictures: They evaluate a design model's validity before it's ever deployed. For example, if you designate that a Web site must use a Secure Sockets Layer (SSL) security certificate, your model warns you if it attempts to deploy your Web site to a Web server that doesn't have an SSL certificate.

Of course, the models can't stop your technical staff from installing the application on the wrong server. The designers create models of logical server configurations. How those logical servers relate to physical servers is something that happens in the physical world.

The set of designers in the Architects edition are collectively known as the Distributed Systems Designers (DSDs). The four new designers are as follows:

✦ **Application Designer** — Model the deployable units of code, such as a Windows application and an ASP.NET Web site that constitute the system under development.

✦ **Deployment Designer** — Map your deployable application systems to logical server configurations in your Logical Datacenter model.

✦ **Logical Datacenter Designer** — Model the logical server configurations on which applications will run.

✦ **System Designer** — Model application systems, which are composed of applications modeled in the Application Designer.

What's so significant about these designers is that the models are linked and can communicate with one another. For example, you can specify that your application needs to run on an IIS server. If you try to deploy your application to a logical server configured to run earlier versions of IIS, the designer will warn you.

Further, the Application Designer can generate the projects defined in your model. When projects are developed, the models are synchronized to reflect any changes. In essence, your system becomes self documenting. As team members go about doing their day-to-day jobs, the documentation takes care of itself.

The DSDs are a component in the Microsoft Dynamic Systems Initiative, which strives to make administering technology systems less costly. You can read more about DSI at

www.microsoft.com/business/dsi/default.mspx

Distributed System Diagrams are solution-level items; they don't belong to any one project in your solution. Figure 2-1 shows the DSD template area in the New Project window.

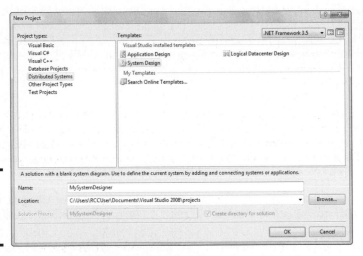

Figure 2-1: You can use a DSD solution.

In most cases, your architects create the DSD models before any coding ever starts. Architects generate Visual Studio projects from the applications they model in Application Diagrams. Figure 2-2 shows an example of an Application Diagram.

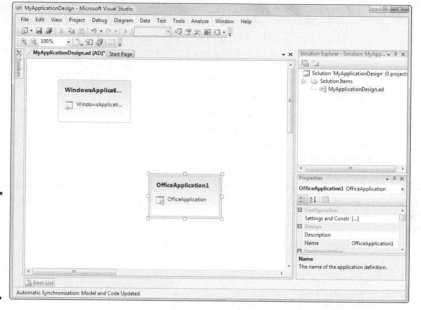

**Book VII
Chapter 2**

Being a Team
Player with Visual
Studio Team System

Figure 2-2:
Model
applications
in an
Application
Diagram.

You can easily create a System Diagram by clicking a set of applications that define a system. For example, your Application Diagram may show a class library, a Web site, and a Windows application. You generate two system diagrams: One shows the Windows application and the class library, and the other shows the Web site and the class library. Figure 2-3 provides an example.

You can test deployment scenarios for your system by using the Deployment Designer. Using either an Application Diagram or a Systems Diagram, you associate a Deployment Diagram with a Logical Datacenter diagram. Create a Deployment Diagram for each Logical Datacenter scenario you wish to evaluate.

Visual Studio Team System for Software Developers

The Developer Edition of VSTS provides additional tools that developers can use to write better code. Many of these tools are available elsewhere as free downloads or open-source software. Visual Studio Team System for Software Developers integrates the following tools into the development environment:

✦ **Static code analysis** — This tool uses rules and patterns to detect errors and bad coding form.

✦ **Dynamic code analysis** — This code-profiler monitors an application's performance while it's running.

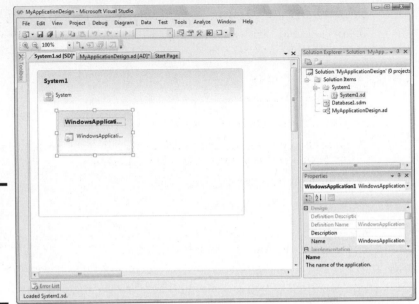

Figure 2-3:
Use Visual
Studio to
generate a
complete
System
Diagram.

✦ **Unit testing** — This is a framework for generating and managing unit tests.

✦ **Code coverage** — This tool provides feedback on how effective your unit tests are at covering all your code.

The testing features in Visual Studio Developer Edition overlap with the Testers Edition. Developers generate unit tests from the Code Editor, as shown in Figure 2-4.

Figure 2-4:
Some
testing
functions
are built
into the
developer
version.

Visual Studio Team System for Software Testers

Team System for Software Testers provides resources for creating and managing many kinds of tests. You can use the Tester Edition to

+ Create unit tests.

+ Record Web tests.

+ Execute a sequential list of tests.

+ Measure your application's performance by running any combination of unit tests and Web tests over and over again.

+ Capture the steps for manual tests.

+ Turn any code into a test.

You organize your tests into projects by using a Test Project template in Visual Studio, as shown in Figure 2-5.

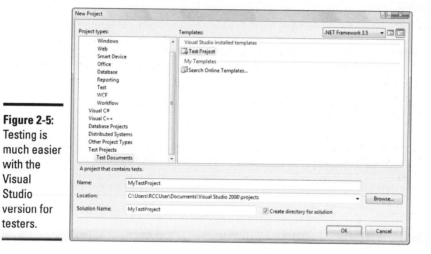

Figure 2-5:
Testing is much easier with the Visual Studio version for testers.

A test run configuration is added by default to the solution when a Test Project is added. Use the Test Run Configuration to configure the testing environment and code coverage, as shown in Figure 2-6.

You add a Test Project just like you would add any project in Visual Studio: from the New Project window.

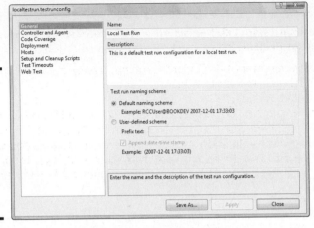

Figure 2-6:
The Test
Run
Configu-
ration is
added by
default for
your con-
venience.

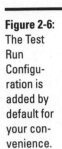

Visual Studio Team System for Database Professionals

Team System for Database Professionals brings the database developer closer into the software-development loop. With the Database Professional Edition, you can do the following:

✦ Refactor database schema objects.

✦ Automate testing with unit tests.

✦ Place database schemas under source control.

✦ Use `SchemaCompare` and `DataCompare` to compare two databases and generate scripts to synchronize the databases.

✦ Populate test databases based on production data, using the `DataGenerator`.

Getting to Know Team Foundation Server

Team Foundation Server — the bedrock of collaboration features in VSTS — provides the following:

✦ **Source control management** — Create check-in policies that define the actions your developers must complete before integrating source code.

✦ **Work item tracking** — Create tasks, assign tasks to team members, and associate tasks with actions, such as code check-in.

✦ **Build automation** — Step through a wizard to create complex auto-mated build processes.

✦ **Reporting** — Generate reports on all activities in your TFS.

✦ **Centralized project site** — Set up a project site where all stakeholders can access project artifacts.

✦ **Project management** — Perform project management tasks in familiar tools, such as Excel and Project.

Many of the features in TFS are possible, using the technologies of WSS. WSS version 3 is available as a free download from the Microsoft Web site. Before you take the plunge with VSTS, install WSS. Also, pick up a copy of *Microsoft SharePoint 2007 For Dummies,* by Vanessa Williams (Wiley). You'll find scenarios that show you how to use SharePoint in many different business contexts.

Accessing Team Foundation Server

You must install the Team Explorer client before you can access TFS. Team Explorer is an add-in for Visual Studio. You can install the client using the Team Foundation Server software or download the add-in from Microsoft Downloads. You don't need to have any edition of Visual Studio to use Team Explorer.

To download the client from Microsoft, access this link:

```
www.microsoft.com/downloads/details.aspx?familyid=
    0ED12659-3D41-4420-BBB0-A46E51BFCA86&displaylang=en
```

Book VII
Chapter 2

Being a Team
Player with Visual
Studio Team System

To use Team Explorer to access an existing project on a TFS, follow these steps:

1. **Choose Team Explorer from the View menu.**

The Team Explorer window appears.

2. **Click the Add Existing Team Project button.**

The Connect to a Team Foundation Server window appears.

3. **Click the Servers button.**

The Add/Remove Team Foundation Server window appears (see Figure 2-7). Alternatively, you can select an existing server from the Connect to a Team Foundation Server drop-down list.

4. **Click Add.**

The Add Team Foundation Server appears.

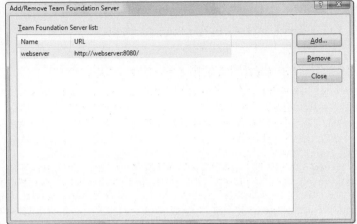

5. Type the server's name in the Name text box.

If your administrator instructs you to use a different port or protocol, enter those in the Connection Details section. Figure 2-7 shows a connection to a server. This shows the default port. In some cases, this port will conflict with other third-party products. For example, Visual MainWin also relies on this port. To ensure there isn't any conflict, you need to change the port used by one of the two products.

6. Click OK.

7. If prompted, type your username and password.

8. Select a project from the list of projects, as shown in Figure 2-8.

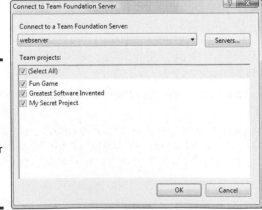

9. Click OK.

The project appears in the Team Explorer.

Creating a new team project

You might wonder why Microsoft didn't create a Team System edition for project managers. It's probably because project managers don't use Visual Studio that often. And VSTS accommodates their style of work by interfacing with Excel and Project.

Some tasks, such as creating new team projects, must be completed by using Visual Studio. Visual Studio provides a group of predefined environment settings specific to project managers. To reset your settings to use the Project Management Settings, use the Import and Export Settings Wizard, as described in Book II, Chapter 1. The project manager environment settings eliminate most of the menu items used by developers and other roles.

The New Team Project Wizard walks you through the process of creating a new team project. To start the wizard, follow these steps:

1. From the File menu, choose New Team Project.

The New Team Project Wizard appears.

Alternatively, you can choose File⇨New⇨Team Project. If you're not connected to a team server, the Connect to Team Foundation Server dialog box appears; refer to Figure 2-8. You complete it to connect to a Team Foundation Server.

2. Type a name for the project in the Name field.

The name must be unique on the team server.

3. Click Next.

The Select a Process Template step appears. The *process template* defines workflow for your project. Team Foundation Server includes two process templates from the Microsoft Solutions Framework; you can extend them or create your own.

4. Select a process template from the drop-down list, as shown in Figure 2-9.

The steps that appear next depend upon the process template you select. Steps 5 through 9 in this list are based on the Microsoft Solutions Framework (MSF) for the Agile Software Development process template.

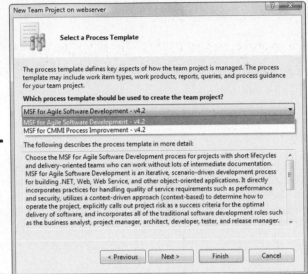

Figure 2-9:
You must
select a
process
template
from the
drop-down
list.

Visit the VSTS Developer Center on MSDN to get more information on using development processes from the Microsoft Solutions Framework at

    http://msdn.microsoft.com/vstudio/teamsystem/msf

5. Click Next.

The Specify the Settings for the Project Portal step appears. The values you enter in this step appear in your SharePoint-based project portal. The URL you use to access your project portal also appears in this step.

6. Type a site title and description in the wizard and then click Next.

The Specify Source Control Settings window appears.

7. Select your settings to establish source control for the project.

8. Click Next.

The Confirmation Page appears.

9. Review your settings and click Finish.

The wizard creates your project.

The project is accessible from the Team Explorer and its project portal. Figure 2-10 shows a sample project portal.

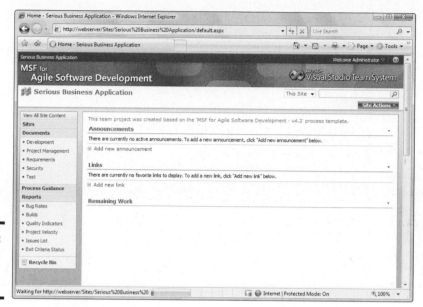

Figure 2-10:
The sample
project
portal.

Browsing with the Team Explorer

Team Explorer is the premier client for browsing resources in a Team
Project. You open the Team Explorer from the View menu. The Team
Explorer displays the following:

✦ **Work items** — Lists the work-item queries in your team project. Click a
   query to expand a list of work orders.

✦ **Documents** — Displays the document libraries from the project portal.
   The project's process template determines which document libraries are
   created.

✦ **Reports** — Displays a list of reports available for your projects. Reports
   are created by using SQL Server Reporting Services.

✦ **Team Builds** — Displays a list of build types for your team project.

✦ **Source control** — Defines check-in policies for the project.

Figure 2-11 shows a work-item query accessed via Team Explorer.

**Book VII
Chapter 2**

Being a Team
Player with Visual
Studio Team System

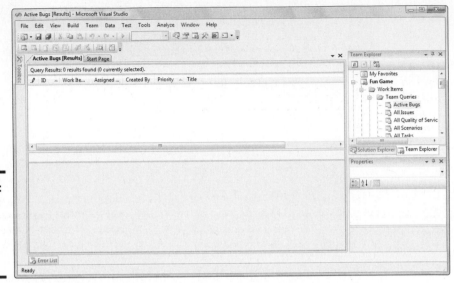

Figure 2-11:
Access the
work-item
query via
Team
Explorer.

Creating work items with Excel

You can connect to projects in a TFS by using Excel or Project. Team
Explorer adds a Team toolbar that you can use to get work items and to publish new or modified items to the server. To connect to a new work-item list
in Excel, follow these steps:

1. **Click the New List button on the Team toolbar.**

The Connect to Team Foundation Server window appears. (Refer to
Figure 2-8.)

2. **Connect to your server, as described in the preceding example.**

3. **Select a team project from the list of projects and then click OK.**

The New List window appears.

4. **Select the Query List radio button to access a list of work items.**

Alternatively, click Input List to enter new work items and get individual
work items.

5. **Click the Select a Query drop-down list.**

A list of predefined work item queries appears.

6. **Select a query from the list and then click OK.**

The query's results appear as a spreadsheet (see Figure 2-12).

Figure 2-12:
You can
select the
query and
see the
results.

The work items are retrieved into an Excel list. You can add new work items
or update existing items. Click the Publish button in the toolbar to save your
changes to the server, and your saved changes are immediately available to
other team members. Figure 2-13 shows a work item being added to a list.

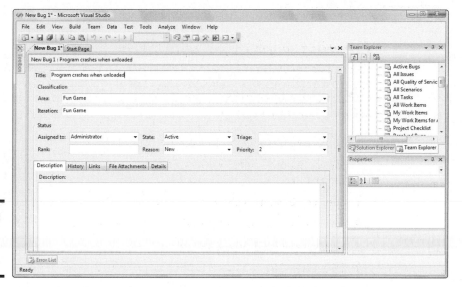

**Book VII
Chapter 2**

**Being a Team
Player with Visual
Studio Team System**

Figure 2-13:
Adding
work items
is easy.

You can add work items in Excel, Project, or Team Explorer; or, during
source-control check-in.

Chapter 3: Using Visual Studio with Vista and Office 2007

In This Chapter

✔ Exploring the technologies of Vista

✔ Using the Windows Software Development Kit

✔ Taking a peek at Windows Workflow Foundation

✔ Starting to develop applications for Office 2007

✔ Running virtual machines

The "next generation" of Microsoft operating systems and productivity software was a long time coming. The latest offerings from Microsoft is a whole slew of software that includes

✦ **Windows Vista** — The newest desktop operating system (OS) from Microsoft

✦ **Windows Server 2008** — A next-generation server platform

✦ **Office 2007** — The latest release of Office products

This chapter hits some of the highlights of this latest software and gives you some hints for how you can get started developing applications that target Vista and Office 2007. Finally, read on to discover how you can use Virtual PC 2007 to cut down on the number of physical servers you need (and the headaches they bring) to run all this software.

Exploring Vista

Windows Vista has several editions. As you might expect, the lower-end editions offer fewer features than higher-end editions; each higher edition is a superset of the lower-end features. The Vista editions are

✦ Home Basic

✦ Home Premium

+ Business

+ Enterprise

+ Ultimate

A simple of list of features can't do justice to Vista. You need to experience Vista in order to get your mind around what it can do. It's completely different than Windows XP or Windows 2000.

The most visible change that Vista offers is its Windows Aero interface, which creates an immersive user experience, similar to what you experience while playing a video game. This change means a learning curve for those migrating to Vista in regard to its interface. Businesses typically don't like learning curves because they cause a short-term loss in productivity. To accommodate this, Vista has four levels of user experience you can choose from:

+ **Windows Classic** — This is the user interface experience that Windows XP offers.

+ **Aero** — This is the latest user interface experience with 3D objects and transparency.

+ **Basic** — This is similar to the Windows Classic version with subtle additions, such as those found in the new Vista toolbars.

+ **Standard** — This is the same as the Aero experience but doesn't have the glass effects, advanced animations, and advanced graphics features.

However, Vista offers more than a slick user interface (UI). With Vista, Microsoft has "componentized" everything — and eliminated overlapping technologies.

In terms of software development, the UI experience is more immersive and graphically intense than anything you could create with Windows Forms in Visual Studio. Before talking about what this means for the future of Windows development, you must first understand some of the technologies that underlie Windows Vista:

+ **Windows CardSpace** — Manages a portfolio of digital identities for use on the Internet. Examples of digital identities include credit cards, user-names, and passwords.

+ **Windows Communication Foundation (WCF)** — Next generation of Web services, intended to be used for all communications among applications. WCF replaced existing communication technologies, regardless of whether the message is moving within the machine, from machine to machine, or across networks.

✦ **Windows Presentation Foundation (WPF)** — The presentation subsystem responsible for user experience in Vista. With WPF, Microsoft separates the UI from the source code into a separate markup file.

✦ **Windows Workflow Foundation (WWF)** — The programming model intended to offer tools for quickly building workflow-enabled applications.

Another key technology that was slated for Vista is Windows File Storage (WinFS). As a major technology that improves search and enables the use of structured data among applications, *WinFS* is a database that sits on top of a standard hard drive and provides access to resources. Unfortunately, WinFS didn't ship with Vista. Microsoft indicated WinFS would ship with Windows 2008 Server and would work on Vista and Windows XP. However, in June 2006, the WinFS team quietly announced that this wouldn't happen. Instead, WinFS will be rolled into SQL Server and ADO.NET. At some point, a relational file system may be made available for Windows.

All the technologies in Visual Studio 2008 are part of version 3.5 of the .NET Framework (and 3.0 for Vista), which works with Windows XP and Windows Server 2003. Even if you don't intend to move to Vista or Server 2008 right now, you can start building applications that can run on them.

With this understanding of Vista technologies, you must be wondering what this means to you as a developer. In the past, you used Windows Forms to create Windows applications. So how do you create Vista applications? You have the same options that you have now:

✦ **Managed** — Create managed applications by using version 3.5 of the .NET Framework (formerly known as WinFX).

✦ **Unmanaged** — Create unmanaged or native applications by using Win32 or COM.

You can still create applications by using Windows Forms. However, Vista provides you with another choice for user interface: Your applications can target the new Aero interface. Similar to how you can create a Windows UI and a Web UI by using a core set of logic, you can add an Aero interface, as well.

When talking about Vista, it's important to discuss both existing and new development. You want to make sure that your existing applications that work fine in Windows XP will continue to work with Vista. For starters, you can download the Application Compatibility Cookbook from the DevReadiness Microsoft community site (`http://devreadiness.org`). The toolkit provides access to videos, presentations, white papers, and tools designed to help you make the transition to Vista.

Getting Started with Vista

You might think getting started with Vista means installing Vista. Oh, no — that's too easy. You want to get *developing* for Vista. Here are a few tools that you need to get started:

+ **.NET Framework version 3.0 or version 3.5** — Formerly known as WinFX, this is the managed application programming interface (API) you use to access all the technologies of Vista. The .NET Framework installs with Visual Studio 2008.

+ **Windows Software Development Kit (SDK)** — This includes documentation, samples, and tools for building managed and unmanaged Vista applications, and can be downloaded from

    `http://msdn2.microsoft.com/en-us/windowsvista/aa904955.aspx`

+ **Visual Studio 2008 Development Tools** — These provide the mechanism for working with Vista technologies.

After you install these tools, you end up with several new project types, as listed in Table 3-1. The templates are available for Visual Basic and C#.

Table 3-1	Vista Project Types and Templates
Project Type	*Project Template*
Windows	WPF Windows Application
	WPF Service Library
	WPF Web Browser Application
	WPF Custom Control Library
Workflow	Sequential Workflow Console Application
	Workflow Activity Library
	State Machine Workflow Library
	Sequential Workflow Library
	State Machine Console Application
	Empty Workflow Project

You create projects using these project types the same way you create any Visual Studio project.

Creating Vista applications

Everything changed in Vista. Of course, your applications don't have to change, but chances are that you'll want to take advantage of those changes.

If you want to get started creating applications for Vista, you should start with the Windows SDK.

The Windows SDK consists of the following:

✦ Extensive documentation on every aspect of the Vista OS and its underlying technologies

✦ Samples that demonstrate every aspect of Vista

✦ Tools to help you create, deploy, and manage all kinds of Vista applications

After you install the SDK, you access its contents via your All Programs menu. Because the SDK can be quite overwhelming, begin with the Getting Started section of the SDK documentation. The documentation appears as shown in Figure 3-1.

**Book VII
Chapter 3**

**Using Visual Studio
with Vista and
Office 2007**

Figure 3-1:
Begin with
Getting
Started.

SDK samples

The SDK offers an amazing number of samples, including samples for Vista and version 3.0 of the .NET Framework. You can find these in the samples folder where you installed the SDK. By default, the SDK installs to `C:\Program Files\Microsoft SDKs\Windows`.

The samples are organized by feature or technology. Pick a technology in which you have some interest and browse through the samples. For example, maybe start with WPF because it represents the most visible change to Vista.

Windows Presentation Foundation

You can find the WPF samples in the file `WPFSamples.zip`. After you unzip the samples, you'll find an Intro folder that contains a number of quick start tutorials. The first quick start is a simple Hello World application. Figure 3-2 shows an example of the output from this sample.

Figure 3-2:
The first example is a very simple Hello World presenta-tion.

Not very impressive — but (as you've likely surmised) the samples in the SDK aren't intended to be sophisticated. Their intent is to demonstrate new features. What you're looking at in Figure 3-2 is an example of a page. You can still use good old-fashioned Windows Forms in your development, but WPF also uses pages to display content.

WPF applications are intended to create immersive user experiences. Think about where you're most likely to see applications with intense graphics, video, and other eye candy — usually on the Web. WPF applications use pages to create rich browser-like experiences on the desktop.

Another way WPF applications are like Web applications is that they use a markup language to describe the UI. Web applications use HTML. In Visual Studio, you use a combination of HTML and ASP.NET markup to create the ASPX file that becomes your Web page. You write your code in a separate code-behind file. The same is true of Vista applications. You could possibly run into problems with Vista where it doesn't work very well with the User Account Control (UAC) in place. If this happens, you can easily turn it off during development with the System Configuration applet.

Extensible Application Markup Language

All Vista applications, whether they use pages or Windows Forms, use markup to describe the user interface. This markup language, created by Microsoft, is Extensible Application Markup Language (XAML; pronounced *zam*-el, like *camel* with a *z*).

XAML is an XML language that you use to describe everything about the user interface. Why XAML? When you describe UIs by using an XML file, you can easily transfer UIs between members of a team. For example, UI designers work on an interface. They can pass off the XAML file to a developer, who is writing the code-behind logic. XAML is used by Visual Studio and Microsoft Expression, which is the Microsoft line of graphics design tools. Designers use an Expression product, such as Microsoft Expression Web Designer, to create rich user interfaces in XAML. Developers consume the XAML in Visual Studio.

Visit the Expression Web site, where you can download trial versions of the new Expression products, at `www.microsoft.com/products/expression`.

Don't worry about having to learn a new language. Visual Studio will still use visual designers. The IntelliSense support for XAML makes it fairly intuitive. Figure 3-3 shows an example of a typical XAML file being edited.

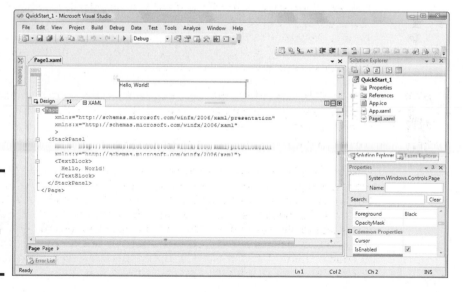

Figure 3-3:
Editing
XAML files
is easy with
the added
support.

Take a look at the Samples Gallery to get more examples of using XAML. You can find the gallery in the Gallery folder of WPFSamples. The Samples Gallery shows code and previews of animation, controls, data-binding, graphics, and layout. It's a great way to get acquainted with WPF. Figure 3-4 shows an example of a control that uses XAML and C#. You can view a description, the code, and a preview.

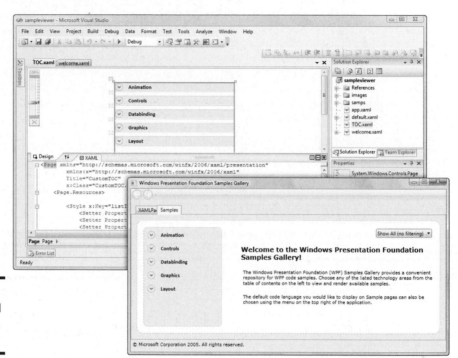

Figure 3-4:
This control
uses XAML
and C#.

If you're starting to feel like you're not in Kansas anymore, you aren't alone. All this Vista stuff is strange new territory. Microsoft has created mountains of documentation to help you figure all this out. Set aside some quality time to read the Vista User Experience Guidelines (UX Guide). The guidelines walk you through the new user interface changes for Vista applications. You can find the guidelines at

http://msdn2.microsoft.com/en-us/library/aa511258.aspx

Creating workflow applications

Version 3.5 of the .NET Framework has a *workflow application,* which is a long-running application that represents a model of a process from beginning to end. For example, think about the workflow required for getting a travel-expense reimbursement at work: It starts when you fill out an expense reimbursement form. The form is routed to your boss for approval, and then it's routed to accounts payable. If there's a problem with the form, AP may kick the form into a separate problem queue. At some point (hopefully, before the credit card payment is due), you get a check. Windows Workflow Foundation allows you to create workflows that model other such processes.

The two parts to WWF applications are

+ **The WWF model:** This defines the workflow itself. Workflows can't be executed directly. Rather, you create an instance of the workflow model inside an application — which can be a Windows, Web, or console application — and host the workflow there.

+ **The application that hosts the workflow:** This is the second part of a WWF application. You need the workflow and an application to host it to create a workflow application.

The basic unit of a workflow is an activity, which you might think of as a step in the workflow. Windows Workflow Foundations supports the following three kinds of workflows:

+ **Sequential** — Activities execute one after another.

+ **State machine** — Activities execute when an event occurs.

+ **Data-driven** — Activities execute when a condition is met.

Workflow models use XAML, C#, or Visual Basic. You can create a workflow by typing XAML markup in a text editor. Visual Studio provides a visual designer for creating workflows.

The mother of all workflow applications is SharePoint. You can host WWF workflows in SharePoint, and visual workflow designers are available in SharePoint Designer. To see SharePoint workflows in action, you can download the Enterprise Content Management Starter Kit from the Microsoft Web site at

```
http://www.microsoft.com/downloads/details.aspx?
    familyid=38ca6b32-44be-4489-8526-f09c57cd13a5
```

The Windows SDK includes a number of samples that demonstrate the technologies of WWF. You can find the samples in the `WFSamples.zip` file in the SDK's samples folder. Figure 3-5 shows a sequential workflow in a designer in Visual Studio.

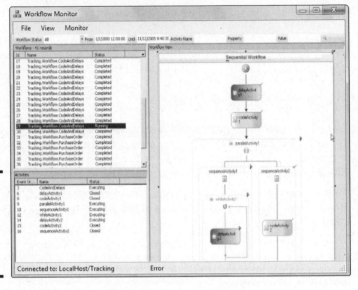

Figure 3-5:
See the
workflow in
the Visual
Studio
designer.

In addition to demonstrating all the features of WWF, the SDK includes a number of applications that show workflows in action. For example, the `OrderingStateMachine` application demonstrates a state machine workflow. The sample has the following four state activities:

✦ `WaitingForOrderState`

✦ `OrderCompletedState`

✦ `OrderOpenState`

✦ `OrderProcessedState`

The workflow's events include `OnOrderUpdated`, `OnOrderProcessed`, `OnOrderShipped`, and `OnOrderCanceled`. When events are fired, the order moves through the state activities like a string of firecrackers. The sample includes a simple host application that you can use to move an order through the states. The buttons in the application fire the workflow's events. Figure 3-6 shows an example.

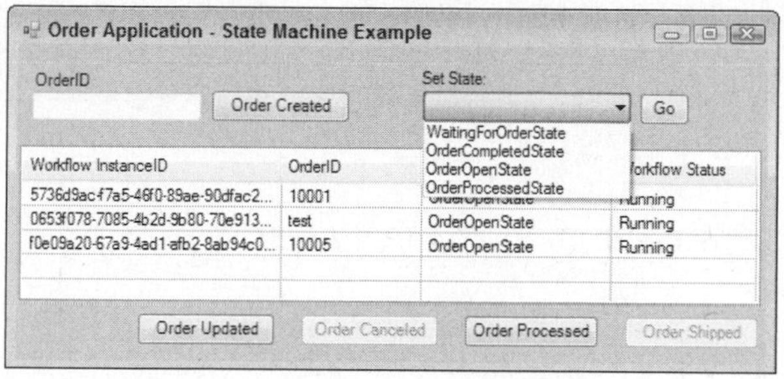

Figure 3-6:
User
interface
objects can
fire the
workflow
events.

Getting Ready for Office 2007

Microsoft released its latest version of Office in early 2007, offering the main-stays you expect (Word, Excel, and the usual crew) along with a few new client applications, such as the following:

✦ **Communicator 2007** — Integrates communication into Office applica-tions to enable a single identity across applications and communication modes

✦ **Groove 2007** — Enables collaboration among team members in a workspace

✦ **InfoPath 2007** — Creates forms that integrate with other Office applica-tions, such as Outlook and Excel

✦ **OneNote 2007** — Takes notes and organizes them in a digital notebook

✦ **SharePoint Designer 2007** — Designs, customizes, and contributes to SharePoint sites

Another development for Office 2007 is the use of server products. SharePoint Portal Server and Project Server have been around for a while, but they're both beefed up. The server offerings in Office 2007 include

✦ **Forms Server 2007** — Serves up InfoPath forms

✦ **Groove Server 2007** — Implements and administers enterprise-level Groove services

✦ **Project Portfolio Server 2007** — Organizes, measures, monitors, and creates workflows for a portfolio of projects

✦ **Project Server 2007** — Manages a project's life cycle

✦ **SharePoint Server 2007** — Provides a portal for collaboration, content management, and process workflow

**Book VII
Chapter 3**

Using Visual Studio
with Vista and
Office 2007

Office 2007 has a completely revamped user interface. A primary feature of this interface is the *Ribbon,* which sits atop applications and is used to access menu commands. The Ribbon allows users to access more commands with fewer mouse clicks; see Figure 3-7.

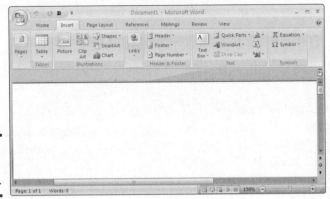

Figure 3-7:
The Office 2007 Ribbon.

Another feature of Office 2007 is the Office Open XML Formats. All your Office data is now saved as XML files instead of using proprietary file formats. Using XML enables data to be moved easily across Web services.

The increased use of servers, XML, and Web services makes it easier for developers to use Office 2007 as a development platform. They make it so easy, in fact, that you can actually create full-blown applications that use Office 2007 clients as their interfaces. The advantage of this approach is that your users are using clients they already use every day and don't need to learn a new interface to use your application.

Microsoft will release a new version of Visual Studio Tools for Office (VSTO) to complement Office 2007. VSTO simplifies Office development by cutting down on the amount of code required to develop Office applications. If you're doing Office development, you should check out VSTO.

You should also check out the Office Developer Center on MSDN for tutorials and downloads for using Visual Studio to develop Office applications at

`http://msdn.microsoft.com/office/default.aspx`

Going Virtual

With the releases of Office 2007, Vista, Visual Studio 2008, and many other products comes the headache of finding enough hardware to run everything. If you're one of the brave souls who ran beta versions of this software, you likely frequently found yourself reformatting your hard drive and installing software.

Instead of running all this software on individual machines, consider running it on virtual machines. With the release of Microsoft Virtual PC 2007, you can create multiple virtual machines on a single physical server.

Virtual PC 2007 includes support for networking, which includes these capabilities:

✦ Create a virtual network that consists of virtual machines only.

✦ Network virtual machines to the local machine only.

✦ Network virtual machines to the larger network.

Virtual servers work equally well in development and production environments. Officially, Virtual Server supports server operating systems, such as Windows Server 2003 and Windows Server 2008. However, it will also run Windows XP and Vista.

You need to have adequate hardware to run virtual machines. Virtual PC 2007 runs as a service, but it isn't necessary to run all your virtual machines at once. For example, Rick has a dozen or so virtual machines configured on one of his test servers. At any given time, he's usually running only, at most, two of those virtual machines.

Virtual PC 2007 is available as a free download from the Microsoft Web site at

www.microsoft.com/windows/products/winfamily/virtualpc/default.mspx

While you're there, be sure to check out other resources, such as the Virtual PC 2007 Application Compatibility Toolkit 5.0 (which you can use to migrate physical servers to virtual servers).

The administration and remote-control features of Virtual PC 2007 are Web-based. You use the administration Web site to do the following:

✦ Create, add, and configure virtual machines.

✦ Create virtual hard drives.

✦ Create, add, and configure virtual networks.

✦ Configure and maintain the virtual server.

Figure 3-8 shows an example of the Virtual PC Settings dialog box.

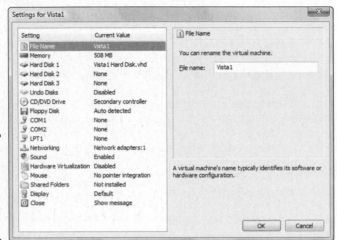

Figure 3-8:
The Virtual
PC Settings
dialog box is
available, as
shown here.

To access the virtual machine, simple select it in the list of virtual machines and then click the New button in the Virtual PC Console window, as shown in Figure 3-9.

Rick made extensive use of Remote Desktop while writing this book. He set up multiple virtual machines so he could run different scenarios in desktop sessions. For example, he often installed beta software and extensions on a virtual machine, including the software listed in the section "Getting Started with Vista" (earlier in this chapter). It worked like gangbusters.

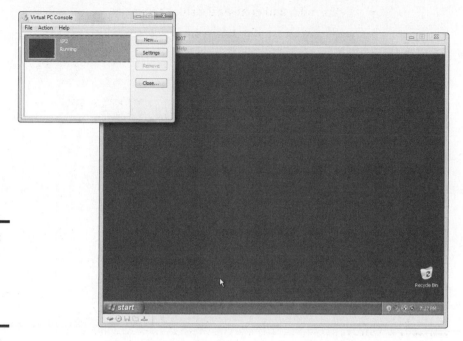

Figure 3-9:
The virtual machines are very easy to access.

Index

Symbol

? (question mark), shortcut operator, 516

A

abstract classes, 582–583
abstraction, 528
Accept button, 150
acceptance tests, 640
AcceptButton property, 150
AccessDataSource control, 328
accessibility, 145, 208
Accessibility properties, 145
accessing data. *See* data access
Action category, 145
Activated event, 560
active processes, finding, 470–471
Active Server Pages (ASP), 188
Active Template Library (ATL), 176
ActiveSync issues, 287
ad hoc development, 31
Add Connections dialog box, 314–317
Add New Data Source command, 311
add-ons. *See* extensions
administration extensions, 739–740
ADO.NET. *See also* Data Source
 Configuration Wizard
 components, 400
 Data Sources window, 293
 Microsoft Access databases, 401
 multi-tiered applications, 401
 overview, 292
 recommended techniques, 433–435
 tools, 293
 XML support, 432–433
ADO.NET, data providers
 accessing, 402
 Command object, 402–403, 414–417
 DataAdapter object, 402–403
 DataReaders, 400, 402–403
 DataSet, 400
 definition, 316

ExecuteNonQuery method, 414
ExecuteReader method, 414
ExecuteScalar method, 414
features and services, 402–403
instances of objects, 403
.NET Framework, 400, 401–403
objects, 403
provider-independent code, 402
queries, executing, 414–417
selecting, 401–402
stored procedures, 415–417
ADO.NET, data sources
 connected model, 293–294
 data binding, 295
 DataReaders, 294
 DataSet method, 294
 description, 292–293
 disconnected model, 293–294
 displaying data, 294–295
 offline storage, 294
 retrieving data, 293–294
 strongly typed DataSet, 294
 TableAdapter, 293–294
 updating data, 295–296
 Web Forms controls, 295
 Windows Form controls, 295
ADO.NET, database connections
 closing, 407–408
 Connection object, 402–403
 connection objects, 403–404
 connection pooling, 404, 408
 connection strings, 408–413
 opening, 404–406
 Using blocks, 407–408
ADO.NET, DataSets
 DataAdapter services, 425–426
 DeleteCommand property, 426, 428–430
 explicit transactions, 432
 filing, 426–428, 432–433
 implicit transactions, 431–432
 InsertCommand property, 426, 428–430
 OdbcDataAdapter object, 426
 OleDbDataAdapter object, 426
 OracleDataAdapter object, 426

ADO.NET, `DataSets` *(continued)*
  retrieving data, 430–432
  `SelectCommand` property, 426
  `SqlDataAdapter` object, 426
  synchronizing with XML documents, 433
  `TableAdapters`, 430–431
  transactions, 431–432
  updating data, 426–431
  XML documents, creating, 432–433
  XML Schema, creating, 432–433
ADO.NET, reading data
  all commands in a row, 424
  by column index, 423–424
  by column name, 423–424
  `DataReaders`
    description, 400
    features and services, 402–403
    `Get` accessors, 421–425
    `GetSchemaTable` method, 425
    `GetValues` method, 424–425
    objects, 417–420
    `Read` method, 420–421
    setting up, 418–420
  firehose cursor, 417
  `GetOrdinal` method, 423
  `Item` method, 423
  in native format, 421–422
  `OdbcDataReader` object, 417–420
  `OleDbDataReader` object, 417–420
  `OracleDataReader` object, 417–420
  schemas, 425, 432
  `SqlDataReader` object, 417–420
  stepping through data, 420–421
  with typed accessors, 421–422
Adventure Works database, 300, 445
Agile Manifesto, 39
Agile process, 34
AJAX (Asynchronous JavaScript And XML),
      62, 217–222, 744. *See also* Atlas;
      extensions
AJAX Control Toolkit, 222–224
Ajax For Dummies, 744
AJAX Web applications
  JavaScript
    document fetch, 216
    interaction with HTML, 215
    versus Java, 215

returned XML data, 217
    server requests, 215–216
    `XMLHttpRequest` object, 215–216
  partial page updates, 214–217
  postback architecture, 214
  postback delays, 214–217
AJAX-enabled WCF services, 29
aligning controls, 138
allocating memory, 52. *See also* garbage
      collection
`AlterSchemaFromDbo.sql` script, 445
`AlterSchemaToDbo.sql` script, 445
analysis stage, 34
analyzing code. *See* FxCop
anchor properties, 145
`Anchor` property, 168, 169–171
anchoring controls, 168, 169–171
anonymous users, 269
`App_Browsers` folder, 198
`App_Code` folder, 198
`App_Data` folder, 198
appearance
  See CSS (Cascading Style Sheets)
  See customizing
  See master pages
  See properties
  See styles
  See themes
`Appearance` properties, 145
`App_GlobalResources` folder, 198
Application Designer, 76
application domain, 562
application events, 562, 564, 566–568
application state, 257–259
applications. *See* software development;
      specific applications
`App_LocalResources` folder, 198
`App_Themes` folder, 198
`App_WebReferences` folder, 198
Architect certification, 113
architecture
  client/server, 42
  evolution of, 42–43
  postback, 214
  VSTS, Software Architect Edition, 76–77,
      751–753
arranging controls, 138

`Array` class, 506
arrays. *See also* collections
  of arrays, 508
  bounds, 507
  declaring, 507
  definition, 506
  elements, 507
  indexes, 507
  iterating through, 511–512
  length, 507
  properties, 507
  rank, 507
  zero-based index, 508–509
articles. *See* publications
artifacts, 715–716
`.ascx` file extension, 204
Ask a Question, 106–107
ASP (Active Server Pages), 188
`.asp` tag prefix, 200
ASP.NET pages
  buttons, adding, 195–196
  characteristics of, 189
  Check Page for Accessibility, 208
  code editing, 211
  Code view, 208
  code-behind code, 211
  Component Designer view, 208
  content, adding, 194–196
  control properties, setting, 195
  Design view, 208
  generated code, changing, 211
  "Hello World" example, 194–196
  hyperlinks, adding, 210–211
  inline code, 211
  partial clauses, 211
  postbacks, 190
  serving, 190
  Source view, 208–211
  syntax, viewing, 193–194
  Target Schema for Validation, 208
  validator commands, 208
  views, 208–211
ASP.NET pages, server controls
  `.asp` tag prefix, 200
  buttons, HTML control, 201, 202–203
  buttons, Web control, 199–200, 202–203
  calendars, 206–207
  composite, 205
  custom, 203
  displaying messages, 203
  `<form>`, 205–206
  HTML, 198, 200–203
  Label Web, 203
  syntax, 199–200
  types of, 198–199
  user, 190, 203–207
  validation, 190
  Web, 198–203
ASP.NET 3.5
  anonymous users, 269
  application state, 257–259
  client-side statement management, 256, 257
  Controls layer, 254
  customizing Web sites, 268–270
  Data Stores layer, 254
  layers, 254–256
  membership, 260–267
  new services, 253–254
  personalization layer, 270
  profiles, enabling, 268–269
  Providers layer, 254
  server-side statement management, 256
  Services layer, 254
  session state, 259
  state management, 256–259
  toolkit, 256
  UI (user interface) controls, 269–270
  UI structure components, 269–270
  upgrading, 118
  view state, 257–259
  Web parts controls, 269–270
ASP.NET Web Service template, 177
`.aspx` file extension, 189
assemblies
  definition, 533
  deploying, 43–46
  DLL hell, 46
  GAC (Global Assembly Cache), 46
  storing, 46
assembly language, 57
assignments, 498–500
associations, creating, 544–545

Asynchronous JavaScript And XML (AJAX).
　　See AJAX
ATL (Active Template Library), 176
ATL Project Wizard, 178
ATL Server Project Wizard, 178
ATL Smart Device Project Wizard, 178
Atlas, 62, 745. *See also* AJAX
　　(Asynchronous JavaScript And XML);
　　extensions
attributes, 381, 530
Auto Hide option, 91
auto-complete, Code Editor, 100
AutoFormat feature, 335–336
AutoSize property, 169, 172
AutoSizeMode property, 172
auto-sizing controls, 169, 172

B

back-end services controls, 135
backwards compatibility, 116–117, 122
base classes, 530
batch files, mobile Web applications,
　　285–287
battery life, smart devices, 288
BCL (Base Class Library), 25, 29
Behavior category, 145
best practices, 33, 36–38
Bin folder, 198
binding data. *See* data binding
BindingNavigator component, 318, 321.
　　See also data binding
BindingSource component, 318, 321–323.
　　See also data binding; data source
　　controls
body, in classes, 531
bookmarks, Code Editor, 484–486
books. *See* publications
Books Online, 443–445
border properties, 145
Bottom element, 247
bounds of arrays, 507
Branch command, 716
breakpoints, 484, 627, 628–630

browsing
　　code, 485–486
　　data types, 517–519
　　files, 153
　　folders, 153
　　servers, 99–100
　　TFS resources, 761–762
build configurations
　　creating, 666–668
　　debug, 660
　　release, 660
　　selecting, 663
build engines, 674
Build menu, 662–663
builds. *See also* projects; solutions
　　automating, 673–674
　　compiler errors, 663–666
　　creating, 662–663
　　description, 660–661
　　integrating new code, 672–673
　　master, 673
　　output, 663–666
　　platform, selecting, 663
built-in value types, 500–502
business object layer, 42
buttons. *See also* controls
　　Accept, 150
　　AcceptButton property, 150
　　adding to pages, 195–196
　　Cancel, 146, 150
　　CancelButton property, 146, 150
　　default, 146
　　DefaultButton property, 146
　　HTML control, 201, 202–203
　　making active, 195–196
　　toggling, 150
　　Web control, 199–200, 202–203

C

C++ language, 26, 59, 280–281. *See also*
　　Visual C++
C++ For Dummies, 60
C# language. *See also* Visual C#
　　classes, 488, 490–491
　　data type declarations, 487

declaring variables, 489–490
executable statements, 487–489, 491
fields, 491–492
getting started, 489–490
`Imports` statement, 486–487
initializing variables, 489–490
`Main` procedure, 489
members, 487, 491–492
methods, 491–492
namespace declarations, 487
non-executable statements, 486–487
objects, 490
organizing programs, 486–489
procedures, 491–492
setup statements, 486–487
statements, 491
using external resources, 486–487
`using` statement, 486–487
wrapper statements, 486–487
CAB files, 276
calendars, 206–207
call stack, 497–498
camel casing, 570
Cancel button, 146, 150
`CancelButton` property, 146, 150
Cascading Style Sheets (CSS), 246–251. *See also* styles
case standards, 570
`CatalogZone`, 270
`Catch` blocks, 619–620
`Catch` statements, 618–619
catching exceptions, 619–622
`.cd` file extension, 536
cell phones. *See* smart devices
centering controls, 138
certification, Microsoft, 112–113
change management. *See* SCM (software configuration management)
`ChangePassword` control, 265
Chart Expert, 734
charts, 734. *See also* reports
check boxes. *See* controls
Check Page for Accessibility, 208
checking files in/out, 711–713
Class Designer. *See also* class diagrams; classes

commands, 537–538
components, 537
data type commands, 537–538
diagram commands, 537
IntelliSense features, 545
member commands, 537
objects, creating, 548–550
refactoring, 591–592
refactoring commands, 545–546
toolbar, 537–538
uses for, 535–536
class diagrams. *See also* Class Designer
`.cd` file extension, 536
creating, 536
definition, 536
viewing, 547–548
class libraries, 119–120, 352–353, 378–379
Class Library template, 177
Class View, 89
classes
abstract, 582–583
adding members to, 540–543
associations, creating, 544–545
C#, 488, 490–491
concrete, 582
creating, 539–540
data type information, viewing, 546–547
definition, 526
displaying in tree view, 89
generating code, 545
importance of, 528
method declaration, 542–543
.NET, 530–535
versus objects, 527
partial, 975–977
static, 548–550
strongly typed `DataSets`, 375
Visual Basic, 488, 490–491
ClickOnce strategy, 677–680
client/server architecture, 42
client-side scripting, validation controls, 228
client-side statement management, 256, 257
CLR (Common Language Runtime), 25, 48–50, 455

CLR Console Application template, 178
CLR Empty Project template, 178
CLR routines, 453, 457–458
Club Site starter kit, 212
code
  browsing, 485–486
  camel casing, 570
  case standards, 570
  code-behind, 211
  commenting, 585–589
  deprecated, 116
  documenting, 585–589
  editing, 211. *See also* Code Editor
  generated, 211, 374, 638
  generating, 55, 545
  Hungarian notation style, 571–572
  indenting, 477–478
  inline, 211
  managed
    definition, 47
    executing, 46–50
    versus native code, 47
    smart devices, 274
    SQL Server projects, 453
    Visual C++, 176
  method stubs, 580
  naming conventions, 569–572
  native
    versus managed code, 47
    smart devices, 274
    Visual C++, 177
  object-oriented, 582–585. *See also* OOP
    (object-oriented programming)
  Pascal casing, 570
  provider-independent, 402
  refactoring, 592–594
  reviews, best practices, 37
  snippets, 577–579
  source, 522–523. *See also* Code Editor;
    source code control
  stepping through, 627, 630–633
  stubs, 580, 648–649, 650
  unmanaged, 182–186, 767
  viewing, 374, 377–378

Code Editor
  bookmarks, 484–486
  breakpoint symbols, 484
  browsing code, 485–486
  colored squigglies, 484
  colors, 484
  description, 100–101
  error indicator, 484
  example, 476
  expanding/collapsing code, 482–483
  features, 476
  find and replace, 479–481
  formatting commands, 478–479
  indenting code, 477–478
  IntelliSense, 483–484
  line numbering, 484–485
  navigating code, 485–486
  Navigation bar, 485–486
  opening files, 476
  outline feature, 482–483
  region directives, 482–483
  smart indenting, 477–478
  symbols, 480
  syntax assistance, 483–484
  tagging comments, 481
  to-do list, 481–482
  visual cues, 484
code signing, 683–687
Code view, 208
collaboration software, 38, 77–78
collections, 506, 509–513. *See also*
    ADO.NET; arrays
ColorDialog dialog box, 153
colors
  Code Editor, 484
  dialog boxes, 153–154
  error indication, 484
  properties, 145
  squigglies in Code Editor, 484
columns, 297, 349–350, 356
combo boxes. *See* controls
Command object, 402–403, 414–417
comment markers, 585
commenting code, 585–589

comments, tagging, 481
Common Language Runtime (CLR), 25,
48–50, 455
Common Type System (CTS). *See* CTS
communities online. *See* online
communities
CompareValidator control, 226
compiler errors in builds, 663–666
compilers
  J#, 61
  JIT (just-in-time) compilation, 14
  .NET, 24
  Visual C++, 60
Component Designer view, 208
component development, 37, 40–42
component management, 43–45
composite controls, 205
concrete classes, 582
concurrent SDLC stages, 35
Configuration Manager, 666–668
Configure DataSet with Wizard command,
  311
configuring
  See also CSS (Cascading Style Sheets)
  See also customizing
  See also master pages
  See also properties
  See also styles
  ASP.NET 3.5 default database, 260–261
  ASP.NET 3.5 membership, 263–264
  databound controls, 328–329
  default database, 260–261
  membership, 263–264
  menus, 155–156
  Professional Edition, 85–87
  projects, 669–671
  solutions, 669–671
  TableAdapter, 365–371
  Web applications for, 123
connected data source model, 293–294
connecting to data sources. *See* data
  binding; databases; Server Explorer
connecting to databases. *See also* data
  binding
  ADO.NET
    closing, 407–408
    Connection object, 402–403

connection objects, 403–404
connection pooling, 404, 408
connection strings, 408–413
opening, 404–406
Using blocks, 407–408
source code, 704–705, 707–708
SQL Server 2005, 448
tables
  change scripts, 463
  columns, 297
  creating, 462–463
  definition, 297
  foreign keys, 298
  fully qualified names, 307
  keys, 297–298
  primary keys, 297–298
  relating to other tables, 297–298
  rows, 297
views, 464–465
Visual Database Tools, 459–465
in Windows applications, 314–317
Connection object, 402–403
connection objects, 403–404
connection pooling, 404, 408
connection string builders, 413
connection strings, 408–413
connection strings store, 317
ConnectionZone, 270
constants, class member, 531
Constraint object, 347
construction and implementation stage, 34
constructors, 531
consuming
  applications, 680–681
  events, 553
container controls, 166–168
containers, 94
Contents feature, 105
context sensitive menus, 90, 150, 155
ContextMenuStrip control, 150, 155
ContextMenuStrip property, 150
contextual menus, 98
control toolbox, 134–136
ControlBox property, 150

controls. *See also specific controls*
  adding to forms, 136–137
  AJAX, 222–224
  ASP.NET, 218–219. *See also* ASP.NET
    pages, server controls
  back-end services, 135
  behavior, setting, 145
  container, 166–168
  Crystal Reports, 135
  data access, 135
  databound, 318–320, 328–336, 340–342,
    379–380. *See also* data binding
  dialog boxes, 135
  flow control, 168
  formatting, 138–140
  grouping, 134, 166–168
  inside controls, 167–168
  layout
    aligning, 138
    anchoring, 168, 169–171
    arranging, 138
    auto-sizing, 169, 172
    centering, 138
    docking, 168, 169–171
    margins, 138, 145, 169, 172–173
    padding, 138, 169, 172–173
    spacing, 138, 169, 172–173
  locking, 138, 141
  menus, 135
  names, 146
  navigation, 232–234
  printing features, 135
  purpose of, 133
  smart tags, 143
  snaplines, 140–141
  tab order, 141–142
  text on, 146
  third-party, 137
  toolbars, 135
  UI (user interface), 269–270
  validation, 226–231
  in Visual C++ applications, 185–186
  Web parts, 269–270
  Web server
    adding, 330
    AutoFormat feature, 335–336
    customizing, 331–334, 335–336
    deleting data, 340–342
    editing data, 340–342
    paging data, 335, 340
    properties, 334–336
    sorting data, 340
    tasks, 334–336
    templates for, 331–334
  Windows
    binding to controls, 318–320
    binding to properties, 324–326, 342–343
    `BindingNavigator` component, 318,
      321
    `BindingSource` component, 318,
      321–323
    definition, 321
    menus for navigation, 318, 321
    navigating to data sources, 318, 321
    to properties, 324–326
  WPF interoperability, 135
Controls layer, 254
conversions
  Java to C++, 59
  Java to .NET assemblies, 61
  JLCA (Java Language Conversion
    Assistant), 59
converters, 124–125
copyright information, on master pages,
    241–242
cradled devices, connecting to, 283–284
`CreateSynonymsDbo.sql` script, 445
`CreateUserWizard` control, 265
CRUD statements, 366, 371–372
Crystal Reports. *See also* reports
  Chart Expert, 734
  commands, 725, 734
  connecting to data sources, 725–730
  creating reports, 720–724
  Data Access, 720
  data binding, 725–730
  Database Expert, 726–730
  databases, connecting to, 725–730
  editions, 719–720
  Field Explorer, 731–734
  Format Editor, 734–736
  Highlight Expert, 735

Report Designer, 720, 730–736
Report Viewer, 720
Section Expert, 735
CSS (Cascading Style Sheets), 246–251. *See also* styles
CTS (Common Type System). *See also* data types
  call stack, 497–498
  heap, 497–498
  new operator, 497
  reference types, 497–503, 516
  root data type, 496
  stack, 497–498
  type hierarchy, 496–497
  value types, 497–502, 516
cursor style, setting, 145
Custom Application Wizard, 178
custom server controls, 203
customizing
  See also configuring
  See also CSS (Cascading Style Sheets)
  See also properties
  See also styles
  control toolbox, 135–136
  with CSS (Cascading Style Sheets), 246–251. *See also* styles
  databound controls, 331–334, 335–336
  Document Explorer, 109–111
  with master pages. *See also* styles; themes
    accessing, 243–245
    adding to Web sites, 240
    content, adding, 240–241
    content pages, adding, 242–243
    converting from Web pages, 243–245
    copyright information, 241–242
    definition, 234
    versus regular pages, 240
    title element, 244
  reports, 731–736
  with styles. *See also* CSS (Cascading Style Sheets)
    menu controls, 156, 160–162
    XSLT, 391–394

with themes
  adding to Web sites, 236–237
  definition, 235
  elements, 235
  images, 235
  skins, 235–239
  as style sheets, 237
Web server controls, 331–334, 335–336
Web sites, 268–270
CustomValidator control, 226

D

data
  deleting, 340–342, 367
  displaying, 294–295
  editing, 340–342, 380
  inserting, 366
  paging, 335, 340
  reading, 367. *See also* ADO.NET, reading data; databases, querying; retrieving data; selecting data
  retrieving
    from data sources, 293–294, 339. *See also* TableAdapters
    storing retrieved data, 311
    transactions, 431–432
  selecting, 367, 401–402. *See also* databases, querying; reading data
  sorting, 340, 372–374
  updating
    with DataSet Designer, 336–339
    TableAdapters, 430–431
    UPDATE command, 367
    Update method, 428–430
    UpdateCommand property, 426, 428–430
Data Access, 720
data access. *See also* ADO.NET
  with drag and drop
    preparing for, 299–300
    Web Forms, 304–308
    Windows Form, 300–304
  Windows Form, 300–304

data access, Web Forms
  creating data sources, 336–339
  data controls, 328
  data source controls, 328
  displaying data, 328
  drag and drop, 304–308
  HTTP (HyperText Transfer Protocol),
    326–327
  processing stages, 326
  retrieving data, 336–339
  updating data, 336–339
  Web server controls
    adding, 330
    AutoFormat feature, 335–336
    customizing, 331–334, 335–336
    deleting data, 340–342
    editing data, 340–342
    paging data, 335, 340
    properties, 334–336
    sorting data, 340
    tasks, 334–336
    templates for, 331–334
data access, Windows applications
  access methods, 309–310
  accessing data, 309–312
  adding data, 312–314
  data sources
    adding, 312–314
    available sources, 316
    connecting to controls, 318–320. *See
      also* data binding
    connecting to databases, 314–317
    connection strings store, 317
    data providers, 316
    databound controls, 318–320. *See also*
      data binding
    datasets, 311
    definition, 310
    managing, 310–311
    protecting, 324
    storing retrieved data, 311
    tree view, 311–312
  default components, 318–319
  managing data, 310–311
  tree view, 311–312

data access layer, 42
data binding
  definition, 295
  source code, 704–705, 707–708
  stored procedures, 370
  Windows controls. *See also* databound
    controls
    binding to controls, 318–320
    binding to properties, 324–326, 342–343
    BindingNavigator component,
      318, 321
    BindingSource component, 318,
      321–323. *See also* data source controls
    definition, 321
    menus for navigation, 318, 321
    navigating to data sources, 318, 321
    to properties, 324–326
Data category, 145
data controls, 328
Data Explorer, 296
data providers
  accessing, 402
  Command object, 402–403, 414–417
  DataAdapter object, 402–403
  DataReaders, 400, 402–403
  DataSet, 400
  definition, 316
  ExecuteNonQuery method, 414
  ExecuteReader method, 414
  ExecuteScalar method, 414
  features and services, 402–403
  instances of objects, 403
  .NET Framework, 400, 401–403
  objects, 403
  provider-independent code, 402
  queries, executing, 414–417
  selecting, 401–402
  stored procedures, 415–417
Data Source Configuration Wizard
  definition, 293
  invalid-object errors, 307
  Web Forms data, 304–308
  Windows Form data, 300–304
data source controls, 328

data sources. *See also* Data Sources pane;
    databases
  ADO.NET
    connected model, 293–294
    data binding, 295
    `DataReaders`, 294
    `DataSet` method, 294
    description, 292–293
    disconnected model, 293–294
    displaying data, 294–295
    offline storage, 294
    retrieving data, 293–294
    strongly-typed `DataSet`, 294
    `TableAdapter`, 293–294
    updating data, 295–296
    Web Forms controls, 295
    Windows Form controls, 295
  creating, 336–339
  setting, 145
  Web Forms, 336–339
  Windows applications
    adding, 312–314
    available sources, 316
    binding to controls, 318–320
    connecting to databases, 314–317
    connection strings store, 317
    data providers, 316
    databound controls, 318–320
    datasets, 311
    definition, 310
    managing, 310–311
    protecting, 324
    storing retrieved data, 311
    tree view, 311–312
Data Sources pane. *See also* data sources;
    Windows Forms Designer
  Add New Data Source command, 311
  adding data, 312–314
  `BindingNavigator` component, 318
  `BindingSource` component, 318. *See
    also* data source controls
  Configure DataSet with Wizard
    command, 311
  connecting to databases, 314–317
  databound controls, 318–320
  `DataGridView` control, 318–320
  default components, 318–319

Edit DataSet with Designer command, 311
  managing data, 310–311
  `Refresh` command, 311
  `TableAdapter` component, 318
  tree view, 311–312
Data Sources window, 293
Data Stores layer, 254
data structures. *See* ADO.NET; collections
data types. *See also* collections; CTS
    (Common Type System)
  accessing in source code, 523–524
  browsing, 517–519
  classes, 504
  converting, 514–515
  creating your own, 503–506
  declarations, 487
  definition, 493
  enumerations, 505–506
  information, viewing, 546–547
  nullable, 516–517
  rules for, 493–494
  strongly typed, 350
  structures, 504–505
  for variables, 494–495
  viewing information about, 519–521
  weakly typed, 350
`DataAdapter` object, 402–403
`DataAdapter` services, 425–426
Database Expert, 726–730
Database Professionals edition, 756
database projects, SQL Server 2005,
    446–449
`DataBase` property, setting, 409
database references, 448–449, 455
databases. *See also* data access; data
    sources
  adding to projects, 461
  choosing a Visual Studio edition, 68
  creating, 459–462
  definition, 297
  deploying, 461
  flat files, 297
  history of, 296–297
  object, 299
  ODBC (Object Database
    Connectivity), 317
  overview, 296–297

databases *(continued)*
    relational, 297–298. *See also* RDBMSs
        (relational database management
        services)
databases, connecting to. *See also* data
        binding
    ADO.NET
        closing, 407–408
        Connection object, 402–403
        connection objects, 403–404
        connection pooling, 404, 408
        connection strings, 408–413
        opening, 404–406
        Using blocks, 407–408
    source code, 704–705, 707–708
    SQL Server 2005, 448
    tables
        change scripts, 463
        columns, 297
        creating, 462–463
        definition, 297
        foreign keys, 298
        fully qualified names, 307
        keys, 297–298
        primary keys, 297–298
        relating to other tables, 297–298
        rows, 297
    views, 464–465
    Visual Database Tools, 459–465
    in Windows applications, 314–317 data
databases, querying. *See also* reading data;
        selecting data
    creating, 371, 464–465
    CRUD statements, 371
    executing, 414–417
    with LINQ, 468–470
    Query Builder, 451–452
    Query Designer, 464–465
    Query tool, 355
    SQL Server 2005, 445, 464–465
    TableAdapter Query Configuration
        Wizard, 371
databound controls, 318–320, 328–336,
        340–342, 379–380. *See also* data
        binding
DataColumn object, 347
DataGridView control, 295, 318–320

DataList control, 295, 328
DataMember property, 321, 323
DataReaders, 294, 400, 402–403
DataRelation object, 347
DataRow object, 347
DataSet Designer. *See also*
        TableAdapters
    creating data sources, 336–339
    data access, 296
    DataTable tool, 355
    Query tool, 355
    Relation tool, 355
    retrieving data, 336–339
    strongly typed DataSets, 355–364
    TableAdapter tool, 355
    toolbox, 355
    updating data, 336–339
datasets, 311
DataSets. *See also* strongly typed
        DataSets; TableAdapters
    Constraint object, 347
    converting to XML, 351
    creating, 337–339, 349. *See also* DataSet
        Designer; strongly typed DataSets,
        creating
    CRUD statements, 366, 371–372. *See also*
        TableAdapter Query Configuration
        Wizard
    as data source, 339
DataAdapter services, 425–426
DataColumn object, 347
DataRelation object, 347
DataRow object, 347
DataTable object, 347
    definition, 400
DeleteCommand property, 426, 428–430
    deleting data, 367
    description, 294
    explicit transactions, 432
    filing, 426–428, 432–433
    implicit transactions, 431–432
InsertCommand property, 426, 428–430
    inserting data, 366
    monitoring, 636
    objects, 347
OdbcDataAdapter object, 426
OleDbDataAdapter object, 426
OracleDataAdapter object, 426

queries, creating, 371
retrieving data, 430–432
reusing, 339
SelectCommand property, 426
selecting data, 367. *See also* TableAdapter
    Query Configuration Wizard
sorting output, 372–374
SqlDataAdapter object, 426
stored procedures. *See also* TableAdapter
    Configuration Wizard
  anatomy of, 366
  binding to existing procedures, 370
  creating, 367–369
  CRUD statements, 366, 371–372. *See also*
    TableAdapter Query Configuration
    Wizard
  definition, 365
  DELETE command, 367
  deleting data, 367
  INSERT command, 366
  inserting data, 366
  naming, 367
  reading data, 367
  SELECT command, 367
  selecting data, 367
  sp prefix, 367
  versus SQL statements, 365–367
  strongly typed DataSets, 362–363
  UPDATE command, 367
  updating data, 367
  usp prefix, 367
structure of, 347
synchronizing with XML documents, 433
table relationships, creating, 355, 357–360
TableAdapters, 430–431
transactions, 431–432
typed versus untyped, 348. *See also*
    strongly typed DataSets
untyped, 348–350
updating data, 367, 426–431
uses for, 346
XML data sources, 351
XML documents, creating, 432–433
XML Schema, creating, 432–433
XML schemas, creating, 378
DataSource property, 321, 323, 409
DataTable object, 347

DataTable tool, 355
date pickers. *See* controls
Davis, Stephen, 60
Deactivate event, 560
debug build configurations, 660
debug mode, 212
debugging
  breakpoints, 627, 628–630
  enabling, 626–627
  generated code, 638
  monitoring DataSets, 636
  PDB (program database) files, 626–627
  special circumstances, 637–638
  SQL Server projects, 458
  starting, 627–628
  stepping through code, 627, 630–633
  stopping, 627
  viewing data, 633–637
  visualizers, 635
  Watch window, 636–637
  windows for, 633–634
default button, 146
DefaultButton property, 146
DELETE command, 367
DeleteCommand property, 426, 428–430
deploying
  assemblies, 43–46
  databases, 461
  overview, 675–676
  precompiling Web sites, 696
  projects, 662
  with Publish Web Site utility, 697–698
  sharing assemblies, 693–695
  Smart Client applications
    accessing applications, 680, 681
    ClickOnce strategy, 677–680
    code signing, 683–687
    consuming applications, 680–681
    publishing options, 682–683
    removing applications, 681–682
    updating applications, 687–688
  software under CLR, 49–50
  strategies for, 676
  unit of deployment, 43–46
  Web applications, 695–699
  web.config files, 698–699
  with Windows Installer, 688–693

deployment stage, 34
deprecated code, 116
`Design` category, 145
design stage, 34
Design view, 208
designers
  See also Class Designer
  See also `DataSet` Designer
  See also Web Forms Designer
  See also Windows Forms Designer
  Application Designer, 76
  Component Designer view, 208
  Crystal Reports, 102
  Logical Datacenter Designer, 76–77
  SharePoint Designer, 187
  for smart devices, 102
design-time properties, 145
.dess file extension, 285
destructors, 531
`DetailsView` control, 295, 328
Developer Edition, SQL Server 2005,
    438–442
developers
  blogs, 743–744. *See also* online
    communities
  building a toolbox, 38
  learning to program, 63–66
  partnerships, 39–40
  roles in a project, 39–40
  VSTS, Software Developers Edition, 77,
    753–754
device emulators, 283–287
dialog boxes, 135, 150–154. *See also specific
    dialog boxes*
Dialog Editor, 184
`Diff` command, 716
disabled persons, help for. *See*
    accessibility
disconnected data source model, 293–294
discovering events, 553–554
displaying
  class diagrams, 547–548
  classes in tree view, 89
  data, 294–295
  properties, 98–99

reports, 720
server configuration, 99–100. *See also*
    Server Explorer
servers in tree view, 90
Solution Explorer commands, 96–98
tabbed documents, 92
DLL hell, 46
`Dock` property, 156, 168, 169–171
Dockable option, 91
docking
  controls, 168, 169–171
  tabbed documents, 91–92
  windows, 91–92
Document Explorer, 109–111
documentation, 585–589. *See also* help
documenting code, 585–589
dot-net community, 22
`DotNetNuke` starter kit, 212
drag and drop
  creating strongly typed `DataSets`,
    360–362
  for data access
    preparing for, 299–300
    Web Forms, 304–308
    Windows Form, 300–304
drag-and-drop events, 145
`DragDrop` category, 145
`DropeSynonymsDbo.sql` script, 445

E

Eclipse, 16
Edit DataSet with Designer command, 311
Edit Items, 156
editing
  ASP.NET code, 211
  data, 340–342, 380
  files in source code control, 711–713
  menu controls, 156–157
editors. *See also* Code Editor
  Dialog Editor, 184
  Eclipse, 16
  Menu Editor, 184
  String Editor, 184
`EditorZone`, 270

Embed in ToolStripContainer, 156
emulating smart devices, 283–287
encapsulation, 528
"The End of DLL Hell," 46
enumerations, 502
environment settings. *See* properties
error indicator, Code Editor, 484
errors. *See* exceptions
event handlers
  creating, 145
  definition, 552
  discovering events, 553–554
  for nondefault events, 558–559
  registering, 557–558
  setting, 148
  Visual C++, 185
  wiring up, 556–559
events. *See also* event handlers
  class member, 531
  consuming, 553
  discovering, 553–554
  drag and drop, 145
  examples of, 551
  focus, 145
  Help documentation, 555–556
  keyboard, 145
  listing, 554–555
  mouse, 145
  nesting, 560
  nondefault, handlers for, 558–559
  sending, 553
  sequence of, 560
  shutdown, 559–561
  startup, 559–561
  tools for, 553
  Web page life cycle, 562–564
  Windows applications, 559–561
  wiring up, 556–559
exception handlers, 618–619
exceptions
  available, listing, 624–626
  catching, 619–622
  definition, 617–618
  properties, 621–622
  structured handling, 618–619
  throwing, 622–624
  unhandled, 618
executable statements, 487–489, 491

ExecuteNonQuery method, 414
ExecuteReader method, 414
ExecuteScalar method, 414
executing
  under CLR, 49–50
  CLR routines, 457–458
  database queries, 414–417
  managed code, 46–50
  scripts, 452–453
  Visual Studio, the first time, 85–87
explicit transactions, 432
Express Edition, 68–69, 71, 438
expressions, binding to properties,
    342–343
Extensible Application Markup Language
    (XAML), 771–772
eXtensible Markup Language (XML). *See* XML
extensions. *See also* AJAX (Asynchronous
    JavaScript And XML); Atlas; plug-ins
  administration tools, 739–740
  AJAX, 217–222
  developer blogs, 743–744
  development resources, 741–743
  new server products, 741–743
  Office, 740–741
  troubleshooting tools, 739–740
  Vista, 740–741

F

fat clients, 129. *See also* Smart Client
Favorites feature, 106
Field Explorer, 731–734
fields
  C#, 491–492
  class member, 531
  in reports, 731–734
  Visual Basic, 491–492
file system sites, 191
files. *See also* items
  browsing from dialog boxes, 153
  formats, 66
  saving from dialog boxes, 153
  source code control
    checking in, 713
    checking out, 711–713
    editing, 711–713

files *(continued)*
  locking, 712
  retrieving, 710–711
  versioning, 710–711, 716–717
  storage, Vista, 767
  types of, 94
filing DataSets, 426–428, 432–433
filtering help, 105, 108
Finally statements, 618–619
financial calculations, data types for, 501
find and replace, Code Editor, 479–481
flat files, 297
Floating option, 91
FlowLayoutPanel control, 166
Focus category, 145
focus events, 145
FolderBrowserDialog dialog box, 153
folders
  adding to Web sites, 198
  browsing from dialog boxes, 153
  reserved, 198
FontDialog dialog box, 153
fonts, 145, 153
FooterTemplate, 331–334
foreign keys, 298
<form> control, 205–206
Format Editor, 734–736
formatting
  Code Editor, 100, 478–479
  controls, 138–140
  reports, 734–736
FormBorderStyle property, 150
FormClosed event, 560
FormClosing event, 560
forms. *See* Web Forms; Windows Form;
    Windows Forms Designer
FormView control, 295, 328
freeing memory, 51–53. *See also* garbage
    collection
from clause, 468–470
FTP sites, 191
fully qualified names, 307
Function statements, 487
FxCop, 572–577

G

GAC (Global Assembly Cache), 46
garbage collection, 50–53
generated code, 211, 374, 638
generations, memory, 52–53. *See also*
    garbage collection
GET requests, 601, 602–603
Getting Started, 89
goals, 641–642
Grasshopper plug-in, 16
gridlines. *See* snaplines
GridView control, 328, 340–342
GripStyle property, 156
GroupBox control, 166
grouping
  controls, 134, 166–168
  items, 94
  tabbed documents, 92
  validation controls, 231

H

HandleCreated event, 559
HasValue property, 516
Hawaii, 28, 78
header, in classes, 530
Header Files folder, 179
HeaderTemplate, 331–334
heap, 497–498
Height element, 247
help
  Ask a Question, 106–107
  collections, 82–83
  for commands, 98
  Contents, 105
  for disabled persons, 145, 208
  Favorites, 106
  filtering, 105, 108
  Getting Started, 89
  How Do I?, 106
  Index, 105
  mobile applications, 277
  MSDN News, 89
  MSDN subscriptions, 71–72

navigating, 105–107
online communities, 111–114, 743–744
opening, 105–107
for properties, 146
Search, 105
searching, 108
smart devices, 277
Sync with Table of Contents, 106–107
topic context, displaying, 107
viewing options, setting, 104
Visual Studio Headlines, 89
Windows Mobile support page, 277
Help Collection Manager, 82–83
Hide option, 91
hierarchical code organization. *See*
    namespaces
Highlight Expert, 735
Holzner, Steve, 744
home page, 89, 110–111
hosting, 562, 749
hotshot development, 31
How Do I?, 106
HTML
    controls, 201, 202–203
    interaction with JavaScript, 215
    server controls, 198, 200–203
HTTP (HyperText Transfer Protocol),
    326–327
Hummel, Joe, 39
Hungarian notation, 571–572
hyperlinks, adding to pages, 210–211

1

`Icon` property, 150
icons
    lightning bolt, 553
    in this book, 9
implementation stage, 34
implicit transactions, 431–432
`Imports` statement, 486–487
indenting code, 477–478
Index feature, 105

indexed data types, 509–511
indexers, 531
indexes, arrays, 507
information hiding, 529
inheritance, 529, 533–534
initializing variables, 495–496
initiation stage, 34
inline code, 211
input from users, validating. *See* validation
    controls
`INSERT` command, 366
Insert Standard Items, 156
`InsertCommand` property, 426, 428–430
inserting data, 366
installing Visual Studio. *See* Professional
    Edition, installing
instances of objects, 403
integration tests, 37, 640
IntelliSense
    Code Editor, 483–484
    code snippets, 577–579
    code stubs, 580
    object-oriented code, 582–585
    `using` statements, 581
interfaces, to classes, 530, 583–584
interfaces, to users. *See* UI (user interface)
`IsMdiContainer` property, 150
items, 94, 98. *See also* files
items, grouping. *See* projects; solutions
`ItemTemplate`, 331–334
iterating through arrays and collections,
    511–512
iterative development, 33
iterative SDLC stages, 35

#

J#, 61–62
Java
    converting to C++, 59
    converting to .NET assemblies, 61
    versus JavaScript, 215
Java Language Conversion Assistant,
    124–125

JavaScript
  document fetch, 216
  interaction with HTML, 215
  versus Java, 215
  returned XML data, 217
  server requests, 215–216
  XMLHttpRequest object, 215–216
JIT (just-in-time) compilation, 14
JLCA (Java Language Conversion
    Assistant), 59
JScript, with AJAX, 62
JVM (Java Virtual Machine), 47–48

K

Key category, 145
keyboard events, 145
keyed data types, 509–511
keys, 297–298
keywords, value types, 500–502

L

Label command, 717
Label Web control, 203
Language Integrated Query (LINQ),
    467–472
languages. *See* programming languages
launching. *See* executing
layers, ASP.NET, 254–256
Layout event, 560
Layout property, 145
Layout toolbar, 138–140
Left element, 247
legacy software, 40–42
libraries
  ATL (Active Template Library), 176
  BCL (Base Class Library), 25, 29
  for C++ applications, 176
  class, 119–120, 352–353, 378–379
  Class Library template, 177
  Visual C++, 60
  Windows Forms Control Library
    template, 178
life cycles
  SDLC (software development
    life cycle), 34–35

Web pages, 562–568
  Windows applications, 559–561
lightning bolt icon, 553
line numbering, Code Editor, 484–485
LINQ (Language Integrated Query),
    467–472
LinqDataSource control, 328
list boxes. *See* controls
Load event, 559
local IIS sites, 191
local working folder, setting, 703–704
locking
  controls, 138, 141
  files in source code control, 712
Logical Datacenter designer, 76–77
Login controls, 265
login page, setting up, 265–267
Login.aspx, 265
LoginName control, 265
LoginStatus control, 265
LoginView control, 265
look and feel
  See CSS (Cascading Style Sheets)
  See customizing
  See master pages
  See properties
  See styles
  See themes

M

macros, Code Editor, 100
Main procedure, 489
MainMenuStrip property, 146, 150
maintenance stage, 35
Makefile Application Wizard, 178
managed applications, 180–181, 767
managed code
  definition, 47
  executing, 46–50
  versus native code, 47
  smart devices, 274
  SQL Server projects, 453
  Visual C++, 176
margin properties, 145
Margin property, 169
margins, controls, 169, 172–173

mashups, 745

master builds, 673

master pages. *See also* CSS (Cascading
Style Sheets); styles; themes
- accessing, 243–245
- adding to Web sites, 240
- content, adding, 240–241
- content pages, adding, 242–243
- converting from Web pages, 243–245
- copyright information, 241–242
- definition, 234
- versus regular pages, 240
- title element, 244

MDI (Multiple Document Interface), 150

members
- adding to classes, 540–543
- C#, 487, 491–492
- list of, 531
- overriding, 533–534, 584–585
- Visual Basic, 487, 491–492

Members.aspx, 265

membership
- configuring, 263–264
- default database, configuring, 260–261
- IIS, setting up, 261–262
- login page, setting up, 265–267
- securing content, 263–264
- user registration, 267

memory. *See also* garbage collection
- allocating, 52
- common errors, 51
- freed, trying to use, 51
- freeing, 51–53
- generations, 52–53
- releasing, 51

menu bar, 90

Menu control, 232

Menu Editor, 184

menus. *See also specific menus*
- adding to forms, 155–156
- configuring, 155–156
- context sensitive, 90, 150, 155
- control, setting, 150
- controls
  - ContextMenuStrip, 150, 155
  - editing, 156–157
  - embedding in a
    ToolStripContainer, 156
  - GripStyle property, 156
  - items, adding, 156, 157–158
  - items collection, editing, 158–159
  - location, setting, 156
  - move handles, displaying, 156
  - multiple per form, 159–160
  - RenderMode property, 156, 160–162
  - smart-tag enabled, 156
  - style, setting, 156, 160–162
  - ToolStrip, 155, 158
  - ToolStripContainer, 155, 156,
    159–160
  - ToolStripManager, 162
- primary menu control, 146
- solutions, 98

MenuStrip control, 155, 158

Merge command, 716

messages, displaying, 203

metadata, 291

method stubs, 580

methods
- C#, 491–492
- class member, 531
- declaring, 542–543
- static, 548–550
- Visual Basic, 491–492

MFC (Microsoft Foundation Classes), 176

MFC ActiveX Control Wizard, 178

MFC Application Wizard, 178

MFC DLL Wizard, 179

Microsoft. *See also specific products*
- Access databases, 401
- certification, 112–113
- Expressions, 187
- mobile strategy, 272
- Office 2007, 740–741, 775–779
- patterns and practices, 38
- Web application tools, 187

mobile applications, 196–198

mobile Web applications. *See also* smart
devices
- automating connections, 285–287
- batch files, 285–287

mobile Web applications *(continued)*
  cradled devices, connecting to, 283–284
  device emulators, 283–287
  "Hello World" example, 282–283
  need for, 275
  overview, 281
  site setup, 281–283
  viewing your site, 284–287
mocks (mock objects), 649–650
modal dialog boxes, 150–151
modeless dialog boxes, 150–151
modifiers, in classes, 530
monolithic software, 41
Mouse category, 145
mouse events, 145
move handles, displaying, 156
MSBuild, 674
MSDN News, 89
MSDN subscriptions, 71–73
MSDN Webcasts, 39
Mueller, John, 535
Multiple Document Interface (MDI), 150
multi-tiered applications, 401
My object, 492

N

Name property, 146, 150
names
  classes, 530
  controls, 146
namespaces. *See also* using statements
  browsing data types, 518–519
  collections, 506
  declarations, 487
  description, 45
  directives, 524
  shortcuts to, 524
  System.Collections, 506, 509–511
  System.Collections.Generic, 511
  System.Collections.
    Specialized, 511
  System.XML, 397
  Web services, 599–600
naming
  code, conventions for, 569–572
  stored procedures, 367

variables, 494–495
  Web services, 598–599
  Windows Form, 150
NAnt, 674
native code
  versus managed code, 47
  smart devices, 274
  Visual C++, 177
navigation
  Code Editor, 485–486
  controls, 232–234
  help documents, 105–107
Navigation bar, 485–486
nesting events, 560
.NET
  communities, 111–114
  compiler, 24
  component management, 43–45
  components, 24–25
  definition, 24
  dot-net community, 22
  future of, 27–28
  history of, 21–23
  new features, 29
  previous versions, specifying, 125–126
  programming languages
    choosing, 62–63
    defaults, 57
    J#, 61–62
    from Microsoft, 26
    Microsoft comparison, 63
    supported, 24
    Visual Basic, 57–59
    Visual C#, 59
    Visual C++, 60–61
  targeting, 24
  versions, 21–22
  XML resources, 396–397
.NET 2.0, 122, 125–126
.NET 3.0, 122
.NET 3.5
  backwards compatibility, 122
  configuring Web applications for, 123
  downloading, 28
  for Vista applications, 27
.NET Framework data providers. *See*
    ADO.NET, data providers

.NET Framework Redistributable, 19
.NET SDK, 14, 24
new operator, 495, 497
New Project dialog box, 94–96
NMock, 655
non-executable statements, 486–487
Northwind database. *See* Adventure Works database
n-tier design, 42–43
null values, 516
NUnit testing framework, 654

O

object databases, 299. *See also* databases
Object Test Bench (OTB), 548–550, 651–654
ObjectDataSource control, 328
objects. *See also* OOP (object-oriented programming); OTB (Object Test Bench); *specific objects*
  ADO.NET, 403
  C#, 490
  versus classes, 527
  creating, 548–550
  instances of, 403
  mocks (mock objects), 649–650
  Visual Basic, 490
ODBC (Object Database Connectivity), 317
OdbcConnectionStringBuilder, 413
OdbcDataAdapter object, 426
OdbcDataReader object, 417–420
Office 2007, 740–741, 775–779
offline data storage, 294
OleDbConnectionStringBuilder, 413
OleDbDataAdapter object, 426
OleDbDataReader object, 417–420
On the Web icon, 9
online communities, 111–114, 743–744
OOA (object-oriented analysis), 526
OOD (object-oriented design), 526
OOP (object-oriented programming), 37, 525–529. *See also* classes; code, object-oriented; objects
OpenFileDialog dialog box, 153

opening
  ADO.NET database connections, 404–406
  files in Code Editor, 476
  help, 105–107
  projects, source code control, 714
  properties, 144
  Properties window, 144
  windows, 90
operators, 531
options. *See* properties
OracleConnectionStringBuilder, 413
OracleDataAdapter object, 426
OracleDataReader object, 417–420
OTB (Object Test Bench), 548–550, 651–654
outlining with Code Editor, 100, 482–483
overriding members, 584–585

P

padding controls, 138, 169, 172–173
Padding property, 169
page events, 562
page setup events, 564
Page_Init event, 563
Page_Load event, 563
Page_PrcInit event, 563
Page_PreRender event, 563
Page_Render event, 563
PagerTemplate, 331–334
PageSetupDialog dialog box, 153
Page_Unload event, 563
paging data, 335, 340
Panel control, 167
papers. *See* publications
partial classes, 375–377
partial clauses, 211
partial page update patterns, 219–222
partial page updates, 214–217
Pascal casing, 570
PasswordRecovery, 265
passwords, 265
patterns, 38, 219–222
PayPal-enabled eCommerce starter kit, 212
PDAs. *See* smart devices
PDB (program database) files, 626–627

performance improvement. *See* AJAX Web
  applications
personalization layer, 270
personalizing. *See* customizing
Pin command, 717
placeholders. *See* stubs
plug-ins, 16. *See also* extensions
Pocket PC versus Smartphone, 272
pocket PCs, 272, 274. *See also* smart
  devices
polymorphism, 529
Position absolute element, 247
Position relative element, 247
POST requests, 601, 603–604
postback events, 564–566
postbacks
  architecture, 214
  avoiding, 190
  definition, 190, 562
  delays, 214–217
.prc file extension, 450
precompiling Web sites, 696
preconfigured dialog boxes, 153
preferences. *See* customizing; properties
presentation layer, 42
previewing reports, 733–734
primary keys, 297–298
primitive data types, 500
print preview, 153
PrintDialog dialog box, 153
printer setup, 153
printing controls, 135
PrintPreviewDialog dialog box, 153
procedures
  C#, 491–492
  Visual Basic, 487, 491–492
Professional certification, 113
Professional Edition
  cost, 71
  description, 70
  installing
    over beta versions, 81
    environment settings, 85–87
    help collections, 82–83
    launching the installed program, 85–87
    with other versions, 81–83

over prerelease versions, 81
step-by-step, 84–85
system requirements, 83–84
profiles, ASP.NET, 268–269
program database (PDB) files, 626–627
programming. *See* code; software
  development; software engineering
programming constructs, 64
programming languages
  See also CLR (Common Language
    Runtime)
  See also JVM (Java Virtual Machine)
  See also .NET, programming languages
  See also specific languages
  assembly, 57
  definition, 13
  file formats, 66
  history of, 57
  learning to program, 63–66
  programming constructs, 64
  syntax, 64–65
  Web development standards, 66
programs. *See* software development;
  specific applications
Project Designer, 669–671
project management, 38. *See also* VSTS
  (Visual Studio Team System)
projects. *See also* builds; solutions
  adding items to, 98
  configuring, 669–671
  contextual menus, 98
  creating, 94–96, 759–761
  definition, 94, 660
  deploying, 662
  help for commands, 98
  properties, 669–671
  property pages, 671
  source code control
    adding to solutions, 707
    default folder, changing, 703
    opening, 714
    retrieving, 714
  templates, 95
  type, specifying, 95

properties. *See also* configuring
  anchor, 145
  binding to data, 324–326, 342–343
  binding to expressions, 342–343
  borders, 145
  cancel button, 146
  class member, 531
  colors, 145
  control behavior, setting, 145
  control names, 146
  control text, 146
  cursor style, 145
  data source, setting, 145
  default button, 146
  design-time, 145
  displaying, 98–99
  elements, 144
  fonts, 145
  help, 146
  layout, 145
  margin, 145
  opening, 144
  setting, 146–147
  size, 145
  Web server controls, 334–336
Properties window, 144–146. *See also*
    events; properties
property pages, 671
Property statements, 487
prototyping, 37. *See also* whiteboarding
provider-independent code, 402
providers, definition, 254
Providers layer, 254
proxy class, 613
public methods, in unit tests, 647
publications
  Ajax For Dummies, 744
  C++ For Dummies, 60
  "The End of DLL Hell," 46
  Visio 2007 For Dummies, 535
Publish Web Site utility, 697–698

Q

Query Builder, 451–452
Query Designer, 464–465
Query tool, 355

querying databases. *See also* reading data;
    selecting data
  creating, 371, 464–465
  CRUD statements, 371
  executing, 414–417
  with LINQ, 468–470
  Query Builder, 451–452
  Query Designer, 464–465
  Query tool, 355
  SQL Server 2005, 445, 464–465
  TableAdapter Query Configuration
    Wizard, 371
question mark (?), shortcut operator, 516

R

radio buttons. *See* controls
RangeValidator control, 226
rank, arrays, 507
Rational Unified Process (RUP), 34, 38
RDBMSs (relational database management
    services)
  elements of, 299
  foreign keys, 298
  keys, 297–298
  primary keys, 297–298
readability, 41
reading data, 367. *See also* databases,
    querying; retrieving data; selecting
    data
reading data, ADO.NET
  all commands in a row, 424
  by column index, 423–424
  by column name, 423–424
  DataReaders
    description, 400
    features and services, 402–403
    Get accessors, 421–425
    GetSchemaTable method, 425
    GetValues method, 424–425
    objects, 417–420
    Read method, 420–421
    setting up, 418–420
  firehose cursor, 417
  GetOrdinal method, 423
  Item method, 423
  in native format, 421–422
  OdbcDataReader object, 417–420

reading data, ADO.NET *(continued)*
  `OleDbDataReader` object, 417–420
  `OracleDataReader` object, 417–420
  schemas, 425, 432
  `SqlDataReader` object, 417–420
  stepping through data, 420–421
  with typed accessors, 421–422
receiving events. *See* consuming, events
refactoring
  C# code, 592–594
  with Class Designer, 545–546, 591–592
  definition, 589
  Visual Studio options, 590–591
reference types, 497–503, 516
reflexive table relationships, 357
`Refresh` command, 311
region directives, 482–483
registering event handlers, 557–558
`Registration.aspx`, 265
`RegularExpressionValidator`
  control, 226
`Relation` tool, 355
relational databases, 297–298. *See also*
  databases; RDBMSs (relational
  database management services)
relationships between tables, 355, 357–360
release build configurations, 660
release mode, 212
releasing memory, 51. *See also* garbage
  collection
Remember icon, 9
remote server sites, 191
renaming. *See* naming
rendering, 562
`RenderMode` property, 156, 160–162
`Repeater` control, 295, 328
Report Designer, 720, 730–736
Report Viewer, 720
reports. *See also* Crystal Reports
  adding content to, 730–736
  charts, 734
  connecting to data sources, 725–730
  creating, 720–724, 731
  customizing, 731–736
  data binding, 725–730
  designer for, 102
  exporting, 720

  fields, 731–734
  formatting, 734–736
  previewing, 733–734
  sections, 730, 732–733, 735
  viewing, 720
`ReportViewer` control, 295
`RequiredFieldValidator` control, 226
requirements gathering, 34
reserved folders, 198
resizing windows, 150
Resource Files folder, 179
resource management, 184–186
retrieving data
  ADO.NET, data sources, 293–294
  ADO.NET, `DataSets`, 430–432
  data access, Web Forms, 336–339
  from data sources, 293–294, 339. *See also*
    `TableAdapters`
  DataSet Designer, 336–339
  storing retrieved data, 311
  transactions, 431–432
reusing code. *See* IntelliSense; snippets
reusing strongly typed `DataSets`, 378
Right element, 247
role-based editions, 748, 750–751
`Rollback` command, 717
root data type, 496
round trips. *See* postbacks
rounding errors, 501
rows, 297
RSS feeds, displaying, 110–111
rules, RDBMSs, 299
RUP (Rational Unified Process), 34, 38

S

`SaveFileDialog` dialog box, 153
schemas
  ADO.NET, reading data, 425, 432
  Adventure Works database, 445
  validating, 208
  XML, 377–378, 387. *See also* XML Schema
SCM (software configuration management),
  715–716
scope creep, 32
`ScriptAs` command, 444
scripts, SQL Server 2005, 444–453

SDKs (software development kits), 14, 24
SDLC (software development life cycle), 35
Search feature, 105
Search page, Document Explorer, 109
second system syndrome, 32
Section Expert, 735
sections, in reports, 730, 732–733, 735
security, smart devices, 288
SEI (Software Engineering Institute), 38
select clause, 468–470
SELECT command, 367
SelectCommand property, 426
selecting data, 367. *See also* databases,
    querying; reading data
sending events, 553
server controls
    .asp tag prefix, 200
    buttons, HTML control, 201, 202–203
    buttons, Web control, 199–200, 202–203
    calendars, 206–207
    composite, 205
    custom, 203
    displaying messages, 203
    <form>, 205–206
    HTML, 198, 200–203
    Label Web, 203
    life cycle, 562
    syntax, 199–200
    types of, 198–199
    user, 190, 203–207
    validation, 190
    Web, 198–203
Server Explorer
    browsing servers, 99–100
    creating databases, 459–462
    displaying, 90
servers
    See also ASP.NET pages, server controls
    See also SQL Server 2005
    See also TFS (Team Foundation Server)
    browsing, 99–100. *See also* Server
        Explorer
    client/server architecture, 42
    configuration details, displaying, 99–100
    displaying in tree view, 90
    new products, 741–743
server-side statement management, 256

Services layer, 254
session state, 259
settings. *See* properties
Share command, 716
SharePoint Designer, 187
shortcut menus. *See* context sensitive
    menus
showing. *See* displaying
ShowInTaskBar property, 150
Shown event, 560
shutdown events, 559–561
Simonyl, Charles, 572
site maps, 232–233
<sitemap> node, 232
SiteMapDataSource control, 328
<sitemapnode> node, 232
SiteMapPath control, 232
sizing
    controls, 145, 169, 172
    windows, 150
skins, 235–239. *See also* themes
Smart Client applications
    accessing applications, 680–681
    ClickOnce strategy, 677–680
    code signing, 683–687
    consuming applications, 680–681
    publishing options, 682–683
    removing applications, 681–682
    updating applications, 687–688
Smart Device Project template, 178
smart devices
    ActiveSync issues, 287
    battery life issues, 288
    CAB files, 276
    categories, 272
    characteristics of, 130
    creating, 131–133
    data access, 275
    definition, 271
    designer for, 102
    development differences, 275–276
    features, 130
    "Hello World" example, 132–133
    help, 277
    history of, 129–130
    managed code, 274

smart devices *(continued)*
  Microsoft mobile strategy, 272
  mobile Web applications
    automating connections, 285–287
    batch files, 285–287
    cradled devices, connecting to, 283–284
    device emulators, 283–287
    "Hello World" example, 282–283
    need for, 275
    overview, 281
    site setup, 281–283
    viewing your site, 284–287
  native code, 274
  platform, selecting, 273–274
  pocket PCs, 272, 274
  security issues, 288
  smartphones
    C++ applications, 280–281
    creating an application, 277–279
    definition, 272
    development issues, 274
    "Hello World" example, 276–281
    platform, changing, 280
    required downloads, 276
    Smartphone versus Pocket PC, 272
    Windows Mobile support page, 277
  special considerations, 274, 287–288
  Tablet PC, 272
  ubiquitous embedded devices, 272
  Windows CE, 272, 274
  Windows devices, 273
  Windows Embedded, 272
  Windows Mobile, 272
smart indenting, Code Editor, 477–478
smart tags, 143, 156
Smartphone versus Pocket PC, 272
smartphones. *See also* smart devices
  C++ applications, 280–281
  creating an application, 277–279
  definition, 272
  development issues, 274
  "Hello World" example, 276–281
  platform, changing, 280
  required downloads, 276
  Smartphone versus Pocket PC, 272
  Windows Mobile support page, 277

smoke test, 644
snaplines, 140–141
`.snippet` file extension, 578
snippet files, 578
snippets, 389–391, 577–579
`SOAP`, 601, 604–608
Software Architect Edition, 76–77, 751–753
software configuration management
    (SCM), 715–716
software developers. *See* developers
Software Developers Edition, 77, 753–754
software development. *See also* code;
    software engineering
  ad hoc approach, 31
  architecture evolution, 42–43
  best practices, 37
  client/server architecture, 42
  code generation, 55
  common problems, 31–32
  component approach, 40–42
  hotshot approach, 31
  legacy software, 40–42
  life cycle, 35
  monolithic software, 41
  n-tier design, 42–43
  readability, 41
  resources, 38–39
software development kits (SDKs), 14, 24
software engineering. *See also* software
    development
  Agile, 34
  best practices, 33, 36–37
  definition, 34
  iterative model, 33
  processes, 33–34
  RUP (Rational Unified Process), 34
  scope creep, 32
  second system syndrome, 32
  test-driven, 34
  waterfall model, 33
Software Engineering Body of Knowledge
    (SWEBOK), 38, 715
Software Engineering Institute (SEI), 38
software factories, 28
Software Testers edition, 755–756
Solution Explorer, 89, 96–98

solutions. *See also* builds; projects; Solution Explorer
  adding items to, 98
  configuring, 669–671
  creating, 94–96
  definition, 94, 660
  menus, 98
  properties, 669–671
  property pages, 671
  source code control, 705–707, 714
  templates, 95
  type, specifying, 95
sorting data, 340, 372–374
source code, 522–523. *See also* Code Editor
source code control
  artifacts, 715–716
  binding source code, 704–705
  code database connection, 704–705, 707–708
  commands, 709, 716–717
  common tasks, 708–709
  default projects folder, changing, 703
  description, 702
  elements of, 701–702
  files
    checking in, 713
    checking out, 711–713
    editing, 711–713
    locking, 712
    retrieving, 710–711
    versioning, 710–711, 716–717
  local working folder, setting, 703–704
  preparing for, 702–704
  projects, 707, 714
  SCM (software configuration management), 715–716
  software for, 38
  solutions, 705–707, 714
  unbinding source code, 707–708
  version control, 710–711, 716–717
  visual clues, 709–710
  work products, 715–716
Source Code Editor. *See* Code Editor
Source Files folder, 179
Source view, 208–211

sp prefix, 367
spacing controls, 138, 169, 172–173
Sphar, Chuck, 60
SplitContainer control, 167
SQL CLR integration, 455
.sql file extension, 450
SQL Server 2005
  Books Online, 443–445
  database projects, 446–453
  database sample, 445
  Developer Edition, 438–442
  editions, 437–439
  Express Edition, 438
  ScriptAs command, 444
  scripts, creating, 444
  SQL Server Management Studio, 443–445
  SQL Server projects, 453–458
  unused features, disabling, 443–445
SQL Server Management Studio, 443–445
SQL Server Project template, 178
SQL Server Surface Area Configuration Tool, 443–445
SQL statements versus stored procedures, 365–367
SQL stored statements. *See* stored procedures
SqlConnectionStringBuilder, 413
SqlDataAdapter object, 426
SqlDataReader object, 417–420
SqlDataSource control, 328
stack, 497–498
stages of SDLC, 34–35
start page, 89, 110–111
starter kits, 212
StartPosition property, 150
startup events, 559–561
state management, 256–259
statements. *See also specific statements*
  C# language, 486–491
  CRUD, 366, 371–372
  executable, 487–489, 491
  non-executable, 486–487
  Visual Basic, 486–491
static classes, 548–550
StatusStrip control, 155, 158

stepping through code, 627, 630–633
stored procedures
  ADO.NET, 415–417
  anatomy of, 366
  binding to existing procedures, 370
  creating, 367–369
  CRUD statements, 366, 371–372
  definition, 365
  DELETE command, 367
  deleting data, 367
  INSERT command, 366
  inserting data, 366
  naming, 367
  reading data, 367
  SELECT command, 367
  selecting data, 367
  sp prefix, 367
  versus SQL statements, 365–367
  strongly typed DataSets, 362–363
  UPDATE command, 367
  updating data, 367
  usp prefix, 367
String Editor, 184
strings, 501–502
strong typing, 350
strongly typed DataSets. *See also*
    DataSets
  classes, 375
  code, viewing, 374, 377–378
  columns, adding, 356
  constraints, adding, 356–357
  creating. *See also* DataSet Designer
    in class libraries, 352–353, 378–379
    from database objects, 360–362
    with drag and drop, 360–362
    in existing projects, 354
    for Windows Form, 378–379
  data types, 350
  with databound controls, 379–380
  definition, 350
  editing data, 380
  extending, 375–377
  generated code, changing and viewing, 374
  partial classes, 375–377
  reusing, 378

stored procedures, adding, 362–363
tables, 355–360
updating data, 380
views, adding, 363–364
versus weakly typed, 350
XML schemas, 377–378
strongly typed languages, 494–495
structured exception handling, 618–619
structures, value types, 502
stubs, 580
styles. *See also* CSS (Cascading Style
    Sheets)
  menu controls, 156, 160–162
  XSLT, 391–394
Sub statements, 487
supplementary content, 392–394
SWEBOK (Software Engineering Body of
    Knowledge), 38, 715
symbols, Code Editor, 480
Sync with Table of Contents, 106–107
syntax, programming languages, 64–65
syntax assistance, Code Editor, 483–484
system tests, 640
System.Collections namespace, 506,
    509–511
System.Collections.Generic
    namespace, 511
System.Collections.Specialized
    namespace, 511
System.Object, 533–534
System.XML Namespace in .NET, 397

T

.tab file extension, 450
tab order, controls, 141–142
Tabbed Document option, 91
tabbed documents, 91–93
TabControl control, 167
Table Designer, 462–463
TableAdapter Configuration Wizard,
    365–372
TableAdapter Query Configuration Wizard,
    366–374

`TableAdapters`, 318, 355, 364–371, 430–431
`TableLayoutPanel` control, 167
tables
  change scripts, 463
  columns, 297
  creating, 462–463
  definition, 297
  foreign keys, 298
  fully qualified names, 307
  keys, 297–298
  primary keys, 297–298
  relating to other tables, 297–298
  rows, 297
  strongly typed `DataSet`s, 355–360
  untyped `DataSet`s, 349–350
Tablet PC, 272
tagging comments, 481
tags, XML, 381
Target Schema for Validation, 208
Team Explorer, 761–762
Team Foundation Server (TFS). See TFS
teams. See developers; TFS (Team Foundation Server); VSTS (Visual StudioTeam System)
Technical Stuff icon, 9
Technology certification, 113
templates. *See also* master pages
  databound controls, 331–334
  `FooterTemplate`, 331–334
  `HeaderTemplate`, 331–334
  `ItemTemplate`, 331–334
  `PagerTemplate`, 331–334
  for projects, 95
  for solutions, 95
  SQL Server 2005, 446
  SQL Server scripts, 446, 449–451
  style, setting, 333–334
  Visual C++, 177–179
  Web Forms, 331–334
  Web server controls, 331–334
  Windows Form, 178
  XML documentation, 586–588
  XSLT, 392–394
test cases, 643

test-driven development, 34
TestDriven.NET, 655
Testers Edition, 77
testing
  code. *See also* unit tests
    acceptance tests, 640
    best practices, 37
    integration tests, 640
    process description, 639–641
    profiles, 269
    smoke test, 644
    system tests, 640
    validation controls, 227–229
    VSTS, Software Testers edition, 755–756
  objects, 548–550, 651–654
  Web services, 601–608
  Web sites, 212
testing stage, 34
text boxes. *See* controls
text on controls, 146
`Text` property, 146, 150
TFS (Team Foundation Server)
  accessing, 757–759
  browsing resources, 761–762
  cost, 71
  features, 756–757
  hosting, 749
  Team Explorer, 761–762
  team projects, creating, 759–761
  work items, creating, 762–763
themes. *See also* CSS (Cascading Style Sheets)
  adding to Web sites, 236–237
  definition, 235
  elements, 235
  images, 235
  skins, 235–239
  as style sheets, 237
thin clients, 129–130. *See also* Smart Client
third-party controls, 137
third-party tools, 38
`throw` statements, 622–624
throwing exceptions, 622–624
Time Tracker starter kit, 212

Tip icon, 9
title bar caption, setting, 150
title element, master pages, 244
to-do list, Code Editor, 481–482
tools. *See also* editors
  administration, 739–740
  ADO.NET, 293
  AJAX Control Toolkit, 222–224
  ASP.NET, 256
  building a toolbox, 38
  configuration management, 15
  database connection, 459–465
  database queries, 355
  `DataTable`, 355
  events, 553
  .NET Software Development Kit (SDK), 24
  project management, 38
  `Query`, 355
  `Relation`, 355
  software development basics, 15
  source code control, 38
  `TableAdapter`, 355
  third party, 38
  troubleshooting, 739–740
  unit tests, 654–655
  Vista development, 768–770
  visual, 299
  Visual Database Tools, 459–465
  Visual Studio, 90, 296
  VSTO (Visual Studio Tools for Office), 28, 69, 71
  VSTS (Visual Studio Team System), 747–749
  Web applications, 187
`ToolStrip` control, 155, 158
`ToolStripContainer` control, 155, 156, 159–160
`ToolStripManager` control, 162
Top element, 247
transactions, 431–432
`TreeView` control, 232
`.trg` file extension, 451
troubleshooting tools, 739–740
`Try` statements, 618–619

U

ubiquitous embedded devices, 272
UDDI (Universal Description, Discovery, and Integration), 609, 612. *See also* WSDL
`.udt` file extension, 451
UI (user interface)
  See also controls
  See also dialog boxes
  See also menus
  See also Windows Form
  controls, 269–270
  MDI (Multiple Document Interface), 162–165
  Office 2007, 776
  Vista, 766–767
UML (Unified Modeling Language), 536–537
unbinding source code, 707–708
unhandled exceptions, 618
unit testing frameworks, 648, 654–655
unit tests. *See also* testing, code
  approaches to, 647–648
  automating, 654–655
  code improvements, 646–647
  code stubs, 648–649, 650
  creating, 642–644
  definition, 639
  displaying results of, 644–646
  goals, 641–642
  mocks (mock objects), 649–650
  public methods, 647
  running, 644–646
  test cases, 643
  tools for, 654–655
unmanaged code, 182–186, 767
untyped `DataSets`, 348–350
`UPDATE` command, 367
updating data, 295–296, 336–339, 367, 380
upgrading to .NET 3.5
  alternatives, 117
  ASP.NET considerations, 118
  deprecated code, 116
  issues, 116–117
  justification for, 115–116

keeping .NET 2.0, 125–126
from pre-.NET languages, 117–118
supporting old code, 116–117
.targets files, 126
undoing, 117
upgrading to .NET 3.5, migration strategies
class libraries, 119–120
copy and paste, 124
.NET Framework version, specifying, 122–124
preparation, 118–119
side-by-side Web applications, 122–124
Visual Studio converters, 124–125
Web applications, 120–124
Windows applications, 119–120
user input, validating. *See* validation controls
user interface (UI). *See* UI
user registration, 267
user server controls, 190, 203–207
Using blocks, 407–408
using statements, 486–487, 581–582
usp prefix, 367

V

validation controls, 225–231
validation server controls, 190
ValidationGroup property, 231
ValidationSummary control, 226
validator commands, 208
Value property, 516
value types, 497–502, 516
variables
C#, 489–490
data type, specifying, 494–495
declaring, 494–496
default values, 495
definition, 493
initializing, 495–496
naming, 494–495
new operator, 495
strongly typed languages, 494–495
Visual Basic, 489–490

version control, 710–711, 716–717
View Designer, 464–465
View menu, 90
view state, 257–259, 562
viewing. *See* displaying
views, databases, 464–465
virtual machines, 777–779. *See also* .NET
Vista
creating applications for, 768–775
development tools, 768–770
editions, 765–767
extensions, 740–741
file storage, 767
FxCop, 573
hardware requirements, 777–779
managed applications, 767
.NET 3.5, 27
SDK samples, 769–770
underlying technologies, 766–767
unmanaged applications, 767
user interface experience, 766–767
virtual machines, 777–779
WinFS, 767
workflow applications, 773–775
WPF samples, 770
XAML (Extensible Application Markup Language), 771–772
Visual Basic
classes, 488, 490–491
data type declarations, 487
description, 57–59
executable statements, 487–489, 491
fields, 491–492
Function statements, 487
getting started, 489–490
Imports statement, 486–487
members, 487, 491–492
methods, 491–492
My object, 492
namespace declarations, 487
non-executable statements, 486–487
objects, 490
organizing programs, 486–489
procedures, 487, 491–492

Visual Basic *(continued)*
  Property statements, 487
  setup statements, 486–487
  statements, 491
  Sub statements, 487
  using external resources, 486–487
  wrapper statements, 486–487
Visual Basic Upgrade Wizard, 124–125
Visual C#, 59. *See also* C# language
Visual C++. *See also* C++ language
  adding controls, 185–186
  compilers, 60
  description, 60–61
  development environment, 60
  elements, 176
  event handlers, 185
  "Hello World" example, 179–180, 181
  interoperability, 177
  libraries, 60
  managed applications, 180–181
  managed code, 176
  native code, 177
  project folders, 179
  resource editors, 184
  resource management, 184–186
  templates, 177–179
  unmanaged code, 182–186
  wizards, 177–179
Visual Database Tools, 459–465
Visual J#, 26
Visual SourceSafe (VSS), 717
Visual Studio
  code name Hawaii, 78
  communities, 111–114
  as development hub, 17–18
  editions. *See also* Professional Edition
    choosing, 71–74
    cost, 71
    database applications, 68
    downloading, 69
    Express, 68–69, 71
    TFS (Team Foundation Server), 70–71
    VSTO (Visual Studio Tools for Office), 69, 71
    VSTS (Visual Studio Team System), 70, 71

    Web applications, 68
    Windows applications, 68
  features, 16
  future of, 77–78, 745–746
  launching the first time, 85–87
  new features, 19–20
  overview, 15–17
  tools, 296
Visual Studio Headlines, 89
Visual Studio Team Suite, 748
visual tools, 299
Visual Web Developer
  ASP (Active Server Pages), 188
  definition, 187
  starter kits, 212
  Web sites, 191–192, 196–198, 212
visualizers, 635
.viw file extension, 451
VSS (Visual SourceSafe), 717
VSTO (Visual Studio Tools for Office), 28, 69, 71
VSTS (Visual Studio Team System). *See also* TFS (Team Foundation Server)
  Application Designer, 76
  architecting software, 76–77
  collaboration features, 77–78
  cost, 71
  Database Professionals edition, 756
  description, 70
  editions, 76–77, 748–756
  hosting, 749
  Logical Datacenter designer, 76–77
  mapping applications to technology environments, 76–77
  products, 747–749
  project management, 75
  resources, 750
  role-based editions, 748, 750–751
  server requirements, 749
  Software Architect Edition, 76–77, 751–753
  Software Developers Edition, 77, 753–754
  Software Testers edition, 755–756
  team tasks, 75
  Testers Edition, 77

testing framework, 655
tools, 747–749
trial editions, 750
Visual Studio Team Suite, 748
whiteboarding, 76

W

Walkowski, Debbie, 535
Warning icon, 9
Watch window, 636–637
waterfall development, 33
WCF (Windows Communication
  Foundation), 23, 27, 29
weak typing, 350
Web applications
  See also AJAX Web applications
  See also mobile Web applications
  See also Visual Web Developer
  See also Web Forms
  choosing a Visual Studio edition, 68
  configuring for .NET 3.5, 123
  connection strings, 411
  deploying, 695–699
  Microsoft tools, 187
  migrating, 120–124
  reserved folders, 198
  starter kits, 212
Web development standards, 66
Web Forms. *See also* ASP.NET pages; Web
    Forms Designer
  data controls, 295
  Data Source Configuration Wizard,
    304–308
  drag-and-drop data access, 304–308
  templates, 331–334
Web Forms, data access
  creating data sources, 336–339
  data controls, 328
  data source controls, 328
  displaying data, 328
  drag and drop, 304–308
  HTTP (HyperText Transfer Protocol),
    326–327
  processing stages, 326
  retrieving data, 336–339

updating data, 336–339
Web server controls
  adding, 330
  AutoFormat feature, 335–336
  customizing, 331–334, 335–336
  deleting data, 340–342
  editing data, 340–342
  paging data, 335, 340
  properties, 334–336
  sorting data, 340
  tasks, 334–336
  templates for, 331–334
Web Forms Designer, 101–102
Web pages. *See also* state management;
    Visual Web Developer
  adding to sites, 196–198
  buttons, adding, 195–196
  characteristics of, 189
  Check Page for Accessibility, 208
  code editing, 211
  Code view, 208
  code-behind code, 211
  Component Designer view, 208
  content, adding, 194–196
  control properties, setting, 195
  Design view, 208
  generated code, changing, 211
  "Hello World" example, 194–196
  hyperlinks, adding, 210–211
  inline code, 211
  life cycle, 562–568
  partial clauses, 211
  positioning elements, 247
  postbacks, 190
  serving, 190
  session state, 259
  Source view, 208–211
  syntax, viewing, 193–194
  Target Schema for Validation, 208
  validator commands, 208
  views, 208–211
Web parts controls, 269–270
Web references, 613

Web server controls
  adding, 330
  ASP.NET, 198–203
  AutoFormat feature, 335–336
  customizing, 331–334, 335–336
  deleting data, 340–342
  editing data, 340–342
  paging data, 335, 340
  properties, 334–336
  sorting data, 340
  tasks, 334–336
  templates for, 331–334
Web services
  in applications, 612–616
  client side, 615–616
  communicating with, 608–609
  creating, 596–597
  data binding, 613–615
  definition, 595
  description, 597–600
  finding, 609–612. *See also* UDDI (Universal Description, Discovery and Integration); WSDL (Web Services Definition Language)
  methods, adding, 600–601
  namespace, 599–600
  proxy class, 613
  renaming, 598–599
  testing, 601, 602–608
  uses for, 595–596
  in Web applications, 615
  Web references, 613
Web Services Definition Language (WSDL), 609–612. *See also* UDDI (Universal Description, Discovery and Integration)
Web sites
  anonymous users, 269
  application state, 257–259
  client-side statement management, 256, 257
  customizing, 268–270
  login page, setting up, 265–267
  pages, adding, 196–198
  precompiling, 696
  profiles, enabling, 268–269
  server-side statement management, 256
  session state, 259
  state management, 256–259

  types of, 191
  user registration, 267
  view state, 257–259
Webcasts, 113–114
`web.config` files, 255, 698–699
`WebPartManager`, 270
`WebPartZone`, 270
well-formed XML, 386
WF (Windows Workflow Foundation), 23
`where` clause, 468–470
whiteboarding, 76. *See also* prototyping
Width element, 247
Win32 Application Wizard, 179
windows
  docking, 91–92
  open, managing, 91–93
  opening, 90
  resizable, setting, 150
  restoring defaults, 91
  setting options, 91
Windows applications. *See also* Windows Form
  choosing a Visual Studio edition, 68
  connection strings, 410–411
  data sources
    adding, 312–314
    available sources, 316
    binding to controls, 318–320
    connecting to databases, 314–317
    connection strings store, 317
    data providers, 316
    databound controls, 318–320
    datasets, 311
    definition, 310
    managing, 310–311
    protecting, 324
    storing retrieved data, 311
    tree view, 311–312
  events, 559–561
  life cycle, 559–561
  migrating, 119–120
Windows applications, data access
  access methods, 309–310
  accessing data, 309–312
  adding data, 312–314
  data sources

adding, 312–314
available sources, 316
connecting to controls, 318–320. *See also* data binding
connecting to databases, 314–317
connection strings store, 317
data providers, 316
databound controls, 318–320. *See also* data binding
datasets, 311
definition, 310
managing, 310–311
protecting, 324
storing retrieved data, 311
tree view, 311–312
default components, 318–319
managing data, 310–311
tree view, 311–312
Windows CardSpace, 23
Windows CE, 272, 274. *See also* smart devices
Windows CE Embedded, 272
Windows Communication Foundation (WCF), 23, 27, 29
Windows Embedded, 272
Windows Form. *See also* UI (user interface); Windows applications
control buttons, toggling, 150
data controls, 295
Data Source Configuration Wizard, 300–304
defining, 145
description, 130–131
displaying in the taskbar, 150
drag-and-drop data access, 300–304
inheritance, 165–166
minimized icon, setting, 150
naming, 150
properties, common, 149–150
properties, setting, 146–147. *See also* properties
reusing, 165–166
start position, setting, 150
status strip, 155
strongly typed DataSets, 378–379
template, 178
title bar caption, 150

Windows Forms Application template, 178
Windows Forms Control Library template, 178
Windows Forms Designer. *See also* Data Sources pane
accessing data, 309–312
data binding
BindingNavigator component, 318, 321
BindingSource component, 318, 321–323. *See also* data source controls
definition, 321
menus for navigation, 318, 321
navigating to data sources, 318, 321
to properties, 324–326
data sources. *See also* data binding; Data Sources pane
adding, 312–314
available sources, 316
connecting to databases, 314–317
connection strings store, 317
data providers, 316
for databound controls, 318–320
datasets, 311
definition, 310
managing, 310–311
protecting, 324
storing retrieved data, 311
tree view, 311–312
description, 101–102
uses for, 131
Windows Installer, 688–693
Windows menu, 93
Windows Mobile, 272
Windows Mobile support page, 277
Windows Service template, 178
Windows Workflow Foundation (WF), 23
WindowStyle category, 145
WinFS, 767
WinFX. *See* .NET 3.5
wiring up event handlers, 556–559
work items, creating, 762–763
work products, 715–716
work-flow enabled services, 29

WPF (Windows Presentation Foundation),
  23, 27
WPF interoperability, 135
wrapper statements, 486–487
WSDL (Web Services Definition Language),
  609–612. *See also* UDDI (Universal
  Description, Discovery and Integration)

X

XAML (Extensible Application Markup
  Language), 771–772
XML (eXtensible Markup Language). *See
  also* XSLT (XSL Transformations)
  ADO.NET support for, 432–433
  attributes, 381
  comment markers, 585
  documentation tags, 586
  documentation template, 586–588
  documenting code with, 585–589
  .NET resources, 396–397
  schemas, 387
  self-describing, 382–383
  snippets, 389–391
  storing data, 382–384. *See also* XML
    documents
  System.XML Namespace in .NET, 397
  tags, 381
XML Designers, 296
XML documents
  creating, 386–387, 432–433
  describing data, 385

linking to XSLT style sheets, 394–395
navigating, 395
synchronizing with DataSets, 433
well-formed, 386
XML files. *See also* XML documents; XML
  Schema; XSLT (XSL Transformations)
  creating, 384–385
  description, 381–382
  size issues, 384
  types of, 384–385
XML Schema
  creating, 388–389, 432–433
  description, 387–388
  strongly typed DataSets, 377–378
  syntax, 388–389
  XML snippets, 389–391
XmlDataSource control, 328
XMLDocument class, 397
XMLHttpRequest object, 215–216
XMLReader class, 397
XMLSchema class, 397
XMLWriter class, 397
XPath, 395–396
XPathNavigator class, 397
XSLT (XSL Transformations), 391–396

Z

zero-based array index, 508–509
Z-index element, 247

Notes

Notes

Notes

Notes